HISTORY
and
GENEALOGY
of
FENWICK'S COLONY

NEW JERSEY

Thomas Shourds
of SALEM COUNTY

HERITAGE BOOKS
2011

HERITAGE BOOKS
AN IMPRINT OF HERITAGE BOOKS, INC.

Books, CDs, and more—Worldwide

For our listing of thousands of titles see our website
at
www.HeritageBooks.com

A Facsimile Reprint
Published 2011 by
HERITAGE BOOKS, INC.
Publishing Division
100 Railroad Ave. #104
Westminster, Maryland 21157

Entered according to Act of Congress, in the year 1876, by
Thomas Shourds and George F. Nixon
In the Office of the Librarian of Congress, at Washington, D. C.

— Publisher's Notice —
In reprints such as this, it is often not possible to remove blemishes from the original. We feel the contents of this book warrant its reissue despite these blemishes and hope you will agree and read it with pleasure.

International Standard Book Numbers
Paperbound: 978-0-7884-4986-4
Clothbound: 978-0-7884-8643-2

INTRODUCTORY.

The earliest attempts at settlement by the Europeans on the shores of the Delaware may be traced to the second decade of the seventeenth century. In 1621 a charter was granted to the West India Company by the United Netherlands, whose purpose was to transport colonists to these new Territories, and establish trade and commercial intercourse therewith. In 1623 Captain Cornelius Jacobson May, under the patronage of the before-named company, made a voyage to America, and sailed up the Delaware river as far as the mouth of Great Timber creek, a few miles below the present site of Philadelphia, and erected a trading post, which was called Fort Nassau. The Swedes and Finns soon followed, as in 1638 Queen Christiana gave her countenance to the sending of a Colony to the same river, and where a settlement was made. Passing over the grant made by Charles I., king of England, to Edmund Ploydon, in 1634, of certain territories in America, and the attempts of the New Haven Colony, under Captain Nathaniel Turner, in 1640, to effect a settlement on the eastern shore of the river, the English emigrants holding the right of government, and title to the soil, under the conveyance made by the second Charles to the Duke of York, 1664, were the next to establish a Colony on the banks of the before-named river. The many political changes, arising from the wars and internal commotions of the home government, added much to the attendant troubles of the colonists, but at no time were they entirely lost sight of, or their nationality obliterated. The language, the customs, and the religions of each were distinctly preserved for several generations, and even at this day have not entirely disappeared.

The Dutch were the least successful in establishing themselves here, for the reason, doubtless, that much greater attractions lay about New Amsterdam, and the many difficulties in which they were involved by the dissentions across the sea. The Swedes and Finns, yielding generally to the condition of things around them, and avoiding as much as possible any participation in quarrels between the Dutch and English, soon made a settlement on the eastern or New Jersey side of the Delaware river; most of which can be traced with some degree of accuracy. In a letter from William Penn, then living in Philadelphia, he says: "The first planters were Dutch, and soon after the Swedes and Finns. The Dutch applied themselves to traffic, and the Swedes and Finns to husbandry. The Dutch have a meeting place for religious worship at New Castle, and the Swedes one at Christiana, one at Tinicum and one at Wicaco, within half a mile of this town. The Swedes inhabit the freshes of the river Delaware. There is no need of giving any description of them who are better known in England than here, but they are a plain, strong and industrious people, yet have not made much progress in the culture or propagation of fruit trees, as if they desired rather to have money than plenty or traffic. But I presume the Indians made them the more careless by furnishing them with the means of profit, to-wit: all kinds of furs for rum and such strong liquors. They kindly received me as did the English, who were few before the people concerned with me came among them. I must needs commend their respect to authority and kind behavior to the English. They do not degenerate from their old friendship between both kingdoms, as they are a people, physical and strong of body, so have they fine children, and almost every house is full; it is rare to find one of them without three or four boys, and as many girls; some of them have six, seven and eight sons, and I must do them justice to say I see few young men more sober and industrious." On the New Jersey shore they had settled near Salem, on Raccoon creek, where Swedesboro now stands, at the mouth of Woodbury creek, and other places on the navigation.

John Fenwick, on his arrival to this country, found much of his territory occupied by the Swedes and Finns and Hollanders, but he settled amicably with them by confirming their title to the land they held in possession. Deeds for the Finnstown tract and the Boughtown tract and other like conveyances appears on record, and are curious documents in their way. Those settled on Raccoon Creek had made their homes on either side of the stream, and extending several miles along the same, with a Church at Swedesboro. This Colony assumed such proportions that the attention of travelers and historians were attracted to it, and many detached sketches of their mode of living, their political arrangement, their success as farmers, dealers in furs and skins, may be found in the old books. Near the mouth of Woodbury Creek a few families of Swedes had their farms and fisheries, but this settlement always remained small, and was eventually overgrown by the English, who established a Friends' Meeting there, and occupied most of the land in that region. At the outlet of Pennsiaukin Creek into the Delaware river at one time stood a small stockade called Fort Eriwonock, surrounded by a few Swedes and Finns. This, like the Colony at Woodbury Creek, soon lost its identity, and the grants of land thereabouts, as made by the proprietors of West New Jersey, took precedence of any previous title to the same, saving always the Indian ownership, which was recognized and compensated for previous to location. The more particularity is given to the description of these localities and names of such as resided there, for the reason that many of the emigrant's families became the ancestors of the present inhabitants living in West Jersey and scattered through the different States of the Union. The use of surnames was not general among the Swedes and Finns for several years after the arrival and settlement of the English under John Fenwick and William Penn. The custom was overcome only by intermarriage with and the rigid usage of the English in this regard, and has rendered it impossible to follow the lines of families which took that direction. The transposition of names, the alteration in spelling, as well as Christain and surnames, is another source of confusion and leads to endless difficulties in geneological research. Among the Indians; names were never hereditary, and one generation could not trace its lines of blood through that of another by this means. When any name could be found it was so utterly unpronouncable and beyond the possibility of being spelled, that our ancestors in despair abandoned all attempts at reconciling the one language with the other.

As early as the year 1684, the proper authorities of Salem County were at much pains to secure a translation of the language used by the Aborigines, and have the same on record in one of the court's books of the Bailiwick, evidence of their purpose to carry out a desirable object, and of how little was accomplished thereby. These impediments are encountered by the genealogist and antiquarian at every step, making dark his pathway, and his progress in some degree uncertain. In following the movements of the first English emigrants, the inquiry very naturally arises why their places of settlement were selected, as they were in this wilderness country, and the causes that contributed such action. The charts of the new world were defective, and knowledge of this particular section, in like degree limited. These people were not surrounded with prestige of any monied corporation, or backed by the royal perogative to assist them in this undertaking. The breaking up of their household was an end of all claims to an inheritance in their native land. The persecutions they had passed through, and the uncertainty of any change for the better, banished all hopes of justice and tolerance for them. Whatever may have been their attachments, or however bitter the feeling incident to separation from friends and home; no hope of return softened their grief or assauged their sorrow. With all their earthly goods (limited among the most fortunate,) their families and such of their associates as would make the venture, left the shores of England never to return. Their departure was not surrounded with any pleasant associations, neither had their approach to the land of their adoption any anticipated welcome. Privations and dangers met them at every step, but no means were at hand whereby they could escape. They only knew that the Delaware river was the western boundary of New Jersey, but the most desirable localities whereat to make their settlement no one had given them any information. The natives, they looked upon as savages in a literal sense, and dreaded the necessity of any intercourse with them; regarding the wild beasts of the forest with less fear, and more easily controlled. Under these circumstances did our ancestors turn their ship from the ocean into Delaware bay and ascend the river, ignorant of where should be their abiding place.

John Fenwick, with his children, his associates and servants, in the little ship Griffin, Captain Griffith master, sailed up the bay, about fifty miles along the eastern shore from Cape May, and anchored opposite the old Swede's fort, Elsborg, near the mouth of Assamhocking river, on the 23d of September, 1675, old style. The day following they ascended the Assamhocking river, now Salem, about three miles, and landed on the south side of the river on a point of land pleasantly located, that being, at the present computation of time, the fifth day of October, 1675. We can readily imagine that their minds were turned to the author of their being in adoration and praise for their safe arrival to their newly adopted country, after a long and tedious voyage in crossing the Atlantic of more than two months and a half. Fenwick soon determined on laying out a town at the place where they landed; it being one of those pleasant autumnal days which are common in this latitude at that season of the year. He gave it the name of Salem, which signifies peace, and which name it still bears, it being the first English town on the Eastern shore of the Delaware. The next in order of time was the ship Kent, bringing the London and Yorkshire commissioners and many families, intending to occupy the lands of West New Jersey. For some reasons never explained the ship passed only about twenty miles higher up the river than where the Griffin anchored, and the passengers went on shore near the mouth of Raccoon creek, and where a settlement of Swedes were found. The destination of the commissioners and many of the emigrants was Yegou's Island, now Burlington City, which point was reached after much trouble and delay. The reason the passengers by this ship went so far up the river is explained by this fact that where Burlington now stands, as early as the year 1668, a Hollander named Peter Yegou built a house of entertainment for travelers. No other settlement to that time had been sustained on the river front above the mouth of Raccoon creek until this point was reached, and, as a consequence, no discretion was left the commissioners if they sought comfortable lodgings. The sale of rum by Peter to the Indians ended in a drunken riot, in which he was driven away from the house, and forced to abandon the place. George Fox and his companion, Richard Lippincott, was of them who rested in the empty dwelling one night on their road from New England to Virginia, which occurrence he mentions in his journal. These are well settled historical facts, and accounts for the procedure on the part of the commissioners, and also explains the name attached to the island before the arrival of the English. Several emigrant ships followed, and proceeded at once to Burlington, where the people landed and soon found homes in the neighborhood. The Newton settlers chartered a vessel for their special use, the ship Adventure, and sailed from Dublin harbor. With them they brought all their worldly goods, and some implements of husbandry, and arriving in the winter season, they only proceeded as far as Salem, where they remained through the cold weather. Their purpose was to settle on the Irish tenth, lying between Oldman's and Pennsahawken creek, and which they examined at once to carry out that object. This was two years before William Penn first visited America. A settlement was made on a stream falling into the river Delaware opposite, and a short distance below the city of Philadelphia, which they called Newton creek, and the same name given to the location chosen. Why this place was pitched upon, and whence the name adopted does not appear. This settlement became allied with the Salem settlement more than any other along the Delaware river; marriages were frequent among the inhabitants of the two locations. The prominent cause of this, I presume, was that very early after the arrival of Fenwick's colony, and the one at Newton, Friends organized a yearly and quarterly meeting, composed of members of both localities, and likewise those of Burlington. The early emigrants, finding in the Aborigines excellent neighbors and reliable associates, the relations brought about marriages between the emigrants and natives, involving the genealogy of a number of families in the Salem tenth, and likewise all West Jersey. It is always to be regretted that so little pains has been taken to trace the Indian blood, distributed in these latter generations, and although much diluted, occasionally crops out, in feature or form. Although, black hair, dark skin, and exact, graceful form, may not always be taken as coming from this line, yet the presumption is a fair one, that the parents of such with several removes, were of this people, and the manor born. Like the Swedes and Finns, however, their customs in regard to names rendered it impossible to follow families in the ascending line, and through neglect, much has been lost in the other direction.

In writing the history and also genealogy of ancient families of Fenwick colony, I have been assisted by a number of persons who have kindly loaned me their family records. Among the most conspicuous is Charles E. Sheppard, of Bridgeton, a young practicing lawyer, of much promise, who has a talent for antiquarian researches. Gideon D. Scull, the eldest son of David Scull, of Philadelphia; Gideon has resided in England for a number of years, a man of literature, has turned attention extensively to the history and genealogy of his native land, and has furnished me with several valuable charts of families, which otherwise would have been difficult to obtain with such correctness in any other way. I am particularly indebted to my valued friend and antiquarian, John Clement, of Haddonfield, who has furnished me with much valuable information in regard to the families and early history of West New Jersey. Without such assistance it would be impractable for any one after a lapse of two centuries to follow the ancient families to the present time with much degree of accuracy.

JOHN FENWICK.

John Fenwick, the proprietor of the one-tenth of West New Jersey, was born in Northumberland county, at Stanton Manor, in England, in the year 1618. He was the second son of Wm. Fenwick, and in the year 1640 he became a member of the church of England. In the year 1645 he was a student of law at Grey's Inn, in London. Soon after he was made captain of Cavalry by Cromwell; he taking such active part against the crown, it has been the opinion of many, that it was the primary cause, after Charles II ascended the throne, that there was so little favor shown him in the affairs of the colony. About the year 1648 he married Elizabeth Covert, of the county of Sapoy. The Coverts as well as the Fenwicks were ancient families, and they can be traced back in English history as early as the 12th century. He had three children by Elizabeth Covert, all daughters; Elizabeth, Anne and Priscilla Fenwick. His second wife was Mary Burdet, the daughter of Sir Walter Burdet, but there was no children by that connection. In 1665 he and his wife Elizabeth became members of the society of Friends. He, like many others of that religious faith and other descendants, were imprisoned for conscience sake. About that time Lord Berkley offered West New Jersey for sale. There appeared to have been an understanding between Edward Billinge and John Fenwick, for John Fenwick to purchase the whole of West New Jersey, and Fenwick to have the one-tenth of the whole. The deed was given by Berkley in the year 1673, and the consideration money mentioned in the deed was soon after the purchase by mutual understanding. The land comprising Salem and Cumberland counties, as now divided, were set off as Fenwick's tenth. He immediately afterwards made preparations to emigrate and take possession of the lands in West New Jersey, in America, and held out inducements for others to emigrate with him. There was a large number accepted the invitation, principally members of his own religious faith. Many of them purchased land and paid him for it before they embarked, which afterwards gave rise to many difficulties between them and the proprietor, because their lands were not surveyed to them as soon as they desired. The following are the names of some of the principal persons who embarked with John Fenwick: John Pledger, Samuel Nicholson, James Nevil, Edward Wade, Robert Wade, Samuel Wade, Robert Windham, Richard Hancock, and their families, and several others. There were several single men, Samuel Hedge, Jr., Isaac Smart, and others. The servants that hired in England to persons above mentioned, and likewise to John Fenwick and his two son-in-laws, were Robert Turner, Gewas Bywater, Wm. Wilkinson, Joseph Worth, Joseph Ware, Michael Eaton, Eleanor Geeve, Nathaniel Chambless, his son, Nathaniel Chambless, Jr., Mark Reeve, Edward Webb, Elizabeth Waiters. Smith, in his history of New Jersey, says in many instances the servants became more conspicuous members of civil and religious society than their employers. I myself, in tracing families, find the remark to be correct. Fenwick's immediate family that came with him were his his daughter Elizabeth and her husband, John Adams, his daughter Anne Fenwick, who married Samuel Hedge, Jr., the spring following, and his youngest daughter, Priscilla, whose husband was Edward Champney. His wife, Mary Fenwick, did not accompany him to his new home in the wilderness, for some cause that has never been explained. The letters passed between them manifested a sincere and filial attachment, and they continued to correspond while life remained. They embarked from London in ship Griffith, Robert Griffith being master, on the 23d of the 9th month. They arrived at the mouth of Assamhockin, and ascended the stream about three miles, and landed at a point of land at a place Fenwick and his friends that were with him thought it a suitable location for a town. He gave it the name of New Salem, because he remarked to one of his intimate friends the name signifies Peace, but it did not prove so to him, as the sequel of his history will show. He, like his great friend and benefactor, William Penn, and also Roger Williams, found in settling colonies that there were more thorns than roses.

As soon as it was practicable after they landed, the proprietor held a council with the Indian chiefs that lived within the compass of Salem county, and purchased all their lands of them, thereby securing perpetual peace with the natives, and the same kind of a treaty was made with them by Billenge or his agents for the remainder of West Jersey. They reserved certain rights for themselves—trapping, fishing, and the privilege of cutting certain kinds of wood for the purpose of making baskets, also in making their canoes and other things. The treaty was faithfully fulfilled. About fifty years ago, the few remaining Indians in this State made application to the New Jersey Legislature to sell all their rights and privileges they held in the State, which was accepted by the Legislature, and they were paid the price they asked. They then removed to the State of New York to dwell with the Mohawks and other scattering tribes that remained in that State.

John Fenwick, after his arrival here, issued a proclamation granting civil and religious liberty to all persons who should settle within his province. In the year 1676, he turned his attention to providing homes for his children, and accordingly directed Richard Hancock, his surveyor, to lay out and survey two thousand acres in Upper Mannington for Samuel Hedge, Jr., and his wife Anne. The said land was called Hedgefield. He also directed him to survey two thousand acres for his son-in-law, Edward Champney, and his wife Priscilla, which land was bounded on the west by John Smith's land, on the north by James Nevel's farm, and Alloways creek on the south. To his son-in-law, John Adams and his wife Elizabeth, he gave all that tract of land located in what is now called Penn's Neck. It is known at the present day as the Sapaney. Fenwick built himself a house in the town of Salem on what he called Ivy Point. From said house he was forcibly taken in the middle of the night by a party of men from New Castle and taken to that town, and from thence sent to New York, and there imprisoned by an order of Governor Andross, under pretence that he was infringing upon the rights of that State, which they claimed to own to the eastern shore of Delaware river. After he was released, he for some time neglected to attend meetings. Accordingly Salem Monthly Meeting, held the 6th of the 3d month, 1678, appointed Richard Guy and Christopher White to visit John Fenwick to inquire of him whether he owned the truth that he formerly possessed, and if he owned it to desire him to come to the next monthly meeting, if not, return his answer to the next meeting. At the next meeting, the Friends that were appointed to visit Fenwick on account of his non-attendance of meetings, reported they had an interview with him, and he informed them that he loved the truth he formerly possessed, and that an answer to a letter he had received from George Whitehead, a distinguished Friend in London, he wished to be forwarded to the meeting. The contents of the letter, I believe, were never preserved, but the proceedings of the meeting shows plainly that difficulties existed between him and some of the members of his own society; which was at fault, they or him, no one can tell to a certainty at the present day. After two or three years more of perplexities and trouble in endeavoring to establish a government in the colony, he wisely abandoned it by selling all the lands he had in the Salem tenth, (reserving one hundred and fifty thousand acres for himself and family,) to Governor Wm. Penn. The deed was given the 23d day of March, 1682. From that time the whole of West Jersey was under one government. The Legislature met at Burlington, and Samuel Jennings, of that place, was elected Deputy Governor at the first Legislature afterwards. John Fenwick was elected one of the members of that body from Salem county, in the fall of 1683, but being unwell, he left his home in Salem and went to Samuel Hedge's, his son-in-law, in Upper Mannington, there to be cared for by his favorite daughter, Anne Hedge, in his last days, for he died a short time afterwards at an age of 65 years. He requested before his death to be buried in the Sharp's family burying-ground, which was complied with. The said ground was formerly a part of the Salem County Almshouse farm, but now belongs to Elmer Reeve. If the ground could be designated where the grave-yard was, although the exact spot where Fenwick lays could not, it would be a grateful deed for his descendents and the citizens of this county to assist in erecting a monument to his memory there on the spot where the grave-yard was, for gratitude for favors received is one of the noblest traits of mankind. His will, made not long before his death, shows no alienation on his part toward the members of his own religious society, for he leaves his friend, William Penn, one of his executors, and also trustee for his three oldest grandsons, Fenwick Adams, Samuel Hedge and John Champney. His other three executors were Quakers, Samuel Hedge, John Smith, of Smithfield, and Richard Tindall, of Penn's Neck. The last named was his surveyor.

John Adams married Fenwick's oldest daughter Elizabeth whilst in England. They had three children born in that country, Elizabeth, Fenwick and Mary Adams. Soon after their arrival in this country he built a house on Ivy Point, near the one that Fenwick built, both of which were located a few rods west of Market street, on a rising ground near where Thomas T. Hilliard's lime kiln is built. They were standing there about fifty years ago, and there John Adams and his wife Elizabeth ended their days, which event took place prior to 1700. Fenwick Adams, their son, married and settled on his parent's property in Penn's Neck. William Adams was his grandson and he had one grand-daughter whose name was Susannah, and she married a man by the name of Townsend, a native of Cape May county. They had two daughters, Susannah and Sarah. Susannah married Thomas Hartly, of Elsinborough, who lived and owned where William Morrison lives at the present time.— Thomas and his wife had four children named Elizabeth, born in the year 1765; Susannah, born 1772; Sarah, born 1774; and Thomas, born 1775. Sarah Townsend married William Nicholson, of Mannington, in 1773. They had seven children —Rachel, Milicent, Samuel, William, Daniel and Ann. The two first mentioned died young. William married Elizabeth Thompson, daughter of Joshua Thompson, of Alloways creek. Daniel married Mary Chambers. Sarah had two husbands, the first Chambless Allen, the second Amos Peasley. Ann married George M. Ward.

The first wife of the late Benjamin Griscom, of Salem, was Susan Adams, a direct descendant of Fenwick Adams. Benjamin and his wife Susan had five children, named Sarah, Andrew, Benjamin, John and Mary. Edward Champney and Priscilla his wife had two children born in England, John and Mary Champneys, also a son born in this county, Edward Champney, Jr. I am inclined to think that John Champney married and died a young man. Edward Champney, Jr., as late as 1720, sold large tracts of land (being part of the 2,000 acre allotment that his grandfather, John Fenwick, deeded to his father and mother) to Abel Nicholson and others. The Tylers became the possessors of a large part of the said allotment, either by marriage or purchase. Samuel Hedge 2d was the son of Samuel Hedge, a merchant and citizen in London. To be a citizen at that period required a person of wealth and influence to have the privilege of voting for members of Parliament. It was the opinion of some persons that there was an attachment formed between Samuel Hedge 2d and Anne, the daughter of John Fenwick, whilst living in their native land. Perhaps on that account he was willing to leave his father's home where wealth and comforts abounded, to seek his fortune and happiness in the wilds of America. By so doing he verified the lines of the poet when he said: "Love is mightier than all." They were married at New Salem, in the spring of 1676, and soon afterwards went and lived in Upper Mannington on a tract of land containing 2,000 acres that Fenwick deeded them in the 11th mo. of the same year. It was called the Hedgefield tract. Samuel and his wife remained there until 1685; he being one of his father-in-law's executors, and having been appointed by

Fenwick to carry out his plans in laying out streets in Salem and Cohansey. He built a brick house on Bradway street, where they resided until their death. The old mansion was removed a few years ago by the late Wm. F. Miller, and he built one of more modern architecture on the site of the old one. The property is now owned and occupied by M. P. Grey.

Samuel Hedge and his wife Anne, died sometime between the year 1694 and 1697, leaving one son, Samuel Hedge 3d, and he married Rebecca Pyle. They had four children— Samuel F. Hedge 4th, John Hedge, who died a minor, William Hedge, who died 1729, leaving his estate to his mother, and Nathan Hedge, who died 8th mo., 1735. The latter, by his will, bequeathed to his mother, (whom he also made his executrix) the greater part of his estate. Her name at the time was Rebecca Cox. Samuel Hedge 3d died 3d of the 11th mo., 1709. His widow Rebecca Hedge, married Daniel Cox, of Burlington, 1712. Samuel F. Hedge 4th, went to Greenwich to reside, and went into partnership in the mercantile business with Nicholas Gibbon. Sometime after the death of Nicholas Gibbon, Samuel married his widow, whose maiden name was Anne Grant, the daughter of Alexander Grant. She had three children by her first husband, Nicholas, Grant and Jane Gibbon. Samuel F. Hedge 4th, and his wife, Anne, had two children, Samuel Hedge 5th, and one daughter, Rebecca Hedge. She was born 1st of the 2d mo., 1728, and her brother Samuel in 1726. In 1728 Samuel F. Hedge deeded one acre of ground on the south side of Market street to the Episcopal church. In 1733 he died, having made his will in 1732, leaving his wife, Anne Hedge, executrix. He devised to his widow a lot of eight acres in Salem, located on the south side of Market street; also sixteen acres of woodland adjoining the first mentioned lot. The woodland was bounded on the south by Nathan Hedge's land. He also bequeathed to her a lot of meadow on Fenwick creek, of four acres, together with one thousand acres of Fenwick's Grove out of 1,900 acres surveyed to him. The whole tract originally contained 15,000 and was located in Upper Mannington, running from Mannington creek to Salem creek. It included the lands owned by the Bassett family at the present time, and extended to Salem creek, and was bounded on the south by the Hedgefield tract. In 1735 Benjamin Acton, a practical surveyor at that time, was employed to survey and set off the one thousand acres to the widow. The balance of the 1,900 acres he devised to his son Samuel Hedge 5th. After the death of Anne Hedge, the widow of Samuel Hedge, she left the property in Salem that she received from her second husband, to Grant Gibbon and Jane Gibbon, the children by her first husband Nicholas Gibbon. Robert Johnson, Sr., married Jane, and she was the mother of Robert G. Johnson. About the year 1758 there was a division of the town lots on the south side of Market street, between Samuel Hedge 5th and Robert Johnson, Sr. Rebecca Hedge, Samuel F. Hedge's daughter, married Giles Smith. He was born the 18th of 2d mo., 1719, and was the son of Samuel Smith, of Mannington, who lived on and owned the southern portion of Hedgefield. Giles and his wife Rebecca had one son whose name was Christopher Smith. Christopher married Rebecca Hancok in 1675. They had five children— Rebecca was born in 1766, Elizabeth was born 1768, John Smith was born 1770; he married the daughter of Benjamin Smith, and left one son whose name was Samuel. Susanna Smith was born 1771; she married Job Ware of Alloways Creek, and left no children. Esther Smith was born 1774, and married Robert Moore of Easton, Maryland. Samuel Hedge 5th married Hannah Woodnutt of Mannington, daughter of Joseph and Rachel Woodnutt. She was born in 1729. Samuel and his wife Rachel resided in Salem in the old family mansion on Bradway street. They had three children—Rebecca, born 20th of 1st mo., 1751, Joseph W. Hedge, born 1756, and Samuel Hedge 6th, born 1758. In 1770, Rebecca Hedge, daughter of Samuel and Rachel Hedge, married Thomas Thompson, of Salem. He was born in 1745, and was the son of Thomas Thompson, and grandson of Andrew Thompson of Elsinborough. Joseph W. Hedge and his brother Samuel Hedge, Jr., died in 1790, at the family mansion in Salem, within a short time of each other, with an epidemic fever that was prevailing at that time. Neither of them was ever married, and consequently their large real estate was heired by their sister, Rebecca Thompson. Thomas Thompson and his wife Rebecca had seven children. Their names were Ann, Hannah, Hedge, Mary, Rebecca, Jane, and Rachel. They lived and owned where the First Baptist church now stands, and they lived together happily nearly sixty years. Thomas died in his eighty-second year. His widow survived five or six years after his death, and was in her eighty-first year at the time of her death. Neither of them were members of the Society of Friends but professors, and regularly attended all of their meetings of divine worship. They were buried in the Friends' burying-ground at Salem, with their ancestors. Fenwick Archer, their grandson, as soon as the Society permitted it, much to his credit, had their graves done up, and his great uncles' graves, Joseph and Samuel Hedge, and his great-grandmother's, Hannah W. Hedge, and a small monument with their names and ages cut upon them placed at the head of each.

Ann Thompson, daughter of Thomas and Rebecca Thompson, married John Firth. They had four children—Elizabeth, Thomas, John and Samuel Firth.

Hannah Thompson's first husband was John Anderson. They had one daughter, Rebecca Anderson. Hannah's second husband was Leonard Sayres, a native of Cumberland county, but at that time his home was in Cincinnati, Ohio. Hedge Thompson, Thomas' son, married Mary Ann Parrott, daughter of Richard Parrott. Hedge and Mary Ann, his wife, had five children—Richard P., Thomas, Joseph H., Rebecca and Mary. Richard P. married Maria Hancock; Thomas married William Johnson's daughter; Dr. Joseph H. married Rebecca Kelly, and Mary married Samuel Starr, an Episcopal minister. Rebecca, youngest daughter of Thomas and Rebecca, married John Holme of Elsinborough. She left one daughter, Rebecca Holme, who married George W. Garrison. Jane Thompson married John Smith, of Mannington, son of Hill Smith. Their children were Ann, Hill, and Thomas T. Smith. Ann married George W. Garrison, being his second wife, and Thomas T. married Elizabeth Hancock, daughter of Joseph Hancock.

Rachel Thompson the youngest daughter of Thomas and Rebecca Thompson, married Dr. Benjamin Archer; they had one son, Fenwick Archer. Mary Thompson, third daughter of Thomas and Rebecca Thompson, died single.

Within a few years there has been different opinions respecting the property in the town of Salem, held by the county. Some persons have contended the land was given for a particular purpose, while others thought it was given to the county without reservation, and held that the representatives of the people of the county had a right to sell or rent any part of the ground, as they should think would be for the interest of the county. Samuel Hedge was left to carry out the wishes and designs in the town of Salem, and also in the town of Cohansey, of his father-in-law, John Fenwick. After the death of Fenwick all the land on the south side of Bridge street, now Market street, extending from Broadway to Fenwick creek, Samuel Hedge and his wife, Anne, became the owners. The following is an order I find in Richard Tindall's book of surveys, eighteenth page. A warrant given 7th of 11th mo., 1688.

"A warrant to Richard Tindall, Surveyor-general for the county of Salem, and to John Woolidge, his deputy, to lay out

JOHN FENWICK.

one acre of land in Salem town, given by John Fenwick to erect a Court House and Prison."

Agreeable to the words of the warrant, it was certainly given for a particular use—to erect a Court House and Prison on—and if the inhabitants of the county should in some future time remove the said buildings from the said ground, it is reasonable to suppose that the property would revert back to the heirs of the donor.

Erick Yearness and Henry Neilson arrived in this country as early as 1640, and located themselves at the first fast land above the mouth of what is now known as Salem creek. They, like their neighbors the Swedes, believing the Indians to be the rightful owners of the soil, purchased a large tract of land of the Indian chiefs and gave it the name of Finn's town point. When John Fenwick arrived in this county, in 1695, he claimed the lands that the Finns and Swedes were located upon. They submitted to his authority, and in the year 1676 Richard Hancock, Fenwick's surveyor, laid off one thousand acres of said land and marsh for Erick Yearness, also a tract of the same size for Henry Neilson, and gave them a proprietary deed for the same. In the year 1688, by the request of Stephen Yearness, son of Erick, James Nevell gave Richard Tindall an order to re-survey the said tract at Finn's town point, and if there should not be the full quantity to report to him at his office in Salem within three months from date that the order was given. I have no records to follow the family of Erick Yearness further than his son, Stephen Yearness. Tradition informs us that Edmund Gibbon married a young woman, owner of a large tract of land at Finn's point, who was a lineal descendant of Stephen Yearness. I believe Edmund and wife left four children; three sons and one daughter.

ACTON FAMILY.

Benjamin Acton, according to the records, was one of the prominent young men in the settlement of Fenwick Colony. There is no record in what year he arrived at New Salem; circumstances make it probable he came to America in company with Christopher White, Henry Jennings, William Hancock and their families and servants, together with a number of other emigrants. They embarked in the ship Kent, from London, Gregory being master, and landed at New Salem 23d of sixth month, 1677. Soon after that time Benjamin is mentioned in public affairs of the Colony. Doubtless he had a good education; was a land surveyor by trade, and also a tanner and currier. He purchased a lot of sixteen acres of John Fenwick, on Fenwick street, now called East Broadway; on that lot he built and made it his home, and carried on the tanning business during the remainder of his life. His worth and ability was early appreciated by the Society of Friends, of which he was a consistent member. As early as 1682 he and another Friend were appointed to repair and build an addition to the house that the Society purchased of Samuel and Ann Nicholson, so that the said house should be large enough in which to hold a Yearly Meeting. When the town of New Salem was incorporated in 1695, Benjamin Acton was chosen recorder. In laying out a public highway, in 1705, from Salem to Maurice River, he was one of the commissioners and surveyors; also, in 1709, to lay out a public highway from Salem by the way of John Hancock's new bridge to the town of Greenwich. John Mason and Bartholomew Wyatt, Sr., were the other two commissioners. There was another ancient highway laid out in 1706. It commenced at the upper end of what is known as Yorke street at this time, through Elsinboro, crossed Ambelbury Swamp, continued on near where the present road is to the brick mansion belonging to the late Redroe Morris, and Benjamin Acton, Walter Heighstin and John Mason were the commissioners. According to the records, Benjamin was principally employed by private landholders to do their surveying. Richard Tindall being surveyor general, and

BENJAMIN ACTON.
Born 1814.

John Woolidge, of Salem, his deputy, they did all the surveying for the proprietor while he lived; after his death they were employed by the executors of Fenwick, and subsequently by James Nevell, William Penn's agent. After the death of Nevell and Richard Tindall, James Logan, the faithful friend of William Penn, became the principal agent of Penn's heirs, and he employed Benjamin Acton and Thomas Miles, of Penn's Neck, to do the surveying for the heirs of Penn in Salem tenth. Benjamin Acton received an order from James Logan, of Pennsylvania (it being near the close of a long and useful life), to re-survey one thousand acres of land, lying on the south side of Gravelly run, it being one of the branches of Stoe creek, where the present village of Jericho is. The order was given by the urgent request of Samuel Deeming, of Maryland, who had previously sold the said land to John Brick. Benjamin Acton made his return on the 13th of 9th month, 1729. He stated in his report that the said land was now re-surveyed, with the assistance of John Brick and his two sons; that it proved more chargeable than he expected. Signed by me, Benjamin Acton, surveyor of Fenwick Colony and Salem Tenth. He married about 1688 or '9. The following are the names of his children: Elizabeth, the daughter of Benjamin and Christianna Acton, was born at Salem, 26th of 12th month, 1690; Mary, born 17th of 10th month, 1692; Benjamim Acton, Jr., the 19th of 8th month, 1695; Lydia, 24th of 11th month, 1697; Joshua, 9th of 7th month, 1700. Benjamin, in his old age, built himself a brick dwelling house on his lot on Fenwick street in 1727, which is still standing; its roof is what is called hip, resembling very much the French or Mansard roof, which is common in this generation. The ancient dwelling is owned at this time by Joseph Test. Benjamin Acton, Jr., in 1729, built himself a much larger dwelling than that of his father's on the same lot of ground. The said house was remodeled by the late George Rumsey, but the ancient walls remain. This property, in the last generation, was owned by the Gibbs family. Elizabeth, the eldest daughter of Benjamin and Christianna Acton, born 26th of 12th month, 1690, married Francis Reynolds, 10th month, 1712. Mary Acton, their second daughter, born 17th of 10th month, 1692, married William Willis, in 1715. Benjamin Acton, Jr., married Elizabeth Hill, the widow of Thomas Hill, in 1727. Her daughter, Sarah Hill, by her first husband, married John Smith, of Amblebury, the grandson of the emigrant. John and his wife had two sons—Richard Smith, born 10th of 11th month, 1743, married Rachel Dennis, of Bacon's Neck, in 1762; they had several daughters. Hill Smith, the second son, born 15th of 4th month, 1745, married Ann Nicholson, daughter of John Nicholson. They lived most of their time in Mannington, on the Tide Mill farm, devised to her by her uncle, James Mason. They had two sons—Hill and John Smith. The latter married Eliza, daughter of Israel Brown. John Smith married Jane, the daughter of Thomas and Rebecca Hedge Thompson, of Salem. Sarah Hill Smith's second husband was Aaron Bradway, of Elsinboro; she was his second wife. (Aaron was the grandson of Edward Bradway, the emigrant.) Aaron and his wife had one son, Thomas Hill Bradway; he inherited the sixteen acre lot at the foot of Broadway street, Salem, which was purchased by Edward Bradway of John Fenwick, in England, 1674. Thomas H. Bradway repaired the old brick mansion built by his ancestor, Edward Bradway, in 1691; the building had long been neglected, there being no windows or doors remaining. At the beginning of the present century it was further fitted up, and a piazza made in front of it by John S. Wood, the son-in-law of Thomas H. Bradway.

Benjamin Acton, Jr. and his wife Elizabeth Hill lived in the large brick mansion built in 1729, which is still standing. He was tanner by trade, and occupied the yard that was devised to him by his father. Benjamin had five children, as follows: John, born 31st of 8th month, 1728; Joseph, born 30th of 9th month., 1730; Benjamin, born 15th of 9th month, 1733; he died in infancy; the second Benjamin, born 28th of 12th month, 1735; and Samuel, born 31st of 6th month, 1738. It is probable that some of the children died young. John Acton, the eldest son, succeeded his father in the tanning business, and married about the year 1752 or '53. There is no account to show that John and his wife had more than one child—Clement Acton. John Acton's second wife was Mary Oakford, of Alloways Creek, the grand-daughter of Charles Oakford, and sister of Aaron Oakford, of Darby, Pa. John and his wife, Mary Oakford Acton, had several children, as follows: Samuel, John, (who afterwards became a sea captain, and traded from Philadelphia to West Indies; he never married); Elizabeth, (who married John Hancock, their descendants being quite numerous in Alloways Creek township at this time); Barbara, (who married Ephraim, the son of Jesse Carll; their family genealogy has been written); Susan, (who married Samuel Hall, of Delaware); and Joseph Acton.

Clement Hall, the second son of Judge William Hall, who emigrated to New Jersey in 1677, was born at Salem, 30th of

6th month, 1706. He inherited part of the sixteen acre lot purchased by William Hall, lying between Samuel Nicholson's lot and Edward Bradway's. Clement Hall died comparatively a young man. He and his wife, Sarah Hall, had two children, Ann and William. Ann married John Mason, of Elsinborough, the son of Thomas and grand-son of John Mason, the emigrant. John and his wife Ann had one daughter, Sarah H. Mason, born 1763. She married Elgar Brown, by whom she had four children, Ann, Elisha, Israel and John M. Brown. Sarah, the widow of Clement Hall, built a large brick dwelling, which is now owned by Morris Hall, who resides there. Sarah kept a store in the dwelling for many years. Her son, William Hall, married Hannah Brinton, of Chester county, Pa., a sister of Caleb Brinton. The Brinton family is one of the oldest in Chester county, and at one time was considered the largest landholders in that section of Pennsylvania.

William Hall located on quite an extensive tract of land in the State of Delaware, near St. Georges Creek, New Castle county, and there he lived. He and his wife, Hannah B. Hall, had four children, Mary, Hannah, Clement and Sarah Hall. Hannah married Clement Acton, of Salem, son of John Acton. Clement Hall, their son, married Ann Darrah, who was a widow at the time of their marriage. Her first husband's name was Darrah, a cousin. Clement Hall lived but a short time after their marriage, leaving no children. His widow afterwards married Col. Edward Hall, of Mannington, she being several years his junior; she had no children by any three of her husbands. She was the daughter of Lydia Darrah, of Philadelphia, of Revolutionary memory.

The youngest daughter of William and Hannah Brinton Hall was Sarah Hall, born 6th of 12th month, 1768, married Samuel, the eldest son of John and Mary Oakford Acton, born 10th of 11th month, 1764. William Hall married his second wife, and by her he had one son, Samuel Hall, who, when he grew to manhood, came to Salem county and subsequently married Susan, the youngest daughter of John and Mary O. Acton; they had several children. Clement and Hannah H. Acton had two children, Benjamin and Hannah. Clement's second wife was Hannah, the daughter of James M. and Margaret Woodnutt, of Mannington, born 16th of 1st month, 1780. By that union there were two children, Margaret and Clement Acton. Benjamin, the eldest son of Clement Acton, married Sarah Wyatt, daughter of Richard and Elizabeth W. Miller, of Mannington. They had ten children: Richard Miller Acton, born

4th of 2d month, 1810; Clement Acton, born 8th of 1st month, 1813; he died young; Benjamin Acton, born in the 9th month, 1814; Hannah T. Acton, born 10th of 2d month, 1816; Elizabeth Acton, born 28th of 10th month, 1818; Charlotte Acton, born 9th of 7th month, 1821; Casper Wistar Acton, born 18th of 10th month, 1823; Letitia Acton, born 17th of 7th month, 1825, Sarah Wyatt Acton, born 3d of 9th month, 1827; Catherine, born 22d of 5th month, 1829.

    Hannah H., the daughter of Clement Acton, was twice married; her first husband was John, the son of Job and Grace Thompson Ware, of Alloways Creek. They had three children, Clement A., William and Catharine Ware. Her second husband was Dr. Charles Swing, by whom she had five children. Charles, the present member of the Legislature from the upper district, John, Hannah, Abigail and Margaret Swing. Margaret, the daughter of Clement and Hannah Woodnutt Acton, married Dr. John Griscom, a resident of Philadelphia. He was the son of William and Ann Stewart Griscom, of Salem, and grand-son of William and Rachel Denn Griscom. The latter was the son of Andrew and Susannah Griscom, born the 10th of 11th month, 1747. There was an error made, when I wrote the Davis family. It was Tobias Griscom, instead of Andrew, the father of Andrew and William Griscom, the latter married Sarah Davis, the eldest daughter of David Davis, and was born in Salem county 30th of 1st month, 1715. Soon after their marriage they moved to the neighborhood of Haddonfield. Tobias, I am inclined to believe, was the son of Andrew Griscom, the emigrant. Dr. John and his wife Margaret Acton Griscom have two sons and one daughter; Clement is the oldest son. Clement Acton, the son of Clement and Hannah W. Acton, left Salem many years ago and went to Cincinnati, Ohio, he and his cousin, Thomas Woodnutt, carried on the mercantile business in that city at the old stand of their uncle, William Woodnutt, for a number of years.

    Richard Miller Acton, the eldest son of Benjamin and Sarah Wyatt Acton, born 4th of 2d month, 1810, was apprenticed to learn the currier business in Wilmington, Delaware. He subsequently carried on the business in Salem for several years. He has been entrusted to do considerable public business to general satisfaction. At one time he was much interested in the public schools in the city of Salem, and represented his county in the Senate of New Jersey. He has recently been appointed one of the Trustees of the State Normal School. He married Hannah, the daughter of Thomas and Hannah H. Mason, formerly of Elsinborough. They have had three children. The eldest, Mary Mason Acton, born 29th of 1st month, 1836, married William C., the son of William F. and Mary Reeve, of Allowaystown. Sarah M. Acton, born 14th of 11th month, 1837, died in 1854. Richard W. Acton, born 26th of 6th month, 1853, died in 1854. Benjamin, the third son of Benjamin and Sarah W. Acton, born in the 9th month, 1814, was for a number of years one of the principal grain merchants in the city of Salem, his place of business being at the foot of Market street. In his younger days he was an active politician, and represented this county in the Senate of the State. A number of years since he relinquished the mercantile business, and soon after was chosen one of the officers of the Salem National Banking Company. At the present and for a number of years he has held the responsible office of cashier of that institution. His wife is Sarah Jane, the daughter of Sheppard and Ann Blackwood. They have had several children: Thomas W., Franklin Miller, Elizabeth, Louisa J., and Charles H. Acton. Thomas W. lived to maturity and died unmarried. Elizabeth married Dr. B. A. Waddington, the son of James Waddington; she did not live long after that event, leaving no issue. The surviving children, Franklin M., Louisa J. and Charles H., are unmarried.

Hannah Thompson Acton, the eldest daughter of Benjamin and Sarah W. Acton, born 10th month, 2d, 1816, married Samuel P., the son of William and Mary R. Carpenter, of Mannington. She is deceased, leaving several children. John R. Carpenter, the eldest son, married Mary, daughter of Joseph and Elizabeth Thompson; they have issue. Sarah Carpenter married Richard, the son of William F. and Mary Reeve. S. Preston Carpenter married Rebecca, daughter of Elisha and Hannah Ann Bassett, of Mannington. William Carpenter is unmarried.

Elizabeth Wyatt Acton, born 28th of 10th month, 1818, married Franklin, the son of William F. and Esther Miller, of Mannington. Franklin and his wife died young, leaving one daughter Hetty Miller, who subsequently married David E. Davis, of Pilesgrove. Charlotte, the daughter of Benjamin and Sarah W. Acton, born 9th of 7th month, 1821, married Richard, the son of Clayton and Mary S. Wistar, of Mannington. They have three children, Clayton, Richard and Elizabeth. Clayton married Rebecca, daughter of Andrew and Mary Thompson. Elizabeth married Richard Thompson, of Mannington. Richard, Jr. is unmarried.

Casper Wister Acton, born 18th of 10th month, 1823, married Rachel, daughter of Thomas and Sarah J. Goodwin, formerly of Elsinborough. They have had eight children—Richard M., Hannah, Henry, George, Catharine, Wyatt, Morris and Thomas, the last deceased.

Letitia, daughter of Benjamin and Sarah W. Acton, born 17th of 7th month, 1825, married John, the son of Clayton and Mary S. Wistar. They died young, leaving one son, John Wister, who is engaged in the iron and implement business in Salem.

Sarah Wyatt Acton, born 3d of 9th month, 1827, married Emmor, the son of William and Letitia Reeve; she is his second wife.

Catharine, the youngest daughter of Benjamin and Sarah W. Acton, born 22d of 6th month, 1829, is deceased.

Samuel, the son of John and Mary Oakford Acton, born 10th of 11th month, 1764, learned the tanner's trade of his father. He married Sarah, the youngest daughter of William and Hannah Brinton Hall, residents of Delaware. Samuel and his half-brother, Clement Acton, were engaged in the mercantile business for some time in Salem, occupying the Thomas Thompson store, on Fenwick street, but afterwards known as the George W. Garrison's. After the two brothers concluded to abandon the business, Samuel purchased the tan yards that belonged to John Ward, at Haddonfield, which has been represented to have been greatly out of order, and he spent a considerable sum upon it for repairs. He died suddenly about 1800 or 1801, leaving a widow and a family of children with limited means. The widow soon after removed to Salem with her young children, and with all her difficulties she never despaired, but persevered to keep her children together until they were old enough to learn trades, so as to enable them to provide for themselves, always having a watchful care over their morals. She died at the home of her daughter, Mary A. Bassett, in Mannington, in 1852, in the 84th year of her age, having survived her husband more than half a century. She lived to see her children not only in good outward circumstances, but considered among the wealthy inhabitants of Salem county—confirming the saying of the wise king of Israel: "I never knew the righteous forsaken or their children begging bread."

Clement, the eldest son of Samuel and Sarah H. Acton, born about 1796, learned the trade of a hatter of Caleb Wood, of Salem, and followed the business for some time after he became of age, at the old shop located on Market street, where David

Smith formerly carried on the hatting business. He soon abandoned his trade and became a trader in fur; purchased largely for a firm in New York for a few years, after which he changed his business and kept a lumber yard. He built a large steam saw mill which was located on Penn street, near Fenwick creek, and carried it on, together with his lumber yard, for several years with profit, until the mill was burned. During that time he purchased the old dilapidated building near the centre of the town, on Market street, where the late John Denn, of Mannington, formerly lived and carried on the hatting business. Clement, soon after he purchased the property, removed the old dwelling and built a large brick building large enough for a commodious dwelling and store; there he and the late Thomas Cattell kept a hardware store for a number of years. Clement was twice married; his first wife was Mary, the daughter of Job and Ruth Thompson Bacon, of Cumberland county; she died a young woman without leaving any children; his second wife was Sarah, the daughter of Owen and Elizabeth Jones, of Port Elizabeth. They had three children—Elizabeth J., Clement and Sarah Hall Acton. Clement is deceased. Their son, Clement Acton, married Martha Ann Wills, of Burlington county; he did not live long after his marriage, leaving a widow and one daughter, Helen Acton. Mary, the daughter of Samuel and Sarah Hall Acton, was born 10th of 8th month, 1798. She learned the tailoring trade and followed it until she married Benjamin Thompson, the son of Joseph and Mary Allen Bassett, of Mannington. Benjamin and his wife had four children—Sarah H., Rachel, Maria and Richard Bassett; the two last mentioned were twins. Benjamin died a few years ago. Mary A., his widow, is still living, at the advanced age of seventy-seven years. Clement A., the eldest son of Benjamin and Mary O. Bassett, born in 1829, died when he was seven years of age. Sarah H., the daughter of Benjamin and Mary Oakford Bassett, born the 20th of 11th month, 1831, married Barclay, the son of Andrew and Martha Griscom. They have four children—Walter D., Clement B., Richard and Henry Griscom. Rachel A., daughter of Benjamin and Mary O. Bassett, born 11th of 11th month, 1834, married Collins, the son of Samuel Allen, of Gloucester county; they have two children—Samuel and Edgar Allen. Maria and Richard Bassett, children of Benjamin and Mary O. Bassett, were born 22d of 8th month, 1837. Maria married Henry M., the son of George and Margaret Rumsey, of Salem; they have three children—Margaret, George and Mary Rumsey. Richard Bassett married Annie, the daughter of Jonathan and

Lydia Grier; there are two children by this union, Benjamin A. and George G. Bassett. Isaac Oakford Acton, the second son of Samuel and Sarah H. Acton, learned the trade of blacksmith in Pennsylvania; not long after he became of age he commenced the business in Salem, his shop being on East Griffith street. By industry and close application to business, he accumulated a considerable fortune in a few years. His first purchase was on Broadway street; the house and land formerly belonged to Thomas Goodwin. Isaac soon afterward removed to the old brick dwelling, and built a large three-story brick building for dwelling and store; he there kept an iron store for some years. He afterwards took a lot fronting on West Griffith street, being part of the Nicholson lot, belonging to Salem Monthly Meeting of Friends, and erected a large iron foundry, which is carried on by him at this time. Isaac married Lucy Ann, the daughter of Jonathan and Temperance Bilderback, of Mannington; they had three sons—Edward, William and Clement Acton. Edward married Mary, the daughter of Jonathan and Mary Woodnutt, of Mannington. Edward volunteered in the army at the time of the Rebellion, and there died, leaving three children—Walter W., Isaac Oakford, and Jonathan W. Acton. William Acton, the son of Isaac and Lucy Ann Acton, married Mary, the daughter of James and Elizabeth Andrews; they have several children. Clement, the youngest son of Isaac and Lucy A. Acton, married Beulah, the daughter of John and Beulah Tyler, of Greenwich; Beulah is deceased, leaving one child—Lucy Ann Acton. Samuel, the youngest son of Samuel and Sarah H. Acton, born about 1801, learned the trade of a house carpenter, and followed his business for several years. He afterwards followed pumpmaking; he, like his two elder brothers, was uncommonly industrious, and applied himself closely to his business, and has accumulated a competency. His wife is Mary Jane, the daughter of Jonathan and Temperance Bilderback; they had one daughter—Sarah Jane Acton, who married Samuel, the son of Caleb and Ann Thompson Lippincott, of Mannington; she died a comparatively young woman, leaving two children—Mary O. and Sarah J. Lippincott. Joseph, the youngest son of John and Mary Oakford Acton, married Grace, the daughter of Peter Ambler, of Mannington; they had two sons—Joseph and Peter Ambler Acton. The latter was a school teacher, and died a young man, unmarried. His eldest brother, Joseph, learned the trade of wheelwrighting. He married Rebecca, the daughter of James Bradway, of Alloways Creek; they had two children—William and Sarah Ann Acton. William follows the same trade as his grandfather, Joseph Acton, being that of a shoemaker. He has been twice married; his first wife was Mary, the daughter of John Bailey, late of Salem. They had three children—Charles, Rebecca, and Emma Acton. His second wife was the widow of Henry Colgin, daughter of John Riley. Sarah Ann, the daughter of Joseph and Rebecca B. Acton, married John Raphine; she is deceased, and left the following named children—Mary Jane, Josephine, Hannah, William, Charles, Fanny, and Elizabeth Raphine.

ABBOTT FAMILY.

George Abbott and his two brothers, John and Thomas, and their sister, Mary Abbott, emigrated from England, to the State of Connecticut, in the year 1690. George left New England with his wife Mary, and his sister, Mary Abbott, and located themselves in the township of Elsinborough, Salem county, New Jersey. In the year 1696, George Abbott purchased of Joseph, the second son of Samuel Nicholson, the emigrant, 136 acres of land, with buildings, out-buildings, and appurtenances thereunto belonging; it being Samuel Nicholson's country seat. It was located on the north side of Monmouth river, now Alloways creek, it being the lowest farm on the north side of said river, to which was added various pieces and parcels of lands, in succeeding years purchased of the Nicholson family. In 1704, George Abbott removed the Nicholson mansion, built a brick dwelling, and in 1724 an addition, also of brick; this house is still standing, in good repair. It remained in the Abbott family to the fifth generation, a period of 150 years. The said property is now owned by Andrew Smith Reeve.

The children of George and Mary Abbott were Benjamin, born 2d of 1st month, 1700; Hannah, born 30th of 9th month, 1702; George Abbott, Jr., born 13th of 10th month, 1704; Sarah Abbott, born 16th of 2d month, 1709; Samuel C., born 20th of 6th month, 1712, and Mary Abbott, born 26th of 8th month, 1714.

George, the parent of those children, died in the year 1729; his will, now in possession of the family, being admitted to probate in that year, devising his real estate to his son Samuel Abbott. His personal property equally between his two daughters, Hannah and Rebecca Abbott. Mary, his widow, survived him eight years. I have no doubt that Benjamin, George, Sarah and Mary died young and unmarried, as the will of their father makes no mention of them in 1729.

Hannah, I presume, died unmarried. Rebecca, the daughter of George and Mary Abbott, married a man by the name of Howell; he belonged to the ancient Howell family, of Gloucester county. By the will made by Mary, widow of George Abbott, in 1747, her property is devised to her two children, Samuel Abbott and Rebecca Howell; from this I infer, that her daughter had died previously, leaving no issue. Mary Abbott, sister of George Abbott, who emigrated with him from the State of Connecticut, married William Tyler, Jr., who emigrated from England with his father in 1685; he was born 5th of 7th month, 1680.

William and Mary Abbott Tyler, had six children. William Tyler, 3d, born in 1712; Edith Tyler, born in 1714; Rebecca Tyler, born in 1716; Mary Tyler, born in 1718; James Tyler, born in 1720; Samuel Tyler, born in 1723; [See the genealogy of the Tyler family and Thompson and Allen family.] William Tyler, Jr., made his will in 1732 and died the following year. Mary Abbott Tyler, widow of William, survived him several years, afterwards married Robert Townsend, of Cape May, in 1735; by this marriage she had one daughter, Rany Townsend, and she subsequently married a man by the name of Stites. The Stites' are one of the ancient families of Cape May county. After the death of Robert Townsend, his widow returned to Salem county, and lived with her Tyler children; the time of her death is not given. I have mentioned heretofore, that family burying grounds in the first settlement of this country was common; the Abbott family had theirs; it was a few rods east of their old mansion in Elsinborough; it, like many others of the kind, has been passed over by the plough, and no trace of the once honored spot is discoverable. Samuel, the sixth child of George and Mary Abbott, was born 20th of 6th month, 1712; he was the only male descendant; married Hannah Foster, born 21st of 10th month, 1715, daughter of Josiah and Amy Foster, of Burlington county, New Jersey, in the year 1733.

Samuel and Hannah F. Abbott had three children— George Abbott, their eldest son, born 29th of 11th month, 1734; William Abbott, their second son, born 4th of 4th month, 1737; and Rebecca, the daughter, was born 26th of 11th month, 1740. Samuel, their father, departed this life 25th of the 11th month, 1760, at the age of forty-eight years, of cancer of the face. In a volume of Memorial of Ministers and the Distinguished Members of Philadelphia Yearly Meeting, that lived during the last century, I find the following account of Samuel Abbott, although he died comparatively a young man. It shows how highly he was appreciated by his fellow members and others: "He was born of believing parents, who carefully educated

"him in the way of truth, laboring in the ability afforded them
"to bring up in the nurture and admonition of the Lord. His
"father dying when he was still young, the care of providing
"for the family fell upon him. In the responsible station to
"which he was thus raised, he endeavored to act with great
"watchfullness, in uprightness and integrity. His orderly,
"consistent walking amongst men, gained him a good report,
"and by his obedience to the inspeaking word of Divine grace
"he obtained the favor of his heavenly Father. As he contin-
"ued faithful to the manifestations of truth, a further increase
"of the day spring from on high was granted him, and about
"the twenty-second year of his age a gift of gospel ministry
"was committed to his charge. He was led by his beloved
"friends to travel in the different neighboring provinces in the
"work of the gospel, and in love to the souls of his fellow
"creatures, and good accounts of his labors in the churches
"abroad were received by his friends at home. His death took
"place 25th of 11th month, 1760, as one entering into a sweet
"sleep." Hannah, his widow, married Samuel Nicholson, of
Elsinborough, she being his second wife, in 1763. She died
in the year 1793, aged seventy-eight years.

Josiah and Amy Foster, parents of the above named Hannah
Abbott, were residents, as before stated, of Burlington county.
They had a large family of daughters, who married in the
families of the Abbotts, Reeves, Newbolds, Millers, and
Whites, and others, whose descendants now in 1876, distantly
connected, are very numerous in Philadelphia and New Jersey.
Josiah Foster died 1st of 9th month, 1770, aged eighty-eight
years. Amy, his widow, died 15th of 8th month, 1783, aged
ninety-eight years, three months and eleven days.

George, son of Samuel and Hannah F. Abbott, born 29th of
11th month, 1734, the family have no knowledge of, other than
that he signed two marriage certificates recorded in the Salem
Monthly Meeting of Friends, in the year 1756 and 1758. The
presumption therefore is, that he never married, and that he
died before his father, at about the age of twenty-four years,
as he is not mentioned in the will of his father, which is dated
8th month, 1759, nor does his name appear on any record
after the year 1758.

William, the second son of Samuel and Hannah F. Abbott,
was born 4th of the 4th month, 1737, married Rebecca, the
daughter of William Tyler 3d, and Elizabeth, his wife; Rebecca
was born 18th of the 2d month, 1743, and they were married
2d of the 2d month, 1763. They had three children—Samuel,

born 27th of 11th month, 1763; George was born 27th of 9th month, 1765, and Josiah Abbott born 23d of 9th month, 1768. William Abbott, their father, after an active life as a farmer, died in the 1st month, 1800, in the sixty-third year of his age, devising by will dated 1st of 12th month, 1799, the old homestead farm of the family, in Elsinborough, to his eldest son, Samuel Abbott; George Abbott, his second son, a farm which he purchased of Christianna Miller, in the township of Mannington; to his son, Josiah Abbott, the plantation purchased of Mark Miller and Benjamin Wynhook; the said farm is located in Mannington, near Salem. Rebecca, his widow, survived him about six years, and died 28th of 7th month, 1806, aged about sixty-four years. Rebecca, the daughter of Samuel and Hannah Foster Abbott, born 26th of 11th month, 1740, married Joseph, the son of John Brick, Jr., and Ann Nicholson Brick, of Gravelly Run, Cumberland county, 17th of 12th month, 1760. Soon after their marriage they settled on a farm in the township of Elsinborough, that was left to his wife by her father, Samuel Abbott, who had purchased it in 1756 of Thomas and Sarah Morris Goodwin. Joseph and Rebecca Abbott Brick had three children—Ann, Hannah, and Samuel Abbott Brick. Rebecca A. Brick, wife of Joseph Brick, departed this life 16th of the 11th month, 1780, aged thirty-nine years. Ann Brick, their eldest daughter, married Joseph, son of Clement and Margaret Hall, of Elsinborough. [See genealogy of Hall family.] Hannah Brick, daughter of Joseph and Rebecca A. Brick, married Anthony Keasby, of Salem. Samuel Abbott Brick married Ann Smart, daughter of Isaac and Ann Smart, of Elsinborough. Samuel, the eldest son of William and Rebecca Abbott, born 27th of 11th month, 1763, married Marcia Gill, daughter of John and Amy Gill, of Haddonfield, N. J. They were married 24th of 11th month, 1791. Their children were William Abbott, born 22d of 8th month, 1792; Rebecca Abbott, born 29th of 7th month, 1794; and Hannah Abbott, born 3d of 4th month, 1796; Sarah, the fourth child, born 1797, died in infancy. William Abbott, son of Samuel and Marcia Abbott, married Rachel Denn, daughter of James Denn, of Alloways Creek; by her had five children— Ann, Hannah, John, Mary, and Amy Abbott. After the death of William's wife, Rachel, he married Martha Reeve, of Cumberland county; they had no issue. William died 20th of the 4th month, 1835, in his forty-second year. Rebecca, the second child of Samuel and Marcia Abbott, married Andrew, the eldest son of Joshua and Rebecca A. Thompson, of Elsinborough. They were married 1st of 4th month, 1818. She died in 1821, aged twenty-seven years, leaving one daughter, Hannah Ann Thompson, who subsequently married Elisha, son of Elisha and Mary Nicholson Bassett, of Mannington. Hannah, the daughter of Samuel and Marcia Abbott, married Jedediah T., son of David and Rebecca Allen, of Mannington; she was his second wife. They had issue, two children—Hannah and Chambless Allen. Their mother survived her husband several years; she died 25th of 12th month, 1866, aged seventy-one years. Marcia, first wife of Samuel Abbott, died 2d of the 1st month, 1798, aged thirty-four years. Samuel Abbott's second wife was Martha Ogden; married 1st of 10th month, 1809. She was the daughter of Samuel and Mary Ann Ogden, of Pilesgrove. She was born 2d of the 2d month, 1779. They had five children—Mary Ann Abbott, born 20th of the 10th month, 1810; Lydia Abbott, born 21st of the 1st month, 1813; Samuel, born 14th of the 3d month, 1815; George, born 13th of 7th month, 1817; Martha Abbott, born 4th of 4th month, 1811. Samuel Abbott was an active and successful agriculturist, and accumulated a fortune. He died 14th of 4th month, 1835, in the seventy-second year of his age. In the division of his estate, he gave his son, George Abbott, the old homestead in Elsinborough; the same property was purchased by George Abbott, the emigrant, in 1696. Samuel Abbott's widow died 4th of the 5th month, 1848, in her seventieth year. George Abbott, son of William and Rebecca Abbott, was born 27th of the 9th month, 1765. He married Mary Redman, of Haddonfield. George, soon after his marriage, sold the farm devised to him by his father, William Abbott, and removed to the city of Philadelphia, and pursued the business of a druggist. He died at Haddonfield, N. J., 15th of 11th month, 1831, aged sixty-seven years. His wife, Mary, died also at Haddonfield, a short time before her husband. They had five children, who attained their majority. First their daughter, Rebecca R. Abbott, born 2d day of the 5th month, 1798. She married Josiah Holmes, and died without issue 6th of 4th month, 1824.

William, son of George and Mary R. Abbott, born 8th of 8th month, 1800, died at Philadelphia, unmarried, 29th of 12th month, 1867. Samuel W., son of George and Mary R. Abbott, born 18th of 10th month, 1807, married Helen Lambert, of Lambertville, New Jersey, and died without issue at Philadelphia, 27th of 2d month, 1868. James, son of George and Mary R. Abbott, born 29th of 3d month, 1811, went to Philadelphia in 1830, there married Caroline Montelius, 21st of 12th month, 1837. Redman, son of George and Mary R. Abbott, born 28th of 10th month, 1813, went to Philadelphia, there married Susan F. Leaming, of Cape May county. William, son of George and Mary R. Abbott, of the firm of Wood & Abbott, of Philadelphia, was a successful merchant. He never married, and died in 1868, in his sixty-seventh year, leaving a large estate. James Abbott, fourth child of George and Mary Abbott, and his wife, Caroline Montelius Abbott, have six children—Montelius, Francis R., Mary H., Harry James, William J., and Helen D. Abbott. Redman, son of George and Mary R. Abbott, and his wife Susan, have three children—Ellen F., William Louis, and Gertrude Abbott. All four of George Abbott's sons were merchants in the city of Philadelphia.

Josiah, the third son of William and Rebecca Abbott, was born 23d of 9th month, 1768. He married a young woman by the name of Wilson. Soon after his marriage he removed to the city of Richmond, Va., and carried on the hatting business; having at Salem served an apprenticeship to that trade. Josiah and his wife had two children, Josiah and Adaline Abbott; they were born about the years 1792 to 1794. Josiah Abbott, Jr., studied law and practiced for some years; he married and left three children, one son and two daughters. Josiah died in 1850, leaving a widow. His sister, Adaline Abbott, married Thomas H. Drew, of Richmond. They had children.

Mary Ann Abbott, eldest daughter of Samuel and Martha Abbott, was born 20th of 10th month, 1810, departed this life 10th of 1st month, 1844, in the thirty-fourth year of her age. Lydia, the second daughter of Samuel and Martha Abbott, born 21st of 1st month, 1813, and died 14th of 6th month, 1845, aged thirty-three years. Martha Abbott the youngest daughter of Samuel and Martha Abbott, born 4th of 4th month, 1819, married Samuel S. Willets 6th of 10th month, 1841, of Haddonfield, New Jersey; she departed this life 13th of 7th month, 1845, aged twenty-six years, leaving one son, Samuel A. Willets, who subsequently married Abby Evans, daughter of Josiah and Hannah Evans, of Haddonfield. Samuel, the eldest son of Samuel and Martha Ogden Abbott, born 14th of 3d month, 1815, married Sarah Wistar 6th of 5th month, 1846, eldest daughter of Casper and Rebecca Wistar. He was born 20th of 6th month, 1818. Their children are as follows: Mary Ann Abbott, born 24th of 9th month, 1847; their son Casper W. Abbott, born 6th of 12th month, 1848, died aged ten months. Samuel Abbott, 4th, was born 28th of 7th month, 1851. Rebecca and Catharine Abbott's twins were born 26th of 2d month, 1853. Mary Ann, the eldest daughter of Samuel and

ABBOTT FAMILY.

Sarah W. Abbott married, 4th of 12th month, 1872, Josiah, son of Clayton and Martha Wistar, late of Mannington. Samuel and his wife Sarah W. Abbott owns and resides in the township of Mannington on the homestead of his father.

George, the second son of Samuel and Martha Abbott, born 13th of 7th month, 1817, married Ruth S. Baker, 9th of the 10th month, 1845, daughter of George W. and Ruth Baker, of New Bedford, Mass. Their children were Henry B. Abbott, born 5th of 8th month, 1846; Charles T. Abbot, born 12th of 4th month, 1848; George Abbott, 5th, born 11th of 9th month, 1849; William Abbott, born 2d of 9th month, 1852, and died 30th of the 12th month, 1862, aged eleven years. Joseph B. Abbott, son of George and Ruth Abbott, born 26th of 2d month, 1857, and died 30th of the 1st month, 1863, aged six years. William Abbott, sixth son of George and Ruth Abbott, born 13th of 2d month, 1868. George, the son of George and Ruth Abbott, married Elizabeth Lippincott, 9th of 10th month, 1872, daughter of Aquila and Sarah Lippincott. They have one son, Edward S. Abbott, born 2d of 9th month, 1873. George, the son of Samuel and Martha Abbott, sold the old homestead of the Abbott's, located in the township of Elsinborough. Said property was devised to him by his father. George purchased a valuable property in Mannington (it formerly belonged to Whittin Cripps), and resides thereon.

EDWARD BRADWAY HOUSE.
Salem, N. J.   Built 1691.

BRADWAY FAMILY.

Edward Bradway and his wife Mary Bradway, and their three children—Mary, William and Susannah Bradway, together with their three servants—William Groon, Thomas Buckel, and John Allen, embarked from London in the 3d month, in the year 1677, in the ship called the Kent. They landed at Salem, in West New Jersey, in the 7th month following. There is no doubt but that Edward Bradway had considerable means. When he came to this country he had purchased one town lot and one thousand acres of land of the proprietor before Fenwick embarked for this country. As early as 1676 the street now known as Broadway was laid out and called Wharf street, and several town lots were laid out and surveyed on said street; one for Edward Bradway before his arrival, containing sixteen acres, commencing near the public wharf at the creek, and running up the street a certain distance, and from the line of said street a northerly course to Fenwick creek. In the year 1691 Edward Bradway built on his town lot a large brick house which is still standing, for size and appearance surpassing any house built prior to that date, and for many years afterward, in Salem. I think it far excels in size and architecture the two houses built in Philadelphia about the same period—one built by William Penn in Leatita court, and the other built by Samuel Carpenter on Second street, corner of Norris alley. The Governor of this State resided in the Bradway house some time after the death of Edward Bradway; hence it went under the name of the Governor's house for many years afterwards. It is still owned by one of the lineal descendants of Edward Bradway, being the seventh generation.

In 1693 the town of Salem was incorporated into a borough, and the authorities of the town changed the name of Wharf street to Bradway street, in honor of Edward Bradway. Edward had two children born in Salem—Sarah and Hannah Bradway. His allotment of land that Richard Hancock surveyed for him in 1676, by order of John Fenwick, was located on the south side of Alloways creek, joining Christopher White on the west and Wm. Malstiff's land on the east, running 800 rods, starting from the creek, course south thirty-one degrees, east until it reached Henry Salter's 10,000 acre tract. Mary Bradway, the eldest daughter of Edward Bradway, married William Cooper in 1687, who was a blacksmith, and was the first that followed that business in Salem. They had three children born in Salem —Mary was born in 1688, Sarah in 1690, and Hannah in 1692. Edward Bradway, about the year before his death, deeded 300 acres of land to his daughter, Mary Cooper, being part of his allotment in Alloways Creek. He mentioned in his deed of conveyance the natural affection he had for his daughter Mary Cooper, and gave her 300 acres of land, and then describes the boundaries. She was to pay for consideration, if demanded, one ear of Indian corn on the first day of the 9th month, each and every year forever. One of the largest branches of Alloways creek runs by the property; hence the name of Cooper's creek was given it. About eighty years ago the grandson of William and Mary Cooper, whose name was Benjamin Cooper, came from Gloucester and resided on the property a few years, and then sold it to different persons and returned to his native county. William and Mary Cooper, soon after the death of her father, which event took place, I think, in 1693, purchased a large tract of land in the county of Gloucester, where the city of Camden now stands, and removed from Salem to that place in 1694. They had two sons born at that place—William and Edward Cooper.

William Bradway, the oldest son of Edward Bradway, married, in 1691, Elizabeth White, the eldest daughter of Christopher White. She was born in London in 1669, and had four children —Edward, the oldest, was born in 1692; William, their second son, died young; Jonathan, the youngest son, was born in 1699; and their daughter Elizabeth was born in 1701. She married the son of Fenwick Adams, of Penn's Neck. Hannah Bradway, the youngest daughter of Edward Bradway, Sr., was born in 1681. She married Joseph Stretch, who had lately arrived in this country from England. They were married in 1701, and from them sprung the large family of that name in this county. Edward Bradway, the oldest son of William Bradway, became the owner of the property in Salem on Bradway street, and was married about the year 1720. It appears he died a young man, leaving one son named Aaron Bradway, who, in 1745 or '46, married a young woman that owned one-half of Middle Neck in Elsinborough. Joshua Waddington now lives on and owns part of said property. Aaron and his wife Sarah had two children

—Joshua and Sarah Bradway. Joshua always remained single, and after the death of his father—his mother having died when he was quite young—he inherited all her real estate. His sister, Sarah Bradway, married Jonathan Waddington, of Alloways Creek. Jonathan Waddington and his wife had six children, all of them sons, named as follows: William, Aaron, Robert, Thomas, Jonathan and Edward Waddington. Aaron Bradway's second wife was Sarah Smith, widow of John Smith, who was the grandson of John Smith of Amblebury. Aaron and his wife Sarah had one son named Thomas Bradway. Aaron Bradway's third wife was widow Rolph, and by her he had one daughter named Hannah R. Bradway, who afterwards became the wife of David Bradway, of Alloways Creek.

Thomas Bradway became the owner of his father's real estate in Salem on Bradway street by will. His wife was Isabella Dunlap, and I believe they had three children. The oldest was Sarah Ann, who married John S. Wood of Cumberland county; Thomas Bradway and Eliza Bradway. William Bradway, Jr., the son of William Bradway, never married and died young. Jonathan Bradway's first wife was Mary Daniels, the daughter of James Daniels, Sr. They had three children—William the oldest, born in 1728; Rachel and Jonathan Bradway. His second wife was Susanna Oakford, the daughter of Charles Oakford, Jr. They had three children—Edward born in 1741; Sarah and Nathan Bradway. William, the oldest son of Jonathan Bradway, and his wife Sarah, had three children—Adna, the oldest, died a minor; William and Mary Bradway. The latter became the wife of John Thompson of Elsinborough, and was the grand-mother of the present William Thompson of that township. William Bradway, Jr.'s, wife was Mary Ware, the daughter of John and Elizabeth Ware. They had five children. The oldest was Sarah, who married Elisha Stretch, and their children were Mary, Joshua, William, Ann and Job Stretch. Anna Bradway married James Stewart, Jr. Two children were born to them—Hannah and Mary Stewart. Hannah died a young woman, and Mary married William Griscom.

William Bradway, the oldest son of Jonathan Bradway, was born in 1728, and married Sarah Hancock; they had three children—Adny, William and Mary Bradway. Mary's husband was John Thompson, of Elsinborough. They were the grandparents of the present William, Joseph and Casper Thompson. William Bradway, Jr., married Mary Ware, daughter of John and Elizabeth Ware, and they had five children—Sarah, Anna,

Rachel, Ezra and John. Sarah, their oldest daughter's husband was Elisha Stretch. They were the parents of Mary, Joshua, William, Ann and Job Stretch. Ann Bradway married James Stewart. Their children were Hannah and Mary Stewart. The latter was William Griscom's first wife. Anna's second husband was Samuel Fogg, and they had one son, the present William Fogg, who resides at Salem. Rachel Bradway's first husband was Joseph Stewart, the son of Samuel Stewart, of Salem township. Their children were Mary, Anna and Lydia Stewart. Rachel's second husband was David Griscom, who was a teacher of Clermont Boarding School, near Philadelphia, for several years. There were two children, Rachel and David. Ezra Bradway married Mary Denn, daughter of James Denn, of Alloways Creek. They had five children, all of them being sons—William, John, George, Mark and Charles. John Bradway's first wife was Hannah Pancoast, daughter of John and Sarah Pancoast; and his second wife was Clarissa Hancock. They had one son John, who is cashier of the Woodbury Bank.

Jonathan Bradway's second son's name was Jonathan, and he married Elizabeth Stewart, the daughter of John and Mary Stewart. Their children were John, Mark and Thomas Bradway. The last mentioned died young. John married and removed to the State of Ohio. Mark Bradway married the daughter of Thomas Hartley, and they had one son named Thomas H. His second wife was Martha Denn, and had one son named Mark Bradway, who was a merchant for several years at Hancock's Bridge. Thomas H. Bradway was by occupation a tailor, and did a very extensive business in that line for many years. His house and shop were located on Fenwick street, Salem, where William Holtz built his large brick dwelling. Thomas' wife was Rachel Worthington, daughter of David and Jail Worthington. Thomas subsequently purchased a large farm in East Notingham township, Chester County, Pa., and removed there. The farm was much reduced when he bought it, but by his industry and good management it proved to be a profitable investment. He lived to a great age. Most of his children reside there at the present time. Rachel Bradway, the daughter of Jonathan, married Samuel Hancock. There were three children, Rebecca, Prudence and Samuel. Rebecca's first husband was Samuel Padgett; her second, Barzilla Jeffres. Prudence Hancock's husband was Thomas Roberts. He was a merchant and a practical surveyor at Hancock's Bridge during the greater part of his life. Few men had more friends and less enemies at the time of their death than he. Those living there at that time testify that they never witnessed such a large concourse of people of all denominations as attended his funeral, showing that his friends and neighbors duly appreciated his goodness of character, and were desirous to pay their last respects to him on this earth. He left two children, Samuel and Sarah.

Samuel Hancock, Jr. married Hannah Pancoast, daughter of Edward Pancoast, of Gloucester county. They had six children, named Rachel, Clarissa, Beulah, Joseph, Edward and Samuel. Rachel lived past middle age and died single. Clarissa married John Bradway. Beulah was the first wife of David Ogden, late of Woodbury. Joseph married Susan Bacon of Philadelphia, and was for several years a member of the Pennsylvania Legislature, and now is one of the Inspectors of Buildings for the city of Philadelphia. Edward Hancock married Susan Thompson, daughter of William Thompson, of this county. Samuel Hancock's wife was Charlotte Gillingham. He is by occupation a lumber merchant, and is considered to have more than ordinary talents. He was a member of the city council for several years, and now holds the responsible office of City Comptroller for the city of Philadelphia.

Edward Bradway, the oldest son of Jonathan Bradway by his second wife, Susanna Oakford, was born in 1741, and married Elizabeth Waddington. They had six children—David, Hannah, Edward, Waddington, Elizabeth and Adna. His second wife was Susanna Barbour. David Bradway's first wife and mother of his children was Hannah Bradway, the daughter of Aaron Bradway. Waddington Bradway's first wife was Mary Bates, and their children were Edward, Elizabeth and Phebe. His second wife was Hannah Stretch, the daughter of Jonathan and Elizabeth Stretch. They had two children—Jonathan and Mercy Bradway. Jonathan, their son, married Dorcas, daughter of Andrew and Sarah Griscom. They have several children. Mercy Bradway married Jacob Ridgway. Mercy is deceased, leaving two children—Kesiah and Waddington B. Ridgway. Kesiah is deceased. Waddington married Anna, the daughter of John and Rebecca Powell. Waddington and his wife have several children—one daughter and four sons. His third wife was Hannah Bainer, the daughter of Elisha and Lydia Bainer, of Cape May. Their children were Waddington, Hannah, Isaac, Lydia, Susan and Josiah.

Adna Bradway's first wife was Sarah Baker, the daughter of Esther Baker. She owned the property where Quinton Harris now owns and lives. His second wife was Lydia Bainer, daughter of Elisha and Lydia Bainer. Their children were Sarah, Elisha, Adna, Jacob, Edward, Lydia, Jonathan and Elizabeth. Sarah Bradway, daughter of Jonathan, married William Adams, of Penn's Neck. They had two children—Susanna and John Adams. John died young. Susanna was the first wife of the late Benjamin Griscom, of Salem. Sarah's second husband was Richard Ware, who owned the property in Quaker Neck where Josiah Wistar lives. They had two children—Sarah and Elizabeth Ware.

The Waddington family were closely connected with part of the Bradway's. William Waddington arrived in this country from England in 1695. He soon afterwards purchased a tract of land of Edward Wade, being the southern portion of his allotment adjoining Anna Salter's line on that property, and built there and made it his permanent home. He had one son, Jonathan Waddington, who married about the year 1728, and lived on his patrimonial estate. He and his wife had four children—Hannah, Jonathan, Elizabeth, and Jane. Hannah, the oldest daughter, married Walker Beesley. Their children were Walker, Hannah, Benjamin, Mary and Abner. Walker was killed at the massacre of Hancock's Bridge during the Revolutionary war in 1778. Hannah Beesley married her cousin John Beesley. They had two children, Walker and David. Mary Beesley was the wife of Peter Townsend, late of Mannington. Benjamin died young; and Abner Beesley married Mary Mason, daughter of John Mason.

Elizabeth Waddington's husband was Edward Bradway. Jane Waddington married Edward Keasby, Jr. She was his second wife. They had one daughter, Sarah Keasbey, whose husband was John Pancoast, son of Edward Pancoast. They resided for some time after they were married on the farm that was left to her by her father below the village of Canton. Richard Irelan now owns it. After a few years they sold it and purchased a farm of Josiah Reeve, which farm is owned at the present time by Luke S. Fogg. After the death of Jane Keasby they sold the property and removed to Mullica Hill, and there ended their days. Their children were Hannah, Achsah, John, Israel, Jane, David, and Aaron.

The father of Jonathan Waddington, 3d, died 1760, by circumstances not common in this country. On the evening of 18th of 3d month, 1760, the wind being south, it commenced snowing and at sunrise the next morning it was clear, and the snow was three feet deep on the level. I have been informed by persons living at the time, that it required great exertions on the part of those owning sheep to extricate them from under the snow. Jonathan Waddington, Jr., in endeavoring to save his sheep, caught a violent cold and died three or four days afterwards. At his death there was but one infant son by the name of Waddington in this county. Watson, in his Annals of Philadelphia, mentions the account of the same fall of snow I have alluded to. It was the greatest that history gives any account of since the first European settlement.

The family of Coopers have scattered in nearly all the States of the Union, I think; nearly all of them are descendants of William and Margaret Cooper, of Coltshill, in the county of Stafford, England; the following are the names of their children: William, the son of William and Margaret Cooper, was born at Coltshill, 26th day of 9th month, 1660; Hannah, daughter of the same parents, born 21st of 9th month, 1662; Joseph, the son of William and Margaret Cooper, born 22d of 7th month, 1666; James Cooper, son of William and Margaret Cooper, born 3d of the 10th month, 1670; Daniel Cooper, son of the same parents, born 27th of 1st month, 1673. William Cooper and wife emigrated with their children in 1682; he settled in Burlington county. The eldest son, William Cooper, was by trade a blacksmith. He settled at Salem about 1684. He married Mary, the daughter of Edward Bradway. They subsequently moved to Gloucester, where the city of Camden is; he died in 1691, leaving one son and two daughters. He left his father, William Cooper, and his father-in-law, Edward Bradway, executors in his will. Joseph Cooper, son of William and Margaret Cooper, married Lydia Riggs, in 1688. Daniel Cooper married Abigail Wood, in 1693; his second wife was Sarah Spicer, daughter of Samuel Spicer; they were married in 1695; she was the sister of Jacob Spicer. Hannah, the daughter of William and Margaret Cooper, married, in 1704, John Wolston.

BRICK FAMILY.

John Brick was a native of England; he emigrated to Fenwick Colony previous to 1680, and purchased a large tract of land on the south side of the town branch of Stoe Creek, called Gravelly Run; the village of Jericho is on the original tract of land. Samuel Demming, of Maryland, bought the land of John Fenwick in 1679; he, Demming, sold the said land to John Brick, Sr., about 1690. The land was reserved by Benjamin Acton in 1729. John had several children; the oldest was John; there was Joshua, who located himself in the neighborhood of Maurice river; he was the father of the late Joshua Brick of Port Elizabeth. Richard Brick, the third son of John, purchased a tract of five hundred acres in the township of Mannington; it lay adjoining to the Hedgefield tract. He was a large farmer; likewise carried on the tanning and currying business very extensively. He left one son, John Brick; I think he never married. At his death his real estate was purchased by his cousin, Joshua Brick, at Port Elizabeth, and Isaac Townsend of the same place, and they conveyed to the late Jesse Boyd. Samuel Brick, the youngest son of John Brick, Sr., married and left issue. His son Samuel lived for a number of years on his cousin John Brick's estate, in Mannington, and followed the tanning business to some extent, and also farming. He was the father of Josiah Brick, of Upper Penns Neck. The eldest son of John Brick, Jr., inherited all of his father's real estate at Gravelly Run; he became a conspicuous and influential person in the colony, was one of the Judges of Salem courts for many years. At the division of the county, the commissioners thought of making the branch of Stoe Creek, where Seeley mill is located on, the boundary line, but John Brick used his great influence, for them to make the Gravelly run the line, thereby throwing his property in the new county of Cumberland, which he deserved. He married Ann, the daughter of Abel and Mary Tyler Nicholson, of Elsinborough, in 1729. She was born 15th of 11th month, 1707. They commenced life together at Cohansey. They had eight children. The oldest, Mary, born 10th of 2d month, 1730; Elizabeth, John, Joseph, Ann, Hannah, Ruth and Jane, born 10th of 1st month, 1743. John Brick, the father of the before mentioned children, died the 23d of the 1st month, 1758, and his widow, Ann N. Brick, in 1778, at the age of nearly seventy-two years. Previous to his death John Brick purchased a considerable quantity of land in Alloways Creek township, lying on the south side of Alloways creek. Part of a neck of land called Beesley Neck, which he devised to his second son, Joseph Brick, who married Rebecca Abbott, the daughter of Samuel Abbott, of Elsinboro, about the year 1758. Joseph and his wife resided for a short time on his property at Alloways Creek, subsequently removed to Elsinboro on a farm that was left to his wife by her father, Samuel Abbott, who had purchased it, a short time previous to his death, of Thomas and Sarah Goodwin, it being part of Lewis Morris' estate. Joseph and his wife Rebecca had three children—Ann, Hannah, and Samuel. His wife, Rebecca, died 16th of the 11th month, 1780, aged thirty-nine years. His second wife was Martha Reeve, daughter of Joseph Reeve, Jr., and Milicent, his wife. Their home was on the south side of Cohansey, opposite the town of Greenwich, Cumberland county. By her he had two sons—Joseph and John. Ann Brick, his oldest daughter, married Joseph Hall, son of Clement Hall. Hannah Brick married Anthony Keasbey, of Salem. I think he was the son of Matthew Keasbey. Anthony and his wife had eight children—Rebecca, Matthew, Edward, Prudence, Hannah, Artemesia, Anthony and Ann. Samuel Brick, the eldest son of Joseph, married Anna Smart, daughter of Isaac and Ann Smart, of Elsinboro, and had five children—Deborah, Rebecca, Ann, Samuel and Joseph. The last two were twins, and after they arrived at some age went to Philadelphia to learn trades. I think they are both deceased at the present time. Deborah always remained single, and lived to an old age. Rebecca married Paul Hubbs, a native of Pilesgrove, but at the time of his marriage was a resident of Philadelphia. He was the son of Charles and Rebecca Hubbs, of Woodstown. Ann, the youngest daughter of Samuel and Ann Brick, married John Stevenson, Jr., son of John Stevenson, of Mannington. John and his wife, a short time after their marriage, removed to the State of New York. His wife died not long afterwards, leaving one or two children. Mary, the eldest daughter of John, Jr., and Ann N. Brick, born 10th of the 2d month, 1730, married Nathaniel Hall, of Mannington. Elizabeth Brick, the daughter of John, Jr., and Ann N. Brick, was born 4th of the 7th month, 1732. She married, in 1753, John Reeve, of Cohansey. Ann

Brick, the daughter of the before mentioned parents, was born 23d of 1st month, 1738. She married Joseph Clement, of Haddonfield, in 1761. Ruth Brick, daughter of John and Ann N. Brick, was born 1st of the 10th month, 1742, married Benjamin Reeve, of Philadelphia, in 1761. He was a clock and watchmaker, and carried on that business in that city. He was the youngest son of Joseph and Eleanor Reeve, of Cohansey; was born 2d of 7th month, 1737. Joseph, the eldest son of Joseph and Martha Reeve Brick, married Elizabeth Smith, daughter of David Smith, a resident of Mannington. He was a native of Egg Harbor. His wife was the daughter of Jonathan and Mary Shourds Pettit. They removed to Salem county when they were about middle age. Joseph and his wife, Elizabeth Brick, had three or four sons and one daughter. His two oldest, I have been informed, learned the brick laying business. They subsequently became civil engineers, Samuel following his business in the city of Philadelphia, and was quite successful in his calling. Joseph, his brother, removed to Brooklyn, State of New York, and amassed a fortune in his adopted city. He is now deceased, leaving a widow but no children living at the time of his death. Samuel married; he and his wife have several children. They reside on Arch street, Philadelphia. John, the son of Joseph and Martha R. Brick, was a tanner and currier by trade; his place of business was in Church alley; the firm was known as Brick & Eldridge. They carried on their business very extensively forty years ago or more. John married; they had one daughter, and she married Clinton Clement, of Salem. She did not live long afterwards, dying leaving no issue. John died recently in the city of Camden, and was brought to Salem and buried in the Friends' graveyard, where his relatives lay.

WILLIAM BASSETT.
Born 1803.

BASSETT FAMILY.

The family of the Bassetts came from England in the ship Fortin in 1621, and settled near Boston, Massachusetts. Their names were William and Joseph Bassett; many of their descendants remain about Lynn, Massachusetts, and in Rhode Island and Connecticut. One of the family, William Bassett, came from Lynn, Massachusetts, in the year 1691, and settled near Salem, N. J., with his three sons, Zebedee, Elisha, and William. Zebedee, the eldest, subsequently settled in the State of Delaware, and was the ancestor of the Bassett branch in that State; He was born about 1680, married, left two children—Daniel and Rebecca Bassett. Daniel married a young woman by the name of Lawrence. They had five children; their names were Daniel, Zebedee, Elisha, Sarah, and Amy. There is no account of any one of these children marrying, excepting Daniel, who was born 5th of 9th month, 1722; he married Mary Lippincott. They had two children—Daniel and Mary Bassett. Daniel's second wife was Sarah Linch, of Pilesgrove; they were married in 1760; they had four children—Hannah, Sarah, Nathan, and Elizabeth. Daniel Bassett, the son of Daniel and Mary Lippincott Bassett, married Mary, the daughter of Gideon and Judith Scull, of Egg Harbor; they had three children—Gideon, Daniel and Mary. Gideon, their eldest son, died in 1779, aged two years and a half. Daniel had five children by his second wife—Hannah, Elizabeth, Mark, Ebenezer and Ruth Bassett. Nathan, the son of Daniel, married Sarah Saunders, had twelve children—Hannah, Ann, Elizabeth, Deborah, Josiah, Mary, Sarah, Beulah, Mark, Rachel. Elisha Bassett, second son of William Bassett, the emigrant, born about 1682, was about ten years old when he came with his father to Salem. In 1705 he was elected a constable for the town of Salem, and continued in that office eight years. He married Abigail Elizabeth Davis, daughter of John and Dorothea Davis, of Pilesgrove; they had thirteen children. Sarah, the oldest, born in 1719, married Thomas Smith, of Mannington, in 1740; they had three sons—William, David, and Thomas Smith. [See genealogy of Smith family.]

Her second husband was Charles Fogg, of Alloways Creek; there were four children—Sarah, Rachel, Charles, and Aaron Fogg. Elizabeth Bassett, the second daughter of Elisha and Elizabeth Bassett, was born 23d of 2d month, 1720. She married Thomas Davis; they had ten children—Abigail, Elisha, Sarah, Isaac, John, Charles, Elinor, and Elizabeth. Elisha married Hester Scott; had five children. Josiah, the son of Elisha Davis, married Ruth Bradway; they had six children—Ann, Edward, Albert, William, Hester, and Hannah Davis. Elisha Bassett, Jr., son of Elisha and Elizabeth Bassett, was born 15th of 12th month, 1822. He married Mary, the daughter of Joseph Woodnutt, of Mannington; they had six children—Joseph and Rachel both died young; Sarah, the third child, was born 10th of 8th month, 1759. She married Joseph Pettit, son of Jonathan and Mary Shourds Pettit, of Tuckinton. Joseph and Sarah B. Pettit's children were Woodnutt, Jonathan, and Mary Pettit. Hannah, the second daughter of Elisha and Mary Woodnutt Bassett, married John Roberts, of Haddonfield; they had two sons—Jacob and David Roberts. Joseph, the son of Elisha Bassett, Jr., and Mary, his wife, was born 26th of 6th month, 1765. He married Mary, the daughter of David and Rebecca Allen, of Mannington; they had nine children—Elisha, Joseph, David, Hannah, Rebecca, Samuel, Benjamin, William, and Mary Bassett. Davis, the son of Elisha and Elizabeth Bassett, was born 1726; married Mary Elwell, of Philadelphia; they had six children. Samuel, the son of Elisha and Elizabeth Bassett, was born in 1728; he married Ann, the daughter of Lewis and Sarah Morris, of Elsinborough; they had six children. Grace, the eldest, was born 16th of the 3d month, 1756; William was born 4th of the 2d month, 1758; Samuel was born 30th of the 8th month, 1760; Morris was born 30th of 4th month, 1763; Davis was born 3d of the 8th month, 1765; Ann Bassett was born 5th of 1st month, 1767.

Rebecca, the daughter of Elisha and Elizabeth Bassett, married John Page. They had nine children—William, the son of Elisha Bassett, was born in 1733, married Phebe Coppethwaite; their eldest daughter, Mary, was born 18th of 9th month, 1762; Abigail was born 16th of 9th month, 1766. Mary Bassett, the daughter of William, married Isaac Snowden. They had six children. Rachel, the daughter of Elisha and Abigail E. Bassett, born about 1736, married Andrew Miller. Isaac Bassett, the youngest son of Elisha Bassett, was born in 1738, married Deborah, the daughter of Zacheus and Deborah Dunn. She was born 6th of 4th month, 1745; they had three children—Deborah, born 3d month, 1765. She subsequently was a recommended minister. Abigail, the second daughter of Daniel and Deborah Bassett, married Joseph Erwin, M. D. Isaac Bassett lived to a great age, about ninety-six years. His father, Elisha Bassett, born in Massachusetts in 1682, died in Salem county, 1786, aged one hundred and four years. His wife, Abigail Elizabeth Davis, born on Long Island, 1698, being sixteen years younger than her husband. She died agreeable to Salem monthly record 30th of the 12th month, 1770, aged seventy-two years.

Elisha, the oldest son of Joseph and Mary T. Bassett, born 26th of 1st month, 1778, married Mary, the daughter of Darkin and Esther Nicholson, of Elsinborough. They had eight children—David, Josiah, Elizabeth, Elisha, Edward, John T., Albert and Mary; the latter died young. Elisha's second wife was Mary, the widow of Samuel Lippincott, of Gloucester county. She was the daughter of Thomas Clark of the same place. They are both deceased, leaving no issue. David Bassett, his eldest son, married Mary, the daughter of Evi Smith. Josiah Bassett died young. Elizabeth Bassett married Biddle Haines. Elisha Bassett's wife was Hannah Ann, daughter of Andrew and Rebecca Abbott Thompson. They have issue. Edward Hicks Bassett's wife is Hannah, daughter of Evi Smith; they have issue. John Thompson Bassett married Susan Humphreys; they have two daughters. Albert Bassett married Mary Shoemaker. Joseph and David Bassett were twins. Joseph's first wife was Lydia, daughter of Jonas and Elizabeth Freedland, of Quaker Neck. They had four daughters, Elizabeth, Hannah, Lydia and Sarah. Their eldest daughter, Elizabeth, married William G. Woodnutt, and has several children. Hannah Bassett married William, the son of Burtis Barbour; they have issue.

Sarah Bassett, the third daughter of Joseph, married Edward, the son of Samuel and Phebe Hall, formerly of Mannington. They have issue. Lydia Bassett, the youngest, married John Zerns, of Pennsylvania. They have two children, William and Elizabeth. Joseph Bassett's second wife was Sarah, daughter of Morris and Lydia Hall, of Elsinborough. They had one son, Morris Bassett. Joseph's third wife was Ann, the widow of Caleb Lippincott. They are both deceased, leaving no issue. Few men left behind them a more enviable character than Joseph Bassett for his industry, integrity and upright dealings with his fellow-men. David Bassett, his brother, married Vashti Davis, of Pilesgrove. They had five children—Joseph, William,

Hannah, Davis and Samuel; I think three of them died unmarried. Hannah married Samuel P. Allen, a native of Gloucester; they have children. Davis Bassett married Martha Lippincott; they had one daughter, Martha Vashti Bassett. David's second wife was Hannah, daughter of Woodnutt Pettit. She lived but a short time, leaving no issue. David's third wife was Ann Packer; she survived her husband several years. By that union there was no offspring. Hannah, daughter of Joseph Bassett, Sr., married Jonathan, son of Samuel and Amy Pettit Cawley; she lived but a short time, leaving one daughter, Amy, who subsequently married Charles, son of Samuel Lippincott, of Pilesgrove.

Rebecca, the second daughter of Joseph and Mary Bassett, married Casper, son of John and Charlotte Newbold Wistar, of Mannington. Their children were named Sarah, Joseph, Charlotte, Mary, Bartholomew, Casper, Catherine, Rebecca, Joseph and John. I think five of them died young—Joseph, Charlotte, Bartholomew, Hannah and John. Sarah married Samuel Abbott, of Mannington; they have issue. Mary Wistar's husband is Casper, son of John and Esther Thompson, formerly of Elsinborough; they have two children—Bebecca and Casper Thompson. The wife of Casper Wistar, Jr., is Emma, the daughter of Aaron Fogg. Catharine Wistar married Job Bacon, of Cumberland county. Joseph Wistar's wife is Anne, the daughter of James Brown.

Samuel, the son of Joseph Bassett, Sr., married Mary Ann, daughter of George Craft, formerly of Gloucester county. There were several children. Amanda Bassett married John Snowdon; her second husband was a Baptist clergyman named Cornell. Rebecca married Richard Ware. Benjamin Bassett married Mary, the daughter of Samuel and Sarah Acton; they had five children—Clement, Sarah Ann, Rachel, Richard and Maria; Clement died young. Sarah Ann married Barclay, son of Andrew Griscom; they have issue. Rachel Bassett married Collins, son of Samuel Allen; they have issue. Richard Bassett's wife is Anne, daughter of Jonathan Grier. Maria Bassett married Henry M. Rumsey.

William, the youngest son of Joseph and Mary Bassett, born in 1803, married Abigail, daughter of Stacy Hazleton, of Mullica Hill, Gloucester county. They had eight children—Stacy, Joseph, Charles, Sarah Ann, Clara, William Irving, Thomas F. and Fenwick.

Mary, the youngest daughter of Joseph and Mary Bassett, born in 1806, married George Craft, Jr., of Gloucester county.

George and his wife are both deceased, leaving four children—Edwin, Beulah, Mary and George. Edwin's wife is Elizabeth, daughter of Aaron Gaskill, of Philadelphia. They have issue. Beulah Craft married Joseph Garretson; they have two children. Mary Craft's husband is Foster Flagg. There are three children—Lydia, Maria and George. George, the youngest, married Ann Jessup; they have one daughter, Ann Craft. There are but two living of the large family of children of Joseph and Mary Bassett at this time, Rebecca Wistar and William Bassett.

7

CARLL FAMILY.

The Carll family is a large and influential one in Salem and Cumberland counties. Ephraim Carll emigrated from Germany to this country about the year 1720, and subsequently married and left two sons—Jesse Carll, the eldest, was born in 1733, and his second son, Phineas, in 1735. The latter subsequently married and removed to Cumberland county, near Cohansey Neck. He and his wife had a large family of children, and their descendants are very numerous. The wife of the late Edmund Davis, of Bridgeton, was one of them. Jesse Carll, born in 1733, married Grace Hancock, in 1756; she was the daughter of Edward Hancock, the son of John and Mary Chambless Hancock. The latter reached America in 1680, in company with her mother, Elizabeth Chambless, who came to meet her husband, Nathaniel Chambless, who had emigrated to this country in 1675, in company with John Fenwick. Jesse Carll lived on a small farm containing about sixty acres of upland, and a quantity of meadow which his wife Grace had inherited from her father. (The property was recently owned by George M. Ward.) They had twelve children—Hannah, Elizabeth, Lydia, Grace, Ephraim, Sarah (who died young), Prudence, Jesse, William, John, Sarah, and Martha. Jesse Carll, their father, died in 1806, and his wife in 1808. Both of them were buried in Friends' graveyard, on the north side of Monmouth river, where his wife's ancestors were interred. By industry and economy, qualities characteristic of the Germans, they accumulated a large personal estate, and supported a large family of children in a comfortable manner. It has been related that John Wood, the father of the late John S. Wood, having purchased one of the large tracts of timber land near his Jericho property, needed a considerable sum of money to meet his payments. Having been unsuccessful in effecting a loan from those whom he believed most likely to have money, he was advised to apply to Jesse Carll. Wood replied that he had little hope of getting it from that quarter, inasmuch as Carll had a large family to support upon the income derived from the small property owned by his wife. He, however, applied to Jesse Carll for the loan, and upon being asked the amount of money he wished, replied: "*Three hundred pounds.*" "I can accommodate you with that sum," said Carll, "and more if you wish," and he accordingly counted out to him the required amount in gold and silver coin, which he had laid away in his own house, as was the custom with those who had money in those days before banks were established. Such a practice at the present day would be very hazardous, notwithstanding the boasted advancement of the present generation in civilization and Christianity. After this event, John Wood was frequently known to remark that when he needed money it was his rule not to apply to those who made the greatest display, but to those of industrious and economical habits, who made no ostentatious show.

Hannah, the eldest child of Jesse and Grace Carll, born 24th of 8th month, 1757, died a young woman, unmarried. Elizabeth, another daughter, born 17th of 11th month, 1758, married Abner Fitzpatrick, whose grandfather emigrated to this country from the north of Ireland; they now spell the name Patrick. Elizabeth and her husband had six children—Mary, Phineas, Abner, Jesse, Samuel and Elizabeth. Lydia, the daughter of Jesse and Grace Carll, born 14th of 12th month, 1760, married Edward Keasbey 3d, son of Bradway Keasbey. Their children were Sarah, Prudence, Grace, Joseph, Elizabeth, and Edward. Grace, the daughter of Jesse and Grace Carll, born in 1762, married Thomas Ware, of Cumberland. They had four children—Asbury, Jacob, Hannah, and Lydia. Ephraim, the eldest son of Jesse and Grace Carll, born 17th of 11th month, 1764, married Barbara, the daughter of Joseph and Sarah Acton. (Joseph was the son of Benjamin Acton, Jr., and grandson of Benjamin Acton, who emigrated to New Jersey from England about the year 1690.) Ephraim and his wife, Barbara, had eight children—Edward H., Joseph A., Hannah, William, Ephraim, Grace, Jesse, and Mary. Ephraim Carll, Sr., died in 1803, and was buried in the same graveyard in which his parents were interred. Sarah, the daughter of Jesse and Grace Carll, born in 1766, died a minor.

Prudence Carll, the daughter of Jesse and Grace, born 14th of 5th month, 1768, married Bradway Stretch, and had one daughter—Martha Stretch. Jesse, son of Jesse and Grace Carll, was born 14th of 12th month, 1760, and his wife was Mary, the daughter of Edward Hancock, Jr. He and his wife lived and owned the property that belonged to her father and grandfather, formerly part of William Hancock's allotment of 1,000 acres, bought by him of John Fenwick, and surveyed to him by Richard Hancock in 1676. At the death of William Hancock, which took place in 1679, he devised all his landed estate to his widow, Isabella Hancock. In 1681 she sold 500 acres to John Maddox, an eminent Quaker, who emigrated to this country in 1680. In the year 1700, John Maddox sold that part of the property lying next to Monmouth river, to Jeremiah Powell, of Salem, and the southern portion adjoining the Salter tract, to John Hancock, the son-in-law of Nathaniel Chambless. Jesse and his wife, Mary Carll, had five children—Rebecca, Elizabeth, Sarah, Lydia and William Carll. William, the son of Jesse and Grace Carll, born in 1773, died a minor. John, the son of Jesse and Grace Carll, born in 1775, died a young man, unmarried. Sarah, the daughter of Jesse and Grace Carll, born 15th of 7th month, 1778, married Job Sheppard; they had two sons—John and William Sheppard.

Martha, the youngest child of Jesse and Grace Carll, born 15th of 8th month, 1780, married William Waddington, the oldest son of Jonathan, Jr., and Sarah Waddington. William and his wife had six children—Anna, Sarah, William, Martha, Hannah and Jesse Carll Waddington. Mary, the daughter of Abner and Elizabeth Patrick, married Washington Smith, the son of Captain William Smith, of Revolutionary memory. Captain Smith commanded a company of the American Militia, which led the advance when the British troops quartered at Judge Smith's house, on the north side of Quinton's Bridge, were attacked by order of Colonels Hand and Holme. He was forced to retreat however, there being a greater number of the enemy's troops in ambuscade than his commander anticipated; but he accomplished his retreat with credit, and to the satisfaction of his superior officers. His horse was shot and killed under him during the engagement. Washington and his wife Mary Smith had ten children—Mary Ann, Peter, Elizabeth, John P., Abner, Lucetta, Phineas, Martha, Lydia and Washington Smith. Peter Smith married Elizabeth, the daughter of James Elliott; they have issue. Samuel Smith, his son, married Priscilla, the daughter of Samuel Kelley; she died young. His second wife was Lydia, the daughter of David and Elizabeth Finley; they had issue. Ephraim, the son of Peter and Elizabeth Smith, married Hannah, daughter of Luke S. Fogg and Ann his wife. Ephraim and his wife have issue. Peter, the son of Peter and Elizabeth Smith, married Ellen, daughter of James and Rachel Baker; they have issue. Thomas Jefferson Smith is a physician, and resides at Bridgeton.

Elizabeth, the second daughter of Washington and Mary Smith, married Oliver Smith; they were first cousins. They had three daughters—Arthalinda, Sarah Elizabeth and Ann. Arthalinda died a young woman unmarried; Sarah Elizabeth married William, the son of Abner and Hannah Patrick; Ann, the youngest, married Philip Y. Keen. The wife of John P., the second son of Washington and Mary Smith, was Hannah, daughter of Joseph Allen. John and his family removed to the State of Illinois many years ago, and both he and his wife are deceased at this time, leaving four sons—Joseph A., Benjamin, Washington and Phineas. Abner, the son of Washington and Mary Smith, married Mary Ann, the daughter of Nathaniel and Susan Stretch. Abner died several years ago, leaving a widow and one daughter, Susan Smith, who married Charles, the son of George Hires, Sr., of Salem. Lucetta, the daughter of Washington and Mary Smith, married Richard, the son of Thomas Mulford. They have four children—Phebe, Ann Maria, Mary and Martha. Phebe Mulford is Luke S. Fogg's second wife; they have no issue. Ann Maria Mulford married Richard, the son of Benjamin and Susan Irelan, she being his second wife; they have issue. His first was Phebe, daughter of Jesse and Mary Carll; she died leaving one daughter, Phebe, since deceased. Mary Mulford's husband is A. Smith Reeves, son of Charles and Mary Reeves; they have issue. Martha Mulford married George A. Githens; they have issue.—Phineas, the son of Washington and Mary Smith, married Margaret, the daughter of Daniel Green; she died young, leaving one son, Phineas Smith, Jr. Phineas' second wife was Phebe Sally; they have one daughter—Margaret Smith.—Martha, the daughter of Washington and Mary Smith, married Abner, the eldest son of Jesse and Ann Patrick. Abner and his wife had one daughter, Elizabeth, who subsequently married George Hires, Jr. Lydia, the youngest daughter of Washington and Mary Smith, married John Mills. They have a large family of children—Martha, who married Elias Hicks Powell, the son of John and Rebecca Powell; Joel, Lucetta, Albert, Chambless, Mary, Filmore, Kate, Washington and Thomas Mills. The wife of Washington, the youngest son of Washington and Mary Smith, was Hannah Sack. They reside in Kansas, and have four children—Elizabeth, Mary Ann, Hannah and Phineas.

William, the son of Oliver Smith, who was a son of Captain

William Smith, was twice married. His first wife was the daughter of Ephraim Carll, Sr. His second wife was Rebecca Finley, daughter of John Finley; they had four children—Mary, the oldest, married Samuel Patrick; they had one son, Winfield S., who married the daughter of Peter Harris; Mary died young. Rebecca, the second daughter of William Smith, married Samuel Patrick, his second wife, and who was a sister of his first wife; they have issue. Hannah S., daughter of William and Rebecca Smith, married Anthony English, the son of David S. English, formerly Sheriff of Salem county. Both died young, leaving three children; their names were William S., David S., and Charles Leslie. Charles Leslie Smith, son of William and Rebecca Finley, married the daughter of Daniel and Phebe Hood; they have had two children—Elmer H., and William. James Smith, the son of Oliver Smith, married Sarah, the daughter of Edward and Prudence Waddington. James is deceased, leaving three sons —Edward W., Oliver and Keasbey Smith; all three of them are married. Edward, the eldest, married Anna, the daughter of Lewis Fox; they have children. Oliver, the second son of James Smith, married Hannah, the daughter of Joseph H. and Rachel A. Fogg; they have two children. Keasbey Smith, married the daughter of Job Thorp; they have children.

Abner, the son of Abner and Elizabeth Carll Patrick, was born the 3d of 2d month, 1788. There was a singular consanguinity in his marriage which does not often occur. His first wife was Barbara Carll, the widow of his uncle, Ephraim Carll. There was no issue by that connection, and she died many years before him. His second wife was Hannah, the widow of his brother, Samuel Patrick, and the daughter of his first wife, she being the daughter of Ephraim and Barbara Acton Carll. Abner and Hannah Patrick had four children—Elizabeth, born in 1822; Margaret, born in 1825; William, born in 1827; and Hannah, born in 1831. Elizabeth Patrick married Lewis, the son of William Fox; they had three children—Anna, the eldest, married Edward, the son of James and Sarah Smith; they have issue. Hannah, the second daughter, married Josiah, the son of Richard Dubois; they have children. Abner, the son of Lewis and Elizabeth Fox, married Amanda Giberson; they have issue. Mary Ann, the daughter of Abner and Hannah Patrick, married Robert, the son of James Butcher. By that union there were four children—Elizabeth, James, Hannah and Arthalinda. Elizabeth married Robert, the son of Job Griscom. James Butcher's wife is Lydia, the daughter of Peter and Mary C.

Harris; they have issue. Hannah, daughter of Abner and Hannah Patrick, married Benjamin O. Robinson, the son of William Robinson, Sr.; they have issue. Abner Patrick, the father of the above mentioned children, died in 1834, aged about forty-four years; his widow, Hannah Carll Patrick, daughter of Ephraim Carll, Sr., departed this life in 1859, aged sixty-four years and a few months.

Edward, the eldest son of Ephraim and Barbara Carll, died when he was about fifteen years old, and William Carll, the second son, departed this life in 1807, aged about eleven years. Ephraim Carll, son of Ephraim and Barbara, born 30th of 8th month, 1798, married Elizabeth, the daughter of John Finley, of Stoe Neck; they had three daughters. The oldest, Rebecca, married William Plummer, Jr.; they have several children. Elizabeth, their eldest daughter, married George Hires, Jr., she being his second wife. Sarah, their second daughter, married George R. Morrison, the son of William and Mary Ann Morrison. George and his wife have issue. The other children of William Plummer are Rebecca, William and Loren. Barbara, Ephraim Carll's second daughter, married James Butcher, Jr.; they have two children—Hannah and Isabella. The latter died young. Hannah, their eldest daughter, married Edward, the son of Joseph and Mary Brown; they have issue. James Butcher, Jr., came to an untimely death by a kick from his horse. Subsequently his widow, Barbara C. Butcher, married Charles, the son of Edward and Catharine Fogg. Charles and his wife have issue. Elizabeth, the daughter of Ephraim and Elizabeth Carll, married William, the son of Jonathan House, of Upper Alloways Creek; they have issue. Ephraim Carll's second wife was Mary Ann, the eldest daughter of Washington and Mary Smith, by whom he had six children, who are now living—Edward, Jessie, Lewis, George, William Henry, and Charles. Edward Carll, their eldest son, married Phebe, the daughter of Reuben Sayres; they have three children—Mary Ann, Milton, and Sarah.

Jesse P., the son of Ephraim and Mary Ann Carll, married Phebe, the daughter of David and Elizabeth Finley. Jesse and his wife had three children—Rosanna, James W., and Isabella Carll; his second wife is Lucetta, the daughter of John and Lydia Mills; they have issue. Lewis, the son of Ephraim and Mary Ann Carll, married Arthalinda, the widow of Henry Clay Miller; she is the daughter of James Baker. Lewis S. and his wife have four children—Luke S., Lucius, Henry M., and Lucy Carll. George C., the son of Ephraim and Mary Ann Carll, is a physician, and resides in the county of Cape May. His wife is Maggie, the daughter of Jonas Miller, of that county. George and his wife have issue. William Henry Carll married Elizabeth, the daughter of Charles and Mary Reeves; they have children. Charles, the youngest son of Ephraim and Mary Ann Carll, married Louisa Githens, the daughter of George Githens, Sr. She is deceased, leaving one daughter—Anna G. Carll. Grace, the daughter of Ephraim and Barbara Carll, was born 10th day of 10th month, 1800; she married William Mulford, of Roadstown, Cumberland county; their children are Mary Elizabeth, George, and Ephraim Mulford. Jesse, the son of Ephraim and Barbara Carll, was born 20th of 1st month, 1803, and married Mary, the daughter of Sylvanus Sheppard; there are five children—Ephraim, Mary, William, Sylvanus, and Hannah Ann Carll. Sylvanus was drowned in Alloways creek before he was of age, whilst going with his father to fish for shad in Delaware bay. Ephraim, the son of Jesse and Mary Carll, married Prudence, the daughter of David and Elizabeth Finley; they had four children—Sylvanus, Winfield, Laura, and Mary. Mary, the daughter of Jesse and Mary Carll, married Peter, the son of Benjamin and Martha Harris; they have four children—Lydia, Hannah Ann, Mary Elizabeth, and Benjamin. Lydia married James Butcher, the son of Robert Butcher. The husband of Hannah Ann is W. Winfield, the son of Samuel Patrick. William, the son of Jesse and Mary Carll, married Mary, the daughter of William Harmer, of Greenwich. His second wife was Harriet Applegate; they had one son—William. Hannah Ann, the youngest daughter of Jesse and Mary Carll, died a young woman, unmarried.

Sarah, the daughter of Edward and Lydia Keasbey, married Aaron Waddington, the son of Jonathan and Sarah Waddington; they had issue—Sarah Ann, Lydia, Joshua, Bradway and Jane Waddington. Sarah Ann Waddington, married John Hill, of Salem, son of Vining Hill, of Lower Penns Neck; they have issue—Sarah, Ellen and John. Lydia, daughter of Aaron and Sarah Waddington, married Jonathan, the son of Samuel and Jerusha White, of Pilesgrove; her husband is deceased, leaving one daughter—Gertrude. Joshua, the son of Aaron and Sarah Waddington, married Anna Vanneman; they have issue—Pauline, Luella, Ernest, Sarah, Florence, Laura and Jane. Bradway Waddington married Mary, the daughter of Samuel and Jerusha White; they had two children—Adelaide and Frank. Jane Waddington married James Fonda; she is deceased, leaving one child—Adelaide Fonda.

CHAMBLESS FAMILY.

Nathaniel Chambless, and his son Nathaniel, embarked for this country in the year 1675. They were servants of Edward Wade. About 1680 he purchased 250 acres of land of his former employer, being a part of the allotment Edward Wade bought of John Fenwick before he embarked for this country. In 1681, his wife Elizabeth and daughter Mary embarked from London in the ship Henry, and landed at Elsinborough in the 7th month of the same year. Soon after his wife came they settled on his property in Alloways Creek. He about that time bought 250 acres more, adjoining his first purchase, of Joseph Wade. Both comprised the greater part of what is now called Alloways Creek Neck. In 1688 their daughter Mary married John Hancock, who emigrated to this country in 1679. He was a native of England. John and his wife had nine children. Their eldest son, John Hancock, was born 10th of 1st month, 1690, in Alloways Creek Neck. The names of their other children were William, Elizabeth, Mary, Sarah, Nathaniel, Edward, Joseph and Grace. Some persons suppose that they were of the same family of Hancock's as those by that name who resided in Elsinborough and Hancock's Bridge. There is no evidence that any relationship existed. Notwithstanding Nathaniel Chambless and his son Nathaniel were servants when they first came to this country, by industry and by maintaining high moral character, both became eminent men in religious and civil society in the early settlement of Fenwick Colony.

Nathaniel Chambless, Sr., was left executor of the great estate of his intimate friend, Rudoc Morris, of Elsinborough, who died in 1701, and also guardian of his minor children. Several other of like trusts he was chosen to do, showing conclusively that the men who lived in that generation had implicit confidence in his ability and integrity. There is no record that he and his wife ever had but two children—Nathaniel, and Mary, who married John Hancock. I think he died about 1710. They formerly spelled their name Chamness, but the family a generation or two afterwards changed it to Chambless.

He deeded, before his death, 100 acres of land to his daughter, Mary Hancock; the residue of his real estate to his son, Nathaniel Chambless.

James Chambless, son of Nathaniel and Eleanor Chambless, was born 22d of the 1st month, 1689. Mary was born in 1692. Elizabeth was born in 1700. Hannah was born in 1702. Nathaniel Chambless, 3d, was born in 1705. Rebecca Chambless, the daughter of James Chambless, was born 3d of 11th month, 1716. She afterwards married Jedediah Allen, son of Ephraim Allen. Soon afterwards Jedediah purchased, I believe, John Rolph's estate in Mannington. It contained 500 acres, and was located on the south side of Mannington creek, adjoining Job Ridgway's land. Jedediah and his wife, Rebecca, had three sons—Jedediah, David and Chambless. The latter's occupation was that of a tailor, and he lived the greater part of his life in the city of Philadelphia. The land in Mannington was divided equally between the two oldest sons, Jedediah and David.

James Chambless, Jr., son of James and Mary Chambless, was born 29th of 1st month, 1721. About the year 1742 he married Mary Fetters. They had three daughters named Sarah, Mary and Rebecca. Sarah's husband was William Smith, the oldest son of Thomas Smith, of Mannington. Mary Chambless' husband was David Smith, the brother of William. They lived in the town of Salem, where he followed his trade, being a hatter, and continued in that business until his death. Nathaniel Chambless, 3d, married Susan Oakford, the daughter of Wade Oakford, in 1725. They had one daughter named Sarah Chambless. When about eighteen years old, she married William Hancock, the son of John Hancock, the man who was instrumental in having a bridge built across Alloways creek as early as 1720—hence the name of the Bridge. The village derives its name from him. He was a large landholder at the time of his death. He had 500 acres that he inherited from his mother, Isabella Hancock, being one-half of William Hancock's allotment that he purchased of John Fenwick in the spring of 1675, before he came to this country. John Hancock purchased in 1720 of James Thompson, of Elsinborough, 250 acres. On said property was the family burying ground of the Thompson family, and by tradition John Hancock himself was buried there, and his son William, and his wife, Sarah Chambless Hancock, were likewise interred there. It afterwards went under the name of the Hancock burying ground. The Thompson family, after the second generation, buried at Salem. A good fence made of boards enclosed the graveyard within the memory of many persons living at the present time. I believe within a few years past the fence has been removed, and the plough has passed over the remains of some of the foremost emigrants in point of intelligence and moral worth that settled in West Jersey. But that graveyard is not an exception; all ancient family graveyards that I know of in this county have shared the same fate. The Sharp's, Bradway's, Stretch's, Oakford's, and Abbott's—all of those families had family graveyards towards the close of the 17th century, not a vestige of which remains at the present day. John Hancock also purchased a large tract of land in Penn's Neck. All his real estate his son William inherited at his death. William Hancock and his wife, Sarah Chambless Hancock, had but one child, named Sarah. She afterwards became the wife of Thomas Sinnickson, of Penn's Neck. Soon after their marriage they became residents of the town of Salem. Thomas' occupation was that of a merchant. They left no children. I have frequently been asked: "Where is the Chambless family at the present time?" The answer is: "The name is lost on account of the last two of the male line. James Chambless, Jr., and Nathaniel Chambless, 3d, having no sons; their children were daughters. Their descendants are the Smiths, Allens, Bassetts, Foggs, and many other families that I could name." William Hancock, in 1755, deeded a half-acre of ground in the village of Hancock's Bridge to the Society of Friends to build a meeting house upon, it being a more convenient location than where the old house stood. The house was accordingly built the year following; it was of brick, and is still standing in a good state of preservation. All accounts of him justify the opinion that he was a man of more than ordinary mental abilities. His father gave him more school education than was common at that time. His wealth and learning enabled him to have a great influence in the county. He was a member of the Colonial Legislature for twenty years in succession. His first wife dying before she arrived at middle age, he in his old age married Sarah Thompson, daughter of Joshua Thompson, of Elsinborough. She was many years younger than himself. During the Revolutionary war part of the American militia quartered in his house at Hancock's Bridge. In the 3d month, 1778, one of the most cruel and murderous massacres of the war occurred at that house; William Hancock himself received a mortal wound. His brother-in-law, Joshua Thompson, the same day took him to his house, about half a mile from the scene of carnage, and there he died of his wounds in a short time, leaving a young widow, and one son by his last wife. The son's name was John Hancock, who, at the death of his father, was about five years of age. John, when he arrived to manhood, married Eleanor Yorke, an amiable and interesting young woman, daughter of Andrew Yorke, of Salem. John and his wife had four children. Sarah Hancock was the oldest; she married Morris Hancock, of Elsinborough. Henrietta married Lewis P. Smith, formerly of Bucks county, Pennsylvania. Thomas Yorke Hancock married Rachel Nicholson, daughter of William Nicholson, a native of Mannington. Maria Hancock married Richard Parrot Thompson, of Salem, son of Hedge Thompson.

CATTELL FAMILY.

William Cattell, it is generally thought, came from Shrewsbury, East Jersey, and settled at Salem about the year 1747. His occupation was that of a merchant. He and his wife had two children, as recorded in the monthly meeting books of Salem. Elijah, the son of William and Ann Cattell, was born 27th of 7th month, 1751. Mary Cattell, daughter of the same parents, was born 24th of 9th month, 1757. Elijah, it appears, was a clerk for his father until the latter's death; their place of business was at the corner of Market and Broadway street. After the death of Elijah's father (William Cattell), Elijah Cattell and William Parrott entered into partnership. During the war of the American Revolution, Elijah left the Society of Friends, of which he was born a member, and took an active part against the mother country; he was considered as ardent a patriot as there was in the town of Salem. He married Hannah Ware, she being a descendant of one of the oldest families of the Colony. There were four children—Ann, Margaret, Thomas W., and Maria Cattell. Ann Cattell, the eldest, married William Mulford, a native of Greenwich, at that time a resident of Salem; they had several children. [See Mulford family.] Margaret, daughter of Elijah and Hannah W. Cattell, married David Williams, of Salem; they had issue—Robert, Anna, and Sarah Williams. Maria, the youngest daughter of Elijah and Hannah W. Cattell, never married, and the only one of their children living.

Thomas Ware Cattell, son of Elijah and Hannah W. Cattell, was born in 1790. He possessed an amiable disposition, and an uncommon active mind; was above ordinary men in mathematics. His fellow citizens of Salem had full confidence in his integrity and ability as a calculator, therefore he was elected Assessor of Taxes, which office he held for upwards of twenty years. He was engaged in the mercantile business, nearly all of his long and useful life; was a partner at one time with his brother-in-law, William Mulford, a good business man, on Market street. Afterward, he and the late Clement Acton kept a hardware store and lumber yard for many years. Thomas, after the firm dissolved, confined himself exclusively to the hardware store, and so continued until near the close of his life. His death occurred in 1867, being seventy-seven years old. He was a great loss to the public, as well as to his immediate family; also to the Presbyterian church, of which he had been, the latter part of his life, an active and consistent member. Thomas, when a young man, married Kesiah, the daughter of Alexander and Esther Gilmore, of Lower Penn's Neck. She died several years before her husband. They had seven children—Alexander G., Elijah, Esther, Thomas, Sarah, William and Samuel Cattell.

Alexander Gilmore Cattell, the eldest son of Thomas and Keziah Cattell, was born in 2d month, 1816. He has been a merchant from early life, first in his native town of Salem, afterwards he and his brother Elijah Cattell went into the grain business on Delaware avenue, in the city of Philadelphia. They at once took a leading part in that especial trade in that city. Alexander in early life, took an active part in the public affairs in his native county and State, being affable, and pleasing in his address, which he inherited from his father, also a ready debator in public assemblies. These qualifications soon made him conspicuous. When the inhabitants of the State of New Jersey believed the time had come to have a new Constitution, Alexander G. Cattell, though a young man, was chosen one of the members of the Convention to frame a new one, so as to submit it to the voters of the State for their adoption, or rejection. He at once became an active member from the southern section of the State. He brought forward a section in which he was anxious to be incorporated in the new Constitution, and advocated it with much ability. That was the biennial session of the State Legislature, but it was rejected by the Convention. If it had become a part of the Constitution, it would have been a great saving to the State in a pecuniary way, besides a great deal of useless legislating. He was subsequently elected a member of the State Legislature, and afterwards chosen a member of the United States Senate, in which he served one term. During the latter part of it his health gave way, but upon becoming convalescent, he was sent by the United States Government on an important mission to England, respecting the finances of the country. After he removed to Philadelphia, he took an active part in the commercial affairs of that city; was one of the first that originated the Corn Exchange Bank, and was elected President of that institution. He married when young, Eliza Gilmore, a lady of refinement, daughter of Samuel Gilmore, of Lower Penn's Neck; she being his cousin; she has been deceased three or four years, leaving no issue. Alexander and Elijah Cattell have each built handsome residences in Merchantville, Camden County, where they reside.

Elijah Cattell, second son of Thomas W. and Kesiah Cattell, married Catharine Hardy of Philadelphia; they have three children—Margaretta, Alexander and Edward Cattell; his occupation I have already mentioned in his brother Alexander's history. Esther, the oldest daughter of Thomas and Kesiah Cattell, married Joseph Fithian, M. D., a resident of Woodbury, Gloucester county. He is a native of Cumberland county; they have two daughters—Josephine and Sallie Fithian.

Thomas, the third son of Thomas W. and Kesiah Cattell, married Anna Ashburner; they have seven children—Jane, Hetty, Mary, Lillie, Sallie, Willie and Fannie Cattell. Thomas Cattell, Jr. as likewise all of Thomas W. Cattell's children, had the talent they inherited from the Cattell and Gilmore families, that of acquiring school learning readily; far superior to the majority of students. He is one of the Professors of Lincoln University, located in Chester county, Pa.

Sarah, the second daughter of Thomas and Kesiah Cattell, married Henry B. Ware, of Salem, son of Bacon and Anna J. Rumsey Ware. Henry was educated at West Point. After he was through with his studies was elected Clerk of Salem Bank; continued in that office until his uncle George Rumsey's death; he was then elected Cashier, in the place of his uncle, which office he filled with credit until his physical health became very much impaired and he resigned, but was continued one of the Directors until his death. Henry and his wife, Sallie Cattell Ware, had three children—Anna, Thomas and Alexander Ware. Sallie, his widow, is still living and holds the office of Postmistress at Salem at the present time.

William, the fourth son of Thomas W. and Kesiah Cattell, married Lizzie McKeen; they have two children—James and Harry Cattell. William holds the important office of President of Lafayette College, at Easton, Pa. Samuel, the youngest son of Thomas and Kesiah Cattell, married Henrietta Malliard; they have ten children—William, Thomas, Samuel, Kesiah, Elijah, Henrietta, Barron, Josephine, Joseph and Frank Cattell.

COLES FAMILY.

The family of Coles, it appears was an ancient family of England; one of them became a member of the Society of Friends; to avoid religious prosecution, he emigrated to West New Jersey and purchased a large tract of land in Evesham township, Burlington county. Samuel Cole, the eldest son married, had two or three daughters. Martha, the eldest, married David, the son of Judge David Davis, of Pilesgrove, Salem county. Samuel's daughter Mary, married a Newbold. David and Martha C. Davis had three children—Jacob, Joseph and Martha Davis. Samuel Cole made his will in the year 1772, leaving a large real and personal estate, after providing liberally for his widow, Mary Cole, he devises the greater part of his estate to his grand-children, Jacob, Joseph and Martha Davis, also to his daughter Mary Newbold's children, and likewise a legacy or two to his nephew Thomas Coles, eldest daughter Mary Coles fifty pounds, and he also directs his executors, his son-in-law David Davis and his friend Abraham Allen, to pay fifty pounds to Haddonfield Preparative Meeting of Friends.

About 1750 Thomas' nephew, Samuel Cole, left Evesham and located in Gloucester county, at a place since known as Coles Mills. He soon afterwards married Alice Collins; they had eight children, their names were: Mary, Hannah, Thomas, Samuel, Kimble, Joseph, Hope and Alice Coles, all of whom grew up, married and had issue. Mary, the eldest daughter of Thomas Coles, married Jonathan Collins, by whom she had seven children, whose names were: Alice, Benjamin, Samuel, Mercy, Elizabeth, Jonathan and Thomas. Hannah, the second child of Thomas and Alice Coles, married Peter Strang; they resided in the immediate neighborhood and raised ten children —Thomas, Sarah, Alice, Margaret, Peter, Charles, John, Deborah, Hannah and David. Thomas, the third child of Thomas and Alice Coles, married Martha Stiles; they raised twelve children—Thomas, William, Bartholomew, Elizabeth, Martha, Ann, Samuel, Joseph, Alice, Mary, Ephraim and Sarah.

He came in possession of the mill property which consisted of about 2,000 acres of land on which he lived until 1808, when he bought a mill property on Oldman's creek at what is now known as Harrisonville. He then moved to that place with his large family of children, where he was engaged in the lumber business until his death, which occurred in the year 1826. Samuel, the fourth child of Thomas and Alice Coles, married Elizabeth, the daughter of Joseph Pimm; they had three children—Joshua, Sarah and Samuel. Kimble, the fifth child of Thomas and Alice Coles, married Kesiah, the daughter of John Lippincott, of Evesham, Burlington county; they had children—Maria, Eliza, Julianna, John, Benjamin, Charles and Harriet. Joseph, the sixth child married Margaret Scott, of Pilesgrove, and settled on a farm near what is known as Richman's Mills, where they raised five children, whose names are: Elizabeth, Joseph, Margaret, Sarah and Esther. Hope, the seventh child, married Abijah Collins, and raised five children—Joseph, Isaac, Abijah, William and Hannah. Alice, the eighth and youngest child, married Israel Locke, of Repaupo, Gloucester county, but afterward moved to Pilesgrove, Salem county, where they raised eight children—Thomas, Susan, Hannah, Elizabeth, Harriet, Alice, Martha and Samuel.

Alice, the eldest child of Mary and Jonathan Collins, married John Peterson, of Pilesgrove. Benjamin and Sarah never married. Mercy, the fourth child, married Jesse Lenard, from near Blackwoodtown, Gloucester county, but left no issue. Elizabeth is living in Philadelphia, not married. Jonathan never married, is living in Philadelphia. Thomas, the seventh and youngest child of Mary and Jonathan Collins, died near Eldridge Hill, in Pilesgrove, and left two children—Mary and Alice; they live in Philadelphia.

Thomas, the eldest child of Hannah and Peter String, married Hannah Albertson, with whom he removed to Ohio in 1815. Sarah, the second child, never married. Alice married Alexander Scott; they lived near to Coles' mill, and raised six children—William, Esther, Hannah, John, Peter, and Thomas Scott. Margaret married Joseph Morgan, of Blackwoodtown, Gloucester county; they had children, but lost them when young. Peter, the fifth child of Hannah and Peter String, first married Elizabeth Pimm, and was the father of four children—Martha, Thomas, Joseph, and William. After her death he married Sarah, the widow of Ephraim Garwood, of Pilesgrove. He lived to an advanced age. The sixth child, Charles, married Rhoda Peterson. He was a farmer and lived at what is now known as Springtown, and raised three children, whose names are Amos, Charles, and Stacy String. John String, the seventh child of Hannah and Peter String, married Amelia Stiles; they had children—Hudson, Margaret, Peter, and Thomas String. Deborah, the eighth child, married a man by the name of Clark, and moved to Ohio soon after. Hannah married George Stiles. David, the tenth and youngest child, married Deborah, the daughter of Micajah Conover, and moved to Illinois.

Thomas, the oldest child of Thomas and Martha Coles, married Rachel Birch, and raised eight children—Richard, Samuel, Ephraim, Asa, Martha, Deborah, Alice, and Thomas Coles. He died in the year 1822, where his brother Bartholomew now lives. William, the second child of Thomas and Martha Coles, married Rebecca, daughter of Samuel Morgan, of Pilesgrove. He lived on the farm now occupied by his son, Richman Coles, until his death, which occurred in 1862. They raised seven children, whose names are Samuel M., Thomas, Rebecca, William, Martha, Richman, and B. Franklin Coles. Bartholomew, the third child, married Anna Wister, and raised nine children—Harris, Thomas, Uz, William, Bartholomew, Chalkley, Joseph, Stacy, and Ira Coles. He is still living, and is over ninety years of age. I visited this aged man recently, and found him quite healthy. He told me he cut, during last winter, fifty loads of wood. Elizabeth, the fourth child, married Elijah Horner, by whom she had eight children, whose names were Susan, Martha, Eliza, Caroline, Alice, George, Mary Anna, and Elma. He was a farmer, and lived near Mullica Hill, Gloucester county. Martha, the fifth child, married Edward Pancoast, of Pilesgrove. She died in a few years, and left one son—Stacy, who died young. Ann, the sixth child, first married Joseph Lippincott, and by him had three children—Joshua, Thomas, and Lydia. She afterwards married John Howey, and had one child—Sarah Ann. Samuel, the seventh child of Thomas and Martha Coles, married Marianna Morgan, of Blackwoodtown, Gloucester county, to which place they moved, and raised three children—Elizabeth Ann, Joseph, and Thomas Coles. Joseph, the eighth child, married Margaret, daughter of Samuel Morgan, of Pilesgrove, but died in a few years after, leaving one child—Martha Ann Coles. Alice, the ninth child, married William Garwood, of Mullica Hill, Gloucester county; had one child—John Garwood, and died soon after. Mary, the tenth child, married Israel Kirby, and raised six children—Eli, Ann, Richard, Thomas, Mary, and Charlotte Kirby. Ephraim, the eleventh child, first married Lydia, daughter of Isaac and Tracy Ridgway, who died without children. He then married Rebecca Lippincott, and raised eleven children, whose names were Lydia, Hannah, Eliza, Lippincott, Emily, Aaron, Charles, Ephraim, Joseph, Rebecca, and Francis. He is still living, near Woodstown. Sarah, the twelfth and youngest child of Thomas and Martha Coles, married Nathan Gaunt and raised four children, whose names are Joseph, Nathan, Sarah, and Alvin Gaunt.

Joshua, son of Samuel and Elizabeth Coles, married, but raised no children. Sarah, their second child, married Daniel Harker, she had three children—Elizabeth, Benjamin and Samuel. Samuel, their youngest child, married Anna Kirby; he died young, leaving one child—Elmer K. Coles. Maria, daughter of Kindle and Kesiah Coles, married William Cassady, and raised six children, whose names are Lippincott, Mariah, Beulah, Elmina, William and Edward. Eliza, the second child of Kindle and Kesiah, married William Jones, by whom she had one son—Hiram Jones; she afterwards married Daniel J. Packer, of Woodbury, and had three children—Daniel J., Edward and Benjamin. Elizabeth, the eldest child of Joseph and Margaret Coles, married Cornelius DuBois, and raised ten children—Benjamin, Mary, Joseph, William, John, Elizabeth, Cornelius, Elwood, Edward and Samuel. Joseph, the only son married Rachel Richman, and have six children—Martha Jane, Henry, Preston, Mary Ella, Resigna and Harriet. Margaret married Joseph Harker, and had two children—James and Amy. Sarah married Matthew Rippe; they moved to Indiana in 1853. Esther, the youngest child of Joseph and Margaret Coles, married Samuel Dickinson, and died, leaving one child—Joseph Dickinson.

Susan, daughter of Israel and Alice Locke, married Amon Peterson, by whom she had six children—Stacy, Joseph, Hannah, Thomas, Amon, and Martha. She lives in Woodstown. Elizabeth married Josiah Smith; she is deceased, leaving several children living in the vicinity of Salem. Alice married Joseph Morgan, (she is deceased,) and raised four children, three of whom are living—Samuel R., Joseph, and Israel Morgan. Samuel Locke married Abigail, daughter of Moses Richman; he died without issue. Martha married Zaccheus Bassett; she lives near Daretown, and has children.

Samuel Coles, son of Thomas and Rachel Coles, married Henrietta Dilks. He by profession is a miller, but lives retired at Mullica Hill, Gloucester county. No children. Ephraim married Phebe, daughter of John Davis; their children's names are Mary, Ann, Lydia, Charles, and Isabella. He is also a miller, and lives at Dickinson's Mills, near Woodstown. His son Charles is associated with him. Charles has been Collector of Pilesgrove township for some years. Asa married Patience Hurff, of Hurffville, Gloucester county. He is a farmer, and lives near Harrisonville; has six children—Anna, George, Charles, Mary, Rebecca, and Asa. Martha married Josiah Duffield, and lives near Sharpstown, Salem county; has three children—James, Benjamin, and Caroline.

Samuel M., the eldest son of William and Rebecca Coles, never married, but lives with his mother at Harrisonville.— Thomas R. Coles, first married Charlotte Watson, who had four children—Charles, Samuel, Henry and Marianna; his second wife is Lydia, daughter of John Duell and widow of Stacy Coles; he is a farmer and lives near Paulding's Station, West Jersey Railroad. Rebecca, married Isaac C. Stevenson, they live at Wenonah, Gloucester county, and have two children —Charles and Sarah. William M. Coles, married Lydia, daughter of Samuel Duell; he is a farmer living in Pilesgrove, and has five children—Ida, Cooper, Ella, Emma and Clarkson Coles, Martha married William Moore, they have four children. Richman married Lydia, daughter of Mark Horner; he is also a farmer living on the homestead farm, and has two children— Ellen and Susanna; Richman is now a member of the Legislature of New Jersey. B. F. Coles, the youngest child of William and Rebecca Coles, married Katurah, daughter of S. H. Weatherby; he is a merchant and lives at Englishtown, Monmouth county.

Harris, oldest son of Bartholomew Coles, married Mary Hurff. He is deceased, leaving several children. Thomas, the second son, died a young man. Us, the third son, first married Hannah Ballenger, and afterwards married Mary Ballenger. He is a farmer, living near Daretown, Salem county, and has five children—Jane, Isaac, Anna, Mary, and Sarah Coles. William, the fourth son, married Louisa Whitaker. He was a farmer, and died recently, leaving two children—William and Nancy Coles. Bartholomew, the fourth son of Bartholomew and Anna Coles, married Rebecca, the daughter of Malachi Horner, of Gloucester county. He is also a farmer, living near Whig Lane, in Upper Pittsgrove, and has six children—Anna, Edward, Eleanor, Martha Amy, George, and Stacy Coles. Chalkley Coles, first married Martha Ann, daughter of Joseph and Margaret Coles; his present wife is Elizabeth, daughter of James and Marianna Horner; they have but one child living—Maggie. Joseph Coles first married Elizabeth, daughter of Asa Moore;

afterwards married Postrema Groff; they have three children by his first wife; he is a farmer and lives in Gloucester county. Stacy Coles married Lydia, daughter of John Duell; he died and left one son—John D. Coles. Ira, ninth and youngest son of Bartholomew and Anna Coles, married Martha Ann Adcock; they have no children; he is a farmer and lives where his father has lived for nearly sixty years.

Joseph, the oldest son of Samuel and Mariam Coles, married Harriet Bateman, of Blackwoodtown; he is a farmer and has no children. Thomas Coles first married Sarah ———. She died and left two children; he then married Eliza Kirkbride; she also died and left one child. Thomas lives at Blackwoodtown. Lydia, the oldest child of Ephraim and Rebecca Coles, married George Carter; she died and left several children. Hannah Coles married Richard Springer, of Bridgeport; she is living a widow with several children. Eliza Coles married John Bishop; they have a farm near Elmer, on which they live with three children. Lippincott Coles married Mary Duell and have two children. Charles Coles is married and lives in Indiana. Aaron Coles married Ella, daughter of Barclay Edwards; has no children. Ephraim Coles married Mary Ann Kirby; he was killed by the explosion of a steam engine; left no children. Joseph Coles married a daughter of Joseph and Rachel Coles. Rebecca married Henry Coles and have children. Francis Coles married William, son of George Avis; he is a miller and lives at Daretown.

DAVIS FAMILY.

John Davis emigrated from Wales and settled in Long Island. He married Dorothea Hogbin, an English woman of large wealth. He belonged to the sect called Singing Quakers, worshiped daily on a stump, and was very pious and consistent. He lived to the extreme old age of one hundred years. A number of years before his death, he moved with his family to Pilesgrove township, Salem county, near where Woodstown is now located, about 1705. His eldest son, Isaac, came to New Jersey first; John soon after, with his family, also came. The latter and all his family subsequently became members of Friends' Meeting. Isaac, his eldest son, married and had one son, who was shot by accident or otherwise, not mentioned in the record; he also had two or three daughters. The names of John Davis' other children were John, David, Malachi, Abigail, Hannah, and Elizabeth; all born on Long Island. David Davis, the third son, became the most prominent of any of his sons, and his descendants are the most numerous. He was appointed, by the Legislature, a Justice of the Peace; an office at that time conferred only on those who had qualifications for the position, intellectually and morally. David was subsequently appointed Judge of Salem county Courts, and was one of the four Friends who assisted in organizing Pilesgrove Meeting, about 1724 or 5, previous to which time Friends in Pilesgrove were members of Salem Meeting. He certainly was a man who left his footprints on the sands of time. His wife was Dorothea Cousins, born in England, 19th of 11th month, 1693, and lived to the age of ninety-six years. David Davis, at the time of his death, was sixty years of age. David owned a large tract of land near the Presbyterian church of Pittsgrove. He built himself a large brick house on his property, which is still standing, and he resided there until his death. Thomas Chalkley writes that in 1740 he had a religious meeting at the house of David Davis, and benches were brought from a neighboring meeting house. I presume it was the Presbyterian church, which was near by, and at that time was built of logs. He further states that the meeting was large, and the people were orderly. David and Dorothea Davis had seven children—Sarah, Mercy, Amy, Hannah, David, born 31st of 10th month, 1730; Abigail, born 20th of 9th month, 1732; and Jacob, born 22d of 4th month, 1734. Sarah, the eldest daughter, married William, the son of Andrew Griscom; they had two daughters—Hannah and Deborah. Hannah Griscom married a Clement; they had two daughters—Elizabeth and Sarah. Elizabeth Clement married James B. Cooper; they had one daughter—Hannah Cooper. Deborah Griscom married John Stewart, of Cumberland county, the son of John and Mary Wade Stewart, of Alloways Creek. She was his second wife, and survived her husband many years. Mercy, the daughter of David and Dorothea Davis, married Thomas Redman, of Haddonfield, being his second wife.

Amy, the daughter of David and Dorothea Davis, married John Gill, of Haddonfield; they had six children. Mary, their eldest daughter, married a Roberts; Elizabeth Gill married a Burroughs; they had issue. Amy Gill married a Willis; they had one daughter—Elizabeth Willis, who married Benjamin Cooper. Mercy Gill, the fourth daughter, married Samuel Abbott, of Elsinboro, Salem county, the son of William Abbott; they had three children—William, Rebecca and Hannah. Sarah Gill married a Whital, at Red Bank. John Gill, the son of John and Amy Gill, married Ann Smith; they had one son—John Gill, Jr., his wife is Sarah Hopkins; John is President of the National State Bank, Camden. Hannah Davis, the daughter of David and Dorothea Davis, married Richard Wood 2d; he was the son of Richard and Priscilla Wood, was born 18th of 1st month, 1728, in Salem, now Cumberland county. When he was married, some say, he resided in Philadelphia, at which place he learned the coopering business, but he lived the greater part of his life in the town of Greenwich, where he followed his trade, and at that place their two children were born. Richard, the son of Richard and Hannah D. Wood, was born 2d of 7th month, 1755, and James, the son of the same parents, was born 30th of 8th month, 1765. Richard Wood, son of Richard and Hannah Davis Wood, married and had one son—David Wood, who died single. Richard's second wife was Elizabeth Bacon, the daughter of Job and Mary Stewart Bacon, the latter was the second wife of Richard Wood 2d. George Bacon Wood, M. D., was the eldest son of Richard and Elizabeth B. Wood; he married Caroline Hahn, who died, leaving no issue. Richard Davis Wood, the second son of Richard and Elizabeth B. Wood, married Julianna

Randolph, of Philadelphia; he is deceased, leaving seven children—Richard, Edward, Randolph, Julia, Mary, George B., Stewart and Walter Wood. Charles, the third son of Richard and Elizabeth B. Wood, married a Randolph, and at his death left five children—Elizabeth, George B., Naomi, Minnie and Francis Wood. Horatio C., the son of Richard and Elizabeth B. Wood, married Elizabeth Bacon; their children were Richard, Horatio, M. D., John, George G., James, Mary Ann and Elizabeth Wood. Horatio's second wife was Abigail Evans, daughter of William Evans, they have one son—William Evans Wood.

Hannah Davis Wood, daughter of Richard and Elizabeth B. Wood, married David Scull, she being his second wife. Ann Elizabeth, the youngest daughter of the above parents, married John E., the son of John and Mary M. Sheppard. She died young, leaving one son—George W. Sheppard. James, the son of Richard and Hannah Davis Wood, married Ruth Clement. He resided in Philadelphia, and was a merchant, and being successful in business, he acquired a competency and retired to Haddonfield. James and his wife had five children, of whom Richard C. Wood, their eldest son, Rebecca and Samuel are dead, the latter died young and single. Hannah Ann Wood married Isaac Tyson, of Baltimore. They had five children—Richard W., Jesse, Isaac, James and Hannah Ann Tyson. James, the youngest son of James and Ruth Wood, married Jane Hicks.

David, the son of David and Dorothea Davis, born 1730, like his father, was a large land-holder. His wife was Martha Cole, by whom he had several children. Joseph, their son married Mary Haines, and they had two daughters—Martha and Anna Davis. Martha's husband was William Folwell; they had one son—Joseph D. Folwell. Anna married David, the son of John and Sarah Pancoast. They are both living at this time in Woodstown, and have several children. David, the son of David and Martha Cole Davis, married a Haines; they had issue. Martha, their daughter, married Andrew Griscom, the son of Benjamin Griscom, of Salem; they had six children. Anna, the daughter of David and Mary Davis, married Allen Fenimore. Joseph Davis, the son of David, married a Collins. The second son of David and Mary H. Davis is named David Davis. Jacob, the son of David and Martha C. Davis, married Elizabeth Coulson; there were four children by that marriage. David C. Davis married Mary Engle, daughter of Asa Engle; they had several children. David is deceased. Mary C. Davis died single.

Jacob, the son of Jacob and Elizabeth Davis, married a Lippincott. Hannah Davis married Jonathan D. Smith; they have issue.

Mary Davis married William Rogers, and their children were Rachel, Joseph, and Grace Rogers. David Rogers married Lydia Evans; Grace Rogers married Thomas Ballinger; Rachel Rogers married Zebedee Willis. Jacob, the son of Jacob and Dorothea Davis, born in 1734, married Esther Wilkins, of Evesham, who was born 1736. Jacob and Esther were married at Woodstown, 21st of 5th month, 1761, and had seven children —Hannah, the eldest, born 30th of 4th month, 1762, died in 1765; David Davis, their son, born 19th of 8th month, 1763; Jacob Davis, Jr., born 5th of 6th month, 1765, died 1767; Thomas Davis was born 13th of 3d month, 1768; Josiah Davis, born 24th of 10th month, 1770, died 1776; James Davis, born 21st of 2d month, 1773, died 1776; Esther Davis was born 18th of 5th month, 1778. Esther Davis, their mother, died 8th of 3d month, 1785, aged about fifty-nine years. Jacob Davis remarried Mary Stratton 10th of 8th month, 1792, and she died 3d of 2d month, 1809. Jacob died in 11th month, 1820, aged eighty-six years and four months. Few men have left behind them as pure and unblemished a character as he. Esther, the daughter of Jacob and Esther Davis, born 1778, married Joshua Lippincott, in 1800. I think he was the son of Joshua Lippincott and grandson of Freedom Lippincott. They had two daughters—Beulah and Lydia Lippincott; the latter subsequently married David Scull. David, the son of Jacob and Esther Davis, born 1763, married Hannah Scull, sister of Gideon Scull. David and his wife Hannah had two sons and one daughter; both of the sons died young, and their daughter, Hannah Scull, married George Hollingshead, and had one son and three daughters, as follows: David S. Hollingshead, who is in the mercantile business at Woodstown; Mary, who died a few years ago; Martha and Margaret Hollingshead, who are also both deceased. David Davis' second wife was Abigail Howey. They had one son, Dr. David M. Davis, who married Sallie Ann Smith, daughter of James and Hannah A. Smith, formerly of Mannington. James, her father, is now living in Salem, at a very advanced age. Dr. David M. and Sallie Ann Davis have eight children. Thomas, the son of Jacob and Esther W. Davis, born 1768, married Esther Ogden, in 1796, and by her had ten children—Samuel, the eldest, died young; Martha died single; Mary Ann Davis married William Johns, of Woodbury, who died, leaving no issue by her; Jacob married Sarah Ann, daughter of Samuel Nicholson, of Mannington. They had three children—William, Martha, and Hannah Davis. Josiah, the son of Thomas and Esther Davis, married Mary Mulford; they had four children—James, William M., Joseph, and Thomas Davis; the latter is deceased. Thomas W., the son of Thomas and Esther Davis, married Phebe Townsend, of Philadelphia. They had five children—Joseph T., Esther, Thomas, Robert, and Henry Davis. Esther, the daughter of Thomas and Esther Davis, died single. There were Richard W. and Sarah Davis; the latter married William Walcott, and they had one daughter —Francis] D. Walcott.

DUBOIS FAMILY.

Lewis Dubois, who emigrated to America, was born about the year 1630, and settled up the North river, in Ulster county, N. Y., where a number of his countrymen had also come to escape religious persecution. They were called Huguenots, being followers of Calvin. The great persecution, amounting almost to extermination of the Protestants, is generally referred to the revocation of the edict of Nantes, which took place in 1685, in the reign of Louis XIV. Lewis Dubois married Catharine Blancon; she was born at Manheim, in Germany, where he had gone to escape persecution. It appears, by the record of him after their marriage, they returned to France again, and in that country their son, Abraham Dubois, was born in 1638; soon after that event they left Strasburg for this country, and settled in Ulster county. Their son, Jacob Dubois, was born in 1662. About the year 1714 Jacob had heard there was a large quantity of good land for sale in the southern part of New Jersey. He left his native county in New York and moved to this State to view the lands he heard so much of. Daniel Cox, of Burlington, after he married Rebecca Hedge, the widow of Samuel Hedge, Jr., came in possession of a large quantity of good land in Fenwick's tenth. He owned large tracts of land in what is now Pittsgrove township. Jacob and his sister, John and Isaac Vanmeter, purchased 3,000 acres of the said Daniel Cox, of this tract. The three last persons in the year 1716 conveyed 1,200 acres to Jacob Dubois as his portion. There is no account of Jacob Dubois ever living in New Jersey, but he divided the property he bought of Daniel Cox among four of his sons. Barrett Dubois, one of his sons, settled at Pittsgrove soon after his father had purchased the land in said township. It appears he was married in the State of New York previous to his coming to Salem county; he had eight children. Catharine, their daughter, was born in 1716; Jacob in 1719; the latter married Janite Newkirk in 1747; he was a prominent church member of the Presbyterian society, and was a deacon and one of the trustees to whom the deed was given for the ground to erect the church building upon. Lewis, the third son of Jacob Dubois, was born at Hurly, in Ulster county, N. Y., in 1695. His wife was Margaret Janson; they were married in 1720. He emigrated to West Jersey in company with his brother Barrett, and soon after became the possessor of real estate amounting to 1,091 acres; his first purchase was in 1726 of 350 acres in Alloways Creek township, having bought it of Joshua Wright. It was the land that William Hall bought of James Wasse, of London, in 1706, being part of the Wasse tract of 5,000 acres that lay on the borders of the head water of Alloways creek. Lewis and his wife were among the first members of the large and influential congregation of Pittsgrove in 1742, at the time of the first organization of the Presbyterian society at that place. At that time he sold to the trustees of the church two acres of land for forty shillings, to erect a church building upon for the use of said society, and in 1761 he sold fifty acres of land for a parsonage for seventy-five pounds proclamation money, in addition to the fifty acres the society purchased in 1744 of Abraham Newkirk. One of Jacob Dubois, Sr.'s sons emigrated about the time his brother came to this county to Lancaster county, Pa., and made it his permanent home and one of his grand-sons became an eminent Presbyterian minister. Jacob Dubois, son of Lewis, had eight children; his oldest son, John, married Sarah Dubois, grand-daughter of Barrett Dubois; Mary, their oldest daughter, married William Robinson, of Lower Penn's Neck; they had six children—Benjamin, William, Rebecca, Margaret, Noah and John. The two last mentioned died single. Benjamin married, I have been told, and left two children. William and his wife left six children—William, Noah, James, Mary, John and Benjamin. Rebecca, the oldest daughter, married a man by the name of Patterson. I have no knowledge whether she left any children. Margaret Robinson's husband was Samuel Copner, the son of Joseph Copner, of Penn's Neck. The Copner's were an ancient family of that township, together with the Dunn family and several others, were the prominent members of the Presbyterian church, located near Pennsville. For some cause I never have learned, he left the church of which he was a member the greater part of his life, and joined the Friends' Society, and near the close of his life made a will, and devised one-half of his homestead farm to the Society of Friends; he left two children—Samuel, and one daughter, who married a Sinnickson; she left two children—Cynice Sinnickson and the late Ann Simpson.

Benjamin Dubois married Mary Robinson, sister of Wm. Robinson, Sr., and had six sons and two daughters. All of them, after their father's death, removed to one of the Western states. Solomon Dubois, the youngest son of Jacob Dubois, was a native of Pittsgrove; he purchased lands in Alloways Creek township, and married the daughter of Richard Moore; they had five children, four daughters and one son; their names were Martha, Mary, Susan, Rebecca, and Richard Dubois. Martha married Benjamin Ireland; she died young, leaving one daughter—Ann. She married a person by the name of Corlis; they had no children. Mary, second daughter of Solomon, died single. Susan Dubois, daughter of Solomon, married Nathaniel, the son of David Stretch. Susan died, leaving one daughter—Mary Ann Stretch. Rebecca Dubois died single. Richard Dubois, son of Solomon, married Sarah, daughter of Ephraim Sayre; she died, leaving one daughter—Ann Dubois. She married Joseph Fogg; she is deceased, leaving issue. Richard's second wife was Hannah Ann, daughter of Thomas Sayre; they had four sons—Solomon, Thomas, Richard, and Josiah Dubois. Solomon, the eldest, married Kesiah Bowen; they had three children—William, Elizabeth, and Ruth Dubois. Solomon, the father of the above mentioned children, was killed by a mowing machine while he was mowing. Thomas, the son of Richard and Hannah Ann Dubois, married Elizabeth Stretch; they had one daughter—Hannah Ann Dubois. Thomas' second wife is Sarah Jane, daughter of John W. and Sarah Ann Maskell; they have no issue. Richard Dubois, Jr., married Elizabeth, the daughter of Thomas Mulford; they have four children—Luella, Hannah, Rachel, and Oakford Dubois. Josiah Dubois, youngest son of Richard, married Hannah, daughter of Lewis Fox; they have three children—Mary Jane, Anna S., and Thomas S. Dubois. Richard Dubois, Sr.'s, third wife is Mary Decroy; they have no issue. Solomon Dubois' second wife was widow Hedley; they had one son, Jacob Dubois, who subsequently married Ann Patterson; they had two children—John and Emeline. Jacob's second wife was Charlotte F. Miller; they had issue, two children—Mary and Charles Dubois. Mary is deceased.

ELWELL FAMILY.

The Elwell family of this county, particularly those who have resided in the township of Pittsgrove, have had a large influence both in religious and civil society. Jacob Elwell, the emigrant, was born in England, in the year 1700. He settled in Pilesgrove township soon after he arrived in this country; he married Catharine Dubois, whose parents were French Huguenots and had left France on account of religious persecution, and settled in Canada on Lake Ticonderago. She and her mother were captured by the Indians, and recaptured by her father, who followed the trial after three days of great anxiety and toil, which we can easily imagine, the party in pursuit succeeded in killing two of the Indians. Soon after that event, Jacob Elwell removed from Canada with his family to Salem county, and soon afterwards purchased land of Daniel Cox, of Burlington, in Pilesgrove township, and settled there. Catharine Dubois, his daughter was at that time about twelve years old. Jacob and his wife, Catharine Dubois Elwell, had five children—David, Samuel, Jonathan, Rhoda and Rachel Elwell. David, their eldest son, married, had five children, their names were Jacob, Cornelius, David, Youmacea and Mary Elwell. Samuel, son of Jacob and Catharine D. Elwell, married Amelia Morgan; they had five children—Samuel, Mary, Sarah, Amelia and Sarah Elwell. Jonathan, son of Jacob and Catharine Dubois, married Peggy Summerill, daughter of William Summerill, the emigrant; they had six children—William, Jacob, Jonathan, Catharine, Rachel and Sarah Elwell. Rhoda Elwell, daughter of Jacob and Catharine D. Elwell, married Henry Richmond; they had three children—Jacob, Henry and Isaac Richmond; they all died minors. After her first husband's death, Rhoda married William Ray; they had two children—Bigee and Henrietta. Rhoda's third husband was Josiah Paullin; there were two children—William and Mary Paullin. William, the son of Josiah and Rhoda Paullin, died recently aged about eighty-two years. I have no knowledge of his family. Mary married. Rachel, the daughter of Jacob and

Catharine Dubois, married James Hutchinson; they had no issue. James turned a tory in the war of the Revolution, and was compelled to leave the country, leaving his wife in charge of his mother. He lived but a short time afterwards; his widow subsequently married Jonathan Sneighin.

Samuel, son of Samuel and Amelia Elwell, married Mary Johnson, [See Johnson family.] Mary Elwell married Isaac Johnson, youngest son of John Johnson. [See Johnson family.] Sarah, the daughter of Samuel and Amelia M. Elwell, married Charles Chambers; they had issue—Charles, James and Richard Chambers. Amelia, the daughter of Samuel and Amelia Elwell, married Andrew Urion; they had four children—Samuel, Elizabeth, Amelia and Sarah Urion. Samuel Urion, their son, is now a resident of Lower Penn's Neck, and a large land owner, and is considered one of the best agriculturists in that section of the country; he married Sarah, the daughter of the late Elisha Wheaton. Sarah, daughter of Andrew and Amelia Urion, married Asa Reeves; they have issue. Amelia, daughter of Andrew and Amelia Urion, married William Brown; they have children. Elizabeth, daughter of Andrew and Amelia E. Urion, married Joseph Reeves; they have issue. Catharine Elwell, daughter of Jonathan Elwell, married Garrett Newkirk; there were three children—Margaret, Garrett and Matthew Newkirk; all three of those in after life became eminent citizens. Garrett and Matthew are successful merchants. Margaret equally as much so as her brothers, as a bonnet maker.

I shall conclude this short and reliable history of Jacob Elwell and his wife, Catharine Dubois; for many of his descendants I have alluded to heretofore in the genealogy of other families. Jacob Elwell, the emigrant, died in Pittsgrove township, aged seventy-three years; his widow, Catharine Dubois Elwell, in 1798, far advanced in years. As far as I have learned, both of those aged persons left an enviable reputation and numerous descendants.

GUY FAMILY.

Richard Guy and his wife, Bridget Guy, were among the first emigrants to Fenwick's Colony. His occupation in his native country was that of a cheesemonger; he resided in the parish of Stepny, London, in Middlesex. He purchased one thousand acres of land in what is now known as Elsinboro. The deed and receipt for the land was dated in the 9th month, 1676; the purchase money was ten pounds. The said land was located bounding on Delaware river, extending from the old Swede's fort to the present mouth of Salem creek. He was not, however, a resident of the county but a few years. And on the same day he likewise bought of Fenwick, for his friend Thomas Pyle, a citizen and upholsterer of the city of London, ten thousand acres of land, for which he paid fifty pounds sterling. The following is the receipt of John Fenwick for said land:

"Received on thirteenth day of the third month, called May,
" one thousand, six hundred and seventy and five, of and from
" Richard Guy, of the parish of Stepny, of the county of
" Middlesex, (chessemonger), the full sum of fifty pounds
" sterling, mentioned and expressed in a Deed, bearing even
" date herewith, and made for me John Fenwick, late of Bin-
" field, in the county of Berks, within the kingdom of England,
" Esq., and early Proprietor of the Province of New Cessavia,
" or New Jersey, in America, to the said Richard Guy.
" Witnesseth present:

" PETER HOFF,   By me, FENWICK.
" SAMUEL NICHOLSON,
" RICHARD MORGAN,
" JOHN SMITH,
" EDWARD CHAMPNEY,
" EDWARD WADE,
" THOMAS ANDERSON,
" EDMUND WARNER,
" RICHARD NOBLE,
" JAMES GARDFILDSER."

The said land was surveyed by Richard Noble in 1676, and

was located in the upper part of Salem tenth, where the township of Pilesgrove is now.

About 1690 Richard Guy and George Deacon removed with their families to the county of Burlington. Richard died in a short time afterwards, leaving a widow, who survived him a number of years. George Deacon lived until 1722, leaving children. Some of his descendants are still living in that county at the present time.

GOODWIN FAMILY.

John Goodwin was the son of John and Catharine Goodwin, of the parish of St. Buttolph, in Algate, London. He was born 25th of 10th month, 1680, and emigrated to Pennsylvania in 1701. From thence, the following year, he removed to Salem, and in 1705 he married Susannah Smith, the oldest daughter of John Smith, of Smithfield; they had four children —John, Mary, Thomas and William Goodwin; the two oldest died young. Thomas Goodwin was born in 1721, and married Sarah Morris, the daughter of Lewis Morris, of Elsinborough, in the year 1743. Thomas and his wife lived on her property that she inherited from her father in Elsinborough until 1656, when they sold it to Samuel Abbott, and purchased the property in the town of Salem of John Mason. The said property was located on Broadway street, and in the spring of 1757 they removed to Salem, and here ended their days. In the 10th month, 1765, Sarah Goodwin, wife of Thomas Goodwin died, aged forty-one years, leaving no children. Thomas Goodwin's second wife was Sarah Smith who lived but a few years after her marriage, and departed this life in the year 1783. Thomas remained single for twenty years, and in 1803 he died, aged nearly eighty-two years, leaving his estate to his great nephews and nieces. William Goodwin, the youngest son of John and Susannah Goodwin, was born in 1723, and in 1744 he married Mary Morris, second daughter of Lewis Morris; they lived in Elsinborough on her share of her father's estate; they had five children—John, Lewis, Susannah, Mary and William Goodwin. John Goodwin, their oldest son, was born in 1745, and in the year 1772 he married Sarah Hall, daughter of Clement and Margaret Hall. It was one of the first marriages that took place at the present Friends' meeting house in Salem. John Goodwin's wife lived but a short time after they were married, leaving no children. Mary Goodwin, the mother of John Goodwin, died in 1776, and consequently the property belonged to him after his father's death. John did not survive his mother but a few years, making a will and leaving his right of the real estate to his nephew, William Goodwin, the son of Lewis Goodwin. Lewis Goodwin, the second son of William and Mary Goodwin, married Rebecca Zanes, of Salem, daughter of Susan Zanes; they had two children—John and Susan Goodwin. John married Abigail Carpenter and had three children—Lewis, William and Thomas Goodwin. Lewis Goodwin's second wife was Rachel Nicholson, the daughter of William Nicholson, of Mannington, and they had three children—William, Thomas and Morris Goodwin. William, the oldest son, married Huldah Townsend, daughter of Daniel Townsend, of Cape May. Thomas Goodwin married Sarah Jefferis, daughter of Joshua Jefferis. Morris Goodwin married Sarah Smith. Susannah Goodwin, oldest daughter of William and Mary Goodwin, was born in 1750, and in 1773 she married John Mason, the son of Thomas Mason, and grand-son of John Mason. He was a widower when he married Susannah Goodwin, his first wife was Ann Hall, daughter of William Hall, Jr.. They lived and owned on Broadway street in Salem, which property is now owned by Morris Hall. John Mason and Ann his wife had one daughter named Sarah, and she married Edgar Brown. John Mason and his wife Susannah had six children—William, Mary, Ann, Thomas, Elizabeth and John G. Mason. Their oldest son, William, died in 1776. Mary Mason married Abner Beesley and had four children—Mary, William, Benjamin and Thomas Beesley. Her second husband was Job Ware, who had two children—Job and Elijah Ware. Ann Mason was born in 1778, and married Joseph Thompson, son of Joshua Thompson; they had four children —Susan, the oldest, married Joseph Pancoast. Elizabeth, their second daughter died in her fifteenth year. Sarah Thompson married Thomas Shourds. Ann Thompson married Thomas Fogg. Thomas Mason, their second son, was born 1780. About the year 1812 he married Hannah Hancock, daughter of Joseph Hancock; he and his wife lived but a short time after they were married, leaving one child—Hannah Mason, and she married Richard M. Acton. Elizabeth Mason was born in 1782, and she died single in the twenty-fourth year of her age. John Goodwin Mason was born in 1785; he never married, and died in 1839 in the fifty-fifth year of his age. John Mason, their father, died about 1787; his widow, Susannah Mason, married Joshua Thompson and had two children—William and Joshua Thompson. William Goodwin, Jr., was born in 1758, and married Elizabeth Woodnutt, of Mannington; he and h wife had six children—Prudence, the oldest, married Atkinson Conrad. Mary Goodwin married Jonathan Woodnutt. Rachel Goodwin married Preston C. Woodnutt. Sarah Goodwin married Henry Dennis, her second husband was Jonathan Woodnutt. Elizabeth and Abigail Goodwin always remained single; they were remarkable for their kind and sympathetic feelings, always willing to assist the poor and afflicted, going and looking after them in the abodes of poverty, and administering to their wants as far as their circumstances would allow; they continued in their noble deeds of philanthrophy until old age and as long as bodily strength permitted them to do it. It seemed that the spirit of the immortal Howard had descended upon them.

HANCOCK FAMILY.

William Hancock, Sr., came from England to this county in the year 1677, with his wife, Isabella Hancock, and two sons, John and William Hancock. He took possession soon after his arrival of allotment of land on the south side of Alloways Creek, containing 1,000 acres. The said land was surveyed by Richard Hancock, by order of John Fenwick, in 1676. William Hancock died and left his estate to his widow, Isabella, who, the year following, sold one half of the allotment to John Maddox. She survived about ten years after her husband. In her will she devised her real estate to her oldest son, John Hancock, and her personal estate to William Hancock; and he purchased 500 acres of land in Elsinborough, adjoining lands of John Mason on the south, Samuel Nicholson on the east, Rudoc Morris' land on the west, and by Isaac Smart's land on the north. In 1705 he built a large brick house; it stood until within a few years ago, and then it was torn down by Richard Grier, the present owner of the property, and a large frame house erected on the site of the old one. I believe William Hancock married Sarah Stafford. Their son, Thomas Hancock, was born 5th of the 12th month, 1714. William Hancock held the office of Justice of the Peace for many years, and he died about the year 1740. His son, Thomas Hancock, married and had two sons—William and Thomas Hancock. At their father's death the landed estate was divided equally between them. William Hancock, son of Thomas, married Hannah Fogg, daughter of Charles Fogg, in the year 1770. William Hancock, their son, was born 4th day of the 7th month, 1771; he died a minor. John Hancock was born the 24th day of 4th month, 1773; Elizabeth Hancock was born the 17th of the 7th month, 1776. John died in 1794, and made a will, leaving his estate to his cousin, William Hancock, son of Thomas Hancock. Thomas Hancock married Mary Goodwin, daughter of William Goodwin; they had five children —Thomas Hancock, Jr., William, Morris, Sarah, and Elizabeth Hancock.

John Hancock, the eldest son of William and Isabella Hancock, inherited by his mother 500 acres of land on the south side of Alloways creek, where the village of Hancock's Bridge is now located. All accounts we have of him go to show that he was a man of great energy in relation to business. He added largely to his estate. In the year 1708 he built a bridge across Alloways creek. I have no doubt he was assisted by the public in the work. It was known for many years as John Hancock's bridge. In 1709 there were commissioners appointed by the Court to lay out a public highway from the town of Salem, by the way of John Hancock's new bridge, to the town of Greenwich. John died about 1725, leaving one son—William Hancock, and he came in possession of one of the largest landed estates in the county; his lands lay mostly in Alloways Creek, Elsinborough, and Penn's Neck. William married Sarah, the daughter of Nathaniel Chambless, Jr., of Alloways Creek. In the year 1734 William Hancock built himself a large and substantial brick dwelling, which is still standing, in good repair. It is an historical house, on account of the horrible massacre which took place in it by the British soldiers on the American militia, who were quartered in it in 1778. William Hancock, then an old man, received a mortal wound, and died in a short time afterwards at the house of his brother-in-law, Joshua Thompson, about half a mile farther down the creek. William had one daughter by his first wife, Sarah Chambless—Sarah Hancock. She married Thomas Sinnickson, of Salem, son of Andrew Sinnickson, of Penn's Neck. Thomas and his wife left no issue. His second wife was Sarah, the daughter of Joshua and Sarah Thompson, of Elsinborough; they had one son— John Hancock, who married Eleanor York, daughter of Andrew York, of Salem; they had several children; four of them lived to grow up, and had families—Sarah, who married Morris Hancock, son of Thomas Hancock, of Elsinborough; Henrietta married Lewis P. Smith; Thomas Y. Hancock married Rachel, daughter of William and Elizabeth Nicholson; Maria married Richard P. Thompson, son of Hedge and Mary Ann Thompson, of Salem. William Hancock done a large amount of public business, was a member of the Colonial Legislature for twenty years in succession, and held the office of Judge and Justice at the time of his death.

OBEDIAH HOLMES FAMILY.

The Holmes family, of the county of Cumberland, are an ancient and numerous family. At this late day it is almost impossible to follow the various branches with any degree of certainty, therefore I will endeavor to confine my remarks to those branches who have kept a correct record of their ancestors. It appears that Obediah Holmes, Sr., was born 1606, at Preston, Lancashire, England, and at the age of thirty-three he emigrated to America, landing at Boston in 1639. He located at Salem, in the State of Massachusetts, and most probably married soon after that event. He was a Baptist clergyman of no ordinary intellect, and for the doctrines he so ably and powerfully enunciated, he was arraigned in 1650, and tried by a court of the rigid Puritans of that day, and was condemned to be publicly whipped, together with a number of Friends or Quakers, who likewise held religious opinions, which they regarded as heresy. I have no doubt the Puritans, in their blind zeal, believed such religious doctrines were detrimental to the peace and happiness of their commonwealth. Soon after that event, Obediah Holmes removed, with his family, to Newport, Rhode Island, where religious liberty was granted by just and liberal laws, made and enacted by Roger Williams. He died at Newport, 15th of 10th month, 1682, aged seventy-six years. There is no mention at what time his wife's death occurred, but I think it was previous to his. They had eight children, most of whom survived their parents; some married in New England, one or more settled on Long Island. Two of their sons, Obediah and Jonathan, came to New Jersey and purchased a tract of land of the Indians, amounting to 1,600 acres, located near where Middletown now is, in Monmouth county. The two brothers were constituent members of the Baptist church at Middletown, which church is said to be the first of that denomination constructed in the State. Obediah, however, remained in Monmouth county but a short period, and removed and settled within Fenwick's Colony, in the Cohansey precinct, on the south side of the river, in Shrewsbury Neck, in 1685. He was one of the nine Baptists that assisted in organizing the first Baptist church in South Jersey, in 1690. It does not appear that he was ever ordained a regular clergyman, but he occasionally preached. He possessed, by nature, a legal mind, and the early inhabitants of that section of country soon appreciated his business capacities, and when the Salem courts were regularly established, in the early part of the reign of Queen Anne, he and Thomas Killingsworth were appointed Judges, and John Mason, Samuel Hedge, and Joseph Sayre, from Cohansey, were the Justices.

Obediah Holmes, Jr., married a young woman by the name of Cole; they had four children—two sons and two daughters. The eldest daughter married a young person by the name of Love, his second daughter married a person by the name of Parvin. Both the Love's and the Parvin's are among the first families that settled in Cumberland county. Obediah's eldest son, Samuel Holmes, was drowned when a young man; his youngest son, Jonathan Holmes, married and died young, leaving one son—Jonathan Holmes. The death of Jonathan Holmes, Sr., occurred 8th of 9th month, 1715. Jonathan Holmes, Jr., in 1729, married Anna Dominick, of Long Island; they had eight children—Mary, born 16th of 10th month, 1731; Susanna, born 3d of 11th month; Jonathan, born 14th of 4th month, 1735; Eunice, born 9th of 5th month, 1736; Phebe, born 23d of 2d month, 1738; Anna, born 23d of 10th month, 1739; Abijah, born 3d of 4th month, 1741; and Rachel, born 14th of of 1st month, 1750. All of these died minors, excepting Abijah and Phebe. Jonathan and Ann Holmes were members of the Presbyterian church, at Greenwich, and Jonathan was a large contributor towards building the old brick meeting house at that place, in 1735. He was, also, one of the elders of the church, and continued to be, I presume, up to the time of his death, and he assisted in purchasing the parsonage in 1749 for the church. His remains lie, as also those of his son, Abijah, in the ancient cemetery of that place. Phebe Holmes, the daughter of Jonathan and Ann Holmes, born 1738, married Dr. Samuel Ward; her second husband was Moses Bloomfield, the father of Governor Bloomfield, of this State. Abijah Holmes, son of Jonathan and Ann Holmes, born 3d of 4th month, 1741, married Rachel Seeley, the daughter of Ephraim and Hannah Seeley, on the 18th of 5th month, 1767. They had five children—Sarah, born 1st of 5th month, 1771; Mary, born 29th of 3d month, 1774; Jonathan, born, 10th of 9th month, 1776; John, born 3d of 8th month, 1778; and Ephraim Holmes, born 13th of 7th month, 1780. These children were all minors at the time of their parents' death. Abijah, their father departed this life 6th of 3d month, 1785, and their mother, Rachel Seeley Holmes, 8th of 1st month, 1789.

Jonathan, the son of Abijah and Rachel S. Holmes, born 10th of 9th month, 1776, was married three times. His first wife was Lydia Watson, born 11th month, 1776, and died 19th of 9th month, 1799, and was buried in the old graveyard of the Baptists, near Sheppard's mill. She left one son—Abijah Holmes, who is living, and is far advanced in years, and resides in the city of Camden. Jonathan's widow, Clarissa Holmes, is living in the city of Bridgeton, aged eighty-nine years. They have one son, living in the town.

John, the son of Abijah and Rachel Holmes, born 3d of 8th month, 1778, was married twice. By his first wife he had a son—Alfred Holmes, who lives at this time in Lower Hopewell township, Cumberland county. John's second wife was a Bowen; by her he had three children; their son John Holmes lives at or near Bowentown.

Ephraim, the son of Abijah and Hannah S. Holmes, was born 13th of 7th month, 1780, and married Harriet Potter Bowen, 13th of 4th month, 1813; she was the daughter of David and Jane Potter Bowen. Ephraim and his wife had five children—Edward B., the first son, born 29th of 7th month, 1815, married Julia Dillingham, and died in New York 17th of 2d month, 1858, leaving a widow and one son. Ephraim, the second son, born 11th of 7th month, 1817, is at this time a practicing physician, and resides in the town of Greenwich. Mary P., the third child, born 20th of 9th month, 1819, married Charles M. Lawrence, and died 26th of 10th month, 1865, leaving three children, two of whom are married. Her husband is still living at Port Jervis, New York, and is a physician. David B. Holmes, the fourth child, born 5th of 8th month, 1833, married Caroline Elizabeth Gibbon, daughter of Charles Gibbon; David and his wife reside at Schuylkill Haven, Pa.; they have three children. Harriet Bowen Holmes, the youngest child of Ephraim and Harriet P. Bowen, born 6th of 7th month, 1825, died 31st of 8th month, 1850; she never married. Ephraim Holmes, the father, died 28th of 5th month, 1848, and was buried in the Presbyterian graveyard at Greenwich. His wife, Harriet Potter Holmes, survived him twenty years, her death taking place 2d of 4th month, 1868, aged seventy-eight years.

Many persons think that the family of Holmes in Cumberland and that of Salem are of one family. I think there is no relationship existing between them. They spell their names differently; the Salem county family write their's Holme, while Obediah wrote his name Holmes, and it is so recorded in the Salem Court records, and I believe all his descendants write their names the same way. Further, Obediah Holmes, Sr., landed at Boston more than forty years before Thomas Holme, the surveyor-general for William Penn, and John Holme, (I presume they were relatives,) arrived from England to the province of Pennsylvania. History informs us that John Holme was one of the first Baptists in that province; that was a few years before he came to Salem county to live.

HOLME FAMILY.

John Holme, emigrated from England, and settled in Philadelphia, soon after the city was founded by William Penn. It appears he had a family—wife and two sons; one of his sons bought a large tract of land within the county of Philadelphia and settled thereon; the place is known at this day as Holmesburg. His brother, John Holme, purchased a large tract of land in Salem county, situated in Monmouth precinct, and settled thereon; that being in 1698; he was one of the first that belonged to the Babtist religious association, that lived near the town of Salem; he died the early part of eighteenth century, leaving one son—John Holme, who subsequently married; he had two sons and one daughter; one of his daughters, Elizabeth Holme, married Joseph, the son of Joseph Fogg, the emigrant; they had nine children—David, Ebenezer, Charles, Hannah, Ann, Elizabeth Holmes, Isaac and Rebecca Fogg. John Holme, the eldest son of John Holme 2d, inherited the homestead of his father's, located near Allowaystown, erected a flour mill, known for many years as Holme's Mill. The said mill and land was subsequently owned by Josiah M. Reeves and brothers. John Holme was at one time Judge of the Salem courts, and an ardent patriot in the days of the American Revolution. Benjamin Holme, the youngest son of John Holme 2d, was born about 1730; his first wife was Jane, the daughter of Daniel Smith, Jr., who resided near the village of Quinton's Bridge; about the year 1762 he purchased what was known as the David Morris estate, it being large and valuable, in the township of Elsinborough, of John Hart, he being half brother of David Morris. Benjamin's first wife, Jane Smith, died young, leaving no issue; he subsequently married Esther Gibbon, whose maiden name was Seeley; her first husband was John Gibbon, son of Leonard Gibbon. John volunteered in the army, and was taken prisoner and died in one of the prison ships of the British, near New York. Benjamin and his wife, Esther Holme, had two children—John G. and Jane Holme. Benjamin Holme was a historical man and a staunch Whig, in the American Revolution, and was appointed a Colonel of the American Militia, of the lower counties, operating with Colonel Hand, of Cape May; by so doing his buildings in Elsinborough were burned, by order of Colonel Manhood, the British commander. After peace was restored he rebuilt his buildings and lived to an advanced age, much respected by his neighbors and friends. John G. Holme, son of Benjamin and Esther Holme, married Rebecca, the daughter of Thomas and Rebecca Thompson, of Salem; she died leaving one daughter—Rebecca Holme, who subsequently married George W. Garrison. John G. Holme's second wife was Margaret, daughter of Clement and Rebecca K. Hall, of Elsinborough. John and Margaret Holme had three children—Benjamin, Jane and Caroline Holme. By this marriage of John Holme to Margaret Hall, (they having issue) was the means of restoring the large landed estate Colonel Holme bought of John Hart, to the Morris family again. Margaret was the fifth generation in lineal descent from Rudoc Morris. Benjamin, son of John G. and Margaret Holme, married Elizabeth, the daughter of Henry and Ann Smith Dennis, of Salem; their children living are Caroline, John, Henry, Lucy, Franklin and Jane Holme. John, the son of Benjamin and Elizabeth Holme, married Lena, daughter of James Woolman, of Pilesgrove; they have issue. Jane, daughter of John G. and Margaretta Holme, married John, the son of Morris and Lydia Hall, of Elsinborough. John is deceased, leaving no issue; his widow, Jane Hall, resides in Salem. Caroline, daughter of John and Margaret Holme, died when she was about ten years of age. Jane, daughter of Colonel Benjamin Holme and his wife Esther, married a man by the name of Harris, who resided at Swedesboro, Gloucester county; she died about a year after marriage, leaving no issue.

CLEMENT HALL.
Born 1819.

HALL FAMILY.

In 1677 William Hall emigrated to this country in company with John and Andrew Thompson, and their families. They landed at Elsinborough the 22d of 12th month, the same year. Before they sailed from Dublin, William Hall hired with John Thompson for a number of years, and soon after his servitude expired he removed to the town of Salem, and kept a small store. In 1688 he married Elizabeth Pyle, daughter of Thomas Pyle, who was a large landholder in the upper part of Fenwick's tenth; one tract alone, bordering on Oldman's creek, contained 10,000 acres. When the different townships were laid off they named the township where he lived, and most of his real estate lay, Pylesgrove; then the largest township in this county, containing 87,000 acres. It is believed William Hall came in possession of considerable property, both real and personal, by his wife. Following are the names of William and Elizabeth Hall's children, and the dates of births: Sarah was born 28th of the 2d month, 1689; Hannah in 1692; Elizabeth in 1694; Ann in 1699. Soon after the birth of Ann his wife, Elizabeth, died. His second wife was Sarah Clement of the county of Gloucester; they had three children—William Hall, Jr., born 22d of the 8th month, 1701; their second son, Clement, was born in 1706; and Nathaniel in 1709; who, when he arrived at the age of twenty-one, left this county and went and resided in the State of Delaware. Clement, I presume, died young.

William Hall was appointed, by the West Jersey Legislature, a Judge of the Court for Salem county about the year 1709, to take the place of Thomas Killingsworth. It is to be regretted that a fuller account of the last named individual has not been written and handed down for the benefit of posterity. According to the limited accounts we have of him he was, undoubtedly, more than an ordinary scholar, for that time, and a man in whose judgment and integrity the first emigrants to this country had implicit confidence. He was one of the first Baptists that came to this county, and a clergyman of that religious denomination. William Hall was Judge as late as 1710, and the greatest landholder in the county of Salem, owning one hundredth part of Fenwick's tenth. His possessions in the town of Salem were considerable; he owned one lot extending from Broadway street to Fenwick creek, bounded on the south by Friend's property of sixteen acres, deeded to them by Samuel Nicholson, in 1681; on the west by Edward Bradway's lot; also on the opposite side of the same street another lot of land, bounded on the west by the public fair grounds, on the south and east by Samuel and Anne Hedge's land. Certainly he was a self-made man; no doubt his natural talents were above the common men. By his industry and good judgment he became one of the foremost men of the Colony. The time of his death I have no positive means to determine; most probably about 1718. I do not remember ever having seen an account of him in the public records after that time.

Soon after his death, his widow, Sarah Hall, being his executor, sold large tracts of land in various parts of the county which the records show. His tract of 1,000 acres in upper Mannington was left to his oldest son, William Hall, Jr., together with the greater part of his real estate in the town of Salem. The said William Hall, Jr., on the 20th day of ninth month, 1723, married Elizabeth Smith, the grand-daughter of John Smith, of Amblebury. They had seven children—Clement, their oldest child, was born 15th of 12th month, 1723; their daughter, Sarah, in 1727; Susan, in 1728; Nathaniel, in 1730; Elizabeth, in 1735; Mary, in 1737; and their youngest son, Edward, in 1740. William Hall built himself a large brick house about the year 1725, on his property in upper Mannington, and at that place he and his wife lived and spent their days. The house still stands, and is owned by Samuel L. J. Miller, one of their lineal descendants. There is an ancient family bible of John Smith's that he brought with him from England in 1675. It was printed with ancient type in England, in 1634. Persons not accustomed to seeing such ancient printing would find it difficult to read it. The book is in a good state of preservation, and belongs to one of the Hall family at this time. I hope some one of the family will prize it sufficiently to preserve it for future generations as a momento of ancient times. In one of the margins Elizabeth Smith Hall in 1730 wrote: "This day John Smith is 106 years old." He was her grandfather. In looking over the records of Salem Monthly Meeting, I find that he was the son of John Smith, born in the county of Norfolk, 20th day of 4th month, 1623. The account shows that there were instances of longevity then as well as at the present day.

William Hall, Jr., made his will in 1750, in which he devises his real estate in Salem to his eldest son, Clement Hall, and his property in Mannington, to his two youngest sons, Nathaniel and Edward Hall. Clement Hall, the son of William Hall, Jr., married Margaret Morris, of Elsinborough, about the year 1748. There were seven children—Ann, Sarah, Clement, John, Joseph, Morris and Margaret, the last mentioned died when she was quite young. The oldest daughter married John Goodwin. She lived but a short time after her marriage, leaving no children. Sarah Hall's husband was Dr. Thomas Rowen, of Salem. They had three children—Sarah Rowen, the late Dr. Thomas Rowen, and Elizabeth Rowen. Sarah married Charles Penrose, of Philadelphia. Dr. Rowen's wife was Hetty Sinnickson, the daughter of John Sinnickson, of Lower Penn's Neck. They are both deceased at this time, leaving no children. Clement Hall's wife was Rebecca Kay, a native of Gloucester county. Clement and his wife had seven children, named respectively Ann, Margaret, Morris, Prudence, Sarah, Deborah and Rebecca. Ann Hall married Samuel Nicholson Thompson. They had six children—Samuel, Joshua, Clement, Charles, Isaac and Ann Thompson.

Margaret Hall's husband was John Holme, of Elsinborough; she was his second wife; there were three children—Benjamin, Jane and Caroline. Benjamin's wife was Elizabeth Dennis, the daughter of Henry Dennis, of Salem. Benjamin is now deceased, leaving a widow and six children—Caroline, John, Henry, Louisa, Franklin and Jane. Caroline died young. Morris Hall married Elizabeth Woodnutt, the daughter of James Woodnutt, of Mannington; there were four children—Margaret, Hannah, Rebecca and James Hall. Prudence Hall, when far advanced in life, married Joseph Ogden, of Woodbury; they are both deceased now, leaving no children. Sarah Hall died at middle age; she never married. Deborah Hall married Samuel D. Ingham, of Pennsylvania, being his second wife. Samuel and his wife are both deceased, leaving three children—William, Rebecca and Mary Ingham. Rebecca Hall married John Sinnickson, the son of Andrew Sinnickson, and was his second wife; they had three children—Howard, Clement and Mary Sinnickson.

John Hall, the second son of Clement and Margaret Hall, married and lived in Salem on the property that was left him by his father. It was purchased by one of the Norris family. Joseph Corliss bought the old mansion. The Hall property formerly extended to the town meadow. John was a merchant and died a young man; whether he left any children I never heard.

Joseph Hall's wife was Ann Brick, the daughter of Joseph and Rebecca Brick, of Elsinborough. Joseph Brick was from an ancient and respectable family at Cohansey, the son of John and Ann Brick, and was born 24th of 3d month, 1735; soon after he was of age he married Rebecca Abbott, the daughter of Samuel Abbott, of Elsinborough; they commenced life on the farm that her father purchased of Thomas and Sarah Goodwin, in 1756; the farm is the one that William B. Carpenter now owns and lives on. Joseph and Rebecca Brick had three children—Ann, Hannah, (who is the wife of Anthony Keasbey, of Salem), and one son, Samuel Brick.

Joseph Hall and his wife had nine children, named respectively Samuel, William, Margaret, Rebecca, Martha, Ann, Edward, James and Hannah. Samuel married Sarah Ware, daughter of Jacob Ware; he died young and left one son—Joseph Hall, who now resides at or near Dunkirk, in the State of New York. William's wife was Hannah Hall, daughter of Jarvis Hall, of Mannington; both are deceased at the present time, leaving three or four children. Margaret Hall married John Denn, Sr., and the names of her children I mentioned in a former number of the Denn genealogy. Rebecca married David Ware, of Lower Penn's Neck, son of Jacob Ware; her husband has been deceased many years; she died recently, quite aged; she possessed good mental abilities, and an uncommon quiet disposition in all of her trials through life—for she had many—and through them all she always manifested a quiet and evenness of disposition, which endeared her to her immediate family and likewise to a large circle of relatives and friends. Ann Hall married David Hall, the son of Morris Hall; they were first cousins; they soon afterwards removed to the State of New York and made it their permanent home. David has been deceased for some time. I have heard his widow is still living; they had several children. Martha Hall, their afflicted daughter, was born blind and always remained so; she lived to an old age, and died a few years ago. Edward Hall's wife was the daughter of David Lloyd, of Lower Penn's Neck; they left their native county soon after they were married, and were for a time at Pittsburgh, Pa. James Hall was a currier by occupation, and resided for some time in the city of Philadelphia. Hannah Hall, their youngest daughter, accompanied her sister Ann and husband when they went to the State of New York; she afterwards became the wife of Judge Orton, of that

State. Joseph Hall, the father of the above named children, died in the prime of his life; he had uncommon physical strength, which was characteristic in the Hall family, and he was likewise endowed with uncommon natural abilities; his death occurred about the time John Wistar died.

Daniel Garrison, who had been Surrogate for a number of years, and was considered to be a good judge of the acquirements of the leading men at that time in the county of Salem, was asked which of the two men, John Wistar or Joseph Hall, possessed the greatest natural abilities. His reply was, "If Joseph Hall had the school education John Wistar possessed, he would have been his equal, if not his superior." Joseph's widow survived him several years.

Morris, the youngest son of Clement and Margaret Hall, was born in 1762. He learned the wheelwrighting trade, but did not follow it when he became of age, but worked as a journeyman house carpenter with Jonas Freidland, and while building a large dwelling house for that eminent philanthropist, Gabriel Davis, in Bacon's Neck, Greenwich township, they became acquainted with two young women—Elizabeth and Lydia Potts, daughters of John Potts, who lived in the same township. Subsequently Jonas married Elizabeth, and Morris, Lydia Potts. The length of time Morris worked at his trade after he was married, I have no knowledge of, but not long before he went to farming. He and his wife had five children—Clement, David, Sarah, John, and Lewis Hall. Clement Hall's wife was Sarah Hancock, daughter of Thomas and Mary Hancock, of Elsinboro. Their children were mentioned in the Hancock family. David's wife was Ann Hall, daughter of Joseph Hall; they were cousins. Sarah Hall married Joseph Bassett, of Mannington. She left one son, Morris Bassett. John Hall's wife was Jane Holme, daughter of John and Margaret Holme. John's death occurred several years ago. His widow resides in Salem. Lewis Hall left his native State and located himself, I think, in the western part of Pennsylvania, at first. Where he made his permanent home, I have never heard. He is now deceased.

Clement and Margaret Hall, parents of the above mentioned children, lived and died in the township of Elsinboro, at the old residence of Margaret's ancestors, situated near the river shore. The property was purchased of Richard Guy by Samuel Carpenter, of Philadelphia, for a country seat, and built a brick house about the year 1690, and in 1694 he sold it to Rudoc Morris. The property is still held by one of his descendants. Clement Hall, Sr., died about the year 1772. In his will he left his real estate in Salem to his son, John Hall, and his daughter, Sarah. His wife survived him several years, and in 1782 she made her will, leaving one-half of her plantation to her oldest son, Clement Hall, and the fishery at Fort Point equally between Clement and her second son, John Hall. At John Hall's death his share of the fishery was sold. Darkin Nicholson, living near the mouth of Salem creek, was the purchaser, and at his death the Hall family bought his right. It is evident that the Morris and Hall families had full jurisdiction over the fishery along that shore for more than one hundred and fifty years, notwithstanding the neighboring State of Delaware undertakes to claim to low water mark along the Jersey shore. If their claim is good and valid now, it was certainly good at that early period, when the owners of the soil along the Jersey shore held undisputed possession of the fisheries, and frequently rented them to persons belonging to this and other States; fisheries being all within the bounds of the twelve-mile circuit.

Margaret Hall willed one-half of her plantation to her two youngest sons, Joseph and Morris Hall. Joseph subsequently sold his share, and purchased part of Middle Neck, of Isaac and Nathan Smart—he and his wife were joint owners; it was on this property where what is called the Elsinborough grape was first discovered. The Smart family, very soon after they bought the land of Fenwick, turned their attention to cultivating grapes; they imported several varieties of English grapes. Soon after they discovered a grape different entirely from any they ever saw growing among their foreign grapes; they supposed it was a seedling, and gave it the name of the Smart grape. The late Morris Hall informed me that was the traditional account of the grape; he was born in the township and his mother before him, and all he ever heard or saw from those much older than himself, came to the conclusion it was not a native of the township, but it originated in the Smart vineyard, on said property; since their death it has been sold to other persons. Morris Hall purchased a farm adjoining his brother's, of the administrator of John Hancock, of Hancock's Bridge, whose grand-father purchased it of James Thompson. Morris and his wife both died there; after Morris' death (for he lived many years after his wife was deceased) the farm went to his son, John Hall, and his daughter, Sarah Bassett. The homestead is owned at this time by his grand-son, Clement Hall.

Nathaniel and Edward Hall, as has been previously stated, became the owner of their father's homestead estate in upper Mannington. Edward was the owner of the old family mansion and a large tract of land adjoining. Nathaniel's share was the western part of the Hall's allotment; the greater part of said land is now owned by Edward H. Bassett. He built himself a commodious brick house about the year 1756, and soon afterwards married Ann, the eldest daughter of Judge John and Ann Nicholson Brick, of Gravelly Run. He died in 1784, aged fifty-four years, leaving five children—William, born in 1758; Ann in 1760; Elizabeth in 1763; John in 1765, and his youngest son Josiah in 1767. Josiah was a clock and watch maker by trade; he followed it in the town of Salem and was for several years Clerk of the county of Salem; his wife was Elizabeth Smith; he owned and lived where Joseph Test now resides and owns; he left no children; his wife survived him several years. Nathaniel left his plantation equally between his two eldest sons—William and John Hall. William was the owner of the homestead; he married soon after he became of age and had ten children—William, Josiah, Hannah, Mary, Martha, Nathan, Ann, Achsah, Samuel and Horatio. John Hall, when he was far advanced in years, married Phebe Edwards, a young woman of Pilesgrove; she lived but a short time after they were married, leaving one son. Soon after that event he removed to Salem, where he died, in a few years, with a cancer in his face. His son died within a short time after his father; his estate, which was considerable, was divided among his relatives.

Elizabeth, daughter of Nathaniel Hall, married Samuel Nicholson, Jr., the son of the eminent philanthropist, Samuel Nicholson, of Elsinborough. They lived on his father's property in the township of Mannington. After the death of his father he became the owner; it now is part of the estate of Joseph Stretch, who lately died. They had five children—John, who married a young woman by the name of Beesley; they left one daughter—Catharine Nicholson. Ann married Daniel Smith; Elizabeth died single; Samuel married a woman by the name of Paullin; Josiah, their youngest son, married Rachel Hall, daughter of Jarvis Hall. He died many years ago, leaving a widow, who is living in Salem at this time, and I believe three children, two sons and one daughter.

Edward Hall, the youngest son of William Hall, Jr., was considered above mediocrity in physical and mental abilities. His affability and pleasing address secured him many friends among a large circle of acquaintances. His first wife was a Willis, and by her he had one son—Howell. At the commencement of the Revolutionary war he abandoned the religious society of which he and his ancestors were members, and enlisted in the army. There are many anecdotes of his sayings and doings while he was in the service of his country. I will mention two which are well authenticated by tradition: The army under Colonel Hand was at Cohansey Bridge, which is now Bridgeton. Edward, on his way down to join it, met his intimate friend, John Reeve, about his own age, who was a public minister, on his way to attend Salem quarterly meeting. After the usual salutation, John remarked, "Edward, I notice thee is dressed in soldier's clothes." "I am," replied Hall, after consideration; "I came to the conclusion it would be right for me to fight for my country." John then replied: "If thee thinks it is right, it may be thy duty. I hope God will be with thee. I bid thee good-by." They then separated and did not meet again until the war was ended. Soon after he went to the army he was made a Colonel in the West Jersey militia. It was the practice in those days among some of the tanners when they had a quantity of leather on hand, to take a load down among the inhabitants along the sea shore and trade it for raw hides. Samuel Austin told me of one of his adventures during the war. He left his home in Mannington with a load of leather, which he had frequently done before, and proceeded to Egg Harbor with it. There was at that time several vessels belonging to England anchored in the bay, one of them having a quantity of boxes of tea aboard. The officer told him he would exchange a few boxes of tea for leather. The love of great gain, which is predominant in the human family, made him yield to the temptation. Thinking he could evade the authorities, he covered up the tea with some hides he purchased, and started for home. Inadvertently he came by the way of Bridgeton, where the American army was quartered, and was soon stopped by some of the soldiers to search his load. He declared his innocence, but they told him their orders were to search all wagons that came from the seashore, and began to throw off his hides. At that juncture, Colonel Hall came out of the tavern and saw Austin, and then told the men to put his load on again, and said: "He is a neighbor of mine, and a true patriot." He then called Austin in to take a drink with him before he proceeded on his journey. Samuel told me it was the first and last time he ever undertook to traffic in contraband goods, and always felt grateful to Colonel Hall, although he did it ignorantly, for his timely interference, as it prevented him from losing his team and load, and likely his life.

Edward Hall's second wife was the widow of David Stretch,

HALL FAMILY.

of Lower Alloways Creek. Soon after he left his native home in Mannington, and went to reside on the farm that his wife had a life-right in, being formerly the Christopher White estate, near Hancock's Bridge. They had two children—Mary and Edward Hall, Jr. After her death he returned to the old family residence in Mannington, In a few years afterward he married his third wife, Ann Darrah, of Philadelphia, the daughter of the celebrated Lydia Darrah, who risked her life in informing General Washington of the contemplated attack of the English army, during the severe winter that the American army was at Valley Forge. I need not state the particulars of her patriotic adventure. I trust most of the American readers have seen the full account of it themselves. His last wife survived him many years. I knew her well; she was intelligent and interesting conversationist. She lived the latter part of her days with her husband's grand-daughter, Hetty Miller. She had one brother, Joseph Darrah, who was a captain in the navy. His home was at New Castle, Delaware. In 1825 his sister, Ann Hall, employed me to take over to his daughter a considable sum of money, Their father I think was deceased at that time. Their residence was located on one of the principal streets of the town. Howell Hall, the eldest son of Colonel Hall, inherited the family mansion and a large portion of the land belonging to it. The balance of the land was divided between Mary and Edward. Mary became the owner of the greater part of the estate, her two brothers leaving no children. Her husband was Samuel L. James. They had six children—Clara, James, Hetty, Caroline, Samuel and Edward James. Clara was the first wife of David Reeves, of Bridgeton. They subsequently removed to Phœnixville, Pennsylvania. Hetty's first husband was Josiah Miller, of Mannington; Caroline married Robert Buck, of Bridgeton. Their three sons, James, Samuel and Edward emigrated to one of the Western States.

In all generations there are noble and intellectual women, who are calculated to make their foot-prints upon the sands of time. Among such was Sarah Clement Hall, of Salem; she descended from an ancient and respectable family, of England; her grand-father, Gregory Clement, was a citizen of London, and also a member of Parliament; was one of the Judges in the trial of Charles I, King of England. About 1670 his son James, and his wife, Jane Clement, emigrated to this country and settled on Long Island; their children were James, born 1670, who subsequently married Sarah Hinchman; Sarah Clement, born 1672, she married Judge William Hall, she being his second wife ; Thomas, born 1674 ; John, born 1676 ; Jacob, born 1678, married Ann Harrison ; Joseph, born 1681; Mercy, born 1683, married Joseph Bates ; Samuel, born 1685, and Nathaniel Clement, born 1687. William and Sarah C. Hall had three sons—William, Clement and Nathaniel, who are the ancestors of the Halls in the county of Salem. After the death of her husband it devolved upon Sarah to settle his large estate, and as far as the record appears she did it admirably.

Aaron Leaming, the ancestor of the large family of that name in Cape May, came from Connecticut when about sixteen years of age, and lived at Salem for a short period of time ; he was poor and friendless, but soon found a friend in Sarah, the the wife of William Hall ; he became a member of the Society of Friends. Aaron's son, in his account of his father, says that Sarah Hall was a lawyer of good ability for those times, and had a large collection of books, and being very rich took delight in my father on account of his sprightly wit and genius, and his uncommon fondness for the law which he read in her library.

RICHARD JOHNSON FAMILY.

The ship "Joseph and Benjamin," Captain Matthew Paine, master, anchored at Fort Elsborg, on the 13th of March, 1675. Hypolite Lafetra, John Pledger and his wife, Elizabeth, with their son, Joseph Pledger, aged three years, John Butcher and Richard Johnson, landed in Elsinborough. Afterwards the ship and other passengers proceeded further up the Delaware. Lafetra, a French Hugeunot, left his native country on account of religious persecution, having imbibed the doctrinces of George Fox, became a zealous Friend, and assisted in organizing Salem monthly meetings, in June, 1676. He and John Pledger bought of the proprietor, John Fenwick, 6000 acres of land in the same year. The land was located in Mannington, including what is now known as Quaker Neck, both branches of Fenwick creek; its southern boundary was a small stream called Mill creek, until it nearly reached Alloways creek. On part of the tract on the north of Pledger creek, John Pledger, Jr., erected himself a large brick dwelling in 1728, which is still standing, and owned by Elisha Bassett. John Pledger, Jr., was born at Salem, 27th of 9th month, 1680. Hypolite Lafetra sold his share of the 6000 acres to Jeremiah Powell and several others. Of the land that lies between the two streams, some 2000 acres, Benjamin Wyncook, an Englishman, became the owner; whether Lafetra left heirs is unknown at this time, and if he did they were daughters, and the name of the emigrant is lost in this county. John Butcher, it has been stated, was a cavalry officer in Cromwell's army. Like Fenwick, he became convinced of the doctrine of George Fox, and eventually became a member of the Society of Friends. His son, Thomas Butcher, located a large tract of land in Cohansey precinct, lying between the Gibbon's and Wood's land, now in Cumberland county, in Stoe Creek township. The late James Butcher, of Alloways Creek, was a lineal descendant, as was also John Butcher, of Salem, and Richard M. Acton's wife, on her mother's side. The first wife of William Griscom, of Woodbury, was a descendant of one of the oldest branches on the male line, and inherited a large share of the Butcher estate.

Richard Johnson was a young man of marked ability and rendered great assistance to the proprietor; he came from the county of Surry, England, and married Mary Grover, 25th of 6th month, 1682, at Salem. The following named persons signed their marriage certificate: James Nevell, his wife, Creseda Nevell, John Wilkenson, Cecilia Morgan, Ellen Robinson, Margaret Haselwood, Thomas Johnson, cousin of Richard, George Haselwood, John Maddox and Henry Jennings. Richard was one of the Burgesses of the town of Salem after it was incorporated as a borough in 1693, and was one of the Judges of the Salem Courts and a Justice of the Quarter Sessions, as also an influential member of the Salem monthly meeting of Friends, and took an active part in building the first brick meeting house in their ancient graveyard in 1699, which was completed in 1700; he paid fifteen pounds towards its erection. There was a subscription for the purpose of aiding poor Friends, in 1697, that belonged to Salem meeting, for which he gave twelve shillings; his place of residence was on Fenwick street where Rumsey's stores are now, the dwelling being built of brick with a hip or mansard roof. William Parrott purchased the property in 1788 or '90. William soon after removed the ancient dwelling and erected in its stead a large substantial two story brick dwelling, one of the first private dwellings in the city. In the year 1707, when men were chosen for their worth and ability, Richard Johnson, William Hall, Bartholomew Wyatt, Sr., and John Thompson, were elected to represent the Salem tenth in the State Legislature of New Jersey, which held its sessions at South Amboy and Burlington alternately. Richard was a large landholder in the town of Salem and other parts of the county; he owned five hundred acres of land on the south side of Alloways creek. Thomas Jones Yorke, of Salem, Samuel Kelty and the Hires' are the owners of the greater part of it at this time. Richard and Mary Grover Johnson had three children—Robert, Elizabeth and Ann. Richard Johnson died 1st month, 1719, aged seventy years; his wife, Mary G. Johnson, died in 1714; they were buried in the Friends' graveyard at Salem. Robert Johnson, their son, married Margaret, the widow of Joseph Sayres, in 1717; they had three children —Robert, Mary and Ann; he died 13th of 12th month, 1728, aged thirty-four years; his widow, Margaret Johnson, died in 1730, aged thirty-seven years. Elizabeth, the daughter of Richard and Mary Johnson, married John Pierson, being his second wife; he was the father of John Pierson, pastor of St. John's Episcopal church, in Salem, by his first wife. Elizabeth

Johnson Pierson died 5th of 5th month, 1720, leaving one daughter—Elizabeth Pierson.

Anna Johnson, the daughter of Richard and Mary G. Johnson, born 1687, married Alexander Grant, of Salem, in 1714, who arrived from England a few years before; his place of residence was located on the west side of Market street, then known as Bridge street; the ancient house is still standing and is owned by Anna G. Hubbell, one of his lineal descendants. Alexander and his wife, Anna Johnson Grant, had two children—Anna and Barbara Grant, the latter died single. Anna Grant, the eldest daughter, married Samuel Fenwick Hedge, the great grand-son of John Fenwick, and soon after their marriage removed to Greenwich. Samuel F. Hedge and Nicholas Gibbon were in the mercantile business together at that place. Samuel and his wife, Anna G. Fenwick, had three children—Samuel, Rebecca and another daughter, who died in infancy. Samuel F. Hedge died in 1731, making his will a short time previous, in which he devised a large landed estate to his widow, Anna G. Fenwick; she afterwards married Nicholos Gibbon, who was a partner in the mercantile business with her first husband. Nicholas and Anna G. Gibbon had five children—Nicholas, Grant, Jane, Ann and Francis. Jane became the wife of Robert Johnson, Jr., which I shall allude to more fully in another place. Ann married Judge Edward Weatherby, by whom she had one son, who died young. Robert Johnson, Jr., whose father died when he was young, lived sometime with his uncle, John Pledger, Jr., in Mannington, to learn the farming business; he married Margaret Morgan, of Chester county, now Delaware. (The romance respecting the marriage alluded to in the Sinnickson family genealogy.) Her parents were consistent members of the Society of Friends and she herself always adhered to the same religious society. The Morgans, Brintons, Palmers and Wades were among the first Quaker families who emigrated and settled in the province of Pennsylvania; they trace their ancestors to the time that William Penn landed at Chester in 1682, excepting Robert Wade, who emigrated with his brother Edward and Samuel Wade in company with John Fenwick. Robert purchased lands of the proprietor in the Salem tenth, but soon afterwards sold the said lands and removed to Upland, now Chester, in 1678, and bought 500 acres of land on the south side of Chester creek. Robert Johnson, Jr., and Margaret Morgan were married 18th of 12th month, 1752, at Marcus Hook; she died young, at the age of twenty-three years and seven months, leaving one child—Margaret Johnson, born 2d of 8th month, 1756. I think Margaret Morgan Johnson always retained her right among Friends, her husband, therefore, had her buried in the Friends' ancient graveyard in Salem, and directed a small marble stone to be placed at the head of her grave with her name upon it, it being the first of the kind that was ever used in the yard. I have no doubt he was actuated by the noblest motives to mark the spot where the object of his first love lay mouldering in the mother earth. Margaret, their daughter, subsequently married Andrew Sinnickson, of Penn's Neck, 26th of 5th month, 1779, the son of Andrew Sinaker, of the same township. Andrew and Margaret I. Sinnickson had one daughter, Mary, and two sons—Thomas and John. Margaret Johnson Sinnickson died 4th of 11th month, 1792, aged thirty-six years and three months; was buried in the Swedes church yard at Penn's Neck. Robert Johnson, Jr.'s second wife was Jane Gibbon, daughter of Nicholas and Ann Gibbon; they were married 3d of 11th month, 1767, and had one son—Robert Gibbon Johnson, born 23d of 7th month, 1771. Robert Johnson, Jr., died 28th of 12th month, 1796, aged sixty-nine years; his widow, Jane Gibbon Johnson, died 16th of 8th month, 1815, aged seventy-nine years and three months. Mary, the daughter of Robert Johnson, Sr. and Margaret Sayre Johnson, married John Pledger, of Mannington; they had issue, one son and a daughter. Joseph Pledger, their son, after he arrived at the age of twenty-one left his native county and settled in North Carolina. Catharine Pledger, their daughter, married John Ewing. Ann, the youngest daughter of Robert and Margaret Sayre Johnson, was married three times; her first husband's name was Hale, it does not appear there was any children by this marriage; her second husband was named Scoggin, I think, a brother to Jacob Scoggin, who married the daughter of William Tyler, 3d; they had one daughter, who subsequently married a man by the name of Smith, and had issue, one son—Scoggin Smith. Ann Johnson's third husband was John Beesley, and they lived on and owned the property that her grand-father, Richard Johnson, bought of the proprietor, located on the south side of Alloways creek, not far from Quinton's Bridge; they had one son whose name was Johnson Beesley. Ann survived all three of her husbands, and in her old age she went under the name of Nanny Beesley, and was considered very skillful in curing many diseases with herbs; her son, Johnson Beesley, married and had one daughter, who subsequently married John, the eldest son of Samuel Nicholson, of Mannington. John Nicholson and his wife had one daughter —Catharine, who married Job Stretch, the son of Elisha and Sarah Bradway Stretch, of Alloways Creek; Job and Catharine Stretch had two or three children. Mary, one of their daughters, married John P. Moore, a native of Cumberland, but now a resident of the city of Salem, and keeps a hardware store on Market street.

Nicholas and Leonard Gibbon were the sons of Arthur and Jane Gibbon, of Gravesend, county of Kent, England.— Arthur became possessed of 5,500 acres of land in Cohansey precinct, now Cumberland county, lying in Greenwich and Hopewell townships. A few years after, Nicholas married Ann G., the widow of Samuel Fenwick Hedge, and they left Greenwich and moved to Salem. He continued in the mercantile business in that town, was Collector of the Port, and Surrogate of the county of Salem, as also Colonel, and had command of all the militia in the lower counties. The place of their residence was on Market street, in the house devised to his wife by her father, Alexander Grant. Nicholas died 2d of 2d month, 1758, aged fifty-five years and three months. His wife, Ann G. Gibbon, died 24th of 3d month, 1760, aged fifty-seven years. Their eldest son. Nicholas, born 5th of 11th month, 1732, and died 7th of 1st month, 1748, aged sixteen years. Grant Gibbon, the second son, born 28th of 11th month, 1734, was engaged in the mercantile business; was Surrogate of the county, and Judge and Justice, and Collector of the Port of Salem after his father's death. He was a man of culture and very prepossessing in his manners, which made him very popular with the people. He was a warm patriot, and a sympathizer in all the measures of the American Revolution. On the 13th of 10th month, 1784, a meeting was held in the county of Salem, in which the inhabitants unanimously proffered their sympathy to their fellow citizens in Boston suffering under the oppression of General Gage. At that meeting they proposed raising money to alleviate the distressed condition of the people of that city, and it was resolved that Grant Gibbon, one in whom the public had entire confidence in his integrity and patriotism, take the burthen and trouble in soliciting money fer their relief from the people. He cheerfully undertook this task, and collected the sum of £157 3s 9d, which was speedily forwarded to the suffering poor in Boston. Grant Gibbon died comparatively a young man, which event occurred 27th of 6th month, 1776, aged forty-one years, being about seven days before the Declaration of Independence was signed in Philadelphia. Jane

Gibbon, his eldest sister, born 15th of 5th month, 1738, married Robert Johnson, Jr.; Ann, the daughter of Nicholas and Ann Gibbon, was born 29th of 4th month, 1741; and Francis, the youngest son of Nicholas and Ann Gibbon, was born 14th of 5th month, 1744, and died 11th of 1st month, 1788, aged forty-three years.

Thomas Carney, born in Ireland in 1709, emigrated to this country early in life, and subsequently married Hannah, the daughter of John Procter, of Penn's Neck. He was a large landholder. His lands were located along the Delaware river, and extended easterly to Game creek. Thomas, the son of Thomas and Hannah Carney, was born in 1740. Peter Carney, their second son, was born in 1742. James, the third son, was born in 1748, and died in the 1st month, 1776, aged about twenty-eight years. John, the fourth son, was born in 1760, and died in 1774, aged about fourteen years. Sarah Carney, their daughter, married George Clark. Naomi, the second daughter of Thomas and Hannah Carney, married John Summerill, of Penn's Neck. Mary Carney, the youngest daughter, was thrice married; her first husband was Henry James, by whom she had one son—Henry; her second husband was John Page; and her third, Joseph Stout. Thomas Carney, the father of the above mentioned children, died in the 5th month, 1784, aged seventy-five years; and his amiable wife departed this life in 2d month, 1778, aged about sixty-three years. They were buried in the old Episcopal church yard at Church Landing in Penn's Neck, and several of their children lie mouldering there in their mother earth. When quite young, I heard several aged people speak of the benevolence of Hannah Carney. By tradition, she was in the practice of getting her husband to slaughter a fattening bullock occasionally in the winter. Then she, with a boy to drive for her, with a pair of oxen and a cart filled with meat and flour, (there were no spring wagons in Salem tenth in those days,) she would go into the woods of Obisquahasset among the poor and laboring classes who lived in small log dwellings, and there on a cold North American winter day, she would dispense to them both flour and meat according to their necessities. And above all, she was enabled, by the kindness of her manners and expressions, to encourage the despondent and administer by kind words to the sick and afflicted among them. Surely she had her reward, when she returned to her home in the evening, of feeling in her own mind that she had endeavored to do something to alleviate the suffering of her fellow beings. On reflecting upon the character of Hannah Carney, the sayings of David, the sweet psalmer of Israel, arrested my attention: "Blessed are those that consid-"ereth the poor, for the Lord will deliver them in time of "trouble." Peter, the second son of Thomas and Hannah Carney, married the daughter of Jonathan Roberts, of Mannington; they had issue, two daughters—Elizabeth and Margaret Carney. Elizabeth died single, and Margaret married John Tuft. They had one son—Sinnickson Tuft, who died single, in his twenty-second year. Thomas Carney, Jr., the oldest son of Thomas and Hannah Carney, married Mary, daughter of Abel Harris; they had three children—Ruth, Harris and Hannah Carney. Ruth was born in the 5th month, 1773, and married Benjamin, son of Whitten Cripps, of Mannington. Whitten Cripps descended from an ancient family on his father's and mother's sides. He married Martha Huddy, in 1759, which took place in the Friends' meeting house that stood in the grave yard at Salem. There were two children—Mary, who married Peter Andrews, and Benjamin Cripps. Whitten took his name from his grandfather, James Whitten, who located on the farm in Mannington, long known as the "John Denn Farm." Benjamin and Ruth Carney Cripps had one son—Thomas Carney Cripps, who died aged about twelve years. Ruth Carney Cripps, wife of Benjamin, died 17th of 2d month, 1794, aged twenty-one years. Harris Carney, son of Thomas and Mary Carney, died young.

Abel Harris, the father of Mary Carney, died in 1789. He made his will in 1779, and devised £100 to the Episcopal church in Penn's Neck, and also the interest of £100 to the township of Alloways Creek, for the schooling of children.

Hannah, the youngest daughter of Thomas and Mary H. Carney, was born 27th of 7th month, 1780; she married Robert Gibbon Johnson, on the 19th of 6th month, 1798. Robert and his wife had four children—Jane Gibbon Johnson, born in 1800; she died young. Mary Jane Johnson, their second daughter, born in 1805, died in infancy. Ann Gibbon Johnson, their third daughter, married Ferdinand W. Hubbell, Esq., of Philadelphia, a lawyer of considerable eminence of that city; he has been deceased several years. They had four children—Robert Johnson, Ann L. Johnson, and Helena. Robert Carney Johnson, the son of Robert Gibbon and Hannah Johnson, married Julia Harrison, the daughter of the late Josiah Harrison, Esq., of Salem. Robert C. lives and owns the palatial dwelling where his father formerly lived, on Market street, in Salem. Robert and his wife had two children—

Robert Harrison, who died in infancy, and Henry Johnson. Hannah Carney Johnson died when her son, Robert, was an infant. Robert Gibbon Johnson's second wife was Juliana Elizabeth, daughter of Paul and Esther Zantzinger, of Lancaster county, Pennsylvania. They were married in 1813; she died in 1854, aged seventy-three years. There was no issue. Robert Gibbon Johnson and his wife, Hannah Carney Johnson, had the largest and most valuable real estate of modern times, in Salem county. Robert inherited a large estate from his ancestors, and his wife became the owner of the great and valuable estate of Thomas Carney, consisting of several farms, most of them located in Upper Penn's Neck. Robert, like his uncle, Grant Gibbon, was pleasing in his address; held in his time several important offices, was a member of the State Legislature two or three times, and was one of the Judges of Salem Courts for several years. In his old age he wrote a history of Salem county, which was published in 1839; it is often referred to at the present time. He at one time informed me that he intended writing and giving a more general history of the settlement of this Colony; but death intervened before he had an opportunity to accomplish it. He died 3d of 10th month, 1850, aged seventy-nine years.

JOHN JOHNSON FAMILY.

The name of Johnson has been familiar in the county of Salem since the first settlement by the Europeans. The Swedish family by the name of Jonanson, located on the eastern shore of the Delaware, now Penn's Neck, in 1640, but was soon merged to Johnson. The first English emigrant that bore the name was Richard and his cousin, Thomas Johnson, who came and located in Fenwick's tenth a few months before the proprietor. John Johnson, who was not any way connected, as far as appears, to the before mentioned, emigrated with his wife, Jane Suayberry Johnson, to Salem county from Ireland, about 1756. John had considerable means at his disposal, and he located a large tract of land in the township of Pilesgrove, now Pittsgrove, and settled thereon. John and his wife had eight children—James, John, Rebecca, Samuel, Phebe, William, Mary and Isaac. John, the father of these children, departed this life the 31st of 3d month, 1802, aged seventy-one years. His widow, Jane S. Johnson, died 28th of 6th month, 1825, aged ninety-two years and eight months.

James, the eldest son of John and Jane Johnson, was born 31st of 10th month, 1757. Soon after the war of the American Revolution commenced, he entered the Colonial army, and was at the battle of Red Bank. He married Christiana Swing, of Pittsgrove, 28th of 2d month, 1781. The year that James rented the large and productive farm in Mannington, that formerly belonged to Bartholomew Wyatt, 3d, of William Carpenter, son-in-law of Wyatt, I have no means of ascertaining. He continued to reside on the Wyatt farm until the Spring of 1809, when having previously purchased valuable real estate in Lower Penn's Neck, located a short distance from the town of Salem. James with his family settled there in the year mentioned. James and Christiana had sixteen children; six of them died young, and his wife, Christiana, died 19th of 3d month, 1825, aged sixty years and four months. James died 9th of 2d month, 1837, in his eightieth year. He, in his time, possessed physical and mental abilities above the average of mankind, and also uncommon energy, combined with a sound and comprehensive mind. He was one of the most successful agriculturists in the county of Salem in his day. Although it appears his parents were members of the Presbyterian Church, he was himself a deacon and a consistent member of the Baptist Church of Salem up to the time of his death.

Ruth, daughter of James and Christiana Johnson, was born 1st of 12th month, 1784; she married John Redstrake, in 1807, and they had six children—Mary, Ann, James J., Edward, Jane, Ruth and Isabella. Mary Ann married William, son of William Hall, of Mannington; they had issue. James Johnson, son of John and Ruth Redstrake, has been twice married, his first wife was the daughter of Edmund Gibbon, of Penn's Neck; she died young, leaving no issue; his second wife was named Brown, a native of Greenwich, Cumberland county. Edward, the second son of John and Ruth Redstrake, married a person by the name of Stout, and his children are Mary Jane and John. John, son of Edward, married Elizabeth, daughter of Michael Allen. Jane, daughter of John and Jane Redstreak, married Thomas Gibbon; they have issue, one son—Thomas Gibbon, Jr. Ruth, the daughter of John and Ruth J. Redstrake, married a man by the name of Jefferson, of Delaware; they had issue, two sons. Isabella Redstrake married a person by the name of Murphy; they have issue. Sarah, daughter of James and Christiana Johnson, was born 11th of 6th month, 1783, married Jonathan, son of John Lindzey, of Upper Alloways Creek, in 1803; they had issue—William, Ruth, John, Mary and James. William went to one of the Southern States. John married Hannah, the daughter of James and Hannah Butcher, of Alloways Creek. John is deceased, leaving four children—James, Charles, John and Sarah Lindzey. Mary, the daughter of Jonathan and Sarah Lindsey, married Lawrence Hoover Boon, of Salem; they have two daughters—Sarah and Maria Josephine. Josephine married Albert H. Slape, a lawyer and Prosecutor of the Pleas for Salem and Atlantic counties. William, son of James and Christiana Johnson, was born 12th of 10th month, 1788, married in 1810, Margaret Lambson, a direct descendant of Thomas Lambson, who emigrated from England, and located land and settled thereon in 1690, in the township of Penn's Neck. William and Margaret Johnson had thirteen children—Isabella, Rebecca, Christiana, Mary Jane, James S., William, Ephraim, Edward, John, Margaret, Robert, Ferdinand and Charles. Isabella, daughter of William and Margaret Johnson, married William Meveling, of Maryland; they have issue. Rebecca, the daughter of William and Margaret Johnson, married Thomas, son of Dr. Hedge and Mary Ann Thompson, of Salem. Thomas is deceased, leaving a widow and two children—Hedge and Isabella P. Thompson. Hedge married Achsah, daughter of Isaac and Achsah Hall Peterson, of Salem; his wife is deceased, leaving no issue. Rebecca Johnson Thompson, widow of Thomas, resides with her son in the State of Maryland. Isabella Thompson, their daughter, married Charles Watson, of Philadelphia; she died without issue.

Christiana, daughter of William Johnson, married George Kelton, and reside near Haddonfield, Camden county; they have six children. James S., son of William and Margaret Johnson, resides in Penn's Neck, on the homestead of his father. He married Sarah, daughter of John and Hannah Lindzey, 11th of 10th month, 1854; they have issue, three sons. William, Ephraim, Edward, and John Johnson, sons of William and Margaret, are deceased. Margaret, daughter of William and Margaret Johnson, married James, son of John and Lydia Flanagan, late of Philadelphia. James and his wife are living in Philadelphia, and have issue.—Mary and William. Charles and Robert Johnson, sons of William, remain single. Abraham, son of James and Christiana Johnson, born 19th of 7th month, 1792, married Mary Conaroe, of Salem. They moved to the western part of New York, and both are deceased; they died in Buffalo, and left two daughters. Mary, daughter of James and Christiana Johnson, born 23d of 5th month, 1790, married Joseph Dennis, in 1810; he was a bricklayer by trade, and a native of Greenwich, Cumberland county. They moved to the State of New York, and both are deceased, leaving four children. One of their daughters married Dr. Smith, of Chicago, Illinois. Rebecca, daughter of James and Christiana Johnson, born 8th of 10th month, 1794, married Edward, son of Henry Mulford, of Lower Alloways Creek; they moved and settled near Fredonia, New York; from thence they moved and settled near Chicago, Illinois; Rebecca is deceased, leaving three children—James, Edward, and Anna Mulford. James and Edward married, and are deceased; they left issue. Anna, their sister, is married, but has no issue. Edward Mulford, Sr., is living, at an advanced age, near the city of Chicago, and possesses a princely fortune. John, the son of James and Christiana Johnson, born 14th of 2d month, 1796, followed the sea in early life, was the captain of the ship Josephine, trading from Philadelphia to New Orleans for a number of years. When he was past middle age he left the seas and settled on the farm that his father left to him in Penn's Neck. His wife was Elizabeth, daughter of John M. and Ann Sinnickson, of Salem; they had issue, one son. John and his wife, and their minor son, are deceased. Ann, daughter of James and Christiana Johnson, was born 7th of 7th month, 1802; married Jonathan, son of John Mulford, of Alloways Creek, in 1826; they have five children, named Christiana, Amanda, James, John, and Anna Mulford. Christiana, their oldest daughter, is married, and resides in Boston, Massachusetts. Lydia, daughter of James Johnson, born in 1804, married James M. Challis, a Baptist clergyman, in 1823; she is deceased, leaving five children—Joseph, William, Luther L., George, and Emma Challis. Joseph, son of James and Lydia Challis, is married, and lives at Frankford, Pa.; has issue. William Challis is a physician, is married, and has issue. George, son of James and Lydia Challis, is married, and has children. Emma, daughter of James and Lydia Challis, married Richard Probasco; they are living in Talbot county, Maryland. Luther, William, and George Challis are among the first inhabitants of the city of Atchison, Kansas, and all three are reputed to be very wealthy. Rachel, daughter of James and Christiana Johnson, born 21st of 4th month, 1805, married Josiah Hall in 1824; they moved to Cecil county, Maryland, and had two children—James and Christiana Hall. Josiah and his wife, Rachel J. Hall, are deceased, leaving a large and valuable estate.

John, son of John and Jane Johnson, of Pittsgrove, born 1st of 10th month, 1759, married Elizabeth, daughter of Cornelius Dubois, in 1783; they had twelve children. Cornelius Johnson, their eldest son, born 12th of 6th month, 1784, married Elizabeth Vick. John, son of John and Elizabeth D. Johnson, born 7th of 4th month, 1788, married Rebecca Jones. Jane, daughter of John Elizabeth Johnson, born 13th of 3d month, 1690, married Robert, son of Samuel Dubois. Ann, daughter of John and Elizabeth Johnson, born 5th of 5th month, 1792, never married. David, son of John Johnson, born 8th of 5th month, 1795, married Hannah, daughter of David Dickinson. Benjamin, son of John and Elizabeth Johnson, born 14th of 4th month, 1799, married Maria, daughter of William Mayhew. Robert, son of John Johnson, born 28th of 4th month, 1801, remains unmarried. Elizabeth, daughter of John and Elizabeth Johnson, born 2d of 4th month, 1807, married Enoch, son of David Mayhew. Three of John and Elizabeth Dubois Johnson's children died young. Cornelius, John's eldest son, and Elizabeth

Vick, his wife, had six children. Cornelius, the eldest, died a young man. Margaret, the daughter, married, but her husband's name is not mentioned. James Johnson, another son, is not married. William married Ann, the daughter of Jacob Hitchner. John and Rebecca Johnson had three children—Caroline, Ruth Ann, and Hiram Johnson. Ruth Ann Johnson married Cobert Iredell; they had issue. Hiram Johnson married Sarah Nixon, daughter of Martia Nixon. Robert Dubois and Jane Johnson, daughter of John, had twelve children—Mary Ann, Ruth, Alfred, Susan, Elizabeth, Belinda, John, Frank, Charles, Enoch, Elma, and Amy. Susan, daughter of Robert Dubois, married Albert Leurz; they had issue. Elizabeth Dubois married Benjamin Lamb; they had children. Belinda Dubois married Frederick Fox; they have issue. Frank Dubois married, his wife's name not known; they had children. Charles Dubois married; they had issue. David Johnson, son of John and Elizabeth Dubois Johnson, married Hannah Dickinson; had five children; their names are Emeline, Edward, Mirah, John, and Elizabeth Johnson. Emeline, the eldest, married John Venal; they had issue. Edward married Rhoda S. E. Taylor; they have children. Mirah married John, son of Isaac Mayhew; they had issue. John, son of David Johnson, married Sarah Campbell; they have issue. Elizabeth Ann Johnson married Alfred Rice; they had issue. Rebecca, daughter of John and Jane Johnson, was twice married; her first husband was Benjamin Harding; he died, leaving no issue. Her second husband was Hugh Maguire; they had three children—Ann, Jane, and Alinda Maguire. Jane Maguire married Isaac Wood; she is deceased, leaving no children. Ann Maguire married a person by the name of Cripps; he died, leaving no issue. Alinda Maguire is still living, unmarried. Phebe, daughter of John and Jane Johnson, married John Stewart; they moved in the State of Delaware; they are both deceased, leaving issue. Mary Johnson, daughter of John and Jane, married Samuel Elwell; they moved to the State of Indiana in 1817; they had three children—Isaac, Elizabeth, and Rebecca; all are deceased, leaving issue.

William, the son of John and Jane Johnson, married Elizabeth Maguire; they had two children—Hugh and Lucretia; they left their native State, and moved to the State of New York. Samuel, the son of John and Jane Johnson, was twice married; his first wife was Nancy McClung, by whom he had five children—Isaac, Samuel, Elizabeth, Mary and one who died young; his second wife was Sarah Martin, by whom he

JOHN JOHNSON FAMILY.

had eight children—Nancy, Sarah Ann, Samuel, Josiah, Charlotte, Ruth, George and Martha. Isaac, son of Samuel and Nancy Johnson, was born 20th of 7th month, 1787, and married Catharine, daughter of Eleazar Mayhew; she was born 10th of 7th month, 1789. Eleazar Mayhew was a land surveyor and conveyancer, and had six sons and one daughter—Catharine, John, Stanford, William, Eleazar, Isaac and Elaw Mayhew. The latter was a physician. Eleazar's family are all deceased at the present time; they all married excepting Eleazar Mayhew, Jr., and left issue; he himself was a large land holder at the time of his death. Isaac and Catharine Mayhew Johnson had seven children, namely—John, Rebecca, Sallie, Harrison, Nancy, Samuel and Doctor Mayhew. Catharine, wife of Isaac Johnson, departed this life 30th of 4th month, 1858, aged about sixty-nine years. Isaac is still living in his eighty-ninth year, and enjoys excellent health, both physical and mental, for one of his age; he has been an uncommon active man, and has done a large amount of public business, having been Sheriff of Salem county a number of years ago.

John, the son of Isaac and Catharine Johnson, left his native country and went to Indiana and there settled, and married Mary Ann Shuster; they have seven children. Rebecca, daughter of Isaac and Catharine M. Johnson, married Garrett Prickett; they have six children. Sallie, daughter of Isaac and Catharine M. Johnson, married Edmund Dubois; they have twelve children. Harrison, son of Isaac and Catharine M. Johnson, married Emma, daughter of Moses Richman, Esq.; they had seven children, five of whom are still living. Nancy, daughter of Isaac and Catharine M. Johnson, married Isaac Newkirk; they had six children, three of whom are deceased. Samuel, son of Isaac and Catharine M. Johnson, married Susan Hitchner; they had nine children, eight of them are still living. Mayhew Johnson, M. D., the youngest son of Isaac and Catharine M. Johnson, has been twice married; his first wife was Isabella Tyngle, by whom he had three children; his second wife was Lizzie Norton, by whom he has three children. Mayhew Johnson, M. D., resides with his family at Pennsgrove, in which section of the county he has quite an extensive medical practice.

Sarah Ann, eldest daughter of Samuel Johnson by his second wife of Sarah Martin Johnson, married a person by the name of Reynolds; they had issue. Samuel and Isaiah, sons of Samuel and Sarah M. Johnson, are both deceased leaving no issue. Charlotte, daughter of Samuel and Sarah M. Johnson, married Henry Carroll; they had issue. Ruth, daughter of Samuel and Sarah M. Johnson, married a person by the name of Taylor; they had children. George, son of Samuel and Sarah M. Johnson, left Salem county and settled in the State of Georgia. Martha, the youngest daughter of Samuel and Sarah M. Johnson, is still living, but never married.

Isaac, the youngest son of John and Jane Johnson, born 21st of 7th month, 1772, married Mary Elwell, born 23d of 5th month, 1778; they were married 24th of 6th month, 1795, and had twelve children, named Harriet, Elizabeth, Isaac, Amelia, Mary, Sarah, John, Samuel, Emma Ann, William, Benjamin F., and James. Isaac Johnson, the father of the before mentioned children, died 5th of 1st month, 1852, aged about eighty years. His widow departed this life 18th of 9th month, 1862, aged eighty-four years, three months and twenty-six days. Harriet, daughter of Isaac and Mary Johnson, born 3d of 10th month, 1796, married William Newkirk. Their children were Mary, Isaac J., and Redma. Elizabeth, daughter of Isaac and Mary Johnson, born 18th of 4th month, 1798, married Isaac Abbott; they had issue—Martha and Mary. Elizabeth, their mother, died in 1871. Isaac, son of Isaac and Mary Johnson, born 1st of 10th month, 1799, married Rachel Dubois; they had twelve children—Rebecca, Joseph, Thomas, Isaac, Elizabeth, Hester, Adaline, Christiana, Mary, Martha, Matilda and Emma. Their father, Isaac Johnson, departed this life 1st of 10th month, 1874. Amelia, daughter of Isaac and Mary Johnson, born 26th of 10th month, 1801, married Daniel Clark; they had seven children—David, Mary Jane, Harriet, Amelia, Isaac J., Charles and Daniel. Mary, daughter of Isaac and Mary Johnson, born 15th of 3d month, 1804, married Samuel Dubois; they had seven children—Rebecca, Adaline, Louis, Jane, Eliza, Emeline and Johnson. Their father, Samuel Dubois, died in 1872. Sarah, daughter of Isaac and Mary Johnson, born 18th of 8th month, 1805, married Henry Elwell; they had issue, seven children—Samuel, Mary, William, Franklin, Charlotte, Eliza and Borden. John, son of Isaac and Mary Johnson, born 5th of 3d month, 1810, married Elizabeth Merrick; their children were Mary, Isaac, William, Clinton, Alonza and Larrie. Their father died in 1864. Samuel, son of Isaac and Mary Johnson, born 19th of 5th month, 1812, died in 1870. Emma Ann, daughter of Isaac and Mary Johnson, born 29th of 9th month, 1814, married Ewalt Richman; they have nine children—Charles, Isaac J., Henry, Wilbert, Clayton, Johnson, Harriet, Sarah and Anna.

Benjamin F., son of Isaac and Mary Johnson, born 15th of 6th month, 1818, married Anna Mickle; they have two children —Woodburn and Ella. James, son of Isaac and Mary Jonnson, born 21st of 2d month, 1820, married Sarah Stull; they have issue—Caroline and Ella. Isaac Johnson, the father of the before mentioned children, was an uncommonly active business man; he was heard to say when a young man, he was determined to possess more broad acres of land than his father owned at the time of his death, all of which he realized, and more. He was the owner of a large tract of excellent land not far from Daretown, containing upwards of 600 acres, together with large quantities of land in other sections, and the owner of one or two flour mills at the time of his death. Besides attending to his own business, which was extensive, he transacted much public business, and was Sheriff of the county of Salem at one time.

JENNINGS FAMILY.

Henry Jennings was a prominent member of Salem Monthly Meeting of Friends, soon after its organization. He was the son of William and Mary Jennings, born the 21st of 7th month, 1642, in the county of Surrey, England. Henry and his wife, Margaret Jennings, embarked for America in the ship Kent, Captain Gregory, and landed at New Salem 23d of 6th month, 1677. In 1682, John Adams, son-in-law of John Fenwick, sold Henry Jennings 200 acres of land. He likewise purchased a considerable tract of land in Cohansey precinct, it being near the town of Cohansey, (now Greenwich). Henry and his wife removed from Salem and located in the city of Philadelphia, about the year 1700, and at that place they ended their days. He was a tailor by trade, and followed it in that city. He died in 1706, and made his will the year previous; and, not having any children, he devised most of his estate to his uncle, Isaac Jennings, of London, and to the daughter of Isaac, Margaret Jennings, his cousin.

Some persons have supposed that Henry and Samuel Jennings were brothers. If they were relatives it was not nearer than cousins. Samuel Jennings emigrated from Coles Hill, in Buckinghamshire, England, and located at Burlington, N. J., in 1680. Soon after his arrival he built himself a large brick dwelling, which stood on the banks of the Delaware. In his house the Yearly Meeting of Friends of Pennsylvania and West New Jersey were held several years. The time-honored house was removed about ten years since. He was a recommended minister some four or five years before he left his native land, and was highly appreciated as such in that Kingdom. Soon after his arrival, Edward Byllings, the Propritary Governor, appointed him his deputy, in which capacity he served up to 1683, when he was chosen Governor for one year by the Assembly of New Jersey, and continued so up to the time of his removal to Philadelphia, in 1692. His abilities were highly appreciated by William Penn. Soon after he moved to the Province he was appointed to the Commission of Peace, in the city of his adoption.

About that time the controversy with George Keith arose, in which Samuel Jennings was much engaged on behalf of the Society. In the early part of 1694 he sailed for London, as a respondent on the appeal of Keith, to the London Yearly Meeting, in which body he ably vindicated the cause of his American brethren from the aspersions of their detractors. Soon after his return from England he removed to Burlington, the place of his former residence. In 1702 the crown of England, to which the government of New Jersey had been transferred by the proprietors, appointed him one of the procinial council; and in 1707, the year preceding his death, he filled the office of Speaker of the Assembly, in which position he distinguished himself by a bold and fearless opposition to the arbitrary misrule of the bigoted Lord Cornbury.

Edward Hyde was the son of the Earl of Claridon, and was one of the first officers who deserted the army of King James. King William, in gratitude for his services, appointed him Governor of New York and New Jersey, in 1702, and conferred on him the title of Lord Cornbury, an office he was entirely unfit for by nature and education; he being a bigoted belligerent, and arbitrary in his disposition, not seeming to understand the wants of the colonists; all which incapacitated him for an executive officer. The inhabitants of the colony of New York, as well as those of New Jersey, became wearied of his misgovernment, and accordingly they determined to send an appeal to Queen Anne for her to remove the Governor. Samuel Jennings had the credit of writing the address, which was forwarded to the home government, and by so doing he incurred the great displeasure of Cornbury, who is reported to have said "Jennings was the most impudent man he ever knew." However, it had the desired effect, and Lord Cornbury was recalled in 1708, the year of Samuel Jenning's death. Proud, the historian, wrote that "Samuel Jennings was worthy of memory, and endowed with both spiritual and temporal wisdom; was suppressor of vice and encourager of virtue." He was one of those rare individuals in whom was concentrated a variety of qualifications and mental endowments, by which, under the sanctifying power of truth, he was made eminently useful to his fellow men, both in his ministerial and civil capacity. He did more than any of his cotemporaries in organizing the civil government of West Jersey. At his death he left no sons to perpetuate his name, but three daughters.

Sarah Jennings, his eldest daughter, married Edward Pennington, in 1699; he was the youngest son of Isaac Pennington, an eminent citizen of London, a man of literature, who wrote extensively in defence of Quakerism. Edward's mother, when Isaac married her, was a widow of Sir William Sprignett, a military officer. William left one daughter—Guielma Maria Sprignett, who afterwards was the first wife of William Penn; there were two children—William and Letiti Penn. The second wife of William Penn was Hannah Callowhill; they had two sons. John, the only American child of William Penn, was born in Philadelphia, in the house that Samuel Carpenter built, on Second street, corner of Norris alley. The second child by his second wife was Richard Penn. Edward Pennington was a half-brother of Guielma Penn; he was a Surveyor-General of the province of Pennsylvania up to the time of his death, which event took place in 1701, two years after his marriage, leaving one son—Isaac Pennington. Ann Jennings, the second daughter of Samuel, married William Stevenson, in 1706, and the third daughter, Mercy, married John Stevenson, the brother of William, in the same year. Thomas, another brother, married Sarah, the widow of Edward Pennington. John Stevenson, the great grand-son of Samuel Jennings, emigrated from Burlington county to Upper Penn's Neck about seventy or eighty years hence, but remained there a few years; he afterwards removed to the township of Mannington, on the Wyatt farm, when the late James Johnson left and moved on his farm in Penn's Neck. John's wife was Emily Newbold, a member of the ancient family of that name in Burlington county. John and Emily Stevenson had several children—William, Mary, Daniel, Charles, John and Emily Stevenson. Mary married Clayton, the son of John and Charlotte Wistar; they had two sons—John and Richard Wistar. Daniel Stevenson married Hannah, daughter of John Adams. Charles Stevenson married Rachel, the eldest daughter of Samuel and Margaret Hilliard. John Stevenson, Jr. married Ann, daughter of Samuel and Ann Brick, of Elsinboro.

16

KEASBEY FAMILY.

Edward Keasbey, first of the Keasbey family in this county, emigrated from England about the year 1694, and settled in the town of New Salem. He was then a young man. I think it probable that he was a member of the Society of Friends before he left his native land, and came here to avoid religious persecution. Soon after his arrival he took an active part in the affairs of the religious meetings of the Society, to which he appeared to be so ardently attached. He gave the sum of twenty dollars towards erecting the brick meeting house in the grave yard on Broadway street. The house was completed in 1701. On 26th of 11th month, 1701, he married Elizabeth, widow of Isaac Smart, of Elsinborough. She was the daughter of Andrew and Isabella Thompson, and was born near Dublin, Ireland, 15th of 8th month, 1666. Edward and his wife, Elizabeth T. Keasbey, had four children—Mary, the eldest, born 11th of 3d month, 1703; Edward, Matthew and Susanna. Matthew Keasbey, born in 1706, married, and had a large family of children, most of whom were daughters, and consequently at this late period the record of them is lost. Edward Keasbey, Jr., eldest son of Edward and Elizabeth T., was born in 1705, and subsequently married Elizabeth, the daughter of Edward Bradway, Jr., and grand-daughter of the emigrant of that name. Edward and Elizabeth B. Keasbey had three children— Edward, Mary and Bradway. Edward Keasbey 3d, was born 1726, and afterwards married Prudence, the daughter of Edward and Temperance Quinton.

Edward Quinton was the son of Tobias Quinton, who emigrated from England and purchased lands on the south side of Alloways creek, where the village of Quinton is now located. He died about the year 1705, leaving one son—Edward. Temperance Quinton was the daughter of Daniel, the son of John Smith, of Almesbury (it is now spelled Amebury). Daniel Smith was born near Norfolk, England, 10th of 12th month, 1660. He came to this country with his father, in company with John Fenwick, the proprietor, in 1675, and subsequently purchased of him 1,000 acres of land on the north side of Alloways creek, opposite the present village of Quinton. At the schism in the Society of Friends, made by George Keith, Daniel Smith became an active partisan with the Keithites, as they were called, and when Keith returned to England many of his followers became members of the Baptist religious association. Daniel Smith became a Baptist, and most of his family did likewise, except his eldest son John, who still adhered to the Society of his ancestors. John Smith left three sons—John, Benjamin, and James. The latter became an eminent merchant in Philadelphia, his partner being the late Jacob Ridgway. James was much the senior of his partner, and retired from business a number of years before his death. He ended his days in the city of Burlington.

Edward Quinton died in 1756, and his wife Temperance departed this life in 1775, aged seventy-five years. Edward and Prudence Q. Keasbey had ten children—Edward, Elizabeth, Matthew, Sarah, Lewis, Phebe, Prudence, Edward the second, Samuel and Anthony. Several of these children died in infancy. After the death of Prudence Q. Keasbey, Edward married Sarah Quinton, sister of his first wife, by whom he had six children—Temperance, Delniz C., Jesse, Rachel, Kizzie and Jane. The father of the above mentioned children died in 1779, aged fifty-four years.

Matthew, the son of Edward and Prudence Keasbey, was born in 1749, and lived to grow to manhood, when he went to sea and was drowned. Lewis, his brother, born 1752, married Sarah Grinnell; he left issue. Anthony, the youngest son of Edward and Prudence Keasbey, born in 1758, married Hannah, the daughter of Joseph and Rebecca Abbott Brick, of Elsinborough. Anthony and his wife had eight children—Rebecca, Prudence, Matthew, Edward Quinton, Hannah, Anthony, Artemesia, and Ann. Rebecca, their eldest child, married Dr. Charles Hannah; she left no issue. Prudence died at middle age, unmarried. Matthew married Ann, the daughter of Michael Fisher, of Woodbury; they had six children—Rebecca, Caroline, Charles, Quinton, John, and Elizabeth. Dr. Edward Q. Keasbey married a young woman by the name of Aertson. They had four children—Anthony, Helen, Anna, and Edward.

Hannah, the daughter of Anthony and Hannah Keasbey, married Thomas, the son of Dr. James and Ruth Vanmeter, of Salem. Hannah is deceased, leaving two daughters—Artemesia and Martha. Anthony, the youngest son of Anthony and Hannah Keasbey, sold his patrimonial estate to his brother, Dr.

Edward Q. Keasbey, and went to one of the Southern States. Artemesia died a young woman, unmarried. Ann, the youngest daughter of Anthony and Hannah B. Keasbey, married James M. Hannah. They had three children—Charles Gilbert, Cornelia, and Percival. Anthony, the father of the above mentioned children, died in the early part of this century, leaving one of the largest landed estates of that period. His wife survived him several years.

Temperance, the eldest daughter of Edward and Sarah Keasbey, married Judge John Smith, who resided near the village of Quinton. They had one son—Edward K. Smith, who was a surveyor of land for some years, and afterwards was elected Sheriff. He married the daughter of Andrew Sinnickson, of Salem. He and his family subsequently removed to one of the Western States. Delzin, the eldest son of Edward and Sarah Keasbey, was a hatter, and followed his trade in Salem for a number of years. His residence was in the ancient brick house of the Keasbey's situated at the upper end of East Broadway. It is still standing.

Delzin Keasbey's wife was Rachel Smith. Jesse, the second son of Edward and Sarah Quinton Keasbey, married the daughter of Thomas Rowen, Sr., of Salem, sister of the late Dr. Thomas Rowen. Jesse and his wife had two children—John and Ann Keasbey. Rachel, the daughter of Edward and Sarah Q. Keasbey, married Leonard Gibbon, the son of John and Esther Gibbon, who was born 15th of 11th month, 1766; they resided near Roadstown, Cumberland county. John was the son of Leonard, who, with his brother, Nicholas Gibbon, emigrated from England in the fore part of the last century; they purchased 6,000 acres of land at or near the town of Cohansey, now Greenwich; they likewise organized the first Episcopal church in that town, and the first of that persuasion in that section of Fenwick's Colony. The house of worship was removed many years ago, and there is nothing remaining to mark the place where it stood but a few tomb stones in the vacant lot near by. John Gibbon's wife was Esther, the daughter of Ephraim Seeley. (The Seeleys are one of the oldest families that settled at what was then called the Cohansey precinct, now Cumberland county.) She had several children by her first husband. Edmund Gibbon married a young woman in Penn's Neck who had large possessions on Finn's Point that she inherited from her ancestors; they had several children—Grant, Thomas, Charles and one daughter, who was the first wife of James J. Redstrake, of Salem; he was at that time a resident of Penn's Neck, his native place.

Esther Seeley's second husband was Colonel Benjamin Holme; she was his second wife, (his first being Jane, the daughter of Daniel Smith; she was killed a few years after her marriage by a horse, and left no children. Robert Johnson, in his history of Salem county, said her maiden name was Smart; he was informed incorrectly). Benjamin and his wife Esther had two children—John and Jane Holme. John's first wife was Rebecca Thompson, of Salem; his second wife was Margaret, daughter of Clement Hall, of Elsinborough; their children have been mentioned before. Jane, the daughter of Benjamin and Esther Holme, married William Harris, a resident of Swedesboro, Gloucester county; she lived but a short time after her marriage. There is some difference of opinion whether the Holme family of Salem county are descendants of Obediah Holme, who settled at Cohansey in the early settlement of the English colony, and was one of the Judges of Salem county for several years; his descendants are numerous in Cumberland county at the present day, and the most reliable information in my possession is that they are a different family and no way connected; their names are different; one is Holmes and the Salem county family spell their names Holme. The ancestor of the latter, John Holme, emigrated to and settled in Philadelphia at an early period; he had two sons born in that city; the eldest son when married went to reside on lands his father bought of William Penn, where Holmesburg is located; it being not far from Philadelphia. The younger son, John Holme, came to this county in 1698, and purchased a large tract of land in what is now Upper Alloways Creek; he had two sons and one daughter—John, Benjamin and Elizabeth Holme. The latter in 1737 married Joseph Fogg, of Fogg's Landing, (he was the son of Joseph Fogg, the first emigrant to this county by that name.) Joseph and his wife had ten children— David, Ebenezer, Charles, Hannah, Ann, Elizabeth, Holmes, Isaac, Rebecca and Ann Fogg. John Holme, the eldest son, inherited most of his father's real estate near Allowaystown; he, like his brother Benjamin, was a zealous Whig during the American Revolution, but I think he was never in the military service. The Holme family were one of the earliest families of the Baptist Society that was organized near Salem.

Leonard Gibbon and his wife Rachel K. had eleven children —Mary, Harriet, Eliza, Mason Seeley, Francis, Robert G., Edward K., Anthony, Leonard, Quinton and Sarah Gibbon. Eliza, the eldest daughter of Leonard and Rachel Gibbon, married Jeremiah Parvin, of Deerfield township, Cumberland county; they had issue, two sons and one daughter—Leonard, Oliver and Harriet; they are all living. Mason Seeley Gibbon, the eldest son of Leonard and Rachel Gibbon, married Mary Brooks, the daughter of James Brooks, of Roadstown. Mason and his wife had six children—Caroline, Robert, James, William Henry, Leonard and Eliza Gibbon; I think they are all living, excepting Leonard. Edward K. Gibbon married twice; he removed to one of the Western States, and had one daughter. Anthony Keasbey Gibbon also went to one of the Western States, and there married, and had issue, one son, who is still living. Quinton Gibbon, the youngest son of Leonard and Rachel Gibbon, is a physician in the city of Salem; his residence is on Market street. Quinton married Sarah, the daughter of Morris and Sarah Hancock; both of her parents were the lineal descendants of William and Isabella Hancock, who emigrated from England to this county in 1677, and settled on his allotment of land, containing 1,000 acres, that he purchased of John Fenwick two years previous. The land lay on the south side of Monmouth river, where the village of Hancock's Bridge now stands. Dr. Gibbon and his wife have one daughter—Henrietta Gibbon. Sarah A. Gibbon, daughter of Leonard and Sarah Gibbon, lives in Salem, with her brother, Dr. Quinton Gibbon; she is unmarried. Leonard Gibbon, the father of the above mentioned children, died when most of his children were minors; Rachel, his widow, died in Salem 12th month, 1851, aged nearly seventy-eight years.

Bradway Keasbey, the son of Edward 2d, and Elizabeth Bradway Keasbey, was born in 1730; he married and settled on part of James Daniels, Sr., estate, but whether he purchased the property of one of the Daniels' family or not, I have no definite knowledge. Neal Daniels emigrated from Ireland to this country in 1681, and purchased a tract of land of Annie Salter, in the forks of Stoe Creek, and it was as good a soil as there is in that section of the county. His son, James Daniels, was born in Ireland; he has left behind him the most interesting and correct account of the Indians, at the time of the first Europeans landed here. He describes them as peacable and quiet people, until spirituous liquor was introduced among them. The alcohol produced a radical change among them, they were then often troublesome and more difficult to get along with as neighbors.

Edward Keasbey and his wife had one son—Edward Keasbey. Bradway Keasbey's second wife was Jane Waddington, the daughter of Jonathan Waddington; they had issue, one daughter, Sarah Keasbey, who subsequently married John, the son of Edward Pancoast. The latter was a resident of Gloucester county. John and his wife lived for a short time on her property, that was willed to her by her father. They, however, in a few years sold it to Samuel Pancoast, and purchased a farm of Josiah Reeves, in the same township, located on the north side of Alloways creek, on the main road leading from Hancock's Bridge to Salem, it being near the former place. John and Sarah K. Pancoast had seven children—Hannah, Achsah, John, Israel, Jane, David, and Aaron Pancoast. John Pancoast, several years before his death, sold his property in Alloways Creek township and purchased a farm of Aaron Pancoast, at Mullica Hill, Gloucester county, and there he and his wife ended their days. At that place, Hannah, the eldest daughter of John and Sarah K. Pancoast, married John, the youngest son of William and Mary Bradway; she died a comparatively young woman, leaving five children—Clayton, Sarah, Achsah, Ann, and Mary Ann Bradway. Achsah, the daughter of John and Sarah K. Pancoast, married James Lippincott; they had issue, two daughters—Hannah Lippincott, who married Jonathan Colson, and Sarah Ann Lippincott, who married William Dunn. John, the eldest son of John and Sarah K. Pancoast, married the eldest daughter of Benjamin and Susan Griscom, of Penn's Neck. John and his wife had seven children—Benjamin, Mary Jane, Beulah, John, Sarah, Susan, and Hannah Pancoast. Jane, the daughter of John and Sarah K. Pancoast, married Andrew, the eldest son of Benjamin and Susan Griscom; she died soon after they were married, leaving no issue. Israel, the son of John and Sarah K. Pancoast, married Sarah Ann Lippincott; they had issue—Stacy Keasbey, Dilwyn, and Mary Ann Pancoast. David Pancoast, son of John and Sarah K. Pancoast, married Ann, the daughter of Joseph Davis, of Pilesgrove; they have issue—Joseph D., Mary, Martha, Anna, David, William, Charles, and Isabella Pancoast. Aaron, the youngest son of John and Sarah K. Pancoast, married Anna Dunn; they have one daughter—Deborah Pancoast.

Edward, the son of Bradway Keasbey, married Lydia, the daughter of Jesse Grace Carll; they had issue—Sarah, Joseph, Prudence, Grace, Elizabeth, and Edward Keasbey. Sarah, the eldest daughter, married Aaron, the son of Jonathan and Sarah B. Waddington; they had five children—Sarah Ann, Lydia, Joshua, Bradway, and Jane Waddington. Joseph, the son of Edward and Lydia Keasbey, married Hannah, the daughter of

David Stretch; he died a young man, leaving no issue. Prudence Keasbey married Edward Waddington, brother of Aaron Waddington. Edward and his wife had eight children—Richard, Sarah, Edward, Prudence, Elizabeth, Joseph, Lydia Ann, and Rebecca Waddington. Grace, the daughter of Edward and Grace Keasbey, married Reuben Dare; I think he was a native of Cumberland county. They purchased a farm in Beesley's Neck, in the township of Alloways Creek, being formerly a part of the Joseph Brick estate. Reuben and his wife left several children. One of their daughters married William, the son of Edward Bradway; they own the homestead and reside thereon at this time. Elizabeth, the youngest daughter of Edward and Grace Keasbey, married William Plummer; they owned, and while they lived occupied part of the homestead of her parents, Edward and Grace Keasbey; they had three sons and one daughter—William, Edward K., Charles, and Elizabeth Plummer. William married Rebecca, the daughter of Judge Ephraim Carll; they have issue. Elizabeth, the daughter of William and Elizabeth K. Plummer, married Isaac, the son of David Allen; they have several children. Charles, the youngest son of William and Elizabeth K. Plummer, married Ann Eliza, the daughter of Henry and Elizabeth B. Miller; they have issue.

Prudence, the daughter of Edward and Lydia Keasbey, married Edward, the youngest son of Jonathan and Sarah Waddington. Edward and his wife had eight children—Richard, Sarah, Edward (who died a minor), Prudence, Elizabeth, Joseph, Lydia and Rebecca. Richard married Mary Ann, the daughter of David Bowen, of Alloways Creek; they have issue—Anna, Edward, David, Elizabeth, George and Mary. Anna married William, the son of Elijah and Beulah Ware; they have issue. Edward, the eldest son of Richard Waddington, married Mary, the daughter of Daniel Hood; they have issue. David Waddington, married Maggie Stretch; they have one child. Elizabeth Waddington married Jonathan, the son of Aaron and Mary Fogg. George Waddington's wife is Mary, the daughter of Charles and Beulah Gaskill; they have issue. Sarah, the eldest daughter of Edward and Prudence Waddington, married James, the son of Oliver Smith; they have three children. Edward, the eldest, married Ann, the daughter of Lewis and Elizabeth Fox; they have issue. Oliver, the second child, married Hannah, the daughter of Joseph H. and Rachel Fogg; they have issue. Keasbey, the youngest son, married Mary, the daughter of Job Thorp; they have issue. Prudence Waddington's husband was Ebenezer Barrett.

A few years after their marriage they removed to Illinois, where, I think, Prudence died, leaving four or five children. Ebenezer, soon after the death of his wife, removed to Kansas with his family; they remained at their new home but a short time, and then emigrated to Nebraska, and settled near Omaha. Elizabeth Waddington married John, the son of Maurice Welch, of Mannington. John and his wife are deceased, leaving two children—Aaron and Lydia. Joseph, the youngest son of Edward Waddington, married Ruth, the daughter of Joseph and Jane Appleton; the latter is the daughter of Hezekiah Hews, and grand-daughter of Benjamin Wright, of Mannington. Joseph and Ruth Waddington had six children—Emma, Jane, who died young, Joseph, Tacy, Lydia Ann and George. Lydia Ann, the daughter of Edward and Prudence Waddington, married Jonathan, the son of Adna and Lydia Bradway; they have one daughter—Lydia P. Bradway. Rebecca, the youngest daughter of Edward and Prudence Waddington, married Samuel Borden, a native of Upper Penn's Neck; they have issue. Edward and his wife, Prudence, were buried in the old grave yard on the south side of Alloways Creek, where all the bodies of their ancestors are mouldering in their native dust, while their souls have entered upon immortality. The great American poet, Longfellow, wrote the following encouraging poem:

> Life is real, Life is earnest,
> And the grave is not its goal;
> Dust thou art, to dust returneth,
> Was not spoken of the soul.

Joseph Keasbey, the eldest son of Lydia Keasbey, married Hannah, the daughter of David and Mary Street Stretch. Joseph, soon after he became of age, purchased land in Elsinborough, being part of the Norris estate, bordering on Alloways creek; it formerly belonged to the Stubbins family. Joseph and his wife Hannah commenced life on the said farm; he lived but a short time afterwards, dying in 1814, with typhus fever, which disease was prevalent and very mortal about that time. He left no issue, but devised about two-thirds of his real estate to his widow, Hannah Keasbey. A certain portion he directed to be sold for the payment of his debts, and the residue he devised to Mark Stretch, a distant relative of his wife. His widow subsequently married Andrew Smith.

Grace, the daughter of Edward and Lydia Keasbey, married Reuben Dare. They owned and lived on property in Lower Alloways Creek, on a point of land lying on the south side of the creek, called Beesley's Neck. I think it formerly belonged to the Brick family. Reuben and his wife had several children. William W. Bradway, the present occupant of the farm, married one of their daughters. Elizabeth Keasbey, the youngest daughter of Edward and Lydia, married William Plummer, Sr. They had four children—William, Edward, Elizabeth, and Charles. William, the eldest, married Rebecca, the daughter of Judge Ephraim Carll. The children of William and his wife, Rebecca Plummer, have been mentioned previously. Elizabeth Plummer, the daughter of William Plummer, Sr., and his wife Elizabeth, married Isaac, the son of David Allen, of Upper Alloways Creek, now Quinton township. Isaac and his wife Elizabeth have issue—David, Sarah, Thompson, and Charles Anna Allen. Charles, the youngest son of Elizabeth and William Plummer, Sr., married Ann Eliza, the daughter of Henry and Elizabeth Miller, of Elsinborough. Charles has been deceased several years, leaving a widow and three children—Elizabeth, Henry, and Anna.

Rebecca, the eldest daughter of Jesse and Mary Carll, married Richard, the son of Robert Moore, Jr.; she lived but a few years after her marriage, leaving issue. Elizabeth, the second daughter of Jesse and Mary Carll, born in 1799, married Jonathan, the eldest son of David and Mary S. Stretch; she also died in early life, leaving no issue. William, the son of Jesse and Mary Carll, born in 1801, married Ann, the daughter of Larry Dowlin; they had seven children—Rebecca, Mary, Ann Elizabeth, Arthalinda, Jesse, Marietta and Janetta. Rebecca Carll married William Allen; she died young, leaving no issue. Ann Elizabeth Carll married Thomas, the son of Ephraim Seeley, a native of Bridgeton; they have issue—Kate and Belford Seeley.

Jesse Carll, the son of William and Ann, married Elizabeth Craig, of Cumberland county; he is deceased, leaving a widow and three children—Lydia Ann, William and Catharine. Marietta Carll married Amos, the son of Aaron and Susan Padgett; they have two children—Arthalinda and Anna. Arthalinda married Daniel Hogate; they reside in Salem. Anna is still unmarried. The Padgetts are one of the oldest families in Salem and Cumberland counties. Arthalinda, Mary and Janetta Carll died minors. Sarah, the daughter of Jesse and Mary Carll, married Joseph, the son of Isaac Mills; she has been dead many years, leaving issue. Lydia, the youngest daughter of Jesse and Mary Carll, married Joseph Bowen; they have no issue. Jesse, the father of the above mentioned children, died in 1814 of the typus fever. Sarah, the daughter of Jesse Carll, Sr. and his wife Grace, married Job Sheppard, and had two sons—John and William. John's wife was Sarah, the daughter of Samuel Ward, of Elsinborough; they have five children—Samuel, Job, Sarah, Rebecca and Mary Jane. Samuel Sheppard married Hannah, the daughter of James Baker; they have issue—Hannah, Alabedia and Isabella. Job Sheppard's wife was Jane Fryant; they had four children—John, Roger, Job and Jenita. John, the eldest, married Rachel, daughter of James and Rachel Baker; they have issue. William, the youngest son of Job and Sarah Sheppard, married Sarah Boyd; there were two children—David and Sarah Ann. David's wife was Rachel Piphran; they removed to Indiana. Sarah Ann Sheppard married William, the son of Mark Stretch; they also went to one of the Western States; she is deceased now, leaving issue. William Sheppard's second wife was Mary Ferrell, a widow, whose maiden name was Smith, a native of Delaware. William Sheppard, when about ten years of age, lost his speech by that scourge, scarlet fever, and he has been a mute, in a great measure, ever since; he and his wife reside at Hancock's Bridge, and both of them are past three score years and ten.

Anna, the eldest daughter of William and Martha Waddington, married Jonathan, the son of Jonathan and Joanna Hildreth. They had one daughter—Joanna Hildreth, who married Dr. Thomas P. Dickinson, a native of Pilesgrove. Their children are A. M. P. V. H. Dickinson, who married Mary Springer; Thomas and Hildreth, the latter is deceased. Sarah, the daughter of William and Martha Waddington, married Daniel, the son of Daniel and Sarah Tracy; they had no issue. William, the son of William and Martha Waddington, married Eliza, the daughter of Davis and Fanny Nelson, of Elsinborough. There were two children—Fanny and William. Fanny's husband is William Jones. She is deceased, leaving one daughter—Eliza. William married the daughter of William Simms; they have issue. Elizabeth Waddington, the daughter of William and Martha Waddington, died a young woman of pulmonary consumption. Martha, the daughter of William and Martha Waddington, married Joseph, the son of John and Elizabeth Hancock. Joseph is deceased, leaving no issue. Jesse C., the youngest son of William and Martha Waddington, married Rachel Scudders. They are both deceased, leaving one daughter, Sarah Waddington, who subsequently married Henry Elwell; they have issue.

LIPPINCOTT FAMILY.

The family of Lippincott, it is said, took its name from Luffencott, a manor and parish at the western extremity of the county of Devonshire, on the borders of Cornwall, England; which remained their property and the place of their residence from the time of King Henry III until the second year of King Henry V, A. D., 1414, or from 1243, or earlier to 1414. One of the family, John Lippincott, between 1430 and 1450, married Jane, daughter and co-heir of John Wyberry, which brought the estate of Wyberrys into the family, and continued their property until about 1775, when Henry Lippincott, the last of the branch, sold it to Charles Cartcliff. There is a strong reason to believe that the first ancestor of the numerous family of Lippincotts in America was Richard Lippincott, born in Plymouth, Devonshire, England. He emigrated to Dorchester, New England, between 1636 and 1640. In 1644 he returned to Plymouth, England, his native land, and about the year 1650 he joined the new religious sect, the Society of Friends, and suffered much therefor. On the 20th of January, 1660, at Plymouth, he was committed to prison by Oliver Creely, mayor, and with others was taken from a meeting house. How long he remained in prison we have no account. In 1663 he and his family left England and located themselves in Rhode Island. In 1669 he removed from Rhode Island and settled in New Jersey, at Shrewsbury, in which place he became a large landed proprietor. He died at Shrewsbury 25th of 9th month, 1683, and his widow, Abigail Lippincott, died 2d of 6th month, 1697. Richard, a short time previous to his death, purchased 1,000 acres of land of John Fenwick, in Cohansey precinct, being on the south side of Cohansey river, in Shrewsbury Neck. Previous to the death of Abigail Lippincott, the widow of Richard, she liberated all her slaves, which act is sufficient to perpetuate her name to the latest posterity.

In the record of the town of Freehold, N. J., mention is made of Richard Lippincott as one of the overseers of the town of Shrewsbury, in 1670. This book of records is said to be the oldest deed book in New Jersey, it having been commenced the 14th of 12th month, 1667. Richard and Abigail Lippincott had six sons and two daughters. Remembrance, their eldest son, was born at Dorchester, New England, in 1641. He was baptized on the 19th of 7th month, 1641, and died 11th of 2d month, 1723. He married Margaret Barber, of Boston; they had issue, four sons and eight daughters. He resided in Monmouth county, N. J. John, their second son, was born at Boston, New England, 6th of 9th month, 1644, and died 16th of 2d month, 1720. He married Janetta Austin; they had issue, four sons and four daughters. They resided in New Jersey. Abigail, their eldest daughter, was born in Plymouth, 17th of 11th month, 1646, died an infant. Restore Lippincott was born at Plymouth, England, 3d of 5th month, 1648, and died at Mount Holly, in the 5th month, 1741. He represented Burlington county in the State Legislature, in 1703, the year that East and West Jersey were united under one government, and continued a member of that body for several years. At his death, Thomas Chalkly mentions in his journal, that he was present at the funeral. He further stated that he was informed that Restore left behind him nearly two hundred children, grandchildren, and great-grand-children. Freedom, their fourth son, was born 1st month, 1650, at Stone House, England, and died in 1697; he was married 14th of 8th month, 1630, to Mary Custin, of Burlington, and had three sons and two daughters. Increase, their second daughter, was born at Stone House, England, 5th of 10th month, 1657, and died 29th of 9th month, 1695. She married Samuel Dennis, who came from England and settled at Shrewsbury, in 1675; he died 7th of 6th month, 1723, aged seventy-two years. He and his wife had two sons and three daughters. Jacob, their fifth son, was born in England, in the 3d month, 1660, and died 6th of 12th month, 1686. He married, and had one son and one daughter, both of whom died in infancy. Preserved, their sixth son, was born in Rhode Island, 25th of 12th month, 1663, and died in 1666. Restore, their third son, married Hannah, daughter of William Shattock, of Boston; they had three sons and six daughters. Samuel was born at Shrewsbury, N. J., and married Ann Hulet, of Shrewsbury, on the 3d of 5th month, 1700. Abigail, the eldest daughter, was born at Shrewsbury about 1678. There is no account of her marriage. Hannah, the daughter of Restore Lippincott, was born at Shrewsbury, in the 9th month, 1676. Hope, their second daughter, was born at Shrewsbury, in the 8th month, 1681. She married William Glading in 1701.

Rebecca, daughter of the same parents, was born 24th of 9th month, 1684. James, their son, was born at Shrewsbury, 11th of 4th month, 1687. James married Anna Eves, in 1707. Elizabeth, daughter of Restore, was born at Shrewsbury, 15th of 11th month, 1690. About that time Restore removed from Shrewsbury to Burlington county, and located himself with his family near the town of Mount Holly, at which place his son Jacob was born, in the 6th month, 1692. Jacob subsequently married Mary, the daughter of Henry Burr, whose wife was Elizabeth Hudson, a native of England. Jacob and his wife had six sons and two daughters. Rachel, the youngest daughter of Restore and Hannah Lippincott, was born near Mount Holly, 8th of 11th month, 1695; she married Zachariah Jess. Jacob, son of Restore and Hannah Lippincott, married Hannah Burr; they located in the lower part of Gloucester county, or Pilesgrove, Salem county, where most of their descendants are residing at the present time, together with the descendants of Samuel Lippincott, who was a public Friend; he was the son of Freedom Lippincott, who was the son of Richard Lippincott, the emigrant. Samuel was born 12th of 12th month, 1728, and married Abigail, the daughter of Joseph and Elizabeth Bates; they had six children—Joseph, Samuel, Joshua, Mercy, Abigail, and Elizabeth. Those two branches of Richard Lippincott's descendants are inhabitants of Burlington, Camden, Gloucester, and Salem counties, N. J., and Philadelphia.

Jacob Lippincott and his wife, Hannah Burr, had eight children—Caleb, Benjamin, Samuel, Joshua, Jacob, William, Mary and Hannah Lippincott. Caleb, the eldest son, married Hannah, the daughter of Daniel Wills, a resident of Rancocas, in 1785. Benjamin, second son of Jacob and Mary B. Lippincott married Hope Wills, the sister of his brother Caleb's wife; they had three children—Elizabeth, Aaron and Benjamin Lippincott. Caleb and his brother Benjamin owned property on the east side of Oldman's creek, in Gloucester county, where they and most of their children after them resided. Samuel, the third son of Jacob, married and left one daughter, who married Isaac Barber; they emigrated to Clark county, Ohio, and were both living in 1848 at a great age. Joshua, the fourth son of Jacob and Mary Lippincott, married Rebecca Wood, and they had two sons and one daughter. Jacob, the fifth son of Jacob and Mary Lippincott, married a young woman of Abington, Pa. William, the sixth son, married Sarah Bispham, whose father was a merchant of Philadelphia; they had two children—Joshua and Mary Lippincott. Joshua married Sarah Wetherill, of Philadelphia; there were three children—Sarah Ann, Mary, and Joshua, who married a niece of James Dundan. Mary, the daughter of William and Sarah Lippincott, married Samuel Yorke, of Philadelphia, and they had seven children—Edward, William, Peter, Sarah, Mary, Joshua and Samuel Yorke. Mary, the daughter of Jacob and Mary Lippincott, married Jacob Spicer, Jr. Hannah, the youngest daughter of Jacob and Mary Lippincott, married a man by the name of Lord. Caleb, the eldest son of Jacob and Mary Lippincott, married Hannah Wills about 1755, and had six children—Letitia, who married Aaron Elkinton, Rebecca, Elizabeth, Hannah, who married John Knight, William and Samuel Lippincott. The latter married Mary, the daughter of Samuel Ogden, of Pilesgrove, and had one son—Caleb Lippincott, who married Ann, daughter of Joshua and Rebecca Thompson, of Elsinborough; they had issue, three sons—Samuel, Clark and David Lippincott; the latter is deceased. Samuel Lippincott's second wife was a Webster, and they had three sons and one daughter—Samuel, Hannah, Josiah and Charles Lippincott. His third wife was Christiana, daughter of John and Mary Black, native of Burlington county, but at the time of their daughter's marriage they resided in Salem county. Samuel and Christiana had no issue. Samuel, the eldest son of Samuel Lippincott by his second wife, Webster, has had four wives; his first was a Zanes, her parents residing near Mullica Hill, and one son, Joseph Lippincott, was born to them. Samuel's second wife, Lydia Iredell, had two daughters—Sarah Ann and Hannah Lippincott; his third wife was Mary Haines, of Burlington county; they had no issue; his fourth wife was Hannah Brown, of Chester county, Pa., and both are living and reside at Woodbury, Gloucester county. Hannah, the daughter of Samuel Lippincott, Sr., has been twice married; her first husband was Asa Moore, and her second Samuel Duell, of Pilesgrove; she had no issue. Josiah, the second son of Samuel Lippincott, married the daughter of David and Hannah Clark Cooper, of Woodbury; they have issue. Josiah and his wife are residents of Philadelphia at this time. Charles, the youngest son of Samuel Lippincott, married Amy, the daughter of Jonathan and Hannah Bassett Cawley.

William Lippincott, the son of Caleb and Hannah Wills Lippincott, married Elizabeth, daughter of Thomas Folwell; they had eight children—Thomas, Samuel, Anna, Elizabeth, Mary, Deborah, Hannah and William. Thomas married Anna Stanger; their children were Joseph, Isaac, Anne, Daniel,

Abigail Scull, Rebecca and Elizabeth. Samuel, the son of William, was twice married; by his first wife he had four children—Ann F., Nathan T., Samuel M., and George Lippincott; the latter is deceased. Nathan T. Lippincott was twice married; his first wife was Mary, the daughter of Caleb Borton; she died, leaving five children; his second wife was Priscilla, the daughter of Ebenezer Wright. Samuel married the daughter of Jonathan Cawley by his second wife. Nathan married Priscilla, daughter of the late Ebenezer Wright, of Mannington. Samuel's second wife was Abbie, the daughter of Thomas Laurie, of Woodstown; they had issue. Anne, daughter of William and Elizabeth Lippincott, married a Buzby; she joined the Shakers. Elizabeth, the second daughter of William Lippincott, married Thomas Borton, of Woodstown; they removed many years ago to Springfield, Ohio. Mary, the third daughter, died single. Deborah, the fourth daughter, is deceased. Hannah Lippincott resided in 1848 with Thomas Borton, in Ohio. William, the youngest son of William and Elizabeth Lippincott, followed the butchering business in Salem for many years; he married Hannah Wright, of Quaker Neck, the grand-daughter of Ebenezer Miller, Jr. William and his wife Hannah had two children—William and Priscilla Lippincott. William married Elizabeth, daughter of David and Mary Engle Davis; they had issue; their daughter, Letitia, married Robert, the son of Aaron and Mary Fogg, of Salem.

Benjamin, son of Jacob and Mary B. Lippincott, married Hope Willis, a sister of his brother Caleb's wife, in 1741. He resided on and owned a large tract of land adjoining Caleb Lippincott, in the lower part of Gloucester, near the Salem county line. Benjamin and his wife Hope Lippincott had three sons—Aaron, Benjamin, and Jethro. Aaron, the eldest son, married, and had two sons—John and Benjamin, both of whom married, and owned and resided on the property that their grandfather purchased. Benjamin H., the second son of Aaron Lippincott, married and had one son—Benjamin P., who subsequently married Ann Dewell, a lineal descendant of Samuel Lippincott, an eminent minister, and a member of the Salem Monthly Meeting of Friends. Samuel was the son of Freedom Lippincott, who was the son of Richard Lippincott, the emigrant. Ann Dewell's mother by her first husband had two sons, Samuel P. and James Lippincott. The latter lived most of his time at Mullica Hill, Gloucester county. Benjamin P. Lippincott's second wife was Rebecca Howe; they had issue—Isaac, Barclay, and Lydia. Barclay was a tailor, and carried on his business on

Market street, Philadelphia. Joshua, the son of Jacob and Mary Burr, married Rebecca Wood, and had three children. James, the eldest, was born 20th of 3d month, 1768; died 17th of 8th month, 1822. Jane, their daughter, born 28th of 3d month, 1770, married Morgan Hollingshead, of Moorestown, N. J. Joshua, the youngest son of Joshua and Rebecca Lippincott, was born 23d of 10th month, 1774, and died 16th of 12th month, 1805. He married Esther, the daughter of Jacob Davis, of Woodstown, the 27th of 11th month, 1800. They had one daughter, Lydia Lippincott, who was born 16th of 9th month, 1801, and married David, the youngest son of Gideon and Sarah Scull, in 1823. The Lippincott family is one of the most numerous in the State of New Jersey. I will not attempt to follow the different branches further. James S. Lippincott, of Haddonfield, I have been informed, intends writing a full history of the large and interesting Lippincott family.

I have recently received information from Gideon Delaphine Scull, now a resident of England, in regard to the ancestors of his family in England. After much investigation he has ascertained that there was a clergyman in London by the name of John Scull in the reign of Charles I, and in the year 1630 was repelled from his living by Archbishop Laud, because he would not conform to the new church rituals. Soon after that event he left England and went to Holland; he likewise writes that he recently found a will of Alice Skull, a widow, of Brinkworth, county of Wiltshire, written in 1649, in which she says that it is reported to her that her son, John Scull, has gone into another country, and she does not know if he will ever return to claim what she leaves him. According to that information, John Scull must have emigrated from Holland about 1660, and located himself on Long Island, in America. By the records, his son John Scull located on a large tract of land at Great Egg Harbor as early as 1690; the said lands lay adjoining John Somers'. John Scull's wife was Sarah Somers, and it is probable she was the sister of John Somers. John and Sarah Scull had several children. Their son, Gideon, married Judith, the daughter of James and Margery Belange; they had several children. At the first settlement of the province of Pennsylvania there was one Nicholas Scull, an eminent surveyor, who resided in Philadelphia, and who left a family of children; it does not appear that they are near connections of the family that lived at Long Island, and afterwards at Egg Harbor; although they might have originated from the same parents in England. Respecting the descendants of Nicholas

Scull my knowledge is limited. There is a record of a family that was buried in Friends' graveyard in Philadelphia, which says that James Scull, son of Edward and Sarah, was buried 29th of 4th month, 1717. Sarah, the wife of Nicholas Scull; was buried 8th month, 1717. Elizabeth Scull, daughter of James, was buried 29th of 6th month, 1740. Sarah, the daughter of Joseph Scull, buried 5th month, 1748. Abigail Scull, daughter of the same parents, buried 9th month, 1749. William Scull, son of William, buried 3d of 10th month, 1768. Comfort Scull, wife of William, buried 14th of 9th month, 1775. Elizabeth, wife of Benjamin Scull, was buried 17th of 4th month, 1792.

LAWSON FAMILY.

John Lawson, from whom the family of that name in Salem descended, was born in Liverpool, England, of Quaker parentage, in the year 1756. In early life he learned the coopering business; it appears soon after he learned his trade, he emigrated to America, and located himself at Salem, and followed his trade together with William Perry as a partner. He also was a member of the Society of Friends. They both continued at that business until the Revolutionary war broke out. John left the religious society, of which he was born a member, and joined the first Battalion of New Jersey, of Captain William Helm's company. Soon after peace was declared, he married Jane White, of Salem, in 1788; they had three sons and one daughter. Edward, their son, born in 1790; was a seaman, and was one of the six Jerseymen that was lost during a heavy gale, on the night of 20th of 12th month, 1819, on the shoals off Barnegat, while taking the Spanish brig, Le Tigre, which had been taken on a voyage from Laguira to Cadiz, by the South American Privateer, Constitution, Captain Brown, who put a prize crew on board, who mutinied and brought her into the Delaware bay and up the Cohansey creek, where she was seized by James D. Westcott, Collector of the Port. The Spanish Consul at New York put in a claim in the United States Court, in behalf of the Spanish Government, for the vessel and cargo, which was decided in their favor. A new crew was put on board to take her from Bridgeton to New York; the company was composed of the following persons: Edward Lawson, from Salem; Howell Mulford, Charles Dare, Thomas Whitney, Talman Mulford and Oliver Russell, from Bridgeton; and two Spaniards, Nicholas Carrega and Gregario Montot. During the storm the vessel went on the shoals and all on board perished. Samuel Lawson, the second son of John and Jane Lawson, born in 1791, was a hatter by trade, and died in 1836; he worked for many years as journeyman hatter for the late Delzin Keasbey. John Lawson, the third son of John and Jane Lawson, was born in 1793; he learned the trade of a blacksmith with James Dennis, of Salem. He showed in early life that uncommon industry which was characteristic of him during his long pilgrimage in this world of care. When he was an apprentice, instead of going about the streets in the evenings as most other apprentice boys did, he sawed wood whenever he could get an opportunity so to do; he husbanded his earnings so much so, when he became of age he had nearly enough means within himself to start the business of blacksmithing; and by close application to his trade he acquired a competency for himself and family, also to educate his children to fit them for business. Mary Lawson, daughter of John and Jane Lawson, was born in 1795, married Thomas James; they had three sons—Edward, James and Samuel James.

To digress, somewhat, there was a young man by the name of William Perry, who learned the trade of a blacksmith about the same time that John Lawson did, and I think with the same man. Perry's father was a partner of John Lawson, Sr., in the coopering business; the two young men were quite intimate. William Perry, sixty years ago or more, went to Cincinnati and followed his trade at that place, and was very successful, and accumulated a large fortune. It appears by the account I have of him that he was greatly respected in his adopted city, so much so that one of the principal streets in Cincinnati was named Perry street to perpetuate his name. He was many years one of the most prominent members of Friends' Meeting in that city. A few years before the death of John Lawson, William Perry and his wife came East, and spent several days at Cape Island; before they returned home he was desirous of visiting his native town, and also to see the friend of his youth, John Lawson, which he and his wife did. He soon found his friend, but they did not know each other at first; but when they did recognize each other, after an absence of more than forty years, their feelings can better be imagined than described. John Lawson served in the war of 1812, for which he received a pension; he married Elizabeth Lummis, of Salem, in 1819, and died 24th of 3d month, 1866, aged about seventy-three years. His father, John Lawson, brought over with him from England one of the first editions of Thomas Chalkly's journal, published in that Kingdom—a work which he much admired and read, and had his children's ages recorded in it. The book is still in possession of the family, which is highly prized as a family relic. John and Elizabeth Lawson had five children— Jane E., Mary, James D., John and Charles S. Lawson. Mary the second daughter, married Powell, the eldest son of William and Mary Carpenter, of Elsinboro. Powell and his wife, Mary Carpenter, had issue, one child, who died young before its father, which event took place in 1850. Mary's second husband is Evan C. Stotsenberg; they were married in 1872; he is a resident of Wilmington, Delaware, and a manufacturer in that city. James D. Lawson is a merchant in Woodstown; his wife is Mary D., the eldest daughter of David and Annie Pancoast, of that town. James and his wife, Mary D. Lawson, have issue, two daughters—Annie P. and Emma S. Lawson. Charles S. Lawson, the youngest son of John and Elizabeth Lawson, married Ann Elizabeth, daughter of Eli S. Mulford; they have four children—Elizabeth, John, Graham C. and Gertrude Lawson. Charles has been Mayor of the city of Salem several years, and makes an energetic and efficient officer. Jane E. and her brother, John Lawson, are single, and occupy the house in Salem where their parents lived.

GRISCOM, MADDOX AND DENN FAMILIES.

Andrew Griscom was a native of England, and emigrated to America in 1680. He purchased a large tract of land where South Camden is at the present day, and married Sarah Dole; they settled upon it and had two children—Tobias and Sarah Griscom. Tobias, his son, married Deborah Gabitas, and they settled on the lands he inherited from his father in Gloucester, now Camden; they had the following children—Andrew, Samuel, William, Tobias and Mary Griscom. Andrew, the eldest, was a blacksmith by trade, and settled near Tuckahoe on lands that his grand-father had purchased several years previous; he married Susanna Hancock, daughter of John and Mary Chambless Hancock, of Alloways Creek, and had three children—Sarah, Everett and William Griscom. Sarah, the eldest, died in 1762, aged twenty years. Andrew, by his second wife, Mary, had three children—Mary, Andrew, born 1755, and Deborah Griscom. Andrew married Letitia Tyler, of Greenwich, and had two sons—Benjamin, who married Susan Adams, of Penn's Neck; his second wife was Rebecca, the widow of Joshua Thompson, of Elsinboro; and Andrew Griscom, who was twice married, his first wife the daughter of Esther Baker; by his last wife, Sarah Griscom, he had four children—Dorcas, Job, Martha and Ruth Ann Griscom. Samuel, the second son of Tobias and Sarah Griscom, was a house carpenter and ship builder; he married, and carried on his trade in the city of Philadelphia, and resided for some time on Arch street, between Third and Fourth streets. It has been said he became in possession of a large landed estate in the city of Philadelphia. He assisted in the erection of Independence Hall. As to his children, and the other branches of the Griscom family I have not much knowledge of, but think his children were daughters. William Donaldson married Sarah Griscom, daughter of Samuel Griscom, about the year 1774 or '75; their daughter, Margaret Donaldson, was born in Philadelphia, 10th of 1st month, 1776, and is still living. In 1793 she married Joseph Boggs; in 1795 her husband died leaving one son, who is now dead.

Margaret Boggs resides with her niece's husband, Dr. Stephen T. Beale, at Germantown. William Griscom, son of Tobias, married Sarah Davis, of Pilesgrove; they settled at Haddonfield, and had two daughters—Hannah and Deborah Griscom. Mary, the daughter of Tobias and Deborah Griscom, married Thomas Holloway.

John Maddox, the son of Ralph Maddox, was born in 1638, and in 1668 he removed to London, and resided in the parish of St. Sepulchre, where he followed the trade of a chandler. In 1669 he married Elizabeth Durham, the widow of Joseph Durham. They had one daughter born in London in 1671, named Elizabeth. In 1678 he and his wife, and their daughter and son-in-law, Richard Durham, and his three servants—Thomas Oder, Thomas Hoatan, and Mary Stafford, sailed from London in the ship Surry, Captain Steven Nichols. They arrived at New Salem in the 9th month following. In 1682, James Maddox purchased one-half of William Hancock's allotment of 1,000 acres, located on the south side of Alloways creek, of Isabella Hancock, widow of William Hancock, who died in 1779. In 1700, James Maddox sold his property to Jeremiah Powell and Edward Hancock, and in the year 1688 Elizabeth Maddox, daughter of James Maddox, married James Denn. They had two children —Margaret and John; Margaret was born 29th of 4th month, 1689, and John in 11th of 6th month, 1693. John married Elizabeth Oakford, daughter of Charles and Mary Oakford, in 1717. She was born at Alloways Creek, 17th of 3d month, 1698. Their children were Naomi, born in 1718, and John Maddox Denn, Jr., born 25th of 7th month, 1721. His wife Elizabeth Denn died about the year 1724. In 1725 he built his brick house which is still standing within a few rods of Alloways creek, now owned by one of his lineal descendants, William Bradway. John married his second wife in 1728, whose name was Leah Paul. There were two children by his last wife —Paul Denn, born in 1728, and their daughter, Leah Denn, born 18th of 8th month, 1731. John Maddox Denn departed this life in 1733. His son, John Denn, married Elizabeth Bacon, of Cohansey, daughter of John and Elizabeth Smith Bacon, in 1744. They had five children—Rachel, born 30th of 2d month, 1745; James, born 19th of 11th month, 1746; John, in 1751; David, born in 1756; Martha, in 1758. Rachel, their oldest daughter, married William Griscom, the son of Andrew Griscom, in 1773. They had six children—John, William, Everett, Samuel, Rachel, and David Griscom. William Griscom, when married, followed the saddle and harness making business in the village of Hancock's Bridge, and after a few years he purchased a farm in the township of Mannington, located near to a place called Guineatown, and at that place he and his wife resided until her death. Their oldest son, John Griscom, commenced teaching school in early life, and subsequently married a young woman by the name of Haskins, and had several children. After her death, and in his old age, he married Rachel Denn, of Salem, daughter of John and Rhoda Denn. Many years of his life he taught school in the city of New York, and was considered one of the best scholars in that city. He was elected a professor in chemistry. When he was past middle age he went to Europe, where his name as a scholar preceded him. On his arrival in England he was at once introduced among the literary people of that Kingdom; also on the Continent—France, Belgium, Germany, and Netherlands. When he returned home he published an account of his travels, called his "Tour in Europe," which was much read at the time, and greatly admired for its easy and beautiful language. I think it is deficient in originality of thought, but upon the whole it is a credit to the author, and will perpetuate his name to posterity as one of the best American scholars in his time. Soon afterwards he traveled through most of the cities and towns of the Eastern and Middle states lecturing on Joseph Lancaster's system of education in common schools. The plan was generally adopted. He might be considered the father of that system in this country, as Joseph Lancaster was in England. His letters addressed to his mother during her last illness, whilst she was suffering with that loathsome disease, the cancer, will always reflect great credit to his memory for that kind and sympathetic feeling they expressed to a kind and affectionate parent in her great affliction.

William, their second son, was a blacksmith by occupation in his younger days; his wife was Ann Stewart, the daughter of Samuel and Sarah Stewart, of Salem; they had six children. Their names were Samuel, William, George, John, Mary and Charles Griscom. Samuel, their oldest son, when quite young opened a boarding school at Clermont, near Frankford, in Philadelphia county, at the same place where his uncle, David Griscom, had taught several years before. Greatly to his character he made a home for his aged parents until he married; his wife was Sidney Gillingham, the daughter of Yearness Gillingham; they had four children. Samuel now resides at Galveston, Texas, with two of his sons. William Griscom, the second son, married Mary Stewart, the daughter of James and

Anne Stewart, of Cumberland county; his wife died young leaving three children—Hannah, Wade and James Stewart; his second wife was Sarah Whitelock, of Frankford, the daughter of Isaac Whitelock; he has three children by his last wife—Isaac, Anne and Sarah. George Griscom is a lawyer, and resides in Philadelphia; he married Mercy Brown; they have two or three children; their names I am not acquainted with. John Griscom is a physician, and had a very large practice in the city of Philadelphia at one time, but his health failing him, of late years he has spent a considerable time in Europe for the purpose of recuperating his failing constitution; he married Margaret Acton, of Salem, the daughter of Clement Acton, Sr. I believe they have three children—Clement, Hannah, the youngest, I believe, is a son, but his name I do not know. Mary Griscom married Samuel Stewart, of Indiana, who was a native of the county of Salem, and son of James Stewart, of Alloways Creek; there were no children by that connection; he died a short time ago, and his widow is now a resident of Woodbury. Charles Griscom's wife was Elizabeth Powell, widow of Joseph Powell, and daughter of William Denn. Charles died within two years ago of the pulmonary consumption, leaving a widow and six children; their names are Carrie, Lillie, Charles, Everett, Mary and William Griscom.

David Griscom, the fifth son of William and Ann Griscom, was above ordinary men in mental abilities, and a teacher the greater part of his life; his first wife was Anne Whitelock; she died young, leaving no children. After that event he resided in the city of New York, as a private teacher for one Joseph Walker, an English friend, to educate his two sons. About the time they were through with their education Joseph made an extensive tour in Europe with his two sons, and David accompanied them, and after their return to this country David married his second wife, she being a sister to the first one; her name was Jane Whitelock. He purchased a farm near Woodbury about that time, and started a nursery; his physical health was never very strong; he died a few years ago with that great scourge of the human family, pulmonary consumption, leaving a widow and six children to mourn their loss; he was very circumspect in his life and conversation, and at his death there was a vacuum in general society in the neighborhood in which he dwelt that is not easily filled.

Everett Griscom, the third son of William and Rachel Griscom, was drowned, while bathing, about the sixteenth year of his age. The whole of that branch of the Griscom family were remarkable for acquiring education above most other children, and he was uncommonly precocious in his studies. The late Dalymore Harris, Esq., told me he went to the same school for some time with John, William, and Everett Griscom, and it was astonishing to him, and he had often reflected upon it during his life, how readily Everett Griscom comprehended any branch of learning he undertook to study. He left all the scholars behind; even his brother John, who was considered an adept in acquiring knowledge, could not compete with his brother Everett. Mathamatics he comprehended without any great effort; his reading he never heard equalled during his long life. This is the testimony of one respecting Everett Griscom, who was an excellent judge, and was himself a good scholar, and a practical surveyor. Persons of inquiring minds would inquire why a whole family of children should be so precocious in acquiring knowledge. I believe their intellect was transmitted from their mother. She was the grand-daughter of John and Elizabeth S. Bacon, both of whom, by all accounts, had more than common intellectual abilities. John was one of the Judges of Salem county for many years before Cumberland was set off from Salem. In those days men were elected to office according to their qualifications, not by political rings, which I fear is too often done at the present day without regard to their abilities, to fill such offices to which they are elected, creditably to themselves and beneficially to the public.

Samuel Griscom, fourth son, was a bricklayer, and followed his trade for many years in Philadelphia. He was subsequently chosen Superintendent of the Schuylkill Canal and Navigation Company. I believe he held that situation at the time of his death. His wife was Ann Powell, the daughter of Jeremiah Powell, of Alloways Creek. They are both deceased at the present time, leaving twelve children—Rachel, David, Sarah, Powell, Elizabeth, Samuel, Edwin, William, Horace, Anne, Chalkley, and Emmeline.

David Griscom, their fifth son, married Rachel Stewart, widow of Joseph Stewart, of Salem. Her maiden name was Bradway, the daughter of William Bradway. David kept the Clermont boarding school, near Frankford, for several years. He afterwards purchased a farm in Chester county, Pennsylvania, gave up his school and removed to it, and there ended his days, leaving a widow and one daughter named Rachel. She afterwards married Artheneal Alsop's son, who, I believe, was a school teacher. Rachel Griscom, William and Rachel's daughter, married, when she was past middle age, John Bullock, of

Wilmington, Delaware, who kept a boarding school in that city.
James Denn, the oldest son of John and Elizabeth Denn, after the death of his father, became the owner of the patrimonial estate; his wife's maiden name, I believe, was Kirby, native of Upper Penn's Neck; they had seven children—Elizabeth, Mary, James, John, Martha, Rachel and William. Their oldest daughter Elizabeth, married Mark Stewart. Mary Denn married Ezra Bradway. James Denn, Jr.'s wife was a Bacon; she left two sons, and one daughter who married William Hunt. His oldest son, Theophilus Denn, died when he was about twenty-one years of age. Job Denn, his other son by his first wife, is still living, and resides in Salem at the present time. James' second wife was Mary Haines; there were five children by his last wife—Franklin, John, who is a carpenter, living in Salem, and three daughters. Martha Denn married Aaron Evans, she left two children—Mary and Charles Evans. Rachel Denn's husband was William Abbott, the oldest son of Samuel Abbott. Rachel left two children—John and Hannah Abbott. William Denn's wife was Mary Stewart, the daughter of James and Mary Stewart; they had seven children—Hannah Ann, Beulah, Clayton, Samuel, Charles, Elizabeth and Mary.

James Denn lived to an advanced life very much at his ease, having all his father's real estate; enjoying the natural privilege which were abundant in his time, living mostly at home in a retired way; his brother John, was apprenticed at an early age in the city of Philadelphia to his uncle, David Bacon, to learn the trade of a hatter, and soon after he became of age he commenced the hatting business in the village of Hancock's Bridge. About that time he married Susan Fitzgerald; her family belonged to Delaware; they had three children—Samuel, John and Rachel Denn. A few years later he removed to Salem and followed his trade on Market street. The house and shop were located where Thomas Hilliard's house now is; he continued at his trade until he purchased the Cripp's estate in Mannington. Soon after he abandoned his trade, removed, and took possession of his farm and soon became one of the most successful farmers in that township—certainly he was one of the best meadow men that ever lived in the county of Salem. About that time his son, John Denn, married Rhoda Shourds, daughter of Benjamin and Mary Shourds. He built, and divided his farm, and his son, John, occupied the part he built on until his death, which took place when he was comparatively a young man, leaving a widow and five children.

Their names were Rachel, Mary, Susan, Anne, and Rebecca, who died young. Rachel, his daughter, married Professor John Griscom, who has since died, leaving her a widow. Mary Denn, the second daughter, died a young woman. Susan remains single. Anne, the youngest daughter living, married William Gibbon, of Philadelphia; he has been deceased several years, leaving a widow and two children—Susan and Henry Gibbon. The son died a few years ago. The daughter resides with her mother in Salem.

John Denn, Sr.'s daughter Rachel, married Jacob Hufty, she being his second wife. She lived but a short time after their marriage, leaving no children. Samuel Denn was a merchant in the town of Salem for several years, and married at an advanced age, Elizabeth Alford, the daughter of Samuel Alford. They are both deceased, leaving no offspring. John Denn, Sr.'s second wife was Margaret Hall, daughter of Joseph and Ann Hall, of Elsinborough. They had five children—Elizabeth, John, Anne, Margaret, and Rebecca Denn. Elizabeth married James Woodnutt, the son of Preston Woodnutt. John sold his real estate in Mannington that was left to him by his father, to George Abbott, and eventually removed to California. Anne Denn remains single. Margaret married Edward Bilderback, now deceased, leaving her a widow with two children. Rebecca married a young man in the State of Maryland, and has been deceased several years, leaving one daughter.

John Denn, several years before his death, made application to the Legislature of New Jersey for a law for him to dig a canal across the bottle of the meadow that he owned in Lower Penn's Neck, opposite his plantation in Mannington. The greater part of said meadow formerly belonged to William Penn. James Logan sold it to James Whitten, the former owner of the meadow, in 1712. He likewise had the power to contract the creek as soon as the canal became navigable. The law was obtained, and he soon afterwards commenced operations. After the canal was completed sufficiently for navigation, it was not of the capacity of the creek for draining the low lands and the large tracts of meadow that lay above the mouth of the canal, consequently the meadows were greatly damaged by not having sufficient fall of water, as great as formerly, before the creek was contracted, accordingly there was a great opposition by the proprietors of land above said canal. Meetings were called to devise some plan to prevent him from proceeding any further in his operations. They insisted he should remove the obstruction he had already made in the creek, but he continued firm in his undertakings, taking the precaution to keep within the limits of the law. He built a bridge across the creek for his own accommodation until such time as the canal would wear sufficiently to vent the water above, so it would not be any great detriment to the meadows. After fifty years or more there is now a permanent dam and road across the creek where his bridge was formerly. Therefore his plans and motives have been fulfilled, notwithstanding he did not live to see it all completed on account of his great age. At his death he was more than fourscore.

David Denn, John's younger brother, lived to old age single. He was a tanner and currier, and carried it on in a small way, I believe, while he lived on his brother James' property, near Hancock's Bridge. His sister, Martha Denn, married Mark Bradway. They had one son, whose name was Mark Bradway. Her second husband was Thomas Thompson. She survived him many years.

MASON FAMILY.

John Mason was a native of Gloucestershire, England, and resided in the parish of Winchcome. He emigrated to America when a young man, and landed at Philadelphia in 1683. Soon afterward he came to Salem to live, and purchased a town lot in the town, containing sixteen acres; it lay on the south side of Broadway, and was bounded on the west by Samuel Hedge's land. He erected a brick house there, and lived in it for some time. In 1686 he purchased 5,000 acres of land, being part of the 32,000 acres that was laid off for Eldridge and Warner, to secure the debt that John Fenwick owed them. James Nevell sold the whole of the tract in the year before stated. About the year 1690, John Mason purchased of Roger Milton 1,000 acres of upland and salt marsh, in the township of Elsinborough; it was bounded on the east by Samuel Nicholson's allotment of 2,000 acres; on the west by Redroc Morris' land. In 1695 he built a substantial brick dwelling, left Salem, and lived on his landed estate before described. In 1704 he built a large addition to it, which made it one of the largest brick dwellings that was in the county at that early day. John Mason married Sarah Smith, daughter of John Smith, of Ambelbury; she was born near London, England, 27th of 10th month, 1671. Their oldest child, John Mason, Jr., was born 19th of 7th month, 1697. Their daughter, Ann Mason, was born 24th of 11th month, 1699; William, the son of John and Sarah Mason, was born 23d of 11th month, 1701; Sarah, daughter of John and Sarah Mason, was born 2d of 2d month, 1704; Samuel, son of John and Sarah Mason, born 15th of the 3d month, 1706; Thomas son of John and Sarah Mason, was born 28th of 5th month, 1708. Rebecca Mason, born 1710, daughter of John and Sarah Mason, owned land in various parts in Fenwick tenth; he purchased considerable tract of land in Monmouth precinct of Anna Salter, erected a flour mill about 1705; it is now known as Maskell mill. He was appointed a Commissioner for public highways in 1706; was a member of the Legislature for two or three years, and one of the Justices of Salem

Courts for a number of years. He was a large landholder in the State of Delaware, likewise in Pennsylvania in the neighborhood of Chester. His descendants are not very numerous; there are none at the present time by the name of Mason of his descendents in this county. John Goodwin Mason, who died in 1839, was the last of the male descendants. There are quite a number in the female line who are direct descendants of John Mason, the emigrant. John Mason, the son of Thomas and grandson of John Mason, Sr., was born about 1729; his first wife was Ann, the daughter of Sarah Hall, of Salem; by her he had one daughter—Sarah Mason, who married Elgar Brown, a native of Pennsylvania; they had four children—Ann, Elisha, Israel and John M. Brown. John Mason's second wife was Susanna, the daughter of William and Mary Goodwin; they had five children—Thomas, Mary, Ann, Elizabeth and John G. Mason; Thomas Mason, their son, married Hannah, the daughter of Joseph and Hannah Butcher Hancock; they had issue, one daughter, who married Richard Miller Acton, of Salem. Mary Mason, daughter of John and Susanna Mason, first husband was Abner Beesley, of Alloways Creek; they had four children—Mary, William G., Benjamin and Thomas Mason Beesley; her second husband was Job Ware; they had two sons—Job and Elijah Ware. Ann Mason, daughter of John and Susannah Mason, married Joseph Thompson, son of Joshua and Sarah Thompson; they had three daughters who lived to grow and settle in life; Susan, who married Joseph Pancoast; Sarah married Thomas Shourds; and Ann Thompson married Thomas Fogg. Elizabeth, daughter of John and Susannah Mason, died a young woman unmarried. John G. Mason, the youngest son of John and Susanna Mason never married, died aged fifty-six years.

Its probable Thomas Mason emigrated from England to West New Jersey, about the same time his brother, John Mason, did, he resided in the town of Salem some length of time. After the death of John Fenwick he purchased 500 acres of land in Upper Mannington, being part of Fenwick's grove; he soon became a citizen of that township and continued to reside there until his death. In 1720 he purchased of Samuel Fenwick Hedge 500 acres of land, being part of Hedgefield. There is nothing to show that he even took an active part in the public affairs of the Colony. I see by the court records he occasionally served as one of the Grand Jurors. The following are the names of Thomas and Elizabeth Mason's children: Mary, was born in Mannington 2d of 7th month, 1701; Aaron, was born in 1702; Martha, was born 12th of 9th month, 1704; Joseph, was born 14th of 8th month, 1706. James Mason, son of Thomas and Elizabeth Mason, born 11th of 6th month, 1709; he became in possession of nearly all of the large landed estate in the township of Mannington that belonged to his father, Thomas Mason. He married a daughter of Abel Nicholson; they had no issue; he devised the greater part of his landed estate to his nephew, James Mason Woodnutt, son of Jonathan Woodnutt. James left his mill and farm adjoining to his wife's niece, Ann, the daughter of John Nicholson.

MILLER FAMILY.

The most reliable information that I have obtained, is that Joseph Miller came from the State of Connecticut in 1698, and settled at Cohansey. His occupation was that of a land surveyor. It is well known that at that time, and for many years previous, New England, excepting Rhode Island, was not a place where the Quakers could meet in peace, and worship God according to the dictates of their conscience. Many of them went to reside in Rhode Island under a more liberal government, created by Roger Williams, and a large number emigrated to the Middle States. Such men as Robert Zanes, Richard Lippincott and their families, and several others, emigrated as early as 1675. Joseph Miller and his wife had one son—Ebenezer, born at Cohansey, in 1702. At the death of Richard Tindall, Joseph was chosen deputy surveyor for the lower section of Fenwick's tenth. There is no mention of him as a public surveyor later than 13th of 9th month, 1729; he re-surveyed at that time a tract of land of 1,000 acres for John Brick, lying on the west branch of Gravelly Run or Stoe Ceeek. The said tract of land had formerly been surveyed by Benjamin Acton, of Salem, for Samuel Dumming, of Maryland, by order of James Logan, agent of William Penn, Governor of the province of Pennsylvania. My opinion is that he died about the year 1730, and his son, Ebenezer Miller was his successor as a public surveyor. In 1724 he married, I think, Sarah Collier, daughter of John Collier; their son, Ebenezer Miller, Jr., was born 15th of 9th month, 1725; their daughter, Hannah Miller, was born in 1728; Josiah Miller, in 1731; their son, Andrew Miller, in 1732; William Miller, in 1735; John C. Miller, in 1737; Mark Miller, in 1740; Sarah Miller, in 1743, and Rebecca Miller, 17th of 5th month, 1747. The father of the above mentioned children died in the town of Greenwich at the age of seventy-two years, with a comfortable hope that all would be well with him in a future state. His daughter, Hannah, in 1740, married Charles Fogg, son of Daniel Fogg, of Alloways Creek; they had two children; their eldest daughter, Sarah Fogg, was born in the 5th month, 1747, and died the following fall. In 1749 their daughter, Hannah Fogg, was was born; she afterwards married William Hancock, son of Thomas Hancock, of Elsinborough, being his second wife. In 1771 their son, William Hancock, Jr., was born, and died within the same year; their son, John, was born 24th of 4th month, 1773, and their daughter, Elizabeth, was born in 1776. William Hancock died when his son John was about ten years of age, leaving his real estate to his son, subject to his mother's thirds. John, before he arrived at the age of twenty-one, went into the mercantile business at Hancock's Bridge, as a partner with the late Captain John Tuft, of Salem; he had a delicate constitution, and there appears to have been an unpleasant feeling between him and his half-sister, who had married a young man by the name of Daniels, of Alloways Creek; he was determined that if he should die his sister should have nothing of his estate, and he accordingly made his will on the day he arrived at the age of twenty-one, leaving his landed property to his cousin, William Hancock, son of Thomas Hancock, and his personal property to his mother; he died in a short time afterwards. His mother's second husband was Aaron Thompson, and they had no children. Hannah survived her husband many years, and in the latter part of her life made her home with Elizabeth Miller, she being a cousin of Elizabeth's husband, Richard Miller. In that family she ended her days at a very advanced age. Not long before her death she met Thomas Jones, Sr., on Salem street, and he accosted her in this way: "Mrs. Thompson, I am sorry to see you "lay aside your old-fashioned bee-hive bonnet that the aged "Quaker ladies have worn generally during my time. I was "in hopes you would adhere to the old-fashioned bonnets "whilst you lived. For my part," he continued, "I expect to "continue in the old custom of having my hair done up in a cue "whilst I live."

Ebenezer Miller, Jr., in 1751, married Ruth Wood, daughter of Richard Wood, of Stoe Creek township, Cumberland county. She was born in 1732. Their children were born in Cumberland. Their daughter Hannah was born 14th of 1st month, 1753; their son Ebenezer in 1761, and died in 1763; Priscilla was born in 1763; their second son Ebenezer Miller, was born in 1766, and their daughter Sarah in 1768. Some two thousand acres of the Pledger and Lafetra allotment of 6000 acres, now known as Quaker Neck, came in possession of Benjamin Wyncoop, he being an Englishman; it's more than probable that the said Wyncoop purchased the land of one of the heirs of

Hypolite Lafetra. The house is still standing that was built by one of the family in the beginning of the last century. The property that the old mansion stands on is owned at present by George Griscom. It is certain, however, that at the commencement of the Revolutionary War he was the owner of the whole allotment which is now known as Quaker Neck. At that period all the land from what is called Stone Bridge, which crosses the branch of Pledger creek, called then the Neck, extending to the Salem line, was covered with heavy timber. It went under the name of Wyncoop's woods. Great changes have been wrought there within 100 years. At the present time there is not less than ten farms on said tract; most of them have large and costly mansions, barns and other buildings, and the lands are highly cultivated. Upon the whole it is one of the most desirable situations for an agriculturalist in the county. Benjamin Wyncoop being an Englishman by birth, had a strong predeliction in favor of his native land. Traditional accounts state he had fears that for the part he took in favor of England his property would be confiscated, and he accordingly offered it for sale.

After selling his possessions here he removed to Philadelphia, and owing to the depreciation in the currency, he became poor, and died a few years afterwards in one of the almshouses of that city. John Mountain, an Irishman by birth, who, by industry and economy, in a short time had become able to stock a farm, was fortunate enough to rent that large and inproved farm of John Mason, called the Mason's Point Farm, in Elsinborough, at a very moderate rent. In a few years he accumulated money enough to purchase the homestead of Benjamin Wyncoop. At the time of his death Mountain left one daughter, Mary, who became the owner of all his real estate. Richard Parrott subsequently married her, and they had two children named Mary Ann and Isabella Parrott. Mary Ann became the wife of Hedge Thompson, of Salem. Their children's names I mentioned in the account of the Hedge family. Isabella remained single and lived to an old age. The landed estate of their mother was divided between them. George Griscom is now the owner of Mary Ann's share, and George Abbott, Isabella's land. George Hall bought a large tract of land of Wyncoop, being part of the Neck, all woodland at the time. Lucas Gibbs' of Salem, purchased about 175 acres, lying next to the town of Salem, and his brother Richard Gibbs bought 200 acres or more adjoining the homestead. Both of the Gibbs were Salem men. Lucas Gibbs' property was afterwards owned by Job Tyler, a native of Cumberland. The Fogg family are now the owners of Richard Gibbs' estate.

Ebenezer Miller, Jr,, purchased a farm of Wyncoop.—Richard Ware, of Alloways Creek, bought land and lived there the remainder of his days; Josiah Wistar is the present owner. Mark Miller, brother of Ebenezer Miller, purchased land known at this time as the David E. Davis farm. William Abbott, of Elsinboro, bought the farm and ended his days where his grandson Samuel Abbott now owns and lives. Benjamin Wright likewise bought 100 acres adjoining the Abbotts.—Benjamin in his will devised the said farm to his grandson, Benjamin Wright; Joseph Waddington is the present owner. Ebenezer Miller and his brother, Mark Miller, removed from Cumberland, and made their homes on the lands they purchased of Wyncoop. Mark's wife was Phebe Foster; they had five children—four daughters and one son—William F. Miller. Mary Miller, their eldest daughter, married John Sheppard, of Greenwich. One married Jacob Wood. William F. Miller's first wife was Esther Cooper, native of Gloucester; she died several years before William, leaving one son named Franklin Miller. William F. Miller's second wife was a Newbold from Burlington county, and she survived her husband several years. Franklin Miller married Elizabeth Acton, daughter of Benjamin and Sarah Acton; both of them died young of pulmonary consumption, leaving one daughter, Hetty Miller, who inherited a large estate from her grandfather and father. She was the wife of David E. Davis, formerly of Pilesgrove, who is now deceased.

Josiah Miller, the second son of Ebenezer Miller, Sr., married Letitia Wood in 1760, daughter of Richard Wood, Sr., of Stoe Creek township, Cumberland county, she being a sister of his brother Ebenezer's wife. They had five children—Josiah Miller, Jr., born 12th of 12th month, 1761; Richard Miller, born 15th of 4th month, 1764; John Miller, born in 1767; Letitia Miller, born in 1769, who subsequently married William Reeve; and in 1774 Mark Miller was born. Josiah Miller about that period purchased a large tract of land in Lower Mannington, which formerly belonged to the Sherron family, it being the southern part of James Sherron's allotment of 1,000 acres that he bought of John Fenwick in 1676, being considered one of the finest tracts of table land within Fenwick's tenth. Josiah soon after his purchase removed with his family from his native county and resided on his land in Mannington; he built the brick house where his great-grand-son, Samuel L. J. Miller, owns and lives. I think his two youngest sons, John and Mark Miller, died young; his wife Letitia survived him several years. Josiah Miller, Jr., never married. After the death of his mother he lived with his brother Richard, and after the death of his brother he continued making his home with his widow whilst he lived. In his will he devised his farm to his sister-in-law, Elizabeth Miller, during her natural life, and afterward to her son Josiah Miller, and to his nephew Josiah Miller Reeve, he devised $2,500, with other legacies to his relatives.

The land Josiah Miller owned in Mannington was divided between his two sons—Josiah and Richard. The latter married Elizabeth, daughter of Richard Wistar, of Philadelphia, by whom he had three children—Sarah, Letitia and Josiah. Andrew Miller, third son of Ebenezer, married Rachel, daughter of Elisha and Abigail Bassett, of Pilesgrove. Andrew died before he reached middle age, leaving a widow, and two children, named Daniel L. and Rebecca. Rachel Miller, a short time after the death of her husband, opened a small store, whilst her son, Daniel, went into partnership with Abram Bois and the late Judge Thomas Sinnickson, in the mercantile business. The store was located where the drug store, known as Ingham's Building, now is. In the year 1809 he withdrew from the firm and moved to Philadelphia, as also did his mother and sister. The two latter kept a boarding house on Arch street and opened a retail dry goods store on Second street, which shows that they possessed more than ordinary business capacities. Daniel L. Miller, the son, and William Nicholson, Jr., who had left his native county in the same year opened a wholesale and retail dry goods store on Second street, under the name of Miller & Nicholson. About that period Daniel married Hannah Nicholson, daughter of Abel Nicholson, a citizen of the upper part of Gloucester county, but whose forefathers were natives of Salem. In 1812 William Nicholson withdrew from the firm, and James Kinsey, of Salem, and a young man by the name of Cooper, of Phildelphia, became partners with Daniel L. Miller. The firm was known as Miller, Kinsey & Co. Daniel and his wife had eight children— Charles, Elizabeth, Daniel L., William, Andrew, Rachel, Ann and Hannah. William, the oldest, married Ann Maria Seth, of Salem. Elizabeth became the wife of William Parrish, the son of the eminent Dr. Joseph Parrish, of Philadelphia.

Andrew married Josephine Bunting. Daniel L. Miller, Jr.'s wife was Ann Ridgway. Rachel's husband was William Biddle, the son of the late Clement Biddle; he kept a large hardware store in Philadelphia. I believe his sons and grand-sons are still in that business, and the firm is one of the wealthiest in that line in the city. Anna married Robert Biddle, the brother of William. Daniel L. Miller continued in the mercantile business until near the close of a long life; his wife is also deceased at the present time.

William Miller, the fourth son of Ebenezer, born 1737, married Mary Magere, a native of Wilmington, Del., about the year 1760, and had three children—William, Jr., Ebenezer and Elizabeth. William Miller, Jr., married Rebecca White, daughter of William White, of Pilesgrove, and they had two children, both daughters—Sarah Ann and Eliza. Sarah Ann married Amos Buzby, the son of Joseph Buzby. Eliza Miller married Lewis Hancock, son of William Hancock, of Elsinborough.

John, fifth son of Ebenezer Miller, married Margaret Bacon, of Greenwich, in 1767; she was the daughter of Joseph and Mary Bacon, and was born 20th of 2d month, 1737. John and his wife had five children; their oldest son, Joseph, was born 16th of 6th month, 1768; their daughter, Mary, was born 1770; John Miller, Jr., was born 15th of 3d month, 1772; William was born 1774, and Isaac 20th of 5th month, 1776. Joseph Miller, John's oldest son, was a tanner and currier, and he and his brother John carried on that business in the town of Greenwich the greater part of their lives. Joseph's first wife was Sarah Dawson, of Mount Holly, by whom he had four or five children. They all died young except Margaret Miller, who is still living, aged more than three-score-and-ten. His second wife was Letitia Matlack, widow of William Matlack, of Upper Greenwich, Gloucester county; she lived only four or five years, leaving no children by her second husband. Joseph's third wife was Mary Allen, daughter of Anthony and Mary Allen, residents of Woodbury; he had one son by his last wife—Joseph Allen Miller. Joseph survived his last wife a number of years. Besides attending to his trade he transacted considerable public business, such as settling estates, for which business he was well calculated. The inhabitants of Greenwich had full confidence in his integrity and impartiality in transacting important public business; he died at a very advanced age, regretted by a large circle of relatives and friends.

His son, Joseph Allen Miller, received a good English education; he married Ann Fogg, daughter of Samuel Fogg, of Stoe Creek township; two children—Joseph and Franklin were born to them. Joseph with his family removed to Salem several years ago, and he was soon after elected teacher of the male department of Friends' School in that city. After a few years he was chosen principal in one of the public schools, and continued in that situation several years; he is now deceased. His wife soon after coming to Salem opened a trimming store, and by good management and close application to her business, has succeeded admirably. Mary, the daughter of John Miller, Sr., married George Brown of Upper Greenwich, Gloucester county, and had six children, four daughters and two sons; their sons names were James and Miller Brown. John Miller, second son of John and Margaret Miller, was a tanner and currier by trade, and carried on that business in partnership with his brother Joseph; he married Margaret Evans, daughter of Joshua Evans, of Haddonfield; he was remarkable for his exemplary deportment in his intercourse with his fellow men, and for his unquestionable piety. It can be said of him, with truth, "Behold a true Israelite without guile." He and his wife had four children—John, Evan, Mary and Mark. John's wife was Mary Andrews, daughter of Josiah and Elizabeth Andrews; they had five children—Elizabeth, Margaret, John, Annie and Franklin. Mary Miller married Mark Rulon, and they both died young, leaving no children. Evan Miller married Ann Lane, a widow, of Cincinnati, Ohio; her native place was Greenwich, and her maiden name was Test.

William Miller, third son of John Miller, Sr., married Susan Goodwin, daughter of Louis Goodwin, of Elsinboro.— There were four children by this marriage—Louis, Rebecca, George and Susan. Louis married Emily Lippincott and removed to the State of Ohio over forty years ago. Rebecca married Charles Harmer, of Greenwich, and she died in a short time afterwards. George Miller went to Philadelphia many years ago and opened a confectionery store on Market street, in which business he has prospered. Susan Miller, the youngest, married William Nicholson, and she and her husband have lived most of the time since their marriage in Philadelphia; she died recently, leaving four children—Rachel, Susan, William and Elizabeth Miller. Isaac Miller, fourth son of John Miller, married Mary Webster, of Stoe Creek; they had three daughters—Phebe, Letitia and Ann Miller. Phebe was a Findley. Letitia married Thomas Brown, of Hopewell township, Cumberland county. Ann's husband was John Putner.

MORRIS FAMILY.

Redroe Morris, son of Lewis Morris, was born in Wales, in the Kingdom of England, about the year 1658. In 1683, Redroe Morris, with several others, emigrated to the province of Pennsylvania; they landed at Philadelphia, in the 9th month, 1683; in a short time afterwards he removed to Salem to dwell, and from thence to Elsinborough, on part of Richard Guy's allotment of land, that Samuel Carpenter, of Philadelphia, had previously purchased. About that time he married Jail Baty, daughter of Richard Baty; she was born in Yorkshire, at a place called Humpford, about 1658. She emigrated in company with Robert Ashton, for Pennsylvania, in the ship called the Shoveld, of Stockton, Captain John Howell, master; they sailed from Hull, on the 8th day of 3d month 1686; and landed at New Castle in the fifth month following. At that time it was in the district of Pennsylvania. Redroe and his wife Jail Morris, had six children, all of them born in Elsinborough. Jonathan Morris, their eldest son, was born 16th of 12th month, 1690, he died a minor; Joseph, the son of Redroe and Jail Morris, was born 6th of 6th month; Sarah the daughter of Redroe and Jail Morris, was born 16th of 12th month, 1693; Lewis, the son of Redroe and Jail Moore, was born 23d of 11th month, 1695; David, the son of the before mentioned parents, was born in 1698. Redroe Morris died in 1701, aged nearly forty-three years; he was an active and useful member of Salem Monthly Meeting of Friends. At the time of his death he was owner of 1300 acres of land in Elsinborough; in his will he directed his real estate to be equally divided among his three surviving sons—Joseph, Lewis and David Morris. He had also a large personal estate, which with his slaves, he left to his widow and daughter, Sarah Morris. His friend, Nathaniel Chambless, of Alloways Creek, was the Executor. His widow Jail Morris, married John Hart, of Salem, in 1703; they had issue, one son—John Hart. Joseph Morris became the owner of the homestead of his father; he married and died young, leaving one daughter—Margaret Morris; she subsequently married Clement, the son of William Hall, Jr., and Elizabeth Smith Hall, of Mannington. Clement and his wife, Margaret Hall, had six children,—two daughters and four sons,—Ann, Sarah, Clement, John, Joseph and Morris Hall. Ann married in 1772, John, the eldest son of William and Mary Morris Goodwin. Sarah, the second daughter of Clement and Margaret Hall, married Dr. Thomas Rowen, of Salem. Clement, the son of Clement and Margaret M. Hall, married Rebecca Kay, of the county of Gloucester. John Hall, the second son of Clement and Margaret Hall, resided in Salem, dying, leaving no issue. Joseph Hall, son of Clement and Margaret Hall, married Ann, the daughter of Joseph and Rebecca Brick, of Elsinborough. Morris, the youngest son of Clement and Margaret Hall, married Lydia Potts, of Cumberland County. Their children are mentioned in the genealogy of the Hall family.

Lewis, the son of Redroe and Jail Morris born 1695, married Sarah Fetters, of Salem. Lewis and his wife left three daughters—Sarah, Mary, and Ann Morris. Sarah, the eldest daughter, married Thomas, the eldest son of John and Susanna Smith Goodwin; the latter was the daughter of John Smith, of Smithfield; Mary, the daughter of Lewis and Sarah Morris, married William Goodwin, brother of Thomas Goodwin. William and his wife had five children—John, Lewis, Susanna, Mary and William Goodwin. John, the eldest son, married a Hall. Lewis was twice married, his first wife was a Zanes; his second, was Rachel, the daughter of William Nicholson, of Mannington. Susanna, the eldest daughter of William and Mary Goodwin, was twice married; her first husband was John, the son of Thomas Mason, of Elsinborough; her second husband was Joshua Thompson, of Alloways Creek, son of Joshua and Grace Thompson, of Elsinborough; Mary, the daughter of William and Mary Goodwin, married Thomas Hancock. William, the son of William and Mary Goodwin, married Elizabeth Woodnutt, of Mannington. Ann Morris, the daughter of Lewis Morris, by Sarah his wife, married Samuel, the son of Elisha and Abigail Bassett, of Pilesgrove; they had six children—Grace, William, Samuel Morris, Davis, and Ann Bassett. Sarah Fetters, the wife of Lewis Morris, was a sister of Erasmus Fetters; he was a tanner and currier; he resided in Salem, on Yorke street; the house in which he lived was a brick, with a hipped roof, it was standing in 1810. Erasmus died in 1760; in his will executed in 1756, he left £10 each to William and Mary M. Goodwin's daughters; the like sum to each of James Chambless, Jr.'s children—Sarah, Mary, and Rebecca Chambless. The two first named became the wives of William and David Smith's of Mannington. Erasmus left to his niece Ann, the wife of Samuel Bassett, £50, and the remainder of his estate, real and personal, to his nephew, Henry Vanmeter, of Pittsgrove. David, the youngest son of Redroe Morris, born in 1698, married. He and his wife Jane Morris, had one son—Joshua Morris, born 3d of 10th month, 1723. The child and mother died in a short time afterwards. David it appears, died comparatively a young man, making a will, leaving his estate to his half-brother, John Hart. The real estate was large, comprising about 400 acres, also a flour mill located at the mouth of Mill Creek, near Fort Point. However there were 160 acres of salt marsh included with the 400 acre tract. John Hart sold his real estate, (that was devised to him by his half brother David Morris), to Col. Benjamin Holme, about 1760. To show what energy and perseverance will accomplish, Margaret Hall Holme, after the death of her husband John Holme, the son of Col. Benjamin Holme, purchased the 160 acres of salt marsh that was owned by her husband, and part of David Morris' estate, formerly; she banked and reclaimed it from the overflow of the tide, notwithstanding great opposition from some of her neighbors, who owned meadow adjoining ; that being over fifty years ago. The said meadow is at the present day as productive and profitable as any other portion of the large landed estate of the Morris'.

NICHOLSON FAMILY.

Samuel Nicholson, lived in Wiseton in the county of Nottinghamshire; he was a husbandman; his wife was named Ann; they had five children, all born in England—Parobale, was born 20th of 2d month, 1659; she married Abraham Strand; Elizabeth Nicholson, the second daughter of Samuel and Ann Nicholson, born 20th of 3d month, 1664; she married John Abbott, and left three daughters—Rachel, Mary and Elizabeth Abbott. Samuel, the son of Samuel and Ann Nicholson, born 6th of 3d month, 1666; Joseph, the son of Samuel and Ann Nicholson, born 30th of 2d month, 1669; Abel, the son of Samuel and Ann Nicholson, born 2d of 5th month, 1672. Samuel and Ann, his wife, with their five children, emigrated in company with John Fenwick. With a number of others they landed at where Salem is, on the 5th of 10th month, 1675. Samuel had purchased, previous to their sailing, 2,000 acres of land; the said land was surveyed to him in 1676, together with sixteen acres for a town lot, in new Salem. He died about the year 1690, on his property in Elsinborough; he was the first Justice of the Peace in Fenwick Colony. His widow, Ann Nicholson, died in 1693; in her will she devised her estate to her three grand-daughters—Rachel, Mary and Elizabeth Abbott, and her three sons—Samuel, Joseph and Abel Nicholson. Samuel Nicholson, Jr., married, and he and his wife both dying soon afterwards; he made a will devising his large landed estate to his two brothers—Joseph and Abel Nicholson; that was about 1695. Joseph parted with his share, which included the old homestead of his parents, located on the northern bank of Monmouth river, now known as Alloways, to George Abbott, Henry Stubbins and John Froth. Joseph Nicholson married and settled near Haddonfield, Camden county. Abel, the youngest son of Samuel Nicholson, and Ann his wife, married Mary, the daughter of William and Joanna Tyler; she was born in England in the 11th month, 1677. Abel and his wife resided in Elsinborough; they were married about 1694. Sarah, their eldest child, was born 19th of 11th month, 1694; Rachel, the daughter of Abel and Mary Nicholson, was born 7th of 7th month, 1698; Abel, the son of Abel, by Mary his wife, was born 13th of 1st month, 1700; Joseph, the son of Abel and Mary Nicholson, was born 4th of 12th month, 1701; William, the son of Abel and Mary Nicholson, was born 15th of 9th month, 1703; he became the owner of 500 acres of Hedgefield, in Mannington; he built a brick mansion on the property, which is still standing; he married, he and his wife had three children—Rachel, Ruth and William Nicholson, the latter married Sarah Townsend, of Penn's Neck. Rachel, their oldest child, was born 9th of 11th month, 1774; Milesant, the daughter of William and Sarah Nicholson, was born 3d of 8th month, 1776; William, the son of William and Sarah Nicholson, was born 8th of 3d month, 1779, he died young; Samuel, the son of William and Sarah Nicholson, was born 2d of 7th month, 1781; William, the son of William and Sarah Nicholson, was born 16th of 11th month, 1783; Sarah, the daughter of William and Sarah Nicholson, was born in 1791; Daniel, the son of William and Sarah Nicholson, was born 19th of 1st month, 1786, and Ann, the youngest daughter of William and Sarah Nicholson, was born in 1793. Ann, the daughter of Abel and Mary Nicholson, was born 15th of 11th month, 1707; Ruth Nicholson, daughter of Abel and Mary Nicholson, was born 9th of 9th month, 1713; Samuel, the son of Abel and Mary Nicholson, was born 12th month, 1716; John Nicholson, the youngest son of Abel and Mary Nicholson, was born 3d of 6th month, 1719. Ann, the daughter of Abel and Mary Nicholson, married John Brick, Jr., of Gravelly Run, it is now known as Jericho, Cumberland county. John was one of the Judges of Salem courts for a number of years; he died 23d of 1st month, 1758; he and his wife, Ann Nicholson Brick, had eight children—Mary, their eldest daughter, who married Nathaniel Hall, of Mannington, was born 10th of 2d month, 1730. Elizabeth, the daughter of John and Ann Brick, was born 4th of 7th month, 1732, she was afterwards the wife of John Reeve, of Cohansey. John, the son of John and Ann Brick, was born 10th of 11th month, 1733; Joseph, the son of John and Ann Brick, was born 24th of 3d month, 1735; Joseph was twice married, his first wife was Rebecca Abbott; his second wife was Martha Reeve. Ann, the daughter of John and Ann Brick, was born 23d of 1st month, 1738; she subsequently married Joseph Clement, of Haddonfield, in 1761. Hannah, the daughter of John and Ann Brick, was born

8th of 3d month, 1741; Ruth, the daughter of John and Ann Brick, was born 1st of 10th month, 1742; she married Benjamin Reeve in 1761. Jane Brick was born 10th of 1st month, 1743.

Samuel Nicholson, the son of Abel and Mary Nicholson, married Sarah Dennis, of Cohansey; they had two children—Samuel and Grace Nicholson, the latter married Andrew, the son of Joshua Thompson, of Elsinborough. Samuel Nicholson, Jr., married the daughter of Nathaniel and Mary B. Hall, of Mannington; there were five children—John, Ann, Mary, Samuel and Josiah Nicholson. John Nicholson, the youngest son of Abel and Mary Nicholson, married Jane Darkin, the daughter of John Darkin. John and his wife lived and owned a large farm adjoining the Tylers on the north side of Alloways creek; they had several children—Ann, Abel and Jane Darkin, and one or two other daughters. Abel became the owner of the real estate of his parents; he died a young man; the property was divided among his sisters. Darkin Nicholson became the owner, by his grand-father's (John Darkin) will, of the large and valuable estate in Elsinborough, known as the Windham estate; it is a point of land adjoining the Salem town marsh; on that point the New Haven colony located in 1640. Darkin married Esther Brown, a native of Chester county, but at the time of her marriage, she lived in Elsinborough with her mother, who had recently married William Goodwin, Sr.; she was William's second wife. The children of Darkin and Esther Nicholson were Mary, Esther, James, Darkin and John Nicholson. Mary was the first wife of Elisha Bassett, of Mannington. Esther Nicholson married John Thompson, of Elsinborough, the son of John and Mary Bradway Thompson.

OGDEN FAMILY.

John Ogden was a native of England. It appears by the record, he was a man of considerable distinction in his native country, and possessed more than ordinary intellect. For his meritorious conduct towards his sovereign, Charles the I., King of England, he was presented with a Coat-of-Arms, from Charles the II., with this motto, "And if I make a show, I do not "boast of it." This John Ogden was one of the persons to whom King Charles the II. granted the Charter of Connecticut in 1662. The record of the family states he lived for a length of time on Long Island. About the year 1673, he settled at Elizabethtown, in East Jersey, when in connection with Bailey Baker and Watson, he purchased a tract of land of the Indians, for which a patent was granted by George Nichols, who was Governor of the colony under the Dutch, while they held New York. The Elizabethtown grant, was the occasion of much contention with English proprietors, and they looked upon Ogden as a leading malcontent. The record of his is correct, he was a true patriot, a leader of the people, an earnest Christian and an acknowledged pioneer of the oldest town in the State, whose house the first white child of the settlement was born. He died in the early part of 1682, leaving many descendants. His wife was Jane Bond, sister of Robert Bond. Judge Elmer writes, (being well acquainted with the history of the State), "that the descendants of John and Jane Ogden have held dis-"tinguished places in the government of the State, among whom "were Aaron Ogden, Governor in 1813, and his son Elias D. B. "Ogden, Judge of the Supreme Court."

The family of the Ogdens are very numerous both in East and West Jersey. John Ogden, the grandson of the emigrant, came to Fairfield as early as 1690, and became a large landholder in that region; he likewise became the owner of a large tract of land of 655 acres, on the north side of Cohansey, in Greenwich township, adjoining lands of Nicholas and Leonard Gibbon. In 1729, the said John Ogden sold part of said land adjoining Pine Mount, to Ebenezer Miller, of Greenwich. Samuel and Jonathan Ogden came and settled in North Cohansey precinct, about the same time that John did; whether they were brothers or cousins, the record of the family does not determine. It is evident that Samuel Ogden settled at Deerfield, as the inscriptions on one of the tombstones in the Presbyterian Cemetery in that place fully confirms. The Samuel Ogden that was buried in Deerfield yard must have been the son of Samuel Ogden, who emigrated to Fenwick's Colony, as inscribed on the tombstone, "died in 1805, in his 72d year." It is generally thought he was a member of the Assembly of New Jersey in 1780, and member of Council in 1781, and of the same body in 1783, and fourteen times afterwards; his last services being in 1800. There was a Samuel Ogden no doubt of the same family, appointed a Captain of the Militia, in 1776, and afterwards a Major, and Lieutenant-Colonel. He died in 1785. The descendants of John Ogden, who settled near Fairton, are very numerous in the County of Cumberland. John, and many of his immediate descendants, lie buried in the ancient yard of the Presbyterians, that is located on the south bank of Cohansey, near the town of Fairton.

The Ogden family of Cumberland, was, as it appears at the time of the Revolutionary War, ardent Whigs, many of them joined the American army among them was one Benjamin Ogden, who was taken prisoner and died in prison in the city of Philadelphia; also John, the son of David Ogden, served in Washington's army at the time he retreated from New York. David Ogden, the grandson of John Ogden, was a large landholder in Fairfield township, likewise owned a flour mill, the said mill was probably erected by John Ogden, his grandfather. It is known at the present time as John Trenchard's Mill, and is located on a branch of the Cohansey, called by the early settlers, North Branch, afterwards Mill Creek. David Ogden had eleven children. His oldest son, John Ogden, was born 1st month, 1755; he married Abigail Bennet 3d of 3d month, 1799. The following are the names of their children—Abigail, born 13th of 12th month, 1779. John, born 21st of 1st month, 1782; the latter owned property at Port Norris, and kept a tavern there; afterwards in Port Elizabeth. Hannah Ogden, daughter of John and Abigail Ogden, was born 12th of 8th month, 1784. Rachel was born 16th of 7th month, 1786; Theodocia Ogden was born on 13th of 3d month, 1791; Aldon, was born on 27th of 3d month, 1793; Elmer was born on 28th of 7th month, 1795; Benjamin was born 4th of 10th month, 1797; Matilda was born 2d of 12th month, 1799, and David Sayre Ogden was born 15th of 5th month, 1803. All of John and Abigail Ogden's children lived to grow to maturity, and married. Abigail, their eldest daughter, married Ephraim Westcott; their daughter Rachel, married George Summers, in 1804; John Ogden married Charlotte Jones, in 1809; Hannah Sayre married John Howell, in 1808; Theodocia Ogden married Joseph Hunt, in 1810, and Adam Ogden married Hannah Thompson, in 1821. Benjamin Ogden, son of John and Abigail B. Ogden, was born in 1797, and graduated at Princeton College in 1817; from 1818 to 1820 he studied for the ministry, in the Theological Seminary; was licensed to preach in 1821, and was ordained the following year. He was settled at Lewes, Delaware, until 1826; from thence he was called to Pennington, N. J. He continued in the latter place until 1838, when he removed to the State of Michigan; afterwards he went to Valparaiso, Indiana, where he died in 1853; his wife was Emily Sausbury; they were married 15th of 10th month, 1821. Matilda Ogden married Harris Matthias, 25th of 11th month, 1821; David, the youngest son of John and Abigail Ogden, married Martha S. Ewing, 2d of 11th month, 1825. Elmer Ogden, son of John and Abigail Ogden, resides at this time, in the town of Greenwich; he has been twice married; his first wife was Sarah, the daughter of Isaac Sheppard; they had seven children—Isaac S., Horace E., Joseph H., Matilda, Henry S., Sarah J., and Amanda Ogden. Elmer Ogden's second wife was the widow of George Hall, of Salem; her maiden name was Matilda Riley; she is deceased, leaving no issue.

Isaac S. Ogden, son of Elmer and Sarah Ogden, married Ann Elizabeth, daughter of Daniel Bacon, they have issue—Mary, Matilda and Elmer Ogden. Horace Ogden married Maria Jorden, they have six children living—Elizabeth J., Edward M., Ella, Clarence C., Sallie S. and Lydia J. Ogden. Joseph married Lydia Fithian, daughter of Joel Fithian; they have one son—George B. Ogden. Matilda Ogden married Jonathan Fithian, their children are Charles, Frank, Rebecca, Joel and Sarah Fithian; Henry S., son of Elmer Ogden, married Lizzie Syder, they have one son, Frank Ogden. Sarah S. Ogden, daughter of Elmer and Sarah Ogden, remains single, and resides with her father; Amanda Ogden is deceased, and never married; Elmer Ogden has been an active business man, and at one time was a member of the State Legislature, he is now in his eighty-second year, having survived nearly all of his brothers and sisters. His mother died in 1818, aged fifty-seven years, and his father, John Ogden, died in 1832, aged seventy-seven years.

Harris Ogden who resides in Fairfield township, Cumberland

county, is the son of Harris Ogden, and his grand-father was of the same name. He is doubtless one of the leading agriculturists in the county at the present day; his farm is located near the old Presbyterian Stone Church; his buildings and fencings are not surpassed in that section. He is likewise prominent in raising and feeding all kinds of stock, particularly cattle, and it is generally considered that he has no equal in that particular in the county of Cumberland, since the late Dr. William Elmer, of Bridgeton.

It appears that one of John Ogden's sons or grand-sons left Elizabethtown, New Jersey, and located in Pennsylvania near the city of Philadelphia, where he and his family became members of the Society of Friends. Samuel Ogden left Pennsylvania in 1767 and settled in Gloucester county, about one mile below Swedesboro, known as Battentown. He being a tanner and currier by trade, there he established his tannery; the same yard was afterwards occupied by his son Joseph Ogden, and his grand-son David Ogden, late of Woodbury; it is still occupied by one of David's son's, he being the fourth generation. Samuel Ogden married Mary Ann Hoffman, of Gloucester county, she was born 19th of 10th month, 1752. Samuel and his wife Mary Ann Ogden had ten children, who lived to grow up, married and had families of children. One of the family has in possession the Coat of Arms, given by Charles the II, similar to the one the family have in the county of Cumberland. Mary, the daughter of Samuel and Mary Ann Ogden, was born 13th of 6th month, 1771; Esther Ogden, their second daughter was born 15th of 2d month, 1773; Joseph, the eldest son of Samuel and Mary Ann Ogden, was born 4th of 8th month, 1775; Martha, daughter of the same parents, born 2d of 2d month, 1779; Hannah born 29th of 6th month, 1781; Ann Ogden born 22d of 11th month, 1783; Sarah born 22d of 7th month, 1787; Samuel born 27th of 4th month, 1790; John Ogden born 20th of 6th month, 1792, and David Ogden born 19th of 2d month, 1796. Samuel Ogden, father of the above mentioned children, purchased a farm near Woodstown, in Pilesgrove, there he and his wife ended their days, he dying 21st of 4th month, 1821, aged about seventy-six years; his wife died three years previously, aged sixty-six years. Mary, their eldest daughter, married Samuel Lippincott, of Gloucester, she died young, leaving one son—Caleb Lippincott, (see Lippincott family). Esther, the second daughter of Samuel Ogden, married Thomas, the son of Jacob Davis, of Woodstown, they had several children, (see Davis family); Esther departed this life 1st of 8th month, 1845, aged seventy-three years.

Joseph, the eldest son of Samuel and Mary Ann Ogden, succeeded his father in the tanning business near Swedesboro, at that place he accumulated a large fortune, and retired many years before his death to the town of Woodbury. He was four times married; his first wife was the daughter of John Tatem, Sr., of Woodbury, she was the mother of his children; their names were David, Samuel, John, Elizabeth and Mary Ann Ogden. One of Joseph Ogden's wives was Prudence Hall, daughter of Clement and Sarah Kay Hall, of Elsinboro, she being his third wife. His last wife I think survived him, he dying 20th of 11th month, 1863, being in his eighty-ninth year. Martha, daughter of Samuel and Mary Ann Ogden, married Samuel Abbott, of Mannington, Salem county, she was his second wife; they had issue; (see genealogy of the Abbott family); she died 5th of 4th month, 1848, aged about sixty-nine years. Hannah, daughter of Samuel and Mary Ann Ogden, married Isaac Townsend, of Cape May county. Soon after they were married they resided at Port Elizabeth; they had issue; the names of their children were Samuel, Isaac, Ann, Hannah, William and Charles Townsend. Isaac and his wife a few years before their death, removed to the city of Philadelphia. Ann Ogden, daughter of Samuel and Mary Ann Ogden, married John, son of Zadoc and Eunice Silvers Street, of Mannington, about 1804 or 1805. He sold his valuable real estate in said township to John Wistar, and removed with his family to the then new State of Ohio, and purchased a large tract of land in what is now known as Columbiana county, and there founded a town which they called Salem, after Salem, New Jersey.

The Street family became one of the wealthiest families in that section of the State. John, the oldest son of Zadoc and Eunice S. Street, carried on a large business for many years as a merchant; he and his wife had several sons, but no daughters. The family of Streets have great energy of character and a literary turn of mind. Aaron Street, the second son of Zadoc, (after the North-West became open to settlers,) left Salem and located in the territory of Iowa, and there founded a town he called Salem, the said town was the capital of the territory for some time. Aaron had a family; one of his sons was named Isaac Street, he also had a family; one of his daughters was named Mary Ann Street, she subsequently married a young man by the name of Duncan, they were of Scotch family; Mary Ann and her husband reside at San Francisco, California. One of the Street family located in Oregon, and there founded a town and called it Salem. Ann Ogden Street, the wife of John, departed this life 31st of 8th month, 1861, aged seventy-eight years.

Sarah, daughter of Samuel and Mary Ann Ogden, married Samuel Holmes, of Upper Penn's Neck; they had four children, their names were Martha, Ann Eliza, Sarah and William Holmes. Sarah Ogden Holmes died 26th of 2d month, 1829, aged about forty-two years. John, the son of Samuel and Mary Ann Ogden, has been twice married; his first wife was Ann Howe, daughter of Isaac and Abigail Howe, of Gloucester county. John and his wife had three daughters—Mary Ann, Martha and Ann Ogden. Soon after the death of their mother, Ann Street who was on a visit to her relatives in New Jersey, asked permission of her brother John to take two of his daughters home with her to Ohio, he gave his consent, and she brought up and educated them as she would have done with her own children. They are both married, and in affluent circumstances, living in their adopted State. John's second wife was Abigail Atkinson, widow of Caleb Atkinson, her maiden name was Antrim; they have four children, two are deceased, Joseph and Clement are living. John lived the greater part of his life on the homestead farm near Woodstown. He sold his farm some years ago, and now resides in the city of Salem; he is the only one left of Samuel and Mary Ann Ogden's children; he is now in his eighty-fifth year. David, the youngest son of Samuel and Mary Ann Ogden, married Sarah Ann Burr, of Burlington county, they have had two children—Wharton and Rebecca Ogden, the latter is deceased; Wharton has a store at Port Elizabeth. David was a carriage maker, and soon after he married, removed to Burlington county, there he followed his trade until his death, which event took place 2d of 7th month, 1825, when he was only twenty-nine years of age.

OAKFORD AND MOSS FAMILIES.

Charles and Wade Oakford emigrated from England to West Jersey about 1695; it is evident by the records of the Wade family they were nephews of Edward Wade, instead of what many supposed, that Charles Oakford's wife was the daughter of Edward. The brothers, Charles and Wade Oakford, had considerable means when they came in 1698, each of them contributed quite a sum of money for that time, towards erecting the first brick meeting house in the town of Salem. Charles purchased of his uncle Edward Wade of his allotment of land, located in Lower Monmouth precinct, quite a large tract, that being about 1696; he married and settled; the following are the names of his children—Elizabeth, born at Alloways Creek, 17th of 3d month, 1698; Charles and Mary Oakford, born 20th of 1st month, 1701, Mary died young; John Oakford, born 12th of 1st month, 1704. Charles' second wife was Margaret Denn, daughter of James and Elizabeth Maddox Denn; their daughter Mary Oakford, was born 21st of 1st month, 1706; Susanna Oakford, was born in 1709. Charles the father of these children, died about 1728. His son Charles inherited the homestead, and subsequently was one of the ablest farmers in the lower precinct of Monmouth. In the Assessor's duplicate made by George Trenchard, Sr., Charles paid the highest tax in the township, excepting William Tyler. In 1742 he built himself a brick dwelling, which is still standing.— Charles died in 1760, leaving several children—Elizabeth, Isaac and Samuel, also one or two other daughters whose names are not given. Elizabeth married Samuel Naylor, they had issue. Their son Charles Oakford Naylor, married, had a son, Joseph Naylor, who resides at Hancock's Bridge at this time, being over seventy years of age. Isaac Oakford, (Charles' eldest son), inherited the homestead and soon after sold the farm to John Ware, and purchased lands near Darby, Pennsylvania, and there ended his days. The Oakfords in the city of Philadelphia are his descendants. Samuel Oakford settled in the State of Delaware; he lived to a very advanced age, and left issue. Mary, the daughter of Charles and Margaret Oakford, married James, the son of Nathaniel Chambless; they had issue.—Susanna Oakford, the daughter of Charles and Margaret Oakford, married Jonathan, the son of William Bradway, she was his second wife; they had issue. John, the son of Charles and Mary Oakford, married Margaretta Colsten in 1733, they had several children; they married in the Acton family of Salem.

Wade Oakford, the emigrant, brother of Charles, purchased a large tract of land in the upper precinct of Monmouth, being part of James Wasse's 7000 acres; I never heard whom he married. His son William Oakford married when he was past middle-age Rebecca Moss, daughter of Abraham Moss; they had two daughters, one of them died a minor. Notwithstanding William's great possessions, he was a man of very industrious habits. One day some of his friends called to see him and he was not at home, they inquired of his housekeeper where he was (his wife was deceased at that time), she told them he was in the woods cutting wood. They went to look for him and found him busily cutting cord wood; they told him he was too old a man to work so hard, and abundantly able to live without, and leave his only daughter well provided for. To which the old man assented and replied, "that he expected some stranger would "reap the benefit of his labors, inasmuch as some Dutchman "would come and marry his daughter one of these days." This proved to be true, for in a short time one of Richard Wistar's glassblowers by the name of Jacob Houseman married her.—The name has since been abbreviated, and is now spelled House. Jacob and Mary Oakford House had one son named William House, who married Sarah, the daughter of Jonathan and Milicent Wood. Milicent was the daughter of Peter Stretch. William House and his wife Sarah left two children—Jonathan and Mary House. Jonathan House who is still living at an advanced age, married Francis, the daughter of John Blackwood; they have issue. Mary House, his sister, married William, the son of James and Catharine Sherron, of Salem.—William and his wife are both deceased; they left three or more children—Samuel, Albert, and a daughter. Albert Sherron resides in Salem and keeps a grocery store, and has been prosperous in his business.

Alexander Moss I think came to this country about 1720, he located in Alloways Creek township; he and his wife Rebecca Moss had four children—Richard, was born in 11th month, 1724; Isaac, was born 18th of 11th month, 1726; Hannah, was born 14th of 7th month, 1730, and Rebecca Moss was born in

1733. Abraham Moss purchased part of Jonathan Smith's estate, about the year 1735; he died about 1750, and his son Richard Moss become the owner. In 1751 Charles Fogg purchased the farm where William Cooper now lives of William Chandler; in 1767 Richard Moss and Charles Fogg exchanged farms. The Smith property or part of it has been in possession of the Fogg family since. Richard Moss had two children—Isaac and Rebecca Moss, both of them lived to old age, never married. Isaac became the owner of his father's real estate, and subsequently sold it to John Vanculer.

PLUMMER FAMILY.

The laws of this country are well calculated to give every young person, no matter how poor or obscure their parentage is, an opportunity to rise in a social and political standing in the community in which they live. Hence, many of the most useful citizens in this section, and likewise throughout this favored country, descended from what is called the lower order of society. Samuel Plummer was the son of an emigrant from England, named David Plummer, as is supposed by the family. Their record seems to have been lost. Samuel Plummer married Amy Johnson; they had seven or eight children; their names were—David, William, James, Sarah, Samuel, John and Hannah Plummer. Samuel, the son of Samuel and Amy Johnson Plummer, was born the 29th of 9th month, 1813; in early life, he was apprenticed to a carriage maker; after he arrived to manhood, he followed his trade for several years, I think at Sharpstown in Salem county. He however, turned his attention to politics, and subsequently was elected Sheriff of the county of Salem. Soon after the expiration of his term of office, he was elected to the State Legislature, and the following year to the State Senate; he now holds the important office of United States Marshal for the State of New Jersey. He married Keziah Woodruff, daughter of Enos Woodruff, of Bridgeton, Cumberland county; she can properly claim as long a line of ancestry as any other one in the county of Salem, being a lineal descendant of Thomas Woodruff, who was the son of John Woodruff, yeoman, in the county of Worcestershire, England. Thomas married Edith Wyatt, daughter of Joseph Wyatt, a gentleman. The said Thomas Woodruff and his wife Edith, left Worcestershire, and removed to London, at which place they had several children born; their names were Thomas, Edith, John and Isaac Woodruff. In the year 1678, Thomas and Edith Woodruff, together with their children, and in company with a number of others, emigrated for West New Jersey, on board the ship Surrey, Steven Nichols, Captain. They arrived at Salem in 4th month, 1679. Samuel Plummer and his wife, Keziah Woodruff, have had eight children, only three of them are living at this time—Charles, John E. and Sallie Plummer. Charles has been twice married; his first wife was Hannah, the daughter of Benjamin Heritage; she died a young woman, leaving one daughter, Wilhelmina Plummer. His second wife is Anna, the daughter of Benjamin M. Black; they have one daughter—Rebecca Plummer. Charles Plummer is a merchant, and resides at Pedricktown, in Upper Penn's Neck, at which place he has an enviable reputation; his future career is promising. He was elected last year to represent Salem county in the New Jersey State Senate.

PRESTON FAMILY.

John E. Preston, M. D., a resident and practicing physician in the city of Salem, New Jersey, is a lineal descendant of Peregrine White, who was the first European born in this country north of Mason and Dixon line. The following was written for one of the Massachusetts' papers a short time since by Susanna French, she being one of the family. "Peregrine
"White was the son of William and Susanna White, who ar-
"rived on board of the Mayflower at Plymouth Rock, 22d of 12th
"month, 1620. Peregrine was the son of the before mentioned
"parents, and was born in the 11th month, 1620, whilst the ship
"was anchored in Cape Cod, between Cape Cod and Plymouth
"Rock. Daniel White was the son of Peregrine White. John
"White, son of Daniel White, married Miss Skinner, they had a
"son—John, who married Mary Grover, he lived many years in
"Mansfield and was a merchant at that place John and Mary
"Grover had nine children, named respectively—John, Abial,
"Otis, Calvin, Mary, Rachel, Lavinia, Aziah and Susanna
"White, the latter, the author of the poem published some time
"ago; she married William French, who was killed at the battle
"of Bunker Hill. At the intercession of his mother, she sub-
"sequently married William's brother, John French, a resident
"of the city of Providence, Rhode Island. They afterwards
"moved to Dublin, New Hampshire. Lavinia, the daughter of
"John and Mary Grover White, married Aaron Preston; they
"had several children. John E. Preston, M. D., the eldest son,
"who resides at Salem, New Jersey, he being the eighth gener-
"ation from Peregrine White, and the ninth from William and
"Susanna White."

REEVE FAMILY.

Mark Reeve was another of those early pioneers of America who was calculated by his mental endowments and high moral character to give a moral force to the neighborhood wherein he dwelt. He turned his attention more to the religious associations than his intimate friend, William Hall, although the latter is frequently mentioned in the early records of Salem Monthly Meeting, showing that he was a consistent member of the Society of Friends. Mark Reeve, in 1684, married Ann Hunt, of Salem, and on the following year the executors of John Fenwick directed John Woodledge, the deputy surveyor, to lay off sixteen acres of land which Mark Reeve had purchased of them in the town of Cohansey. It is most probable that Mark made that place his home for a short time, but a few years later he purchased a large tract of land on the south side of Cohansey creek, opposite Cohansey (known at the present time as Greenwich). In the year 1705, a four rod road was surveyed from Salem to Maurice river, which, after crossing the Cohansey, passed between James Pierce's and Mark Reeve's land. The Reeve family held large tracts of land in that section for more than a century and a half, but at this time the family have disposed nearly or quite the whole of it. As early as 1698 James Duncan and Mark Reeve made application to Salem Friends for assistance to build a meeting house. There was one erected, having been built of logs, near the banks of the Cohansey, on the main street, where the present brick meeting house now stands. The exact time of Mark Reeve's death does not appear in the records, but circumstances go to show that it was about 1716 or 1717. He left one son, Joseph Reeve, who married Ellinor Bagnall, in 1722; they had five children—Mark, Joseph, John, Mary and Benjamin. Mark, the son of Joseph and Ellinor Reeve, born 28th of 12th month, 1723, became a highly esteemed minister in the Society of Friends in early life. He married about the year 1761 when he was past middle age. The following are the names of his children—Josiah, Ann, Mark, William and George Reeve. Josiah, his eldest son, was born

23d of 9th month, 1762. His father purchased a tract of land in Alloways Creek township, situated on the north side of the creek, and built a substantial brick building on the property. (It is now owned and occupied by Luke S. Fogg.) At that place Josiah went to reside, and soon afterwards married. At the death of his father the said property was devised to him, but he sold it soon afterwards to John Pancoast, and removed to Burlington with his family to reside with his wife's relatives. She, I think, was a Newbold, and by her he had two or more children. Martha, their daughter, married Clayton, the son of John and Charlotte Wistar, she being his second wife. They had one son—Josiah. John Reeve, the son of Josiah, married Priscilla, the daughter of John and Mary Sheppard, of Greenwich. They had children.

The Sheppard family is one of the oldest and most numerous in the county of Cumberland. David Sheppard emigrated from England about the year 1683, and with the Swing family and a few others organized the Cohansey Baptist church, which is considered the mother of the Baptist churches in this section of the State. John and Mark, the grandsons of David Sheppard, having become converted to the principles of the Society of Friends, left the religious society of their father and became members of the Friends' association, but far the largest portion of the Sheppard family still adhere to the Baptist society, while a number of them are members of the Presbyterian church at the present time. William, the son of Josiah and Hannah Reeve, was born 11th of 12th month, 1766, and subsequently married Letitia, the daughter of Josiah and Letitia Miller, of Mannington; they had eight children—Josiah Miller, Anna, Elizabeth M., Letitia, William F., Mark M., Priscilla and Emmor Reeve. Josiah M., the eldest son, married a young woman in Pennsylvania, by the name of Garrigues. She died not many years after their marriage, having two daughters—Hannah and Emma. His second wife was Mary, the daughter of Jonathan Dallas, of Port Elizabeth. Josiah and his wife are both deceased at the present time, leaving one son—Dallas Reeve. Few men that have lived in this county possessed a more energetic character than Josiah M. Reeve; his judgment was above that of ordinary men, and he was of pleasant and agreeable temperament. He more than once represented his county in the State Legislature. He with his two younger brothers, William F., and Emmor, carried on ship building with success for a number of years at Allowaystown. They did not however, confine their attention exclusively to one particular business, but bought largely of land in that neighborhood, considered not worth farming, which through their energy and judicious management has been made to produce more than four-fold. They also enlarged and beautified the town of their adoption, with large and substantial buildings, and no village in this section of the State has superior improvements. I will here state that William Reeve and his wife, after marriage, like his brother Josiah, removed to the county of Burlington and made it his permanent home. Their children were born and raised to maturity. Anna, the daughter of William and Letitia Reeve, married William Hilliard, who lived near Rancocas. Elizabeth M. Reeve, married Jesse Stanger; I believe they had issue. Letitia M. Reeve remains single. William Foster Reeve's wife was Mary, the daughter of William Cooper, of Camden; they have four children living—William Cooper, Augustus, Rebecca and Richard H. Reeve. William, the eldest, married Mary, the daughter of Richard M., and Hannah Acton, of Salem. Richard, the son of William F., and Mary Reeve, married Sarah Ann, the daughter of Samuel P. Carpenter; they reside in the city of Camden. Mary, the mother of the before mentioned children, died sudden recently, whilst on a visit to her relatives in Camden, her native city. William F. Reeve is the only one of the three brothers, who still remains at Allowaystown, a place they did so much to improve. Josiah M., his elder brother, died at that place several years ago, and Emmor his younger brother, left with his family a few years since and resides in the city of Camden. Mark M. Reeve, the son of William and Letitia Reeve, died a few years ago, unmarried, in one of the Western States. The first wife of Emmor, the youngest son of William and Letitia Reeves, was Susan the daughter of William Cooper; they had issue—Mark, Benjamin and Sarah Cooper. Emmor's second wife is Sarah, the daughter of Benjamin and Sarah Acton.

Joseph, son of Joseph and Ellinor Reeve, was born 5th of 7th month, 1725, and subsequently married Milicent, daughter of Joseph and Hannah Wade, 29th of 6th month, 1729; they had three children—Samuel, Martha and Joseph. Samuel, their eldest son, inherited the landed estate of his father, located on the south side of Cohansey, a part of which his great ancestor purchased of the executors of John Fenwick, and there he ended his days. His wife was Ruth, the daughter of Gideon and Judith Scull. The latter were residents of Egg Harbor, and likewise the parents of Gideon Scull, who purchased land near the head waters of Oldman's creek, in Salem county, and carried on merchandising. It was known for many years as Sculltown, but is now called Auburn. Gideon and his wife, Judith Belange Scull, died in the winter of 1780 with the smallpox, which disease they contracted in attending Salem Quarterly Meeting, and both died with it a short time after they returned to their homes at Egg Harbor. Samuel Reeve and his wife Ruth had seven children—Joseph, Rachel, Ruth, Martha, Mary, Samuel and Benjamin. Four of them died in childhood.— Samuel died a number of years before his wife, and she subsequently sold the property and removed to Philadelphia with her children. Her daughter Rachel married Henry, son of Thomas P. Cope; they had issue. Henry and his wife are both deceased at this time. Martha Reeve married a man by the name of Pleasant; her second husband was Lloyd; she was several years his senior.

Joseph, the youngest son of Joseph and Milicent Reeves, was born 26th of 9th month, 1756, and married Martha, the daughter of Preston and Hannah Carpenter, of Mannington. Soon afterward he left his native county, Cumberland, and resided for a while in Salem, where he taught the public school on Margaret's Lane, as it was called at that time. The name of this was derived from an old lady who lived there in a small tenant house belonging to William Parrott. I believe the name of the street has been changed two or three times within the memory of some of the present generation. At one time it was called South street, but at the present time it is known as Walnut street. Joseph Reeve subsequently purchased a small farm in Mannington, being part of his father-in-law's (Preston Carpenter) property, a part of James Sherron's great estate.— He removed there and established a fruit nursery, and continued in that business whilst he lived. His son Samuel carried it on a number of years after his father's death. Joseph and his wife had five children—Samuel, Milicent, Thomas, (who died several years before his father,) Mary and Joseph Reeve.— Joseph their father, was a religious man, and possessed a large share of the milk of human kindness. His death was a great loss to his immediate family, and to the religious society of which he was a useful member. His eldest son Samuel in time purchased his brother's and sister's share of the farm, and carried on farming and the nursery business until within a short period of his death. He died not many years ago, being over four score years. He married, when he was far advanced in life, Achsa Stratton, of Burlington county; they had no issue. Milicent, the eldest daughter of Joseph and Martha Reeve, married Joseph Owen, of Gloucester. She has been deceased some years, leaving no children. Martha, the daughter of Joseph and Milicent Reeve, was born 29th of 9th month, 1754, married Joseph, the son of John and Ann Nicholson Brick; she was the second wife of Joseph Brick. They had two sons —Joseph and John R. Brick. Joseph, the eldest, born 13th of 8th month, 1785, married Elizabeth, the daughter of David Smith. Joseph and his wife had several children—Samuel, Martha, John E., Edward K. and Hannah Reeve. John Reeve Brick married Elizabeth Kinsey; they had one daughter who married Clinton, son of Samuel and Eliza Clement, of Salem. She died young, leaving no issue.

John, the son of Joseph and Ellinor Reeve, born 5th of 1st month, 1730, married Elizabeth, daughter of John and Ann N. Brick, in 1753. They had three children—John, who was born 3d of 11th month, 1754, Ellinor and Peter Reeve. John and his wife lived on and owned a large landed estate in Cohansey Neck, not far from what is now known as Sheppard's mill. He and his elder brother Mark, and his younger brother Benjamin, were recommended ministers, members of Greenwich Monthly Meeting of Friends, as was also the celebrated James Daniels, Jr., who belonged to Alloways Creek Particular Meeting.— James Daniels, Jr., traveled extensively in this country, as also in England and Ireland, in the ministry. He died in Alloways Creek township in 1776, and was considered one of the greatest ministers the society ever had in West Jersey. All four of these men were eloquent in their discourses, and their lives corresponded with their precepts, hence the Greenwich meeting was denominated the "school of the prophets." John Reeve's second wife was Jane West, of Woodbury, Gloucester county. After that event he left his native place and went to reside with his wife, and at that place ended his days at a very advanced age. He was naturally an energetic business man, and those habits of industry continued during his life. There are many persons so contracted in their views of the duties of this life, that they expect those who make a high profession of religion, must necessarily abstain from the business concerns of life, and put on sackcloth and go mourning on their way to the grave. Such was not the opinion of John Reeve, as the following well authenticated anecdote that has been handed down by tradition proves. It took place in an aged counsellor's office in Woodbury, not long before John's death. One of the members of his own meeting remarked to the lawyer that he thought friend Reeve attended too much to the things of this world for his age and wealth. The attorney promptly replied that "during his long acquaintance with mankind he never knew "a person so well adapted for this world and the world to come "as Mr. Reeve." His son, John Reeve, born 3d of 11th month, 1754, inherited a large estate, both real and personal, from his father. He married and had one or more children. John Reeve, his eldest son, married Sarah, the daughter of Jonas and Elizabeth Freedland, of Mannington. They subsequently removed to one of the Western States. I think Ellinor, daughter of John and Elizabeth Reeve, was born 15th of 6th month, 1757, and died unmarried. Peter Reeve, John's youngest son, born 1st of 2d month, 1759, married and had issue—William, who married Martha Bacon; they left no children. Benjamin, the youngest son of Joseph and Ellinor Reeve, was born 2d of 7th month, 1737. He was a clock and watch maker, and followed his trade in the city of Philadelphia. In 1761 he married Ruth, the daughter of John and Ann N. Brick. I have been informed they have a number of descendents living in the city of Philadeldhia at the present day.

ROLPH FAMILY.

James Rolph, it is generally thought, first settled in East Jersey; he came to Salem about the year 1700, and was a man of considerable means. He purchased a lot on the west side of Bridge street, and erected a brick dwelling thereon, it having a hip-roof; he also purchased a large farm in the township of Mannington. He, John Vining, Alexander Grant, and Edmund Whetherby, organized the first Episcopal Church in the town of Salem. He died at Salem in 1732, leaving his estate to his son, John Rolph, who purchased some 300 acres of land in the township of Elsinborough, being part of the Robert Windham estate, known in more modern times as "Richard Darkin's land;" it was the part that was Joseph Darkin's, the son of Richard Darkin. John Rolph, agreeably to tradition, married the daughter of Joseph Darkin; they resided in Elsinborough until his death, which occurred early in life, leaving one daughter—Elizabeth Rolph. His widow subsequently married Aaron Bradway, an inhabitant of the same township. They had one daughter, who married David Bradway of Alloways Creek. (See Bradway family).

Thomas Clement, a native of Gloucester county, and a lineal descendant of Gregory Clement, of England, who was one of the Judges that tried Charles the I., King of England, married Elizabeth Rolph, daughter of John Rolph, of Elsinborough. Thomas and his wife, Elizabeth R. Clement, had three children—Joseph, Ruth, and Samuel Clement. Thomas Clement's second wife was Elizabeth Goodwin, widow of William Goodwin, Jr.; they had no issue; her maiden name was Woodruff. Thomas' second wife also died several years before him. He resided on his farm in Elsinborough the greater part of his time; it belonged to his first wife. He was a merchant for several years in the town of Salem. His business was on Market street, where his son Samuel Clement afterwards occupied; he became one of the most eminent merchants that ever did business in Salem. Thomas Clement lived to an advanced age, with his daughter, Ruth Clement, who tenderly cared for him until the last. He could be justly styled "nature's nobleman ;" his manly deportment and his upright dealings with his fellow man fully warrants that assertion. He was born a member of the Society of Friends, but lost his right by marrying his first wife, although she was a professor. The rules of the society at that time were much more strict than at present. He nevertheless maintained a strong attachment towards the society of his birth, and was a steady attender of meeting during his long life. Not many years before his death, his daughter Ruth mentioned to him the propriety of his becoming a member again. He made this significant reply, "All I want in my old age is to be a member of "the Church militant." Joseph, the eldest son of Thomas and Elizabeth R. Clement, was born 17th of 7th month, 1777 ; he died at his son's, Thomas K. Clement, in Upper Pittsgrove, 10th of 4th month, 1861, aged eighty-three years, and was buried in Friends' yard at Salem by request, where his ancestors were buried. He married Mary, daughter of Colonel Aaron Levering, of Baltimore. She was born in Baltimore, Maryland, 23d of 11th month, 1782, and died at the residence of her daughter, Elizabeth Pratt, at Lancaster, Ohio, 25th of 1st month, 1864. Aaron Levering, her father, descended from an ancient German family of that name, who formerly belonged to the Frankford Company, that settled at Germantown in 1684. The Leverings were large landholders in Roxbury township, near Germantown. Joseph Clement and Mary Levering were married in the city of Baltimore, 17th of 4th month, 1803. Joseph was a merchant for a number of years in the town of Salem ; his place of business, also his dwelling, was located on Fenwick street. He with his wife and most of his children, removed to the State of Ohio. They had seven children—Aaron, William, who died young, Thomas Rolph, Charles B., Elizabeth, William Lawrence and Joseph Clement, Jr. Aaron L. Clement, their eldest son, never married. Thomas Rolph Clement studied medicine, graduated in 1832, and settled in Upper Pittsgrove, and is a practicing physician up to the present time; he married in 1847, Rebecca B. Elwell. They have had seven children— Jerome, born 23d of 2d month, 1848; Mary Levering, born 18th of 6th month, 1849, died in 4th month, 1868 ; Annie, born 8th of 2d month, 1851 ; Arabella, born 23d of 9th month, 1853 ; Howard born 23d of 12th month, 1857 ; Thomas Rolph, born 15th of 3d month, 1868, and S. De Witt Clinton, born 13th of 1st month, 1869.

Charles, son of Joseph and Mary Clement, married Martha Welch, of Cincinnati ; they have six children—Aaron L., Wahaen, Joseph William, Mary Elizabeth, Sarah Ellen, and Charles Clement; two of their children are deceased—Sarah Ellen and Charles. Elizabeth, daughter of Joseph and Mary Clement, has been twice married; her first husband was George Creed; they had four children—Mary Levering, George W., John M., and Charles Creed. Mary L., the eldest, married Frederick Lowe in 1857; they reside in San Francisco, California; he has filled several important offices, among which are United States Senator, Governor of California, United States Minister to China; and at present he is President of the Bank of California. Elizabeth Clement's second husband is James M. Pratt; they have two children—James Arthur and Jennie Creed Pratt. William Lawrence Clement, son of Joseph and Mary Clement, married Pauline Reben; they have four children—John R., Mary, Charles and William Lawrence Clement. Joseph, son of Joseph and Mary L. Clement, married Maria Paul; they have two children—Creed and Charles Clement. Joseph's second wife was Lucy Drake; they had two children—John and Clinton Clement. They reside in Iowa. Ruth Clement, daughter of Thomas and Elizabeth Clement, resided in Salem the greater part of her life, dying when she was past middle age; she never married. Samuel, youngest son of Thomas and Elizabeth Rolph Clement, was a merchant in Salem the greater part of his useful life; he was so upright in all his dealings that he received—and that justly—the name of "honest Samuel Clement." He was for many years in partnership with Gideon Scull, Jr.; they did a large business, particularly as grain merchants; perhaps the most extensive ever done in the city of Salem. Samuel married Eliza, daughter of Jacob Hufty; they had two sons—Samuel and De Witt Clinton Clement. Samuel Clement, Jr., married a daughter of David and Martha Smith; he has been deceased several years, leaving no issue. De W. C. Clement has been twice married; his first wife was the daughter of John Brick of Philadelphia; she died young, leaving no issue; his second wife is the daughter of Thomas J. Yorke, of Salem; they have children.

SINNICKSON FAMILY.

The Sinnickson family is one of the oldest in South Jersey. Originally they spelled their name Cinca, corrupted to Sinaker. There is no definite account that I know of fixing the year when Anders Seneca left Sweden and settled on the shores of the Delaware, but circumstances convince me that he and his family came in company with Minuit, the first governor of New Sweden, in 1638; Anders Seneca had two sons born in Sweden, Broor and Anders. At what period Anders Seneca, Jr., came and settled on the eastern shore of the Delaware is uncertain, but it is safe to presume that it was soon after their arrival in this country, for Anders Nilsson, Jonas Nilsson, Michael Nilsson, Hans Peterson, Van Nemans (now Vanneman) and several other families were inhabitants of Penn's Neck as early as 1640, and the Dahlbo family were likewise residing on the eastern shore of the Delaware about that period. The mortality among the Swedes in the first settlement was very great. Ferris, who had an excellent opportunity to examine the records of the First Swedes' Church, gives a list made by Charles Springer, in 1693, of the number of inhabitants or residents of New Sweden at that time, and the number in each family. The whole number was 945, about 40 of whom were born in Sweden, and among these were Broor and Anders Seneca. The church referred to was built near the mouth of the Christine creek for the convenience of the brethren in Penn's Neck (as it was afterwards called), who had to cross the Delaware in open boats to attend service. Their parents, Anders Seneca and his wife, I suppose, were deceased at that time, as they are not mentioned in the census roll. Broor Seneca and his family, I think, made a home on the western shore of the Delaware river, perhaps near the head waters of the Christine. At the time Charles Springer took the census of New Sweden, Broor Seneca had seven persons in his family. It is reasonable to suppose that most of the number were his children. The Swedes that settled along both sides of the river Delaware believed that the lands rightly belonged to the native inhabitants, hence most of them purchased the lands

THOMAS SINNICKSON.
Born 1786. Died 1873.

they wished to occupy of the Indian chiefs, thereby securing perpetual peace between the aborigines and Swedish settlers; so much so that there never was known any bloodshed in a contentious way between the Scandanavian and Indian races. Anders Seneca, Jr., like his brethren, adopted that humane policy, and bought a large tract of land in Obisquahasit, now known as Penn's Neck, of the natives, and settled thereon; that being about thirty years prior to Fenwick's arrival with his English colony. Soon after his arrival in this country to take possession of his tenth of West New Jersey, in 1675, the Swedes, and Anders Seneca among them, acknowledged his claim, and in 1679 Fenwick deeded all of Anders' former possessions that he got from the natives to him, he stipulating to pay the proprietor or his heirs the sum of three shillings yearly for quit rent. Anders Seneca, Jr., it would seem, left two sons —Sinick and John. Sinick Seneca, the eldest son, married Margaret Wigorvie, 21st of 9th month, 1718. She, too, was of Swedish descent, as the name would imply. They had one son named Andrew, and three daughters—Sarah, Anna, and the third's name is unknown at this time.

John, the youngest son of Anders Seneca, married Anne Gill Johnson. William Gill Johnson bought land in Penn's Neck of William Penn and Michael Lecroa in 1684, it being two years after William Penn purchased all of John Fenwick's right and title of Salem county. William Gill Johnson left two sons who inherited his property, Thomas and John Gill Johnson. Thomas died in 1721, leaving a widow and six daughters— Christina, Rhina, Alice, Sarah, Catharine and Rebecca. Eleanor Gill Johnson, the widow of Thomas Gill Johnson, married Thomas Miles about the year 1723. Thomas and his wife bought of Christina, Rhina, and Alice their shares of the lands inherited from their father. Thomas and Eleanor Miles had one son, Francis, to whom they left the greater part of their landed estate. He left a farm for educational purposes to the township of Lower Penn's Neck, which is a part of the land William Gill Johnson bought of William Penn. Rhina Gill Johnson married Erick Gill Johnson, supposed to be the son of John Gill Johnson. Erick and Rhina had four daughters. Alice married Erick Skeer. Mary died intestate without issue. Sarah Gill Johnson married Andrew, the son of Sinnick Sinnickson—the first of that family writing his name Sinnickson. I think Andrew and Sarah Sinnickson were married about 1745 or 1746. They had three sons, Thomas, Andrew and John, and four daughters, Mary, Sarah, Eleanor and Rebecca. Andrew resided on the patrimonial estate called Fenwick's Point.

At what time the death of Sinnick Seneca, the father of Andrew and his brother John, took place, I have no means of determining—I think not earlier than 1740. In 1734 both of them purchased large tracts of meadow and woodland of the heirs of William Penn, as the following order, given to Thomas Miles, the deputy surveyor for James Logan, will show: "An "order to Thomas Miles to survey to Sinnick and John Seneca, "the marsh called Mud Island, and 100 acres of land adjoining "to their other tracts, and for William Philpot the point of land "and marsh between his plantation and Salem creek, and for "Oneifferds Stanley, Margaret Bilderback and Thomas Bilder- "back, 100 acres at a place called Hell-gate. Dated 7th of 4th "month, 1733. The price of the marsh is five and twenty "pounds and 100 acres of woodland, thirty pounds for a 100 "acres clear of quit rents." Andrew Sinnickson, 3d, held important offices in the colonial government in the town and county in which he dwelt. He filled the office of Judge of the Court and Justice under George III., and was an ardent Whig during the American Revolution. He died 20th of 8th month, 1790, aged seventy years, leaving to his heirs a large real estate, which is considered as good and productive land as there is in the county of Salem.

The Sinnicksons had a family burying ground on their property in Penn's Neck, where most of them were buried for three generations or more; whether the yard is kept in repair, or neglected as many others of the like throughout the county, the fence been removed and the plough passed over it, I have not heard. The family, like most of the Scandinavian settlers, belonged to the Swedish Lutheran Church, and were members of the church located on Christiana in the State of Delaware; regular in attending their meetings, by tradition they were remarkably so considering that they had to cross the Delaware river, in open boats, in Summer and Winter when the ice would permit. There was no edifice for worship on the eastern shore of the Delaware nearer than the church located at Swedenborough; at what time that was erected is uncertain, but most probably in 1644 or 1645. In the year 1744, or about that time, the Swedes, inhabitants of Penn's Neck and a few French Hugenots, the Jaquetts and some others, erected an edifice for Divine worship at a place which is known at the present day as Church Landing, it being near the river. It has been said that in the latter part of the seventeenth century there was a large congregation belonging to the said church; at the present time but a small number belong to it. Like other Swedish churches on the shores of the Delaware such as those at New Castle, Christiana, Wiccacoe or the church at Philadelphia and Swedenborough, all have become Episcopal Churches. I presume their church Rituals are nearly the same.

Thomas Sinnickson, the oldest son of Andrew, 3d, and Sarah Sinnickson, took an active part in the Revolutionary war; and commanded a company in the Continental army. On account of his writings and bitter opposition to British tyranny, he was outlawed by Lord Howe, and a heavy reward was offered for him, dead or alive. At the organization of this government, he warmly approved of Alexander Hamilton's views, and hence he became the leader of the Federal party in this section of country, during the administrations of Washington and the elder Adams. He frequently represented this county in the State Legislature; was a member of the First Congress of the United States, which met in New York City, and also a member of Congress from 1796 to 1798. For a number of years, he was a Judge, and a Justice, and likewise County Treasurer. His wife was Sarah Hancock, daughter of Judge William Hancock, who was massacred in his own house at Hancock's Bridge, in 1778 by the British troops. Thomas Sinnickson resided the greater part of his life in the town of Salem. I think he, or his father bought lands of John Mason, and he built the house where Jonathan Ingham lives at present, and made it his home. He was a merchant in the early part of his life. His place of business was where is now the Drug store of Eakin & Ballinger. He died at an advanced age, leaving a widow who survived him several years. Having died intestate, a large real and personal estate was left to be divided among his numerous relatives. Andrew Sinnickson, 4th, son of Andrew and Sarah Sinnickson, was born 2d of 3d month, 1749. He had four wives; the first was Margaret, daughter of Henry Bilderback. By her he had two sons— Henry and Andrew Sinnickson, 5th. Henry Sinnickson married Elizabeth the daughter of Andrew McCollan, by whom he had one son—John M. Sinnickson, who married Ann the daughter of Jonathan Dallas, of Port Elizabeth. They had three children, two sons and one daughter—Henry, Dallas and Elizabeth. Henry Sinnickson married Harriet Wells, of Woodbury. He was the second Mayor of Salem. Dallas, the second son of John M. and Ann Sinnickson married Mary E. Sinnickson, daughter of John and Rebecca K. Sinnickson. Elizabeth Sinnickson married John Johnson, son of James Johnson, of Lower Penn's Neck. He died in a few years after their marriage, leaving a widow and one son, James D. Johnson, who are both deceased.

Andrew Sinnickson, 5th, married Margaret Walker. They had four sons and two daughters—Henry, Robert, Thomas, Andrew, Maria, and Catharine Sinnickson; the oldest son Henry, died in infancy. Thomas married Clarrisa M. Stretch, daughter of Daniel Stretch, in 1821, by her there were three sons and six daughters—Hannah Ann, Margaret, Robert, Ruth, Thomas, Maria, and Jane, who died young; Andrew likewise died in infancy. Hannah Ann married Henry D. Colley, and has four children—Henry, Mary, Georgianna and Margaret Colley. Margaret Sinnickson married in San Francisco. Robert is unmarried and is a printer by occupation. Thomas married Caroline, daughter of Benjamin Lloyd. They have one son—Lloyd Sinnickson. Maria married Wesley Stretch; they had one daughter—Clara Stretch. Kate is unmarried.

Robert, the third son of Andrew Sinnickson, married Tabitha Burton, in Arkansas, 1846. He died in a short time, leaving one son—Andrew Jackson Sinnickson. The widow and child reside in MacDonough County, Missouri. Maria Sinnickson married Joseph B. Chew, who came from an old and respectable family of Gloucester county. They had eight children—Arabella, Charles, Henrietta, Sinnickson, Edwin, Joseph R., Henry and Mary Chew. Arabella married William Penn Chattin; they have one daughter—Hannah Maria Chattin. Charles married Elizabeth King; they have six children. Henrietta married John the oldest son of Calvin Belden; they have three children, one son and two daughters. Edwin Chew's wife was Elizabeth Hewes; they have three daughters. Sinnickson Chew is a printer by trade, he was for a few years, a partner with William S. Sharp, in publishing the "National Standard;" but has for several years edited and published a paper in the city of Camden; he was three years Clerk for the Legislature of New Jersey. He married Sallie, the daughter of Samuel W. Miller, of Upper Alloways Creek. Joseph R. Chew, Jr., married Cornelia Mulford, and Mary married Thomas Dunn, of Salem. Henry Chew married Marietta Fogg, daughter of James Fogg, of Salem. Andrew Sinnickson married in Windsor, State of New York, in 1858; died without issue. Caroline Sinnickson married Eli Sharp, and had eleven children—William, (Benjamin F., and Sinnickson deceased,) De Witt Clinton, Harriet, Irene, (Maria, and Eli deceased,) Louisa G., Elizabeth R., and Kate Sharp. William's occupation is that of a printer. He was the Editor and Publisher of the Salem "Standard," for a number of years; at this time he publishes a paper in the city of Trenton; he married Indiana Leatherbury, from Maryland. De Witt Clinton Sharp, married Ann Waddington, they have two children—Kate and Eli Sharp. Harriet Sharp married William Davis; they have four children—Sallie, Clinton, Louisa, and Harriet, the others are unmarried. Andrew Sinnickson's second wife was Margaret Johnson, daughter of Robert and Margaret Morgan Johnson; the latter was a native of the town of Chester, Delaware county, Pennsylvania, a descendant of a Quaker family of that State, and was herself a member of that society. Margaret Morgan fearing the distance which would separate her from her family and friends, if she should marry and reside in Salem, at first declined the offer of Robert Johnson's hand. Impelled possibly by disappointment he made a tour in Europe. On his return his ship stopped at Chester where he recognized a slave of the Morgans, who told him that his young mistress was still unmarried. Mr. Johnson renewed his addresses, was accepted and shortly afterward they were married.

The late Judge Thomas Sinnickson, a few years before his death, invited me to walk in the Friends' grave yard, in Salem, with him, to point out the grave of his grandmother, it having been the first grave there to which a marble monument had been placed. It was put there by the direction of her husband Robert Johnson, Sr., and merely mentioned the time of her death, and her age. Andrew and Margaret J. Sinnickson had four children, three sons and one daughter; their names were Mary, Robert, Thomas and John Sinnickson. Robert Sinnickson died in Philadelphia in 1803, unmarried. Mary married John, the son of John and Millicent Smith, of Alloways Creek; they had three children—Thomas S., Margaret J., and Mary Smith. Thomas S. Smith married Mary, daughter of Morris and Sarah Hancock; they have two children—Maria and Thomas Smith, Jr. Margaret J. Smith married Edward G. Prescott, son of Judge William Prescott, of Boston. She was killed by a railroad accident in 1856, and left no children. Mary Smith married Oliver B. Stoughton, of Salem; they have two children—Mary and Margaret Stoughton. Her husband has been deceased several years. Thomas Sinnickson married Elizabeth, the daughter of John and Mary B. Jacobs, of Chester Valley, Pennsylvania. The Jacobs were an old family of that place; his wife, Mary Brinton, belonged to an ancient, respectable and wealthy family of that name of Chester county. Elizabeth Jacobs was a member of Friends' Meeting at the time of her marriage. Thomas Sinnickson and his wife

Elizabeth had four children, three sons and one daughter—John, Charles, Andrew and Margaret Sinnickson. John, the oldest son, is a physician, unmarried. Charles, the second son, married Caroline Perry, the grand-daughter of Jacob Hufty, of Salem. Jacob Hufty was a self-made man; raised himself to distinction by his own exertions, and was Sheriff of the county of Salem at one time. I think that at the time of his death he was a member of Congress. Charles Sinnickson and his wife have two sons—Charles and Thomas Sinnickson. Andrew is Counseller-at-Law, he married Louisa Booth, of Reading, Pennsylvania. They have two daughters. Margaret J., the daughter of Thomas Sinnickson, married Thomas Jones Yorke, and has by him five children—Mary, Lizzie, Thomas J., Margaret and Caroline Yorke. Judge Sinnickson had the misfortune to lose his amiable wife when she was little more than middle age, some twenty years before his death. He was Judge of the court for many years; was at one time a member of Congress; and sustained an excellent character in the community in which he dwelt. He was a native of the township of Lower Penn's Neck, but resided in Salem for nearly eighty years.

John Sinnickson, the youngest son of Andrew and Margaret J. Sinnickson, was active both in body and mind. He, like his brother Thomas, was above common men in muscular strength. His first wife was Mary Howell, the daughter of Dr. Ebenezer C. Howell. She was considered an accomplished lady, and was unusually comely in appearance. John and his wife had four children—Harriet, Robert, Thomas and William H. Sinnickson. Harriet H. Sinnickson married in 1838, Jonathan Ingham, son of Samuel D. Ingham, of Pennsylvania, a man that stood high in his native state, and the possessor of superior abilities. At one time he was a member of Andrew Jackson's Cabinet. Jonathan and his wife have four children—George Trenchard, Sarah A., William Henry and Mary Rebecca Ingham. Thomas Sinnickson married Adeline Wood, daughter of John S. and Sarah Ann Wood, of Cumberland county; they have two children—John and Mary Sinnickson. Robert and William Henry Sinnickson died unmarried. John Sinnickson's second wife was Rebecca K., the daughter of Clement and Rebecca Hall, by whom he had three children—John Howard, Mary E. and Clement Hall Sinnickson. J. Howard married S. E. Foreman, of Freehold, Monmouth county, by whom he had three children—Fanny, Harriet J. and John Foreman Sinnickson. Mary E. Sinnickson married Dallas Sinnickson before mentioned. Clement H. married Sarah M. Smith, daughter of Lewis P. and

Henrietta Hancock Smith. He is at the present time (1876) a member of Congress. Colonel John Sinnickson died in 1862, of a lingering disease, after an active and useful life. He was a farmer by occupation and resided the greater part of his life in the township of Lower Penn's Neck, on the property he inherited from his father. Some years before his death he removed to Salem, and at that place ended his days. He represented his county in the State Legislature, and at one period of his life occupied a seat on the bench as Judge and Justice. Andrew Sinnickson's third wife was Sarah Sinnickson, widow of Andrew Sinnickson, the grandson of John Sinnick, the brother of Sinnick Sinnick. She was the daughter of Joseph Copner, and had one son by her first husband, named Sinnick Sinnickson, who inherited a large real estate from his father, adjoining Fenwick Point, in Lower Penn's Neck. He married a young woman in Burlington county by the name of Bruer, sister of Richard Bruer. Sinnick Sinnickson and his wife had four children, named James, Joseph, Richard and Mary Sinnickson. Mary is deceased at this time, and was never married.— Richard removed to Cincinnati, and went into business with the Longworth family, in the manufacture of wine, and it is said became a millionare. James, I think, resides in Penn's Neck at this time. Andrew, 4th, and his wife, Sarah Copner Sinnickson, had one daughter, whose name was Ann Sinnickson. She subsequently married Sheppard Blackwood. They had four children—Joseph, Eliza, Jane and Margaret Blackwood. Eliza married Thomas D. Bradway, son of Thomas and Isabella Bradway, and had three children— Thomas, Charles and Isabella Bradway. Joseph Blackwood married a young woman by the name of Sheppard, a native of Cumberland county, and had several children. Jane Blackwood married Benjamin Acton, Jr., of Salem. From this union there were six children—Thomas W., Annie, Lizzie, Frank M., Louisa and Charles H. Acton. Thomas and Annie died single. Lizzie married Dr. B. A. Waddington, son of James Waddington; she is now deceased, leaving no offspring. Margaret Blackwood, the youngest daughter of Sheppard and Ann Blackwood, married Charles Cass Clark, the son of the late Dr. Clark, of Cumberland county; they have two children— Charles C., Jr., and Emma Clark. Ann's second husband was John Simpson, of Salem, the son of James Simpson. John died recently at an advanced age, and was remarkable through a long life for his honesty of dealing with his fellow men and was greatly respected by his fellow citizens. His wife died a few years ago of a long and tedious disease. They had no issue.

Andrew Sinnickson's fourth wife was Elizabeth, the youngest daughter of Thomas Norris, of Salem; they had two daughters—Rebecca and Sarah Sinnickson. Rebecca married Edward, the son of Judge John Smith and Temperance Keasbey Smith, They had three children—two sons and one daughter. Edward and family subsequently removed from Salem, to the western part of Pennsylvania, or to one of the Western States, I am not certain which. Joel Fithian, of Cumberland married Sarah; they had two sons and three daughters. They removed to one of the Western States. Andrew Sinnickson was an ardent Whig. During the American Revolution he raised a company of men, commanded them at the battles of Trenton and Princeton. After the war was over he held a commission as Judge and Justice, and lived to an old age, and was greatly respected. His death occurred in 1819, much regretted by his large family. John Sinnickson, his brother and the youngest son of Andrew and Sarah Sinnickson, married Susan, daughter of Daniel Bilderback. They had one son, Frank, who died a young man unmarried, and a daughter, Esther Sinnickson, who subsequently married Dr. Thomas Rowan, of Salem. They never had any children. John's second wife was a widow named Delfant, daughter of Dr. Jonathan McWright, of East Jersey. They had no issue. He died a widower at Biddle's hotel in Penn's Neck after a short illness, leaving to his heirs one of the largest landed estates in the county. Eleanor, the second daughter of Andrew and Sarah Sinnickson, married William Mecum. They had seven children—George, Andrew, Sarah, Margaret, Rebecca and Ellen Mecum. William, George and Ellen died unmarried; Andrew Mecum married Ann, daughter of James Wright. They had one son, James Wright Mecum, who subsequently married Lydia Ann Harrison. They have several children. Sarah Mecum had three husbands—Robert Clark, Captain William Medham, of New Castle county, Delaware, and a third. She had no children. Margaret Mecum, daughter of William and Eleanor Sinnickson Mecum, married Antrim Connarroe, a descendant of Roger Connarroe, who emigrated from the county of Devonshire, England, and landed at Elsinborough Point in 1681, with his wife Elizabeth Stevenson, Connarroe and several other emigrants.* Roger and his wife settled at Salem, and at

---

* Roger spelled his name Conars. Isaac Conars, one of his descendants, removed to Burlington county in 1740. Thomas Connaroe, great-grandfather of the present George M., Esq., of Philadelphia, was the first, who changed the spelling to the present style.

that town they ended their days. Some of their descendants afterward removed to Burlington county. Antrim and his wife Margaret Connarroe had one son and four daughters—George, Sarah, Mary, Margaret and Rebecca Connarroe. George, early in life, removed to the city of Philadelphia. His wife is Charlotte West; they have three children—George, Maria an Ellen. When quite young he displayed a natural genius for the fine arts, and has succeeded admirably in landscape and portrait painting; so much so that he is a credit to the county which gave him birth. Sarah Connarroe married Archibald Little, and had seven children. Mary Connarroe's husband was Abraham Johnson, the second son of James Johnson, of Lower Penn's Neck. They have three children. They removed to Erie county, Pennsylvania. Margaret's husband was George Rumsey, who, I think, was a native of Wilmington, Delaware. He came to Salem a young man, and after a few years became a successful merchant. He appeared to prosper in all his undertakings, and the public had great confidence in his judgment. He was elected Cashier of Salem Bank, which office he filled to the credit of the institution until the close of his useful life. George Rumsey and his wife Margaret had one son, Henry M. Rumsey, who married Maria, the daughter of Benjamin and Mary Bassett. Rebecca Connarroe married a young man by the name of Lawrence; they had no issue.

Mary Sinnickson, the eldest daughter of Andrew and Sarah Sinnickson, and sister of Eleanor Mecum, married George Trenchard, Jr. I think they had two daughters—Jane, who died unmarried, and Rebecca, who subsequently married James Kinsey. They had no children, and ended their days in Salem at the residence where Jonathan Ingham lives at this time. Sarah, the youngest daughter of Andrew and Sarah J. Sinnickson, married Dr. Samuel Dick, of Salem, New Jersey.

Among the patriotic men of the last century, who took an active part in troublous times of our country, was Dr. Samuel Dick, of Salem, New Jersey. Dr. Samuel Dick was of Scotch-Irish descent; his paternal grandfather was a Presbyterian minister, and resided in the north of Ireland. His father, John Dick, married Isabella Stewart, a Scotch lady of superior mind and cultivation. It is supposed that John Dick and his wife came to America between the years of 1730 and 1740. Samuel Dick, their third child, the subject of this memoir, was born the 14th day of 11th month, 1740, at Nottingham, Prince George's county, Maryland. His father, John Dick, in 1746 was settled in New Castle, Delaware, as minister of the Presbyterian Church in that place, and the churches in the vicinity, until his death in 1748. His son, Samuel Dick, was educated by President Samuel Finly, Governor Thomas M. Kean and Dr. McWhorten, and under their pupilage, laid the foundation of a classical knowledge, which few in our country have surpassed. He spoke and wrote five different languages besides his own with ease and correctness—Hebrew, Greek, French, Spanish and Latin. His medical education, according to the State medical report, was received at one of the medical schools of Scotland. He served in Canada, in the Colonial army as Assistant Surgeon, in the French war, which was terminated in 1760, by the conquest of that province by the English, and was present at the surrender of Quebec. In 1770 he came with his mother to Salem, New Jersey, and settled there as a Physician, and purchased property on Fenwick street, corner of Walnut street, and there he ended his days; his descendants occupy it at the present time. It is an ancient and substantial brick building built in 1730. In 1773 Dr. Dick married Sarah Sinnickson, the youngest daughter of Judge Andrew Sinnickson, of Penn's Neck. In 1776 he was a member of the Provincial Congress of New Jersey, and was one of the committee of five appointed to prepare a draught of the Constitution of the State, and by that Congress was also given a commission as Colonel of the militia, in which character he was an active and zealous officer in the Revolutionary War. In 1780 Dr. Dick was appointed Surrogate of Salem county, by Governor Livingston, who highly esteemed him both as an officer and a man. This office he held for twenty-two years. In 1783 Dr. Dick was elected by the State of New Jersey to represent them in the Congress of the United States of America, and was a member of Congress when the treaty was ratified the 14th of 1st month, 1784, by which Great Britain acknowledged our independance. [See Journal of Congress, Vol. IX, page, 21, 22–30.] In the years 1783, 1784, 1785 was a member of Congress held at Annapolis, New York, and Philadelphia, and was selected by Congress with others, to transact important business. He was made one of the committee in 1784, consisting of Jefferson, Blanchard, Gerry, Howell, Sherman, De Witt, Dick, Hand, Stone, Williamson and Read, to revise the institution of the Treasury Department, and report such alteration as they might think proper. He was also a member of the Committee of the States, to sit during the recess of Congress, consisting of some of the first men of the country as to talents and influence. He was also appointed by Congress on other committees, which showed the estimation in which he was held as to ability and integrity.

In private life Dr. Dick was greatly respected in word and deed, and was never known to speak ill of any person; the latter is inscribed on his tomb stone in the Episcopal Church yard, in Salem, New Jersey. His character is described by one that knew him, in these words: "He was a man of brilliant "talents and great requirements, refined taste, and polished "manners, a skillful surveyor and physician; a profound "scholar, a discerning politician and zealous patriot." He departed this life in Salem, 16th of 11th month, 1812, leaving a widow and six children; their names were Sarah, Isabella, Anna, Samuel Stewart and Maria Dick; all of whom are deceased. His only descendants now living are the children and grand-children of his daughter Isabella, who married in 1804, Josiah Harrisson, a lawyer, now deceased. Josiah and Isabella D. Harrisson had four children, all of them were daughters. Maria and Henrietta Harrisson are single woman. Lydia Ann Harrisson married James W. Mecum; they have four children—George, Ellen, Maria H. and Charles Mecum. Julia Harrisson married Robert Carney Johnson; they have one son—Henry Harrisson Johnson.

Sarah, the daughter of Sinnick Sinnickson, Sr., married a person by the name of Pichard. It does not appear that she left any issue. Anna Sinnickson, Sarah's youngest sister, married a person by the name of Peterson, who was also of Swedish origin. They left children, but their record has not been handed down to the present generation. John Sinaker and his wife Ann Gilliamson Sinnickson had three children—Sarah, Elizabeth and Sinnick Sinnickson. The latter had one son, Andrew Sinnickson, who subsequently married Sarah Copner, daughter of Joseph Copner, of Lower Penn's Neck. They had one son—Sinnick Sinnickson. Reference to his wife and children have been made previously. Sarah Sinnickson, the eldest daughter of John and Ann G. Sinnickson, married William Philpot; they had issue. Their two grandsons, William and Francis Philpot came into possession of a large landed estate, located in the township of Penn's Neck, bordering on Salem creek. They parted with it more than fifty years ago and left their native county and located in one of the Southern States. Elizabeth Sinnickson, sister of Sarah Philpot, married Dennis Murphy; they had three children—John, Sarah and Catharine. Her second husband was Robert McCasson, and had three children—Joseph, Margaret and Mary McCasson. Elizabeth's third husband was Richard Fitzgerald; there was no issue. John Murphy, the son of Dennis and Elizabeth S. Murphy, died a young man unmarried. His sister Sarah married John Powers, and had five children—Catharine, Eleanor, Samuel, Judith and Mary Powers. Catharine died young, leaving no issue. Eleanor married Thomas Dunn; the Dunn's are an old family in Penn's Neck. Soon after the revocation of the edict of the Nantes by the order of Louis XIV. in 1684, many Huguenots emigrated to this country to avoid religious persecution. There were two brothers, Zaccheus and Thomas Dunn, most probably natives of one of the Rhenish Provinces, either Alsace or Lorraine, emigrated to this country. Zaccheus settled in the upper part of Pilesgrove. He had a son Zaccheus Dunn, born 2d of 12th month, 1698. Seven of his children lived to grow up and rear families. Thomas Dunn, his brother, located himself in Penn's Neck, and had numerous descendants. He purchased 100 acres of land of William Penn in 1689, which was surveyed to him by Richard Tindell; the said lands joined Hans Corneleus and widow Hendricks near Finn's Point. Thomas was a Calvinist, and some of his descendants with the Copners and other families organized the Presbyterian Church near Pennsville. His brother Zaccheus became a member of the Society of Friends. Thomas and Eleanor Dunn had three children—Sarah, Elizabeth and Mary Ellen Dunn.

Samuel Powers' wife was Rebecca Hancock; they had five children—Catharine, Margaret, Georgiana, Atwood and John Powers. Judith Powers married Ephraim Shaw. They had issue. Mary, the youngest daughter of John and Sarah Powers, married John G. Elwell, they had one daughter—Elizabeth Elwell. Catharine, the youngest daughter of Dennis Murphy, married John Patterson, and their children were—Martin, Margaret, Elizabeth, Ann, William and Jane Patterson. Martin Patterson's wife was Elizabeth, daughter of David Fogg, formerly a resident of Upper Alloways Creek. They have four daughters—Mary, Elizabeth, Margaret and Martha Patterson. Margaret, the daughter of John and Catharine Patterson, married John Callahan. Their issue was John, William and Samuel Callahan. Catharine's second husband was Richard Sparks. She had two daughters by her last husband—Jane and Anna Sparks. The husband of Elizabeth, daughter of John and Catharine Patterson, was Samuel Garrison. Their issue was one daughter—Hannah Garrison. Ann Patterson married Jacob Dubois, and left two children—John and Caroline Dubois. William Patterson, their second son, married Lydia Ann Goodwin. They had three children. William's second wife was Mary Finlaw, by whom he had two children—Horatio and Lucy Patterson. Jane Patterson married Joseph Shourds. Their children are William and Sarah Shourds. William Murphy, the son of Dennis and Elizabeth Sinnickson Murphy, married a young woman by the name of Berry. Their children were Sarah, Elizabeth, Thomas and John Murphy. The Sinnickson family, for three generations after their settlement in New Sweden, married with the Scandinavian race. It is evident by the family record that their first connection in marriage with the English emigrants was with Thomas Miles. The Gill Johnsons, who early connected themselves with the Sinnicksons by marriage, were Swedes. Circumstances clearly indicated that they were of the first families that settled at the mouth of the Christine. In 1693 there were two of that family resident in Penn's Neck, Erick Gill Jonsson and William Gill Jonsson as they spelled the name of Johnson at that period. The Sinnicksons, as a family, have maintained a respectable standing for more than seven generations in this county.

SHEPPARD FAMILY.

The Sheppard family is the most numerous of any, excepting the Thompsons, in the ancient county of Salem. There were three brothers—David, Thomas and John Sheppard; they came from Tipperary, Ireland. On their arrival in America, they probably resided for a short time at Shrewsbury, East Jersey. In 1683 they settled in what is now Cumberland county, on the South side of the Cohansey, it being a neck of land bounded on the north by the Cohansey river, on the south by a small creek called Back creek. It is not improbable that they gave it the name of Shrewsbury Neck, after the township in East Jersey, where they first settled. The Sheppard family, I have no doubt, were English; their name implies as much. The Sheppards were members of the Baptist Church of Cleagh Keating, in the county of Tipperary, Ireland. They were also among the few persons that organized the First Cohansey Baptist Church, in 1690, at Shrewsbury Neck. David Sheppard's first known purchase was fifty acres of land of Captain William Dare, he afterward purchased fifty acres, on which he lived and died. I have no doubt he became the owner of a large quantity of land in the Neck.

The Sheppard, Westcott and Reeves families, during the last century and the fore part of the present, were the principal owners of Back and Shrewsbury Necks. David Sheppard, Sr., agreeable to the most authentic account, had six children—David, born as early as 1690; John, Joseph, Enoch, Hannah and Elizabeth Sheppard. Hannah married a young man named Gilman. She died 1722, leaving one son—David Gilman. John, the son of David Sheppard, Sr., died about the year 1716, without issue, leaving his property to his brothers and sisters. David, the son of David Sheppard, the emigrant, was born about the year 1690, and inherited the homestead property of his father, in Back Neck. He married about 1719. The children of David Sheppard, Jr., and his wife, Sarah Sheppard, were Philip, born 1720; Ephraim, born 1722; David, 1724; Joseph, 1727, and Phebe Sheppard. Philip, the eldest, inherited a large landed estate in Back Neck, on which he resided. The property is now owned by one of the heirs of the late Ephraim Mulford. Philip was twice married, his first wife was Mary ———, his second Sarah Bennett. He was considered one of the largest and most successful farmers in that neighborhood. Tradition has it that he was the first, in that section, that owned a covered wagon. I do not suppose that it was an elliptic spring carriage, but plain as it was I have no doubt it was considered by the inhabitants a great innovation. It was then the custom to travel on horseback. Philip died 5th of 1st month, 1797, aged seventy-seven, leaving a large real and personal estate to his children. His widow, Sarah Sheppard, married John Remington, in 1801. Philip was buried in the Baptist cemetery, near Sheppard's mill; he was a deacon in the church, and was considered one of the most prominent citizens in that section of Cumberland county. The inventory of his personal property at the time of his death amounted to £580 and 6s. His children by his first wife, Mary, were Amos, Hannah, Mary and Naomi Sheppard. By his second wife Sarah B. Sheppard—Ichabod, Harvey, Phebe and William Sheppard. Ephraim, the son of David Sheppard, Jr., born 1722, was married three times. His first wife was Kesiah Kelsey; his second was Sarah Dennis; third, Rebecca Barrett. He lived in Hopewell township, on the road from Bowentown to Roadstown, and was owner of a large landed estate in that section; leaving at his death large farms to all four of his sons, all adjoining one another on the straight road from Bridgeton to Roadstown. He was a highly respected citizen, and like his brother Philip, was one of the deacons of Cohansey Church. He died 8th of 5th month, 1783, aged sixty years, and was buried in the Baptist yard adjoining the church, near Sheppard's mill, by the side of his wife Sarah Dennis, who died 21st of 1st month, 1777. She died in her fifty-first year. His third wife, Rebecca Barrett, survived him twenty years. She was buried at Shiloh, being a Seventh-day Baptist. Ephraim had ten children, all by his second wife, Sarah Dennis. The oldest was Joel, born 1748; Abner, born 28th of 5th month, 1750; James, born 25th of 12th month, 1752; Hannah and Rachel. Phebe married Wade Barker, who was the grandson of Samuel Wade, Jr., of Alloways Creek. She died young leaving no issue. Wade was buried in the old Baptist yard at Mill Hollow, near Salem. Sarah, Elizabeth and Hope Sheppard, who afterward married Reuel Sayre, were the other children. Sayre subsequently moved to the State of Ohio. Ephraim's youngest child was Ephraim Sheppard. David, the son of David Sheppard, Jr., was born in the year 1724. He married Temperance Sheppard, daughter of Jonadab and Phebe Sheppard. They lived in the township of Downe, Cumberland county. He was a member of Cohansey church, as was also his wife, and both became constituent members of the Dividing Creek Baptist Church at its constitution, 30th of 5th month, 1761; at that time he became deacon of the church and afterwards a colleague of the pastor, Samuel Heaton. David Sheppard died 18th of 6th month, 1774, aged fifty years; his widow subsequently married a man by the name of Lore. She was born in 1731 and died 28th of 7th month, 1796, aged sixty-five years; she and her first husband, David Sheppard, were buried at Dividing Creek Baptist graveyard. The following are the names of David and Temperance Sheppard's children—Hosea, David, Owen, Jonadab, Tabitha, Temperance and Mary Sheppard. Joseph, the son of David Sheppard, Jr., was born in 1727; he married Mary Sayre. They lived in Back Neck, and owned a large quantity of good land, which he left to his children. I have been informed that most, if not all, of said land has now passed out of their possession. He also left a large personal estate for that time, amounting to £647 and 12s. He and his wife were members of the Cohansey Church. It seems he was a prominent man in that section. He was chosen 22d of 12th month, 1774, one of the Committee of Safety, for the county of Cumberland, to carry into effect the resolutions of the Continental Congress, and in whose hands rested the supreme authority after the war commenced, until the formation of the new State Government gave an organized power in New Jersey. He died 8th of 1st month, 1782, aged fifty-four years, and was buried on his own farm in an old family burying ground, now long disused. His wife, Mary Sayre Sheppard, died in 1790, aged fifty-eight years, and was buried in the same yard. Their daughter Lydia, also lies there; all three of them have tombstones at the head of their graves. This family graveyard is an exception to the general rule. It was the practice, in the early settlement of Fenwick's colony, to have family burying grounds, but the plow has passed over nearly all of them, so no man knoweth where many of our ancestors lie. I have been informed that the ancient Swedish family, the Sinnicksons, cleared their old family graveyard a few years ago, in Obisquahasett, and their intentions are to keep it in good order—a noble deed. Dr. George B. Wood has likewise recently caused to be erected a monument to his great grandfather, Richard Wood, who died in 1759, in the family graveyard in Stoe Creek township, county of Cumberland. Joseph

Sheppard, the year before his death, built a large brick house on his property, and died soon afterwards; the house is still standing, and the place is now owned by that enterprising citizen, Richard Laning, the son of John Laning. The following are the names of Joseph Sheppard's children:—David born 1758; Lydia, 1760; Ruth, 17th of 11th month, 1763; Isaac, 1766; Mary, and Lucy 11th month, 1773.

Amos, the son of Philip Sheppard, born about 1750, subsequently married Hannah Westcott, and died in 1788, at middle age; his widow married John Mulford. Josiah, the eldest son of Amos and Hannah W. Sheppard, born 14th of 9th month, 1778; his wife was Charlotte Westcott, daughter of Henry and Jane Harris Westcott. He died 4th of 10th month, 1850. His son Henry was born 3d of 6th month, 1808, married and lives in Fairfield township, near Cedarville; they have a family of children. Jane, the daughter of Josiah, born in 1811, and died a young woman in 1828. Hannah, the daughter of Josiah and Charlotte W. Sheppard, born 23d of 10th month, 1813, married Ephraim Glaspey; they have a family of children, and reside near the city of Bridgeton. Harriet, the fourth child of Josiah and Charlotte W. Sheppard, born 19th of 2d month, 1816, married James Sheppard Kelsay in 1837; they have seven children. Martha, the daughter of Amos and Hannah W. Sheppard, born in 1780, subsequently married Charles Westcott, of Sayre's Neck, Cumberland county. She and her husband afterward moved to Covington, Kentucky, where she died in the winter of 1868, leaving children. Hannah, daughter of Philip and Mary Sheppard, married Ephraim Shaw; they had three children— Harvey, Mary and Lydia. Lydia, the youngest, in 1810 married Henry Whitaker. They reside at Millville, and have a large family of children, most of whom are married. Mary, daughter of Philip and Mary Sheppard, never married, and died 17th of 5th month, 1799, aged about fifty years.

Naomi, daughter of Philip, married William Conner; they had three children. Abigail, the eldest, born 31st of 8th month, 1764, married Thomas Brooks in 1789; they had ten children. Thomas died 16th of 9th month, 1829, and his widow, Abigail Brooks, died 19th of 8th month, 1841, aged seventy-seven years. Prudence, born 1766, and her first husband was James Sheppard, son of Elias and Susanna Sheppard, (James was a nephew of Mark Sheppard, who was one of the first of the Sheppard family that became a member of the Society of Friends.) Prudence had one daughter by her first husband, James Sheppard, which died in infancy. Her second husband was

William Johnson. William and Prudence Johnson had eight children. She died 2d of 9th month, 1860; her last husband, William Johnson, died 17th of 2d month, 1831. David Conner, son of Naomi, left his native state and went to North Carolina, and there married and had a large family of children. Ichabod, son of Philip and Sarah Bennett Sheppard, born 11th of 12th month, 1769, married Ruth Sheppard, daughter of Joel and Hannah Jenkins Sheppard, (Joel was the cousin of Ichabod, being the son of Ephraim Sheppard.) Ichabod and his wife had two children—Phebe and Naomi. Ichabod died 22d of 4th month, 1799, and his widow, Ruth Sheppard, married David Bateman, a minister in the Baptist denomination; they had three sons— Isaac, Daniel and David Bateman. Ruth, their mother, departed this life 29th of 7th month, 1806. Soon after that event David Bateman and his three sons—Isaac, Daniel and David—removed to Ohio, where their children, or some of them, are still living. Phebe, daughter of Ichabod and Ruth Sheppard, married 28th of 3d month, 1819, John Reeves. There were two children by that connection—one daughter living at this time in the city of Bridgeton, and a son residing near Shiloh. Naomi, second daughter of Ichabod and Ruth Sheppard, born 17th of 9th month, 1800, and in 1817 she married Jonathan Young, who was afterwards drowned at sea; they had five children, all of whom died young, excepting Lewis Young, who is a resident of Bridgeton.

Harvey, son of Philip and Sarah B. Sheppard married in 1797, Hannah Smith, of Greenwich, daughter of Isaac and Cynthia Smith; he had one daughter—Hannah, by his first marriage. She married in 1818, John Test, the son of Francis Test, Jr. John and his second wife, Hannah S. Test, removed to Indiana. He studied law, and was elected to Congress during Andrew Jackson's administration. He was an uncle to Joseph Test, who resides in Salem. The second wife of Harvey Sheppard was Ruth Ogden, daughter of Elmer and Charlotte Ogden, of Fairfield township; they had three children—Philip, Abi and Ruth. The third wife of Harvey Sheppard was Amelia Davis, of Shiloh; he and his last wife went west in 1818. Phebe, daughter of Philip Sheppard, married Joseph Newcomb. They lived in Back Neck, and had two children—Joseph and Sarah S. Newcomb. William, son of Philip Sheppard, born 29th of 11th month, 1778, married 8th of 2d month, 1803, Matilda Westcott, daughter of Henry and Jane Harris Westcott; they had six children—Ichabod, William, Sarah, Harris, Phebe and Elmer Ogden Sheppard.

Joel, son of Ephraim and Sarah Dennis Sheppard, born in 1748, married Hannah Jenkins, who was born 1749 and died in 1807; she left seven children, Dennis, Ruth, Sarah, Lydia, Amy, Elizabeth and Reuben Sheppard. Joel's second wife was Letitia Platts, widow of David Platts and daughter of David Gilman; they had no issue. His third wife was Sarah Davis, of Shiloh; they had no children. Joel was deacon in the old Cohansey Church, and was a large farmer, living in Hopewell township, and was a prominent citizen. Dennis, son of Joel and Hannah Sheppard, married a young woman by the name of Ayars. They moved to one of the Western States in 1817. Ruth, daughter of Joel Sheppard, married Ichabod, son of Philip and a cousin of her father. Sarah, daughter of Joel and Hannah J. Sheppard, born 1775, married in 1799 Samuel Bond Davis, son of Elnathan and Susannah Bond Davis. Elnathan was the greatest surveyor in his generation in this section of the State, for many years after the Revolution. The late Josiah Harrison, of Salem, who died aged over ninety years, who was a surveyor in his early life, told me a short time previous to his death that he regarded Elnathan Davis as captain general of the surveyors of Salem and Cumberland counties. Samuel B. and Sarah Davis had several children, one of whom, Jarman A. Davis, lives in Shiloh, and is a Justice of the Peace. Lydia Sheppard, daughter of Joel, married in 1804 Oswell Ayars; they had children but they are all deceased. Amy, daughter of Joel and Hannah Sheppard, born 15th of 2d month, 1780; in 1803 she married Oliver Harris, son of Robert Harris. Oliver and Amy Harris had seven children—Hosea, Hannah S., Mary, Eliza, Samuel S. and Robert. Eliza was born 14th of 10th month, 1808, and in 1826 married Hezekiah Johnson; they moved to Oregon and are still living. One of their children is Franklin Johnson, D. D., pastor of a Baptist Church, at Newark, New Jersey. He is the author of several commentaries on the International Sunday School Lessons, now in general use. Samuel, son of Oliver and Amy Harris, was born 24th of 11th month, 1813. Elizabeth, daughter of Joel and Hannah Sheppard, in 1805 married Eli Bereman. Soon after their marriage they moved to Highland county, Ohio; they had issue. Reuben, son of Joel and Hannah Sheppard, married Elizabeth W. Dare. Reuben and his wife moved to Ohio in 1817; they had one son—William Alfred Sheppard, who was a physician at New Vienna, Clinton county, Ohio. He died in 1871, leaving children, one of whom, Henry A. Sheppard, is a lawyer at Hillsboro, Ohio.

Abner, second son of Ephraim and Sarah Dennis Sheppard,

born 28th of 5th month, 1750; his first wife was Mary Dowdney, who died about fifteen months after their marriage, leaving one child. Abner's second wife was Ruth Paulin; she died 1st month, 1797. His third wife was Mary McGear, widow of John McGear; she died 29th of 4th month, 1809, and his fourth wife was Elizabeth Fithian. Abner was a farmer, and lived in Hopewell township the greater part of his life. At the time of the American Revolution he was in the Militia, and was in Colonel Hand's regiment at the fight of Quinton's Bridge, and took part in the battle; he died 12th of 3d month, 1824. The following are the names of his children—Mary, Ephraim, (who died young,) Henry, Temperance, Phebe, Prudence, Delanah, Lafayette, Ruth, Mary and Ephraim Elmer Sheppard.

James Sheppard, the son of Ephraim and Sarah Dennis Sheppard, was born 25th of 12th month, 1752. His wife was Hannah Brooks, whom he married 23d of 1st month, 1774; she died in 1777. His second wife was Keziah Barber; they were married in 1778. She died 11th of 6th month, 1824, and James, her husband, 3d of 6th month, 1825. He was a deacon in Cohansey Baptist Church, a farmer and a large land owner in Hopewell township, and had an excellent character for uprightness in his dealings with his fellow men, and was greatly respected by all who knew him. The children of James and Hannah B. Sheppard were David and Phebe Sheppard, and by his second wife, Keziah Barber Sheppard, Hannah, Rachel, Mary, Joseph, William, Prudence, Rebecca, Phebe and Hope. Most of these children lived to grow up and marry. William, the son of James Sheppard, born 30th of 7th month, 1785, married 23d of 3d month, 1808, Ann Husted, daughter of Henry and Ann Sheppard Husted, of Shrewsbury Neck. William was an ordained minister of the Baptist denomination, but never had charge of a church. He was a farmer, and preached as he had opportunity. They had thirteen children.

Hannah, the daughter of Ephraim and Sarah Sheppard, born about 1754, married Daniel Moore; she died about 1784. Rachel, another daughter, born in 1761, married James Sayre, who was wounded at the massacre at Hancock's Bridge in 1778. Ephraim, son of Ephraim and Sarah, moved to Salem, and married Elizabeth, widow of John Challis, and mother of John and James Challis; (the latter afterward became an ordained minister among the Baptists.) Elizabeth Milbank, mother of these children, was born at Waltham, England, 2d of 5th month, 1770. Ephraim and his wife, Elizabeth M. Sheppard, had one daughter, Mary W., born in 1809.

David, son of Joseph and Mary Sheppard, born 1758, married in 1783, Phebe, daughter of Providence and Sarah Ludlam; she died in 1799, leaving six children. Sarah, the eldest child, married in 1803, William Walker, a resident of Upper Alloways Creek, Salem county; they had three children. Phebe Walker, their eldest daughter, married Thomas Bilderback, of Allowaystown; they have children. William Sheppard, a son, married Ann Stow, and lived on the homestead farm until his death; since that event his widow and his daughters have resided in Salem. Charles H. Walker owns and resides upon the homestead farm.

Joseph, the son of David and Phebe L. Sheppard, born 9th of 1st month, 1786, was elected pastor of the First Baptist Church at Salem, in 1809, and was pastor of said church until 1829, and then removed to Mount Holly, where he continued as pastor seven years, but his health failing him he resigned his pastoral charge and moved to Camden. He never took another pastoral charge, but preached occasionally when health permitted; he died in Camden in 1838, in the fifty-third year of his age. His wife was Hannah F. Budd; they had four children—Mary, Phebe Ann, Hannah and Josephine Sheppard; they all married but Hannah. Phebe Ann lived in the state of Georgia. Josephine lived in Washington, D. C., but died a few years ago. David Sheppard's second wife was Miriam Smith, widow of Isaac Smith; she died in 1815, and David in 1827. He was a deacon of Cohansey Church, and was a prominent citizen. For many years he lived on the homestead farm in Fairfield township, but in later years he moved to Bridgeton, and built a large brick mansion on the west side of the Cohansey, where his son, Isaac A. Sheppard, lived and died. The dwelling is now known as Ivy Hall Seminary for ladies. Providence Ludlam, son of David Sheppard, born 21st of 2d month, 1788, married Mary Letson, of New Brunswick, New Jersey. One of their children, Ebenezer L. Sheppard, lives in Pittsgrove township, and is a member and clerk of the Pittsgrove Baptist Church. He has recently written and published a historical sketch of that church. William Ludlam and David were twin sons of David Sheppard, and were born 6th month, 1790. William died in 1823, and never married. David, his brother, studied for a physician, but died suddenly about the time he was ready to commence the practice of his profession. Ercurius, the son of David, married Martha Lupodius, of New Brunswick. She is still living, but Ercurius is deceased. He left three children—Mary, Sarah and Martha. Ebenezer, the son of David, born 23d of 7th month, 1798, died 6th month, 1814. Mary, the daughter of David and Miriam Sheppard, his second wife, married in 1824, Jonathan J. Hann; they had two children—Maria and Mary Hann. The latter married Joseph Moore, homeopathic physician, of Bridgeton; she died in 1860. Isaac A. Sheppard, son of David, born in 1806, married 8th of 4th month, 1828, Jane H. Bennett; she died in 1839, aged thirty-five years. Isaac's second wife was Hannah B. McLean, whom he married in 1841, but she only lived a little over a year. His third wife was Margaretta E. Little, who is still living; they were married in 1850. Isaac A. Sheppard died suddenly in his office in 1863, having been found dead sitting in his chair. He was a deacon of the First Baptist Church of Bridgeton. His oldest son, Isaac A., born in 1829, died 11th of 4th month, 1832. Jane B., daughter of Isaac A. Sheppard, born in 1831, married in 1868, Horatio J. Mulford, the eldest son of the late Henry Mulford, of Bridgeton. Horatio, with his brother Isaac W., and his sisters, were the originators and principal benefactors of the South Jersey Institute, a school for both sexes, located in Bridgeton. The cost of the building has been estimated at $60,000. It has a fine corps of teachers, and has been in operation six years, during which time it has established a reputation equal to the best educational institutions in the country. Horatio's wife, Jane Mulford, like her father, died suddenly, and was found dead sitting in her chair, on the evening of 9th of 2d month, 1874. She was a woman of great usefulness in the church and in the community, and her loss was deeply felt by all. She left one child, a son, Horatio Jones Mulford, Jr., who was born in 1869. There were seven other children of Isaac A. Sheppard's—Miriam, Theodore, Francis, Charles, Elizabeth, Frank and Frederick.

Isaac, son of Joseph and Mary Sheppard, born in 1766, married Sarah, daughter of Jeremiah Bennett; she died in 1797. Isaac's second wife was Jane Harris Westcott, the widow of Henry Westcott, and daughter of Ephraim and Jane Harris, of Fairfield township. His third wife was Abigail B. Husted, widow of Henry Husted, and daughter of Ichabod Bishop. Isaac Sheppard died 16th of 12th month, 1815. He had five children—Isaac, the eldest, never married; Henry, the second son of Isaac and Sarah Sheppard, married 27th of 3d month, 1811, Eunice Westcott. Soon after their marriage they moved to one of the Western States, and Henry died there. His widow returned to her native state and died in 1868. They had a family of children. Sarah, daughter of Isaac and Sarah

Sheppard, born 23d of 11th month, 1797, married 17th of 3d month, 1819, Elmer Ogden; she died 21st of 12th month, 1853; he lives in Greenwich, and has several children. Ephraim, the son of Isaac and Jane H. Sheppard, born 15th of 8th month, 1801, married in 1819, Jane, daughter of Jehiel and Mary Westcott; she died in 1823. His second wife was Mary, daughter of John and Mary B. Westcott, of Fairfield; she died in 1842, and he died 9th of 7th month, 1848. His children by his first wife were Ephraim, the eldest, who went west, and died there; and Elias Sheppard, who died young.—Mary Jane, daughter of Ephraim and Mary Sheppard, married Charles Campbell. Isaac Aplin Sheppard, son of Ephraim and Mary Sheppard, went to Philadelphia to live, and subsequently was elected a member of the Pennsylvania Legislature for several sessions. Isaac is the head of the great stove firm of I. A. Sheppard & Company. Joseph, the son of Ephraim Sheppard, married Sarah Flanagin, of Sculltown; he now lives in Camden county, between Haddonfield and Camden.

Lucy, the daughter of Joseph and Mary Sheppard, born in 11th month, 1773, married Isaac, son of Isaac and Judith Wheaton, in 1792; Isaac was born in 9th month, 1769. By that connection there were seven children—Joseph, the eldest, born 17th of 3d month, 1795, died 3d of 3d month, 1871, never married. Their second son, Providence Ludlam Wheaton, born 21st of 4th month, 1798, died 1st of 3d month, 1867; his wife was Ruth Foster; they had one son—Andrew Evans Wheaton, who resides at Greenwich with his mother. Mary Sheppard Wheaton, the eldest daughter of Isaac and Lucy S. Wheaton was born 20th of 11th month, 1799; she was the second wife of Henry Mulford. Their three oldest children were Anna, Maria, Hannah and Isaac W. Mulford. William Wheaton, the son of Isaac and Lucy Wheaton, was born 18th of 4th month, 1801, is living in Hopewell township, and has a large family of children. Isaac Wheaton, born 26th of 2d month, 1803, died 6th of 7th month, 1846, leaving no children. Hannah, the daughter of Isaac and Lucy S. Wheaton, born 25th of 3d month, in 1805, married in 1823 Gabriel Davis Hall, of Bacon's Neck, son of Ebenezer Hall. Gabriel and his wife had several children. She died 31st of 8th month, 1849.

Henry, son of Abner and Ruth Sheppard, was born in 1787, and married in 12th month, 1815, Margaret Lummis; she died 11th of 8th month, 1817. Henry's second wife was Sarah B. Ogden, widow of John B. Ogden. They were married in 3d month, 1819; she died in 1858, and her husband, Henry

Sheppard, in 30th of 7th month, 1867. He was a hatter, and followed the business many years in Bridgeton, where he settled early in life. He was postmaster for several years in that town. All his children were by his second wife, Sarah B. Ogden. Jane Buck, daughter of Henry and Sarah B. Sheppard, born 11th of 12th month, 1819, married in 1840, to Lorenzo Fisler Lee; he died 17th of 7th month, 1848, leaving a widow and four children—Henry Sheppard, Jr., born 8th of 11th month, 1821, married 3d of 4th month, 1845, Rhoda S. Nixon, daughter of Jeremiah Nixon. A short time after their marriage they moved to Springfield, Green county, Missouri; and he has prospered there. For many years he and his brother Charles did the leading mercantile business of the place, but both have now retired from active business. Henry commanded one of the regiments of the militia of the state, and was out several times during the Rebellion. That part of the state suffered much from the war. They have four children—Francis Henry, John Nixon, Mary Thompson and Margaret Sheppard. Charles, son of Henry and Sarah Sheppard, born 5th of 9th month, 1823, married 5th of 11th month, 1856, Lucy Dow, daughter of Ira and Mary Dow, of East Hardwick, Vermont; Charles and his family are living at Springfield, Missouri; he being cashier of Greene County National Bank. There are three more children of Henry Sheppard, Sr.—Sarah, Margaret and Joseph Ogden, who reside in Bridgeton. Joseph is a physician, and during the Rebellion for a time served as a surgeon in the army.

Ephraim Elmer, son of Abner and Mary Sheppard, born 2d of 10th month, 1804, married 1st of 5th month, 1828, Jane Elizabeth Dare, daughter of David and Rebecca Fithian Dare.— They reside in Bridgeton. Ephraim was elected Clerk of the county of Cumberland in 1852 and served to 1857. He was appointed a Judge of the Court of Common Pleas for said county in 1863, and re-appointed in 1868, and was elected Mayor of Bridgeton in the spring of 1873. His term expired in 1876. Ephraim and his wife had eight children. Ephraim Elmer, Jr., born 19th of 3d month, 1830, married 2d of 4th month, 1856, Cinderilla Maxson Bonham, daughter of Hezekiah Bonham, of Shiloh. They had several children, four of whom are living. They reside at Elmer, Salem county. Elizabeth R. Sheppard, born 6th of 4th month, 1832, married in 1850 George W. Elwell. They live in Bridgeton, and have one son, Albert Sheppard, born 17th of 3d month, 1853, who is a druggist. Ruth N. Sheppard, daughter of Ephraim, born 21st of 12th month, 1834, is not married. David Dare Sheppard, son of

Ephraim, born 15th of 6th month, 1836, married 18th of 10th month, 1866, Cornelia Albertson, daughter of Amos Buzby, of Pilesgrove. He was in the dry goods business in Bridgeton until 1870, when he moved to Springfield, Missouri, and went into business with his brother, William D. Sheppard, John Caldwell Calhoun, son of Ephraim Sheppard, born 23d of 4th month, 1840, married in 1861, Jane Elizabeth Smith, of Philadelphia, and resides in that city. William D. Sheppard, son of Ephraim, born 28th of 2d month, 1842, married 18th of 3d month, 1869, Josephine M. Trull, daughter of Nathaniel Trull, of North Tewsbury, Massachusetts. He moved to Springfield, Missouri, in the fall of 1866, and is in business with his brother, David Sheppard. Enoch Fithian Sheppard, son of Ephraim, born 21st of 8th month, 1843, died in 1846. Charles E., son of Ephraim and Jane Elizabeth Sheppard, born 1st of 11th month, 1846. He is a lawyer, and resides in Bridgeton.

The descendants of John and Thomas Sheppard, the emigrants from Ireland, are more difficult to follow than the descendants of David, the emigrant. John married, and his eldest son, Dickinson, was born as early as 1685, and became a large landholder. In 1722 he purchased 1,400 acres of land on the south side of Antuxet creek. In the following year he made another purchase of 1,600 acres adjoining his first purchase, all in the township of Downe, Cumberland county. Dickinson and his wife, Eve Sheppard, had seven children—Patience, Stephen, Dickinson, Jr., John, Jonadab, Ann and Eve Sheppard.

Mark Sheppard, son of John, (probably the John who was the son of Dickinson, and grandson of John, the emigrant,) was born in 1728. His parents were members of the Baptist Church, but he, when a young man, was convinced of the principles of the Society of Friends, applied for membership, and was received by the Society. By his first wife he had a daughter, Mary Sheppard, who married James, son of John and Mary Stewart, of Alloways Creek. She died young, leaving no issue. Mark Sheppard's second wife was Mary Craven, whom he married in 1760. By that connection there were four children—Thomas, born 12th of 11th month, 1764; Sarah, born 2d of 5th month, 1769; William, born 7th of 2d month, 1772, and Josiah, born 5th of 4th month, 1774. Mark Sheppard, the father, died the 16th of 5th month, 1780, aged fifty-two years. During his life he resided in Bacon's Neck. His son, William Sheppard, afterward married the widow of Ebenezer Hall, by whom he had five children, as follows: William married a young woman at Shiloh, a Seventh-day Baptist; Mary married Zebedee Clement; Charles married the daughter of Isaac Jones, of Conshohocken; Richard's first wife was Ann, daughter of Rachel Stewart, of Salem. She died young, leaving one daughter, Rachel Ann, who married Anthony Conard, near Wilmington, Delaware. She is deceased. Richard's second wife is Martha Holmes, daughter of Samuel Holmes, formerly of Upper Penn's Neck. Richard and his wife live at this time at Westfield, Burlington county. Casper W., the youngest son of William Sheppard, married the daughter of the late Henry Mulford. Casper died several years ago.

David Sheppard, who lived in Bacon's Neck, was probably a brother of Dickinson. David and his wife, Ann Sheppard, had six children—David, Abel, Thomas, Prudence, Lucy and Phebe. David, their father, died in 1771, and his son Abel succeeded his father on the homestead in Bacon's Neck. Abel and Abigail Sheppard had nine children. Caleb, their son, born 1757, lived in Bacon's Neck on his father's property during his life.

Job Sheppard, born 1706, was the first pastor of the Baptist Church, at Mill Hollow, near Salem; he died with the small-pox, 2d of 3d month, 1757, and was buried in the graveyard at that place. He and his wife, Catharine Sheppard, had thirteen children. Elnathan, their oldest son, married and lived in Hopewell township, near the old Cohansey Church. Job Sheppard, Jr., was born 6th of 7th month, 1735, married Rachel, daughter of Thomas Mulford, of Cumberland. Job and his wife lived in Hopewell, near Bowentown. They had seven children. Belbe Sheppard, son of Job and Catharine Sheppard, was born about 1737, married and resided in Alloways Creek. He died in 1764, and from him the Sheppard family in Lower Alloways Creek descend. Elizabeth, daughter of Job and Catharine Sheppard, married, but died young and left no issue. Jemima Sheppard, daughter of Job, married and left no issue. Daniel, son of Job and Catharine Sheppard, married a young woman, a resident of Salem. They had one son—Daniel Sheppard. Kerenhappuch, daughter of Job Sheppard, lived in Lower Alloways Creek. Rebecca, daughter of Job and Catharine Sheppard, married Jonathan Bowen, of Bowentown, she being his first wife. She died young, leaving one child, which died in infancy. Her husband was the grandfather of the late Dr. William S. Bowen, of Bridgeton. Catharine, daughter of Job, died when about sixteen years old. Cumberland Sheppard, son of Job and Catharine, married Amy Matlack, of Gloucester county. He lived and died there with his wife. They had several children. Martha, daughter of Job, married Isaac Mulford, of Hopewell. She did not live more than a year or two after that event. She left one child.

Keziah, daughter of Job and Catharine Sheppard, married William Kelsay. Robert Kelsay, their oldest son, followed the sea. Daniel, their second son, married Grace Bacon, and had one daughter, Tabitha Kelsay, who married a man by the name of Jerrell. They settled in one of the Western States. Daniel Kelsay's second wife was Lovisa Mulford. They had two children—Daniel Kelsay, Jr., who was a Baptist minister, and a pastor of Pittsgrove Church, and Maria Kelsay, who married Noah Flanagin, and removed West. Daniel Kelsay's third wife was Hannah, daughter of James and Keziah Sheppard. They had three children. Martha Kelsay, daughter of William and Keziah, married Jacob Richman, and lived in Greenwich, and had four children—Joseph, Jonathan, Lydia and Mary. Ruth, youngest child of Job and Catharine Sheppard, never married, but died about the age of twenty-two years.

Moses, son of Thomas Sheppard, the emigrant, was born in Fairfield township in 1698, and married in 1722, Mary, sister of Philip Dennis, of Bacon's Neck. Mary was born in 1701. They had six children—Rachel, born 1723; Nathan, born 1726; John, born 1730; Sarah, born 1732; Moses, Jr., born 1737, and Mary D., born 1741. Moses was a prominent member of the Baptist Church, but it is probable his wife inclined towards the Friends, as her brother, Philip Dennis, was an influential member of the Society, and a member of Cohansey meeting, as it was then called. John Sheppard, their son, born 1730, subsequently became a prominent member of the Society of Friends, and married in 1756, Priscilla Wood, the youngest daughter of Richard and Priscilla Wood, of Stoe Creek, Cumberland county. Priscilla was born 4th of 3d month, 1734. Mark Reeve, in 1689, sold his lot of sixteen acres, it being on the east side of the main street of Cohansey, adjoining the river, that he purchased of the executors of John Fenwick in 1684, reserving his family burying ground, where his wife, Ann Hunt Reeve, was buried. Joseph Browne, a merchant in Philadelphia, purhcased the property for £80, a considerable sum for such a small lot of land at that period. The said Joseph Browne died in Philadelphia about the year 1711, leaving two sons—Joseph and Isaac. The eldest afterward lived on his father's property, in Cohansey, and a number of his descendants are at this time residents of Cumberland and Salem counties. Joseph's widow was Martha Spicer, sister of Jacob Spicer, and was born in the state of New York on the 27th of 11th month, 1676. In the year 1714 she married Thomas Chalkley, an eminent minister of the Society of Friends, being his second wife. His first wife was

Martha Betterson, of London, in which city they were married in 1699. She died in Philadelphia in 1711. Joseph's youngest son, Isaac, I believe, lived and died in London, England. Joseph Brown, Jr., conveyed the lot in Cohansey to his father-in-law, Thomas Chalkley, in 1738, and he to John Butler, who sold it to Thomas Mulford. In a short time Mulford sold it to William Conover, and in the year 1760 Conover sold it to John Sheppard, son of Moses and Mary Dennis Sheppard, and the property is still owned by the Sheppard family. John and Priscilla Wood Sheppard had six children, born as follows: Rachel, 2d of 7th month, 1762; Mary, 4th of 11th month, 1764; John, 29th of 1st month, 1767; Priscilla, 25th of 11th month, 1769; Richard in 1771; Sarah, 22d of 8th month, 1775, and Moses 3d of 2d month, 1777. John, son of John and Priscilla W. Sheppard, married Mary, daughter of Mark, son of Ebenezer Miller, deputy-surveyor for Fenwick's Colony, after the death of Richard Tyndall. John and his wife had ten children. Thomas R., born 29th of 4th month, 1789, married Letitia, daughter of Richard and Elizabeth Wistar Miller, of Mannington. Thomas and his wife are deceased, leaving one daughter—Sarah Sheppard, second wife of Samuel P. Carpenter. Mark Miller Sheppard, born 12th of 1st month, 1791, never married, and died 15th of 5th month, 1876, in his eighty-sixth year. Charles R. Sheppard, born 10th of 2d month, 1793, died young. Benjamin Sheppard, born 14th of 3d month, 1795, married Mary R. Saunders, daughter of James Saunders, of Woodbury. Benjamin and his wife had eight children—Letitia, Samuel, Sarah, James, Morris, Mary, John and Anna. Charles Sheppard, born 24th of 2d month, 1798, married Rachel Redman Carpenter, daughter of William and Mary R. Carpenter, of Mannington. They had two children—William and Mary. The latter died young, and William Sheppard married a young lady named Zerns, of Pennsylvania. They live in Mannington. Priscilla Wood Sheppard, born 15th of 5th month, 1800, married John M. Reeve, of Burlington county. He was the son of Josiah Reeve, a native of Shrewsbury Neck, below Cohansey, and great grandson of Mark Reeve, the emigrant. John and his wife Priscilla had ten children. The first wife of John E., son of John and Mary Sheppard, born 25th of 11th month, 1802, was Ann Elizabeth Wood, the eldest daughter of Richard and Elizabeth Bacon Wood, of Greenwich. Their children are George and Elizabeth. Elizabeth died young. George Wood Sheppard married Ruth, daughter of Moses and Ann Sheppard. They have issue. John

SHEPPARD FAMILY.

E. Sheppard's second wife is Margaret Garrett. The Garrett family is one of the oldest English families that first settled in Pennsylvania. Their forefather came in the same vessel with William Penn, and landed at Chester in 1682. John and Margaret have three children—Philip G., Ann E. and Margaret. Clarkson, the son of John and Mary Sheppard, born 14th of 4th month, 1813, married Ann Garrett, daughter of Philip Garrett; Clarkson and Annie have three daughters living—Rebecca C., Mary M. and Martha G. Clarkson's second wife was Lydia Warrington, of Burlington county. He is a highly esteemed minister of the Society of Friends. Richard, the son of John and Priscilla W. Sheppard, born 1771, married Lydia Foster, daughter of Josiah Foster, of Burlington county; they had seven children. Moses, the son of John and Priscilla Wood Sheppard, married Rachel, the daughter of Charles and Rebecca Miller Bacon, of Bacon's Neck, Greenwich township. Rachel Bacon's ancestors were among the first families in that part of the colony. Her father, Charles Bacon, was the grandson of John and Elizabeth Smith Bacon, one of the judges of the Salem Courts for a number of years. His wife, Elizabeth, was the youngest daughter of John Smith, of Smithfield, and Rachel's mother was the youngest daughter of Ebenezer Miller, Sr.; she was born in the town of Greenwich, 17th of 3d month, 1747. Moses and his wife, Rachel B. Sheppard, had two children—Moses and Beulah; the latter died young. Moses, the son of Moses and Rachel B. Sheppard, married Ann, the daughter of Job and Ruth Thompson Bacon; they had three daughters, as follows—Ruth, who married George B. Sheppard; they reside in Stoe Creek township. Rachel, who married Job, the son of John and Ann Bacon, of Bacon's Neck; Rachel is deceased, and left children, and Ann, who is not married. Moses' second wife was from West Chester, Pennsylvania; they had no issue.

28

SCULL FAMILY.

John Scull emigrated from Long Island about 1690, in company with others, who took up large tracts of land along the sea shore. He was called a whaleman; and a number of persons at that time followed the business of catching whales from Sandy Hook to the Capes of Delaware; whales, at the first settling of Jersey, being numerous enough to make the business profitable. At the present time they are rarely seen. John Scull was the owner of a large tract of land not far from Great Egg Harbor. John Fothergill, an eminent minister of the Society of Friends, visiting the provinces in 1722, writes that he had a religious meeting at the house of John and Mary Scull, at Great Egg Harbor, which was well attended. Thomas Chalkly also mentions having a meeting at John Scull's house in 1725. John and his wife had thirteen children, eight sons and five daughters. John, their eldest son, was stolen while an infant, by the Indians, and was never recovered. They likewise had a son named John Recompence Scull, who lived to a great age. The tribe of Indians who lived around Great Egg Harbor, belonged to the Delawares, or Lenape or first people. In the year 1758 the celebrated Indian Chief, Isaac Still, claimed land from the mouth of Great Egg Harbor river to the head branches, except the Somers', Steelman's and Scull's tracts of land. John Scull owned 550 acres of land, purchased of Jacob Valentine; it being on Patounk creek. He died 1745. His son, Gideon Scull, married Judith Bellanger. The Bellanger family, which name has been corrupted into Bellangee, came from the province of Poitou, in France, and emigrated first to England and from thence to America, between the years 1682 and 1690. In the early work of French Heraldy, the name is written de Bellinger. The arm borne by them, are given with very emblazonment, and a shield, azure, with a chevan. This coat of arms has been in possession of the family in New Jersey, since their first arrival in America, and was given by Judith Bellangee to her niece, the late Hannah Smith, of Woodstown, whilst on a visit to Philadelphia, sixty years ago; and by her given to her grandson, Smith Bowen, of Philadelphia. Judith Bellange and her sister Christiana, who married Daniel Shourds, lived to be over ninety years of age. The father of Ives Bellange was shot during the dragonnades of Louis XIV., and his wife and five children fled for refuge to the caves and forests of their native province, where they were concealed for several months, until an opportunity presented for them, in company with others, of escaping to England, most likely to Dover, as in the year 1687 Theophilus Bellanger arrived there out of France, as the record states. By reason of the late trouble, yet continuing in the same year, the name of John Delaplaine, linen weaver, is also found among the records, as living as a refugee, at Dover, and it is likely he proceeded to America in company with the Bellange family. Ives Bellange, a weaver, and Christiana Delaplaine, a spinster, were married in 1697, at Friend's meeting, on Market street, Philadelphia. Among the witnesses of their marriage were James and Hannah Delaplaine, and thirty-nine others. There were others of the name of Bellange besides Ives in America at that time. James Bellange, in 1696, appears to have been a Friend residing in Burlington, New Jersey, where he held some town lots. There was a Henry Bellange, who, in 1684, located 262 acres of land in Evesham, Burlington county. The general opinion is, that Henry, James and Ives Bellange were brothers. This belief is founded on the tradition, that the Huguenot children emigrated to America. There is reason to believe that all the families in West Jersey, named Bellanger, are the descendants from those above named. The change in the orthography having taken place during the lapse of time. In the old records of London, it is stated that Adrian de Bellange, in the reign of James I., about 1622, was one of the householders, being strangers within the liberty of St. Marlins le Grand, London.

In the first report of the French Relief Committee in London, dated December, 1687, fourteen months after the revocation of the edict of Nantes, 15,400 refugees had been relieved during the year. Of these, says Weiss, the historian, of the Huguenots, 13,050 were settled in London, and 2000 in different seaport towns, where they had disembarked 140 persons of quality, 143 ministers, 144 lawyers and physicians, traders and burghers, the rest artisans and workmen, for 600 of whom no work could be found, and they were sent to America. Ives Bellange and his wife, Christiana Bellange, soon after their marriage removed from Philadelphia to Egg Harbor. They had two children— James and Ives Bellange. James married 9th month, 1727, at

Great Egg Harbor, to Margery Smith, grand-daughter of Richard Smith, the wealthy patentee of Smithtown, on Long Island. There is a tradition of the Smith family of Egg Harbor, that Richard Smith, the patentee, had nine sons, two of whom purchased lands at Great Egg Harbor and there resided. Three of their descendants about seventy years ago, David, Jonathan and Robert, died at Egg Harbor; but the latter's widow, Dorothea, and her five children, removed to Salem county. James and his wife, Margery, had eight children—Phebe, Judith, Susannah, Christiana, Ruth, Margery, Thomas and James Bellange.

Phebe Bellange married John Ridgway, and had five sons and two daughters. Susan Bellange married John Ridgway, Jr.; they had five children. Christiana Bellange married Daniel Shourds; she died in 1822, aged ninety years, leaving six children. Ruth Bellange married Job Ridgway; they had five children. Thomas Bellange married Mary Barton; there were six children. James Bellange married Grace Ingle. Gideon Scull, son of John and Mary Scull, born in 1722, married Judith, the second daughter of James Bellange; they had four sons and six daughters. They died in 1776, of the small-pox, which disease they contracted while attending Salem Quarterly Meeting. William Lawrence, the second of the brothers, born in Hertfordshire, England, in 1623, emigrated under the charge of Governor Winthrop, Jr., to New England, with his elder brother, John Lawrence, in the ship Planter, in 1635. The younger brother Thomas Lawrence came to America. William Lawrence removed to Long Island, and became one of the patentees of Flushing, in which town he resided during the remainder of his life, dying in 1680, leaving a large estate—his own plate and personal property alone being valued at £4,430. His second wife was Elizabeth Smith, a daughter of Richard Smith, before mentioned. His son William, by his first wife, married in 1680, Deborah Smith, the youngest sister of his father's second wife, Elizabeth. By this marriage they had, among other children, Samuel, who married Mary Hicks, living at Black Stump, Long Island. They had nine children, the youngest of whom was Abigail, born 14th of 3d month, 1737. She married at Newtown, Long Island, in 5th month, 1758, to James James, of Philadelphia. She died at Woodstown, 6th of 5th month, 1770, and was interred in the Friends' burying ground at that place. James James died at Sculltown, 16th of 5th month, 1807, aged seventy-eight years. James and Abigail L. James had five children. James James married Kerranhappuck Powell, who lived in Sunbury,

Georgia; they had three children. William died single in one of the Southern States. Abigail James married Judge Francis Child, of Morristown, New Jersey, where their descendants reside. Hannah married William Wayman, of Long Island, and subsequently moved to Woodstown; they had five children. Sarah married Abram Canfield. Mary James married Daniel Harker, of Philadelphia; they had one child—Abigail. Samuel Lawrence James, the youngest child of James and Abigail L. James, married Mary Hall, the daughter of Colonel Edward Hall, of Mannington, grandson of William Hall, the emigrant, who was a Justice and the second Judge of the Courts of Salem county. Edward Hall's mother was Elizabeth Smith, granddaughter of John Smith, of Almsbury, who died at his granddaughter's in his one hundred and seventh year. He landed at Salem in company with John Fenwick, in 1675. Samuel and Mary James had eight children; the eldest was Clara, who married David Reeve, of Bridgeton, and subsequently removed to Phœnixville, Pennsylvania; they had one son—Samuel, and three daughters—Mary, Rebecca and Emily Reeve. Hetty James, the second daughter of Samuel L. and Mary H. James, married Josiah, the son of Richard and Elizabeth W. Miller; they had three sons—Richard, Samuel L. J. and Wyatt W. Miller. Hetty was the second wife of David Reeve. James James, the eldest son of Samuel, married Beulah Arney, of Johnstown, Pennsylvania, daughter of Daniel Arney. They went to Tennessee. They had children, one of whom, Samuel James, married a daughter of a large cotton dealer, in Louisiana. The fourth child of Samuel and Mary James was Samuel, who lives in Missouri, unmarried. The fifth child, Sarah, married Joseph Pierson, of Baton Rouge, Louisiana; they had children. After the death of Pierson, she married David Reeve, being his third wife. Caroline James, the sixth child, married Robert Buck, of Bridgeton. He is one of the proprietors of the nail and iron works of that city. They have several children. Edward, the seventh child, married and lived in Missouri; they had several children. Mary Hall James, the eighth child, I believe, remained single.

Gideon Scull, the grandson of John Scull, was born at Great Egg Harbor, in 1756, married Sarah James, the eldest child of James James, 29th of 4th month, 1784. Gideon sold his share of the patrimonial estate to his brother, Mark Scull, and removed to Salem county to Lockheartstown, being the Swedish name of a place on Oldman's Creek; and at that place he followed the mercantile business. It was called Sculltown for upwards of sixty years, but has been changed to Auburn. Gideon and his wife had nine children, the eldest was Abigail, who died young. The second child was named Abigail, who died in Philadelphia, in 1867, at an advanced age; she never married. James Scull died at sea in 1820. Gideon Scull married Lydia Ann Rowen, the daughter of Dr. Thomas Rowen, Sr., by his last wife; they had five sons and five daughters. Gideon was an enterprising business man. He and Samuel Clement were in the mercantile business together on Market street, Salem, for a number of years, and their's was the leading store in the town at that time. He subsequently removed to Philadelphia and went into the wholesale grocery business; the firm was known as Thompson & Scull. Paul, the third son of Gideon and Sarah J. Scull, married Hope Kay, whose parents resided near Woodbury. Paul and his wife lived on the Plainfield farm, as it was called, located about two miles from Woodstown. He was considered one of the greatest agriculturalists in the county, energetic and full up in all the modern improvements in the way of fertilizing the exhausted virgin soil. He died before he was far advanced in life, with pulmonary disease, and his death was a public loss. He had one son and three daughters. Offly, the fourth son, died young; Sarah, the third daughter, died single, in the city of Philadelphia. David, the fifth son, married Lydia, the daughter of Joshua and Esther Davis Lippincott, in 1823. She was born in 1801, and died in 1854. They had eight children; three sons and five daughters, who are all living except two, who died young. Their names are Caroline, Gideon Delaplaine, Hannah, Jane Lippincott, Lydia L., David, Jr., Edward Lawrence, and Mary Scull. Hannah, the youngest child of Gideon and Sarah J. Scull, married William Carpenter, Jr., the son of William and Mary P. Carpenter, of Mannington; she died the first year after her marriage, leaving no issue. David Scull's second wife is Hannah D., daughter of Richard and Elizabeth Bacon Wood, formerly of Greenwich, Cumberland county.

Gideon Scull, before mentioned, was born in 1756, and died in 1825, aged sixty nine years; and his wife, Sarah J. Scull, born in 1759, died in 1836, aged about seventy-seven years. She was a recommended minister in the Society of Friends. The family belonged to Pilesgrove Monthly Meeting. David Scull, their youngest son, born in 1799, left his native place, Sculltown, many years ago, together with his family, and went to Philadelphia, where he kept a wholesale wool store on Market street. His business capacity, and close application to business, enabled him to acquire a competency, and he has retired from the business, two of his sons having taken his place. Caroline, the eldest daughter of David and Lydia Scull, died young. Gideon Delaplaine, the eldest son, born in 1824, married in 1862, Anna Holder, of England. They have two children—Walter Delaplaine Scull, born in Bath, England, and Edith Maria Lydia Scull, born at Great Malvern, England. At this time G. D. Scull and family reside at the Laurels, Hounslow Heath, near London. Hannah, the second daughter of David and Lydia Scull, remains single. Jane Lippincott, the third daughter, married William D. Bispham; they have one son—David Scull Bispham. Lydia Scull, daughter of David and Lydia Scull, died young. David Scull, Jr., married Hannah Coale, of Baltimore, who is deceased; she left one son—William Ellis Scull. Edward Lawrence Scull is single, and is in business with his brother David, on Market street, Philadelphia. Mary, the youngest daughter of David and Lydia Scull, married Paschal Harker; they have no issue.

SMITH AND DARKIN FAMILIES.

The original name of Elsinborough township was Elfsborg, called thus by the Swedes. The name was derived from a fort that was erected on the south side of Assomhocking creek, so called by the Indians. The Swedes named the stream Varickenkill, but it was afterward called by Fenwick's colony Salem creek. The fort alluded to was built in 1643, by order of Governor Printz. Ferris, in his history, of the early settlement on the Delaware, which is the most reliable that I know of, says it was erected on the south side of the creek, at its junction with the Delaware river. If that is correct, which I have no reason to doubt, the mouth of the creek must have been a mile or more further down the river than it is at the present time. The Swedes made no permanent settlement there. After they abandoned their fort, which took place in 1651, their settlement was further up and on both sides of the Delaware river; on the Jersey side as far as the mouth of Raccoon creek, on the opposite shore from the mouth of Christiana creek to Weccacoe, where Philadelphia is now located. The first English settlement in the county of Salem was in Elsinborough, on a point of land which now belongs to Amos Harris, and to William, Joseph and Casper Thompson. The said point was called by the aboriginal inhabitants Assomhocking point. An exploring company from New Haven, Connecticut, reached here in the year 1640. They were not over two years in this county, but whilst here they explored a stream about four miles below Salem creek, and named it Cotton river on account of the cotton wood that they found growing in the low ground along the shores of the stream. It is now known as Alloways creek. They were looked upon by the Swedes and Indians with considerable jealousy, and in the winter of 1642 an epidemic broke out among them, which they called the pleurisy, and more than half of their number died of the disease, and those that escaped returned in the summer to New Haven again. It does not appear that there was any other settlement in the township until John Fenwick arrived with his colony in the Spring of

1675. Robert Windham, in the fall of the same year, purchased 1,000 arces of land of the proprietor, it being the same that the New Haven colony had partly cleared and left over thirty years before. The said land was bounded on the west by Salem creek, on the east by Alemsbury creek, south by John Smith's land, south-west by Middle Neck, as it was afterward named. Robert Windham and his wife lived there until their death, which took place about the year 1686, leaving one daughter. Her name was Ann Windham. She shortly afterward married Richard Darkin, who emigrated to this country from England in 1683. He seems to have been a man above mediocrity, and rendered great assistance to the new colony in their civil affairs. He was likewise a consistent and useful member of the Society of Friends. Richard and his wife Ann Darkin had four children—Joseph Darkin, their eldest son, was born at Windham, near New Salem, 8th of 1st month, 1688; their daughter, Hannah Darkin, was born 3d of 9th month, 1691; their son, John Darkin, was born on the 9th of 6th month, 1694, and Ann Darkin was born 31st of 1st month, 1700. In 1717 John Darkin, son of Richard Darkin, married Sarah Thompson, daughter of Thomas Thompson. They had two children—Jale Darkin, born 11th of 10th month, 1718. She married John Nicholson, son of Abel Nicholson. John Darkin, son of John and Sarah Darkin, was born in 1720. The last mentioned John Darkin left no children, but left his Windham estate to his nephew, Darkin Nicholson. In the year 1719 Joseph Darkin, son of Richard Darkin, married Ann Smart, daughter of Isaac Smart. They had one daughter. Her name was Hannah, born 18th of 10th month, 1722.

John Smith was the son of John Smith. He was born in the county of Norfolk, in England, 20th of 7th month, 1623. The said John Smith married Martha Craffs, daughter of Christopher Craffs, of Northamptonshire. They were married in 1658. The following are the names of their children born in England: Daniel Smith, born 10th of 12th month, 1660; Samuel Smith, born 8th of 3d month, 1664; David Smith, born 19th of 12th month, 1666, and Sarah Smith, born 4th of 12th month, 1671. John Smith, his wife and children, sailed for West New Jersey, in America, on board the ship Griffith, Robert Griffith being master, and landed at a place they called New Salem, 23d of 6th month, 1675. The names of their children born in this country are as follows:—Jonathan Smith, born in New Salem, 27th of 10th month, 1675; Jeremiah Smith, born at Alemsbury, 14th of 9th month, 1678. John Smith purchased 2,000 acres of John Fenwick, the purchase extending from the head of Alemsbury creek to Alloways creek, and bounded on the east by Edward Champney's land, on the west by Samuel Nicholson. After the townships were laid off, one-half of said allotment of land was in Alloways Creek township. Daniel Smith, the eldest son, bought 1,000 acres in in Alloways creek township, near what is now called Quinton. The land lay on the north side of the creek. He built and lived on the property that was owned by the late Ann Simpson. This Alemsbury estate was divided between Samuel, David and Jonathan Smith. His daughter, Sarah Smith, married John Mason, of Elsinborough.

SAYRES FAMILY.

The Sayres family, it has been said, is of Swedish origin, but at what time their forefathers arrived in this country, is a matter of uncertainty. About the year 1716, Thomas Sayres, son of Jonas Sayres, purchased a large tract of land, tradition says, of William Hall. I think it not improbable, inasmuch as Hall, about that time was the owner of a vast quantity of land in this county, including what is now Cumberland county. The Sayres land was located near Masons, now known as Maskell's Mill. Thomas Sayres and his wife Rachel, had several children—Thomas, James, Leonard, Lot and Ruth. The latter afterwards became the wife of James Daniels, an eminent preacher in the Society of Friends; he died in 1776, leaving Ruth, who was several years younger than himself, a widow; they had no children. Thomas Sayres and Rachel Abbott were married in 1742; they had eleven children—Abbott, born in 1743, Reuben, Hannah, David, Reuel, Joseph, Dennis, Rachel, Thomas, Dorcas and William. Abbott Sayres married, and died a young man, leaving one daughter—Hannah Sayres. The Sayres family, generally, were ardent Whigs during the American Revolution. Reuben Sayres, the second son of Thomas and Rachel, born 5th of 11th month, 1746, married Hannah, the daughter of Bradway Stretch, who was several years older than himself. He volunteered in the army under Colonel Holmes, stationed at Hancock's Bridge. The morning of the bloody massacre at that place he was killed. He succeeded in escaping from the house with his musket, but was pursued by several of the Tories, and one or two of the English soldiers. He ran for a large tract of woodland that was about a half mile distant from the house of William Hancock where the carnage took place, and reached it in safety. His pursuers followed him closely, and he then ran towards a swamp called the Holly Swamp, but as he climbed upon the fence his pursuers shot and killed him. His remains were not found for several days afterwards. He had two cousins who took part in the same engagement. One of them, John Sayres, was killed in the house whilst asleep, and James Sayres was severely wounded, but finally recovered. Reuben left a large real and personal estate, which was appraised at £1,345 8s. 9d. It appears there was considerable difficulty in apportioning his personal estate between his relatives and widow. The law at that period in reference to personal estates were not easily to comprehend, owing, I have no doubt, to the unsettled condition of the country. The administrators and heirs agreed to leave it to three disinterested men as arbitrators, and Andrew York, William Smith and Edward Hancock were chosen. The following is their verbatim return. "We the undersigned being "respectfully chosen to settle the personal estate of Reuben "Sayres, deceased, between the administrators and the several "heirs, this fourth day of February, 1779. We received the "papers and heard the allegations and proofs respecting premises "and the statement of the amount. We do agree and determine "the annexed statement is just and true for settling between the "heirs and the administrators. Witnesses our hands, that is "the widow should have the sum of £445 16s. 8d. Andrew "York, William Smith, Edward Hancock." The widow, Hannah Sayres, afterwards married Wade Barker; they had one daughter—Hannah Barker. After the death of her second husband, she married James Sayres, the cousin of her first husband.

David Sayres, the son of Thomas and Rachel Sayres, was born 3d of 11th month, 1751. I have been informed by the family that he died a young man. He married and left one son, whose name was Abbott Sayres. Reuel, the son of Thomas and Rachel Sayres, born 4th of 10th month, 1754, inherited the farm which now belongs to Robert Butcher, and built the present house on the premises; it has been rebuilt within a few years by the present owner. Reuel Sayres and his wife, I think, sold it to Henry Mulford, the father of the late Charles Mulford, of Salem. Reuel and his family removed to Ohio. Henry Mulford, I think, retained the property whilst he lived, and it was then sold, James Butcher being the purchaser; hence the property was brought back into the Sayres family. James Butcher's wife, Hannah Sayres, was the daughter of Abbott Sayres, a direct descendant of Thomas and Rachel Sayres. William, the youngest son of Thomas and Rachel Sayres, born in 1767, subsequently married Amy Evans; they had issue—Reuben Sayres, born in 1798, and Evan Sayres, born in 1800, he died a minor. Samuel and Thomas Sayres were born in 1802. Reuben, the son of William and Amy Sayres, married Clarissa Press; they have issue. Their daughter Amanda

Sayres, was born in 1825. James Sayres, their son, was born in 1829, subsequently married Martha, the daughter of Silas Harris, of Salem; they had issue, two daughters and one son. He removed to Camden several years ago and followed his trade of house carpentering. Amy Sayres, Reuben and Clarissa Sayres' second daughter, married Edward, the eldest son of Ephraim and Mary Ann Carll; they have issue—Mary Ann, Milton and Sarah Carll. Sarah D. Sayres, the youngest daughter of Reuben and Clarissa Sayres, born in 1837, is unmarried, and remains at home. She has the charge, in a great measure, of her aged and honorable parents, who have long been consistent members of the Baptist Church at Canton. Paying a visit to the aged couple, at one time, and observing the solicitous care of their daughter towards her parents, it brought to my mind the saying of a wise man in ancient times, in addressing his son: " Go my son and observe the young stork of the " wilderness. See he bears on his wings his aged sire, he carries " him, lodges him in safety, and supplies him with food."

Thomas, the son of Thomas and Rachel Sayres, was born in 1763, and came in the possession of part of his brother Reuben's real estate; he married and had two daughters and one son— Anna, Rachel and Thomas B. Sayres. Anna Sayres, daughter of Thomas Sayres, Jr., married David Bowen; they had four children—J. Madison, Rachel, Mary Ann and Thomas Bowen. J. Madison Bowen came into possession of the homestead farm, but afterwards sold it to Eliakim Smith, and removed to Cumberland county. Rachel, the daughter of David and Anna Bowen, married Jervis Butcher, who was a hatter and followed his trade in Salem. He died many years ago, leaving a widow and one son—Jonathan Butcher. Mary Ann, the second daughter of David and Ann Butcher, subsequently married Richard, the son of Edward and Prudence Waddington; they had six children—Anna, Edward, David, George, Elizabeth and Mary Waddington. Mary Ann, the mother of the above mentioned children, has been deceased for several years.— Thomas, the youngest son of David and Anna Bowen, removed to one of the Western States when a young man. Rachel, the second daughter of Thomas Sayres, Jr., married David Elwell. Her second husband was Benjamin Garrison, of Pilesgrove. I have been informed they lived in Camden for some time, and eventually removed to one of the Western States. Thomas B. Sayres, the son of Thomas Sayres, Jr., married the daughter of Sylvanus Sheppard; they had issue. He and his family went to one of the Western States many years ago.

James, the son of Thomas Sayres, the emigrant, was born about 1720. The most reliable account I have is that he lived, after he married, in Stoe Creek township, Cumberland county. He had three sons—James, John and Ephraim Abbott Sayres. James and John enlisted in the army of the American Revolution and served under Colonel Hand. They were stationed at Hancock's Bridge, at the time of the bloody massacre at that place in 1778. John was killed while he was lying on the floor asleep, and his brother James was thought to be mortally wounded by having a bayonet thrust through him, but he finally recovered. James' first wife's name I do not know, but they had issue—James Sayres, 3d. His second wife was Hannah, the widow of Wade Barker, and the daughter of Bradway Stretch. Her first husband was Reuben Sayres, cousin of her third husband. James and his wife Hannah had one daughter, Rachel, who subsequently married Daniel Gilman, of Cumberland. James Sayres' third wife was Sarah, widow of Job Smith. Her maiden name was Sarah Mulford, and she had by her first husband seven children—John, Jane, Sarah, Samuel, Mary, Eliakim and Job. The latter is a cabinet maker and undertaker, and carries on his business at Hancock's Bridge. James and Sarah Sayres had one daughter, Hannah, who subsequently married Edmund, son of Conrad Hires, of Bridgeton. Abbott Sayres, the son of James, married and had two or more children—Hannah, who married James Butcher, and a son—Abbott, Jr. The latter married Mary Harris, and had one son, Abbott, who at the present time resides in Cumberland county.

Ephraim, the son of James Sayres, Sr., married and had one son—Ephraim. The last named purchased a farm in Stoe Creek township, Cumberland county, being originally part of Richard Wood's landed estate, and resided there until his death. He had two children by his first wife—Mary and Abbott. His daughter Mary married Reuben Dayton; her second husband is Edward, the son of Edward and Catharine Fogg, and they have several children. His son, Abbott Sayres, married and at this time resides at Bridgeton.

Ananias Sayres, brother of Thomas, the elder, married Mary, the daughter of Richard Gibbon, living near Roadstown. Mary, it appears, inherited a farm from her father on which she and her husband dwelt. They had issue—Hannah, Rachel, Mary, Sarah, and Leonard G. Sayres. Hannah, their eldest daughter, married Job Remington, of Greenwich; they had one son—Job, who was apprenticed in Philadelphia to learn the house carpenter trade. He subsequently kept a lumber yard below

Green street wharf, in that city, known as the George Knox lumber yard, and accumulated a large fortune. He retired many years before his death with a competency. His mother, Hannah Remington, married John Adams, a native of Egg Harbor, but at the time of their marriage followed his trade, that of a carriage maker, in the town of Greenwich. John and his wife had three children—Hannah, Joseph and John.

Rachel, the daughter of Ananias and Mary Sayres, married Job Tyler, of Greenwich. They had issue—Benjamin, Job, Mary and Richard, all of whom are noticed in the sketch of the Tyler family. Mary, the daughter of Ananias and Mary Sayres, married David Mulford. They had eleven children—Hannah, born 9th of 2d month, 1776; Ephraim, Mary, Thomas, Nancy, David, Sarah, Rebecca, William, John and Elizabeth. Hannah, Nancy and Sarah died minors. John Mulford died unmarried at the age of twenty-six. Ephraim, the son of David and Mary Mulford, born 8th of 10th month, 1778, married Ruth Wheaton, the second daughter of Isaac Wheaton, who lived at Cohansey Neck, near the town of Greenwich. The said Isaac Wheaton and his eldest daughter were drowned off Billingsport, in the Delaware river, with several others from on board the Greenwich Packet, Rachel, during a violent gale on the night of the 15th of 2d month, 1802. Ephraim and Ruth had issue—Ananias, William, Isaac and David Mulford. Ephraim's second wife was Rhoda, daughter of John Laning; they had three children—Ruth, Ellen and Alfred Mulford. Ephraim, their father, lived far beyond the age allotted to man, having died at the age of ninety-two years, leaving a large estate to his children. Mary, the daughter of David and Mary Mulford, was born 27th of 10th month, 1780, and married Dr. Charles Hannah, of Hancock's Bridge. She died a young woman, leaving one son—James M. Hannah.

Thomas, the son of David and Mary Mulford, was born 19th of 12th month, 1782, and married Phebe Butcher, sister of the late James Butcher; they had issue—Richard and Charles Mulford. His second wife was a widow, Rachel Evan Scudder; they had one daughter, Elizabeth Mulford, who subsequently married Richard Dubois, Jr. Richard, the son of Thomas and Phebe Mulford, married Lucetta, the daughter of Washington Smith; they had issue—Phebe, Ann, Maria, Mary and Martha. Rebecca, the daughter of David and Mary Mulford, born in 1794, married Asa Couch. William, the son of David and Mary Mulford, was born in 1792; he married Grace Carll, the daughter of Ephraim Carll, Sr., and left several children.

Sarah, the daughter of Ananias and Mary Sayres, married Richard Cole. They lived a number of years on the Isaac Norris farm near Salem, and had four sons and one daughter, Sarah Cole, who with her two eldest brothers, Charles and Richard, died in early age of consumption; soon after that event Richard and his wife removed to Gloucester county, and there ended their days. Leonard G. Sayres, the son of Ananias and Mary, appears to have left his native county and settled in the state of Ohio, when the city of Cincinnati was a village. Whether he married before he went West I have no knowledge. He is reported to have prospered in his adopted State, and to have accumulated a large fortune. Leonard's second wife was Hannah Anderson, a widow, and the daughter of Thomas and Rebecca Thompson, of Salem. Lot, the youngest son of Thomas Sayres, married the daughter of John Warner, a member of the Society of Friends. He, like many of that persuasion, became a strong Whig, and at the battle of Quinton's Bridge, in the revolutionary struggle, (notwithstanding he was an old man like John Burns of Gettysburg memory,) took his musket and volunteered in the skirmish. Lot and his wife had one son, Job Sayres, who was born in 1765, and subsequently married Sarah Padgett; they had issue; their eldest child was Street Sayres; he was born in 1791, and died a minor. Rachel, the daughter of Job and Sarah Sayres, born in 1793, married Captain Daniel Dixon; their children were Thophilus Beesley, Job S. and Daniel. Job Sayres' second wife was Mary Tuft, sister of the late Captain John Tuft, of Salem. By that union there were three children—Margaret, William and Rebecca Sayres. Theophilus B. Dixon married Harriet, the daughter of Daniel Dorrell; they have six children—John F., Sarah, Mary, Bilbe, Martha and Theophilus B. Jr. Job Dixon married Eliza F. Brown, one of the descendants (on her mother's side) of Joshua Carpenter, of Philadelphia, being the seventh generation. She was the daughter of Zaccheus, Jr. and Eliza Fogg Brown. Job and his wife have four children—David Fogg Brown, Zaccheus B., Daniel and Rachel Dixon. Daniel, the son of Daniel and Sarah S. Dixon, married Mary, the daughter of Edward Orr; they have nine children—William, Thomas V., Joseph, Charles, George, Helen, Hannah, Mary and Albert Dixon. Margaret, the daughter of Job and Mary T. Sayres, married Japhet Somers, of Penn's Neck; they have issue—William, Mary and Ann Somers. William, the son of Job and Mary T. Sayres, married Eliza Pendgar, of New York; they have no issue. Rebecca, the youngest daughter of Job and Mary T. Sayres, married William Simkins; they have issue.

THOMAS SHOURD'S RESIDENCE.
Built by one of his ancestors (Joseph Ware, 2d,) in 1730.

SHOURDS FAMILY.

History informs us soon after William Penn purchased the province of Pennsylvania he traveled through parts of Germany and Holland on horseback, inviting the inhabitants of those countries to emigrate to his newly acquired province in North America. Among those that accepted his invitation was Cornelius Shoverde, a stadtholder of one of the provinces of Holland. He and his family arrived at Philadelphia in 1684. They lived in a cave for a short period of time, near Germantown. Subsequently he purchased 300 acres of land of the proprietor; the said land was located in Penn's manor, nearly opposite where Bordentown now is in New Jersey. There was a large stone placed at one corner of the allotment, with his initials cut on it, and the writer, in company with the late Hector Ivins, who at that time resided near by, visited the place of his ancestor, where he lived and ended his days. His wife's maiden name was Sophina Weimar, and most of their children were born in Holland. Their names were Samuel, Catharine, Esther, Sarah and Sophina. Sophina, the youngest, married Zebulon Gaunt, in 1715; their children were Samuel, Zebulon, Israel, Hannah, Mary and Sophina Gaunt. Samuel, the son of Zebulon and Sophina Gaunt, married Hannah Woolman; they had seven children—Judah, Asher, Reuben, Elihu, Peter, Sereptha and Elizabeth.

Samuel, the son of Cornelius and Sophina Shoverde, married Sarah Harrison, of Philadelphia; and he and his wife, Sarah Shoverde, had a large family of children. Two of the youngest located themselves at Tuckerton, and that generation of the family changed the spelling of their name from Shoverde to Shourds. Mary, the daughter of Samuel and Sarah Shourds, married Jonathan Pettit. They resided at Tuckerton, and their house was standing a few years ago in a commanding situation, near Barnegat bay. Their son, Joseph Pettit, married Sarah, the daughter of Elisha and Mary Woodnutt Bassett, of Mannington; they had issue—Woodnutt, Jonathan and Mary Pettit. Daniel, the son of Samuel and Sarah Shourds, married

Christiana Bellange, who died 21st of 10th month, 1822, aged ninety years. They had six children—Samuel, John, Daniel, Shady, Hannah and Amy Shourds. Samuel, the eldest, married Hannah Gray;* they had nine children—Gray, Thomas, Samuel, Benjamin, John, Asa, Job, Daniel and Elizabeth Shourds. John, the son of Daniel and Christiana B. Shourds, married Sarah Johnson; they had five children—David, Joseph, Hannah, Reuben and Ruth Shourds. Samuel and his brother, John Shourds, sold their property at Tuckerton over fifty years ago. Samuel rented a farm in Back Neck, Cumberland county, and resided there for several years, and John Shourds rented property of the late Dr. Thomas Rowen, in Penn's Neck, and he and his family resided there several years. Samuel and his brother John subsequently removed to New York with their families, excepting David, the eldest son of John Shourds, who married and settled in the township of Lower Penn's Neck; he was the father of the present Joseph Shourds, of that township.

Samuel Shourds and his brother John purchased large tracts in parts of Munroe and Genesee counties, New York. The greater part of their land was then in its primitive state, it being soon after the Erie canal was completed, but their property advanced rapidly in value, and the natural result was they became quite independent in a few years. An uncommon circumstance occurred a few years before Samuel and John's death. They felt desirous to visit their native place once more before their death, and accordingly they came to Woodstown to visit Jonathan and Hannah Smith, the latter being their sister, and all four of them went to Tuckerton by land. Samuel was then in his eighty-ninth year, his brother, John, two years younger, Jonathan Smith in his eighty-eighth year, and his wife, Hannah, eighty-two years old. When they arrived at the place of their nativity what pleasing and also sad reflections

---

* Samuel, the son of Daniel and Christiana Shourds as stated in the Shourds genealogy, married Hannah Gray. She was a sister of Samuel Gray. The Gray family I think were natives of Monmouth county. Samuel Gray and his wife had four children—Charles F. H. Gray, Jesse, who now resides near Pemberton, New Jersey, Hannah and Charity Gray. Charles F. H. Gray came to this county in company with his father many years ago, and married a daughter of the late Joseph C. Nelson, an eminent land Surveyor of Pittsgrove. Charles and his wife have several children. He has filled many and various township offices. His father, Samuel Gray, ended his days at his son's house. Charles' grandfather and one of his uncles, emigrated to Genesee county, State of New York, more than half a century since, in company with Samuel and John Shourds.

they must have had in recurring back to the days of their youth. How many of their former friends and associates had gone to their final resting place. There was one, however, who resided at Great Egg Harbor, their brother Daniel, who was still living to receive his aged relatives. Daniel, the son of Daniel and Christiana Shourds, married Rebecca Leeds; they had issue—William, Phebe, Matilda and Daniel, 2d. Shady, the daughter of Daniel and Christiana Shourds, married Walter Wilson, of Burlington city; they have issue—William, who died a minor. Hannah, the daughter of Daniel and Christiana Shourds, born about the year 1765, married Jonathan Smith, a lineal descendant of Richard Smith, of Long Island; they had three children—Jerusha, Elizabeth and Jonathan Smith. Jerusha married Samuel, the son of William White, of Woodstown; their children were Mary, Samuel, William, David, Wilson and Jonathan. Jonathan married Lydia Waddington, the daughter of Aaron Waddington, of Elsinboro. Elizabeth was twice married. Her first husband was Clement Hinchman; they had issue, one daughter—Clemence Hinchman. Her second husband was William Cawley, son of Samuel Cawley, Jr. Elizabeth, the daughter of Jonathan and Hannah Smith, was twice married. Her first husband was Daniel Bowen, M. D., a native of Bridgeton; they had one son—Smith Bowen, who married Ann Bisham, daughter of Samuel Bisham, of Philadelphia; they have three children—Mary, Elizabeth, Anna Stoke and Samuel Bisham Bowen. Elizabeth Smith's second husband was Hosea Fithian, M. D., son of Jonathan Fithian, of Cumberland county; they had three children—Hannah, Mary and Elizabeth. Elizabeth, their mother, died in 1854. Jonathan, the son of Jonathan and Hannah Smith, married Hannah, daughter of Jacob Davis, of Pilesgrove; they had four children—Mary E., Samuel, who died young, Jonathan and Ellen Smith.

Samuel, the son of Samuel and Sarah Shourds, was born 24th of 7th month, 1718. The latter was a clock and watch maker, and followed his trade in Bordentown, New Jersey. His wife was Taminson, the daughter of John and Elizabeth Pancoast, of Burlington county. Taminson was born 29th of 11th month, 1725. Benjamin, the son of Samuel and Taminson P. Shourds, was born 7th of 1st month, 1753. He subsequently married Mary, the daughter of William and Rachel Silvers, of Pilesgrove; they had seven children—Thomas, Rachel, Samuel, Rhoda, William, Mary and Benjamin. Thomas, the eldest, died 23d of 11th month, 1778. Rachel, the eldest daughter of

Benjamin and Mary Shourds, married Jervis Hall, of Mannington; she was his second wife. There were two children—Casper and Rachel Hall. Rachel, their mother, died when her children were young. Casper Hall died in 1819, when he was about eighteen years old. Rachel, the daughter of Jervis and Rachel S. Hall, married Josiah, the youngest son of Samuel Nicholson, of Mannington; they had two or three sons and one daughter—Hannah Nicholson, who married George Radcliff; they have issue. Josiah Nicholson has been deceased many years. His widow, Rachel Hall Nicholson, resides in the city of Salem, and is a teacher in one of the public schools of that city. Rhoda, the daughter of Benjamin and Mary Shourds, married John, the son of John and Susan Denn, of Mannington; they had five children—Rachel, Mary, Susan, Ann and Rebecca. The latter died young. John Denn, Jr., died in Mannington before he arrived to middle age. Soon after that event Rhoda Denn removed to the town of Salem with her children. She was above mediocrity in intellect, and remarkable for self-denial. She was a recommended minister in the Society of Friends for a number of years. Her communications in public meetings were not extended to much length, but she possessed a faculty of condensing and saying much for her hearers to reflect upon in a few words. She has been deceased a number of years. Her daughter, Rachel Denn, married Professor John Griscom, the son of William and Rachel Denn Griscom; she was his second wife. They resided in the city of Burlington until his death. Soon after that occurred his widow, Rachel D. Griscom, returned to Salem to live. Mary, the second daughter of John and Rhoda Denn, died a young woman, unmarried. Susan Denn, the third daughter of John and Rhoda Denn, remains single. She and her sister, Rachel D. Griscom, keep house together, on Broadway, in Salem. Anna, the fourth daughter of John and Rhoda Denn, married William Gibbons, of Philadelphia; they had two children—Susan and Henry Gibbons. William, their father, has been deceased several years. Their son, Henry, died in the West Town boarding school. He was a promising and interesting youth, and if his life had been spared I have no doubt he would have made his mark on the sands of time; but such is life. Anna Gibbons and her daughter, Susan, reside in the city of Salem.

William, the son of Benjamin and Mary Shourds, married Martha, the daughter of Peter and Mary Andrews, of Mannington. Peter was a native of Great Egg Harbor; his wife, Mary, was the daughter of Whitten and Martha Huddy Cripps, of Mannington.* William and Martha Shourds had four children—Rachel, Mary, Benjamin and William Shourds.—Rachel, their eldest daughter, married Thomas Mullineux, of Ulster county, New York; her husband is deceased, and she now lives at Mount Holly, Burlington county. Mary Shourds lives in the city of Philadelphia, and remains single. Benjamin, the eldest son, resides in Philadelphia, and is a brick layer by trade. He is married and has several children. William Shourds has been twice married; his first wife was Hannah Yardly, by whom he had three children—Martha, Letitia and Hannah. His second wife is Rebecca Rainer. Mary, the daughter of Benjamin and Mary Shourds, married Samuel Hewes, of Delaware county, Pennsylvania; they are both deceased, leaving one son—Charles Hewes. Samuel Shourds, the second son of Benjamin and Mary Shourds, was born 6th of 9th month, 1781; he married Elizabeth, the daughter of Jacob and Mary Carpenter Ware. Jacob was the great grandson of Joseph Ware, the emigrant, who came to this country in the ship Griffith, as a servant, and landed at Salem 5th of 10th month, 1675. Jacob's wife was Mary Carpenter, the daughter of William and Mary Powell Carpenter. William was the grandson of Joshua Carpenter, of Philadelphia. He was born in the State of Delaware, and came to this county about the year 1745 or '46, and married Mary, the daughter of Jeremiah Powell, Jr., who was several years younger than her husband; they had four children—Mary, William, Powell and Abigail. Samuel and Elizabeth Shourds had three children—William, Mary and Thomas. William died young. Samuel Shourds,

---

* I have frequently alluded to the Cripps family without stating their ancestry. It is an old family of England. Nathaniel, the first that I have knowledge of, was the son of John Cripps, born about 1656. He married, in England, Grace, sister of James Whitten, who located land in Lower Mannington, at the first settlement of Salem county. Nathaniel and his wife, Grace Cripps, came to America in 1678, and settled in Burlington county. By tradition he was the founder of Mount Holly. Nathaniel and Grace Cripps had six children—John, Benjamin, Samuel, Virginia, Theophla and Hannah Ann Cripps.—John, the eldest son, married Mary Eves, of Haddonfield. Benjamin, the second son, married Mary Hough. Their children were Whitten, who in 1759 married Martha Huddy; John, their second son, died a minor; Hannah, married Samuel Mason, of Mannington, in 1756, son of Thomas Mason, of the same place; Cyntha married James Bonsall, of Darby, Pennsylvania. Whitten Cripps subsequently was the owner of the landed estate of his great-uncle, James Whitten; he had two children—Benjamin, who married the daughter of Peter Carney, of Upper Penn's Neck; and Mary Cripps, who married Peter Andrews, a native of Egg Harbor.

the father of the before mentioned children, died in 1807, in his twenty-sixth year. He resided, at the time of his death, in Lower Penn's Neck, where his children were born. Mary Shourds married William Bradway, the son of Ezra and Mary Denn Bradway, of Lower Alloways Creek; they have six children—Elizabeth, Sarah, Mary, Anna, Rachel and Ellen Bradway. Thomas Shourds was born 28th of 2d month, 1805, and married Sarah, the daughter of Joseph and Ann Mason Thompson, 10th of 1st month, 1828. Joseph Thompson, her father, was the son of Joshua Thompson, a native of Elsinboro, and the great grand-son of Andrew Thompson, the emigrant, who landed at Elsinboro in 1677. Ann Mason, wife of Joseph Thompson, was the daughter of John Mason, who was the son of Thomas Mason, and he was the son of John Mason, who emigrated from England and landed at Philadelphia in 1684; (he, however, came and settled at Salem soon afterwards.) Thomas and Sarah Thompson Shourds had eight children—Anna T., Samuel, (who died when about twenty months old,) Thompson, Samuel, 2d, Thomas M., Elizabeth T., Sarah W. and Mary Carpenter Shourds. Samuel Shourds, 2d, died when he was in his nineteenth year. Sarah Ware Shourds died when she was in her twenty-first year. Elizabeth Thompson Shourds died when she was about thirty-one years old. Thompson, the son of Thomas and Sarah T. Shourds, is a carpenter and builder, and follows that business in Philadelphia. He married Rachel, the daughter of Comly and Susan Tyson; they have had three children—William, Anna T. and Susan T. Rachel, his wife, is deceased, as also their oldest child, Willie Shourds. Thomas Mason Shourds, the son of Thomas and Sarah T. Shourds, married Anna, the daughter of Joseph and Mary Brown, of Alloways Creek; they have three children—Sarah W., Mary and Thompson Shourds.

SUMMERILL FAMILY.

The Summerill's are a large and ancient family of Upper Penn's Neck. The most reliable account of the family is that William Summerill and Thomas Carney emigrated from Ireland about 1725, and settled in Penn's Neck, Salem county. William Summerill, soon after his arrival, purchased a large tract of land near the present brick mill at the head of Game creek, extending to Salem creek. He and his wife, Mary Summerill, resided on that part now owned by Benjamin and Rebecca Summerill Black, (she having inherited the property from her father.) They had two sons—Joseph and John. When his children were young he had the misfortune of losing his wife; soon after which he left the township of Penn's Neck and settled in Pittsgrove, and there married a widow by the name of Elwell. By this wife he had two daughters, one of whom subsequently married a Newkirk, the parents of Garrett and Matthew Newkirk, of mercantile fame of Philadelphia. An incident, relating to the introduction of those eminent men into business life in Philadelphia, was related to the writer more than thirty years ago by an aged physician, then a resident of Pittsgrove. He said the father of Garrett and Matthew Newkirk was in the practice of going to Philadelphia market with his poultry once in a year, which was common among the farmers of Salem county at that time. On one of his trips his eldest daughter accompanied him for the purpose of buying a new bonnet, soon after they arrived in the city, she went to one of the milliners and purchased herself one, and whilst waiting for it to be trimmed to her liking, she was impressed with the idea that she would be glad to have the opportunity of learning the trade before she left. She asked the milliner in attendance if she would be willing to take her to learn the trade; the milliner replied in the affirmative, but when she mentioned the matter to her father he discouraged and desired her not to undertake it. But her mind was settled upon it; she told her father that if he would pay her board whilst learning the trade, that would be all of his estate she wanted. He at last consented. After she had learned the business she set up on her own account, and in a few years accumulated a fortune. At the death of her father she obtained a situation in one of the dry good stores for her eldest brother Garrett, and in a short time afterwards she found a situation for her younger brother, Matthew; both of them eventually became successful and wealthy merchants in their adopted city. William Summerill, the emigrant, died in Pittsgrove, at a very advanced age.

Joseph, the eldest son of William and Mary Summerill, settled in Wilmington, Delaware, and engaged in the shipping and blacksmithing business. He married and had two sons and two daughters; both of his daughters married sea captains. His sons, Joseph and Nehemiah, became merchants in Philadelphia, but finally failed, causing, also, the failure of their father. After which they removed to the interior of Pennsylvania, where, it is said, some of their family still remains. John, the youngest son of William and Mary Summerill, married Naomi Carney, daughter of Thomas and Mary Carney, of Carney's Point. The Carney's purchased a large tract of land on the Delaware river, being part of the Bowtown tract of 1640 acres, that formerly belonged to Matthias Nelson, he being a Swede. John and his wife, Naomi C. Summerill, owned and lived on the property that his father purchased when he first settled in New Jersey. It is now owned and occupied by Benjamin and Rebecca S. Black, as before mentioned. The old mansion house was burned during the war of the Revolution by a marauding party from the British fleet that was lying in the Delaware river opposite Helms Cove. There is now a large iron pot in the possession of the Summerill family, that was in the old family mansion when it was burned; it certainly is quite a centennial relic. John Summerill, 1st, died comparatively a young man, leaving a widow and four sons—John, Jr., Joseph, Thomas and William, and two daughters—Mary and Rebecca. Naomi, their mother, proved a parent indeed. She remained and carried on farming, and raised and educated her six children. She never married again.

John Summerill, 2d, married Christiana Holton; they had nine children. James and Josiah died minors. Their father was a successful agriculturist, and at his death was the owner of a large quantity of excellent land in the township of Upper Penn's Neck. He lived to be nearly fourscore years, leaving four sons and three daughters—John, 3d, Naomi, Garnett, William, Ann, Rebecca and Joseph C. Joseph Summerill, the second son of John, 1st, married Mary Linmin; they had two children—William and Mary; both of whom are deceased. William Summerill, son of Joseph, married Elizabeth A. Crispin. He purchased the James Mason farm, in Mannington, near Salem, and resided thereon until his death. He left a large family of children. Most of William Summerill's children's names I have no knowledge of, excepting three of his sons—James, Robert and Henry, who are residents of Upper Pittsgrove. William's widow is still living. Mary, the daughter of Joseph and Mary L. Summerill, married Stephen Straughn. He is deceased. Thomas, the son of John and Naomi Carney Summerill, married Elizabeth Borden; they are both deceased, dying young, and leaving a family of young children, who are all deceased excepting two daughters—Hannah and Elizabeth Paul. One of the sons was married, and left two sons, who are in business in Philadelphia. Hannah, the daughter of Thomas and Elizabeth B. Summerill, married Samuel Holton; she is deceased, leaving one son. Elizabeth, daughter of Thomas Summerill, married Somers Barber; the latter is deceased, and leaves two children, both living. William, son of John and Naomi Summerill, died a young man, unmarried. Mary, daughter of John and Naomi Summerill, was twice married; her first husband's name was Clark, and after his death she married John Holton; they left three sons—Thomas, Samuel and Andrew Holton; the last named is living; the two oldest brothers are deceased.

John Summerill, 2d, died in 1854, and left seven children. The eldest son, John Summerill, 3d, died in 1865, aged sixty-two years. He was above mediocrity in mental abilities. In early life he became an active politician, was elected to the State Legislature when a young man, and was subsequently chosen a State Senator and served the full term with entire satisfaction to his constituents. He was affable and very pleasing in his manner. His wife was Emily Parker. At his death he left two sons—John, 4th, and Joseph C. Summerill, both of whom are store keepers and large dealers in grain at Helms Cove, a short distance below Pennsgrove. There their father commenced the same business in 1829.

Naomi, the daughter of John, 2d, and Christiana H. Summerill, married Robert, the son of James and Elizabeth Newell. Robert and his wife since their marriage, reside in the township of Mannington. They have three sons and one daughter living. John S. Newell, their eldest son, married Emma, the daughter of William Morris, late of Sharpstown; they have one child—Robert. Their daughter, Josephine, married Edward A. Vanneman, of Upper Penn's Neck; her husband is deceased, leaving children. The two younger sons of Robert and Naomi Newell are Robert, Jr., and James. Garnett, the second son of John and Christiana Summerill, is a farmer, and owns and resides on the property that was formerly owned and occupied by Peter Carney, the youngest son of Thomas Carney, Sr. Garnett married Mary Borden, of Sharpstown. They had four children—James, Annie, William G. and John, M. D. James is deceased; Annie married Henry M. Wright; William J. and John M. Summerill are unmarried. William, the third son of John and Christiana Summerill, married Hannah Vanneman. He resides in Upper Penn's Neck. He and his wife have two sons—Josiah and Daniel V. Summerill, both of whom are married, and reside on farms near Pennsgrove. William Summerill does a large amount of public business in his native county, having been, and is at the present time, one of the Judges of the Salem County Courts, and is also one of the Directors of the Canal Meadow Company. This canal was projected as early as 1801 by John Moore White and Michael Wayne, two eminent lawyers of West Jersey, who, at that time, owned a large tract of low lands and meadow bordering on Salem creek. They, in conjunction with the late Joseph Reeve, who resided near Sharpstown, made an application to the State Legislature for a law to cut a navigable canal for a two-fold purpose. The said canal was intended to carry off the waters that flowed down the upper branches of Salem creek into the river, instead of a circuitous route of more than twenty miles to the Delaware river by the course of Salem creek, and only two miles and four rods by the canal. The contemplated canal was dug, but proved a failure. It was attempted about thirty years ago to open it deeper, but it was soon abandoned as impracticable. Some seven years since, there was an application made to the State Legislature for a new law for the purpose of taxing all the owners of the low lands and meadows that lay above John Denn's canal to the head of tide water, for the purpose of defraying the expenses of digging a canal large enough for navigation, and also, to stop the creek some distance below the contemplated canal. The meadow was surveyed by three commissioners chosen for that purpose, which survey amounted to seven or eight thousand acres, and a tax assessed on said meadow by a second set of commissioners elected for that purpose, agreeable to their law. The Directors decided in cutting the new canal on the site of the old one, about half a mile below Hawk's Bridge, that was dug nearly seventy years previous. Through the energy and perseverance of Elisha Bassett, William Summerill, George Biddle, David Pettit and Robert Walker, the work was commenced and the canal was completed so as to be navigable, and Salem creek completely stopped about fifty rods below the canal, where it empties into Salem creek. This public work was undertaken through great opposition by some of the owners of land that lay bordering on Salem creek, notwithstanding it is likely to prove one of the greatest public benefits that was ever undertaken and fully consummated of the kind in Salem county. In regard to navigation it enables owners of land in Upper Penn's Neck, a large part of Mannington and Pilesgrove townships, as well as the owners of extensive meadows and low lands, that lie below the dam, to send the products of their farms to market without much cost, or labor. The complete draining by the canal makes their meadows more than two-fold profitable than heretofore.

Ann, the daughter of John and Christiana Summerill, married Elias Kaighn, of Camden. The latter is deceased, leaving one daughter, but his widow is now living at Helm's Cove, Upper Penn's Neck. Rebecca, the daughter of John and Christiana Summerill, married Benjamin Black; they own and reside on the old homestead farm of the Summerill's, as heretofore mentioned. They have two sons and two daughters. Joseph, the youngest son of John and Christiana Summerill, is a Methodist clergyman, of which religious society, I think, most of the Summerill family are members. Joseph married Sarah I. Vanneman, and has six children, three daughters and three sons—Hannah, Christiana, Louisa, Joseph C., Thomas C. and Daniel Vanneman Summerill. At the death of Thomas Carney, 1st, he left two sons—Thomas and Peter Carney, and two or three daughters. He, as was the custom in that day, devised all his real estate to his sons; his daughters, particularly Naomi, his eldest daughter, who married John Summerill, 1st, did not heir any of her father's real estate. Thomas Carney, Jr., left one daughter to inherit his large estate, who afterward married the late Robert G. Johnson, of Salem. Peter Carney, the brother of Thomas, left two daughters; one of them married Benjamin Cripps, of Mannington; the other daughter married John Tuft, of Salem, but died young, leaving one son—Sinnickson Tuft. There is a singular circumstance connected with the Carney and Summerill families that does not often occur. Naomi Carney Summerill's descendants, now, after a lapse of nearly a century, owns the larger part of the landed estate that belonged to her two brothers, Thomas and Peter Carney, including several large and valuable farms.

SHARP FAMILY.

The Sharps are an ancient family of the South of England. They held a large landed estate in Tilbury, in Gloucester, near the city of Bristol. Anthony Sharp, the subject of this sketch, being the eldest son of that lineage of the Sharps, inherited the great landed estate of the family, in the county of Gloucester. He was born about 1630, and early in life became convinced of the doctrines of George Fox; likewise one or two of his younger brothers became members of the persecuted religious sect, called Friends or Quakers. Anthony Sharp, the eldest brother, emigrated from Tilbury, England, in the time of Cromwell, and settled in Queens county, Ireland, and purchased a large county seat called Roundwood, near Mount Mellick. That was his home, although he resided and did an extensive mercantile business in the city of Dublin. The estate called Roundwood is still in the possession of the Irish branch of the Sharp family to this day. Anthony Sharp purchased a large landed estate in East and West Jersey. On the 22d of 4th month, 1681, he bought of Roger Roberts, of Dublin, the one-tenth part of the one-hundredth part of West New Jersey. Again in a deed, dated 16th of 9th month, 1700, he purchased of Henry Mason and Elizabeth his wife, and William Barnard, the sixteenth of the twentieth part of the one-hundredth part; he likewise bought of the same parties the following day the tenth part of the one-hundredth part of West New Jersey. Anthony Sharp also purchased of Thomas Warner, of Dublin, the one-third part of the one-half part of John Haywood's, one of the East Jersey proprietors. The deed was dated 14th of 10th month, 1682. The said John Haywood, William Penn, Gwinn Laurie, Robert Barclay, and eight others, all being members of the Society of Friends, bought from George Carterett East New Jersey. The said John Haywood sold his one-twelfth to Thomas Warner, of Dublin, for £350 sterling; not for himself alone, but including in that transaction, as equal parties, were Anthony Sharp and Samuel Claridge; both of these were citizens of Dublin. A division was made of the one-third part each owned, that being in 1682. Afterwards Anthony Sharp purchased of Samuel Claridge one-half part of his original one-third of John Haywood's moiety, as one-half part of the original one-twelfth of East New Jersey. This deed bears date 20th of 2d month, 1694.

Anthony Sharp, the elder, had three sons—Isaac, Joseph and Daniel, and one daughter—Rachel Sharp. He died in the year 1707, and was buried in the ancient Friends' burying-ground in the city of Dublin. Isaac, the eldest son of Anthony, married and had three sons—Anthony, Isaac and Joseph Sharp, and four daughters; their names were Mary, Sarah Mason, Rachel and Margaret Sharp. Anthony, the eldest son of Isaac Sharp, married and had two children, one of whom whose name was Isaac, died during his minority. The daughter, Francis Sharp, married Luke Flood, of Queens county, Ireland. The family of Floods are an ancient family of both England and Ireland Francis and her husband resided on the great landed estate called Roundwood, that was owned by the first Anthony Sharp. Mary, the daughter of Isaac Sharp, probably died unmarried. Her sister Sarah Mason Sharp, married a person by the name of Daniel Delaney, and Margaret, the youngest daughter of Isaac Sharp, married a man by the name of Hill; they afterwards emigrated to America. Anthony Sharp, 1st, bequeathed to his third son, Daniel Sharp, and his heirs in male line in the order of primogeniture, one-fourth part of his lands in East Jersey. He bequeathed to his second son Joseph, and his heirs in the male line, one-fourth part of all his lands in East New Jersey, and in default of such issue to his eldest son Isaac Sharp.

Joseph Sharp, second son of Anthony, married Catharine Sewage of Ireland, had one daughter. Isaac, the second brother of Anthony, 2d, emigrated to America, and settled in West Jersey, at a place called Blessington, now known as Sharpstown. He brought the frame of his house with him from Ireland, and the site where he built his house is on the farm owned at the present time by Joseph Robinson. The tract is known as " The Park" to this day by the old inhabitants in that section. It is probable that the said Isaac Sharp emigrated about the year 1730. He was appointed Judge of the Court of Salem county, by George II., King of England, 1741. This is the copy:
"George the Second, by the Grace of God, of Great Britain,
"France and Ireland, King, Defender of the Faith, and to our
"trusty and well beloved Isaac Sharp, Esq., Greeting: We,
"reposing especial trust and confidence in your integrity, pru-
"dence, and ability, have assigned, constituted and appointed,

"and we do by these presents assign, constitute and appoint you, the said Isaac Sharp, to be our officer, Judge of Inferior Court of Common Pleas, to be held in and for our county of Salem, in our Province of New Jersey, giving and hereby granting to you the said Isaac Sharp, full power and authority to exercise and enjoy all power and jurisdiction, belonging to the said Court, and to hear, try and determine all causes, and quarrels which is recognizable in our said Court, and to award execution therein accordingly. In testimony whereof, we have caused the Great Seal of our said Province of New Jersey to be hereunto affixed. Witness our trusty and well beloved Lewis Morris, Esq., Captain General and Governor-in-chief over our said Province of Nova Cesaviea, or New Jersey, and the territories therein depending in America, and Vice Admiral in the same, and at our city of Perth Amboy, the sixteenth day of August, in the eighteenth year of our reign, Anno Domini, 1741.   HOLME."

Isaac Sharp married a daughter of Thomas Lambert, who resided near the falls of the river Delaware, in the county of Burlington, previous, however, to the marriage of his father. Isaac, then residing on his country-seat, in Ireland, called Roundwood, made a settlement on him, it being six hundred acres on land at Blessington, situated in the township of Pilesgrove, in the county of Salem, and all other (his) the said Isaac Sharp's lands in the said county of Salem, and likewise one moiety, or half of all other the said Isaac Sharp's lands within the said province of East and West New Jersey, in America, except 1050 acres of land on Cooper's creek, in the county of Gloucester, known by the name of Rush Hill; also all the said Isaac Sharp's personal estate in the county of Salem, or elsewhere in America. Isaac Sharp, the emigrant and his wife, had three sons and five daughters; their names were Samuel, Edward, Anthony, Mary, Jaiel, Hannah D., Sarah, Rachel Wyncoop, and Elizabeth Sharp. The time of the death of Isaac Sharp, the father of the above mentioned children, is not mentioned; probably before the year 1770. I think his name is not mentioned in Salem County Court records after that date. He had a birth right in the Society of Friends, and he continued to be a member during his long and active life.

Anthony, the youngest son of Isaac Sharp, of Sharpstown, espoused the part of the patriots during the Revolutionary struggle. He lay concealed in the barn whilst the British were in the neighborhood of his home, and Samuel Humphries, the projenitor of the present families of Humphreys, then a small boy, carried provisions to him in his place of refuge. He, however emerged from his retreat, and went with Dr. Ebenezer Elmer, (the father of Judge L. Q. C. Elmer,) of Bridgeton, to Fort Ticonderoga, to participate in the engagements on the frontier. It was here that, although a Quaker, he attained the rank of Colonel in the army; and his name now stands coupled with the above grade on the roster of the officers of the American forces. When driven from their home the silver plate and other valuables of the Sharps, of Sharpstown, were conveyed across the Delaware river to their relatives, the Delaneys, who resided at Wilmington, Delaware. The man who rowed the boat was named Jonas Keen, and he related the circumstance on his death bed as one that had made a deep impression on his memory. The said Jonas Keen lived to the very advanced age of ninety years, and has descendants now residing in Salem.

Edward, the second son of Isaac Sharp, the emigrant, as stated before, married Martha Thompson, of Sussex county, East Jersey. She was the daughter of Colonel Mark Thompson, of Marksboro, in the above county, and who served with the rank of Colonel in the Revolutionary army. Whilst engaged under General Dickinson, at the battle of Princeton, he was severely wounded, and was carried under the same tree to which the soldiers had taken General Mercer. Dr. Jacob Thompson Sharp, formerly of Salem, grandson of Colonel Mark Thompson, alluded to above, was (until children were born to him by his wife, Hannah Ann Smith, of Philadelphia,) the sole surviving representative of the family of Sharp's, who emigrated to Salem county from Ireland; which is confirmed by the report of Mr. Gifford before the Historical Society of New Jersey, at Newark, several years ago, which expressly states that the above assertion is true. There are other families bearing the same name in Salem county, likewise in New Jersey, which are remote from the Sharps of Blessington, or Sharpstown. Edward Sharp alone married, the others dying without issue. He married the daughter of Mark Thompson, as before stated; they had four sons—Samuel, Jacob Thompson, Breckenridge and Edward Sharp, and one daughter—Mary; all of whom died before attaining their majority, except Jacob Thompson Sharp, who studied medicine and practiced that profession many years, in both East and West Jersey; and now resides in Cumberland county. He married, as before stated, Hannah Ann, daughter of Edward Smith, a prominent merchant of Philadelphia, and a native of Salem county, as were likewise his ancestors for several generations. Dr. Jacob Thompson and his wife, Hannah Ann Sharp, had six children, four of whom are still living, viz: Dr. Edward S. Sharp, of Salem; Sallie M. Westcott, of Bridgeton, Alexander Henry Sharp, a lawyer of Atlantic county, and Thomas M. Sharp, Esq., of Port Elizabeth, Cumberland county Martha Thompson Sharp and Jacob Thompson Sharp are deceased.

Joseph Sharp, younger brother of Isaac Sharp, of Blessington, near Salem, resided at the same place and doubtless emigrated from Ireland simultaneously with his brother Isaac. Isaac Sharp, 1st, did by his last will, bearing date 15th of 3d month, 1734, give to his two sons, Isaac and Joseph, all his lands whatsoever in East and West Jersey, ratifying and confirming the above mentioned conveyance to his father by Thomas Warner to his heirs and assigns forever.

William, the younger brother of Anthony Sharp, born in Gloucestershire, England, married a young woman by the name of Covert; they had a son by the name of Thomas Sharp. Anthony Sharp, his uncle, gave to him, who was then about emigrating to America, and in consideration of his, Thomas Sharp, looking after Anthony Sharp's possession, there for his ease and best advantage; he, the said Anthony Sharp, granted and confirmed unto him, and his heirs, something over 1,000 acres that Anthony Sharp bought of Roger Roberts, of Dublin, in 1681; and the deed of conveyance was made the same year. This property was located on the King's Highway; Salem County Alms House farm is part of it. Thomas Sharp had a son Isaac, who built in the first decade of the eighteenth century a large and substantial brick dwelling, which is still standing, in good repair. William Austin is now the owner. That family of Sharps, like those of Sharpstown, had a large deer park, which is still visible.

Thomas, the father of Isaac Sharp, had a family burying ground, which was common at the first settlement of this country. John Fenwick was buried there; the reason assigned was—Fenwick was desirous to lay with his wife's relatives, the mother of his children, she being a cousin of Thomas Sharp. Isaac, the son of Thomas Sharp, was one of the Justices of Salem court from the year 1709 to 1739; he was an active and useful member of Salem Meeting of Friends. Thomas Chalkley mentions in his journal being at the house of his worthy friend Isaac Sharp, in 1730. Isaac's descendants are not numerous; he had a grandson that married Grace Bassett; their children were—Abraim and William Sharp. Dr. Griffith who resided in Salem a number of years ago, married a lady of that family. No part of the large and valuable estate of the Sharp's family belong to their descendants at the present time.

JOHN SMITH (OF SMITHFIELD) FAMILY.

John Smith, the son of William Smith, was one of Fenwick's executors. He was born in the county of Kent, in England, in the year 1645. In 1673 he married Susannah Marcy, daughter of Edward Marcy, and in 1685 he and his wife, together with a number of emigrants, embarked for America on board the ship Ariel, Edmund Baily master. They landed at New Castle in the 4th month of the same year. In the 6th month following, he came to Salem, in West New Jersey, and purchased 1,000 acres of land of Samuel and Anna Hedge, in Upper Mannington, it being one-half of the Hedgefield allotment, and there he made his permanent home. From that time it was known as Smithfield. It has been said he was a relative and also an immediate friend of John Fenwick. I presume this was the reason he was made one of Fenwick's executors, notwithstanding he had not arrived in this country at the time of his death. It is generally admitted by those familiar with the characters of the first settlers, that he had more than ordinary intellect and business capacities. He and his wife had two children born in England, who died the first year after they arrived in this country. Their children born in America were Susanna Smith, born in Mannington 8th of 8th month, 1689; Joseph Smith, their eldest son born in 1691; John Smith, Jr., born in 1693; Samuel Smith, born in 1696; and Elizabeth Smith, born 3d of 3d month, 1703. She married Judge John Bacon, of Bacon's Neck. Joseph Smith, the son of John and Susanna Smith, married and had one son—Thomas Smith, who in 1740 married Sarah, the daughter of Elisha and Abigail Bassett, of Pilesgrove; they had three sons, the eldest was William, born 31st of 8th month, 1741. He married Sarah, the daughter of James Chambless, Jr., of Alloways Creek; their children were Mary, Charles, William, James, Beulah, Clement and Atilla Smith. Mary, the eldest, married John Ellet, son of Charles and Hannah Carpenter Ellet; their children were Hannah C. and Maria Chambless Ellet, the latter remains single and resides in Salem. Hannah Carpenter Ellet was twice married, her first husband was George W. Smith, of Virginia; they had issue, one son—Charles P. Smith. Her second husband was Joseph E. Brown, the son of Joseph and Ann Allen Brown; they had issue, two sons. James Smith, son of William and Sarah Chambless Smith, married Hannah, the daughter of Jediah and Hannah Carpenter Allen, of Mannington; their children are Sarah Ann and Mary Smith. Clement, the youngest son of William and Sarah Smith, married Hannah, the daughter of William and Catharine Low Tyler, of Salem; they had one son—Clement Smith. Beulah, daughter of William and Sarah Smith, married Joseph H. Wilson, of Philadelphia; their children were Mary, William, Emeline, James, Harlin, Louisa and Sarah Wilson. Charles, William and Atilla Smith, never married.

David Smith, the second son of Thomas and Sarah Bassett Smith, was born 17th of 7th month, 1744. He married Mary, the daughter of James, Jr., and Mary Oakford Chambless, sister to his brother William's wife. They had no issue. David was a hatter by trade and followed his business in the town of Salem during his life. He adopted his nephew, the son of Thomas Smith, and made him the heir of his estate. David, the son of Thomas, married Martha, the daughter of Thomas Jones, of Salem. They had issue, three children—Mary, James and Arabella; one of whom married Samuel, the eldest son of Samuel and Eliza Clement; the other married a son of Judge Hornblower, of East Jersey.

Thomas, the youngest son of Thomas and Sarah Bassett, was born 25th of 1st month, 1747. He married Hannah Shillis; their children were Elisha, Stephen and David Smith. Elisha married and left heirs—Stephen, Eliza and Ellen Smith. Stephen married Mary W. Jones, of Philadelphia; their children were Sarah, James, Thomas, Charles, Elizabeth, Chambless, Clement and Isaac Smith.

In 1718 Samuel Smith married Hannah Giles. Their son, Giles Smith, was born 18th of 10th month, 1719, and their daughter Hannah Smith was born in 1721. She, in 1742, married Preston Carpenter, the son of Samuel Carpenter, and grandson of Samuel Carpenter, Sr., who arrived in Philadelphia in 1683, in company with his brother, Joshua Carpenter, and other emigrants, and who was one of the first merchants in that city, and in the year 1700 was computed to be the richest man, except the proprietor, in the province of Pennsylvania, but towards the close of his life he met with several heavy losses, and his estate was considerably reduced before he died.

Preston Carpenter and his wife had, I think, seven children—Thomas, Elizabeth, William, Hannah, Margaret, Mary and Martha. Thomas married a young woman in Gloucester whose maiden name was Tonkins. They were the grand-parents of Judge Thomas Carpenter, of Camden. Willim Carpenter's first wife was Elizabeth Wyatt, daughter of Bartholomew, 3d. His second wife was Mary Redman, daughter of John Redman. Elizabeth Carpenter married Ezra Firth, son of John Firth. Margaret Carpenter married James Mason Woodruff. Hannah Carpenter's first husband was Charles Ellet; her second husband was Jedediah Allen. Mary Carpenter married Samuel Tonkins. Martha Carpenter married Joseph Reeve.

Elizabeth Smith, youngest daughter of John Smith, of Smithfield, was born in 1703, and married John Bacon, of Cohansey, in 1720. He was, I believe, the son of Samuel Bacon They had seven children, named respectively Thomas, John, Elizabeth, David, Martha, Mary and Job. Thomas Bacon, the oldest son, was born in 1721, and was the father of Charles and John Bacon. Charles married and settled on his father's property in Bacon's Neck, Greenwich township. They had five children. Thomas, married a young woman in Mannington by the name of Wright. They both died young, and left one son, the present Thomas Bacon, formerly of Mannington. Benjamin's second son married a young woman in Gloucester county by the name of Allen. They had two children. His second wife was Susan Dallas, daughter of Jonathan Dallas. David Bacon, their third son, never married, and was a merchant in the town of Salem for several years, but after a time he removed to Woodstown and there ended his days, leaving a legacy to Pilesgrove Monthly Meeting for them to erect a school house, which is now known as Bacon's School. Charles Bacon never married, and died at an advanced age on his farm in Bacon's Neck. Rachel Bacon married a Sheppard. She was the mother of the late Moses Sheppard of Greenwich. John Bacon came to this county and made it his home. After a time he married Hannah Denn, daughter of Paul Denn, of Alloways Creek. They had five children—Thomas, Eleanor, Martha, Hannah and John.

Elizabeth Bacon married John Denn of Alloways Creek, and was the mother of the late John Denn, of Mannington. David Bacon learned the hat trade in Philadelphia, and made his permanent home in that city, where he followed his trade the greater part of his life and amassed a fortune. He married and left two children—Joseph and Hannah Bacon. Joseph Bacon the son of David Bacon, married and had four sons named Thomas, David, Joseph and Samuel Bacon. Hannah the daughter of David Bacon, married Jonathan Evans. They were the parents of the late Thomas Evans, who married Catherine Wistar, the daughter of John Wistar, of this county. Job Bacon, the youngest son of John and Elizabeth S. Bacon, was born 1735, and married Mary Stewart, daughter of John Stewart, of Alloways Creek. They had three children—Job, Elizabeth and George Bacon. Job Bacon, their son, had two children by his first wife—John and Martha Bacon. His second wife was Ruth Thompson, daughter of John Thompson, of Elsinborough. They had four children named respectively Mary, Sarah, Ann and Josiah Bacon. Mary was the first wife of Clement Acton, of Salem; Sarah remains single and resides at Greenwich; Ann married Moses Sheppard; Josiah Bacon went into the mercantile business in Philadelphia. It is believed that he has accumulated a large fortune. He is one of the Pennsylvania Railroad directors. The widow of Job Bacon, Sr., Mary S. Bacon, married Richard Wood, Jr. He was born in Stoe Creek township, Cumberland county, as it is now called, in 1728. He was the son of Richard Wood, who purchased 1,000 acres of land and built himself a brick house, as early as 1725, which is still standing. He died in the year 1759, and was buried in his own family burying ground on his farm. I have been informed that his great grandson, Professor George B. Wood, of Philadelphia, has erected a small marble monument in the old family graveyard to the memory of his great ancestor.

Elizabeth, daughter of Job and Mary Bacon, married Richard Wood, 3d. He was born 7th of 2d month, 1755. Elizabeth was his second wife. He was a successful merchant in the town of Greenwich, and had six children—Professor George Bacon Wood, Richard, Charles, Horatio, Ann Elizabeth and Hannah Wood. At the death of Richard Wood, 3d, the poor and afflicted lost a valuable friend. He was ever ready to administer to their necessities; so much so that his name in Greenwich and in the country around is held in grateful remembrance by the inhabitants to the present day. He told his wife a few years before his death to always look after the poor, and remarked that there was no danger but there would be enough attention paid to the rich. The case of this truly great man reminds me of the wise man, who said he never knew the righteous forsaken or his children begging bread. This saying has been verified respecting Richard Wood's children, as they have all been successful in life in a remarkable degree as to this world's goods, also a very respectable standing in general society.

George Bacon, son of Job Bacon and Mary, his wife, married Naomi Tyler. They had four children—Ezra, George, Francis and Mary Bacon. He was a partner in the mercantile business with his brother-in-law, Richard Wood, several years, and he was far above ordinary men in his conversational powers, easy in his address, and without ostentation, which made his company very agreeable and interesting. He wielded a great influence for good in the town of Greenwich, and in society generally in which he associated. He died at an advanced age greatly regretted by all who knew him.

STRETCH FAMILY.

Joseph Stretch emigrated to this country from England about the year 1695. In the year 1700 he married Hannah, the youngest daughter of Edward and Mary Bradway, who was born in New Salem, the 7th of 7th month, 1681. Joseph and his wife settled on the southern portion of a tract of land which her father had purchased of the heirs of John Fenwick, containing 900 acres of fast land and meadow. The said tract was below the Salter line, now known as Stoe Neck. About the year 1720, William Bradway, the son of Edward, had a brick dwelling erected on his part of the property, and his nephew, Bradway Stretch, built himself a brick dwelling about the size of his uncle's, on the property he inherited from his mother, about the year 1740. There are standing at this time six brick dwellings, all in sight of each other, which were erected in the fore part of the last century,—Daniel's, Bradway's, Stretch's, Padgett's, Butcher's and Richard Wood's. They are located on the head of the tide waters of the Unknown or Stoe creek. The early emigrants universally made the first clearings and settled on the navigable streams. I presume for two good causes—the first was there were but few public highways, and they poorly kept up for traveling, and what traveling they did do was on horseback; the second was by living near to navigation they could more readily get their produce to market in vessels and boats. There was a more important cause than either before mentioned: our hardy pioneers of the wilderness being men of judgment and enterprise, soon discovered the most fertile lands lay bordering on the navigable streams and their tributaries, which, I think, is the case in the counties of Salem and Cumberland.

Joseph and Hannah Stretch had two sons—Bradway, born 11th of 3d month, 1702, and Joseph, born in 1704. Bradway subsequently married Sarah, the daughter of John and Mary Chambless Hancock, born 15th of 11th month, 1701. They were married in 1724, and had eight children—Hannah, William, David, James, Sarah, Mary, Bradway and Eleanor

Stretch. William, the eldest son of Bradway and Sarah, married and left one son, John Stretch, who married a Finley. He afterwards sold his part of the Stoe Neck property to his nephew, John Finley. James, the son of Bradway and Sarah, born 4th of 4th month, 1793, married Elizabeth Evans. She inherited the brick house farm which belonged to her father, a short distance below Harmersville. (The farm belongs at the present time to Peter E. Harris.) At that place James and his wife commenced life. They had three children—James, Dorcas and Rachel. James' second wife was a widow by the name of Allen; they had no issue. James lived to reach about eighty-seven years. His son James had two wives. The name of the first I never learned; she lived but a short time after marriage. His second wife was Mary, daughter of Asa Jefferies; they had several children. A short time after his father's death he sold the property inherited from his parents and removed with his family to Indiana. He and his wife are both deceased, leaving, I understand, a large estate to their children. Two of their sons studied law, and are successful in their profession. Dorcas, the daughter of James and Elizabeth Stretch, married Samuel, the son of Edward and Hannah Pancoast. They were natives of Burlington county, but subsequently removed to Gloucester, and there ended their days, leaving a family of eleven children—Joseph, Elizabeth, Eliakim, James, Hannah, Samuel, William, Dorcas, Josiah, Charles and Anna. Joseph married Susan, the daughter of Joseph and Ann Thompson; their children are mentioned in the Thompson family. Elizabeth's husband was Malichi Horner, of Gloucester, who is deceased; they had no issue. Eliakim kept a feed and flour store for a number of years in Philadelphia, and married Tacy Roberts, of Byberry; they had issue. John and Mary Pancoast both died young. The parents of the above mentioned children are deceased. James was a bricklayer, and followed his trade in Philadelphia during his life. He married and left several children. Hannah, the second daughter, possessed great natural abilities, a logical mind, a remarkably mild temperament, and conversational powers above mediocrity. The poet truly wrote:

> There is many a gem that is born to bloom unseen
> And waste its sweetness on the desert air.

She married Townsend, the son of Reuben Hilliard. He was a carpenter, and carried on his trade in Philadelphia. They had nine children—Elizabeth, Samuel, Joseph, Hannah, Reuben,

Anna, William, Mary and Charles. Hannah P., the mother, died several years ago of that loathsome and painful disease—cancer, which appears to be hereditary in the Pancoast family. Her husband is still living. All of their children (each of whom evinced uncommon intellect) are deceased excepting Anna, who married Bennett Smedley. Samuel, the son of Samuel and Dorcas Pancoast, was sent in early life to Philadelphia to learn the carpenter trade. After his term of apprenticeship expired, he followed the business several years with success. He married Mary, the daughter of Enoch and Beulah Allen; she lived but a short time, leaving no issue. His second wife is Malenia Skirms, whose parents lived near Trenton, New Jersey. Samuel and his wife have four children—Allen, Mary, Eveline and Charles. Allen Pancoast's wife is Eliza Denfield; they have issue. Mary Pancoast married Oliver Lund; they have issue. The younger children are unmarried. Samuel was a member of the Legislature of Pennsylvania for two or three terms. For many years of his life he pursued the business of buying and selling real estate in the city of Philadelphia. He has now retired from business and from public life, possessed of a competency, and lives at his country seat at Tioga. William Pancoast, his brother, died a young man unmarried. Dorcas, the daughter of Samuel and Dorcas Pancoast, is living with her relatives in Philadelphia, unmarried. Josiah Pancoast removed when a young man to one of the Southern States, and died in a short time unmarried. Charles, the youngest son of Samuel and Dorcas Pancoast, resides in Philadelphia, where he has been an Alderman for a number of years. He married Harriet Merrill, a widow, a native of Massachusetts. Charles and his wife have no issue. Anna, the youngest daughter of Samuel and Dorcas, was very precocious in acquiring an education, and was a teacher in the Philadelphia schools the greater part of her life. She subsequently married William Keyser, an eminent teacher in that city, a native of Bucks county, Pennsylvania. They had one daughter—Eveline Keyser. William died not many years after his marriage of pulmonary consumption. Her second husband was Henry Maguire; they had one child—Jenny. Anna is now deceased, dying of the same disease of which her husband died. Samuel Pancoast, father of the above mentioned children, died in Elsinborough, in 1833, of Asiatic cholera, which he contracted while in Philadelphia on a visit to his children. Soon after that event his widow, Dorcas Pancoast, removed to Philadelphia and made her home with one of her daughters; she lived to nearly fourscore years.

Hannah, the daughter of Bradway and Sarah Stretch, born 6th of 2d month, 1725, married Wade Barker. They had issue, a daughter, Hannah Barker, who subsequently married Robert Watson; her second husband was James Sayres. Rachel Sayres, their eldest child, married a man by the name of Gilman, a native of Cumberland county. Sarah, the daughter of Bradway and Sarah Stretch, born 14th of 2d month, 1736, married Samuel Scudders; they had issue. (They were the great-grand-parents of William Evans Scudder, who keeps store at Hancock's Bridge at the present time.) Mary, the daughter of Bradway and Sarah Stretch, born 24th of 2d month, 1736, married a Corliss. They had issue, Jacob Corliss, who subsequently married and died a young man, leaving one son, Benjamin Corliss, who inherited the farm that Jervis Hires now owns, located near the village of Canton. Mary S. Corliss, the mother of Jacob, departed this life 2d of 6th month, aged over sixty-seven years. Eleanor, the daughter of Bradway and Sarah Stretch, born 16th of 3d month, 1745, married a man by the name of Evans; she died in 1770, aged twenty-six years, leaving issue.

Joseph, the son of Joseph and Hannah B. Stretch, was born 12th of 8th month, 1704; from him there are numerous descendants. He purchased more than two-thirds of the Christopher White allotment of 1,000 acres bought of John Fenwick in 1676. The greater part of said estate was inherited by Josiah White, the grand-son of Christopher. Joseph Stretch, Jr., was the purchaser of a large part of it, including the old brick mansion that was built by Christopher White in 1691. Joseph and Deborah Stretch had eleven children—Sarah, Mary, Peter, Joseph, Samuel, Jonathan, Joshua, Martha, Nathan, Aaron and Rebecca. Sarah, the eldest daughter, born about 1725, married Solomon, the son of Joseph Ware, Jr., and Elizabeth Walker Ware. There were eight children by that union—Peter Stretch, Elizabeth, Job, Hannah, Elisha, Barsheba, Sarah and Solomon. This large family of children all died minors excepting Sarah, who was born 14th of 6th month, 1756. She subsequently married Joshua Thompson, of Elsinborough, but died young, leaving three children—Joseph, John and Elizabeth. John died soon after his mother's death, aged about ten years. Those whom Joseph and Elizabeth married, and their offspring, are mentioned in the genealogy of the Ware and Thompson families.

Joseph Stretch, 3d, born 3d of 9th month, 1732, married Sarah, daughter of Joseph Ware, 3d. She was born 2d of 8th month, 1737. They had issue—Jael, born in 1762, and Martha in 1763. Samuel, the son of Joseph and Sarah Stretch, born 8th of 7th month, 1736, had two wives; their maiden names do not appear in the family records. The issue by his first wife was Joseph Stretch, who subsequently married and left one son —Jonathan Stretch. Samuel by his second wife had two sons —Samuel and Luke Stretch. Samuel died a young man unmarried, and devised all the estate he inherited from his parents to his brother Luke. The latter subsequently married Sarah, daughter of Joseph and Mary Street Fogg. Luke and his wife had three children, two of them died young during the lifetime of their parents. The other son, Aaron, became possessed of a considerable estate, which had belonged to his parents. He died young, and leaving no near relations of the Stretch family, excepting the issue of Joseph Stretch, half brother to his father, there originated a long contested law controversy for the possession of the property. The real estate was taken possession of by Jonathan Stretch, a son of the half blood of Luke Stretch. The personal property was decided by the legal adviser to belong to Joseph Fogg, he being an own brother of Sarah F. Stretch, the decedent's mother. The real estate, I believe, was finally decided to belong to David Stretch, he being a descendant of the oldest male line of Samuel Stretch, and from him to his son Nathaniel.

Sarah Stretch married Samuel Test in 1768. They lived on a small property she inherited from her parents, about a mile below Hancock's Bridge, containing about 50 acres. They had issue, two sons. Samuel, the eldest, was born in 1768, and learned the hat business. His brother Mark, I think, married Dorcas Keasbey. The property after their parent's death was divided equally between the two brothers. Samuel's share was where his parents lived; Joseph Brown is at the present time the owner. It appears that Samuel Test, soon after the death of his parents, sold his estate to Barzilla Jeffers, and removed to Indiana, and settled in Richmond, which at that time was a small village, and there he followed his trade the greater part of the remainder of his life, and acquired a competency. He was a leading member in his middle and old age of the largest Society of Friends on the Continent of North America—the Indiana Yearly Meeting. After he reached nearly four-score years he made a pilgrimage to his native State and county, and in company with his friend, the late Josiah M. Reeve, visited the house in which he was born, located in Alloways Creek township. We can well imagine his emotions as he went from room to room of the home of his youth. It doubtless brought back pleasing remembrances of his affectionate parents as he again stood in that ancient building where he first uttered that endearing name, mother, which the good and wise in all ages have delighted to venerate. When he looked around his native home, and the generation of men he was familiar with in the days of his youth, he realized that the friends and neighbors of his parents had gone to their final home, and had been succeeded by another generation whom he knew not. Such a visit and his own reflections were amply sufficient to repay him for the long and toilsome journey to his native home. I have been informed he lived but a short time after he returned. Of his immediate family I have no means of knowing. His brother Mark and his wife Dorcas Test had one son—Mark. He sold the estate he inherited from his parents more than forty years ago to Morris Hancock, and settled near his uncle Samuel in the vicinity of Richmond, Indiana.

Jonathan, the son of Joseph and Deborah Stretch, born 8th of 8th month, 1737, married Hannah, the daughter of Joseph and Elizabeth Ware, born 4th of 7th month, 1739. They had issue, seven children The eldest was Sarah, who was born in 1759, David, Deborah, Mark, Elizabeth, Rebecca and Jonathan. Hannah W. Stretch, their mother, departed this life 18th of 12th month, 1775. Jonathan Stretch's second wife was Elizabeth Fogg. They had issue—Hannah Stretch. David, the son of Jonathan and Hannah Stretch, born 25th of 5th month, 1762, married Mary, the widow of Joseph Fogg. Her maiden name was Mary Street, and she held a large tract of land in her own right located near the village of Canton. David and his wife had six children—Hannah, Jonathan, Nathaniel, David, Mark, and Jael. David's second wife was Rachel Baker, of Mannington. She was a widow, the daughter of Jedediah Allen. David and his second wife had no issue.

Hannah, the daughter of David and Mary Stretch, was born in 1778. Her first husband was Joseph Keasbey; there was no issue. Her second husband was Andrew Smith. They had four children—Mary, Hannah, Catharine and David. The latter married Elizabeth, the eldest daughter of Thomas and Rachel Hancock. They had issue—Morris and Sarah Smith. Mary, the daughter of Andrew and Hannah Smith, married Charles, son of Thomas Reeves. Charles B. and his wife had issue—A. Smith, Elizabeth and Thomas. A. Smith Reeves married Mary, the daughter of Richard and Lucetta Mulford; they have issue. Hannah, the daughter of Andrew and Hannah Smith, married Hiram Harris. They have two children—David and Catharine. Catharine, the youngest daughter of Andrew and Hannah Smith, married Amos, the son of Stretch and Rebecca Harris. They have two children—Rebecca and Stretch Harris.

Jonathan, the eldest son of David and Mary Stretch, born in 1790, married Elizabeth, the daughter of Jesse and Mary Carll; they had no issue. His second wife was Hannah Sheppard. He died not long after marriage, leaving no offspring. His widow subsequently married Dr. David Jayne. Nathaniel the son of David and Mary Stretch, was born in 1792. His first wife was Susan, the daughter of Solomon Dubois. By that connection there were three children—Mary Ann, Sarah F. and Susan. (The last mentioned child died young). Mary Ann Stretch, born in 1815, married Abner, the son of Washington and Mary Smith. Abner and his wife had one daughter—Susan, who married Charles Hires; they have three sons. Nathaniel's second wife was Elizabeth, the daughter of John Harris. The said John Harris served as a soldier during the whole of the Revolutionary war, and was in the regular army the winter that Washington and his army lay at Valley Forge. He married after he returned home, and he and his wife had four children—Benjamin, Lydia, Elizabeth and Clara. Nathaniel Stretch has been deceased for several years, leaving a widow, but no issue by his last wife.

David, the son of David and Mary Stretch, was born in 1795. His wife was Sarah, the daughter of Moses Hadley; by that connection there were five children—George, Aaron, Jonathan, Lydia Ann and Mary. The wife of George Stretch was Mary, the daughter of David S. English. Aaron and Jonathan Stretch removed in early life to Nashville, Tennessee. Lydia Ann Stretch married William H. Nelson; he died several years ago leaving a widow but no issue. Mary, the youngest of David and Mary Stretch's children, married Richard Sailor. She is a widow at this time, her husband having been deceased for a number of years. Mark, the youngest son of David and Mary Stretch, was born in 1797. He, in after life, married Elizabeth, the daughter of Jonathan and Joanna Hildreth. Mark and his wife had four children—Joseph, Mary, Elizabeth and Joanna. His second wife was Tamson Finley; they had one daughter—Deborah. Mark is deceased, and his son, Joseph H. Stretch, lived beyond middle age. He died recently, leaving a large landed estate; he never married. Mary, the daughter of Mark and Elizabeth Stretch, married John H., the son of William Morris, of Pilesgrove. John and his wife have one son—William. The husband of Elizabeth, the daughter of Mark and Elizabeth Stretch, is William A., the son of Joseph Casper. They have issue—Hildreth, William J., Annie, Elizabeth and John. Joanna, the daughter of Mark and Elizabeth Stretch, married Charles B. Reeves. She was his second wife, and by that connection there were two sons. Joanna is deceased at this time. Jael, the youngest daughter of David and Mary Stretch, born in 1799, married David, the son of George Grier, Sr. She was his second wife, (his first wife was Lydia, the daughter of Jonathan and Joanna Hildreth, who left no issue.) David left two sons by his last wife,—George and Richard Grier. George, the eldest, died a minor. Richard subsequently married Amanda, the daughter of David and Mary Davis, of Pilesgrove. Jael's second husband was William H., the son of Davis and Francis Nelson. She was a dutiful wife, and an affectionate and loving mother. She died many years before her husband, leaving no issue by the last marriage.

Joshua, the son of Joseph and Deborah Stretch, born 28th of 12th month, 1740, married Lydia, the widow of Paul Denn, and daughter of John and Mary Stewart. They were married at Alloways Creek in 1762, and had three children—Job, Milicent and Elisha Stretch. Job, the eldest son, was born 6th of 12th month, 1763. I think he died a young man unmarried. Milicent was born 10th of 11th month, 1766, and married James Hance; she died not many years after that event, and left no issue. Elisha, the son of Joshua and Lydia Stretch, was born 17th of 12th month, 1768. His wife was Sarah, the daughter of William and Mary Ware Bradway. They had eight children, three of whom died young; Mary, Joshua, William, Ann and Job Stretch all lived to mature age. Mary, the eldest, married Mark, the son of Mark and Martha Bradway. She lived but a short time after marriage, leaving no issue. Joshua married Elizabeth, the daughter of Waddington Bradway, Sr. There was one son by that connection, Joshua Stretch, who studied medicine, and practiced his profession in Salem for a time. He married Lydia, the daughter of Mark Bainer, of Philadelphia. He left Salem and removed to Philadelphia, where he died soon after of that insidious disease so destructive to the human family, pulmonary consumption. He left a widow and two or three children. His father, Joshua Stretch, was remarkable for his high moral character. For a number of years he taught school in Salem with great credit to himself, and with the approval of those who patronized him. William, the second son of Elisha and Sarah Stretch, learned the tailoring business, and followed it after he became of age in Salem. He was very proficient in his calling, and his customers were the best in the town and county. Toward the close of his life he left Salem with his family and removed to Jersey City. He married several years before he left Salem, but the name of his wife I have never learned. He died not long after, leaving several children.

Ann, the youngest daughter of Elisha and Sarah W. Stretch, married John D., the son of Mark and Elizabeth Stewart. They had seven children—Elizabeth, Charles, Elisha, Sarah, James, John and Ann. Elizabeth, the eldest, died before her mother, who died in 1857, aged over fifty-two years. Charles, Elisha, Sarah, James and John died soon after they had arrived to the age of maturity—a time when life is full of hope and pleasure—leaving behind an aged and kind father and a beloved sister to mourn their untimely end. Job, the youngest son of Elisha and Sarah Stretch, was apprenticed to his brother William to learn the tailoring business, and he followed that occupation in Salem during the remainder of his life. His wife was Catharine, the daughter of John Nicholson, a lineal descendant of the fifth generation of that eminent Friend, Samuel Nicholson, who in 1675 emigrated to this country in company with John Fenwick and his family from the county of Northamptonshire, England. Job and his wife Catharine had three children —Eliza, Charles and Mary. Eliza, I have been informed, married Joseph Paul; they reside in Philadelphia. Mary Stretch's husband is John P. Moore, who keeps a hardware store on Market street, in the city of Salem. He was a partner several years in that business with the late Thomas W. Cattell, the father of Alexander G. Cattell. Job Stretch, the father of the above mentioned children, died a number of years ago of consumption, which is hereditary in his mother's family. Elisha Stretch's second wife was Mary, the widow of Ezra Bradway, the daughter of James Denn. They had three daughters— Beulah, Mary and Sarah. Beulah, the eldest, married Nathan Kiger; by that connection there were four children—Alfred, Mary, Anna and Nathan. Her second husband is Simon Wallen. Mary, the second daughter of Elisha and Mary Stretch, died a young woman, unmarried. Sarah, their youngest daughter, married Joseph Mitten. I think they are at this time residents of California.

Rachel, the daughter of James and Elizabeth Stretch, married

Jonathan Butcher. She died in early life, leaving one daughter, Ruth Butcher, who subsequently married George Grier, Jr., the son of George and Rebecca Ware Grier. I shall digress somewhat to mention the families that organized the first Presbyterian Church in Lower Alloways Creek. Richard Moore came from Pittsgrove and purchased land near what was called Logtown about 1840. He had five children—Robert, Joanna, Rebecca, Mary and Hannah. Robert, Jr., married and died young, leaving two children—Richard and Rebecca. Joanna Moore married Jonathan, the son of Joseph Hildreth. They had five children—Lydia, Hannah, Elizabeth, one who married Joseph Corliss, (being his first wife,) and Jonathan Hildreth, Jr. Rebecca married George Grier, and had three sons—Richard, George and David. Mary Moore married Solomon Dubois; they had three or four children. Hannah Moore married Daniel, the son of Peter Stretch; they had several children which I shall mention hereafter. These families, together with the Sayres, Woodruffs and Padgetts, were the principal families which constituted the Presbyterian congregation. The church stood on the old road leading from Hancock's Bridge to the village of Canton, a short distance below Harmersville. They also purchased a lot of ground for a graveyard adjoining the Baptist graveyard at the present time. I have been informed that both yards are enclosed with one fence. The Presbyterian church was reduced to one or two families at the beginning of this century, and they finally abandoned it, and the house was removed after standing little over half a century.

George and Ruth B. Grier had five children—Richard, the eldest, died a young man unmarried; Jonathan B., Rachel, Robert and Charles. Jonathan B. Grier married Lydia, the daughter of David and Hannah Fogg. I think they have five children—David, George, Rebecca, Anna and Jonathan B. Grier. David Grier married Gulielma, the daughter of Josiah and Sarah Engle, of Pilesgrove; they have issue. George Grier married the daughter of Allen Wallace. Rebecca Grier, married James, the son of John and Hannah Lindsey, of Lower Penn's Neck; they have issue. Anna Grier married Richard, the son of Benjamin and Mary Bassett; they have issue. Jonathan, the youngest son, married Anna, the daughter of Samuel P. and Hannah Allen, of Mannington. Robert, the son of George and Ruth Grier, married Sarah, the daughter of William and Elizabeth Thompson, of Elsinborough. They have five children—Ruth, Georgiana, Abigail, Richard and William T. Ruth, their eldest daughter, married Robert, the son of George and Hannah C. Boon. Georgianna married Joseph, the son of Aaron Lippincott, of Mannington. Rachel, daughter of George and Ruth B. Grier, married John, the son of Jesse and Ann Patrick. They had four children—Richard, George, Charles and Morris. Charles, the youngest son of George and Ruth Grier, died a young man unmarried. At the death of James, the son of Bradway Stretch, he devised his landed estate which he had inherited from his father (being one-half of Stoe Neck farm), to his daughter, Dorcas Pancoast, and his granddaughter, Ruth Butcher, afterwards Grier. Samuel Pancoast and George Grier sold the said property to John Finley, who some years before had purchased one-half of the Bradway Stretch farm of John Stretch.

Peter Stretch was advanced in years when he married, and there is no definite record of the maiden name of his wife, but tradition says it was Temperance Howell, which I think quite probable. (She named a son by her second husband, Howell Hall.) Peter was a large landholder, and the greater part of his real estate was located near Hancock's Bridge, and was originally the Christopher White estate. Peter, the son of Peter and Temperance Stretch, born 16th of 2d month, 1767, married, but died a young man, leaving issue—Elizabeth Stretch, who died a minor. Anthony, the son of Peter and Temperance Stretch, born 11th of 1st month, 1769, died at the early age of three years. Daniel, the son of Peter and Temperance Stretch, was born 7th of 9th month, 1770. Peter Stretch died about the year 1774, leaving a widow and two minor children—Peter and Daniel. Temperance, his widow, subsequently married Colonel Edward Hall, of Mannington, and they had two children—Sarah, born 9th month, 1779, and Howell, born 18th of 1st month, 1785. Temperance, their mother, died about 1787. Daniel, the son of Peter and Temperance Stretch, subsequently married Mary Stretch, a distant relative; they had two sons—Peter and Robert. Peter Stretch died without issue in 1797, and the large estate, both personal and real, descended to his brother Daniel. Daniel's second wife was Hannah, the daughter of Richard and Mary Moore, who was born 15th of 4th month, 1776. They had six children—Daniel, Clarissa, Edward, Ann, Richard and Temperance. Daniel and his wife Hannah died in 1813 at the village of Canton, while their children were all minors. His estate at the time of his death was larger than that of any other person living in the township. Peter, his eldest son, married Phebe, the daughter of Moses Hadley. They had six children—Emily, Elizabeth, Richard, Josiah, Wesley and Phebe. Peter and his wife are both deceased at this time, and most of their children died young. One of his sons, Wesley Stretch, I have been informed, resides in Philadelphia, and is concerned in the celebrated drug store of the late Dr. David Jayne, on Chestnut street.

Daniel, the son of Daniel and Hannah M. Stretch, born 3d of 11th month, 1799, married Eliza Hadly, sister of his brother Peter's wife. They had two sons—Edwin and Richard. I think Edwin married the daughter of Joseph Boon; they have issue. Richard Stretch married Lydia, the daughter of Edward and Eliza Smith; they have several children.

Clarissa, the daughter of Daniel and Hannah M. Stretch, born 26th of 1st month, 1802, married Thomas Sinnickson, of Salem. They had issue, all of whom were noticed in the genealogy of the Sinnickson family.

Edward, the son of Daniel and Hannah M. Stretch, born 3d of 7th month, 1804, married the daughter of William Nixon. There were three sons and one daughter by this union—William, Edward, Peter and Hannah. William married Mary Ann, widow of Robert Hancock, and the daughter of James Fisher. William and his wife have several children.

Ann, the daughter of Daniel and Hannah M. Stretch, born 11th of 9th month, 1806, married Josiah Paullin; they have issue—Anne, Josiah B., George M. and William Henry. Ann subsequently married William Hunter. George M. was a surgeon in the army during the late rebellion, and is now a practicing physician in Canton. He married Annie, the daughter of John H. and Elizabeth Lambert; they have issue. Richard M., the son of Daniel and Hannah M. Stretch, was born in 1809. He has for many years been in the mercantile business at Allowaystown. He married Rebecca, the daughter of Robert and Anna Coe. They have four children—Charles, Anna, Robert and Mary. Charles married Hannah Gray, of Philadelphia; they have issue. Anna married Benjamin I. Diament. Robert is connected with the West Jersey Express Company, in Philadelphia.

Aaron, the son of Joseph and Deborah Stretch, born 14th of 10th month, 1746, married Elizabeth Reeves; they had one son, Reeves, and two or three daughters. Aaron died a comparatively young man. His widow afterwards married a man by the name of Mills, by whom she had two children—Joel and Keziah. Elizabeth's third husband was William Bradway, of Stoe Neck; they had no issue. Reeves, the son of Aaron and Elizabeth Stretch, married a Glaspey. They had five children—Job, Rachel, Sarah, Rosanna and Reeves. Job, the eldest son, married Rebecca, the daughter of Joseph Deal; they had issue. Elizabeth married Enoch, son of Richard Garrison, of Cumberland; they have three or four children. Job Stretch, Jr.'s wife is Sarah, the daughter of Isaac and Martha Harris; they have five children. Richard, the youngest son of Job and Rebecca Stretch, married Sarah, the daughter of Job Thorp. Job Stretch, Sr.'s second wife was Charlotte, widow of Jacob Dubois, and daughter of John Finley.

Reeves, the youngest son of Reeves Stretch, Sr., married the daughter of Richard Garrison. He died a young man, leaving three minor sons—Richard, Charles and Reeves. Rachel, the daughter of Reeves Stretch, married Daniel Barnes. Sarah, the second daughter of Reeves Stretch, married Elisha Bonham, the son of Justice Bonham; they had two or three children. She is deceased at the present time. Rosanna Stretch's husband was George A. Githens of Greenwich. They had five children—Hannah, Louisa, Cecelia, George A. and William H. George and his wife Rosanna Githens are deceased at the present time. Georgh A. Githens' wife is Martha, daughter of Richard and Lucetta Mulford. For several years past he has resided in Salem, and is in the mercantile business. Louisa Githens became the wife of Charles, the youngest son of Judge Ephraim Carll. She lived but a short period after her marriage, dying of pulmonary consumption, leaving one child. Hannah, her sister, has paid the debt of nature since of a similar disease. I think Cecelia is still living.

TYLER FAMILY.

The Tylers in this country are descended from an ancient English family. Their ancestors came with William, the Conqueror, into England, and fought in the battle of Hastings in 1066. They were residents of England for five hundred years. About that period there were three brothers, branches of the old English family, who emigrated to America. One settled in New England, one in the state of Virginia, (the ancestors of the ex-President, John Tyler), and the other, William Tyler, came to West Jersey about 1688, and purchased a large tract of land on the north side of Monmouth river of John Champney, being part of the 2,000 acres that John Fenwick deeded in 1676 to James Champney, and his wife Priscilla Fenwick Champney. William Tyler, whilst he was in his native country, married as nearly as can be ascertained in 1676, Johanna Parson. They had four children born in England as follows—Mary Tyler, at Walton, in the county of Somerset, 11th month, 1677; William Tyler, 5th of 7th month, 1680; John Tyler, in the 5th month, 1682, and Johanna Tyler in 1684. The following certificate given him by his friends in England show conclusively where his residence was in his native land: "Whereas, William Tyler,
"of Walton, in the county of Somerset, Yoeman, intends to
"transport himself and family into the province of Pennsylva-
"nia, in America, if the Lord will, and has desired a certificate
"on his behalf. We therefore, whose names are subscribed, do
"hereby certify that the said William Tyler hath professed the
"truth for several years past, and that we do not know but that
"his conversation hath been answerable to his profession, and
"that we do know that he hath been ready and willing to con-
"tribute to the service of truth, as opportunity hath offered and
"occasion required, and that as to his dealings with the world,
"he has been punctual and of good report as far as any of us
"know or have heard, and we know nothing of debts or other
"entanglements on his part but that he may with clearness
"prosecute his intended voyage. In testimony whereof we
"have hereunto subscribed our hands. Dated the eleventh day

"of seventh month, called September, in the year 1685. Signed "by Edward Chanyles, William Lidden, Thomas Howell, John "W. Ridder, and ten others." It is evident that William Tyler's wife, Johanna, lived but a short time after their arrival in this country. His second wife's first name was Elizabeth; her maiden name I never heard. He had three children by Elizabeth. Their oldest was named Catharine, who was born 13th of 6th month, 1690; their son, Philip Tyler, was born in the 6th month, 1692, and Elizabeth Tyler, 1694. William Tyler, the father of the above mentioned children, was a farmer, and likewise carried on the tanning business. He made his will in the 2d month, 1700, in which he bequeathed a large landed estate to his sons. The Champney property, where he resided, he left to his oldest son, William, it being about 400 acres, and to his second son, John Tyler, 800 acres situated in the lower part of Alloways Creek township, together with some other lands in the same township. The witnesses to the will were William Hall and John Firth. There appears no reliable record of any time of his death, but it is thought by the family to have occurred in 1701. Mary Tyler, daughter of William Tyler, Sr., married Abel Nicholson, the son of Samuel Nicholson. They had eight children—Sarah, Rachel, Joseph, William T., Ann, John, Ruth and Samuel.

John Tyler, the second son of William Tyler, married Hannah Wade, the daughter of Samuel Wade. He inherited a large landed estate from his father, which I think was located in Alloways Creek township, not far from the village of Harmersville, being part of Annie Salters' allotment. John and his wife Hannah W. Tyler, had one son—Benjamin by name. The year he was born is uncertain, probably about the year 1720. Soon after he arrived of age, he sold his patrimonial estate at Alloways Creek, and purchased some 400 acres near the town of Greenwich, now Cumberland county, being part of the Gibbon estate. In 1746 he married Naomi Dennis, the sister of Philip Dennis, of Bacon's Neck. They had four children—Elizabeth, born 28th of 2d month, 1748; Rachel, born in 1751; John in 1753; Letitia, 9th of 11th month, 1755. The last mentioned was young when her mother died. In 1759 Benjamin married his second wife, Mary Adams by name, and he had four children—Job, born in 1760; Lydia, in 1763; Hannah, in 1765, and Benjamin, 30th of 10th month, 1771. John Tyler, the son of Benjamin, married Abigail Lippincott. They had three children—Samuel, Benjamin and Naomi. His second wife was Nancy Hall, but she died in a short time afterwards leaving no issue. Benjamin's third wife was Hope Sharp, by whom he had one daughter—Hannah Y. Tyler. Elizabeth, the oldest daughter of Benjamin Tyler, married John Dunham. They had two children—John and Elizabeth Dunham. The latter afterwards became the wife of Job Tyler, Jr. Letitia's first husband was Andrew Griscom. They had two children—Benjamin and Andrew Griscom. Her second husband was James English, and they had two children—Martha and Tyler English. Martha afterwards became the wife of Benjamin Harris. Rachel Tyler's husband was John Potts, Jr., of Bacon's Neck. They left children. Job Tyler, the oldest son of Benjamin Tyler by his last wife, married Rachel Sayre. Soon after they were married he sold his farm that was left to him by his father, and his first purchase in Salem county was the James Sterling farm in Mannington, which property now belongs to John T. Bassett. Job Tyler did not own the property long before he sold it, and bought Lucas Gibbs' large farm in Quaker Neck. He was a man of considerable energy, and was considered one of the best farmers of his time in Salem county. His attention was turned to grazing and feeding cattle; perhaps he has never been equalled in this section of the country in that particular. He raised the fattest, but not the largest, bullock that was ever exhibited in Philadelphia. Its neat weight was 2,165 lbs. The inhabitants of Salem county considered it a credit to the place, and the directors of Salem Bank honored him by using the impress of the Tyler ox on their one dollar notes for many years. Job and Rachel Tyler had four children—Benjamin, the oldest, married a young woman by the name of Burden, and had by her one son named James, who subsequently married a woman by the name of Penton, by whom he had two children, a son and daughter, named Rachel and James Tyler. The latter married one of the daughters of John H. Lambert, and Rachel is the wife of John Lambert, Jr. Job Tyler, Jr., married Elizabeth Dunham, she being his cousin. He inherited the homestead farm in Quaker Neck. A few years after the death of his father he sold it to Andrew Griscom and moved to Salem. He and his wife had no children. His wife died some length of time before him. At his death he willed the greater part of his estate, being principally in money, to his brother Benjamin's grandchildren, Rachel and James Tyler.

Mary, daughter of Job Tyler, Sr., married John Bacon, son Job Bacon, of Greenwich. She lived but a short time after her marriage. Richard Tyler, the youngest son of Job and Rachel Tyler, was one of the most promising young men, of his time, in the county. Remarkably pleasing in person and address, he attracted to himself many friends. He died unmarried about 1819, with that distressing disease, the bilious dysentery, which became an epidemic complaint in that year and the season following in this county, and many, particularly the young, fell victims to it.

Samuel Tyler, the son of John Tyler, married Rachel Peck, by whom he had eight children—Abigail, Benjamin, Martha, Samuel, Clarissa, Nancy, Rachel and George. Abigail died unmarried. Benjamin, his son, embraced the Presbyterian faith. He studied for the ministry, and became a highly esteemed clergyman of that sect. His wife was Mary Seeley, the daughter of Richard Seeley. Benjamin died a comparatively young man, leaving a widow and three children—Charles, Joseph and Benjamin, who are living. Martha Tyler, daughter of Samuel, married Oliver H. Williams. Samuel Tyler, Jr. married Elizabeth Burden. Rachel Tyler married Auley B. Wood. Clarissa and Nancy Tyler were twin children, both of them died unmarried. George Tyler, the youngest son of Samuel, married Emily Moore. But one of the eight children of Samuel survived him, and that was Samuel, who has been dead several years.

Bemjamin Tyler's, son of John Tyler, first wife was a Thompson. By her he had six children—Hannah Ann, John, Mary, Ebenezar, Lydia and Benjamin. His second wife was Hope Allen, but they had no issue. His third wife was Martha Owen, a widow, whose maiden name was Buzby, the daughter of Nathaniel Buzby, of Port Elizabeth. She survived Benjamin several years. Hannah Ann Tyler, daughter of Benjamin, married Josiah Harmer. Her second husband was Evi Smith. John Tyler married Beulah Griscom, daughter of Benjamin Griscom, of Salem. Mary Tyler married Charles Harmer. Her second husband was Andrew Thompson, of Mannington. Ebenezar Tyler married Sarah Stewart, daughter of James Stewart, Jr., of Alloways Creek. Lydia Tyler married Reuben Hilliard, of Mannington, son of Samuel Hilliard, of the same place. Benjamin Tyler, Jr. married Alice Woolman, of Pilesgrove. Naomi Tyler, the daughter of John Tyler, married George Bacon, of Greenwich. Their children were Eliza, George, Richard, Francis and Mary Bacon.

William Tyler, Jr., the oldest son of William and Johanna Tyler, was born at Walton, in England, 5th of 7th month, 1680. At the death of his father he was about twenty-one years of age. It appears that his father had much confidence in him, as he directed in his will that he should have charge of the younger children, some of whom were not more than two or three years of age, and was left executor to his father's will. Among his papers that have been preserved by his descendants is a manuscript inventory of his father's goods, which is as follows: "An inventory of the goods and chattels of William Tyler, "deceased, as they were brought before us. Rudoc Morris, "Joseph Parson and John Parson, this 25th of 2d month, 1701, "being appraisers." The amount of the personal estate of William Tyler amounted by the appraisement to £519, 9s, 2d, and was recorded the 20th of 6th month, 1701, in Salem, by Samuel Hedge, 3d, recorder. William Tyler, Jr., received as executor to his father's will, through Elias Osborne, of England, agent of his uncle, Thomas Parsons, of Philadelphia, a considerable amount of money from England. It appears from a letter dated 10th month, 1688, three years after William Tyler, Sr., emigrated to America, that Abraham Grundy was placed in charge of his estate which he had left in England, and his son William also kept up the correspondence after his father's death. A letter dated 5th of 10th month, 1702, he writes to the executor of Abraham Grundy to pay him £20 sterling. I presume it was the balance of his father's estate in England. William Tyler, Jr., married Mary Abbott, sister of George Abbott, the emigrant, and by her had six children. Their oldest, William Tyler, 3d, was born 2d of 5th month, 1712; Edith, their daughter, born 24th of 11th month, 1714; Rebecca, born 29th of 3d month, 1716; Mary, born 16th of 1st month, 1718; James, born 30th of 12th month, 1720; and Samuel, born 26th of 10th month, 1723. The mother of these children survived their father, and afterwards married Robert Townsend, of Cape May, in the year 1735. By this marriage she had one daughter, Rany Townsend, who subsequently married a man by the name of Stites. After the death of Robert Townsend, his widow returned and lived with her Tyler children. William Tyler, 2d, died in 1733, aged fifty-three years. A short time previous to his death he made his will, in which he bequeathed the plantation on which he lived to his son William, (it is owned at the present day by William Robertson and Thomas Vanmeter,) for which William was to pay £50 to his daughter, Edith Thompson, the wife of Samuel Thompson, and the like sum to his daughter, Rebecca Tyler. The said sums to be paid by William in four years after the decease of his father. He left to his second son, James Tyler, a farm of 234 acres, which he bought of William Hall. Richard McPherson and

Aaron Fogg are the present owners of the said property. He gave to his youngest son, Samuel Tyler, a tract of land commonly called Smith Neck, containing 150 acres. He also willed to his two sons, William and Samuel Tyler, a tract of land lying between the first mentioned messuages and the said Smith Neck, containing 100 acres more or less. The said land formerly belonged to John Maddox Denn. He further bequeathed to his wife, Mary Tyler, and his daughters, Edith and Rebecca, all his personal estate, after his funeral expenses and just debts were paid, to be equally divided among them. He also willed that his wife should have the privilege and use of one-half of his best mansion house to dwell in during her natural life, and also to keep a horse and cow upon the first mentioned messuage so long as she continued to dwell thereon. He nominated and appointed his wife, Mary Tyler, and his son, William Tyler, and his son-in-law, Samuel Thompson, executors of his last will and testament. The will was made 29th of 11th month, 1732. The inventory of his personal estate amounted to £271, 13s. The appraisers were Abel Nicholson and Thomas Taylor. William Tyler, 3d, married Elizabeth Thompson. She was the daughter of Joseph and Sarah Thompson, and they lived where Allowaystown is now located. She was born 1st of 8th month, 1716. They had three daughters. The oldest, Sarah Tyler, married Samuel Stewart, the son of John and Mary Stewart, of Alloways Creek. Their children were Joseph, Mary, Mark and Ann. The last mentioned married William Griscom. Joseph Stewart married Rachel Bradway. Mark's wife was Elizabeth Denn, daughter of James Denn, and Mary died unmarried.

Rebecca Tyler, William's second daughter, married William Abbott, the son of Samuel Abbott, of Elsinborough. Their children were Josiah, Samuel and George. Mary Tyler, his youngest daughter, married Jacob Scoggins, whose children were Tyler, Jonas, Mary, Phebe, Rebecca and Elizabeth. I believe Tyler Scoggins died a young man and single. Rebecca lived to an old age and died unmarried. Mary married Joseph Piper and had three children. Elizabeth Scoggins' husband was James Dennis. Their children were Mary, Naomi, Jonathan and Rebecca. It is probable that Jacob Scoggins and his wife Mary bought the share of the homesterd farm of her two sisters, Sarah and Rebecca, that their father, William Tyler, inherited from his father. Sometime after the death of Jacob and Mary Scoggins, their children sold the farm to John Lindsey, after having been in the Tyler family four generations.

After the death of Lindsey the farm was divided between his two sons, John and Joseph. Thomas Jones, Sr., purchased Joseph Lindsey's farm, which was part of James Vanmeter's wife's share of her father's estate. John Lindsey, Jr.'s farm was sold some time after his death, and William Robertson was the purchaser, the father of the present William Robertson.

Edith Tyler, daughter of William Tyler, 2d, married Samuel Thompson, who was born 6th of 9th month, 1707. He was the son of William Thompson and grandson of Andrew Thompson, who emigrated to this country in 1677, and purchased land of Richard Guy in Elsinboro, and settled thereon; whilst his son William bought a large tract of land in Upper Monmouth, where Allowaystown is now located, and at that place he resided until his death. From them sprung numerous descendants. Samuel and his wife had five children. The oldest was Samuel Thompson, Jr. He was the grandfather of the late Joshua Thompson, who died recently in Salem at an advanced age. Aaron Thompson, their second son, married Hannah Hancock, widow of William Hancock, of Elsinborough. Aaron and his wife left no children. Hannah's maiden name was Fogg, daughter of Charles Fogg. Their oldest daughter, I think, was Sarah, she married Josiah Kay. He lived in Gloucester county, about three miles above Woodbury. They had one son, and a daughter—Rebecca Kay. She married Clement Hall, of Elsinboro, the eldest son of Clement and Margaret Hall, of the same township. They had seven children—Ann, Margaret, Prudence, Sarah, Morris, Deborah and Rebecca. Edith Thompson, daughter of Samuel, married Jedediah Allen, of Mannington. He was the oldest son of Jedediah Allen and grandson of Nathaniel Chambless, of Alloways Creek. Their eldest son, Samuel T. Allen, went to Philadelphia and became an eminent merchant and shipper, and accumulated a great fortune. One of his cousins paid him a visit on one occasion, and remarked to him whilst he was at his house upon the splendor in which he lived, Samuel replied, "It does not produce "happiness." Samuel married Maria Wilkins. They had four daughters, one of whom married, and she and her husband emigrated to South America. Rebecca Thompson, the third daughter of Samuel and Edith Thompson, married David Allen, the brother of Jedediah. From that union there were ten children —Hannah Allen, born 5th of 3d month, 1767, whose first husband was Aaron Fogg; second, David Bradway. Mary Allen, born 1768, married Joseph Bassett. Ann Allen, born 1770, married Joseph Brown. Rebecca and David Allen, twin children, born in 1772; Rebecca's first husband was Joshua Thompson; second, Benjamin Griscom; David Allen went to the West Indies and there died. Edith Allen, born in 1775, died I think unmarried. Beulah, born in 1779, died unmarried. Samuel, born in 1781, married a young woman of Gloucester county. Jedediah, born in 1784; his first wife was Sarah Austin, his second wife Hannah Abbott. Chambless Allen, born 1786; his wife was Sarah Nicholson, the daughter of William Nicholson, of Mannington. David Allen died when most of his children were minors. His widow, Rebecca Allen, by her great energy and perseverence made herself adequate to the great charge that was committed to her in raising such a large family of children. Rebecca Tyler, daughter of William Tyler, 2d, died a young woman, unmarried. Mary Tyler, daughter of the same parents, died young, before her father.

Johanna Tyler, daughter of William Tyler, was born at Walton, England, in 1684. She married Jonathan Waddington, son of William Waddington. From this union sprung a line of descendants. Old receipts still exist for the payment of her paternal inheritance, which were given thirty years after the death of her father. "Be it known to all men of these presents "that we, Jonathan Waddington and Joan Waddington, his "wife, which is the daughter of William Tyler, deceased, do "acknowledge we have received of her brother William Tyler, "2d, executor of the last will and testament of her father, Wil-"liam Tyler, aforesaid, deceased, the sum of one hundred and "twenty-nine pounds in full satisfaction of a legacy left said "Joan by said father, of which said one hundred and twenty-"nine pounds, by us received as aforesaid, we do acknowledge "ourselves fully satisfied and paid. Of every part and parcel "thereof we do clear, exonerate, and forever, by these presents, "from the beginning of the world unto this day, as witnesses "our hand and seal the 14th day of May, 1731. Signed, sealed "and delivered in the presence of

"Jonathan Waddington,
Her
"Joan ⋈ Waddington."
Mark.

Philip Tyler, son of William Tyler, 1st, was born 1692, near Salem, New Jersey. His first wife was Elizabeth Denn, the daughter of John Maddox Denn, and by her he had two children—Enoch and Elizabeth Tyler. His second wife's name was Moore, and by that connection were two daughters, the elder was named Rachel, the younger one's name is unknown at the present time. Two of Philip's descendants were living in 1847. The description of their ancestor, as handed down to them, was that he had been in person a tall and spare man. He speculated in land largely, likewise in other business, was unsuccessful, and died poor, about the year 1777, nearly eighty years of age, and was buried in the ancient burial ground of Friends, on the north side of Monmouth river, near Hancock's Bridge. His son Enoch Tyler died a minor. His daughter Elizabeth Tyler married a man by the name of Watson; they had three sons—Thomas, John and Tyler Watson. Rachel Tyler, daughter of Philip by his last wife, died single; her sister married Ephraim Sayre, and numerous descendants sprung from that union.

Rebecca Tyler, daughter of William Tyler, 1st, was born near Salem in 1698, and married William Murdock. The Murdocks are said to have married into the Whital family near Woodbury, the Whitals being recorded in the Tyler's family Bible seems to corroborate it.

James Tyler, the son of William Tyler, 2d, and Mary his wife, was born 30th of 12th month, 1720, and resided all his life on the property on Alloways creek, that was left to him by his father. He built himself a brick house on the said property about the year 1745. His wife was Martha Simpson; they had two children—James Tyler, Jr., and Ruth Tyler. He died at the age of eighty years, and was succeeded on the farm by his son James, who married a young woman by the name of Acton. Their children were Catherine, William, Samuel and John Tyler; the sons so far as known left no children. Catherine Tyler married William Walker, a man of peculiar character, who, after passing through a variety of changes here, emigrated about 1818 to Cincinnati, then to Indiana, where he lived until the war with Mexico. Being strongly allured by the military spirit with which he was surrounded, he applied to the Government for a Captain's commission. It was at first refused him on the plea that he was too old, but was subsequently granted, and he, when more than seventy years of age, marched at the head of his company into Mexico; was present at the battle of Buena Vista, where he fell in 1847. He had several children, who are still living in the West; one a doctor, another son a lawyer. Ruth Tyler, daughter of James Tyler, Sr., married John Ware, the son of John and Elizabeth Ware, of Alloways Creek Neck. Ruth inherited one-third of her father's real estate. When they were first married they lived on the farm that was left him by his father, and subsequently he built on his wife's property, and resided there until his death. When her brother James' children offered for sale the property that they inherited from their parent, John Ware sold his farm in Alloways Creek to Mark Townsend, of Cape May, which enabled him to purchase the whole of the property that once belonged to his father-in-law, James Tyler. John and Ruth Ware had two children—Martha and Eleanor. Martha died a young woman whilst on a visit to her uncle David Ware, near Darby. Eleanor Ware married Jeremiah Tracy, who was many years younger than herself; there was no issue from this union. She, during their marriage, deeded all her real estate to her husband, and died a short time afterwards. This indenture conveyed the last of 700 acres on Alloways creek that was purchased by William Tyler, 1st, one hundred and seventy-five years ago.

Samuel Tyler, youngest child of William Tyler, 2d., and Mary his wife, was born 26th of 10th month, 1723. He was about ten years old at the death of his father. When he was nearly eighteen years of age he apprenticed himself to Benjamin Acton, of Salem, to learn the tanning business. An indenture found among his papers, dated 1741, signed Samuel Tyler, and witnessed by his mother, Mary Tyler, and George Trenchard, specified that he was to serve four years at the business. Soon after the expiration he sold his possesions on Alloways creek, that he inherited from his father, and bought of Rebecca Edgil, of Philadelphia, the property of the upper end of Salem, since known as Tyler street. In the deed for this purchase, dated 1746, the house is called "a new brick "house," making it at the present time more than one hundred and twenty years old. It is now owned by William Davidson. At this house he carried on the tanning business. In 1751 he married Ann Mason, the daughter of John Mason, Jr., and granddaughter of John Mason, the emigrant. Their children, five in number, were named William Tyler, born 3d of 11th month, 1752; John, born 7th of 9th month, 1755; Mary, born 11th of 8th month, 1756; Samuel, born in 7th month, 1758; and Rebecca, born in 6th month, 1764. Samuel lived to see most of his children grow up, and died 26th of 11th month, 1778, at the comparatively early age of fifty-five years. Ann Tyler, his wife, died 23d of 2d month, 1777, nearly a year before her husband. William Tyler, 4th, administered on the estate of his father. The property was appraised 5th of 1st month, 1779; Samuel Stewart and Samuel Thompson were the appraisers. The whole of his personal property amounted to about £1,500, a large sum for that period. William Tyler was twenty-six years old when his father died—his mother dying the year before. He and his brothers and sisters were thus deprived of both parents. They however, found a parent in their maternal aunt, Mary Mason, who went to live with them, and remained with some of the family until her death. According to the law at that time, William Tyler, 4th, as the oldest son, was entitled to all the landed estate. He was not, however, unmindful of his brothers and sisters, but assigned them a share of their father's property. It appears the family all remained at their native home until William's marriage with Beulah Ridgway, in 1792. I think she was the daughter of Job Ridgway, of Mannington. The Tyler family then separated, and he continued at the paternal mansion. His wife lived but a short time after they were married, and died leaving no issue. In 1796 he married his second wife, Catherine Low, daughter of Hugh Low, of Philadelphia. She was born 5th of 2d month, 1765, and died in 1825. Hugh Low was the son of English parents, members of the Society of Friends, who came over to this country with their family when he was an infant and settled in Philadelphia. He was considered to be a man of good natural abilities and strict integrity, liberal in his feelings, and became a firm friend to the country of his adoption.

John Mason Tyler, son of William Tyler and Catharine Tyler, was born 28th of 5th month, 1797. Hannah Gillespey Tyler, was born 30th of 8th month, 1798. Hugh Low Tyler, was born 20th of 3d month, 1800. Mary Tyler, was born 21st of 11th month, 1801. Annie Tyler, was born 1st of 3d month, 1805. William Tyler, fifth son of William and Catharine Tyler, was born 16th of 9th month, 1806. William and Catharine Tyler, the parents of the above mentioned children, lived together more than twenty-seven years, it is said, with great conjugal felicity. He was a man of retiring disposition, of few words and was considered honest and impartial in his dealings with his fellow men. He died after an illness of about two weeks in 1823, in his seventy-second year. Catharine Tyler, his wife, survived him fifteen months. Her death took place 23d of 3d month, 1825, when she was about sixty-nine years of age. She was considered a discreet and sensible woman, with warm sensibilities and devoted piety, sprightly in character and was anxious that her children should be brought up aright, that they might become useful and worthy citizens. John Mason Tyler, the eldest son of William Tyler, in his youth left his parents' home and was adopted by his uncle, John Tyler, and went to live with him. At this home he continued, succeeded his uncle in business, and married Dorothea Graham Hoskins, of Radnor, Pennsylvania, in 1832. They had two children— Catharine Low Tyler, born in 1833, and William Graham Tyler. Joseph Hoskins, the father of Dorothea Tyler, was a native of New Jersey. He went to Delaware county, Pennsylvania, settled on a farm and married Mary Graham, a descendant of an old and respectable family at Chester. Hannah G. Tyler married Clement Smith, of Mannington, in 1818. He was the son of William Smith, and a lineal descendant of John Smith, of Smithfield. Clement and his wife Hannah Smith had one son—Clement William Smith. He was born 28th of 9th month, 1819. Clement Smith, his father, died about the year 1820, leaving a young widow and an infant son. Hugh Low Tyler, second son of William Tyler, was born in 1800. In 1835 he married Mary Shiply Miller, daughter of George Miller and Mary Levis Miller, of Delaware county, Pennsylvania; he was a large landholder in that county. Hugh and his wife had three children—William Levis Tyler, born in 1836; George M. Tyler, in 1838, and John Edgar Tyler, in 1842. His wife at the death of her father becoming possessed of a valuable farm in that county, he left the farm at Salem and he and his family moved to Delaware county and subsequently sold the Tyler farm which had been in the family for more than one hundred years. Mary Tyler, the second daughter of William and Catharine Tyler, was born in 1801. She is considered by those persons that know her to be above mediocrity in point of intellect. I think she is still living. William Tyler, youngest son of William Tyler, when a young man made a long tour through the Western States. After his return he established himself in 1832 in the leather business in Philadelphia. There it was that his sister joined him and made one household until he married. He was persevering and diligent in his business, and it is said by untiring application became prosperous in his circumstances. He married in 1847 Ann Painter, daughter of Enos Painter, a farmer and extensive landholder in Delaware county, Pennsylvania. He and his wife have two sons—William Enos Tyler, born in 1848, and John J. Tyler, born in 1851.

John Tyler, son of Samuel and Ann Tyler, was born in 1755. At the time of his brother William's marriage he bought property in the town of Salem, on Fourth street where his tan-yard was situated; he built himself a dwelling house on said property in which he and his sister Mary resided. He followed the tanning business all his life, and at it he acquired considerable property. He was very unostentatious in his manners. A cotemporary said of him at his death " An honest man is gone." Late in life he became a member of the Society of Friends in whose mode of worship he was educated. He never married and died in 1825 aged more than seventy years. Mary Tyler, his sister, was born in 1756; she never married and spent most of her life with her brother John. She died in the meridian of life aged forty-eight years and a few months. Samuel Tyler, the youngest son of Samuel and Ann Tyler, was born in 1758. He married in 1796 Grace Acton, she being a widow. Her maiden name was Ambler. She was the daughter of Peter Ambler, of Mannington. Samuel Tyler about that time purchased a small farm adjoining his native home and went to farming, the said farm belongs at this time to Thomas B. Stow, of Salem. Their children were Ann and Elizabeth Tyler. Ann married Mark Smith, and by him had five children. Rebecca the oldest, married William Davidson; Beulah Smith, the second daughter, married William Dorman; Samuel Tyler Smith, Sarah Ann Smith and Elizabeth Smith. Samuel Tyler's daughter, Elizabeth, married John Miller, of Gloucester county. They have seven children—Abigail, Lydia, Samuel Tyler, Emily, John Mason, Anna and Edward Miller. John Miller, father of the before mentioned children, lived near Paulsboro'; he was a popular man in his native county, and was several times elected to the State Legislature, lastly was elected a Judge of the Court of the county.

Rebecca, the youngest daughter of Samuel and Ann Mason Tyler, was born in 1764. She lived in great retirement with her brother John Tyler until his death. She never married. At the death of her aunt, Mary Watson, and her sister Mary Tyler, she fell heir to a considerable sum of money. She built herself a house on Broadway, Salem, where she lived several years, but subsequently removed to Gloucester county, and spent the last years of her life with her niece, Elizabeth Miller. She died in 1843, aged seventy-nine years.

Nearly every family has an inclination for some particular occupation. This was the case to a remarkable degree in the ancient and respectable Tyler family. Their ancestor who emigrated to this country was a tanner, and his descendants for four or five generations, particularly the Samuel Tyler line, have followed and are to the present time following the occupation of manufacturing leather. It is likewise true of Benjamin Tyler's lineage, that many of them became eminent agriculturists; particularly Job Tyler, and his son Job Tyler, Jr., late of Mannington or Quaker Neck. They are, as a whole, a family of retiring disposition, avoiding ostentatious show.

TINDALL FAMILY.

Richard Tindall was one of Fenwick's executors and surveyor-general, chosen to that office in the year 1680 by John Fenwick, after the disagreement between him and Richard Hancock. He was also chosen by James Nevell to survey the lands belonging to Governor William Penn, within the bounds of Fenwick's tenth. Richard Tindall emigrated to this country in 1678, and soon afterwards purchased 500 acres of land being part of the allotment of land that was deeded to them in Penn's Neck in 1676 by their father John Fenwick. Part of the said land is now owned by Firman Lloyd, and was known formerly as Tindall Grove. His immediate family I have no knowledge of. His grandson, Benjamin Tindall, was born about the year 1720. Joseph Tindall, son of Benjamin and Hester Tindall, was born 16th of 6th month, 1749; and Mary Tindall, their daughter, was born in 1751. She married Elijah Ware, of Alloways Creek, he being a minister of the Society of Friends, and remarkable for his meek and quiet disposition. He and his wife left no children. By his will he devised that, after his widow's death, a small farm located in Penn's Neck should go to the Salem Monthly Meeting of Friends. Joseph Tindall, the brother of Mary, married and left two sons—Benjamin and Elijah W. Tindall. Benjamin married Rachel Thompson, the daughter of Andrew Thompson, of Elsinborough. She inherited a small farm in Penn's Neck from her grandfather, Samuel Nicholson, and on that farm Benjamin and his wife lived most of their time. A few years before his death Benjamin and his wife removed to Elsinborough on a farm formerly belonging to his wife's grandfather, Samuel Nicholson. Benjamin in a few years afterwards died there, leaving four or five children. Joseph Tindall, their eldest son, married Eliza Hancock, daughter of Thomas Hancock, Jr., and they had one daughter named Lydia Ann, who married Ebenezer Dunn, of Salem.

THOMPSON FAMILY.

John Thompson, the son of Thomas Thompson and Elizabeth his wife, was born in Yorkshire, England, in 1635. Andrew Thompson, son of the same parents, was born in 1637. In 1658 Thomas and his wife Elizabeth, with their two minor sons, John and Andrew, removed from England to Ireland and located near Dublin. In the year 1665, John, the eldest son, married Jane Humbly, daughter of Thomas Humbly. John and his wife, Jane Thompson, had three children born in Ireland. James, the son of John and Jane Thompson, was born in 1666. Ann, the daughter of John and Jane Thompson, 1st of 9th month, 1672. Mary, the daughter of John and Jane Thompson, was born 25th of 10th month, 1675; Thomas Humbly, the father of Jane H. Thompson, was a native of the county of Durham, England; but at the time of his daughter's marriage, resided in Ireland.

Andrew, the son of Thomas Thompson, married Isabella Marshill, daughter of Humphry Marshill. Andrew and his wife, Isabella Thompson, had three children born in Ireland. Elizabeth, the daughter of Andrew and Isabella Thompson, was born 15th of 8th month, 1666. William, the son of Andrew and Isabella Thompson, was born 9th of 8th month, 1669. Andrew, the son of Andrew and Isabella Thompson, was born 13th of 11th month, 1676.

In the year 1677, John and Andrew Thompson, with their wives and children, (John had one man servant, William Hall, who subsequently became one of the most eminent characters in Fenwick's Colony), set sail on the 16th of 9th month, in the ship called the Mary, of Dublin, John Hall, Captain, and landed at Elsinborough Point, in West Jersey, 22d of 12th month, the same year. About the year 1680, the brothers, John and Andrew Thompson, purchased of Richard Guy one-half of his allotment of land that he had purchased of John Fenwick, some few years previous. Andrew's location was near the mouth of Salem creek; he built himself quite a commodious house there. The said house was standing since the memory of the writer, and was known as the " emigrant house." John built and settled on the property that is known at the present time as the Morris Hall farm. John Thompson was a farmer, likewise a brewer, which he carried on extensively for home use, and also sent considerable quantity to Philadelphia and New Amsterdam. The old brew house was standing until about 1850. On his farm was the family burying ground of the Thompson family; and after the property was sold in 1725 to John Hancock, of Hancock's Bridge, the family of Hancocks buried there for a number of years, and kept it in good repair; but it, like other family burying grounds in Salem county, has been neglected of late years. The fence has gone down, and the plow has passed over the remains of some of the most useful emigrants that ever settled in the Salem tenth.

John Thompson, it appears, never took very active part in the civil affairs of the Colony; but was an active, useful member of Salem Monthly Meeting, and was an elder of the church many years previous to his death. He took an active part in erecting the first brick meeting house in West Jersey that there is any record of, on the Nicholson lot, in Salem. He had in a great measure, the care and oversight in building it, and gave £30 towards it, being the largest sum contributed by any one. He died about 1710, aged about seventy-nine years, leaving a son—James Thompson, who married a young woman resident of New Castle, State of Delaware. By that connection there were several children; all died young, excepting one son.

James Thompson, son of James and Ann Thompson, was born in Elsinborough, the 26th of 8th month, 1712; when he became of age he sold the homestead of his grandfather, John Thompson, to John Hancock, of Alloways Creek, and went to the State of Delaware to reside, and married Sarah Wood. She possessed a large tract of land in her own right, it being near the state line, between Delaware and Pennsylvania. The property is still owned by some of the Thompson family. They are quite numerous at the present day.

Andrew, the brother of John Thompson, was more of a public man than his brother. He was appointed by Fenwick as one of his Justices of the Peace of the Colony; from him the numerous family of the Thompsons in this county originated. Andrew and his wife Isabella Thompson had one son born in America—John Thompson. Their son was born in Elsinborough 23d of 4th month, 1684. Andrew died about 1696 aged nearly sixty years. Elizabeth, the eldest daughter of Andrew and Isabella Thompson, was born in Ireland in 1666. She married

Isaac Smart, who was the son of Roger Smart. Isaac was born in the county of Wiltshire, England, in 1658. He came to America in the ship Griffith, in company with the proprietor, in 1675. He and Elizabeth Thompson were married 25th of 2d month, 1683. Isaac and his wife owned and lived on Middle Neck, in Elsinborough, adjoining the Thompson property. They had five daughters and one son—Mary Smart, their eldest, was born 20th of 10th month, 1685; Sarah, the daughter of Isaac and Elizabeth Smart, born 29th of 1st month, 1687; Nathan Smart, son of Isaac and Elizabeth Smart, born 20th of 6th month, 1690; Hannah, the daughter of Isaac and Elizabeth Smart, born 8th of 6th month, 1692; Rebecca Smart, daughter of the same parents, born 23d of 12th month, 1695; Ann, the daughter of Isaac and Elizabeth Smart, born 20th of 6th month, 1697. Isaac Smart died in 1700, and his widow, Elizabeth Thompson Smart, married Edward Keasbey in 1701; by him she had two sons and one daughter. [See Keasbey Family.]

William Thompson, the eldest son of Andrew and Isabella Thompson, purchased a large tract of land in Monmouth precinct, where Allowaystown now is, and settled there. He was three times married. Joseph Thompson, the son of William and Sarah Thompson, was born 22d of 1st month, 1693; William, the son of William and Jane Thompson, was born 16th of 3d month, 1795. Jane, the daughter of William by his third wife, Hannah Thompson, was born 29th of 7th month, 1700. Susanna, the daughter of William and Hannah Thompson, was born 26th of 8th month, 1704. Samuel Thompson, son of William and Hannah Thompson, was born 6th of 9th month, 1707. Mary, the daughter of William and Hannah Thompson, was born 21st of 11th month, 1710. Rebecca, the daughter of William and Hannah Thompson, was born 19th of 12th month, 1714. Benjamin, the son of William and Hannah Thompson, was born 11th of 8th month, 1719.

Andrew Thompson, 2d, son of Andrew and Isabella Thompson, married and settled on his father's property in Elsinborough. Jonathan, the son of Andrew, 2d and Rebecca Thompson, was born 16th of 9th month, 1697. Hannah, the daughter of Andrew and Rebecca Thompson, was born 12th of 1st month, 1699. Isabella, daughter of Andrew and Rebecca Thompson, was born 22d of 10th month, 1700. Andrew, the son of Andrew and Rebecca Thompson, was born 2d of 2d month, 1704. Thomas, son of Andrew and Rebecca Thompson, was born 28th of 11th month, 1707. Sarah, the daughter of Andrew and Rebecca Thompson, was born 8th of 2d month, 1709.

Abraham, son of Andrew and Rebecca Thompson, was born 26th of 10th month, 1710. Joshua Thompson, son of Andrew by his second wife, Grace Thompson, was born 2d of 2d month, 1713. Thomas, son of Andrew and Grace Thompson, was born 21st of 7th month, 1719. Abraham, son of Andrew and Grace Thompson, was born 27th of 5th month, 1721. Jonathan, Isabella, Andrew and Thomas Thompson, children of Andrew by his first wife, Rebecca Thompson, died young.

Nathan Smart, the son of Isaac and Elizabeth Thompson Smart, was born 20th of 6th month, 1690; was married in 1713. Mary, their oldest daughter, was born 22d of 5th month, 1714; about that time he built an addition to the brick mansion that was built by his father in 1696, which is still standing. Elizabeth, the daughter of Nathan and Deborah Smart was born 4th of 1st month, 1716. Hannah, the daughter of Nathan and Deborah Smart, born 23d of 12th month, 1718. Isaac, son of Nathan and Deborah Smart, was born 4th of 2d month, 1721. Edward, the son of Nathan and Deborah Smart, was born 14th of 5th month, 1724. Isaac, the eldest son of Nathan and Deborah Smart, married Ann Wilson in 1756. Isaac inherited the homestead farm in Elsinborough; he and his wife resided there whilst they lived, and raised a large family of children. Mary, the eldest child of Isaac and Ann Smart, was born 1st of 10th month, 1757; she lived to an advanced age and died in Salem. Nathan Wilson Smart, son of Isaac and Ann Smart, was born 20th of 12th month, 1759. Nathan remained single, and died in middle age. Isaac, the son of Isaac and Ann Smart, was born 2d of 3d month, 1761, and married Rebecca, the daughter of John and Mary Thompson, of Elsinborough. Isaac and his wife had nine children—Ann, Nathan, Mary, John, Deborah, Rebecca, Hannah, Isaac and William Smart. Not one of the large and ancient family of the name of Smarts is a resident of Salem county at this time. Robert, the son of Isaac and Ann Smart, was born 19th of 11th month, 1763. Ann Smart, the daughter of the same parents, was born 25th of 11th month, 1765. She died in 1766. Ann Smart, daughter of Isaac and Ann Smart, was born 25th of 9th month, 1768. She married Samuel, the son of Joseph and Rebecca Abbott Brick. [See the Brick Family]. Jane, the daughter of Isaac and Jane Smart, was born 26th of 10th month, 1775. Some of the children of Isaac and Rebecca Thompson Smart are married and settled in the Western States.

Joseph, the son of William and Sarah Thompson, was born in 1693. He owned property not far from Remster's Mill, where he built a brick dwelling, which was removed by James Fries, and a new frame dwelling was erected near the site of the old one. The property at this time is owned and occupied by Daniel Dial. Elizabeth, the daughter of Joseph and Sarah Thompson, was born 1st of 8th month, 1716. Jane, the daughter of Joseph and Sarah Thompson, was born 7th of 8th month, 1718. William, son of Joseph and Sarah Thompson, was born 30th of 8th month, 1720. Joseph, the son of Joseph and Sarah Thompson, was born 30th of 1st month, 1723; he married Mary Conden, of Mannington, in 1747; they had children. Samuel, the son of William and Hannah Thompson, was born in 1707, and married Edith Tyler, the daughter of William Tyler, 2d; they had issue. Their son Samuel Thompson, was a tanner and currier, and carried on his trade in the town of Salem; they were the grandparents of the late Joshua Thompson. Rebecca, the daughter of Samuel and Edith Thompson, married David Allen, of Mannington. David and his wife, Rebecca T. Allen, had eight children—Hannah, Mary, Rebecca, Edith, Beulah, Samuel, Jedediah and Chambless Allen. Benjamin Thompson, son of William and Hannah Thompson, was born 11th of 8th month, 1719; he married Elizabeth Ware, daughter of Joseph Ware, 2d, and Elizabeth Walker, his wife, in 1745. Benjamin Thompson did a large amount of public business; had also the charge of Richard Wistar's Glass Works near Allowaystown, whilst it was in existence. He and his wife had issue. His son, Benjamin Thompson, married a Willis; they were the parents of the late James Thompson, of Upper Penn's Neck. William Thompson, the son of William and Hannah Thompson, married, and settled near Allowaystown; left children. His son, William, succeeded his father to the old homestead. The property was located near Stephen Reeve's Mill.

Joshua, the eldest son of Andrew Thompson, 2d, by his second wife, Grace Thompson, was born 2d of 2d month, 1713. He was twice married, and by his first wife he had two children. Andrew, the son of Joshua and Sarah Thompson, was born 29th of 5th month, 1739. Sarah, the daughter of Joshua and Sarah Thompson, was born 24th of 12th month, 1742. Joshua's second wife was Elizabeth Gibson, of Woodbury, Gloucester county, where her parents resided. Joshua and Rebecca Thompson, children of Joshua and Elizabeth Thompson, were born 8th of 6th month, 1748. John, the son of Joshua and Elizabeth Thompson, was born 7th of 4th month, 1752. Joseph, the son of Joshua and Elizabeth Thompson, was born 26th of 3d month, 1756. Joshua was left a widower several years before his death. He was an elder and leading member of

Salem Monthly Meeting for a number of years. It has been said of him, "that he was a true Israelite, without guile." He was more than four-score years old, at the time of his death. Andrew, the eldest son of Joshua Thompson, married Grace Nicholson, of Elsinborough, the daughter of Samuel and Sarah Nicholson, of the same township; she was born 11th of 9th month, 1746. Andrew and his wife, Grace Thompson, had five children—Joshua, born 19th of 9th month, 1767; Sarah, born 20th of 1st month, 1769; Grace, was born 12th of 2d month, 1771; Rachel, born 7th of 5th month, 1773, and Samuel Nicholson, born 23d of 5th month, 1777.

Joshua, son of Andrew and Grace Nicholson Thompson, married Rebecca, daughter of David and Rebecca Allen, of Mannington; they had three children—Andrew, Ann and David Thompson. Andrew, their eldest son, was thrice married; his first wife was Rebecca, the daughter of Samuel Abbott, of Mannington; they had one daughter—Hannah Ann. Andrew's second wife was Ann Elkinton, of Port Elizabeth, daughter of John Elkinton; Andrew and his wife had issue, four sons—Joshua, Clark, John and Andrew Thompson. Andrew's third wife was Mary Horner, widow of Charles Horner, and daughter of Benjamin Tyler, of Greenwich; they had four children—David, Richard, Anna and Rebecca Thompson. Ann, daughter of Joshua and Rebecca Thompson, was twice married; her first husband was Caleb, son of Samuel Lippincott, of Gloucester county; they had three children—Samuel, David and Clark Lippincott. Her second husband was Joseph, son of Joseph and Mary Bassett; they are both deceased, leaving no issue. David, son of Joshua and Rebecca Thompson, when a young man left his native county, went and resided in the western part of the State of New York, where he ended his days; he never married.

Sarah, the daughter of Andrew and Grace Nicholson Thompson, born 20th of 1st month, 1769, married Jacob, the son of John and Elizabeth Ware, of Alloways Creek; she was his second wife; they had three children that lived to maturity—Sarah, David and Samuel Ware. [See the Ware Family.] Grace, daughter of Andrew and Grace N. Thompson, born 12th of 2d month, 1771, married Job Ware, brother of Jacob Ware. He died young, leaving one son—John Ware. Rachel, daughter of Andrew and Grace Thompson, was born 7th of 5th month, 1773; she subsequently married Benjamin, son of Joseph Tindell, of Penn's Neck; they had several children—Joseph, Andrew, Sarah and Benjamin Tindell. Samuel Nicholson Thompson, son of Andrew and Grace Thompson, was born 23d of 5th month, 1777. He became the owner, by will, of his grandfather's (Samuel Nicholson) homestead farm in Elsinborough. Samuel married Ann, the daughter of Clement Hall, of Elsinborough; they had six children—Samuel N., Joshua, Charles, Clement, Ann and Isaac Thompson.

Sarah, daughter of Joshua and Sarah Thompson, married William Hancock, of Hancock's Bridge. He was killed at the massacre in his own house during the Revolutionary war in 1778; leaving a widow and one son, John Hancock, the father of Thomas Y. Hancock. Joseph, the son of Joshua and Elizabeth Thompson, kept a store with his brother-in-law, William Hancock, at Hancock's Bridge, and was killed at the same time with his partner. Joshua married Sarah, the daughter of Solomon and Sarah Stretch Ware, of Alloways Creek, in 1773; there were three children—Joseph, John and Elizabeth Thompson. Joshua's second wife was Susanna Mason, widow of John Mason, and daughter of William and Mary Morris Goodwin. By her there were two sons—William and Joshua Thompson. Joshua's third wife was Mary Shourds, of Salem, widow of Benjamin Shourds; there was no issue. She died several years before her husband. He died in 1831, aged nearly eighty-three years.

Joseph, the eldest son of Joshua and Sarah W. Thompson, was born 27th of 10th month, 1774. He married Ann, the daughter of John and Susanna Mason; they had six children (two sons who died young), Susan, Elizabeth, Sarah, and Ann Thompson. His second wife was Elizabeth Powell; they have no children living. John, the son of Joshua and Sarah Thompson, died when he was three years old. Elizabeth, the daughter of Joshua and Sarah W. Thompson, born 13th of 11th month, 1778; married William, the son of William and Sarah Nicholson, of Mannington; they had eight children—Elisha, Ruth, Rachel, Beulah, Elizabeth, William, Joshua and Sarah Ann Nicholson.

William Thompson, the eldest son of Joshua, by his second wife, Susanna Thompson, married Elizabeth Carpenter, the daughter of William and Elizabeth Ware Carpenter, of Elsinborough. William and his wife, Elizabeth Thompson, had nine children—Susan, Eliza, Sarah, Joshua, William, Thomas, Abigail, Lewis and Ann Elizabeth Thompson. William, the father of the before named children, has been deceased for a number of years; their mother is still living at the age of nearly fourscore years. Joshua, the son of Joshua and Susanna Thomp-

37

son, died in 1820, in Salem, where he taught Friends' School for a number of years; he never married.

Rebecca, the daughter of Joshua and Elizabeth Gibson Thompson, born in 1748, married Isaac Jones, of Philadelphia; they had issue, one son—Isaac Jones, born in 1773, who was a merchant in that city. John, the son of Joshua and Elizabeth G. Thompson, was born 7th of 4th month, 1752. In early life he learned the blacksmithing business, and followed his trade many years in the town of Salem; he and Jacob Hufty were in partnership together. He afterwards purchased a farm in Elsinborough, being part of the Windham estate, but is generally known as Richard Darkin property. He soon after abandoned his trade, and went and settled on his farm; there he and his wife remained, until old age. Both of them ended their days in the town of Salem. His wife was Mary, the daughter of William and Sarah Hancock Bradway, of Stoe Neck, Alloway's Creek township. John and his wife had four children—Rebecca, Ruth, John and William B. Thompson. Rebecca, their eldest daughter, married Isaac Smart; the names of their children are mentioned in the Smart family. Ruth, the second daughter of John and Mary Thompson, married Job Bacon, of Greenwich, Cumberland county; they had four children—Mary, Sarah, Ann and Josiah Bacon. Mary married Clement Acton of Salem, and died young, leaving no issue. Sarah remains single. Ann married Moses Sheppard, of Greenwich; they had three daughters—Rachel, Ruth and Mary Ann Sheppard. Rachel, the eldest, married Job Bacon, the son of John and Ann Bacon, of Bacon's Neck. Rachel is deceased, leaving children. Ruth married George Wood Sheppard. Mary Ann Sheppard remains single.

Josiah Bacon, the son of Job and Ruth T. Bacon, went to Philadelphia when young; he afterwards became an eminent merchant in that city, and has been for some years one of the Directors of the Pennsylvania Railroad.

John, the son of John and Mary Thompson, married Esther, the daughter of Darkin and Esther Nicholson, of Elsinborough. They had eight children—Ann, William, John, Joseph, Casper, Mary, Elizabeth and Rebecca Thompson. Three of their children are deceased—John, Ann and Rebecca. William, their eldest son, married Rachel, daughter of Daniel and Mary Nicholson; they have no issue. Joseph married Elizabeth, the daughter of William and Mary B. Carpenter; they had two children—Mary and John Thompson. Casper Thompson, their youngest son, married Mary, the daughter of Casper and Rebecca Wistar, formerly of Mannington; they have issue. Elizabeth Thompson, daughter of John and Esther Thompson, married Nathaniel, a son of James and Millicent Buzby Brown;

Thomas, the son of Andrew, 2d, and Grace Thompson, was born 21st of 7th month, 1719. Thomas Thompson learned the tailor trade, and followed it in the town of Salem, on Broadway street. His dwelling and shop were located where the First Baptist Church is now situated. He married, had one son and one or two daughters. Thomas Thompson, the son of Thomas and Mary Thompson, was born 19th of 10th month, 1745. He also learned the tailoring business of his father, and followed it at the old homestead until about 1795. Thomas Thompson, Jr., married Rebecca, the daughter of Samuel Hedge, 4th, and Hannah Woodnutt Hedge. Thomas and his wife Rebecca Thompson had seven children—Ann, Hannah W., Hedge, Mary, Rebecca, Jane and Rachel Thompson. Ann Thompson, the eldest daughter of Thomas and Rebecca Thompson, married John Firth; they had issue. Their sons who married were Thomas and John; there were two or more daughters.

Hannah, the second daughter of Thomas and Rebecca H. Thompson, was twice married; her first husband's name was Anderson; they had issue. Her second husband was Leonard Sayres; at the time of their marriage he was a citizen of Cincinnati, State of Ohio. He was a native of Cumberland county. He was a son of Ananias Sayres, the first Sheriff of that county, when it was set off from Salem in 1748. Hedge Thompson, the son of Thomas and Rebecca H. Thompson, was a physician, and practiced it some years in his native town and county; but he abandoned his profession before middle age. He was a Member of Congress at one time, also one of the Judges of Salem Court. His wife was Mary Ann Parrott, the daughter of Richard Parrott. Hedge and his wife had five children— Richard P., Thomas, Joseph, M. D., Mary and Rebecca Thompson. Mary, the daughter of Thomas and Rebecca H. Thompson died past middle age; never married. Rebecca, daughter of Thomas and Rebecca H. Thompson, married John Holme, the son of Colonel Benjamin Holme, of Elsinborough. Rebecca died young, leaving one daughter—Rebecca Holme. Jane, the daughter of Thomas and Rebecca H. Thompson, married John, the son of Hill and Ann Nicholson Smith, of Mannington. John and Jane T. Smith had three children— Ann, Hill and Thomas T. Smith. Rachel, the youngest daughter of Thomas and Rebecca H. Thompson, married Doctor Benjamin Archer, at that time was a practicing physician, residing in the city of Salem; but he was a native of Swedesboro, Gloucester county. He was a lineal descendant of one of the oldest Swedish families that located on the eastern shore of the Delaware river. Benjamin and his wife had one son, Fenwick Archer, who is now living, and resides in Salem, where his parents formerly lived. Thomas and Redecca Hedge Thompson lived happily together more than fifty years; he dying first, aged about eighty-two years. Rebecca, his widow, died at about the same age.

Thomas, the son of Thomas and Elizabeth Thompson, was born near Dublin, Ireland, about 1659; at which place his parents had removed from Yorkshire, England, with their two sons, John and Andrew, in the year 1658. In what year Thomas emigrated to New Jersey is uncertain; I think it more than probable that he came in company with his brothers, John and Andrew, on board the ship Mary of Dublin, and landed at Elsinboro, 22d of 12th month, 1677; there was frequent mention of him soon after that time up to the fore part of the eighteenth century. He paid £18 in 1699 towards erecting a Friends' Meeting House in Salem. Where his residence was is somewhat of an uncertainty, but circumstances indicate that it was in Elsinboro. He died about 1714. His son, John Thompson, purchased a tract of land in Alloways Creek, it being part of Ann Salter's allotment, lying on the western branch of Stoe creek, and lying between John Mason's Mill, now Maskell's, and John Chandler's Mill, now known as Wood's Upper Mill. The road that crosses the present mill-pond, was originally the dam erected by John Thompson to raise a head of water for his fulling mill; which business he followed for many years. He left three sons and one daughter—Thomas, Andrew, Jacob and Hannah Thompson. Hannah married Philip Dennis, of Greenwich, Cumberland county, in 1761; they had a large family of children. Thomas married Deborah Oakford, in 1762. Andrew Thompson and Elizabeth Bassett were married in the same year, 1762; they lived but a short time together. Elizabeth Thompson departed this life 9th of 7th month, 1770, and Andrew Thompson, her husband, 15th of 1st month, 1775. He was called Alloways Creek Andrew in the records to distinguish between him and Andrew Thompson of Elsinboro. Thomas Thompson had one son—Thomas, born 1763, who subsequently married, and had five or more children. Jacob, the eldest, married Mary, daughter of Thomas Hartly, of Salem; they had two children—Mary and Mark Thompson. The daughter died a minor, but the son is still living.

Andrew, the second son of Thomas Thompson, married Rachel, the daughter of Charles Shields, a native of Ireland; there were two sons—Josiah and Charles Thompson. Josiah's first wife was Sarah, daughter of Jacob Thompson, who was a distant relative, by whom he had three children—Ephraim and two daughters. His second wife was the daughter of Edward Bradway. She died in a short time after her marriage. Soon after his marriage with the third wife he left his native State and moved with his family to the State of Illinois; he afterwards sent for his aged mother, who lived a few years and then passed away. Josiah possessed good business capacities, and was soon appreciated in his adopted home, and did considerable public business; he was appointed postmaster in the town in which he lived. He died several years ago.

Thomas, the youngest son of Thomas Thompson, married Rebecca, the daughter of Richard Moore, of Alloways Creek. Thomas and his wife had seven children—Lewis, Richard, Eleanor, Ann, Thomas, Rebecca and George Thompson. Eleanor, the oldest daughter, married Asbury Stiles. Ann married Isaac Thompson, of Salem; he was the youngest son of Samuel Nicholson and Ann Thompson, of Elsinboro. Rebecca, the youngest daughter, married Samuel, the son of Jonathan Taylor, of Alloways Creek; she died several years ago. Thomas' sons, I believe, left their native county for the purpose of bettering their condition in some other parts of the country.

Jacob Thompson, son of John, was born about 1735; married Hannah Harris. The forefather of the Harris family, as I have been informed, by the late Dalymoore Harris, located near Roadstown, about the year 1700. The children of Jacob and Hannah Thompson, were Phebe, Hannah, Samuel, Rachel, Jacob and Mary Thompson. Phebe, the eldest daughter, married William Finlaw; they had six children—John, Sarah, Hannah, Phebe, David and Rachel Finlaw. John, their eldest son, married Sarah, the daughter of Joshua Moore; they had issue—Hiram, Charlotte, Sarah and Isaac Finlaw. Hiram married, and in a few years afterwards removed to the State of Delaware. Charlotte was twice married; her first husband was named Miller, of Philadelphia; they had three children. Her second husband was Jacob, the youngest son of Solomon Dubois. Sarah, the daughter of William and Phebe T. Finlaw, married Daniel Ashton; they had issue. Hannah, the daughter of William and Phebe T. Finlaw, was twice married; her first husband was Samuel Padgett, and her second Abram Dilks. Phebe, the daughter of William and Hannah T. Finlaw, married William Padgett. David, the second son of William and Hannah T. Finlaw, married Elizabeth, the daughter of Elijah and Lydia Sayres Fogg. He was the son of Samuel and Prudence Fogg, born 12th of 6th month, 1775. David and his wife, Elizabeth Finlaw, had three daughters—Prudence, Phebe and Lydia. Prudence, married Ephraim, the son of Jesse and Mary Sheppard Carll; they had seven children, four of whom lived to man and womanhood—Sylvanus, Winfield, Laura and Mary. Phebe, the daughter of David and Elizabeth Finlaw, married Jesse P. Carll, the son of Ephraim and Mary Ann Carll. Phebe is deceased, and leaves four children—James W., Rosanna, Laura and Isabella Carll. Lydia, the youngest daughter of David and Elizabeth Finlaw, married Samuel P. Smith, the son of Peter Smith, of Mannington. Their children are David F., Fanny, Phebe, Franklin and Peter Smith. Rachel, the youngest child of William and Phebe Finlaw, married Joseph Corliss; she was his second wife. His first wife was the daughter of Jonathan and Joan Hildreth. Joseph and Rachel Finlaw Corliss had two children—Mary and Phebe Corliss; the latter died young, unmarried. Mary Corliss married Smith Robinson, who is now deceased. She has two children living—Rachel F. and Joseph Corliss Robinson.

William Mulford married Prudence Maskell, of Greenwich, Cumberland county. They had six children, the eldest being Abigail, who became the wife of Isaac Hall, of Philadelphia. Jacob Mulford, their eldest son, was twice married; his first wife being Hannah, the daughter of Jacob and Hannah H. Thompson, and his second wife was Tamson Mulford. Hope, the third child of William Mulford, married Stephen Mulford, who resided in Salem. William, the son of William and Prudence Maskell Mulford, married Ann, daughter of Elijah Cattell, of Salem. Rachel Mulford, the daughter of William, married Captain Benjamin Sheppard. Maskell, the son of William and Prudence Mulford, married Rachel Ewing, a cousin of Judge Ewing, who died at Trenton of cholera morbus more than thirty years ago. William Mulford's second wife was Sarah Ewing, who was born 10th of 7th month, 1750. She was a grand-daughter on her mother's side of Thomas Maskell, who emigrated from New England about 1700 and settled at Cohansey; and daughter of Samuel and Abigail Fithian, of Greenwich. William and Sarah Mulford had two sons—Thomas E. and James W. Mulford. Thomas E. Mulford resided many years in Salem, and followed the coopering business; he married Abigail Clark. James W. Mulford also resided in Salem; his first wife was Sarah Alford, and his second Abigial Woodruff. Jacob, the eldest son of William Mulford, lived the greater part of his life in the city of Salem, and his occupation was that of a dry goods merchant. His place of business was where his grandson's (Dr. Patterson) new buildings are located, on Fenwick's street. Jacob in early life left the religious association of his parents (Presbyterian) and became an ardent member of the Methodist Society, and continued to the end of his days a consistent member thereof. He was very exemplary in his deportment, and in his intercourse and dealings with his fellow men. He twice married, his first wife being Hannah, daughter of Jacob and Hannah Thompson, of Alloways Creek. Her ancestors were members of the Society of Friends from the first settlement of Fenwick's Colony. Jacob and his wife Hannah Thompson Mulford had six children, who all lived to be men and women—Clarissa, Prudence, Hannah, William T., Charlotte and Jacob W. Mulford. Clarissa married Edward Stout, a Methodist clergyman, by whom she had five children—Joseph T., Hannah, Sarah Ann, Clarissa and Dr. Daniel M. Stout. Prudence, the second daughter of Jacob and Hannah Mulford, married in 1817, James, the son of James Patterson, who emigrated from the north of Ireland. He was born in 1749 of Scotch parentage, and circumstances go to show that he left his native country when young. There was a family of that name and nationality who located themselves in Philadelphia. John Patterson also came from Scotland, settling in the city of Baltimore, and became an eminent and wealthy merchant. Jerome Boneparte married his daughter, Elizabeth Patterson. The Salem family have no knowledge that there is any relationship existing between the above mentioned families, but their nationalities are the same, and their emigration took place about the same time. I think it not improbable that there is a relationship between them.

James Patterson, the Scotch-Irish emigrant, married Martha Kent, a lineal descendant of Thomas Kent, who purchased a lot of ten acres of the executors of John Fenwick, in 1686. The said lot was at the junction of Nevell street (now Kent) with Yorke street. The family owned a large farm and brick mansion with a Mansard roof. Anthony Keasbey became the owner of the property, and his grandson, Quinton Keasbey, holds the property at the present time. James and Martha K. Patterson had five children—John, Elizabeth, Mary, Rebecca and James Patterson. James, the father of the above mentioned children, died in 1806, aged about fifty-seven years. His wife survived him about six months. Their occupation was farming. James and his wife, Prudence Mulford Patterson, had five children—William, James Kent, Jacob Mulford, Theophilus, M. D., and Mary Jane Patterson. James, their father, died in 1865, aged seventy-three years, and his wife, Prudence Mulford Patterson, died in 1844, aged fifty-two years. William Patterson, their son, married in 1846, Amelia Rumsey Ware, the daughter of Bacon and Anna J. Ware. Bacon was the son of Job and Hannah Ware, of Bacon's Neck, Cumberland county. His wife Ann T. Rumsey, was the daughter of Benjamin Rumsey, of Maryland. William and Amelia had three children—Anna, Henry Ware, and George R. Patterson, who died in infancy. William is a clock and watch maker, and his place of business is on Broadway, nearly opposite Market street, in Salem. James K., the second son of James and Prudence M. Patterson, resides in Salem, and at present is largely concerned in a canning establishment. He is unmarried. Jacob Mulford Patterson, the son of James and Prudence M. Patterson, married Clementina F. Lloyd, in 1854. They have four children—Theophilus, George Walter, William M. and Pamela Patterson. They reside in Woodbury, Gloucester county. Theopilus Patterson, M. D., married in 1858, Caroline R. Ware, daughter of Bacon Ware. They have four children—James Allen, George C., Carrie Ware and Amella Rumsey Patterson. Dr. Theopilus Patterson is much interested in the cause of education, and for several years was Superintendent of the Public Schools of the city of Salem. His services and labors in that direction were duly appreciated, as was shown at his last election, when he was chosen without any political opposition by his fellow citizens. At the last annual election he declined a re-election owing to his pressing professional duties. Mary Jane, youngest child of James and Prudence Patterson, married John C. Coote, in 1866.

Hannah, the daughter of Jacob and Hannah T. Mulford, married Charles Rumsey, a silversmith, formerly of Wilmington, Delaware. Charles and Hannah T. Rumsey had five children—Charles, James, Jacob M., George Augustus and Hannah Ann. Charles, the father, has been deceased several years. His eldest son, Charles Rumsey, was a merchant in Salem for a number of years, but he is now living in Philadelphia. He has been married twice; his first wife was Emma Michner, of Philadelphia, by whom he had two children—Emma G. and Anna

G. Rumsey. His second wife was Fanny Sovereign; they have six children—Jennie, Fanny, Belle, Fred S., Horace M. and Charles Leslie. The last two births were twins. James M., the second son of Charles and Hannah M. Rumsey, resides at Portsmouth, Ohio. He married Harriet Gaffy, and has four children—John, James, Eliza and Willie. Jacob Mulford Rumsey married Mary Stanger in 1857; they have one child—Edward Smith Rumsey. George Augustus Rumsey married Cornelia, daughter of James M. and Ann K. Hannah. They lived several years in the State of Ohio, but are now residing in their native town of Salem. They have five children—Walter, Eugene, Anna, George A. and Carrol Livingstone. Hannah Ann Rumsey married Samuel L. J. Miller, son of Josiah and Hetty Miller, formerly of Mannington. They have one child—Wyatt W. Miller. Hannah Mulford, the widow of Charles Rumsey, is still living at an advanced age.

William Thompson Mulford, eldest son of Jacob and Hannah T. Mulford, succeeded his father in the mercantile business several years. He married Eliza Fisler, and by her had one daughter, Emma D. Mulford, who subsequently married Jonathan J. Broome, a merchant in the city of New York. They had one daughter—Alice Broome. Charlotte, the youngest daughter of Jacob and Hannah T. Mulford, born about 1803, was uncommonly apt in acquiring education, and was generally at the head of her class in school. She married Peter Bilderback, 21st of 7th month, 1824, and died at an early age, leaving one son—Edward M. Bilderback, who married Elizabeth Heishon, in 1845. Edward and his wife have five children—Charles H., Joseph H., Peter, Lorenzo Dow and Edward Bilderback. Charles H. Bilderback, their eldest son, married Mary Elwell. Joseph H. Bilderback, the second son, married Kate Robinson, of Ohio; they have one child—Elizabeth. Peter, the third son, is a traveling minister of the Methodist denomination in one of the Western States, where he married. Edward Bilderback and his family recently removed to the State of Ohio. Jacob W. Mulford, the youngest child of Jacob and Hannah T. Mulford, like his sister Charlotte, possessed more than ordinary intellect. At one time he resided in the city of Philadelphia, and was in the mercantile business, but towards the close of his life he returned to his native town of Salem. His wife was Jane Fisler. He left one son, Jacob, who is a lawyer residing in Camden, N. J. The second wife of Jacob Mulford, Sr., was Tamson Mulford, and by her had one son, James W. Mulford, who married Emily L. Ford, of Delaware. James and his wife are both deceased, leaving no issue.

Samuel, the son of Jacob and Hannah Thompson, removed to one of the Western States. Rachel Thompson, daughter of Jacob, married Jacob Ware, of Cumberland county; there were two children by this union—Beulah and Theophilus, but they both died single. Jacob, the second son of Jacob and Hannah Thompson, married Mary Finlaw, and by that union there were six children—Rachel, Hannah, Sarah, Mary, Margaret and Susan. Hannah, the second daughter, was married twice, her first husband being Samuel, the son of Elijah Fogg, and her second William Kates. Sarah Thompson was the first wife of Josiah Thompson, son of Andrew; Mary Thompson married Hugh Pogue; Margaret Thompson married Horatio Emerson. Susan Thompson, the youngest daughter of Jacob and Hannah Thompson, married William Sheppard.

Jacob Thompson's second wife was Elizabeth Plummer; they had three children—Elizabeth, John and Margaret. Elizabeth, the eldest, married James Harris; there were three children—Jacob, Mary and Isaac Harris. John, the son of Jacob and Elizabeth P. Thompson, married Abigail McPherson; they had five children—Rebecca, Ellen, John, Jacob and Eliza. Margaret, youngest daughter of Jacob and Elizabeth P. Thompson, born 24th of 12th month, 1781, married David Allen, 4th of 3d month, 1801. She departed this life 15th of 1st month, 1843. She and David Allen had four children—Kent, David, Sophia and Isaac. David, their second son, came to an untimely death, in 1841. He was chopping wood, and while falling a tree, a limb fell from one of the upper boughs and struck him on the head, which caused his death in a short time. Sophia, the daughter of David and Margaret Allen, married William Robinson, Jr.; they have five children—two sons and three daughters—William, George, Sarah, Margaret and Rebecca. They are all married excepting Rebecca, who remains single. Isaac, the youngest son of David and Margaret Allen, married Elizabeth, the daughter of William and Elizabeth Keasbey Plummer, of Lower Alloways Creek; they have several children. Mary, the youngest daughter of Jacob and Hannah Thompson, married Jason Garrison, of Cumberland county.

James Patterson, the emigrant, had a sister, Elizabeth Patterson, who accompanied him to America; she afterwards married Raneir Penton, of New Castle, Delaware. They had several children, one of whom, John Penton, married and left one daughter, Eliza Patterson Penton, who subsequently married Thomas

W. Belville, Esq., of St. Georges, Delaware; they had seven children—Penton, Edward M., Thomas C., Lucy M., Sarah W., Georgianna and Belville. Elizabeth Patterson's second husband was Henry Rowen, of New Castle, Delaware; she died about 1806. John Patterson, the son of John and Martha Kent Patterson, married Sarah Beard; they had five children—Anna, Elizabeth, James B., Rebecca and John. Anna Patterson married a Casperson; she died young, leaving one child—Eliza Casperson. Elizabeth, the second daughter, is not married. James B. Patterson, the son of John, married Ann Skees, in 1832, of Pittsburg, Pa., and have six children—Sarah, William S., John, Elizabeth, Mary and Harriet A. Patterson. James B. Patterson, their father, died at Pittsburg, in 1833.

Elizabeth, the daughter of James and Martha K. Patterson, married James Robinson in 1806, and died in 1820. They had six children—Mary, Benjamin, Prudence, Ann, James P. and John, who died in infancy. Mary, the eldest daughter of James and Elizabeth P. Robinson, married John Fowler, of Mannington; they had four children. John R. Fowler married Theodocia, the daughter of Benjamin and Theodocia Griscom, of Salem. John and his family reside in Philadelphia; he is a commission merchant. Mary, the daughter of John Fowler, Sr., married John Dawson. Benjamin married Elizabeth Linch, and Susan Fowler married John McAllister. Benjamin, the son of James Robinson, died in 1830. Prudence S., daughter of James Robinson, married George T. Kelch; she died in 1844. Ann Robinson married John Taylor. James P., the son of James and Elizabeth P. Robinson, married in 1839, Elizabeth Franklin, daughter of Benjamin Franklin, of Mannington; she died young, leaving one daughter—Mary Emma Robinson, M. D. James' second wife was Anna A. Hass, of Philadelphia; they were married in 1846, and have two children now living—Ann Eliza and Lavinia. Ann Eliza married George Coles, and Lavinia married Lewis R. Jessup, of Gloucester county.

Mary, the daughter of James and Martha K. Patterson, married David Fogg, of Upper Alloways Creek, in 1808. They had four children—Martha A., Elizabeth, James P. and Isaac Fogg. Martha, the eldest daughter, married Thackara Dunn. Elizabeth, the second daughter, married Martin Patterson, of Penn's Neck; they have issue. James P. Fogg married Sarah Dunn; they had issue. Isaac Fogg married Mary Dewer.

Rebecca, the daughter of James and Martha K. Robinson, married William Robinson, of Lower Penn's Neck, in 1811, and died in 1827, leaving six children—William, Noah, John P., James T., Mary and Benjamin. The eldest married Sophia, the daughter of David Allen; their children were mentioned in the Allen Family. Noah Robinson married Jemima Foster, daughter of Joseph Foster, of Salem. Noah is deceased, leaving children. James T. Robinson married Kerinhappuck Harris, daughter of Isaac Harris, of Alloways Creek, the 3d of 3d month, 1848. They had three children—Mary Ellen, Sallie E. and Isabella. James' second wife is Sarah H. English, daughter of David and Sarah Ann English, the daughter of Judge Anthony Nelson, one of Salem county's self-made men. His pleasing address and correct language were far above the generality of mankind, and it is remarkable when we consider what little opportunity he had in early life to acquire an education. When quite young he was apprenticed to the late Samuel Brick, of Elsinboro. Those who have a knowledge of how bound children were treated a half century or more ago, will readily agree that Anthony Nelson was, by nature, a superior man. He represented his native county at three or four different periods in the State Legislature, and was one of the Judges of Salem Courts for a number of years. James and Sarah H. Robinson have nine children—Caddie L., Emma Stretch, John Douglas, Kerinhappuck Harris, Jael E., Frank L., James T., Fannie H. and Hattie S. Mary, the daughter of William and Rebecca Robinson, married Jonathan, the son of Joseph and Mary Hildreth Corliss; they have no children.

EDWARD VAN METER.

Born 1811. Died 1875.

VANMETER FAMILY.

The VanMeters in company with several other families, emigrated from Holland to the State of New York, between the years 1650 and 1660, settling at what is now known as Ulster county. Between the years 1712 and 1714, a company of the citizens of the Dutch Reformed, or Presbyterian faith removed from the neighborhood of Esopis, to Pilesgrove now Upper Pittsgrove, their minister David Evans accompanied them, and his tombstone, with appropriate inscriptions, can be seen in the Presbyterian burial ground at Daretown, in Upper Pittsgrove, Salem county, New Jersey. That these emigrants were families of respectability, may be inferred from the standing of their pastor, who was recognized as a man of learning and piety. These families seemed to have been mindful also, of the advantages of education, inasmuch as a first-class school for that early time, was established by them, and the most competent teachers procured. Parents from long distances sent their children to this school, and some of the most distinguished men in the State, in subsequent years, were proud of the learning obtained at the Pittsgrove College, as it was termed. John Moore White, one of West Jersey's ablest lawyers, was educated there. He was one of the Associate Judges of the Supreme Court for many years, and also Attorney General. Among the company who left New York, were three brothers, and their families by the name of VanMeter. Some of the family settled in East Jersey, chiefly in Monmouth county; one of the brothers, Joseph VanMeter settled in that county, and the other two brothers John and Isaac settled in Pilesgrove township, Salem county. Occasional intercourse, as one of the family writes, and visiting continued between the East Jersey and Salem county VanMeters, for some years, but as the older members of the family died, communication between the younger branches of the family gradually ceased. For some reason the name in East Jersey has been changed in spelling to Vanmater, and Vanmartin, but in West Jersey it is uniformly spelled VanMeter. The first and earliest records of the family to be seen in the Clerk's Office at

Salem in 1714 is spelled in that way, and ever since, in all the public records it appears the same.

The Presbyterian Church at Pittsgrove was organized 30th of 4th month, 1741, David Evans being the pastor. The church covenant was signed by the following members: Isaac VanMeter, Henry VanMeter, Cornelius Newkirk, Abraham Newkirk, Barnett Dubois, Lewis Dubois, Garrett Dubois, John Miller, Francis Tully, Jeremiah Garrison, Eleazer Smith, William Alderman, John Rose, Simon Sparks, Thomas Sparks, Richard Sparks, John Craig, William Miller, Nathan Tarbel, Hugh Moore, Peter Haws, James Dunlap, Jacob Dubois, Jr., Joshua Garrison, and Jost Miller. Tradition of a reliable nature states, that the above families did not constitute themselves a church organization, or connect with any Presbytery from the time of their settlement. Religious services were held in their school house and families, from 1714 until 1741, when they erected a log church, and in 1767 the substantial brick church, which is still standing, was erected. A new church opposite the parsonage was dedicated 15th of 8th month, 1867. Many of those early settlers seem to have been men of means. John and Isaac VanMeter located in company with the Duboises, a tract of 3,000 acres of land, from Daniel Cox, of Burlington, New Jersey, the record of which can be seen in the Clerk's Office in Salem, recorded in 1714. These parties divided their lands by the compass, the Duboises taking theirs on the north side of a line, the VanMeters the south side. The VanMeters continued to purchase until they owned a very large portion of the land, reaching from the Overshot Mill in Upper Alloways Creek near Daretown, southerly, south-east to Fork Bridge, about 6,000 acres in all, and most of the titles to the lands held by the present occupants go back to the VanMeter titles. The early VanMeters were noted for their desire to reach out, and obtain broad acres of land, and their love of good horses, the latter is characteristic of the family to the present time, although careful of display. At the organization of the church in 1741 or 1742, John VanMeter's name does not appear, he had no doubt died previously to that date, leaving a son Henry to represent him, and in that Henry most, if not all of the VanMeters who now reside in the county of Salem, can properly claim their ancestorship. Isaac VanMeter was one of the founders of the original church; he had a son, Garrett, who married a daughter of Judge John Holme, in 1774. Garrett emigrated to Virginia with his family, and some of his descendents are there still.

Henry VanMeter, son of John, was married four times. The following named children are mentioned in his will—Joseph, Ephraim, John, David, Elizabeth, Rebecca, Jacob and Benjamin VanMeter. The two last were children of his last wife, Mary Fetters, of Salem. About the year 1685, Erasmus LaFettre and wife emigrated from England to West Jersey, and settled in the town of Salem. They lived on Yorke street, near Elsinborough line, it being so near it was sometimes called Amblebury. Doubtless some of the elder inhabitants of the town of Salem remember in the early part of the present century an old hip-roof brick house, standing where David Fogg's apple orchard is now. That was, I have been informed, LaFettre's mansion. Erasmus LaFettre was a French Huguenot; he left his native country, together with thousands of others, soon after the revocation of the edict of Nantz, by order of Louis XIV., and fled to England. Erasmus and his wife were members of the Society of Friends. They had several children—Erasmus, Thomas, Sarah, Mary, Hannah and one other daughter, whose name is not given, who married James Sherron's son; they had two children—Roger and Griffith. Thomas Fettres, for that generation of children omitted La when writing their names, and spelled it Fettres. Thomas located in the city of Philadelphia, became a mariner in 1722, and settled on one of the Bermuda Islands. In the same year he gave his intimate friend, Captain Benjamin Vining, a citizen of Philadelphia, and likewise a mariner, a general power of attorney to have charge of his estate in America, personal and real, and to sell and forward the proceeds to him. The instrument of writing was executed in the city of Philadelphia the 8th of 8th month, 1722, before James Logan. Sarah Fettres married Lewis, son of Rudroe and Jael Morris, of Elsinborough; there were five daughters—Sarah, who married Thomas, son of John and Susanna Smith Goodwin, of Salem; Mary married William, brother of Thomas Goodwin; Jael Morris married William Shipley; Ann married Samuel, son of Elisha and Abigail E. Bassett; Hannah Morris married John Whittal. Mary Fettres, as before stated, married Henry VanMeter.

Erasmus Fetters, the eldest son of Erasmus, was a tanner by trade and carried it on in the town of Salem at the old mansion on Yorke street. In 1739 he purchased of John Acton, on Fenwick street, a house and tan yard, containing one acre and a half of ground as set forth in the deed; he was twice married, his last wife was the widow of James Chambless, Jr., of Alloways Creek. Erasmus died in 1757 without issue, making his will in 1756 and disposing of his estate in the following manner: gave the house and premises bought of John Acton to his nephew John Whitel; to Roger Sherron £56; to Griffith Sherron £10; to John, son of William Goodwin, £10; Susanna Goodwin £10; Lewis Goodwin, £10; to his last wife's three daughters, Rebecca, Sarah and Mary Chambless, £10 each, also their mother's wearing apparel; to his niece, wife of Thomas Goodwin, £10; to Mary Goodwin, wife of William, £10; to his niece Jail Shipley, wife of William, £10; to his niece Ann, wife of Samuel Bassett, £10; to John Whitel's two daughters, Hannah and Sarah Whitel, £5 each; his negro boy Dick he bequeathed to William Goodwin for ten years, on condition that at the expiration of that time he should be set free. The remainder of his estate both real and personal was bequeathed to his sister Mary VanMeter's two sons, Jacob and Benjamin VanMeter. William Goodwin and John Whitel were his executors. His personal estate, after his just debts were paid, amounted to £1119 18s. 5d., as was filed in the ———— office at Burlington in 1758 by his executors.

Jacob VanMeter settled in Genesee county, New York, and left a family, who in former days visited the home of their ancestors. Benjamin VanMeter married Bathsheba, daughter of Captain James Dunlap, of Pittsgrove; he was the son of Captain James Dunlap, Sr., of Penn's Neck. The Dunlaps came from Delaware to Penn's Neck, and are supposed to be of Irish descent. James Dunlap's will was written in 1758; he died the same year, leaving three sons and one daughter—John, James, Thomas and Mary Ann. James, Jr., married Anna Hunter, and died 19th of 9th month, 1773; his wife died 16th of 1st month, 1780. The Hunter family were from East Jersey; a branch removed and settled in Salem county. Robert Hunter died, leaving a widow and two daughters—Anne and Mary. His widow married Hugh Moore; they had issue, one son, Richard Moore, who settled at Lower Alloways Creek; he died, leaving one son and five daughters. One of the daughters married George Grier. Johanna married Jonathan Hildreth. One married James Sayres, one married Solomon Dubois, one married Daniel Stretch. As has been stated Anne Hunter married James Dunlap, Jr.; they had one son and two daughters—Bathsheba and Mary Dunlap. Bathsheba, the eldest daughter, married Benjamin, the son of Henry and Mary Fetters VanMeter. Mary, daughter of Robert Hunter, married Samuel Purviance; left one son and three daughters. Mary, the eldest daughter of Samuel and Mary Purviance, married Samuel Eakin, a Presbyterian pastor, their children were Samuel, James, Ann, Susan and Johanna. The latter married Isaac Hazelhurst; she died in 1809, leaving five children—Richard Hunter, Samuel, Isaac, Jr., Andrew Purviance and Mary. The other daughter of Samuel and Mary Purviance married William P. Leigh, of Virginia. These Hunters are believed to be the descendants of Robert Hunter, one of the Colonial Governors of New Jersey, who held office from 1710 to 1720. The Hunters were distinguished in early history for their prominence in the pulpit, and State offices, and for their learning and eloquence. Benjamin VanMeter, as before stated, married Bathsheba Dunlap. He settled in early life on his ancestral estate, and was a useful man in his time, being a ruling elder in the Presbyterian Church at Daretown. He was the owner of a number of slaves, but becoming convinced in his own mind that it was an evil to hold his fellow man in bondage, he liberated all of them a few years before his death. At that time there was no law to compel him to do it, and he had been so kind a master that some of his slaves refused to leave, and accordingly ended their days with him. Benjamin VanMeter departed this life 15th of 10th month, 1826, aged eighty-two years; his wife died 7th of 11th month, 1831, aged eighty-four years. Their children were James, Mary, Ann, Sarah, Erasmus Fetters, Robert Hunter and Bathsheba. James, the son of Benjamin VanMeter, was a physician, and commenced practicing medicine at Alloways Creek when a young man. He boarded with John Hancock. However he remained there but one year, and then removed to the town of Salem, and soon afterward married Ruth, the daughter of Thomas Jones. He had a very extensive practice as a physician, perhaps greater than any other one physician that ever resided in the town of Salem, particularly so among the members of the Society of Friends. He was one of the founders of the Presbyterian Church in that place, and died in 1847, aged eighty years. His wife died a few years before him, aged sixty-three years. They left an only child, a son, Thomas Jones VanMeter, who graduated in early life as a physician. He never practiced to much extent. He married Hannah, daughter of Anthony and Hannah Keashey, of Salem. Their children are Artemisa K., Martha J. and James Anthony VanMeter (the latter died in childhood). Hannah, wife of Dr. Thomas VanMeter, died in 3d month, 1871.

Mary, daughter of Benjamin and Bathsheba VanMeter, married Matthew Newkirk, and died in early life, 7th of 7th month,

1802, leaving four daughters, Bathsheba, Elizabeth, Ann and Sarah Newkirk. Bathsheba, the eldest, married Jeremiah Stull, and had several children. John married Julia, daughter of Daniel Garrison of Salem; Mary Stull married a person by the name of Cloud, of Maryland. Caroline Stull married Dr. Wallace. Sarah married James Johnson. Bathsheba married Jacob Mench —all of them have children. Elizabeth, daughter of Matthew and Mary Newkirk, married a person by the name of Effinger, and had several children. Ann, daughter of Matthew and Mary Newkirk, married Henry VanMeter; they had one daughter, who afterwards married a person by the name of Carruthers, and had several children. Sarah, the daughter of Matthew and Mary Newkirk, married a person by the name of Olmstead; they had several children. Ann, daughter of Benjamin and Bathsheba VanMeter, died 10th of 9th month, 1851. Sarah and Fetters VanMeter, children of Benjamin and Bathsheba VanMeter, died in infancy. Erasmus, son of Benjamin and Bathsheba VanMeter, married Mary Burroughs; he inherited the family homestead, and died 7th of 11th month, 1842, aged sixty-six years. He was a ruling elder in the church of his fathers at the time of his death; his wife died 10th of 8th month, 1860, aged seventy-five years. Their children were Benjamin, John, William, James, Elizabeth and Bathsheba VanMeter. Benjamin VanMeter married Hannah McQueen; they had several children, and removed West. John VanMeter, son of Erasmus, married and died, leaving children. William VanMeter, son of Erasmus, went West, married there, and has several children. Elizabeth, daughter of Erasmus VanMeter, married Samuel Swing; they had four children—Erasmus V., Mary Jane, Ruth Ann and Alfred. Erasmus V. Swing is a practicing physician. He married a Burroughs, and settled in Pennsylvania. Alfred was killed in the late rebellion. Bathsheba, daughter of Erasmus VanMeter, married Thomas Brooks; they had two children—Rebecca and Benjamin Brooks. Rebecca married James Robinson, and Benjamin married Amanda Johnson. James, the son of Erasmus and Mary VanMeter, married a sister of James and William Coombs; they settled in the State of Ohio. Robert Hunter, son of Benjamin and Bathsheba VanMeter, graduated as a physician in 1799, and settled in Pittsgrove. His first wife was Rachel Burroughs of the same place; she died three months after marriage; his second wife was Sarah Leake Whitaker, daughter of J. Ambrose and Rachel Leake Whitaker. They moved to Salem in 1809. Dr. Robert VanMeter was also one of the founders of the Presbyterian Church in Salem, and a ruling elder in the church at the time of his death; their children were Emma, Mary, James, Robert, Edward, Mason, Josiah and Harriet.

Emma, daughter of Robert and Sarah VanMeter, died near Baltimore 16th of 11th month, 1869. Mary, daughter of Robert and Sarah VanMeter, married Enos R. Pease, of Connecticut, and died 17th of 4th month, 1834, leaving one child, Alvin Robert Pease, who died in Alleghany City, Pennsylvania, in his seventeenth year. James, Robert and Josiah, children of Robert and Sarah VanMeter, died in infancy. Edward, son of Robert and Sarah VanMeter, married Caroline, daughter of Isaac and Ann Whitaker. They had three children—Mary Caroline, Harriet Fetters and Anna Hunter VanMeter. Edward VanMeter died 4th of 1st month, 1875. He studied law in early life in his native town of Salem, and it appears at that time he was not much attached to his profession, for he soon after went into the mercantile business at Hancock's Bridge. The firm was known as VanMeter & Dubois. Soon after leaving the store he was employed by Jonas Miller as his book-keeper. Jonas was the proprietor of one of the largest public houses at the time on Cape Island. Edward continued with him two or three seasons. Soon after he was married, he turned his attention to his first calling, that of law, as attorney and solicitor in chancery. He did a large amount of public business in his time, and was considered one of the best business men in the city of Salem.

Mason, son of Robert and Sarah VanMeter, is still unmarried, living in Salem. Harriet, daughter of Robert and Sarah VanMeter, married R. J. Cone, of New York, a clergyman. They had two children—Norris Hunter and Charles Kirtland Cone. Norris Hunter Cone graduated from Lafayette College 6th month, 1872, and went to Colorado where he now resides. His brother, Charles Kirtland Cone, died at the age of nine years.

Bathsheba, daughter of Benjamin and Bathsheba VanMeter, married William Mayhew; they had one daughter, Maria, who married a person by the name of Johnson, and had one daughter, Anna, who married Charles Burroughs. After the death of Maria's first husband she married James Richman, and has several children. Bathsheba Mayhew died 17th of 9th month, 1866.

CHRISTOPHER WHITE FAMILY.

Christopher White, son of Thomas White, was born at Omnar, in the county of Cumberland, England, in the year 1642. From thence he removed to London in 1666, and in 1668 he married Elizabeth Leath. She was a widow, and was the daughter of John Wyatt, of the county of Yorkshire. They had one daughter Elizabeth, who was born in Shadwell, near London, in 1669. His first wife Elizabeth died about the year 1671. It appears he married his second wife in the year 1674, whose first name was Esther, but her last name is not given in the records. Josiah White, son of Christopher and Esther White, was born in London, in 1675. Christopher and his wife and their two children, and their two servants, John Brinton and Jane Allen, emigrated to America, and landed at Salem 23d of 6th month, 1677. They had one son—Joseph White, born in Salem 5th of 11th month, 1678. Christopher White, like several other emigrants, had purchased one town lot in Salem, together with 1,000 acres of land, of the proprietor before he left his native country. He resided on his property in Salem until about the year 1682, and he then removed and took possession of his allotment of land in Alloways Creek. In 1690 he built a large brick house on his property in said township, the King's Highway from Salem to Cohansey running through his lands, the house was built near said road, not far from the meadow. There is a tradition in the neighborhood that he sent to England for an architecture, and likewise had the brick imported from that country for the house. The following is the description and size of the building, given to me by Judge Ephraim Carll, who had an excellent opportunity of knowing—he and his family having resided there for several years, and was also present when the building was taken down:

The main building was thirty-two by eighteen feet, and two stories high. The walls were eighteen inches in thickness up to the second story, and the joist of that story projected beyond the walls five feet, making a projection of that width on three sides of the building, and the walls from that point were twelve inches in thickness. The joist in the main building were clear yellow heart pine, and floor boards were of the same material, being one and a half inches in thickness. Beyond the main walls of the building was an extension from the foundation built, being eight by ten feet, for a stairway to the second story and garret. On top of said walls was an arch roof which gave the building a singular appearance. There was also a cellar under the whole of the main building, which was paved by square English brick. The basement floor, and likewise the second and attic floors, were supported by large beams twelve by fourteen inches, which extended across the middle of each floor. The main entrance to the main building on the west side of it, took five large stone steps from the ground to enter the building, and on the east side there was a one-story kitchen attached, which likewise was built of brick, sixteen by twenty feet in size. There was a good sized yard around the house which, at one time, was paved with square brick, but at the time the house was removed many of the yard bricks had been broken up and removed. I have been more particular in describing this building on account of the interest the old inhabitants of the township had respecting it, and when it was erected. The late Robert G. Johnson told me the year after it was taken down, that he regretted very much that there was not a photograph drawing of the building for the Historical Society of New Jersey.

Israel Harrisson married Esther, the daughter of Christopher and Esther White, of Monmouth precinct, about 1693. Israel and his wife Esther had two children. Joseph, their son, born 1694, and Sarah, the daughter of Israel and Esther Harrisson, was born 14th of 12th month, 1696. Israel died in 1704.

Christopher White died about the year 1698, leaving a widow and three children—Elizabeth, Josiah and Joseph White. Christopher White appears to have been a man of an energetic turn of mind, and a high moral tone of character, and those traits were transmitted to his descendants for several generations. His daughter Elizabeth married William Bradway, in the year 1689. Josiah White, son of Christopher, I believe, married Hannah Ashbury in 1698. Their son Christopher White, was born 23d of 6th month, 1699, and died a minor. Their son, Josiah White, was born in 1705. Hannah White, daughter of Josiah and Hannah White, was born at Alloways Creek in 1710. Josiah White, Sr., died about the year 1726, leaving his landed estate to his son, Josiah.

As early as 1698, the owners of the meadows and low lands

bordering on Alloways creek obtained a law from the West Jersey Legislature to enable them to put a dam across the said creek, and to put a sufficient sluiceway to drain all the low lands lying above the present Hancock's Bridge. For some cause which has never been explained, the work was not undertaken until the year 1723, at which time the Company contracted with Josiah White to build the dam. He was the son of Josiah White, and grandson of Christopher White, the emigrant. Josiah was born 21st of 6th month, 1705, at the old homestead of the family, called at that time Monmouth Precinct. He made a contract to erect a dam and put in a sufficient sluiceway for a specific sum, the amount of which I have never learned, and guaranteed it to stand one year before he was to receive his pay. But the meadow owners above the dam soon discovered that their lands did not drain as well as before, and besides losing the navigation of the creek, which was an incalculable loss, for there was as much valuable timber on the land bordering the creek at that time as in any part of West Jersey. Before the expiration of the year the dam broke. Since that day immense quantities of the best quality of ship timber, and thousands of cords of fire wood, together with products of the farms, have been sent to market from the lands bordering the creek above the dam, by the navigable highway which nature designed Monmouth river to be. Within a few years past, by the wear of the creek, many of the ancient piling and other timber on the south side became a hindrance to navigation, and the Freeholders of the county determined to have the timber removed out of the stream. They offered proposals for the lowest bidders to clear the navigation. Edward and Lewis S. Carll agreed to do it, they being the lowest bidders, for the sum of $210. Many of their friends were fearful they would incur a loss by the undertaking, but by good management and perseverance they have been successful in removing a large quantity of heavy timber.

The dam was constructed with two cribs, twenty feet each, making the width of the embankment full forty feet wide. About fifty or sixty feet from the south side of the creek, which, I presume, at that time, was near the channel, they found large quantities of wood cut in lengths to cord tightly in between the three rows of piling and land ties, which, I have no doubt, was used as a tumbling dam until such time as the other part of the enbankment could be raised above tide water. Many of the piling, drawn by means of a stump puller, were imbedded fifteen and some nearly twenty feet in the mud and gravel. The land ties drawn to the shore from the bottom of the creek, were over fifty feet in length, and squared twelve to fourteen inches, they being to all appearance as sound as when put there—one hundred and fifty-six years ago. They were of white oak. The creek since that time has changed its channel northerly fully sixty feet. The first bent on the south side of the stream, with the piling and land ties, are at this time imbedded under the mud fully three or four feet deep, extending under the present tide bank.

I previously mentioned that the work was done by contract by Josiah White. Tradition says the dam was cut on the night before the year expired. The company contended that the stopping broke, but their statement found little or no credit, and was never believed except by those persons who were interested in the meadow company, and they decided not to pay him. Josiah was under the necessity of selling his large patrimonial estate to pay the debt he had incurred in erecting the works for their benefit. At that time he was only twenty-three years old. Many persons in the same adversity would have become dispirited, but not so with one who had inherited from his father and his grandfather those qualities of heart and mind, which made him capable of withstanding more than ordinary trials. After disposing his estate to Joseph Stretch and others, he was enabled to pay his indebtedness and have £500 left. He then determined to leave his native county, not having any family. His widowed mother, Hannah White, had died a short time previous. He went and settled in Burlington county, at or near Mount Holly, and there purchased land on the head waters of Rancocas creek. Soon after he made a dam across the creek for the purpose of raising a head of water, and then built a fulling mill, in which, I think, he carried on the manufacturing of cloth the greater part of the remainder of his life. He married 1st of 10th month, 1734, Rebecca, the daughter of Josiah and Rebecca Foster, a highly respected family of Burlington county; she was a descendant of the Borden family, from whom Bordentown, on the Delaware river, derives its name. She was born 1st of 10th month, 1702.

Josiah and his wife, Rebecca F. White, had six children. Their eldest daughter, Amy, born 13th of 5th month, 1737, died when she was about thirteen months old. Hannah, the second daughter, born 28th of 11th month, 1739, married Thomas Prior, in 1763; her second husband was Daniel Drinker. Josiah, son of Josiah and Rebecca White, born 24th of 4th month, 1752, died when two years of age. Rebecca, the daughter of Josiah and Rebecca, born 15th of 3d month, 1745, married a young man by the name of Redman, of Haddonfield. John, the son of Josiah and Rebecca, born 9th of 7th month, 1747. Josiah White, the youngest son of Josiah and Rebecca, was born 20th of 8th month, 1750. The father of the above named children was a minister in the Society of Friends, recommended as such in the year 1743. On the same day the celebrated John Woolman was also recommended by the Mount Holly Monthly Meeting. Josiah had the happy faculty of condensing what he desired to express either in his public communications or his private conversation, and his company was much sought after. He and Dr. Benjamin Franklin were on quite intimate terms, as he was also with Governor William Franklin, the son of Dr. Franklin, whose country seat was near Mount Holly. Josiah imbibed the idea similar to Homer, the father of poets, that there were plants and herbs that grew to cure all diseases the human family is liable to. I have been informed that for a number of years of his life he used no other medicine in his family but what he made of herbs, and he was frequently sent for by his neighbors to administer the same to their families. He received the appellation of herb doctor. He certainly was a man of clear and comprehensive judgment, and was well calculated to leave his foot-prints on the sands of time, and those great qualities were transmitted to his descendants to a remarkable degree to the first, second and third generations, as their lives and their undertakings for the public good (all of which they accomplished) fully demonstrate.

Josiah lost his wife about nine years before his death; she died 6th of 12th month, 1771, aged nearly sixty-three years. He was born at Alloways Creek, 21st of 6th month, 1705, and died at Mount Holly, 12th of 5th month, 1780, aged nearly seventy-five years. He descended from an ancient family of the name of White, in the county of Cumberland, in England. Thomas White, his great-grandfather, became converted to the principles of George Fox, and soon after that event left his native county and removed to London. In the year 1664 he was taken from the Bull and Mouth meeting, in that city, and taken before Alderman Brown. He told the Alderman that he thought he had filled up the measure of his wickedness, at which the Alderman, incensed, struck him in the face, kicked him and sent him to Newgate prison. His grandfather, Christopher White, also suffered much violence and persecution in the city of London on account of his religious opinions. It is probable for that reason he concluded to leave his native country and emigrate to the wilds of America, where he could enjoy civil and religious liberty. He accordingly purchased 1,000 acres of land of John Fenwick before he left England, in the early part of the year 1675, and with his family arrived at New Salem in the 6th month, 1677. He became an active and useful citizen in Fenwick's infant colony. He died on his plantation in Monmouth Precinct, now Alloways Creek township, about the year 1696. His son, Josiah White, who was born in London in 1675, succeeded him and became the owner of his real estate in said township.

John, the son of Josiah and Rebecca White, born 9th of 7th month, 1747, married 7th of 6th month, 1775, Rebecca, daughter of Jeremiah Haines, of Burlington county; she was born 28th of 7th month, 1744. John and his wife Rebecca White had four children. John, the eldest, lived to grow up to manhood and died unmarried; Christopher, their second son, died a minor; Josiah was born 4th of 3d month, 1781; and Joseph, the youngest, was born 28th of 12th month, 1785. John, their father, died 22d of 8th month, 1785, aged about thirty-eight years.

Josiah White, well known as the pioneer of introducing the Schuylkill water for the use of the inhabitants of the city of Philadelphia, also one of the first projectors of the Schuylkill canal, and also the Lehigh Coal and Navigation Company. The latter he commenced and completed nearly or altogether by his own individual exertions, so as to enable the different coal companies, which were then organizing in the anthracite coal regions, to carry it to the Philadelphia market for common use as fuel. Before that period it was not much used, owing in a great measure to the high price of transporting it to market, which put it out of reach of the common people, it being from $25 to $40 per ton. Josiah was the third son of John and Rebecca H. White, and was born 3d of 4th month, 1781. He was married twice; his first wife being Catharine Ridgway, of Burlington county, whom he married in 1805. She died a few years after her marriage, leaving no issue. Josiah's second wife was Elizabeth, the daughter of Solomon and Hannah White, of Philadelphia. There were five children by that connection— Hannah, the eldest, married Richard Richardson, of Wilmington, Delaware; she is still living. Their next child was a son, who died young. Solomon, their third child, lived until he was in his nineteenth year. He has been represented as a young man of uncommon promise, and was possessed of a mind above mediocrity, and consequently his untimely death was a great loss to his aged and beloved parents. Josiah and Elizabeth

White's fourth child was a son, who died young. Rebecca, their youngest child, is still living, unmarried. Josiah White, the father, died 14th of 11th month, 1850, aged nearly seventy years.

Joseph White, the youngest son of John and Rebecca H. White, was born 28th of 12th month, 1785. Like his elder brother, Josiah, he inherited from his ancestors that great energy of character and a cast of mind which made them pioneers in new and important improvements for the benefit of mankind. He married Rebecca, the daughter of Daniel D. and and Elizabeth Schooley Smith, of Burlington county. Daniel D. Smith was a descendant of Richard Smith, M. D., who was baptised 18th of 5th month, 1593, and died at Branham, Yorkshire, England, in 1647. Elizabeth Schooley Smith was the great-grand-daughter of Samuel Jennings, first Governor of West New Jersey. Rebecca Smith, her daughter, was born 29th of 3d month, 1787. Joseph and Rebecca S. White had eight children—John Josiah, Daniel S., Elizabeth, Sarah S., Anna (who died young), Howard, Barclay and Anna Maria. John J. White, the eldest son, resides in Philadelphia, in the house on Arch street that was formerly occupied by his uncle, Josiah White. He is a lawyer by profession. He has been twice married, his first wife being Mary Kirkbride Shoemaker, and his second wife Abigail Weaver.

Daniel S. White, the second son, married Rebecca L. Shreve. Elizabeth, the eldest daughter, married Joshua Lippincott, of Philadelphia. Sarah S. White died unmarried; Howard died unmarried; Barclay married Rebecca Merritt Lamb, daughter of Restore Lamb, of Burlington county. She died several years ago, leaving issue. His second wife was Beulah Sansom Shreve. Barclay at this time is one of the Government's Superintendents of Indian Affairs, and is located at Omaha, Nebraska. Anna Maria, the youngest child of Joseph White, married J. Gibbon Hunt, M. D. During the year 1808 Joseph White and Samuel Lippincott purchased Josiah White's stock of hardware and commenced business as importer of and dealer in hardware, under the firm of White & Lippincott, at No. 111 Market street, Philadelphia. The following interesting narrative of Joseph White, written by his youngest son Barclay, and forwarded to me a few months ago, shows that his life had been extended to threescore years and ten; he had the ability and energy to have risen as high on the pinnacle of fame in the history of his country as his elder brother. He died at the age of forty-one years in the prime of his life.

In the year 1811 Joseph left Philadelphia with the intention of traveling on horseback to St. Louis, Missouri, and other places in the Western and Southern country, for the purpose of extending the business of the firm, and collecting debts due to it. Stopping at Brownsville, Pennsylvania, he stabled his horse and strolled through the streets to view the town. Passing a store, he noticed a man standing in its door, clad in such custom as denoted he was a member of the Society of Friends; and being a stranger in a strange place, Joseph was attracted towards this member of his own religious Society. Asking for some trivial article of merchandise as an excuse for opening a conversation, he entered the store. This new acquaintance proved to be Elisha Hunt, who, with his brother Caleb, were conducting a mercantile business there. The conversation that ensued was interesting to both Friends, and when supper was announced, Joseph was invited to join the family circle. The Hunts made a proposition that if Joseph White would give up his journey on horseback and assist them in building and freighting a keel boat, Caleb Hunt would in the spring join him on the trip to St. Louis, thus making a more pleasant journey, with favorable prospects of a successful mercantile venture. Such an arrangement was agreed upon. Joseph White spent the winter at Brownsville, the boat was built, and freighted with general merchandise, and in the spring of 1812, Caleb Hunt and Joseph White, with a crew of French-Canadian boatmen, started her from the landing at Brownsville, Pennsylvania, bound for St. Louis, Missouri. During the previous 11th month an earthquake, which is known as the "earthquake of New Madrid," had changed and rent the banks of the Ohio river, adding to the risks and labors of the voyage. As they pursued their course with the current of the river, there was much leisure time, and the boatmen noticed that Joseph frequently interested himself by reading from a volume which he carried in his pocket, and they asked that he would read to them. The volume was the Bible, and by commencing his readings with the narrative portions, they became so interested in the book that the readings were made regular and systematic during the remainder of the voyage.

As far as the mouth of the Ohio the voyage was comparatively easy, requiring only watchful care to keep the boat in the current and avoid obstructions, but from the Ohio's mouth to St. Louis, against the rapid current of the Mississippi river, was another kind of labor. They now doubled the number of their men, and pulled the boat up stream with a long rope, a number of hands on shore dragging it. This was called "cordelling" and "bushwhacking," as the men would catch a bush with one hand and pull the rope with the other. This arduous labor was well calculated to lead the reflective mind to consider if some other power could not be successfully applied for propelling boats against such a current.

After reaching St. Louis the merchandise was sold, partly for cash, the balance to be paid for in lead, which was to be delivered at St. Genevieve, Missouri, during the spring of 1813. Having successfully disposed of their goods, and ascertained that the St. Louis merchants, who were indebted to White & Lippincott, were unable to pay the debt, the friends turned their keel boat down the Mississippi river homeward bound. They entered the mouth of the Ohio river, and proceeded up it as far as Smithland at the mouth of the Cumberland river, where, not finding an opportunity to sell their keel boat, it was committed to the charge of Joseph Wood, to sell, freight or charter.

Joseph White bought a horse of Wood for $50, and with Caleb Hunt, left Smithland on the 6th of 7th month, 1812, at six o'clock A. M., on horseback for the journey home. From the notes of this journey, which are now before me, they passed through Louisville, Kentucky. At Hopkinville they received the intelligence of war being declared with England. The diary notes:—"We were much shocked thereat; this un-"expected intelligence overclouded my prospects, and makes "my ride gloomy." "At Bowling Green, Kentucky, I fell in "with the proprietor of a cave, who wanted me to purchase it. "He asked $10,000. With five men he makes one hundred "pounds of saltpetre per day; to manufacture it costs him from "five to six cents per pound; it is now worth twenty-five cents "per pound in Lexington, Kentucky."

At Sheppardsville, Kentucky, the friends separated, and Joseph White proceeded to Louisville, where he found considerable commotion on account of a man being arrested on suspicion of being a British spy, and fomenting the negroes to insurrection. He passed through Frankford, the seat of government, which he describes as "a smart town, containing about one "hundred and fifty houses." "Cynthina contains about fifty "houses," thence to Lexington, which he found to be "a delight-"ful place, with hospitable people and luxurious soil." Passing through the gap of the Cumberland range of mountains, he traveled on to Knoxville, Tennessee, which is mentioned as "a "lively town, with from two hundred to three hundred houses; "here I was introduced to the Governor of the State and several "principal people." "Near Rogersville I exchanged horses "with William Lyons, gave him $50 to boot, and am to pay $10 "more if he should think it a hard bargain." From Abington, Virginia, he passed up the Valley of Virginia, or Shenendoah Valley, through Lynchburg, stopping to view the Natural Bridge; then on to "Strasburg, containing sixty or seventy "houses," through "Winchester, a fine place with about four "hundred houses," passing by Harper's Ferry, where he found an extensive manufactory of arms, producing nine hundred stand per month, rating at $12 each. Thence to Frederickstown, Maryland, which he supposes "contains eight hundred or one thousand houses," thence through Columbia, Lancaster and Downington, in Pennsylvania, arriving in Philadelphia, 16th of 8th month, 1812. This horseback journey from Smithland, Kentucky, to Philadelphia, appears to have occupied forty-one days.

During the autumn of 1812 Elisha Hunt visited Philadelphia, and while there arrangements were made and a stock company formed to construct steamboats and carry passengers and freight by steamboats between Pittsburg and New Orleans. The stock of this company was divided into six shares, of which Joseph White owned two or one-third of the whole amount of stock. Daniel French, a Connecticut man, owned a patent for steamboats, and had built a little stern wheel steamboat on his plan, which was then running as a ferry boat between Cooper's Point, Camden, New Jersey, and Philadelphia.

French said he could construct steamboats that would run five miles an hour, against the current of the Mississippi river, and an arrangement was made with him by which he sold to the company the right to use his patent west of the Alleghany mountains. The services of French were engaged, shops were erected at Brownsville, Pennsylvania, tools for working in iron were made, logs were cut into plank with whip saws, and with the ferry boat above mentioned as their model, they constructed the steamboat Enterprise, costing about fifteen thousand dollars, and in the latter part of the summer of 1813 she left Pittsburg for New Orleans, under the command of Captain Henry Shreve, who was the son of Israel Shreve, of Burlington county, New Jersey, a Colonel in the Revolutionary army.

The Enterprise reached New Orleans, and was there seized by the State Marshal, at the instance of Fulton and Livingstone, for coming within the limits of Louisiana, they having obtained from the Legislature of that State a charter, granting them the exclusive privilege of running steamboats on the waters of that State. Captain Shreve gave security for trial, the Enterprise was released, and returned up the river with a full cargo of freight and passengers. The charge for carrying freight was eight cents per pound, and one hundred and twenty-five dollars for each passenger. It was announced in the Pittsburg papers, and copied into Cramer & Spears' Almanac that the steamboat Enterprise had just arrived with a full cargo of passengers and freight, in the remarkable short passage of twenty-six days from New Orleans, thus proving the practicability of navigating the Mississippi river by steam.

The Steamboat Company labored under a great disadvantage on account of fuel and had axemen on board to chop wood, which they took on the banks of the river and from drifts, as they could find it. This occasioned great detention, but arrangements were made for a supply at several landings against the next trip. The next time the Enterprise landed at New Orleans, General Jackson pressed her into the service of the United States, and sent her up to Alexandria, on the Red river, with provisions, &c., for the army there.

The Enterprise made about three round voyages between Pittsburg and New Orleans, when peace was declared between the United States and England. Passengers and freight then went around by sea. The Enterprise finally reached Shippins Port, below the Falls of the Ohio river, and the river being low above, and freights dull, the Captain anchored the boat in deep water, and hiring two men to take care of her, went by land to Pittsburg. One of the men went ashore and the other got drunk and neglected the pumps, the weather was hot, the seams of the boat opened, and the Enterprise filled and sank to the bottom, where, as Elisha Hunt, in a letter written during the year 1851, says "she still is." Elisha further states that while he was down in Kentucky, in 1818, a man offered him $1,000 for the wreck, as he thought he could get her engine out to run a saw mill.

Fulton & Livingston obtained judgment against the Company in the State Court, but on appeal the United States Court set that decision aside and left the navigation of the Mississippi free, and open to all. Said suit cost the Company between $1500 and $2000.

The Steamboat Company then built a second boat called the Despatch, designed for shoal water, she soon sank in the Ohio river, after which the stockholders became discouraged, and the Company dissolved.

The Enterprise was the first steamboat that ever went out of the Monongahela river to New Orleans, and returned up against the current.

One of Elisha Hunt's letters says: "The amount of dividend "paid to the stockholders out of the profits of the boats I am "not able to give, for no book account was ever kept by the "Captain. On his return to Brownsville he brought his funds "in several shot bags, of Spanish dollars, which were poured "out on the counter of E. & C. Hunt's store, and laid off into "six piles to the stockholders, with which they were satisfied at "the time."

In consequence of the sinking of the boats, the stockholders lost all their investment, which was about $20,000. The Steamboat Company manufactured the tools necessary for the construction of steam machinery, and also constructed a cotton mill at Brownsville, in which they placed a steam engine, manufactured in their shops. After the close of the war the cotton mill failed.

After Captain Henry Shreve left the service of the Steamboat Company, he constructed a boat at Wheeling, called the Washington. Shreve was employed by the government to remove the snags out of the river, and afterwards entered into an engagement with the United States to remove the Red river raft. He invented a powerful snag boat, and with it improved the navigation of the Red river to Shreveport, which town was named after him.

One of Elisha Hunt's letters states: "The little office con-"nected with our Brownsville store was the rendezvous of many "intelligent and enterprising young men, and there all the "recent inventions for improving travel, etc., were argued and "discussed." Among the regular visitors there he mentions Neal Gillespie Blaine, grandfather of Ex-Speaker Blaine, of the House of Representatives, Robert Clark, Stephen Darlington and others.

The lead which was to be delivered at St. Genevieve in part payment for the keel boat merchandise, was on hand according to contract, when the Enterprise stopped for it. The boat carried it to Pittsburg, whence it was freighted to Philadelphia in Conestoga wagons, and there sold, netting over one hundred per cent. profit on the keel boat venture.

In 1813 or 1814 Elisha Hunt sent to Joseph White one barrel of "Seneca Oil" gathered at Oil Creek, Pennsylvania, which Joseph sold to Daniel Smith, a druggist in Philadelphia. The oil was gathered by damming up the rivulets, and spreading a blanket over the water to absorb the oil. The blanket was then wrung over barrels, which caught the oil.

Joseph White was extensively engaged in coal operations in

the Lackawanna region during the latter years of his life, and died in Philadelphia 25th of 5th month, 1827, aged forty-one years.

After many years of mercantile life at Brownsville, Elisha Hunt returned to his native place, Moorestown, New Jersey, where he passed many of his later years, and died in the summer of 1873 in the ninety-fourth year of his age. It was my privilege and pleasure on several occasions during those years to converse with him upon his social and business connections with my father, and the incidents above narrated have been chiefly derived from such conversations.

It is more than probable that if Josiah White, Jr., had not been defrauded of his just dues by the inhabitants of the Upper Precinct of Monmouth, he would have remained in his native county of Salem, a district of country for which nature has done so much. The inventive genuis and uncommon energy of character possessed by him and his descendants would have been an incalculable advantage to this section of the State; for as William Penn wrote in one of his maxims respecting human life: "Great minds were destined by Providence to be the pio-"neers of all that is good and useful for the benefit of "mankind."

Josiah White, while in his twenty-eighth year, sold all his goods to his brother, Joseph White, and Samuel Lippincott, he having by this time obtained the amount of property he desired as being sufficient for him. It appears he was out of business about two years, and in 1810 he married his second wife Elizabeth, the daughter of Solomon and Hannah White. Her father had been a successful merchant in Philadelphia, but was then deceased. Notwithstanding his plans of life, it seems he was designed for active life, and about two years after he sold out his interest in Market street, there was a water power offered for sale at the Falls of Schuylkill, belonging to Robert Kennedy, comprising about four feet available fall, with all the water of the river, with the right to construct a lock for navigation, charging fifty cents toll on each boat for passing; also, there was four acres of ground on the east side of the river, and seven or eight acres and an old tavern house on the west side adjoining the bridge. He built a large mill for the manufacture of wire, and a smaller one for making nails, and entered himself in the manufacture of these articles about that time. He associated with him Erskine Hazard, who became a partner in the manufacture of wire. In 1801 he took out a patent for rolling iron, and in 1812 another patent for making wire and heading nails. In 1817 he and Joseph Gillingham endeavored to make arrangements with the City Council. They offered to furnish the city with three millions of gallons of water every twenty-four hours for twenty years, at twenty-five thousand dollars a year, and then three millions of gallons every twenty-four hours at three thousand dollars a year forever. But it appears they were not successful in making a contract with the City Council at that time.

About the year 1812 they made an experiment of anthracite coal in their rolling mill. They procured a cart load of it which cost them one dollar per bushel. This quantity was entirely wasted without getting up the requisite heat, and another cart load was obtained, and a whole night spent in endeavoring to make a fire in the furnace, when the hands shut the furnace doors and left the mill in despair. Fortunately one of them left his jacket in the mill, and returning for it in about half an hour, noticed that the furnace door was red hot, and upon opening it was surprised to find the whole furnace of a glowing white heat. The others were summoned, and four separate parcels of iron were heated and rolled by the same fire—before it required renewing. The furnace was then replenished, and as letting it alone had succeeded so well, it was concluded to try it again, and the experiment was repeated with the same result. Coal at that time was $40 per ton.

White & Hazard applied to the Legislature in 1813 to grant them the privilege of making the Schuylkill navigable so as to bring the coal to market, and supply their own wants at a cheaper rate, but the idea was ridiculed. The members from Schuylkill county said in the Legislature, that although they had a black stone in their county it would not burn, and they were unsuccessful in obtaining the law for that purpose at that time. [See Hazard Report, page 302]. White & Hazard called a meeting for all those that were interested in the navigation of the Schuylkill to meet at the tavern, corner of Fifth and Race streets, Philadelphia, in 1815. Josiah White opened the business of the meeting by proposing the application to the Legislature for a company to improve the Schuylkill for slack water navigation by dams and locks. This was the commencement of the present Schuylkill Navigation Company. The Company was incorporated in 1815, showing clearly that he was the originator of that inland navigation which has been millions of dollars benefit to the city of Philadelphia and State of Pennsylvania.

In 1819, White & Hazard sold their water-power at the

Falls of the Schuylkill to the city of Philadelphia. They then turned attention to the coal regions at Mauch Chunk. They left the city on horseback, and the greater part of the way they had to travel through the wilderness, particularly in the mountainous regions, and arrived at Summit Hill in safety, a short distance from Mauch Chunk.

In 1792 a company was formed called the Lehigh Coal Mine Company, who took up a large tract of land contiguous to that on which the coal had been found. White, Hazard & Company rented ten thousand acres of land of said company for twenty years, for one ear of corn a year, if demanded, and from and after three years to send to Philadelphia at least forty thousand bushels of coal per annum on their own account. So as to be sure of introducing it in the market, they immediately set to work to improve the navigation of the Lehigh, with a capital of two hundred thousand dollars, and afterward the stock was increased to a million. In the year 1820 the dams and locks being completed, the first anthracite coal was sent to market by artificial navigation. The whole quantity, says Josiah White, was three hundred and sixty-five tons. This, he said, proved more than enough for family supplies in Philadelphia. In 1823 the navigation of the Lehigh was completed, and was inspected by commissioners who reported it finished, and the Governor issued his licence on the 17th of 1st month, 1823, authorizing them to take toll.

Josiah White removed his family from Philadelphia, in 1821, near Mauch Chunk. Next year a comfortable house was provided for his family upon the hill-side above the beautiful river, with spacious grounds, adorned with rocks and forest trees. An extensive inclosure, called the Park, contained elk and deer, for the amusement of his children, and at that place his mother closed her life in the family of her son, in the eighty-second year of her age. In 1831 the works of the company being so far completed as not to require his constant attention, the family returned to Philadelphia, and resided at the corner of Seventh and Arch streets. Soon after a heavy domestic affliction was experienced by the parents in the loss of their only remaining son, a prominent young man in his nineteenth year.

From 1820 to 1871 the production of coal from the Lehigh Coal and Navigation Company from official reports amounts to 13,705,298 tons.

Josiah White was much interested in the subject of education, particularly desiring its diffusion among the lower classes of the people, in a way to make them self-reliant and self-supporting, often contributing liberally of his means for such purpose. He bequeathed funds for the establishment of two manual labor schools in the West—one in Indiana and the other in Iowa—especially having reference to the religious training of the pupils.

A short time before his death he visited Salem, and in company with Robert G. Johnson, visited the native place of his ancestors at Alloways Creek. He died in Philadelphia the 14th of 11th month, 1850, in the seventieth year of his age.

Notwithstanding his life was a busy one and vast his undertaking in improving the inland navigation of his adopted State, which, by his perseverance and good management he completed, and his mind appeared to be centred to the great first cause. He wrote the following touching expressions, among others of a similar nature, in his religious reflections not long before his death: "When I consider the relationship of man to his Maker, "how depending he is before him, yea, nothing but a cloud of "dust, and the life he lives is only by the will and power of the "Holy One; it is even He that created this dust, and gave it "life and being and capacity to serve him, and to do his will "and life forever." He left three daughters, two of whom are still living. Hannah married Richard Richardson and Rebecca remains single.

I close the short account that I have written of this truly great man by copying the remarks made by Charles V. Hagner, from a work he wrote of some of the leading men that lived near the Falls of Schuylkill. After mentioning the various and great undertakings Josiah White had accomplished for the benefit of the city and State, he says: " Have I not shown good "reasons for saying that I know of no man to whom the citizens "of Philadelphia are so much indebted for substantial benefits "they have so long enjoyed as they are to Josiah White. First "we see him in company with Mr. Hazard, making experiments "with the anthracite coal, and succeeding in bringing it into "practicable use in the rolling mill. Next in successfully con- "triving gates to make it applicable for domestic use. Then "starting the Schuylkill Navigation Company to bring down a "supply of coal. Originating the idea of the Fairmount Dam, "resulting in giving to the citizens of Philadelphia such a plen- "tiful supply of water as they never dreamed of before, and "finally originating the Lehigh works. The warrior who slays "thousands of his fellow creatures is lauded and glorified, high "monuments are erected to his memory, on which are embla-

"zoned his deeds of blood, but the modest, plain, unassuming
"citizen who does so much good for his fellow men, and who
"neither seeks or courts notoriety, sleeps his last sleep, compar-
"atively unnoticed or forgotten."

JOSEPH WHITE FAMILY.

Joseph White descended from an ancient family of Northamptershire, England. He was the son of Samuel and Elenor White, and was born the 20th of 1st month, 1651. He left his native place in England and removed to Ireland, in 1672; soon after that event, he married Elizabeth, daughter of Anthony and Elizabeth Church, who had removed from Staffordshire, England, to Ireland, a few years before, and they became members of New Garden Monthly Meeting, near Dublin. In said meeting, about the year 1679, Joseph White and Elizabeth Church were married. They, in company with a number of friends, among whom were Hugh Middleton, from Gloucestershire, England, Allen Matthias and Hannah Ashbury, all originally natives of England, set sail from Dublin harbor, and after a passage of eight weeks and two days, they landed at Elsinborough Point in West Jersey, on the 17th day of 9th month, 1681. The same day they landed, they had a daughter born, which they named Rema White. Joseph White located on land in Elsinborough and resided thereon. He was an active man in the civil affairs of the Colony; and likewise an influential member of Salem Monthly Meeting. Joseph White, Jr., son of Joseph and Elizabeth White, was born in Elsinborough, 29th of 11th month, 1692. I think that Joseph White, Sr., died about the year 1703. I find no mention of him after that date in public records, or in the meeting books. The family soon after his death left Elsinborough and settled in the upper part of the county.

Joseph White, 2d, married and had several children. John White, son of Joseph and Mary White was born 19th of 3d month, 1717. Joseph White, 3d, son of Joseph and Mary White, was born 21st of 10th month, 1719. William White, son of the same parents was born in 1722. Here appears a discrepency in the records. I have heard stated there were two or three daughters. William White, son of Joseph, 3d, married, and had several children, six daughters and one son. William was born in 1751; he subsequently became an eminent land Surveyor. He died 18th of 11th month, 1836, in his eighty-fifth year. He enjoyed remarkable health, and was never known to be sick during his long life, until a few days before his death. He was married three times. His first wife was a Fisher, by whom he had one daughter—Hannah White. She married Benjamin Heritage, of Gloucester county. Benjamin and his wife had ten children, four sons and six daughters. William White's second wife was Anne Paul, daughter of Samuel Paul, of Gloucester; they had ten children—William, Samuel, Ann, Rebecca, Mary, Joseph, Sarah, Isaac, John and Joel White. William White's third wife was Mary Silvers, widow of Thomas Silvers; they had no issue.

William, the son of William and Anne White, married Susan Bates, of Gloucester county; they had five children—William, George, Samuel, Charles and Susan White. They are all married and scattered in the Western States. Samuel, son of William and Anne White, married Jerusha, daughter of Jonathan and Hannah Shourds Smith, of Pilesgrove. Samuel and his wife had eight children—Elizabeth, Jonathan, William, Mary, Samuel, Caroline, David and Wilson White. Elizabeth, daughter of Samuel and Jerusha White, has been twice married. Her first husband was Clement Hinchman, he however died a short time after marriage, leaving one daughter—Clemence Hinchman. Her second husband was William Carll, son of Samuel Carll, Jr. Jonathan, the eldest son of Samuel and Jerusha White, married Lydia, daughter of Aaron and Sarah Waddington, of Elsinboro. Jonathan died young, leaving one daughter—Gertrude White. William, son of Samuel and Jerusha White, married Emily Buzby; he died without issue. Mary, daughter of Samuel and Jerusha White, married Bradway, son of Aaron and Sarah Waddington. Bradway died a young man, leaving two children—Ada and Frank Waddington. Ada married a person in New York. Samuel and Caroline, children of Samuel and Jerusha White, died minors. David, son of Samuel and Jerusha White, married a young woman of Gloucester county; they have children. Wilson White, married a Loveland; they have issue.

Ann, daughter of William and Anne White, married William Haines, of Gloucester county; they had five children—Joshua, William, Ann, Sarah and Samuel Haines. Joshua, the son of William and Ann White Haines, married Hannah Albertson, of Burlington county; they had three children—Chalkley, Abigail and Rebecca Haines; Chalkley and Abigail are married. William, son of William and Anna Haines died recently; his wife was Rachel Lippincott. William was a recommended minister, and a member of Upper Greenwich Meeting; like his grandfather, he was an eminent Surveyor. He and his wife had four children—Job S., William, Emily and Hannah Ann Haines. Job married Ellen Holmes; they have four children—Jacob, Stacy, Idella and Jesse Haines; William, son of William and Rachel Haines, remains single. Emily married Joseph Livyley; they have five children; Samuel, son of William and Anna Haines, married Ann Eliza Holmes, of Upper Penn's Neck; they had one son—Howard Haines. Ann, the daughter of William and Anna Haines, married Champion Atkinson; she died leaving no issue. Sarah Haines, sister of Ann, married Champion Atkinson, former husband of her sister; they are both deceased, leaving no issue. Rebecca, daughter of William and Anne White, was twice married; her first husband was William Miller, of Greenwich, Cumberland county; they had three daughters—Sarah Ann, Eliza and Mary Miller. Sarah Ann Miller, their eldest daughter, married Amos, son of Joseph Buzby; they have ten children—Edward, Chambless, Joseph, William, Samuel, Franklin, Emily, Elizabeth, Rebecca and Cornelia Buzby. Eliza, daughter of William and Rebecca Miller, married Lewis, son of William and Martha Hancock, of Elsinboro; they had two daughters—Mary and Martha Hancock. Mary, the daughter of William and Rebecca Miller, married Caleb Borton; they had three children—Omar, Mary and Phebe Ann Borton. Omar, son of Caleb and Mary Borton, is a successful Apothecary in Woodstown; his wife is the daughter of John and Sarah Albertson, of Baltimore, Maryland. Omar and his wife, have one daughter—Izetta Borton; she married Dr. Lafayette Allen. Mary, daughter of Caleb and Mary Borton, married Nathan Y. Lippincott; they had five children—George, Edward W., Ellen, Hannah and Emma Lippincott. George, son of Nathan and Mary Lippincott, married Rachel, the daughter of Allen Wallace; they have issue. Edward W. Lippincott, married Emma, daughter of the late Henry Ridgway, of Croswicks, Burlington county; they have no issue. Ellen, daughter of Nathan Y. Lippincott, married Daniel Taylor; they have two daughters. Emma, daughter of Nathan Y. and Mary Lippincott is not married.

Joseph, son of William and Anne White, was twice married; his first wife was Deborah, daughter of James Hewes; he was a lineal descendant of William Hewes, who purchased a large tract of land of William Penn in Upper Penn's Neck, in 1689; the said land was surveyed by Richard Tyndall, by an order of

James Nevill, of Salem. Joseph and Deborah White had three children—James H., Ann and Edward White. Joseph White's second wife was Lydia Moore, of Woolwich, Gloucester county; they had five children, namely—Reuben, Hannah, Deborah, Thomas and Martha. James, son of Joseph and Deborah White, married Mary Ann Holmes, daughter of Samuel Holmes, of Upper Penn's Neck; they had nine children; their names are—Esther, Sarah, Samuel, Ann, Joseph, James, Franklin, Martha and William White. Ann, the daughter of Joseph and Deborah White, married Aaron Lippincott, and have five children, four sons and one daughter. Joseph, married Georgianna, daughter of Robert and Sarah Given, of Salem; they thave no issue. Deborah, daughter of Aaron and Ann Lippincott, married Charles Ballenger; they have two children. Edward, Benjamin and David Lippincott are single.

Edward, son of Joseph and Deborah White, is at the present time Surrogate of Cumberland county. He married Ann, daughter of Jonathan and Fanny House, of Upper Alloways Creek; they have issue, two daughters—Fanny and Mary White. Isaac, son of William and Anne White, left his native State, and went to the city of New York. John and Joel White, sons of William, settled in one of the Southern States. The family have not heard from them for a number of years.

WARE FAMILY.

Joseph Ware came to this country in 1675 as a servant of Edward Wade. Robert Wade, in 1678, sold his allotment of land on the south side of Alloways creek, prior to his purchase in Pennsylvania near the ancient Swedish town of Chester. James Denn and Anthony Page were the purchasers. Soon afterwards Page sold 250 acres to Joseph Ware, who subsequently bought another 250 acres adjoining his first purchase, of Edward Wade, making in all 500 acres. In 1683 he married Martha Groff, and their children were Joseph, born 1684; Sarah, born 5th of 7th month, 1686; and John, born about the year 1688. The latter settled at Cohansey, and became a member of the Baptist Society. He had a son named John, born in 1722, who died in 1773, and was buried in the ancient Baptist grave-yard at Cohansey. His son, Job, born in 1761, was also interred in the same grave-yard in which his father was buried. From this family there is a large number of descendants., Maskell Ware, of Salem, being one of them. Joseph Ware, Jr., in 1707, married Elizabeth Walker. They had three sons and one daughter, Elizabeth Ware, who married Benjamin Thompson, near Allowaystown. Their sons were Joseph, 3d, Solomon and John Ware. Joseph Ware, 3d, married Elizabeth, daughter of Philip Blanchard, born 20th of 8th month, 1716. Joseph and his wife had six children; the eldest, Mary, born 22d of 8th month, 1735; Sarah, Hannah, Rebecca, Joseph, 4th, and Elijah Ware, born 30th of 1st month, 1748. Elijah's wife was Mary, the daughter of Benjamin Tindall, of Penn's Neck, and great-grand-daughter of Richard Tindall, of Tindall's Grove. Elijah and his wife had no issue. He died several years before his wife, and made a will which, after the death of his widow, devised a small farm to Salem Monthly Meeting. He was considered one of nature's noblemen—an honest man—and was an approved minister of the Society of Friends, meek and humble in his deportment, and wielded great moral influence in the neighborhood in which he lived. Sarah Ware, the sister of Elijah, was born 2d of 8th month, 1737, and married Joseph

Stretch, 3d, in 1761. They had two daughters, Jael, born in 1762, and Martha, born 11th month, 1763. Solomon, the second son of Joseph Ware, Jr., was born in 1717. His wife was Sarah Stretch, whom he married in 1740. They lived on the homestead farm of his father, the property upon which I now reside. The house was built by Joseph Ware, Jr., in in 1730, more than one hundred and forty years ago. Solomon and his wife had eight children. Peter, the eldest, born 25th of 8th month, 1741; Elizabeth, Job, Hannah, Elisha, Sarah and Solomon; they all died minors excepting Sarah. Solomon Ware died in 1761, at the age of forty-five years, and his widow departed this life in 1765, four years after her husband. Only two of their children, Elisha and Sarah, were living at that time, and Elisha died with the pleurisy the year after his mother, in his eighteenth year.

The whole of the estate of Solomon Ware, consisting of a farm of 250 acres, and a considerable personal estate, came into the possession of the surviving daughter. Sarah was born 12th of 6th month, 1756, and married Joshua Thompson, of Elsinborough, in 1773. They had three children—Joseph, born 27th of 10th month, 1774; John, born in 1776, and died in 1779, and Elizabeth, born 13th of 11th month, 1778. The latter married William, son of William and Sarah Nicholson, of Mannington, and had eight children—Elisha, Ruth, Rachel, Beulah, Elizabeth, William, Joshua T. and Sarah Ann Nicholson. Elisha went as supercargo on a voyage to the West Indies, and died of yellow fever on the passage home. He never married. Ruth Nicholson's husband was Joseph Edgar Brown, and they did not live together more than two or three years. She died in 1827, and was regretted by a large circle of relatives and friends for her many admirable qualities. She possessed a fine intellect, pleasant and agreeable manners, and warm sympathies for the afflicted. She left no children. Rachel Nicholson married Thomas Y. Hancock. There were five children. Elizabeth, the eldest's, first husband was David, the son of Andrew Smith, of Elsinborough; her second husband was Samuel Fowser. She died several years ago. Ellen, the second daughter, married Dr. Henry Childs, of Philadelphia. William N., the third child, married Beulah, daughter of William Fowser. Cornelia, the third daughter, has not yet married. She conducted herself most admirably during the late rebellion, having served with the army of the Potomac the greater part of the war, attending to the sick and wounded, and continued to assist in the hospitals until the rebellion closed. Since the war ended she has been at

Charleston, South Carolina, teaching a school of colored children. Thomas Hancock, Jr., the youngest child, was drowned while bathing when he was not more than ten years of age.

Beulah, daughter of William and Elizabeth Nicholson, died a young woman, in 1819 or 1820. Elizabeth, another daughter, died in infancy. William Nicholson, their son, married Susan, the daughter of William Miller, and had four children—Rachel, Susan, William and Elizabeth. Rachel, the eldest, married Thomas Mathers, near Germantown; Susan married James Gaskill. William, Jr.'s wife is Florence Earl, and Elizabeth's husband is Sylvester Garrett. Joshua Nicholson married Eliza Smith, daughter of Stephen Smith, and moved to Illinois many years ago. When the war broke out he enlisted in the Western army, and from exposure was taken sick, I believe, near Nashville, Tennessee, and died in one of the army hospitals, leaving a widow and one son—Alexander Nicholson, Sarah Ann Nicholson married Dr. Henry Childs. She has been deceased many years, leaving two children—Elizabeth and John. Joseph, the eldest son of Joshua and Sarah Thompson, was born 27th of 10th month, 1774. His first wife was Ann, the daughter of John and Susanna Mason. Joseph and his wife had five children—Elisha, who died when about two years of age, Susan, Elizabeth, Sarah and Ann. Susan married Joseph Pancoast, son of Samuel and Dorcas Pancoast, and had seven children—Ann, Samuel, Elizabeth, Joseph, Thomas, Hannah and John. Elizabeth Thompson, died in 1820, in her sixteenth year.

Sarah Thompson, their third daughter, born in 1807, married Thomas Shourds, 10th of 1st month, 1828. Ann, the youngest daughter of Joseph and Ann Thompson, born in 1809, married Thomas, son of Aaron and Hannah Fogg, in 1827. They have twelve children—Susan, Joseph, Elisha, Elizabeth, William, Morris, Rebecca, Ann, Mason, Clarkson, Emily and Albert Fogg. Ann Mason Thompson, the wife of Joseph Thompson, departed this life in 1810, and in 1815 he married Elizabeth, daughter of Jeremiah and Sarah Powell. They lived together in conjugal felicity for more than thirty years. In the autumn of 1845 he was attacked with inflammation of the bowels, and after great suffering for upwards of two weeks, his strong constitution gave way and death ensued. He was in the seventy-first year of his age, and his death cast a gloom over a large circle of relatives, neighbors and acquaintances. He was kind and hospitable to the poor and needy, always ready to contribute to their necessities, and in the latter part of his life he became greatly interested in pleading the cause of bondmen—

the bleeding slaves of our land. It can truly be said of him,—
"Mark the perfect and upright man, for the end of that man
"shall be peace, and assurance forever." His last wife was
nearly thirteen years younger than himself, and left no issue.
She departed this life in 1864, being the possessor of talents of
high order, and if her early education had been attended to, few
women in the country would have equaled her. She, like her
husband, was kind and sympathetic in her feelings. Always
ready to plead the cause of the oppressed, she was a co-worker
with her two Friends, at Salem, Elizabeth and Abigail Goodwin,
against the institution of slavery.

John, the youngest son of Joseph and Elizabeth Ware, was
born 3d of 3d month, 1720. He inherited the property from
his father where Samuel C. Pancoast resides at the present time.
He was a farmer and weaver. In 1750 he married Elizabeth,
sister of Joseph Fogg, who was born about 1730. They had
eight children, all of whom lived to grow up. They all married
and had children. John, the eldest, born 16th of 7th month,
1751, married Ruth, the daughter of James Tyler, and two
children, Martha and Eleanor, were born to them. Milicent,
the eldest daughter of John and Elizabeth Ware, born 12th of
10th month, 1753, married John Smith, the great-grandson of
John Smith, of Amblebury. He owned and lived upon the
property in Lower Alloways Creek township, now belonging to
Robert Grier, which was part of the Smith allotment of 2,000
acres. John Smith and his wife Milicent had one son, John,
who subsequently married Mary, the daughter of Andrew Sinnickson. They had two sons and two daughters, named respectively, Robert, Margaret, Thomas and Mary. Robert died in
infancy. Thomas married Mary, the daughter of Morris and
Sarah Hancock. Mary married Oliver B. Stoughton, a native
of Connecticut, who came to Salem in company with his friend,
the late Calvin Belden, upwards of fifty years ago, and they
commenced the hardware and tinning business together in that
city. By industry and careful attention to business they each
acquired a competency, and became useful and respected citizens
of their adopted town and State. Oliver and his wife had
several children. He died several years ago, but his widow is
still living. Margaret, the eldest daughter of John and Mary
Smith, married Edward G. Prescott, an eminent Episcopal
clergyman. He was a native of Boston, Massachusetts, and a
brother of William H. Prescott, one of America's favorite
historians. I have been informed that Edward had symptoms
of pulmonary consumption before he came to Salem. He was

a man of great acquirements in the way of learning, and possessed considerable oratorical powers. He bore an enviable reputation as a Christian minister. His physicians recommended a sea voyage, thinking it would be the means of arresting the fatal disease lurking within him. He repaired to his native city to bid his aged father and family adieu. I have been told that within a few days after the vessel sailed he died and was buried at sea. I think he and his wife had no children. Margaret, his widow, was killed near the city of Burlington, together with several other passengers, at the terrible railroad disaster in 1856. Mary Sinnickson Smith, the widow of John Smith, is still living, being more than ninety years of age. I think she is the oldest person living at this time in the city of Salem.

David Ware, the second son of John and Elizabeth Ware, was born 5th of 4th month, 1755. He commenced life on a farm that was left him by his father, of which James Baker is the present owner. His first wife was Sarah Oakford; they had one daughter—Sarah Ware. Her mother died when she was young. David Ware's second wife was Letitia, widow of William Craig. He owned and lived about two miles above Allowaystown, which is now known as Remster's Mill—it formerly belonged to Richard Wistar. Letitia's maiden name was Morrison. She was an approved minister among Friends. David sold his farm at Alloways Creek soon after his second marriage, to his brother Job Ware, and purchased a farm near Grey's Ferry, Philadelphia county, where he went with his family to reside. His daughter Sarah Ware married Aaron Ashbridge; they had three children—Anna, David and Samuel Howell Ashbridge. Anna Ashbridge married John Firth, of Salem, son of John and Ann Firth. Jacob Ware, son of John and Elizabeth Ware, was born 28th of 11th month, 1759; he married Mary Carpenter in 1780, the daughter of William and Mary Carpenter.

I think it would be right to digress to give the history of the Powell family, as they are closely connected with the Ware and Carpenter families by marriage. William and Jeremiah Powell, brothers, emigrated to America and settled in Philadelphia in 1684. William, the eldest, purchased of the proprietor a large tract of land on the west side of the Schuylkill river. West Philadelphia occupies part of the land that he purchased. He established a ferry where the present Market street bridge stands. [See Watson's Annals.] William's family after several generations was narrowed down to one individual, a widow. Her possessions were great and valuable. Tradition says that a young man by the name of John Hare, a distant relative of her husband, lived with her. She gave him to understand that if he would make application and have the name of Powell added to his name, he should be her heir. This being accordingly done, he become the owner of that large estate called Powellton. Jeremiah Powell, the younger brother of William, settled in this county. Whether he was a married man when he came to Jersey I am not certain; most probably he was. He was one of the contributors towards building the Friends' Meeting House which was erected in 1700 where the grave yard is now in the town of Salem. In that year he purchased a tract of land near Hancock's Bridge of John Maddox, formerly part of William Hancock's allotment, and leaving the town of Salem settled thereon. His son, Jeremiah Powell, was born at Alloways Creek, 18th of 3d month, 1701, and Samuel Powell, his second son, was born in 1704. I presume they were the only children he had, no others being mentioned in the records.

Robert G. Johnson, in his history states that the Friends' meeting at Alloways Creek was established by the Powells and others—it was a mistake. The meeting was organized in 1684, several years before Jeremiah Powell was an inhabitant of the county of Salem. Jeremiah Powell, Jr., in 1735 married Jane Blanchard, the daughter of Philip and Mary Blanchard, who resided in the township of Alloways Creek. They had three children—Elizabeth, Mary and John Powell. Samuel Powell, the brother of Jeremiah, married before his brother and settled on the homestead farm in 1730. George Trenchard, Sr., was chosen an Assessor for the whole township of Alloways Creek, and William Tyler was the Collector. Samuel Powell was assessed for the Powell property. Samuel died a young man leaving no children. Elizabeth Powell, the eldest daughter of Jeremiah and Jane Powell, was born in 1736, and married Benjamin Smith, the grand-son of Daniel Smith. Benjamin and his wife resided in the township of Mannington. They had three children—Joshua, Powell and Elizabeth. The last married John Smith, the son of Christopher Smith. They left one son—Samuel. Joshua Smith married a young women a native of Gloucester; they left two or three children. Powell Smith married Sarah Ambler, daughter of Peter Ambler; they had two children—Sarah and Isaac Smith. Mary Powell, daughter of Jeremiah and Jane Powell, was born 13th of 11th month, 1738; she married William Carpenter, a native of the State of Delaware, and grandson of Joshua Carpenter, of Philadelphia. His age is not definitely known, but I think he was several years older than his wife. They had four children —Mary, Powell, William and Abigail. John, the son of Jeremiah and Jane Powell, was born in 1740, and became a farmer and weaver. When he was about twenty-three years of age he married Ann Dickinson, whose parents lived in Upper Alloways Creek township. John and his wife had one son, Jeremiah Powell, 3d, born in 1764. John Powell possessed a weak constitution, and died while young, leaving a young widow and an infant son. He was pious, of strict integrity, and possessed more than ordinary abilities. Though young he frequently was called upon to settle difference among his neighbors. Like many persons in this country who have clear intellectual minds, he fell a victim to that scourge of mankind, the pulmonary consumption

Jacob Ware and his wife Mary, had two children—Elizabeth and Millicent. The latter died young, and unmarried. Elizabeth Ware married Samuel, the son of Benjamin and Mary Shourds. They had three children. William, the eldest, who died young; Mary and Thomas Shourds. Mary Shourds was born in the 1st month, 1804, and married William Bradway, the son of Ezra Bradway; they had six children—Elizabeth, Sarah, Mary, Anna, Rachel and Ellen Bradway. Jacob Ware's second wife was Sarah Thompson, daughter of Andrew and Grace Thompson, and grand-daughter of Samuel Nicholson. A short time after they were married they went and lived on her grandfather's property, in Lower Penn's Neck. Samuel Nicholson in his will left his large and valuable estate in said township to Sarah Ware and Rachel Tindell, the wife of Benjamin Tindell, they being his grandchildren; Sarah was to have her share during her life, and it then went to her oldest son, David Ware. She died several years before her husband, leaving three children—Sarah, David, and Samuel Ware. Jacob's third wife was Sarah Reed, the daughter of Robert Reed, who formerly was a resident of Pittsgrove township, and by her he had two children—Ann and Jacob Ware. After the death of her husband, Sarah Ware with her two children, removed to the State of Ohio, in company with her father, Robert Reed. Jacob Ware, her son, I believe, is still living near Columbus, Ohio. Sarah Ware, the daughter of Jacob Ware, married Samuel Hall, the son of Joseph Hall; by him she had one son—Joseph Hall, who resides near Lockport, New York. Her second husband was John Vanculan, who owned and lived where William Cooper now resides; they had four children—Eliza, Sarah, John and Samuel Vanculan. Her third husband was Sirge Ayres, a native of Cumberland county. They had one daughter—Emeline Ayres. David Ware's wife was Rebecca Hall, daughter of Joseph and Ann Hall; they had ten children—Sarah, Ann, Samuel, Joseph, Mary, Charles, Emeline, John, David and Rebecca. Samuel Ware, son of Jacob and Sarah Ware, married Ann Fox, daughter of Jacob Fox. They had one son who removed West, and two daughters—Mary Jane and Annie. Both of them are deceased.

Mary, the second daughter of John and Elizabeth Ware, was born in 1757, and married William Bradway, Jr.; they had five children—Sarah, Anna, Ezra, John and Rachel Bradway. Sarah, the eldest, married Elisha, the son of Joshua Stretch, and their children were Mary, Joshua, William, Ann and Job Stretch. Anna, daughter of William and Mary Bradway, married James Stewart; they had two children—Hannah and Mary. Hannah died a young woman, unmarried. Mary married William, the son of William Griscom, Jr., and Ann Griscom. Their children were Hannah, who married Charles Marott, of Philadelphia; William Wade Griscom, whose wife was Sarah Cooper, the daughter of James Cooper, who resided near Woodbury; and James Griscom, who married Hannah Borton, daughter of William Borton, of Woodstown. Samuel Fogg married Anna, the widow of James Stewart. By him she had one son, William Fogg, who married Mary Hall, the eldest daughter of Clement and Sarah Hall, of Elsinborough. William and his wife have resided in Salem for several years.

Hannah, the third daughter of John and Elizabeth Ware, was born 17th of 1st month, 1761. She subsequently married her cousin, Edward Fogg. They had five children—Samuel, Elizabeth, Ebenezer, Edward and David. Samuel's first wife was Anna, the widow of James Stewart; his second wife was Rebecca, the daughter of Joseph and Letitia Harmer, of Greenwich. Samuel and Rebecca Fogg had four children, named respectively—Ann, Joseph, Rebecca and Caroline. Ann married Joseph Miller, Jr., of Greenwich, and had two children—Joseph and Franklin. Joseph, the son of Samuel and Rebecca Fogg, married a young woman at Shiloh. She was a member of the Seventh-day Baptist Society. Rebecca, the daughter of Samuel and Rebecca Fogg, married a young man by the name of Tomlinson, of Stoe Creek township, Cumberland county. She has been deceased many years. Caroline, daughter of Samuel and Rebecca Fogg, married Franklin Dare, son of James Dare, of Greenwich. Franklin has lived in Bridgeton for a number of years, where he has followed the drug business.

They have one son—Charles Dare, a physician practicing in the village of Shiloh.

Elizabeth, daughter of Edward and Hannah Fogg, died at middle age, unmarried. Ebenezer Fogg's wife was Abigail Hancock, the grand-daughter of William and Mary Powell Carpenter. By her he had one daughter—Eliza Fogg, whose first husband was Zaccheus Brown, Jr. Eliza, Ebenezer and Zaccheus were the names of their three children. Her second husband was Abner Penton, by whom she had three children—Abner, Albert and Rachel Penton. Eliza's third husband was Firman Blew, who followed the sea in his younger days, but towards the latter part of his life he purchased a farm near Bridgeton, and at that place he and his wife in their declining years lived together happily. They are both deceased at the present time. Eliza, the eldest daughter of Zaccheus and Eliza Brown, married Job Dixon. They live together at Hancock's Bridge, and have several children. Ebenezer Brown married Milicent, the daughter of James Holliday, and they had two or three children. Edward Fogg, the third son of Edward and Hannah Fogg, married Catharine Hartley, by whom he had seven children—Mary, Casper, Thomas, Richard, Edward, Charles and David Fogg. Mary Fogg, their daughter, married Joseph, the son of Joseph Brown. They have two children—Anna and Edward Brown. Anna married Thomas M. Shourds, and Edward's wife was Hannah, the daughter of James Butcher, Jr. Casper Fogg resides in New Orleans. He is married and has a family of children. Thomas Fogg died several years ago unmarried. Richard Fogg's wife was Mary Woolman, of Pilesgrove; they have several children. Edward Fogg married widow Hunt's daughter, who resided in the town of Salem; she left one daughter. Edward's second wife is Mary Sayres, the daughter of Ephraim Sayres, of Cumberland county. Charles married Barbara Butcher, widow of James Butcher, Jr. David, the youngest son of Edward Fogg, married Sarah Green. Edward Fogg, Sr.'s second wife was Sarah, daughter of Mark Stewart; there was no issue. They are both deceased at the present time. David, the youngest son of Edward and Hannah Fogg, married Henrietta Davis. They are both deceased at the present time, leaving no children.

Eliza, the eldest daughter of Zaccheus and Eliza Brown, married Job Dixon. They live near Hancock's Bridge, and have several children. Ebenezer Brown married Milicent, the daughter of James Holliday, and they had two or three children. Elizabeth, the daughter of John and Elizabeth Ware, was born 2d of 3d month, 1763, and married William Carpenter, the son of William and Mary P. Carpenter. She was an uncommonly energetic woman, very zealous in attending religious meetings, and was desirous that her children might be so trained as to become useful and moral citizens in their day and generation. Her husband, a few years after they were married, upon an improving lease, rented a large farm of Samuel Nicholson, Sr., in the township of Elsinborough, for a number of years. He was to bank and improve a large number of acres of meadow, now known as the Mason Point Meadow Company, that lay adjoining the upland. Upon that farm he and his wife ended their days. William and his wife had seven children—Samuel, Mary, Abigail, William, Elizabeth, Powell and Sarah Carpenter. Samuel Carpenter, their eldest son, married Mary, the daughter of James and Rebecca Mason, of Mannington. They had three or four children, three of whom were named William, Elizabeth and Rebecca Carpenter. Samuel and his wife removed West a short time after they were married. He is living at the present time, and is about ninety-two years of age. Mary Carpenter, the eldest daughter of William and Elizabeth Carpenter, married Thomas Hancock, of Elsinborough. They had four children, three daughters and one son—Eliza, Lydia, Susan and Morris Hancock. The latter was accidentally killed, when a lad. Eliza married Joseph Tindall; Lydia's husband was George Bowen, of Salem. They did not live together many years. I believe she died with pulmonary consumption. Subsequently George married Susan Hancock, sister of his first wife. Mary's second husband was Samuel Cooper. They are both deceased at the present time, and leave no children. Abigail Carpenter, the daughter of William and Elizabeth Carpenter, married John Goodwin, of Elsinborough. Soon after their marriage they settled in the State of Ohio. She died comparatively young, leaving three sons—Lewis, William and Thomas Goodwin. Lewis, I think, is still living in one of the Western States; William Goodwin is a wealthy citizen of Philadelphia; Thomas Goodwin, the youngest son, died several years ago. William Carpenter was the second son of William and Elizabeth Carpenter. He married Mary Beesley, daughter of Abner and Mary Beesley, and had by her six children—Elizabeth, Powell, Anne, William B., Morris and John M. Carpenter. Elizabeth Carpenter married Joseph Thompson, the son of John and Esther Thompson; they have two children—Mary and John Thompson. Powell Carpenter's wife was Mary Lawson, the daughter of John Lawson, of

Salem. Powell fell to the pavement from near the eaves of a Baptist Church, which he was building, and died of congestion of the brain. He left no children. He was a kind and affectionate husband, a dutiful son, and his loss to his family and relatives was great. He had uncommon business capacities, and his death was considered a public calamity to the town of Salem.

Anne, the daughter of William and Mary Carpenter, has been deceased several years; she never married. She was afflicted many years previous to her death, but she bore all her sufferings with Christian fortitude, and when the time of her departure from this life came she could say with sincerity, "Lord, thy servant is ready." William Beesley Carpenter, the second son of William and Mary Carpenter, married Martha Gaskill, the daughter of Josiah and Eliza Gaskill, formerly of Burlington county. William and his wife had seven children—Howard, Mary, Elizabeth, William, Louisa, Anna, Martha and Rebecca Carpenter. Three of the before mentioned children, Howard, William and Rebecca, are deceased. The wife of William B. Carpenter died in 1868 of pulmonary consumption. She was a dutiful wife, an affectionate parent, and a great loss to her family. Her death was much regretted by a large circle of relatives and acquaintances. William's second wife is Nancy Pease, a native of Connecticut. They have two children—William and Julia Carpenter. Morris H. Carpenter is a resident of the city of Philadelphia, and is unmarried. John Mason Carpenter, the youngest son of William and Mary Carpenter, married Ann Harvey, daughter of Minor and Lydia Harvey. John and his wife live in Salem. They had two children—Powell who died young, and George Carpenter.

Elizabeth Carpenter married William Thompson, son of Joshua Thompson. Their children I noticed in the Thompson family's genealogy. Powell, the son of William and Elizabeth Carpenter, resided the greater part of his life in Philadelphia. His first wife was Eliza Slaughter; she died leaving one son, Charles Carpenter. His second wife was Ann Slaughter, sister of his first wife. Their children were Ann, William and Caroline. Sarah, the youngest child of William and Elizabeth Carpenter, married Joseph Hancock, of Mannington. They had four children—Chambless, Elizabeth, Caroline and Hannah.

Job Ware, the youngest son of John and Elizabeth Ware, was born 16th of 1st month, 1766. His first wife was Grace, the daughter of Andrew Thompson, of Elsinborough. She died young, and left one son—John Ware. John married

Hannah, the daughter of Clement Acton, of Salem. He died young, leaving one son—Clement Ware. Job Ware's second wife was the daughter of Christopher and Rebecca Hancock Smith, of Mannington, who lived but a short time, and left no children. His third wife was Mary, the widow of Abner Beesley, by whom he had two children—Job and Eliza Ware. Job Ware, Jr., married Elizabeth Waddington; they are both deceased, leaving one daughter—Sarah Ellen Ware. Elijah Ware married Beulah Powell; they have five children—Sarah, William, Mary, Anna and Charles.

Sarah, the youngest daughter of John and Elizabeth Ware, was born 11th of 4th month, 1769. She was four years old at the time of her father's death, which occurred 21st of 2d month, 1773, when he was fifty years old. He was buried with his ancestors in the grave yard situated on the north side of Alloways Creek. Sarah Ware married Jeremiah Powell, 3d, in 1785. He was the son of John and Ann Powell.— Jeremiah and his wife lived on the property that he inherited from his father; the said property lay adjoining the village of Hancock's Bridge, where their grandson, Jeremiah Powell, now owns and occupies. Jeremiah and his wife lived together more than fifty-seven years in great unity. He was above ordinary men in intellect, and had great argumentative powers. His wife was an agreeable companion to him, industrious, frugal, and possessing a sympathetic nature. They had four children who lived to maturity—Elizabeth, Ann, John and William. Elizabeth was the second wife of Joseph Thompson. Ann married Samuel Griscom; they had twelve children, whose names are given in the account of the Griscom family.

John Powell married Rebecca, the daughter of John Mowers, of Upper Alloways Creek. They had ten children—Sarah, Jeremiah, William, Joseph, Samuel, John, Elias, Hicks, Elizabeth and Rebecca. Four of the above mentioned children are dead—William, Joseph, Elizabeth and Rebecca. John Powell died in 1843 or 1844 in Elsinborough, with a cancer in his stomach. His widow, Rebecca Powell, died four or five years ago. Sarah, daughter of John and Rebecca Powell, married Chalkley Griscom, of Pennsylvania. There are several children from this union. Jeremiah Powell's wife was Elizabeth, daughter of William and Mary Bradway. They had four children— Sarah, Ann, Louisa and John. Joseph Powell married Elizabeth, daughter of William and Mary Denn. He died young, leaving one son—Joseph Powell. Samuel Powell's wife is Sarah Jane, daughter of Josiah and Elizabeth Smith. They have three children—one daughter named Anna, and two sons, Samuel and Franklin. The wife of John Powell, Jr., was Emma Sutton; several children were born to them. Elizabeth Powell married Quinton Harris. She died young, and left one daughter—Elizabeth Harris. Ann, the daughter of John Powell, married Waddington, the son of Jacob and Mercy Ridgway. They have five children—Lydia, John P., William, Henry and Edwin.

William, the youngest son of Jeremiah and Sarah Powell, married Sarah, the daughter of Aaron and Hannah Fogg. They had one daughter, Beulah Powell, who subsequently married Elijah Ware. William died several years since, but his widow is still living, and resides with her daughter in the city of Salem.

WADE FAMILY.

Robert Wade was a citizen and carpenter of the city of London. He purchased of the proprietor of West New Jersey, before he left England, 500 acres of land, which was surveyed for him by Richard Hancock, in 1676, adjoining his brother, Richard Wade's, and William Hancock's allotments of 1,000 acres each. The said lands lay on the south side of Monmouth river, also a lot in the town of Salem, on the north side of Market street. He never built on said lot, it being the same, I believe, that Alexander Grant purchased afterward and built himself a brick house on the premises, and there lived. Samuel Fenwick Hedge's wife was his daughter. Robert Wade sold his landed estate at Monmouth early in the year 1678 to James Denn and Joseph Ware. He then went to Upland, now known as Chester, and bought 500 acres of land on the south side of what is known as Chester creek, of one of the early Swedish settlers who had purchased a large tract of land of one of the Indian chiefs, some thirty years previous to that date, and on that land he erected a large and commodious house for the purpose of entertainment, and gave it the name of the Essex house. Some historians called it the emigrant's house. About that time there were several families of Friends, emigrants from England, that had bought lands in that neighborhood and settled there. Robert fitted up part of his house for the purpose of holding meetings in, and in that house was the first regular Quaker or Friends meeting held in Pennsylvania.

When William Penn on his first arrival in the Delaware river in 1682, landed at Upland, (at that time it was a village of considerable size) Robert met him there at the landing. The proprietor turned to his intimate friend Pierson, and asked: "What shall we name this place?" He replied, "Call it Chester, after my native county, Chestershire." William Penn and family were the guests of Robert Wade for a few days. Robert was likewise one of the members of the Provincial Assembly that the Governor convened for the purpose of organizing a provincial government, and was a member of that body for several years afterwards. Respecting his descendants I have no definite information, but I have been told some of them are living in the neighborhood of Chester at the present day.

Edward Wade was a cloth maker and citizen of London, and with his wife, Prudence, arrived in this country in 1675. He was one of the leading emigrants in Fenwick's colony, and purchased of the proprietor a town lot on Bridge street, now known as Market street, on the north side. Fenwick retained the land on the south side of said street for himself and his heirs. Edward Wade erected a brick house on his lot, and it was standing about forty years ago. By tradition it was the first that was ever built on said street. Edward and his wife ended their days at that place, which event took place before the beginning of the eighteenth century. There is no account that they ever had any sons, but they had one daughter—Mary Wade.

In the year 1676, on the first 2d day in the 6th month, a few Friends met together to organize a meeting of business, it being the first of the kind held on Continent of North America.— The following is the minute of their organization "It is unan-
" imously considered that the first 2d day of the week, in the
" 6th month, that Friends do meet in the town of New Salem,
" in Fenwick's Colony ; and all Friends thereunto do monthly
" meet together, to consider of outward circumstances and bus-
" iness, and if such that has been convinced, and walked
" disorderly, that they may in all gravity and uprightness to
" God, and in tenderness of spirit and love to their souls, be
" admonished, exhorted, and also reproved. And their evil
" deeds and practices testified against in the wisdom of God, and
" in the authority of truth, that may answer the witness of
" God within them." Signed by John Fenwick, Edward Wade, Samuel Wade, Francis Nebo, Samuel Nicholson, Richard Guy, Edward Champney and Isaac Smart.

Women at the first rise of the Society of Friends did not participate in meetings of business for more than a quarter of a century afterward. The early sons of the morning of the Quaker Society were not prepared to condemn what Jehovah had declared in the beginning, " that he had made man in his own image," but his evil deeds and practices.

I have digressed somewhat to show that Edward Wade participated largely in religious as well as in the civil organization of Fenwick's Colony. It appears he always was a firm and steady friend of the proprietor, and was willing to make a due allowance for his foibles and the impetuosity of his disposition, believing his heart was right.

The brothers, Edward, Robert and Samuel Wade, were born in Northamptonshire, England. They emigrated to this province in company with John Fenwick. Samuel, the youngest, was born in 1645, and in the year 1668 he married Jane Smith, the daughter of Thomas Smith, of the same county. They had three children born in England, named respectively Henry, Andrew and Ann, and one son born after they arrived in this country, Samuel Wade, Jr., who was born at Alloways Creek in 1685. Their first three children died young. Edward Wade, Samuel's brother, gave him a deed for 100 acres of land, being part of his 1,000 acres of land that he purchased of John Fenwick. In the year 1680 Samuel and his family settled at Alloways Creek on his property, and in 1686 he built himself a one story brick house, it being one of the first of the kind built in South Jersey. Samuel and his wife died in the early part of the eighteenth century, leaving one son, Samuel Wade, Jr., who married and lived on his patrimonial estate until his death in 1733. He left four daughters, his two sons, Joseph and Samuel, having died the year before their father. One of his daughters married James Barker, and they had one son, John Barker, whose occupation was that of a tailor. He resided in Philadelphia, and at the breaking out of the Revolutionary war joined the army, and was in a short time promoted to a colonel, and continued in the army until the war was ended. Soon after he was elected Mayor of the city of Philadelphia, he being the Republican candidate and Robert Wharton the Federal candidate. The contest for that office was kept up between these two men for many years. Barker was elected three or four different times, and Wharton also was elected to the office for several terms.

Esther Wade, the third daughter of Samuel Wade, Jr., married Samuel Lewis, and she left one son—James Lewis. He followed his trade, which was that of a tailor, in the village of Hancock's Bridge. He left two children. Esther Lewis lived the greater part of her life with her uncle, John Barker, in Philadelphia, and after his death she came to Salem and taught school for several years. Solomon Lewis was a chair maker, and carried on that business several years in the town of Salem. He married a young woman by the name of Brown in the county of Gloucester, and purchased a farm in that neighborhood and became a farmer. Some of his children are living there at the present time. Samuel's fourth daughter married John Tyler, of Cumberland county, and she left several children.

John Stewart was born in Scotland in 1709. His parents belonged to the nobility of Edinburgh, and he consequently received a liberal education. He left his native land in company with two other young men of the same standing in society, unknown to their parents. They arrived in West New Jersey in 1728. John Stewart at that time was about nineteen years of age. Soon afterwards he hired as a farm laborer with George Abbott, Jr., in Elsinborough, and remained with him until he married Mary Wade, the eldest daughter of Samuel Wade, Jr. He by that time, it is believed, received some remittances from Scotland which enabled him to buy the three other shares of the homestead farm of the Wades. Accordingly he and his wife commenced life at that place, and both lived to be over four-score years. He raised another story on the old brick house that Samuel Wade had built more than fifty years before. John Stewart having more education than was common for men to have at that time, was called on frequently to transact business for the public. The community had great confidence in his ability and integrity. He was also pleasing in his address and a good conversationalist. That latter trait of character was transmitted to his children and grand-children generally. He and his wife Mary had nine children—Elizabeth, Lydia, Samuel, John, Mary, Ann, James, Milicint and Joseph. I believe two of them, Ann and Milicint, died minors. Elizabeth, the oldest, married a Bradway, which I mentioned in the genealogy of the Bradway Family. Lydia, their second daughter, married a Duell of Pilesgrove, the grandmother of the present John and Samuel Duell of that place.

Samuel Stewart married Ann Tyler, the daughter of William Tyler. He and his wife bought what is known as the Cow Neck farm, in the township of Salem, and at that place they spent their days. He was much esteemed in general society for his kindness and evenness of temper, and by reason of his clear and excellent judgment, he was frequently called upon to settle differences between persons in the neighborhood in which he lived. He likewise often served as commissioner in dividing lands in this and neighboring counties. It was in acting in that capacity, dividing the great estate of Benjamin B. Cooper, in the lower part of Cumberland county, that he took a severe cold and died a short time afterwards, leaving four children—Ann, Mark, Mary and Joseph. Ann Stewart married William Griscom, and they had six children—Samuel, William, George, John, Charles and Mary Griscom.

Mark Stewart's first wife and mother of his children was Elizabeth Denn, the daughter of James Denn. Their children's names were John, Samuel, Sarah, James, Joseph, William, Elizabeth and Mary Ann Stewart.

Joseph Stewart's wife was Rachel Bradway, the daughter of William Bradway. John Stewart's wife was Hannah Butcher, of Cumberland. They left one son—James Stewart. Mary Stewart married Job Bacon, of Cumberland; they had three children—Job, Elizabeth and George. James Stewart's first wife was a Sheppard. She lived but a short time after marriage. His second wife was Mary Ballinger, whose parents resided near Woodbury. They had five children—James, Deborah, Beulah, Mary and Samuel. There were three men about of an age, natives of the township of Alloways, who were above ordinary men in intellect. Their names were Professor John Griscom, William Waddington and James Stewart, Jr. The latter followed the sea most of his life, and was considered an excellent navigator. He married Sarah Smith, and left five children—Ann, William, Mary, Sarah and James Stewart.

The grandfather of the above mentioned children died with the cancer in his face about the year 1835. I went to see him a few days before his death. The old man was sitting up in his bedroom apparently comfortable and quite cheerful. In our conversation I remarked the room looked ancient, and he said it was, for his mother was born there and lived eighty-five years and died in the same room she was born in, and eighty-five years and a few days over, I was born in the same room and expect to die here in a short time, which he accordingly did. Joseph Stewart, the brother of James, was by trade a hatter, and followed that business in the town of Greenwich, where he died in the prime of his life of hemorrhage of the lungs.

WADDINGTON FAMILY.

William Waddington was a French Huguenot, and emigrated to this country about 1690. He purchased of Edward Wade 1,000 acres of land, it being the southern portion of his allotment, and settled thereon. The said property was held by one of the branches of the Waddington family until about ten years ago. William and his wife had one son, Jonathan Waddington, who subsequently married and had four or five daughters and one son—Jonathan, Hannah, Ann, Elizabeth and Jane Waddington. Hannah, the eldest daughter, married Maurice Beesley; they had five children—Walker, Hannah, Mary, Benjamin and Abner Beesley. Walker, the eldest son, was killed at the massacre in the Revolutionary war at Hancock's Bridge. Hannah, the daughter of Maurice and Hannah Beesley, married John Beesley, her cousin; they had two sons—Walker and David Beesley. The latter died a young man, unmarried. Mary, the daughter of Maurice and Hannah W. Beesley, married Peter Townsend, of Cape May; they had no issue. Benjamin, the son of Maurice and Hannah W. Beesley, died a young man. Abner, the youngest son of Maurice and Hannah Waddington Beesley, married Mary, the daughter of John and Susanna Mason, of Elsinborough; they had issue—Mary, William, Benjamin and Thomas Beesley. [See Mason Family.] Ann Waddington, daughter of Jonathan Waddington, married in 1750 John Baracliff.

Elizabeth, daughter of Jonathan Waddington, married Edward, the son of Jonathan Bradway, in 1760; they had four sons and two daughters—David, Hannah, Waddington, Edward, who died young, Adna and Elizabeth; the latter married Abraim Silvers. Hannah Bradway, her sister, married Job Stretch; they had issue, Jane, the youngest daughter of Jonathan Waddington, married Bradway Keasbey, she being his second wife; they had one daughter, Sarah Keasbey, who married John, the son of Edward and Hannah Pancoast. John and his wife Sarah K. Pancoast had six children—Hannah, John, Israel, Jane, David and Aaron Pancoast.

Jonathan Waddington, Jr., I think, married the grand-daughter of John and Mary Chambless Hancock. He died in 1760, leaving an infant son—Jonathan Waddington, 3d. He was the only one at the death of his father that bore the name of Waddington in this country, and he subsequently married Sarah, the daughter of Aaron Bradway, of Elsinborough. Jonathan and Sarah B. Waddington had six sons—William, Robert, Aaron, Jonathan, Thomas and Edward Waddington. William, their eldest son, married Martha, the daughter of Jesse Carll; they had six children—Anna, Sarah, William, Martha, Hannah and Jesse Waddington. Robert, second son of Jonathan and Sarah Waddington, married, and died a young man, leaving three sons—Aaron, Samuel and James Waddington. Aaron, the son of Jonathan Waddington, 3d, married Sarah, the daughter of Edward Keasbey; they have three daughters and two sons—Sarah Ann, Lydia, Joshua, Bradway and Jane Waddington. Jonathan, the son of Jonathan and Sarah Waddington, died unmarried. Thomas, son of the before mentioned parents, was twice married. By his first wife he had five children—Elizabeth, Sarah, Mary, Jonathan and Thomas Waddington, and his second wife was Hannah Davis; there were two children—Beulah and Jane Waddington. Edward, the youngest son of Jonathan and Sarah Bradway Waddington, married Prudence, the daughter of Edward and Lydia Keasbey; they had eight children—Richard, Sarah, Edward, Prudence, Elizabeth, Joseph, Lydia Ann and Prudence Waddington.

WHITACAR FAMILY.

The Whitacars are an ancient English family. Richard, the ancestor of the Whitacars in West Jersey, was a native of London. By tradition, he came to America at the time of the plague, in 1665, or in the following year, after the great fire. The record of the family in England is supposed to have passed into the hands of other branches. About a hundred years ago, an Englishman who was traveling in this country told a member of the Whitacar family that he knew a place in England called Whitacarsfield, which was doubtless the family property. The early Whitacars were very particular about the spelling of their names, this having been enjoined upon them by Richard, the emigrant, who stated that there were landed estates in England belonging to the Whitacars, which they might inherit at some time were they careful to keep up their record and the olden way of spelling their names. In latter years, however, the last syllable was changed from "car" to "ker," and it is now generally spelled Whitaker.

I have no doubt, if their tradition is correct, that Richard landed in Maryland, and in company with some others entered the Delaware bay in a small vessel, and ascended up the river as far as Billingsport, he being the first of the company that reached the shore, and was therefore the first Englishman that set foot on West New Jersey. He sprang on shore, and with a hatchet cut down a bush, according to the ancient mode of taking possession, in the name of King Charles II. He doubtless remained in America but a short time before he returned to England. It is probable that soon after his return he became a member of the Society of Friends. When Fenwick was fitting out his expedition to West New Jersey, together with a number of emigrants who had previously bought land of him, I find Richard Whitacar was one of the number. William Hancock, of the county of Middlesex, purchased 1,000 acres and one building lot of 16 acres in the town that the proprietor should lay out when he arrived in West Jersey; the said Hancock appointed his friend Richard Whitacar his Attorney until he came to take charge of it, which he accordingly did in 1677. The power of Attorney reads: "Be it known unto all men by these "presents, that I, William Hancock, of the parish of St. Len-"ard, Shoreditch, county of Middlesex, to Richard Whitacar, "of ye city of London, to be my lawful Attorney, deputy for "me, in my name, for all my lott or lotts of land situate, lying and "being in New Jersey, or Nova Cæsaria, America in ye parts. "And I the said William Hancock, shall and will ratify, allow, "confirm all and whatsoever my said Attorney or his substitutes "shall lawfully do or cause to be done in or about the Premises, "by virtue of these presents. In witness whereof, I, the said "William Hancock, have hereunto sett my hand and seal the "sixth day of July, Anno Domini, 1675. And in ye 27th year "of Reign of our Sovereign Lord. King Charles ye second, "over England. William Hancock. Sealed and delivered in "ye presence of us, Thomas Sramodmo and William Johnson, "Esq., Notary Public." It is said that this paper was executed the day previous to the sailing of the ship Griffin, which is a further confirmation that John Smith and Samuel Nicholson were correct in stating that the ship anchored opposite Elsinborough Point 23d of 9th month, 1675, that making them two months and sixteen days on the passage.

The power of Attorney, and a black morocco book in which Richard Whitacar carried it over the sea, is still in the possession of the family, which I have no doubt they highly prize.— Richard Whitacar was made one of Fenwick's Council of Proprietors to govern West Jersey, which office he held from 1676 to 1702, at which time the Colonial Government was formed. He resided most of his time in the town of Salem until about 1690. On 17th of 1st month, 1679, he and Elizabeth Adkin of Alloways Creek, were married in Salem at Friends' Meeting, in the old log meeting house on the Nicholson lot. In 1690 he and his wife moved to the South Cohansic precinct, where about that time there was a considerable emigration from parts of New England and East Jersey, and at that place he located on a large tract of land not far from New Englandtown, and there they settled. The land lay in Fairfield township.— Richard, soon after he settled in the township, built himself a substantial brick dwelling. This property, I have been informed, belonged to the family until after the old French war.— The house was taken down some ten years ago; the piles of old bricks were to be seen in various places in 1873—all that remained of the old Whitacar mansion.

Richard Whitacar and Henry Buck kept a store for several

years near New Englandtown, where they owned a large sloop and traded with New York and Boston. The firm doubtless transacted a great deal of business, this being the only store of any importance in that region. The place where the present thriving city of Bridgeton is now was then a wilderness. The old store book of the firm is still in possession of the family. The writer had an opportunity of looking through it some time since, and it is particularly interesting to the antiquarian, giving as it does a knowledge of the names of many of the early inhabitants of that section of Cumberland county which otherwise probably would have been lost. The first entry in the book is dated October 9th, 1704, and in the page before is written, " We sailed from Boston September 18th, 1704." It appears by the day book that they kept dry goods, groceries, ready-made clothing, liquors and books, particularly school books, bibles and psalm books, and farming implements. Richard Whitacar and his partner, Henry Buck, did considerable public business, as their names frequently appear in the Court minutes to be seen in the Salem Clerk's Office, beginning with 1706, but after 1709 Richard's name is missing. He doubtless died the following winter, and is thought to have been about sixty-six years of age. Henry Buck died about 1726. Richard Whitacar left a number of children. One of his sons, Richard, married and had issue; his oldest child was Nathaniel, whose descendants are given. Of the other children of Richard, Sr., and Elizabeth Whitacar and their branches it is impossible to speak of with certainty. One of their daughters, however, probably married Samuel Alexander, of Fairfield. Their daughters were merged into other families, but there have always been sons enough to keep up the name. They are scattered over the country, and it would be no easy task to collect their genealogies. Silas Whitacar, one of the celebrated party who burned the tea at Greenwich 22d of 12th month, 1774, was a descendant of Richard.

Although Richard Whitacar, Sr., and his wife, Elizabeth Adkin Whitacar, and their children when young, were members of the Society of Friends, most of their descendants at the present time are Presbyterians. Nathaniel Whitacar, son of Richard, Jr., married Mary Ann Dixon, 18th of 11th month, 1729. Their children were Ambrose, Lemuel (who died young,) Lewis W., who married but died at an early age, leaving three children, whose names were Lydia, Lemuel and Lewis. Lydia married her cousin, Nathaniel Whitacar; Lemuel settled near Muskingum, in Ohio, and died there, leaving several children, being about eighty years of age at the time of his death. Lewis settled at Muskingum, Ohio; from thence to Henepin, Illinois, and died there leaving several children. One of his children, John Whitacar, was one of the framers of the Constitution of Illinois, in 1818. Mary, the wife of Nathaniel Whitacar, died 13th of 9th month, 1738, Nathaniel's second wife was Ruth Buck; their children were Sarah, who died unmarried about 1808; Hannah, their second daughter, married Ephraim Foster; Daniel Whitacar, their son, died a single man; Ruth, the youngest daughter, married Josiah Harris, by whom she had two sons—Enos and John Harris; Josiah died. Ruth's second husband was a Davis, by whom she had two children, one of whom was named Sarah, who married a young man by the name of Mench; they settled at Cincinnati, Ohio. Nathaniel Whitacar died in 12th month, 1752, aged about fifty-eight years.

Ambrose Whitacar, the eldest son of Nathaniel, married Freelove Stratton 16th of 1st month, 1755; the children were Freelove, Mary, Nathaniel, Abigail and Catharine. Freelove, wife of Ambrose Whitacar, died in her thirty-third year. On the 10th of 12th month, 1766, Ambrose married Ruth Harris, by whom he had the following children—David, Hannah and Lewis. Ruth died, 5th of 10th month, 1772, in her thirty-ninth year. Ambrose married his third wife, Rachel Leake; their children were Recompence, Oliver, Freelove, Isaac, Sarah and Leake. The last named married Dr. Robert H. VanMeter. [See VanMeter Family.] Ambrose Whitacar departed this life 5th of 11th month, 1796, in the sixty-sixth year of his age. Rachel, his last wife, died 30th of 1st month, 1823, in her eightieth year; both are buried in the same grave in the Presbyterian church yard at Daretown.

Freelove, daughter of Ambrose and Freelove Whitacar, married, when young, Butler Thompson; she died while young, leaving one daughter, Mary Thompson, who subsequently married Thomas Sheppard, by whom she had four children—Lydia, Sarah, Ann and Mark. Lydia Sheppard married Evi Smith, son of David Smith, of Mannington; they had three children—Charles, Mary and Hannah. Mary married David, the son of Elisha and Mary Bassett. Hannah married Edward H. Bassett; Hannah is deceased. Charles, the son of Evi and Lydia Smith, married and resided in Philadelphia; he is deceased and left issue, two sons. Sarah, daughter of Thomas and Mary Sheppard, married Anthony Taylor; they had six children—Mary, Sheppard, Samuel, Joseph, Anthony and Sarah. Mark, the son of Thomas and Mary Sheppard, married Patience

Buzby; their children were Joseph, John, Lydia and Mary Sheppard. Ann, the daughter of Thomas and Mary Sheppard, married Joseph Harmer, of Greenwich; they had six children—Mark, Ruth, Sarah, Richard, Elwood and Letitia Harmer. The second husband of Mary, the widow of Thomas Sheppard, was Samuel Silvers; they had one son, Thomas Silvers, who resides in the city of New York. He married Anna V. Bird, of Philadelphia; they have three children—Helena, Isabel and Melbourne Silvers. Thomas is quite an inventive genius; his most noted invention is the steam governor. His family resides in the city of New York, but he himself spends most of his time in London. Mary's third husband was William White, of Woodstown; he died many years before her. After his death she resided at Greenwich with her relatives, but died at Woodstown over four-score years of age. Mary, daughter of Ambrose and Freelove Whitacar, married Jedediah Ogden, in 1783; they had five children—Isaac, Ambrose, Jedediah, Ruth, Neve and Daniel. Isaac Ambrose Ogden is a Presbyterian minister, settled in Ohio, and has several children. Jedediah and Daniel Ogden settled near Fairfield, Indiana, and have several children. Ruth Ogden married Obediah Bennett, and in 1854 was a widow with children. Neve Ogden died, leaving children. Nathaniel, son of Ambrose and Freelove Whitacar, married his cousin Lydia, in 1784; they had five children—Jael, Ruel, Anna, Nathaniel and Lydia. Jael and Nathaniel settled near Henepin, Illinois. Ruel married and had a number of children, among whom are Abigail, Clara, Ephar and Harriet. Abigail died unmarried. Clara has been twice married; her first husband was a Harris, and her second husband is Judge Whitacar, of Fairton. Ephar is a Presbyterian minister, settled in Southhold, Long Island, and has several children. Harriet married Professor Clark, of Tennessee. Anna Whitacar married Prescott Bishop. Lydia married James Craig, and settled near the home of her ancestors in Cumberland county.

Abigail, daughter of Ambrose and Freelove Whitacar, married Jeffrey Parvin, in 1785, and died in 1794, leaving two children—Sarah and Abigail Parvin. Sarah married Daniel Simkins and died, leaving three children. Abigail married Moses Riley and was left a widow with two children. Catharine, daughter of Ambrose and Freelove Whitacar, married Joshua Reeve, of Bridgeton, in 1782 and died in 1796, in her thirty-fourth year, leaving several children; their names were Samuel, Elizabeth, Joshua, Thomas, Catharine, Harriet and Maria. Samuel, the eldest, died young; Elizabeth married

George Johnson, settled in Philadelphia and died in 1848, leaving children; Joshua enlisted in the army and died; Thomas married Eunice Bishop and died near Cincinnati, Ohio, in 1838, leaving six children—Daniel, Charles B., Caroline, Mary, John B. and Horace. Catharine, the daughter of Joshua and Catharine W. Reeve, married Benjamin Forbes and died, leaving several children; Harriet married David Husted; Maria married Vickers Harris and was left a widow in 1853.

David, son of Ambrose Whitaker, by his second wife Ruth, married Catharine DuBois in 1788, and died 29th of 7th month, 1807, aged forty years. They had six children—Peter, Ruth, Elizabeth, Lewis, David and Rebecca. Peter married Nancy Riley. Their children were Lorenzo, Lucius, William, Louisa and James Lambert. Lorenzo, the eldest son, married Sarah Cake; died and left two children—Lucius and Anna Whitaker. Lucius Whitaker married Ruth Nixon. There were three children. William died unmarried. Louisa Whitaker married William Cole, of Woodstown; he is now deceased. They had two children—Annie and William Cole. James Lambert Whitaker married Fannie Reeves, and settled in Bridgeton. He died 8th month, 1875, leaving one child. Ruth, daughter of David and Catharine DuBois Whitaker, married David VanMeter; both of them are deceased leaving children—Isaac W., David, Phebe and Enoch VanMeter. Elizabeth Whitaker, daughter of David, married Isaac Mayhew; both are deceased, leaving children. Lewis and David Whitaker, sons of David, settled near Logansport, Indiana. Rebecca, the youngest daughter of David, married Joseph Heward. They also settled at Logansport.

Hannah, the daughter of Ambrose and Ruth Whitaker, married Ephraim Foster, by whom she had the following children—David, Ephraim, Nathaniel, Jonathan, Jeremiah, Phebe, Ruth, Hannah, Elizabeth and Esther Foster. Phebe Foster married Hosea Sneathen, and died without issue. Jonathan Foster died a young man, unmarried. Ruth Foster married Samuel Thompson, and died, leaving several children. Their names were Samuel, Newcomb, Phebe, Harriet and Elizabeth Thompson. Hannah, daughter of Ephraim and Hannah Foster, married John McQueen. She died in 1854, at an advanced age. Their children were Ephraim, Rebecca, Elizabeth, Sarah and Hannah. Rebecca married Jonathan Swing, of Pittsgrove. They had several children. Elizabeth McQueen married John Garrison; they lived near Deerfield. Elizabeth died leaving one child. Hannah married Benjamin VanMeter. There were several children by this union. Sarah McQueen never married. Elizabeth, the daughter of Ephraim and Hannah Foster, married Matthew Newkirk, of Pittsgrove, (Newkirk's station); being his second wife. She had children—Matthew, Nathaniel and Mary Newkirk. Matthew married and died young, leaving one son, Matthew, who married and resides in Ohio. Nathaniel, son of Matthew and Elizabeth Newkirk, was a physician, and married Martha, daughter of John and Ann Bacon, of Greenwich, Cumberland county. He died at Bridgeton, leaving issue. Mary Newkirk, daughter of Matthew, is living, unmarried. Elizabeth, widow of Matthew Newkirk, married Samuel Thompson. She died at Bridgeton, leaving no issue by her last husband. Esther Foster married Ethan Osborne; he was an eminent Presbyterian minister, of Fairfield church. She was his second wife, and died without issue.

Lewis, son of Ambrose and Ruth Whitaker, was married to Mary DuBois, in 1797, and died 1st of 10th month, 1828, in his fifty-eighth year. Their children were Ambrose, Hannah and John Whitaker. Ambrose is unmarried, and lives near Swing's Corner, in Pittsgrove. Hannah Whitaker married Benjamin Burroughs. They settled near Cincinnati, Ohio, and left children. John Whitaker married and died at Pittsgrove, leaving issue. Lewis Whitaker was married the second time, and had issue—Mary, Nathaniel, Benjamin B. and Ruth Whitaker. Mary, daughter of Lewis Whitaker, married John G. Sweatman, and died in 1854, at Watson's Corner, leaving no children. Nathaniel Whitaker married and died in Pittsgrove. Benjamin B. Whitaker is unmarried. Ruth married John Mounce, they have no children.

Recompence, son of Ambrose and Rachel Whitaker, (Rachel was his third wife,) married Rachel Moore 6th of 3d month, 1800, and died in his thirty-sixth year, leaving five children. Their names were Abigail, Enoch, Hannah, Caroline and Rachel Leake Whitaker. Abigail, daughter of Recompence Whitaker, married Buckly Carll, a Presbyterian minister. Her husband is deceased, and buried at Daretown. Abigail is still living. Hannah Whitaker, daughter of Recompence, married George Hires; she is still living, having no children. The other children of Recompence Whitaker died young.

Oliver, son of Ambrose and Rachel Whitaker, married Mary Summerill, 2d of 2d month, 1799. The children by this marriage were Rhoda, Summerill, Rachel, Ruth and William. Rhoda married William Biggs, of Cincinnati. They have a large family of children. Summerill married early in life, and went to the State of Illinois. Rachel Whitaker married Jacob

Johns; they reside in Iowa, and have issue. Ruth married William Villers, near Cincinnati; they have a large family of children. William is deceasd, leaving no issue. Mary Summerill, wife of Oliver Whitaker, died aged twenty-four years, and in 1807 Oliver married Elizabeth Kirby. Their children were Ambrose, Phebe, Oliver, Ephraim K., Joseph and Mary Jane Whitaker. Phebe, daughter of Oliver, married James Buck, by whom she had one child—Sarah Elizabeth Buck. Oliver Whitaker married Hannah R. Hollingsworth; their children were Isaac, Martha, Ann, Sarah Jane, Mary, Elizabeth, Joseph B., Charles H., William A., and Abraham Whitaker. Ephraim K. Whitaker married Mary Vanderoot; their children were Phebe, Sarah Elizabeth and Isaac Newton. Joseph Whitaker married Rebecca McBriant; they had four children—Mary L., William Oliver, Ephraim K. and Elizabeth Ann. Mary Jane died in childhood. Oliver Whitaker, Sr., soon after his marriage with Mary Summerill, settled in Clinton county, Ohio. His descendants are numerous, and scattered through the West. He died 11th of 12th month, 1831, aged about fifty-six years.

Freelove, daughter of Ambrose and Rachel Whitacar, married David DuBois, 23d of 4th month, 1804. Their children are as follows: Henrietta, Jonathan, Jedediah, Edmund, Asher, Janetta and David DuBois. Henrietta DuBois married James Coombs, of Upper Pittsgrove. They had issue—Mary Ann, Albert, Edwin, Jane, Oliver, Isabella and Henry Coombs. Albert, Jane and Isabella are deceased. Jonathan DuBois married Martha Adcock; he died, leaving two sons—Henry and George DuBois. Jedediah DuBois married Ann Adcock, and died, leaving three sons. Edmund DuBois married Sarah Johnson; there are children. Asher DuBois married ———— Swing, and died, leaving children. Janetta DuBois married Edward Shute, and died leaving issue. David DuBois married a daughter of Adam VanMeter, they had one daughter. David DuBois, Sr., died in 5th month, 1837; Freelove, his wife, died in 1st month, 1842, aged sixty-four years. Both are buried in the old church yard at Daretown. Isaac, the son of Ambrose and Rachel Whitacar, married Ann, daughter of Jonathan Fithian, of Deerfield, 10th of 3d month, 1814; they had twelve children—Isaac, Ann, Mary, Sarah, Caroline, Oliver, Enoch, Charles, Eliza, James, Lydia and Lewis Whitacar. Isaac, son of Isaac and Ann Whitacar, settled in Carlinville, Illinois, about 1840. He married there Virginia B. Bement, formerly of New York. He was known as Captain Whitacar. His wife died leaving six children—Mary Ellen, Harriet B., Edna Caroline, Virginia, Charles and Clara Whitacar. Mary Ellen, married Victor Hoyt. Harriet B. married James Gand. Ann married Jacob Webb; they had five children—Harriet, Alexander, Charles, Isaac W. and George Smith; two survive, Alexander and George; both of whom are married and have children. Ann and husband are deceased. Mary married Edward Burton, of Bunker Hill, Illinois; they have one child, named Joseph. Sarah Whitacar, daughter of Isaac, Sr., married Daniel Smith; she died in her forty-second year, leaving the following children—Anna B., Elizabeth L., Caroline W. and Franklin Smith. Anna B. and Franklin are the only surviving ones. Caroline, fourth daughter of Isaac and Ann Whitacar, married Edward VanMeter, of Salem. [See VanMeter Family.]

Oliver, son of Isaac and Ann Whitacar, married Sarah A. Fisher; they had one child—Mary Whitacar. Enoch Whitacar married Ruth Diamond; they had three children—Lewis, Edward V. and Richard W. Whitacar. Charles, son of Isaac and Ann Whitacar, died in his nineteenth year. Eliza died in infancy. James Whitacar, son of Isaac and Ann, married Louisa Izard; they had five children—Joseph, Frank, Louisa, Charles and Coleman Whitacar. Lydia Whitacar, married Jonathan D. Ayres. Their surviving children are as follows: Harriet W., Robert S., Caroline V. and Florence Ayres. Lewis, the youngest son of Isaac and Ann Whitacar, married Mary Elizabeth Shove; they have four children living —Harriet, Anna, Elizabeth and Lewis Whitacar.

Isaac, son of Ambrose and Rachel Whitacar, when he was about eighteen years of age, attended school at Woodbury, New Jersey. Among his classmates was James Lawrence, afterwards Captain James Lawrence, of the Chesapeake, whose dying words, "Don't give up the ship!" have often been quoted. When Lawrence received his commission he tried to induce Isaac Whitacar, with whom he was very intimate, to accompany him on his vessel, promising to get him a commission also, but Isaac knowing his mother would never consent to such a thing, declined, although very anxious to go. As a keepsake, James Lawrence drew on a piece of paper, a ship in full sail, and presented it, before leaving school, to Isaac Whitacar, his chosen friend. This is now in possession of the family, and is highly prized by them.

Isaac Whitacar, Sr., departed this life 23d of 2d month, 1857, in his seventy-eighth year. Ann, his wife, died 23d of 4th month, 1855, in her sixty-third year. Both are buried in the Presbyterian church yard at Deerfield. Most of their family are living at the present time in Illinois.

WYATT FAMILY.

Bartholomew Wyatt emigrated to this county about the year 1690. I believe he came from the county of Worcestershire, England. Soon after his arrival he purchased 1200 acres of land in Mannington, of John Fenwick's heirs. The said land was bounded on the east by James Sherron's land. The first house he built on his property was a log house of considerable size, as I was told by Samuel Austin, who was considered in his time as the most correct antiquarian in that part of the county. The said house stood upon the point of land near the meadow, not far from a small creek, (called Puddle Dock), nearly half a mile from where, a few years later, he built himself a large brick house, it being not far from Mannington creek, which was navigable at that time. He was a prominent man in his time in the civil affairs of the Colony, frequently serving as a Grand Juror, as the records of the Court show; also an active member of the Society of Friends, and was one of the largest contributors to the fund for the erection of the Friends' brick meeting house in the present graveyard in Salem. He and his wife, Sarah Wyatt had two children—Bartholomew, who was born 4th of 1st month, 1697, and Elizabeth who was born in 1706. There is no mention in the records of the county, or of the meeting's records later than the year 1728; therefore I presume he died somewhere near that period. His son Bartholomew inherited all his father's real estate. He married about the year 1730, Elizabeth Tomlinson, who was born in 1706. He and his wife Elizabeth resided in Mannington during their lives, and in the year 1731 their son Bartholomew Wyatt, 3d, was born. Their daughter Sarah Wyatt was born in the year 1733, and subsequently became the wife of Richard Wistar, of Philadelphia. Bartholomew Wyatt, Jr., the father of the before mentioned children, lived what was considered at that time quite aged. He died in 1770, aged seventy-two years; his wife had been deceased many years before. It is probable that the disease with which most of the Wyatts and several of the Wistar family died with (being pulmonary consumption), was hereditary in his wife's family.

Bartholomew Wyatt, 3d, in physical appearance, I have been informed by persons that knew him, was tall, and remarkably pleasing in his address. He was considered one of the best English scholars, at the time in which he lived, in the county of Salem. The late Casper Wistar, when young, it is said, looked very much like his great-uncle as to his size and the features of his face. His company was very much sought after; and being of a benevolent turn of mind, he gave largely to the poor and needy; and when the Society of Friends at Salem and vicinity thought it would be a benefit to them to build a larger meeting house, he was the largest contributor, excepting Samuel Nicholson, of Elsinborough. Bartholomew died in the prime of his life, at the age of fifty years, leaving one daughter, Elizabeth, who, a short time before her father's death, had married William Carpenter, the son of Prescott Carpenter. William and his wife Elizabeth had two children—Mary and Hannah. The last named child died in infancy. Elizabeth Carpenter, their mother, died before she arrived at middle age. Mary Carpenter, their daughter, afterwards married James Hunt, a son of John Hunt, of Darby, Pennsylvania. I believe she left three daughters and two sons, and they disposed of the greater part of the real estate of their ancestors in Mannington, to Andrew Thompson, of Elsinborough.

Casper Wistar was the first of that name in this country. He emigrated to the province of Pennsylvania in the year 1717, and as Watson states, was naturalized in 1722 as a citizen of the province of Pennsylvania. His native place was Germany. It appears he had three children—Richard, Casper and Sarah Wistar, and was by trade a button maker. As soon as he had sufficient funds by working by day's work at any employment he found to do, he commenced business at his trade in manufacturing buttons. They were small brass buttons, being nearly round, and were used on short clothes which were the common wear at that time, and they were much sought after and readily sold at renumerative prices. He would invest his money in lands within the city limits, and as the town increased in size the property became valuable, consequently his heirs became wealthy by the increased value of property.

Casper Wistar, Jr., I have been informed, only left one daughter, Elizabeth Wistar, who became the wife of Abram Sharpless, of Chester county, Pennsylvania. She and her husband resided near Concordville, in Delaware county. Abram owned a large tract of land in that neighborhood, and together with his wife's property in the city of Philadelphia, enabled them to leave to their two sons, Abram and Casper Wistar Sharpless, princely estates. Both of them died a few years ago with much reduced estates, fulfilling the old saying:—"The "first gets it, the second keeps it, and the third spends it."

Sarah Wistar, I am informed, never married, and lived to a very advanced age. In her will she left four of her great-nephews, all of them named Casper, £11,000 a-piece, and after the specific legacies were paid, there was left £44,000 to her legatees. Richard Wistar, the eldest brother, purchased a large tract of land in Alloways Creek township, most probably from William Hall, Jr. Soon afterwards he erected a glass factory about two miles above the village of Allowaystown, and commenced the manufacture of glass. Johnson, in his history of this county, stated it was the first of its kind in the United States, but I think he was mistaken in that statement. Massachusetts claims the first, which was started in 1742. The most reliable account I have ever seen respecting Richard Wistar fixes the time he commenced operation in 1744, it being two years later than the Massachusetts enterprise. Richard's glass works, it has been stated, proved to be a very profitable investment. His own time was very much taken up in looking after his great estate in the city of Philadelphia, and consequently he employed Benjamin Thompson, a young man of great business capacity, the son of William Thompson, of Allowaystown, to be the overseer of his glass works. He filled the position, it has been stated, during the time the glass works were in operation, much to the satisfaction of the proprietor. About the year 1750 Richard married Sarah Wyatt, the daughter of Bartholomew Wyatt, Jr., of Mannington. I think they had six children—Richard, Casper, John, Thomas, Elizabeth and Catharine. Richard Wistar, Jr., married and left two children. Richard and Sarah died a few years ago. Casper became one of the most eminent physicians of his time in the city of Philadelphia, and I believe he left a family of children. John married Charlotte Newbold, the daughter of Clayton Newbold, of Burlington county.

At the death of Bartholemew Wyatt he owed his son-in-law, Richard Wistar, £1,000. In making his will he devised one-half of his real estate in Mannington to Richard and his wife Sarah, provided he would cancel the debt, which was accordingly done, and Richard Wistar became the owner. His son, John, after his marriage, settled thereon, and at the death of his father the said property became a part of his share of his father's great estate.

John Wistar, it can be truly said, was one of Nature's noblemen. He had an intellectual mind which he inherited from his mother's family, and a large share of the milk of human kindness. It has been stated, and I do not doubt the correctness of it, because it was in accordance with his feelings toward suffering humanity, that he was the first to advocate the establishing of the Salem County Alms House. He and his wife had, I think, eight children; their names were Mary, Bartholomew, Clayton, Charlotte, Casper, Hannah, Catharine and John. Their father, John Wistar, died in his fifty-sixth year, of pulmonary consumption. It could be truly said of him he was lost too soon for his family and his own religious society, and to the community generally. His widow survived him several years. Their oldest daughter Mary married Isaac Davis, of Philadelphia. Bartholomew married a young woman by the name of Newbold. He was a merchant in Philadelphia. Clayton Wistar's wife was Mary Stevenson, the daughter of John Stevenson, who was a lineal descendant of that eminent man, Samuel Jennings, of Burlington. Clayton and his wife had two sons—John and Richard Wistar. His second wife was Martha Reeve, the daughter of Josiah Reeve, of Burlington, formerly of Cumberland. By this connection they had one son, Josiah Wistar, of Mannington.

Charlotte Wistar married Jonathan Freedland, the son of Jonas Freedland, who was one of Salem county's favorite sons. Charlotte has been deceased several years, leaving no children; her husband is still living.

Casper Wistar's wife was Rebecca Bassett, daughter of Joseph Bassett. Casper is now deceased, leaving a widow and five children—Sarah, Mary, Casper, Joseph and Catharine. Hannah Wistar married Dr. Theophilus Beesley. He had an extensive practice in Salem when he was married, and a few years afterward he and his wife removed to Philadelphia. In that city he stood high in his profession. They are both deceased now. Catharine Wistar married Thomas Evans, the son of Jonathan Evans, of Philadelphia. Thomas, whilst living was an eminent minister in the Orthodox branch of the Society of Friends. John Wistar, the youngest, was left the homestead of his father. In a few years he became of age, he sold it to Thomas Bacon and removed to Philadelphia.

Elizabeth Wistar, the daughter of Richard and Sarah Wistar, married Richard Miller, the son of Josiah and Letitia Miller, of Mannington. They lived most of the time after they were married on the property where their grandson, Wyatt W. Miller, now owns and lives. Richard died in the prime of his life, leaving a widow and three children. Their names were Sarah, Letitia and Josiah Miller. Elizabeth W. Miller was considered in her time more than ordinary in her physical and mental abilities. She, when quite young, had an attack of scarlet fever, which impaired her hearing, and before she reached middle age she was entirely deaf; but it often occurs when a person is deprived of hearing, the other senses are much stronger and it was true with her to a remarkable degree. I well remember when young in seeing her in Friends' meeting, at Salem, taking her seat fronting the gallery, and if any one spoke she would watch the lips of the speaker, and if the one that was speaking remained motionless, it has been said she would get as good understanding of the discourse as others did who had their hearing. Also in conversation, particularly with persons she was accustomed to, there appeared to be no difficulty for her to understand them. She resided in Mannington on the farm for a few years after her husband's death, and then removed to Salem, and died there aged over ninety years.

Sarah Miller married Benjamin Acton, son of Clement Acton, of Salem. Benjamin and his wife Sarah had eight children— Richard M., Benjamin, Hannah, Letitia, Elizabeth, Charlotte, Sarah Wyatt, and Casper W. Acton. Benjamin and his wife are both deceased, although she survived her husband several years.

Letitia Miller's husband was Thomas B. Sheppard, the son of John Sheppard, of Cumberland county. She died young, leaving one daughter.

Josiah Miller, the son of Richard and Elizabeth Miller, in physical and mental abilities, was above the ordinary man, and if he had cultivated his mind, with his wealth and family influence, he would have been one of the most useful men in his generation.

Josiah married Hetty James, daughter of Samuel L. James. She was amiable in her disposition, and was well calculated to make home pleasant and agreeable. He died a comparatively young man, leaving a widow and three minor children—Richard, Samuel and Wyatt Miller. The two youngest own and reside on their patrimonial estate in Mannington. The said property has been in the Miller family four generations.

Hetty Miller, the widow of Josiah lived until she was advanced in life, and then married David Reeves, of Phœnixville,

Chester county, Pennsylvania. He was formerly a resident of Bridgeton, Cumberland county, New Jersey, and was the son of Thomas Reeves, of Gloucester county. That connection was of short duration, however, as she was taken away by a short and severe illness in a short period after they were married, and he survived her only a few years.

WHITTAN FAMILY.

James Whittan purchased property in Mannington the latter part of the seventeenth century, adjoining lands of Richard Woodnutt on the west, lands of Wheoeby on the east. He and his wife, Sarah Whittan, had two children—Ann, their daughter, was born in 1707, and their son, Joseph Whittan, was born in 1709; he died a minor.

James Nevell and Richard Tindell died about the year 1703 or 1704. Nevell was a lawyer, and acted as agent for William Penn in disposing of his lands lying in Fenwick's tenth. It appears that Penn had implicit confidence in his ability and integrity. The settlements he made with the proprietor for lands he disposed of for him fully justify that opinion. Richard Tindell was considered in his time to be remarkably correct in his surveying and in his calculations; so much so, that I have been informed the surveyors at the present time have no difficulty in following the various lines of the numerous tracts of land that he run and calculated more than one hundred and eighty years ago. I call the attention of the reader to one tract of meadow and swamp Richard Tindell re-surveyed by an order from James Nevell in 1685, it being the town marsh which was given by John Fenwick to the inhabitants of Salem town in 1676, and was surveyed by Richard Hancock the same year. Some five or six years ago the present owners of said meadow agreed to have a general survey of it again. They employed Belford Bonham, of Cumberland county, who is considered one of the most correct surveyors in this part of the State. The number of acres that Belford made of the meadow was about the same that Richard Tindell surveyed one hundred and eighty years ago, it being 560 acres. After the death of these two eminent men, Nevell and Tindall, James Logan, the faithful secretary of William Penn, took upon himself the task of disposing the lands that belonged to the proprietor within the boundaries of Fenwick's tenth. He accordingly appointed Benjamin Acton, Jr., to be his surveyor. The said Benjamin Acton resided in Salem, on the property formerly belonging to his father. The property was on East Broadway, opposite Johnson street. Benjamin Acton, Jr., built a large brick house on the lot of ground in 1727. The foundation is still remaining. George Rumsey rebuilt it a few years ago.

After somewhat of a digression, I now come back to the Whittan family again in 1712. James Logan gave an order to Benjamin Acton to survey 100 acres of meadow for James Whittan, the said marsh being over the creek, opposite said Whittan's plantation, for which he paid £20 pounds, new currency. James Whittan, I think died in 1730, leaving his estate to his daughter, Ann Whittan. She married Benjamin Cripps, and their son, Whittan Cripps, became the owner of the real estate of his mother, Martha Huddy.

William Cripps married and had two children—Benjamin and Mary. Mary married Peter Andrews. He was a native of Egg Harbor. Soon after their marriage they purchased a farm of Robert Johnson, being part of the Pledger property in Mannington. Clark Lippincott is the present owner. On that farm Peter and his wife resided. Whilst they lived they had four children. Their names were Clara, Martha, Isaac and Thomas Andrews. After the death of Peter Andrews his widow and daughter, Clara, lived in Salem. Both of them died there at an advanced age. Martha Andrews' husband was William Shourds. They left four children—Rachel, Mary, Benjamin and William Shourds. They all reside in Philadelphia except Rachel, her home is in Mount Holly. Isaac married the daughter of John Woodside, of Mannington. They subsequently removed to the State of New York, near Rochester. Thomas Andrews, likewise, went to the same neighborhood with his brother. He, I believe, studied law, and afterward located himself and family in the State of Michigan. Whittan Cripps was considered above mediocrity as to his native talent. At the breaking out of the war of the American Revolution he left the Society of Friends, of which he was born a member, and devoted all his energies in assisting to carry it on in this part of the county, and at the close of the Revolution he became an active politician as a member of the Republican party as it was then called, but afterwards known as Jeffersonian Democrats and was considered to be the leader of that party in this county. He was elected two or three times in succession to the office of Sheriff. During his last term of office a law was passed by the Legislature of this State, prohibiting any person holding the office of Sheriff more than one term in succession, and his son, Benjamin Cripps, was chosen Sheriff at the next election.

According to the accounts we have, men were much more easily excited in politics the latter part of the last century, during the organization of the government, and party feeling was more acrimonious than it has been since. It was during one of the strongly contested elections, Jacob Hufty was a candidate for the office of Sheriff on the Republican side. A person on the opposite side of politics being at the polls at the time of voting, asked what Mr. Hufty done with his broad-axe, he being a ship carpenter. Whittan Cripps, who was within hearing, quickly said that Hufty had buried it under the walls of Quebec, where such a coward as you dare not show his head. After Whittan's death the property in Mannington was left to his son, and he, not having the management of his father, became intoxicated with politics, neglected his business, and it is said, became involved in debt, and that fine estate was put in market. John Denn that time followed his trade in Salem, he being a hatter. By industry and frugality he had accumulated a sufficient amount of money to warrant him in buying it and in a few years he had the property paid for. He was likewise one of the best meadow men that was ever in this county.

Nathaniel and his wife, Grace Cripps, came to America in 1678, and settled in Burlington county. By tradition he was the founder of Mount Holly. Nathaniel and Grace Cripps had six children—John, Benjamin, Samuel, Virginia, Theophla and Hannah Ann Cripps. John, the eldest son, married Mary Eves, of Haddonfield. Benjamin, the second son, married Mary Hough; their children were Whittan, who in 1759 married Martha Huddy; John, their second son, died a minor; Hannah married Samuel Mason, of Mannington, in 1756, son of Thomas Mason, of the same place. Whittan Cripps and his wife settled on the landed estate of his great-uncle, James Whittan, in Lower Mannington, Salem county. He and his wife had two children—Benjamin and Mary Cripps. Benjamin married the daughter of Peter Carney, of Upper Penn's Neck, and Mary married Peter Andrews, a native of Egg Harbor.

WOODNUTT FAMILY.

Richard Woodnutt, the first one of the family of whom there is any record, came from England about 1690. It is supposed he first settled in Philadelphia, but in 1695 it appears he located at Salem. He was a bricklayer by occupation, and was a member of the Society of Friends, and a man of considerable means. He paid $75 towards erecting the first brick meeting house in West Jersey, which was built on the Nicholson lot on West Broadway, in Salem. Most probably he was the master brick-layer of the said building. He came into possession of a large tract of land in Mannington, being part of John Pledger's allotment, by marriage or purchase, I think in 1696. He married Mary Pledger, some antiquarians think, but there is no record of his having done so; the names of his children, however, seem to indicate it. Richard Woodnutt and his wife Mary had four children. Joseph, the eldest son, was born 5th of 7th month, 1697; Richard was born 22d of 12th month; 1700; Grace in 1703, and Sarah in 1708. Joseph in 1722 married Rachel Craven, and they commenced life on his patrimonial estate in Mannington, near the town of Salem. Most of said estate is owned at the present time by Richard Woodnutt, of Salem, he being the sixth generation from the first emigrant of that name. The old mansion house was burned down upward of fifty years ago, while in tenure of James Elliott. Joseph and his wife Rachel had five children—Thomas was born in 1724, Mary in 1727, Hannah in 1730, Richard in 1732, and Joseph in 1735. Thomas died a young man, unmarried. Mary married Elisha, son of Elisha and Abigail Davis Bassett, of Pilesgrove. Elisha and his wife Mary had six children—their eldest son, Joseph Bassett, died in infancy; Rachel, their eldest daughter, died a young woman, unmarried; Sarah Bassett was born 10th of 8th month, 1759. She subsequently married Joseph Petitt in 1779, and her children were Woodnutt, Rachel, David, Jonathan, Thomas and Mary. Hannah, daughter of Elisha and Mary Bassett, born in 1762, married John Roberts, near Haddonfield, and had two children—Benjamin and David Roberts. Joseph Bassett, 2d, born 26th of 6th month, 1755, married Mary, the daughter of David and Rebecca Allen. By that union there were nine children—Elisha, Joseph, David, Hannah, Rebecca, Samuel, Benjamin, William and Mary. Joseph and his wife lived above the age that is alloted to man, he being more than four-score at the time of his death. He was one of the most successful agriculturalists that Salem county ever produced. David Bassett, his brother, died a young man, unmarried.

Hannah, the youngest daughter of Joseph and Rachel Woodnutt, born in 1729 married Samuel Hedge, 5th. They had four children—Rebecca born in 1751; Mary born in 1753 (she died a young woman unmarried in 1775); Samuel, born in 1775, and Joseph in 1758. Neither of the sons married, and both died in 1797, in the old Hedge house on Broadway street, in the town of Salem. Their great landed estate fell to their sister Rebecca, who was at that time the wife of Thomas Thompson, the son of Thomas Thompson, and grandson of Andrew Thompson, the emigrant, of Elsinborough. The children of Thomas and his wife Rebecca were noticed in the genealogy of the Hedge and Fenwick families.

Richard Woodnutt, the son of Joseph, married Elizabeth, daughter of William Hall, Jr., of Mannington. Richard died when he was about twenty-eight years of age, leaving one daughter—Elizabeth, who married William Goodwin, Jr., of Elsinborough, the youngest son of William and Mary Morris Goodwin. By that union there were six daughters—Prudence, Mary, Rachel, Sarah, Elizabeth and Abigail. Their genealogy has been traced with the Goodwin family. Elizabeth's second husband was Thomas Clement. Joseph, the youngest child of Joseph and Rachel Woodnutt, was born in 1735. I think he died, leaving no issue. The second husband of Rachel Woodnutt, the widow of Joseph, was Daniel Garrison. Grace and Sarah, daughters of Richard and Sarah Woodnutt, I think died unmarried.

Woodnutt, the eldest son of Joseph and Sarah B. Pettit, married Sarah Jess; they had ten children—Rachel, Hannah, David, Joseph, Samuel, Samuel C., Ann, James, Ruth and Sarah. Rachel married William G. Beesley, who has been deceased more than thirty years, leaving no issue. Hannah married David Bassett; she is deceased, and left no issue. David Pettit's wife is Martha B. Engle; their children are Mary, Woodnutt, William, Franklin, Hannah and David. Joseph Pettit, son of Woodnutt, married Caroline, daughter of

Aaron Pancoast. They have four sons—George, Charles Eliu and Joseph. Samuel Pettit died young ; Samuel C. died a young man ; Anna married Eliu Roberts, of Philadelphia, and had three children—Woodnutt, Charles and Hannah Roberts. James Pettit married Elizabeth W. Ridgway. Their children are Clarkson, Ruth and Dillwyn. Ruth died a young woman. Sarah, the youngest child of Woodnutt and Sarah Pettit, married Edward P., son of David and Hannah Cooper, of Woodbury. They have three sons—David, Courtlandt and William. Rachel, the daughter of Joseph and Sarah Pettit, married Benjamin Hewitt; she died young, and I think she left no issue. David Pettit, son of Joseph and Sarah, died a young man, unmarried. Jonathan Pettit married Ann, daughter of George Woolly, of Philadelphia; her children were Charles, Charlotte, Huldah, Lewis, Sarah Ann and Jonathan. Thomas, the youngest son of Joseph and Sarah Pettit, died young. Mary Pettit, their youngest daughter, married Nehemiah Hogbin, and had one son, Charles Hogbin, now deceased. The mother of Joseph Pettit, father of Woodnutt, was Mary Shourds. Woodnutt's wife's (Sarah Jess) grandmother was Ruth Silvers; therefore Woodnutt and his wife were both relatives of my family.

James Mason Woodnutt married Margaret Carpenter in 1776: They had ten children—Sarah, Hannah, Thomas, Jonathan, Preston, Elizabeth, William, Margaret, Mary and Martha. Sarah, the eldest child, born 1777, died unmarried ; Hannah, born in 1780, married Clement Acton, Sr., of Salem, being his second wife. They had two children—Clement and Margaret Acton. Clement went to Cincinnati many years ago and engaged in the mercantile business, at the old stand of his uncle, William Woodnutt. He married Fanny Biddle, and they have two children—Helen and John Acton. Margaret, daughter of Clement and Hannah W. Acton, married Dr. John Griscom, of Philadelphia, son of William and Ann Griscom. They have three children—Hannah, John and William W. Thomas Woodnutt was born in 1782, and died single. Jonathan, the second son of James and Margaret Woodnutt, born 12th of 10th month, 1784, married Mary, the daughter of William and Elizabeth Goodwin. They had four children—Richard, William, Thomas and Mary Woodnutt. Richard, their eldest son, married Lydia, the daughter of Clement and Sarah Hall, late of Elsinborough. They have six children—Mary, Emily H., Sarah H., Elizabeth G., Mary and Richard H. Woodnutt.

William Goodwin Woodnutt, Jonathan's second son, married

Elizabeth, daughter of Joseph and Lydia Bassett. They have seven children—Emily C., Joseph B., Jonathan, Thomas, Anne E., Howard C. and William Woodnutt. Thomas, the youngest son of Jonathan and Mary Woodnutt, removed to Cincinnati, Ohio, and went into the mercantile business with his cousin, Clement Acton. He married Hannah Morgan, a resident of Richmond, Indiana, where he resides at the present time. They have three children—Abbie, William, and Clement A. Woodnutt.

Mary, the daughter of Jonathan and Mary Woodnutt, married Edward, the son of Isaac and Lucy Ann Acton. They had four children—Walter W., Isaac Oakford, Elizabeth, and Jonathan Acton. Jonathan Woodnutt's second wife was Sarah, the widow of Henry Dennis, (her maiden name was Goodwin, the sister of his first wife). They lived together in much unity to an advanced age, and in their death the poor and afflicted lost kind and sympathizing friends.

Preston, son of James M. and Margaret Woodnutt, was born 24th of 1st month, 1787. His wife was Rachel, the daughter of William and Elizabeth Goodwin, and a sister to his brother Jonathan's wife. Prescott and his wife Rachel died about middle age, leaving five children—James, Elizabeth, Hannah Ann, Edward and Preston. Their eldest son, James, married Elizabeth, the daughter of John and Margaret Denn, who were residents of Mannington. John and his wife had five children—Charles, Henry, Franklin, Preston and Margaretta.

Charles Woodnutt, the son of James, married Mary Garretson. They have three children—Clifford, James and Edward. Henry, the second son of James Woodnutt, married Anna Frost. They have five children—Hannah, Thomas, Elizabeth, Henry and Clifford. Franklin Woodnutt, the third son of James, married Eveline Ware; they have one daughter, Elizabeth. Preston and Margaret remain single. Elizabeth G. Woodnutt, daughter of Preston and Rachel, married Amsley, the son of Benjamin Newlin, of Chester county, Pennsylvania. They had two children—Francis and Benjamin. Hannah A. Woodnutt, daughter of Preston and Rachel, married Nathan Baker; there were two children—Mary E. and Henry Preston Baker. I think Preston's two youngest sons, Edward and Preston Woodnutt, remain single.

Elizabeth, the daughter of James M. and Margaret, married Morris, the son of Clement and Rebecca Hall, formerly of Elsinborough. They had five children—Margaretta, James, Franklin, Hannah and Rebecca. Margaretta married John W.

Righter, and their children were Elizabeth, James, William and Charles. William, the son of James and Margaret Woodnutt, was born in 1792. In early life he sold his patrimonial estate in Mannington, and removed from his native county to Cincinnati, Ohio, where he embarked into the mercantile business which he pursued successfully, accumulating an ample fortune. Some years before his death he sold out his interest in that city to his two nephews, Clement Acton, Jr. and Thomas Woodnutt, and ended his days in Philadelphia, leaving a large estate to be divided among his relatives. I think he never married.

Margaret, the daughter of James M. and Margaret Woodnutt, born in 1794, married William J., son of Isaiah Shinn, of Pilesgrove. William and his wife had six children—Emeline, Joseph, Samuel, Elizabeth, Sarah and Martha. The last mentioned child married Dr. Isaiah Clawson. Sarah Shinn married Dr. Thomas Reed. Mary Woodnutt, the daughter of James M. and Margaret, born in 1767, married Benjamin Newlin, of Chester county, Pennsylvania. They had one daughter, Martha, who married Thomas Travilla; they had one daughter—Martha. Martha Woodnutt, the daughter of James M. and Margaret, born in 1799, married Joshua Reeves, the son of Biddle Reeves, of Gloucester; she was his second wife. They had two children—Margaret and William Reeves. The latter married Ruth, the daughter of James J. Pettit; their children are James P., Frank and Martha Pettit Reeves.

Henry, the second son of Richard and Ann Wamsley Woodnutt, born 4th of 12th month, 1736, married Eve Wood; they had three children—Ann, Margaret and Joseph Woodnutt. Ann Woodnutt, Henry's oldest daughter, married John Williams; by that union there were six children—John, Henry, Margaret, Joseph, Thomas and Sarah Williams. The first wife of John Williams, Jr., was Hester Harris; his second, Elizabeth Lambson; his third, Hannah Bradway. There were fourteen children—John, Rebecca, Elizabeth, David, Amanda, Anne Maria, Sarah, Margaret, Hester, Ann, William, Charles, Sarah Ann and Moses Williams. John by occupation was a shoe maker; I believe he followed it during his life in the city of Salem, and he had an excellent reputation for integrity and uprightness in all his transactions with his fellow men. Henry, the second son of John and Ann W. Williams, was a tailor. His wife was Rachel Hutchinson; their children were Woodnutt, Maria, Charles and Henry Williams. Margaret Williams, the eldest daughter of John and Woodnutt Williams, has lived a life of great usefulness as a faithful and tender nurse; she remains single. Joseph, the third son of John Williams, married Ann Welsh; they had four children—Sarah, Emeline, Margaret and Thomas Williams. Thomas Williams married and had one child—Joseph Williams. Sarah Williams, their youngest daughter, it appears died single.

Margaret, the second daughter of Henry and Eve Woodnutt, married Isaac Elwell; they had two children—John and Mary Ann Elwell. The latter subsequently married a man by the name of Dolbow. The numerous branches of the Woodnutt family at the present day, as far as I have the means of judging endeavored to live so as to bring no reproach upon their ancestors, and it should be the duty of the present generation to adopt the many good, benevolent and christian acts they did in their time, so that true civilization and christianity may advance in this and succeeding generations higher than it has ever yet obtained.

WOODRUFF FAMILY.

The Woodruffs are an ancient family in Worcestershire, England. Thomas Woodruff, son of John Woodruff, was born, in Worcestershire, about 1630. In early life he became a member of the Society of Friends, and married Edith Wyatt, daughter of Joseph Wyatt, who located on a large tract of land, in the township of Mannington, at the first settlement of the province. Thomas Woodruff and wife, soon after their marriage, removed to London, where they had several children born, their names were Thomas, Edith, John and Isaac Woodruff. In the year 1678, Thomas and his wife Edith Woodruff, and their aforesaid children, together with one man-servant, named Allen Hanway and his sister, children of Leonard Hanway, of Weymouth, set sail for America. They had a daughter born on the sea, named Mary Woodruff; the name of the ship was Surrey, Stephen Nichols was the captain. They arrived at Salem in 4th month, 1679, at which place it is most probable, Thomas, and his wife Edith Woodruff ended their days. Their descendants are found in most of the States of the Union. The family of Woodruffs is numerous in the county of Cumberland at this time; this circumstance will justify the belief that some of Thomas Woodruff's sons located in the Cohansey precinct, and became citizens of that part of Fenwick's Colony. I called a short time since to see the venerable Daniel M. Woodruff, (a lineal descendant of Thomas Woodruff,) at his home in Bridgeton; although his sight was nearly gone, on account of his great age, being nearly ninety, in other respects he retains his physical and mental faculties remarkably. He entered into conversation in a lively and interesting manner, inquiring after those with whom he was formerly acquainted, and particularly those, of whom he formerly bought cattle, when he followed the butchering business in the city of Bridgeton. He mentioned John Denn, William Carpenter, Wistars and Bassetts; he supposed they were all deceased. I answered him in the affirmative. He then said, "They were all honest "men." Daniel at one time was Sheriff of Cumberland county, also Clerk of the county and Judge of the Court of Common

Pleas, and for many years the principal auctioneer of Bridgeton and the surrounding county. Mr. Woodruff, although not the oldest person, is now the oldest living resident of Bridgeton.

YORKE FAMILY.

The Yorke's sprung from an ancient English family. Thomas Yorke was high Sheriff of England three different times in the reign of Henry the VIII. Simon Yorke was born at Calme, in Wiltshire, England, and owned a large landed estate in that county. He left Wiltshire soon after the death of Charles I, with the intention of leaving his native land on account of the prominent part he had taken on the side of that unfortunate monarch. It seems he changed his intention and settled at Dover, in the county of Kent, and died there 2d of 3d month 1682, aged seventy-six years, and was buried in the Church of St. James, at Dover. He had five sons and one daughter. One of his sons was the father of Simon Yorke, who lived at Ething, in Derbyshire, and died 28th of 7th month, 1767, leaving issue, the late Philip Yorke, a man not unknown to the literary world; he died 19th of 2d month, 1804, aged sixty-one years. He married Elizabeth, sister to Lord Brownlong, in 7th month, 1770 and had issue, Simon Yorke, formerly a member of Parliament for Grantham. Philip the second son of Simon and Elizabeth Yorke, born in Wiltshire in 1651, left his native place and settled in the county of Kent, and there married Elizabeth Gibbon, a young woman of ancient family, daughter and heiress of R. Gibbon, of Dover. Lord Chancellor Hardwick always quartered the Gibbon arms, as may be seen in the middle of Temple Hall.

Thomas Yorke arrived from England and settled in Salem as early as 1685. In 1687 Richard Tindell received an order from James Nevell to resurvey a tract of land containing 500 acres, lying on Nicomer's Run, a part of Fenwick's Grove, in Mannington, known at that time as White's Vineyard. It was owned by Thomas Yorke and Mary White, the faithful housekeeper of John Fenwick. (He made an honorable mention of her in his will, and devised to her a large landed estate). Thomas Yorke resided in the town of Salem in 1690. I presume he died without issue. The Yorke family, it seems, had forgotten him.

THOMAS JONES YORKE.
Born 1801.

Thomas Yorke, the ancestor of the present Yorke family in the United States, came from Yorkshire, England, about 1728. He left in England a brother, two sisters, and his uncle, Joseph Yorke, who was Lord Mayor of Dover, and ambassador to Hague in the reign of George II. John Potts, founder of Pottstown, Pa., married Ruth Savage. John and his wife Ruth had three daughters—Elizabeth, Mary and Martha Potts. Elizabeth, the eldest daughter, married Joseph Walker, and Mary Potts, their second daughter married Deniah Cleaver. Thomas Yorke, soon after he arrived in this country, went into partnership with John Potts in the iron business. In 1736 he married Martha Potts, the youngest daughter of his partner. They had two sons—Edward, the eldest, born 20th of 9th month, 1738, died 12th of 4th month, 1781; and Stephen, born about 1740. Thomas Yorke's second wife was Margaret Robeson, a member of the Robeson family of New Jersey. Secretary of Navy Robeson remarked recently in Salem that he could trace his family in New Jersey for six generations. Thomas and Margaret R. Yorke had two sons—Andrew, who was born 26th of 11th month, 1742, and died in 1794, and Thomas, born 16th of 11th month, 1740. He joined the Royalists at the breaking out of the Revolutionary war, and at its close went to England. He was Mayor of Hull, England, for several years. He died without issue. Thomas Yorke's third wife was Mary Robeson, a niece of his second wife, who was a cousin to his first wife, Martha Potts. Thomas and Mary Yorke had four children— Robeson, Samuel, Martha and Margaret Yorke. Thomas Yorke was Justice of the Peace in Pottstown in 1745; in 1747 he was Lieutenant-Colonel in the French and Indian wars, and in 1757 and 1758 he represented Berks county, Pennsylvania, in the Provincial Assembly. A short time afterwards he removed to Philadelphia, and was appointed Judge of the Courts by the crown of England.

Edward, the eldest son of Thomas and Martha P. Yorke, born about 1738, married Sarah Stille, and had nine children— Thomas, Eliza, Stille, Stephen, Gustavus, Samuel, Peter, Martha and Edward Yorke. Thomas, the eldest son, died a young man, single. Eliza, the eldest daughter, married a man by the name of Cole; they had one daughter, Eliza Cole, who died without issue. Eliza's second husband's name was Farquhar, and they had issue—Isabel, George, Emma (who married Andrew Jackson Donaldson) and Edward Farquhar. Samuel, the son of Edward and Sarah S. Yorke, married Mary Lippincott; their children were Peter, Edward (who married Sarah Hawn, of Louisiana), Samuel and William (who married Mary Murphy).

Peter, the son of Edward and Sarah Yorke, married Sarah Haines; they had issue, three children—Marian, Sarah and Jane. Marian married an Adams. Sarah's husband was Andrew Donaldson Jackson, the adopted son of General Andrew Jackson, and now resides at the "Hermitage," Tennessee.— Their issue was Rachel Jackson, who married Dr. Canrum, of Tennessee; they had issue—Andrew Jackson and Samuel Wetherill Jackson Canrum. Jane was married twice; her first husband was S. M. Wetherill, and her second husband's name was Taggart. Marian Yorke and —— Adams had one son— John Adams. Jane Yorke, by her first husband, S. M. Wetherill, had five children—Ellen, Jane, Alfred, Sarah and Martha Wetherill; and by her second husband, —— Taggart, she had two children—Edward and Rebecca Taggart.

Martha Yorke, the daughter of Edward and Sarah Stille, married Mordica Wetherill; they had one son, Samuel M. Wetherill, who married Jane Yorke, as before stated. Stephen Yorke died single.

Andrew Yorke, the second son of Thomas and Margaret Robeson Yorke, born in the city of Philadelphia 26th of 11th month, 1742, came to Salem in 1773, and lived and kept store in the old brick building which is still standing at the corner of Yorke and Magnolia streets. His wife was Eleanor Coxe, of Manayunk, Pennsylvania. Their issue was Andrew, Eleanor, Martha, Lewis and Thomas Yorke. At the commencement of the Revolutionary war, Andrew took an active part in favor of the Colonies, and was an aid to General Newcomb in the Revolutionary Army. Andrew died at Salem, New Jersey, in 1794, and was buried at St. John's Episcopal church-yard in that city. His son, Andrew Yorke, Jr., died without issue. Eleanor, the daughter of Andrew and Eleanor C. Yorke, married John, the son of William and Sarah Thompson Hancock, of Hancock's Bridge. They had six children—William, Sarah, Henrietta, Thomas Yorke, Maria and Caroline Hancock. William, their son, died young. Eleanor Y., a short time before her death, moved from Hancock's Bridge to Salem, to reside with her daughter, Sarah, but died soon afterwards, and was buried in the Episcopal grave-yard where her parents were interred, her husband, John Hancock, having been deceased a number of years previous. Sarah, the oldest daughter of John and Eleanor Hancock, married Morris, the son of Thomas and Mary Goodwin Hancock, of Elsinborough; they had issue—

Morris, Eleanor, Mary, Sarah, John and Henrietta Hancock. Eleanor, the eldest daughter, married Daniel Stratton, a Presbyterian clergyman, and a native of Bridgeton; they had issue—Morris H. and Daniel P. Stratton. The latter married Isabella Barnes, daughter of the late Joseph Barnes, of Woodstown. Daniel and his wife reside in the State of Missouri. They have issue—Eleanor H. and Rebecca Stratton. Mary, the daughter of Morris and Sarah Hancock, married Thomas Sinnickson Smith, son of John and Mary Smith, of Salem; they have two children—Maria and Thomas S. Smith. The latter is a lawyer and resides in Salem. Maria, their daughter, married Constant M. Eakin; they have issue—Eleanor Y. and Constance Eakin. Sarah, the daughter of Morris and Sarah Hancock, married Dr. Quinton Gibbon, of Salem; they have issue—Henrietta Gibbon.

Henrietta, the daughter of John and Eleanor Hancock, married Lewis P. Smith, of Bucks county, Pennsylvania; they had four children—Henry, Louisa, Genovie (who is now deceased) and Sarah M. Smith. The latter married Clement Hall Sinnickson. He is a lawyer, and has an extensive practice in Salem. He was elected to Congress from the First District of New Jersey in 1874. Clement and his wife had issue—M. L. Sinnickson, deceased. Thomas Y., second son of John and Eleanor Hancock, married Rachel, daughter of William and Elizabeth Thompson Nicholson, formerly of Mannington. Rachel's mother was a first cousin of Thomas Y. Hancock's father, John Hancock; they had issue—Elizabeth, Ellen, William, Cornelia and Thomas Hancock.

Elizabeth, daughter of Thomas Y. and Rachel Hancock, was twice married; her first husband was David, the son of Andrew and Hannah Stretch Smith, of Elsinborough. David and Elizabeth Smith had issue—Morris and Sarah M. Smith. Morris died young, and Sarah married Nathan, the son of Belford M. Bonham, of Cumberland county. Elizabeth H. Smith's second husband was Samuel, the son of William and Ann Fowser. Elizabeth has been deceased several years. Ellen, the second daughter of Thomas Y. and Rachel Hancock, married Dr. Henry Childs, the son of John and Rachel Childs, of Philadelphia. They have three sons—William, Edward and Thomas. William, the son of Thomas Y. and Rachel Hancock, married Beulah, the daughter of William and Ann Fowser; they have issue—Anna F. and Ellen M. Hancock. Cornelia, daughter of Thomas Y. and Rachel Hancock, has great energy of character. During the recent rebellion, directly after the battle of Gettysburg, she hastened there, and rendered great assistance in caring for the sick and wounded in the hospitals. She continued in the army hospital until the final overthrow of the rebellion, after which event she volunteered in the praiseworthy undertaking of teaching school for colored children, near Charleston, South Carolina, where she is still in the same employment. Thomas, the youngest son of Thomas Y. and Rachel Hancock, was drowned whilst bathing in Alloways creek, when he was about seven or eight years old. Maria, daughter of John and Eleanor Hancock, married Richard P., the eldest son of Hedge and Mary Ann Parrott Thompson; they had issue—Isabella Thompson.

Louis Yorke, second son of Andrew and Eleanor C. Yorke, married Mary, the daughter of Thomas and Mary Jones, of Salem. Thomas was of those men that made his own fortune, beginning with small means at his disposal, by industry and close application to his business acquired a competency; lived to an advanced age, and was greatly respected by his fellow citizens. Louis and his wife, Mary J. Yorke, left Salem soon after their marriage and located in the village of Hancock's Bridge. Louis kept store with Lewis Paullin as partner in John Hancock's store house, near the bridge, now occupied by Carll & Brother. Louis and his wife had issue—Andrew, Thomas Jones and Louis S. Yorke. Their father died in Philadelphia in 1809, and was buried in Christ Church burying ground in that city. Andrew, the eldest son of Louis and Mary Yorke, died young. Their second son, Thomas J. Yorke, was twice married. His first wife was Mary, the daughter of Jonathan and Elizabeth Smith, of Bucks county, Pennsylvania. Mary died a young woman, leaving one son—Louis Eugene Yorke. The second wife of Thomas J. Yorke was Margaret Johnson Sinnickson, daughter of Thomas and Elizabeth Jacobs Sinnickson. She was from Chester county, Pennsylvania, and her parents were consistent members of the Society of Friends, descendants of the Jacobs' and Brinton's being among the first Quaker families of Chester county. Thomas and his wife, Margaret J. Yorke, have issue—Mary A., Elizabeth S., Thomas J., Jr., Margaret and Caroline P. Yorke. The eldest daughter, Mary A., married DeWitt Clinton Clement, son of Samuel and Eliza H. Clement; they have issue, one daughter—Eliza H. Clement. Margaret J. Yorke married Dr. J. B. Parker, a surgeon in the United States Navy, and their issue is Mary S. Parker. Caroline P. Yorke married William F. Allen, editor of the "Travelers' Official Guide," their issue is Yorke and Frederica W. Allen.

Thomas J. Yorke, early in life, went in the store of his grandfather, Thomas Jones, in Salem. In 1817 he removed to Philadelphia, and was clerk in one of the dry goods stores until 1821, when he returned to Salem and entered into the mercantile business with his uncle, Thomas Jones, Jr., in the same store house that his grand-father, Thomas Jones, formerly occupied. It is now known as the Star Corner building, corner of Market and Broadway streets. The building is one of the oldest store houses in the city of Salem. It was built by William Cattell, and his son, Elijah Cattell, occupied it as a store during the greater part of his life, and soon after his death it was sold to that eminent philanthropist, Isaac Moss, who, in a short time afterwards, conveyed it to Thomas Jones, Sr. Thomas Jones Yorke continued in business with his uncle until 1847. He was elected a member of the State Legislature in 1835, and in the succeeding year he was elected to Congress, taking his seat in 1837, and continued a member of that body up to 1843. In the year 1853 he was elected a Director and Secretary and Treasurer of the West Jersey Railroad Company, which offices he held until 1866, when he was elected President and continued in that position until 2d month, 1875, when, on account of his failing physical strength, which is incident to old age, he resigned the office. The Company, however, retained him as one of its Directors. His eldest son, Louis Eugene Yorke possessed more than ordinary abilities. He was educated as a civil engineer at the Renselar Institute, in the State of New York, and early in life he entered the service of the Pennsylvania Railroad Company, and assisted to locate the tunnel through the Alleghaney mountains. He was a resident engineer of the Memphis and Charleston Railroad, and soon afterward was employed with the Hoboken Land Improvement Company, and also had charge of the Bergen tunnel in 1860. At the breaking out of the war of the rebellion the martial spirit he had inherited from his ancestors was aroused, and in 1861 he entered the army as a private in the Seventh Regiment of the New York Volunteers. By his great energy and bravery he was soon promoted to Captain in the Fourteenth Regiment of the Regular Army. He was on General Sherman's staff, and later, chief officer to General Logan. He was wounded at Arkansas Point, and made the march with General Sherman from Atlanta to the sea. He resigned at the close of the war with a commission as Brevet-Colonel in the Regular Army. His wife was Mary Miller, of Cincinnati, Ohio. Eugene died in that city in 7th month, 1873, aged forty-one years. Thomas

Jones Yorke, Jr., second son of Thomas J. Yorke, by his second wife, Margaret J. Sinnickson, assisted his father several years in the Railroad Company, and was appointed Secretary and Treasurer of the West Jersey Marl Company. He subsequently entered into the coal business with his uncles, John and Charles Sinnickson, in the city of Philadelphia, under the firm name of Sinnickson & Co. Louis S. Yorke, the third son of Louis and Mary Yorke, married Adelaide Patton, of Philadelphia; their issue was two sons and one daughter—Patton Jones, Louis A. and Adelaide P. Yorke. Patton J. Yorke, their eldest son, married Rebecca Coleman, of Louisana; their issue is Catharine C. and Louis S. Yorke. His second wife was Lizzie Little, of Albany, New York. Louis A., second son of Louis and Adelaide Yorke, married Emma M., daughter of Robert Smith, Esq., of Philadelphia.

Adelaide, the daughter of Louis and Adelaide P. Yorke, married Charles King, of the United States Navy; they have one daughter—Adelaide King. Louis S. Yorke, the son of Louis and Mary Yorke, in early life had an inclination to follow the sea. Accordingly in 1818 his first voyage was in a brig, commanded by Captain Woodhouse, of the United States Navy, from Philadelphia to Rio Janeiro and the river La Platte, in South America. Afterwards he made frequent voyages to Monte Vidoe and Buenos Ayres as mate and master. Afterwards at different times he commanded several large ships in the European and East Indian trade, going to India by the Cape of Good Hope and returning through the Pacific by the way of Cape Horn. He returned from the sea a number of years ago, and resided in Salem and Philadelphia. When the war of rebellion broke out, he again went to sea and entered the United States Navy as paymaster. At the end of the war he went to Louisiana to reside with his eldest son, Patton. Patton Jones Yorke, his eldest son, entered the service of the United States as a volunteer before he was twenty-one years of age. He continued in the army through the war, and was promoted to Colonel of the Second Regiment of New Jersey Cavalry. After the war he married Rebecca Coleman, of Carroll Parish, Louisiana, and there he settled. He has been several times a member of the Legislature of his adopted State, and is a member of that body at the present time. Louis A., the second son of Louis A., and Adelaide Yorke, is paymaster in the United States Navy, and is now in the East India squadron.

Thomas, the third son of Andrew and Eleanor Coxe Yorke, was born at Salem. When young he went to Philadelphia in the dry goods store of M. Herbenton, in South Second street. In the war of 1812 he joined the privateer Shadow as purser, the ship being commanded by his relative, Captain Taylor. When the war was ended Thomas traded to the West Indies as captain of a merchant vessel. He afterwards went into the European and East India trade as captain of a merchantman, and continued in that business a number of voyages. When he left the sea he came back to his native county, and made his home with his sister, Eleanor Hancock, at Hancock's Bridge. He lived but a short time afterwards, and was buried in the Episcopal church yard at Salem. Nature had done much for Thomas Yorke. He was blessed with good abilities and above the average of mankind, was prepossessing in looks, and dignified in his manners and address—the latter being characteristics of the Yorke family.

Martha, the second daughter of Andrew and Eleanor C. Yorke, soon after her father's death, removed from Salem to Hancock's Bridge, and resided at the latter place most of her life. I think she never married.

The third wife of Thomas Yorke, the emigrant, was Mary Robeson, as before mentioned; they had four children. Their eldest son, Robeson Yorke, died without issue. Their second son, Samuel, married Tabitha Keen, of Dover, Delaware, and had issue, Thomas Yorke, who married a young woman by the name of Cox, by whom he had five children—Mary, Samuel, Anna, Emma and William Yorke. Martha, the daughter of Thomas and Mary Robeson Yorke, married James Humphreys; they had issue. Susan Humphreys, their eldest daughter, died without issue. Their son, James Y. Humphreys, married Louisa McAuley, and had one daughter—Sarah Humphreys. Mary Y. Humphreys married Captain Graham, by whom she had one child, Ella, who married John Armstrong, and had issue — Mary Armstrong. Lewis Yorke Humphreys died without issue. His sister, Martha Y. Humphreys, married a man by the name of Madara; they had issue, one child—Mary Madara.

Margaret, the youngest daughter of Thomas and Mary R. Yorke, married Ludwig Sprogell, and had issue. John, their eldest son, died single. Their daughter, Mary Sprogell, died young. Louis Sprogell was Captain in the United States Army. Thomas Sprogell married Mary Stretch, and had issue. Georgianna, their daughter, married Dr. J. Peaco, of the United States Navy; they had children. Their eldest son, John Peaco, died young, and their daughter, Virginia Peaco, married Dr. J. Henderson, of the United States Navy. Dr. J. Henderson and his wife, Virginia P. had six children—John Augustus, George, Virginia Mary, Sylvanus and Caroline.

LOCKE AND ROCKE FAMILIES.

There have been many of the African race born and raised in Fenwick's Colony, that have shown considerable mental intellect. Among those, there were two young men in modern times, who grew up among us, manifesting uncommon abilities, considering their opportunity. Ishmael Locke was one of them; being born of poor parentage he was bound out to John Ballinger, a farmer residing in Upper Alloways Creek, near Quinton's Bridge. Ishmael was sent occasionally to a common country school, during the winter season, but even with that limited opportunity, he applied himself closely to his studies. Being an excellent and careful workman, as a farm laborer, he found no difficulty in procuring good places, and likewise the highest wages. Soon after he arrived at the age of twenty-one, he hired with the late William Carpenter, of Elsinborough, at which place he continued several years; by his orderly conduct and close attention to business, he endeared himself to the family, always studying in his leisure hours. Upon leaving Elsinborough, he taught the colored school at Salem for some time. From Salem, he went to Camden, and there taught the colored school. Subsequently he went to Liberia for the purpose of educating his race in that distant land. The climate was not congenial to his health, and he returned to the United States, after being absent a few years; he again opened a school in Camden, but his health being much impaired whilst in Liberia, he did not live long after his return. As a mathematician he was seldom equalled by any one that was ever raised in Salem county, and in the other branches of learning, there were very few his superiors. His application was wonderful. The late Richard P. Thompson, when he was State Attorney, remarked to me once—" If I had when young, the indomitable application " that Locke possessed, it would have been incalculable advantage " to me in my profession."

John Rocke, Jr., possessed a fine intellect. He was born in Elsinborough. His father, John Rocke, was a good citizen and an honest laborer. He had a natural turn for reading, and was above the ordinary men of his race in intelligence. His wife was Maria Willetts. The Willetts were formerly slaves to one of the ancient Quaker families in this county. Their son, the subject of this sketch, showed in early life a thirst for knowledge, and was by nature an elocutionist, being very fond of reading. His parents, though poor, gave him every opportunity in their power for an education; but as soon as he was able to work he labored for a livelihood among the farmers in his neighborhood, but when an opportunity afforded he was always found endeavoring to improve his mind by reading and also in mathematics. When Ishmael Locke left the colored school at Salem, John Locke, Jr., succeeded as a teacher. He remained in that situation a few years, and then left his native county and State, and went to Boston, Massachusetts. In a short time after that event he studied medicine with one of the noted physicians of that city. After due course of study he received his diploma. There was a disease lurking about him, for which he had to undergo a surgical operation, but without success. He was induced by Charles Sumner to go to Paris, to the celebrated surgeon that had operated on him a short time previous with such good results. He accordingly went and was operated upon. Rocke informed the writer, after his return to this country, when on a visit to his parents, that the surgeon told him "he had better turn his attention to some other call-"ing, that his physical disease was against his being a prac-"titioner in medicine." He studied Law, and was admitted to practice some two or three years afterward. He was a pleasing and interesting speaker; his oratory was not declamatory. He showed great learning in his speeches, was cool and deliberate in his address, so much so, that he attracted the attention of the lawyers of his adopted city. He was a great favorite of the eminent statesman, Charles Sumner, to such an extent, that by his intercession he was admitted to practice in the United States Courts, thereby being the first of his race that ever received such a distinguished honor. Through all his high attainments, he was not unmindful of filial duties. He employed in Salem county an agent, and furnished him funds to assist his parents in procuring the necessaries of life. Soon after the death of his aged father, he took his mother to Boston with him, and maintained her in a comfortable manner, until her death. He survived her but a few years, being a victim of that insidious disease, pulmonary consumption. He was a credit to his race, and an honor to the State and county of his birth.

HISTORY

OF THE

RELIGIOUS BODIES OF FENWICK'S COLONY.

Comprising Sketches of their Places of Worship, and the Lives of their most Prominent Members, carefully prepared by the Author, and arranged in their seniority.

FRIENDS SOCIETY.

I will endeavor to give an account of the first religious organizations within Fenwick's Colony, and a short notice of the conspicuous members of the different societies when they were established.

The Swedes no doubt were the first, but their place of worship appears to have been at Christiana until about 1746, when the Swedes and a few French Hugeunots, Jaquetts, Philpotts, and others, built a church in Penn's Neck, at the place now known as Church Landing. The principal families who were members of the church were the Joansons, Wolversons, Hendricksons, Tonsons, Hans Jeansons, Nielsons, Wolleysons, Sinnicksons, and several others. In all probability the first house erected in West Jersey for Divine worship was at Maurice River, where there was a settlement of Swedes. Being zealous Protestants, and a long distance from their mother church, they built a place of worship near Mauricetown about 1640, more than thirty years before Fenwick, with his Colony, arrived at Elsinborough Point, which was on the 26th of 8th month, 1675, according to the present computation of time. Fenwick ascended the Assamhocking up to the place where Salem is now, and at that point of land he and the emigrants that were with him permanently landed. The greater number of the persons who accompanied him from England to his possessions in New Cæssaria were members of his own religious Society.

At that place he determined to lay out a town to be the seat of government for his colony. He named the town New Salem, as he observed the name signified Peace. He chose from the number of emigrants Richard Noble as his Surveyor General, and directed him to lay out a street ninety feet in width from the creek, which he named Salem, to run in a south-eastern course. The street was called Wharf street, but afterwards called Bradway street, and at the present time it is known as Broadway street. There was another street laid out starting from Fenwick creek, a branch of the Salem creek, also to be ninety feet wide, until it reached the town marsh, but for some reason it was never opened further than Bradway street. It was then called Bridge street, but is now known as Market street. Probably the cause that Fenwick's plans were not carried out, is that he died at an early date of the history of Salem, and left the direction of the improvement of the town to his favorite son-in-law, Samuel Hedge, particularly respecting the streets. He died in a few years after the death of Fenwick (which event took place in the year 1693) before he could consummate the proprietor's plans upon these two main streets. The emigrants first settled upon Wharf street, where the first religious organization took place of the English Colonies in West New Jersey.

Samuel Nicholson, one of the wealthiest emigrants who arrived with John Fenwick, and his wife, Ann Nicholson, with their five children, came from Northamptonshire, England. Soon after their arrival he purchased a lot on Wharf street containing 16 acres, also a tract of land in Elsinborough containing 2,000 acres, and built himself a house on his lot in Salem, principally of hewn logs. At his house, in 1676, the first religious organization in Fenwick's Colony took place, and it is interesting to examine the records of that early time to see the difficulty which the Friends had to find a permanent place for public worship. On 2d of 4th month, 1979, Richard Guy, Edward Bradway, Isaac Smart and Edward Wade were appointed to select a place for a meeting house and burying ground. It appears they were not successful, and at a meeting held 5th of 11th month, 1679, Edward Wade, James Nevell, John Maddox and George Deacon were appointed to treat with Samuel Nicholson and William Penton for their houses and plantations in Salem, and also to see Ann Salter, widow of Henry Salter, about her lot of ground.

At a meeting held in 12th month, 1679, George Deacon, John Maddox and Henry Jennings were appointed to take a view of Edward Bradway's house, and see whether it was suitable for a meeting house. A minute was made at that time fixing upon the 1st and 4th days of the week for religious worship, the meetings to be held first at Samuel Nicholson's, next at Robert Zane's, and next at Richard Guy's house.

In the 9th month, 1680, there was another committee appointed to endeavor to purchase a lot of ground of Edward Champney to build a meeting house upon and for a burying ground. They did not succeed in getting a lot to suit them, and finally in 1681, in the 6th month, Samuel Nicholson and

FRIENDS' MEETING HOUSE.
Salem, N. J.   Built 1772.

his wife Ann deeded the whole of the 16 acres of land situated on Bradway street, in Salem, for the use and benefit of Salem Monthly Meeting forever, for a meeting house and grave yard and other purposes. As soon as the deed was given, John Thompson, of Elsinborough, and Robert Zane, of Salem, were appointed by the meeting to repair the house, and get it fit for Friends to meet in. About a year afterwards the same persons were directed to enlarge the meeting house by adding sixteen feet in length, and height equal to the old frame building, with a chimney and a pair of stairs. For some reason this was not done until the next year, in 1683, at which time Benjamin Acton was employed to build the addition. There was a proposition to have the floors of the house made of boards, but that failed, and on 27th of 12th month, 1687, Benjamin Acton and Thomas Wood were appointed to have the old and new house floored with a good clay floor, and have it ready before the Yearly Meeting should convene.

The first Yearly Meeting was held at Salem 15th of 2d month, 1684, and included the Friends of Haddonfield and Burlington. It was held at Salem and Burlington alternately, and was known as the Half Yearly Meeting. These meetings were continued several years.

At the Yearly Meeting held at Salem in the 2d month, from the 27th to the 31st, 1693, George Keith appeared with his friends and laid before the meeting their proposals for the settlement of the differences among them. These were in the shape of several propositions covering the points at issue, and discussing the reasons for their adoption, which led to much controversy, and final separation of many members from the Society. These proposals were signed by Jeremiah Colbert, John Penrose, Nathaniel Sykes, Anthony Taylor, Samuel Cooper, Isaac Tause, James Shattock, Samuel Adams, George Keith, Thomas Budd, Henry Furness, Nicholas Pierce, Thomas Withers, Andrew Griscom, and others. Thomas Sharp, member of Newton Meeting, was Clerk of the Yearly Meeting at that time. The Friends who adhered to George Keith, had great influence in the Society, and most of them after Keith returned to England became members of the Baptist Church. Andrew Griscom became reconciled with his former friends, and died a member of the Society, and many of his descendants have been active and useful membersthereof.

The account I have of George Keith fully proves that he possessed an uncommon intellect, was a forcible writer, and a pleasing and interesting speaker. The nature of the proposition that he and his followers offered to the Yearly Meeting at Salem, I have never fully understood, but it appears there was no fault found of church discipline, the matter of dispute being on religious dogmas. Keith advocated his peculiar views so ably that he drew forth the ablest minds in the Society of Friends in England and in this country to confute his views. After his return to his native land he joined the Church of England.

Among the early Friends of Salem, William Cooper was was quite prominent for a young man. He and his father, William Cooper, emigrated to America about the year 1678, the father settling in Burlington county, whilst the son located at Salem, and followed his trade, which was that of a blacksmith. In the year 1682 he married Mary, the eldest daughter of Edward and Mary Bradway, and had three children—John, Hannah and Mary Cooper. As near as can be ascertained, William and his family left Salem in 1688 and purchased land where Camden is now located, and resided there until his death, which took place in 1691. In his will he named his father, William Cooper, and his father-in-law, Edward Bradway, his executors. John, the son of William and Mary B. Cooper, married Ann Clark. Hannah Cooper married John Mickle. Mary Cooper, their youngest daughter, married Benjamin Thackray. John Cooper died in 1750, leaving a widow and the following named children—James, John, David, Mary, Ann, Sarah and Hannah. My estimable friend, Judge John Clement, of Haddonfield, who as a genealogist and historian has no superior in West Jersey, informed me that one of the collateral heirs of James Fennimore Cooper, the celebrated novelist and publicist, recently came from his home in New York to trace the connection of the Cooper family of West Jersey with his family. He found by examining the wills and deeds that his ancestor, Fennimore Cooper, was a descendant of William and Mary Bradway Cooper.

Robert Zane, who was active in organizing the first Friends Meeting at Salem, purchased of the proprietor a 16 acre lot on Fenwick street, the junction with the street now known as Yorke street, located on the west side. The old house which his son built and occupied is still standing, and has what is called a "hip roof," which resembles in some measure the modern French mansard roof. Such roofs were common at that time in this country. Robert Zane left Salem before the year 1690, and purchased a large tract of good land near the old Newton Meeting House, bordering on Newton creek, and there he and his wife died. Most of his landed estate is still owned by his descendants, particularly in the female line. A part of the family remained at Salem. Robert's great-granddaughter married Lewis, son of William and Mary Morris Goodwin, of Elsinborough, about 1778 or 1779. There were two children—John and Susanna Goodwin.

The minute of the first organized Monthly Meeting of Friends in West Jersey, was as follows: "At a meeting held last day "of the fifth month, 1676, it was unanimously considered that "the first second day of the week in the 6th month, that Friends "do meet in the town of New Salem, in Fenwick's Colony, and "all Friends thereunto, do monthly meet together, to consider "of outward circumstances, and business. And if such that has "been convinced, and walked disorderly, that they may in all "gravity and uprightness to God, and in tenderness of spirit "and love to their souls, be admonished, exhorted, and also re- "proved, and their evil deeds and practices testified against in "the wisdom of God, and in the authority of truth, that may "answer the witness of God within them. Signed,

"SAMUEL NICHOLSON,
"ROBERT ZANES,
"ROBERT WADE,
"EDWARD WADE,
"RICHARD GUY,
"ISAAC SMART,
"JOHN FENWICK,
"RICHARD JOHNSON,
"and others."

After Samuel Nicholson and his wife sold their Salem lands to the Society of Friends they removed to Elsinborough, on the 2,000 acre tract of land that he purchased of the proprietor in 1676, and there ended their days. The precise time of his death is uncertain, but events which occurred soon after indicate that it was about 1690. Their eldest daughter, Parable, born in England 20th of 2d month, 1659, married Abraham Strand, at New Salem, 25th of 9th month, 1677. Joseph, their second son, born at Northamptonshire, England, 30th of 2d month, 1669, married a young woman at Haddonfield. At the death of Samuel Nicholson he devised that his landed estate in Elsinborough should be divided between his eldest son, Samuel Nicholson, Jr., and his youngest son, Abel Nicholson. Samuel Nicholson, Jr., married, and died in a short time afterward, leaving no issue, and he devised the whole of his real estate to his brother, Joseph Nicholson, who resided near Haddonfield. Joseph, in 1696, sold about one-half of it to George

Abbott, who had recently emigrated from New England. The balance was purchased by Samuel Stebbins and John Firth. Joseph Nicholson died in 1702, intestate, leaving but two children—George and Samuel. George, in 1717, married Alice Lord. Samuel had three wives. His first wife was Sarah Burroughs, whom he married in 1722. In 1744 he married Jane, widow of William Albertson, and daughter of John Engle. Their descendants are numerous in the vicinity of Haddonfield. Samuel Nicholson died in 1750, leaving the following children—Joseph, their eldest, who married Catharine Butcher, of Burlington county, in 1738; Samuel, who married Rebecca, daughter of Aaron Aaronson; Abigail, who married Daniel Hillman, in 1743 (her second husband was John Gill, whom she married in 1769); Hannah, who married John Hillman; and Sarah Nicholson, who died unmarried in 1756.

Abel Nicholson died in 1761 before his first child was born. It proved to be a son, who was named Abel, after his father, and subsequently married Rebecca, the daughter of Isaac Ellis. From this son sprung the immediate family of the name of Nicholson in the neighborhood of Haddonfield at the present time. Abel Nicholson, the youngest son of Samuel Nicholson, the emigrant, was born in England 2d of 5th month, 1672, and he resided on his estate in Elsinborough which he inherited from his father, the greater part of his life. He married Mary, the daughter of William and Joanna Tyler, who was born in England in the 11th month, 1677. Their children were—Rachel, born 7th of 7th month, 1698; Abel, born 13th of 1st month, 1700; Joseph, born 4th of 12th month, 1701; and William, born 15th of 9th month, 1703. (The latter subsequently became the owner of 500 acres of land in Mannington, being part of Hedgefield.)

Ann Nicholson was born 15th of 11th month, 1707, and married John Brick, Jr., of Gravelly Run, in the county of Cumberland. Ruth was born 9th of 9th month, 1713. Samuel was born 10th of 12th month, 1716, and he became the owner of all his father's real estate in the township of Elsinborough. He married Sarah Dennis, of Greenwich, in 1742. John, the youngest child, was born 6th of 3d month, 1719, and his wife was Jael Darkin, of Elsinborough. The descendants of Abel Nicholson I have mentioned heretofore.

Friends of Salem continued to hold their meetings in the house purchased of Samuel Nicholson until the year 1700, at which time they built a new brick house where the present grave-yard is. It stood east of the oak tree. The meeting increased in numbers so much that the house was not large enough to accommodate them, and in 1770 members of Salem Monthly Meeting bought a lot of ground on Fenwick street, of Thomas Hancock and Robert Johnson, and erected the present commodious building, which was completed in 1772.

There was an "Indulge Meeting," as is known in the Society, in Elsinborough as early as 1680. The house stood on the property of Richard Darkin (Casper W. Thompson owns the land at this time.) There was a regular meeting of Friends held at Alloways Creek, at the house of James Denn, in 1679, and continued until 1685.

In the year 1684 Edward Champney and John Smith each deeded half an acre of ground to Christopher White and Samuel Wade—one for a meeting house and the other for a grave yard. The ground was a corner of each of their lots on Monmouth river. The same year Salem Monthly Meeting of Friends agreed with Christopher to build a meeting house on one of the said lots, the cost of the building not to exceed £40. He was also directed to clear a road from the King's Highway to the meeting house, for which he charged £10 more. In 1685 the first religious meeting was held there, and so continued until 1718. The greater part of the members resided on the south side of the creek, and there being no bridge at that period, they were put to great inconvenience in getting to meeting.

Joseph Ware gave the Friends a lot of ground on his plantation on the south side of the creek, the deed having been given in 1717. As soon as the meeting house was finished, the members on the north side of Monmouth river were attached to Salem Particular Meeting. The families were the Abbotts, Stubbins, Moss and Tylers. The meeting house was abandoned about that time, but the grave-yard was used for a number of years after the meetings ceased to be held at that place. The Friends subsequently purchased a lot of ground on the south side of the creek, near Harmersville, for a burying ground, which has been the principal place for interment up to this time. A number of persons, however, have been buried in the ancient grave-yard since the members of the Society, in a measure, abandoned it; such families as the Waddingtons, Hancocks, Carlls, and a few others, were desirous to be lain with their ancestors. The principal families that were members of Alloways Creek Meeting at the time alluded to were the Whites, Bradways, Denns, Wares, Chambless, Oakfords, Wades, Daniels, Hancocks, Stretches, Barbers, and several others. Friends continued to hold their meeting in the house built on the Ware property until the year 1756. In 1753 William Hancock deeded a lot of ground to the members of Alloways Creek Particular Meeting for a meeting house, as it was a more convenient location. The house was built at two different periods of time, the oldest in 1756, the new, as it is called, in 1784.

The Friends meeting at Lower Greenwich was established at an early period in the settlement of the English Colony. Mark Reeves, William Bacon, James Duncan and others, made application to Salem Monthly Meeting in 1698 for assistance in building a meeting house. Previous to that time meetings were held at private houses. Members of Greenwich Meeting, with the assistance of Salem Monthly Meeting, built a meeting house that year. It stood where the present meeting house is located, near the Cohansey, for the purpose of accommodating the Friends that resided on the south side of the river in Fairfield township. Greenwich Meeting, in the fore part of the last century, increased largely in the number of its members, so much so that it was deemed necessary to build a larger house for their accommodation. There was a substantial brick house erected on or near where the old frame house formerly stood. The influential persons and their families that were members of Greenwich Particular Meeting during the middle and latter part of the 18th century, were the Reeves, Davis, Millers, Woods, Sheppards, Tests, Bricks, Dennis, Harmers, Bacons, Tylers, Stewarts, and several others. Several of those mentioned above were conspicuous men in the generation in which they lived. The Reeves, whom I mentioned in the genealogy of their families, and the Woods have left an enviable reputation. There were four Richard Woods born in Cumberland county, three of them being influential members of Greenwich Meeting. The fourth Richard Wood left his native town and eventually resided and died in Philadelphia, and became an eminent merchant, and left a large estate. The first Richard Wood that we have account of in this country, resided on Gravelly Run, known at this time as Stoe Creek township, Cumberland county. The Wood family owned a large tract of land at that place. Richard's wife, I think, was Priscilla, the daughter of Mark Reeve, the emigrant, born about 1700. They had five children—Jane, Richard, Letitia, Ruth and Priscilla Wood. The father of these children died in the year 1759, and was buried on his own farm in the Wood's family burying ground. His son, Richard Wood, was born 18th of 1st month, 1728, and he learned the trade of a cooper and followed it in the town of Greenwich, and he has been represented to have possessed unusual business capacities. Notwithstanding his industrious habits, he never let worldly affairs prevent him from attending to his religious meeting. He traveled with his friend, Mark Reeve, as companion, on a religious visit through the New England States. He married twice. By his first wife he had two children—Richard and James Wood. His last wife was Mary, widow of Job Bacon, and the daughter of John and Mary Wade Stewart, born 6th of 1st month, 1746. She had three children by her first husband—Job, Elizabeth and George Bacon. Richard and his last wife, Mary Wood, had no issue. I have been told that he retired, in a great measure, from business, and purchased the large brick house and a number of acres attached, property formerly of Nicholas Gibbon, and at that place he spent the evening of his days, dying several years before his wife. After his death the widow continued to reside there, and her house was a resort of her numerous relatives and acquaintances. She lived to an old age, and was truly a mother in Israel.

Richard Wood, 3d, born 7th of 6th month, 1755, married twice. There were two sons by his first wife. David, the eldest, in after life, became largely interested in the iron works at Millville. Richard's second wife was Elizabeth, the daughter of Job and Mary Stewart Bacon. There were six children by that marriage—George B., Richard, Charles, Horatio, Ann Elizabeth, and Hannah Wood. It is but justice to the memory of Richard Wood, 3d, to say that he is still held in grateful remembrance by the old inhabitants of Greenwich, through his many acts of kindness and benevolence to his fellow creatures.

The Davis family were distinguished members of Greenwich Meeting. I have no definite knowledge at what time Charles Davis went to Cohansey to reside, but he became a large landholder in Greenwich township, at the place known as Bacon's Neck. In 1739 he married Elizabeth Dennis, of the same place. There was one son, Gabriel Davis, who subsequently came in possession of a large tract of excellent land that belonged to his father, and in the year 1767 he married Sarah, the daughter of Ebenezer Miller, Sr., born at Greenwich 17th of 3d month, 1746. They had no issue. Gabriel Davis was one who did a great many acts of kindness in assisting young men who had but little means, by loaning them money to commence business with. Such acts of benevolence and kindness gave him a name as a benefactor to the poor and needy in the section of country in which he lived. In his will he devised the greater portion of his landed estate to his nephew, Ebenezer Hall, who subsequently married, and at his death, left three children—Gabriel, Elizabeth and Ann Hall. Elizabeth married Thomas Bacon, of Philadelphia. Ann, the youngest daughter, married John, the son of Job Bacon.

There was a Friends Meeting established near the head of Alloways river, at the village of Thompson's Bridge. The name of this place has since been changed to Allowaystown. The meeting house stood on the north side of the creek, adjoining the farm owned by William F. Reeve at this time. There was a burying ground near the meeting house, where most of the early settlers in that section where interred. The house was removed many years ago, but the lot is still enclosed. The persons that belonged to Allowaystown Particular Meeting were members of Salem Monthly Meeting, and the names of the principal members were William Thompson, Thomas, Benjamin, Samuel, Joseph and William Thompson, Jr., Joseph Fogg, and his three sons, Joseph, Daniel and Samuel Fogg, and their families, William Oakford and family, William Craig, the Noblets, and a few other families. Samuel Fogg subsequently purchased land in the lower part of the township, which is known at this time as Lower Alloways Creek. He and his family became members of Alloways Creek Particular Meeting. William Thompson, from whom Thompson's Bridge derived its name, was the son of Andrew and Isabella Thompson, and was born near Dublin, Ireland, 9th of 8th month, 1666. He emigrated with his parents in 1677, and landed in New Jersey at Elsinborough Point the same year. Benjamin Thompson, son of William and Hannah Thompson, was born 11th of 8th month, 1719, and subsequently married Elizabeth, daughter of Joseph Ware, Jr., the marriage having taken place in 1745. Benjamin was considered the best business man of his day in that section of country. He had the principal oversight of Richard Wistar's glassworks the greater part of the time it was in operation. The said glass works were located about two miles east of Allowaystown, on the property now owned by Jacob P. Reeves. The most authentic account I have seen gives this factory as the second one of the kind in the English Colonies in America. There was one started in Massachusetts two years previous to Wistar's in Salem county. Benjamin Thompson died about 1775, and his wife died in the same year.

William Oakford, another distinguished member of Friends Meeting at Thompson's Bridge, was a descendant of Wade Oakford, and he had large possessions in landed estate near that place. Jonathan House, who owns and resides on part of the Oakford estate, is a lineal descendant of William Oakford, as is also Albert W. Sherron, of Salem, on his mother's side.

About the year 1725 there was a Friends Meeting established at Woodstown, which was then called and still bears the name of Pilesgrove Meeting, after the name of the township in which it is located. The principal families which composed Pilesgrove Meeting at the time of its organization were the Lippincotts, Davis, Barnes, Dunns, Silvers, and a few years later Samuel and William Bassett, and several others, became members. Although Pilesgrove Meeting was small in the beginning it is at the present time the largest Friends Meeting in what is known as Fenwick's Colony.

About the year 1760 there was a meeting established at Port Elizabeth, the principal families of which were Jonathan Jones and family, the Dallas, Buzbys, and several others.

In the fore part of this century, Coates and Britton, of Philadelphia, banked a large tract of meadow land lying on the lower side of Maurice river, and extending down the bay nearly or quite to West creek. After the said meadow and low lands were completely reclaimed from the overflow of the tide, they divided the property into small farms, and held out inducements for persons to settle thereon. There were several families, members of Friends Meeting, from Gloucester county and Cape May settled there. George Craft, Sr., of Gloucester, was hired by the proprietors to superintend the whole property, and most of the persons that were tenants under Coates and Britton were members of the Society of Friends. By that means the meeting at Port Elizabeth was greatly increased in numbers. The enterprise of reclaiming such a large body of swamp and salt marsh appeared to answer admirably for some years, but there came a terrible storm and a great swell of the ocean in the 9th month, 1819, which carried and swept away miles of their tide bank along the bay shore, and the inhabitants barely escaped with their lives, whilst a large number of horses and cattle perished. That disaster entirely broke up the little settlement, and many families returned to their former homes. Although the meeting at Port Elizabeth was diminished in numbers by the catastrophe, it was kept up for a number of years afterwards by the families of the Jones, Buzbys, Dallas, Elkintons, Townsends, Bradways, and others. Several of the heads of those families have long since paid the debt of nature, whilst the younger branches have moved to other parts of the country.

At this time there is no Friends Meeting kept up at PortElizabeth.

About the middle or latter part of the last century there was a Friends Meeting established at Pedricktown, in the township of Upper Penns Neck, it being a branch of Pilesgrove meeting. The principal families that composed the meeting were the Pedricks, Somers, Taylors, Greens, Kirbys, and a few others. The Pedrick family is one of the oldest in the county of Salem.

On the 22d of 3d month, 1689, James Nevell gave an order to Richard Tindall to resurvey for Roger Pedrick, at Oldman's Creek, 1,000 acres, which the said Roger Pedrick had purchased of the proprietor in the fore part of 1676. The Somers family emigrated to this county from Great Egg Harbor.

Although somewhat foreign to the subject that I have written upon, there has been much speculation respecting Jacob Spicer. Some have thought he emigrated to New Jersey from England, but he was born at Long Island, of Quaker parentage, his parents, Samuel and Hester Spicer, having resided at Gravesend, L. I. They had six children—Abram, born 27th of 8th month, 1666; Jacob, born 20th of 1st month, 1668; May, born 20th of 8th month, 1671; Sarah, born 19th of 4th month, 1674; Martha, born 27th of 11th month, 1676; Sarah, born 16th of 2d month, 1677; and Abigail, born 26th of 1st month, 1683. Hester Spicer, the mother of the children mentioned, was born in 1647, and was a daughter of John and Mary Tilton.

Samuel Spicer, the father of Jacob Spicer, purchased lands about the year 1683, near Gloucester Point, Gloucester county, and he settled thereon. It is well known that his son Jacob become conspicuous in the affairs of West Jersey, and died near Cold Spring Inlet, Cape May county. His son Jacob was equally as useful a man as his father. He and Leaming wrote the laws of West New Jersey.

As early as 1720 there was a Friends Meeting established at Cape May composed of the founders of Egg Harbor, the Somers, Sculls, Leeds, and a few other families; the members of Cape May were Richard Townsend, Peter Corson and Aaron Leaming. The latter was a native of Connecticut. He came to Salem when a boy and was early noticed by Sarah, the widow of William Hall. He spoke of her as being very intelligent and wealthy, and of having an excellent library, which she invited him to her house for the purpose of reading. Whilst Aaron resided at Salem he joined the Friends Society. Soon after that event he went to Cape May and located a tract of land at Goshen, and married Lydia Shaw, also a member. They had four children—Aaron, Jeremiah, Mathias and Elizabeth.

At a monthly meeting of Friends held in New Salem, in Fenwick's Colony, the 29th of 6th month, 1698, John Thompson, Sr., Isaac Smart, Ruthro Morris and Richard Darkin were appointed to superintend the building of a meeting house, to be of brick, for the use of Salem Monthly Meeting, and to raise money by a voluntary subscription for that purpose.

The following are the names of Friends that contributed, and the different sums of money each gave opposite their respective names:

	£ sh.		£ sh.
John Thompson,	30 00	Edward Goodwin,	4 00
Richard Darkin,	25 00	Joseph White,	2 10
William Tyler,	20 00	Esther Harrison,	2 06
Isaac Smart,	18 00	John Mason,	10 00
Richard Johnson,	15 00	John Remington,	5 00
Thomas Thompson,	18 00	Wade Oakford,	2 10
John Smith, of Smithfield,	18 00	William Bradway,	3 03
Bartholomew Wyatt,	18 00	Edward Keasbey,	4 00
Ruthro Morris,	16 00	Jeremiah Powell,	2 00
William Rumsey,	15 00	James White,	1 10
Nathaniel Chambless, Sr.,	15 60	John Maddox,	10 00
Nathaniel Chambless, Jr.,	15 00	William Savage,	3 10
Josiah White,	7 00	William Hall,	5 00
John Hancock,	10 00	John Smith, of Arbebbury,	10 00
Benjamin Thompson,	10 00	Daniel Smith, son of the	
William Thompson,	10 00	above,	10 00
A. Thompson, Jr.,	10 00	Charles Oakford,	5 00
Joseph Ware,	8 00	Samuel Wade,	7 00
Abel Nicholson,	7 00	Esther White, widow of	
Richard Woodnutt,	6 00	Charles H. White,	5 00
John Shales,	3 00	James Daniels, the elder,	2 02

The names of Friends that contributed toward erecting the building of dwellings in other places:

	£ sh.
Samuel Carpenter, Philadelphia,	15 00
Edward Shippen, Philadelphia,	5 00
Samuel Jennings, Burlington,	5 00
Bridget Guy, widow of Richard Guy,	5 00
Robert Ashton, of Delaware,	5 00
Thomas Smith, of Darby, Pennsylvania,	2 00
	37 00

Report of the Committee to the Monthly Meeting:

	£ sh.
Cost for brick, stone and lime, and workmanship,	188 11
For timber, boards, shingles and glass,	194 03
Iron work, nails and glazing,	37 17
Paying John Thompson for his trouble and expenses, and overseeing the work,	5 00
	425 11

The house was erected a few rods east of the large oak tree. At that time, several of the ablest and oldest emigrants were deceased, such as Fenwick, Samuel Nicholson, John Pledger, Edward Bradway, Edward Wade, Andrew Thompson, Sr., Robert Windham, Christopher White. All of them lay in the yard, except John Fenwick and Christopher White; the former, by his request, was buried in the family burying ground of the Sharp family, in Upper Mannington, near the Alms House; Christopher White was buried in the ancient burying ground of Friends, at Alloways Creek, not far from Hancock's Bridge. Said yard is situated on the north side of Monmouth river. It was deeded to Christopher White and Samuel Wade, by Edward Champny, the son-in-law of John Fenwick, in 1684.

There in that ancient yard stands a white oak which has belonged to Salem Monthly Meeting of Friends for nearly two centuries. Its life has been in accordance with the laws which have always governed it, and has to a remarkable degree retained the vigor of its early life. It has been a close attender of all the meetings held for worship or discipline in the old meeting-house, which formerly stood in the grave yard for upwards of seventy years, and has been present at all the funerals which have taken place in the yard from 1681 up to the present time; it has likewise been a large benefactor to the human race, never having turned any one away who came for protection or shelter from the storms or scorching rays of the noonday sun. The laws which governed this ancient member are unchangable, always standing upright among men, and not heeding their conflicting opinions, and while the earth, with all its allurements, was kept firmly beneath him, his watchword seemed to be upward and onward, with each succeeding year; it has been nourished by its friends who lie buried there, and watered by the tears of their mourners. The size of this ancient member at this time—the trunk is twenty feet in circumference, the branches parallel with Broadway street one hundred feet, from Broadway to the east one hundred and ten feet.

FRIENDS' GRAVE YARD.
Salem, N. J.   First used in 1681.

BAPTIST SOCIETIES.

About the year 1683 some Baptists from the county of Tipperary, in Ireland, settled in the neighborhood of Cohansey. Among these, the early accounts name David Sheppard, Thomas Abbot and William Button. They were members of a Baptist Church at Cleagh Keating in Tipperary county. This church was still in existence in 1838, but has since been disbanded. Thomas and John Sheppard, brothers or cousins of David, settled in the same neighborhood at the same time, and were doubtless also members of this church. In 1685, Obadiah Holmes and John Cornelius arrived from Rhode Island. In 1688, Rinear Van Hyst, John Childe and Thomas Lambson were baptized by Rev. Elias Keach, pastor of the Pennepeck Baptist Church, Pennsylvania.

About this time, Rev. Thomas Killingsworth settled in Fenwick's Colony, and was the first Baptist clergyman who located in South Jersey. He owned a fine tract of land on the King's Highway from Salem to Maurice River, nearly all of which lay in the present limits of Salem township. After his death, the property was owned by the Keasbey family. He was not only a clergyman of considerable reputation, but was the first judge of Salem courts. Through the troublesome time of Cornbury's administration as the first Governor of East and West Jersey, Killingsworth maintained the dignity of the Bench through all opposition. Obadiah Holmes, who came from Rhode Island, as already mentioned, was the son of Rev. Obadiah Holmes, who was publicly whipped in Boston for his religious opinions by the Puritans of that day, and who removed to Rhode Island, and died at Newport, October 15, 1682, aged seventy-six years. Two of his sons, Obadiah and Jonathan, removed to Middletown, Monmouth county, where they purchased a tract of 1600 acres from the Indians, and were constituent members of the Middletown Baptist Church, the oldest in this State. Obadiah soon removed to Fenwick's Colony, and settled in Cohansey Precinct. He occasionally preached, though it does not appear that he was a regularly ordained clergyman. He possessed by nature a legal mind, and represented the Cohansey Precinct as Judge of Salem Courts, acting with Killingsworth from the year 1700 to 1709.

I have no doubt the Baptists held meetings in private houses prior to 1690, in the spring of which year they organized a church, now known as the First Cohansey Baptist Church at Roadstown. This was the first church of this denomination in this part of the State. The first meeting house was built on land of David Sheppard, in Shrewsbury Neck, on the south side of the Cohansey, now owned by William Mulford. Killingsworth was the first pastor, and served as such until his death in the spring of 1709.

A company of Baptists emigrated to Cohansey Precinct from Swansea, in Massachusetts, about the year 1687, and settled about what is now known as Bowentown. Among them were the Bowens, Brookses, Barretts, Swinneys, &c. They had a log meeting house at Bowentown, and maintained a separate organization on account of the differences of opinion concerning predestination, laying on of hands, &c. Their pastor was Rev. Timothy Brooks, who came with them. After the death of Killingsworth, through the efforts of Rev. Valentine Wightman, of Groton, Connecticut, they united with the Cohansey Church, and Rev. Timothy Brooks became the second pastor of that church in 1710, and continued such until his death in 1716, in the 55th year of his age. The meeting house on the south side of the Cohansey was soon after abandoned, and land was purchased 23d of 12th month, 1713, on the north side of the river, in Hopewell township, near what is now known as Sheppard's Mill, and a meeting house erected. The new site was chosen, doubtless, as a compromise between the old one on the south of the river and the one where Mr. Brooks' company had worshipped at Bowentown. Quite a number of Mr. Brooks' company afterwards became Sabbatarians, and were among those who organized the Shiloh Seventh-Day Baptist Church in 1737.

After the death of Mr. Brooks, the church was without a pastor for several years. Rev. William Butcher, from Chester county, Pennsylvania, became the third pastor in 1721, but after a short service of three years, died 12th of 12th month, 1724, in the 27th year of his age.

Rev. Nathaniel Jenkins became the fourth pastor in 1730. He was born in Caerdicanshire, Wales, 25th of 3d month, 1678, came to this country in 1710, and settled at Cape May in 1712 as pastor of the church there. He was a man of talents and education, and served also as a Trustee of the Loan Office and as a member of Council, as the State Legislature was then called. A bill being introduced into the Council in 1721, "to punish such as denied the doctrine of the Trinity, the "Divinity of Christ and the Inspiration of the Scriptures," he stood boldly forth on the platform of "soul liberty," declaring that although he believed these doctrines as firmly as the warmest advocate of the bill, yet he would never consent to oppose those who rejected them with law or with any other weapon than argument. The bill was accordingly quashed. During his pastorate branches of the Church were established at Salem, Pittsgrove, and Great Egg Harbor. A new meeting house was also built in 1741, on the same site as the last, a frame building thirty-six by thirty-two feet, which has since been removed. The old grave-yard, which adjoined it, is still kept up in ordinary repair. I visited the ancient cemetery some two years ago and saw many names that were quite familiar; such as John and Job Ware. They were the lineal descendants of Joseph Ware, who emigrated to this county in company with John Fenwick, the proprietor, in 1675, and located himself in Monmouth precinct. On one of the tomb stones in said yard is a historical record, "In memory of Deborah Swinney, who de-"parted this life the 4th day of April, 1760, in the 77th year of "her age. She was the first white female child born in Cohan-"sey." Mr. Jenkins died 2d of 6th month, 1754, in the 77th year of his age, and the 25th of his pastorate.

He was succeeded by Rev. Robert Kelsey. He was born in Drummore, Ireland, in 1711, came to Maryland in 1734, and to Cohansey in 1738. Having become a Baptist he was ordained in 1750, and preached for the branch at Pittsgrove, and on the death of Mr. Jenkins was, by his recommendation on his dying bed, called as their pastor. He declined at first, but afterward accepted and became pastor in 1756, and served the church until his death, 30th of 5th month, 1789, in the 79th year of his age.

Rev. Henry Smalley became the sixth pastor 3d of 7th month, 1790. He was born at Piscataway, New Jersey, 23d of 10th month, 1765, and graduated at the College of New Jersey, at Princeton, in 1788. A new brick meeting house was completed and dedicated in 1802, and is the one now used by the Church, situate in the village of Roadstown. Its dimensions are forty-five by sixty-three feet, with galleries, and is capable of seating five hundred persons. The Church has, during the last year, erected a commodious chapel adjoining. Mr. Smalley was a man of sterling worth, and was well known and honored throughout the whole community, and the Church greatly prospered under his care. He died 11th of 2d month, 1839, in the 74th year of his age, and in the 49th of his pastorate.

Since him Rev. Isaac Moore, Rev. Edward D. Fendall, Rev. Jonathan G. Collum, Rev. Joseph N. Folwell, Rev. James M. Challis, Rev. Thomas G. Wright, Rev. Thomas O. Lincoln, and Rev. W. F. Basten, the present pastor, have served this ancient church. The present number of members is two hundred and sixty-six.

John Holme resided for a while in the city of Philadelphia after he emigrated from England. He purchased a large quantity of land of the proprietor where Holmesburg now is, and one of his sons became the owner and resided on the property. John Holme, about 1690, bought a tract of land in Alloways Creek Precinct, not far from Allowaystown. In a short time he left Philadelphia with his family and made that place his home until his death, in the year 1701. He was the grandfather of Benjamin Holme of Revolutionary memory. I think he and Thomas Killingsworth were the first members of the Baptist Church who lived in the neighborhood of Salem near the time of its first settlement. Baptist meetings were sometimes held at the house of Thomas Killingsworth, at Salem, and at other times at John Holme's, and were continued until the death of Killingsworth, in 1709. In 1705, Killingsworth also had a preaching place at the house of Jeremiah Nixon in Penns Neck. After the death of Holme and Killingsworth, meetings were continued at the houses of Samuel Fogg and Daniel Smith, the last named being a son of John Smith, of Almesbury. Daniel was a follower of George Keith, but afterwards became a Baptist. He was born in the county of Norfolk, England, 10th of 2d month, 1660, and was a great favorite of John Fenwick, who made an honorable mention of him in his will.

The Baptists of this section were connected with the Church at Cohansey. Timothy Brooks, pastor of the Cohansey Church, preached occasionally for them up to the time of his death, in 1716. Their meetings were frequently held at the house of Edward Quinton. After the death of most of the old members, the new converts united with the Cohansey Church, and attended the mother church until about the year 1741. After the membership from the vicinity of Alloways Creek and Salem became more numerous, they prevailed upon Nathaniel Jenkins, pastor of the Cohansey Church, to come and assist them occasionally. About this time three of the younger members of the Church who lived at Cohansey, Abraham Garrison, Robert Kelsey and Job Sheppard were called to the ministry, and were permitted to visit and preach to the branches of the church. About this time the Baptists turned their attention towards building a meeting house. A quarter of an acre of land was given them by Daniel Smith, Jr., lying between Salem and Quinton's Bridge, near the King's Highway that led to Maurice River. The place was called Mill Hollow, and a meeting house was built there in 1743. In the 12th month, 1748, by the urgent request of the congregation of the new church, Job Sheppard, their minister, moved his family from Cohansey to what is known at this time as the township of Quinton. They held regular meetings every week. It was not until sixty-five years after the commencement of Baptist meetings in and around Salem, and twelve years after they had built their church at Mill Hollow, that the church was constituted. It appears that in 1754 the question of separation from the Cohansey Church and organizing a new church at Mill Hollow came up for serious consideration. The members of the church made an appeal to the mother church to that effect. Their brethren at Cohansey, after some time for consideration, sent the following answer:

"To our dear brothers in and near Alloways Creek, being in
"Church membership with us:—We, the Church of Christ, and
"Cohansey, baptized upon profession of our faith, holding and
"maintaining the baptism of believers by immersion, the laying
"on of hands, the resurrection of the body, and eternal judgment,
"return this to you as our answer."

Then followed the consent that the Baptists of Salem and Alloways Creek, who met at Mill Hollow, should form a distinct Gospel Church. The names of the following constituent members are signed to the church covenant: Job Sheppard, pastor; Catharine Sheppard, Edward Quinton, Temperance Quinton, Edward Keasbey, Prudence Keasbey, Abner Sims, Sarah Sims, John Holme, Daniel Smith, Jr., Seth Smith, Samuel Simms, Joseph Sneathen, John Whittal, Sarah Smith, Phebe Smith, Rachel Sneathen, Patience James, and Kerenhappuch Blackwood. This was the first Baptist Church constituted within the present limits of Salem county. The Baptists continued to hold their meetings at Mill Hollow until about 1790, when the old meeting house was sold, and moved into Salem and used as a barn for several years. The colored Methodists bought it finally and moved it to their lot on Fenwick street, where they used it as a place of worship until recently.

It stands now in the rear of their new brick church, and is used at this time as a school for colored children.

About the year 1670 the Baptist Society purchased 100 acres of Abel Smith for a parsonage. The property was located about one mile from Salem, on the Quinton's Bridge road. When the church was built on Yorke street, in the town of Salem, the Society was in debt about four hundred and seventy-one pounds. The incorporation fully agreed to dispose of the parsonage for the relinquishment of the debt, and Anthony Keasbey, one of the trustees, was the purchaser for about six hundred pounds. The property is known, at the present time, as the "Hannah farm," and is one of the most valuable in this county. On the fifth day of the 8th month, Mary Dunlap, a widow, deeded to John Holme, Thomas Sayre, Benjamin Holme, Anthony Keasbey, John Briggs, Samuel Vance and Howell Smith, a lot containing one acre and a half, located on Yorke street, and joined on the east by lands formerly belonging to Thomas Killingsworth, but at that time owned by Anthony Keasbey. The lot was conveyed to the before mentioned trustees of the Anti-Pedo-Baptist Society to build a meeting house upon, and also for a graveyard for said Society. It was stipulated in the conveyance that the Society should pay, as a consideration for the property, one ear of Indian corn yearly, if demanded. The house was completed about the year 1790, at a cost of fourteen hundred and thirty-four pounds and some shillings, leaving a debt of four hundred and seventy-one pounds and eleven pence unpaid. The Baptist church at Salem, during the latter part of the last century, increased slowly in numbers, and up to 1801 there were but seventy-four members. From that date, however, to 1869 they numbered nearly seven hundred members. After a time it was thought advisable, to have a meeting house more in the central portion of the town, and the majority of the trustees purchased a lot on Broadway of the heirs of the late Thomas Thompson, and they erected on this lot a large and substantial brick church, with a clock in the cupola, the first, I think, that was ever placed in any building in the city of Salem. The building was completed in 1845, and it is known, at the present, as the First Baptist Church of Salem. C. E. Cardo is the pastor, and it has a membership of 452. The congregation increased so greatly in numbers that some of the members believed it would be advantageous to the church to build another house for worship, which was accordingly done. The church was erected and completed in 1870 and stands at the corner of Parrot and Fenwick streets, fronting on the latter. The building is large and elegant in appearance, and is quite an addition to that part of the town; it is called the Memorial Baptist Church, and has 208 members. A. C. Williams is the pastor.

An old manuscript book, which at one time belonged to Thomas Killingsworth, the first Judge and Baptist clergyman in Fenwick's colony, dates back to the 18th of January, 1690; and at the death of Killingworth it was delivered to Cornelius Copner, an inhabitant of Penn's Neck, on the 16th of August, 1709. About 1725 or 1730 Thomas Miles, the celebrated surveyor, became the possessor of it. In it it appears that Killingsworth kept a genealogical record of a number of families that adhered to the Baptist faith, some of whom can be traced accurately up to this day; and others, whose children have either left the State, or the name has been lost in the female line. Most of the English families that he chronicled were inhabitants of Penn's Neck.

Thomas Baldwin was born in Oxfordshire, England, in December, 1657. His wife, Mary Baldwin, was born in the Parish of Macefield, in the county of Sussex, England, 24th of 8th month, 1653. They emigrated to America soon after they were married, and located in Fenwick's colony, in the township of Penn's Neck, about the year 1683. Their stay in this county was of a short duration, for in 1685 they removed to Chester county, Pennsylvania. Thomas and Joseph Baldwin, the twin sons of Thomas and Mary Baldwin, were born at Chester, August 26th, 1685; William Baldwin, son of Thomas and Mary Baldwin, born 19th of December, 1687; Anthony Baldwin, born 10th of February, 1690; Mary, their daughter, born 25th of February, 1692; Martha and Mary, their daughters, were born the 16th of December, 1694.

The Lambson is an ancient family of Penn's Neck. Thomas and his wife, Ann Lambson, emigrated to America and located in Penn's Neck, in 1690, and agreeably to Killingsworth, they were of the Baptist faith. Giles, the son of Thomas and Ann Lambson, was born the 22d day of July, 1692; Eleanor, their daughter, was born the 21st day of March, 1694; Thomas was born the 29th of December, 1696; Joseph was born the 15th of September, 1700; Catharine, their daughter, was born the 21st of March, 1703; Mathias Lambson, son of Thomas and Ann, was born 31st of May, 1705; Michael was born 29th of September, 1707; Mary, their daughter, was born 13th of April, 1710; Daniel was born the 1st day of February, 1715. Many of the large families of Lampson, as well as the Copner family, adhered to the religion of their ancestors, although a number became active members of the Presbyterian Church that was organized in the township, in 1760. Mathias Lampson, of the present century, lived in and owned the ancient brick dwelling that was built by his ancestor about 1730, which stands near Salem creek. He had two or more children. His daughter married the late Charles Swing, being his first wife. His son, Thomas Lampson, not being contented to remain on the farm, turned his attention to mercantile business. He bought property at the foot of Broadway street, Salem, and erected the spacious brick house that is now standing, which belongs to the Steamboat Company. The old mansion and farm in Penn's Neck is owned by the late John Lindzey's heirs.

Cornelius Copner was one of the active English citizens of Penn's Neck as early as 1695 up to his death, in 1731, as the public records of Salem county fully corroborate. He was twice married. By his first wife, whom he married April 28th, 1701, he had the following named children—Edmund, born 2d day of February, 1702; Ann, born 16th of January, 1703; Elizabeth, born 7th of April, 1705; Cornelius, born 25th of July, 1707; John, born 11th of November, 1709; Edmund, born 23d of February, 1712; Christian, third daughter of Cornelius and Christian Copner, was born 17th of June, 1714. Christian Copner, the wife of Cornelius, departed this life 18th of June, 1714. Sarah, the second wife of Cornelius Copner, was born 15th of September, 1696, and married on the 21st of December, 1714. Christian, daughter of Cornelius and Sarah Copner, was born 3d of January, 1716, and died two days later; Tobias, the son of Cornelius and Sarah Copner, was born 11th of February, 1717. Tobias was the father of Joseph and Ebenezer Copner. Samuel, the son of Cornelius and Sarah Copner, was born 17th of February, 1719; Sarah, daughter of Cornelius and Sarah, was born 9th of February, 1720; Samuel, 2d, son of Cornelius and Sarah, born 20th of November, 1721. Joseph Copner, at one time of his life, belonged to the Presbyterian Church, but in his old age, became a member of Salem Monthly Meeting of Friends. Cornelius Copner owned a large tract of excellent land, part of which still belongs to his family. Benjamin Acton, of Salem, is the owner of a part of it, whose wife is a lineal descendant of Cornelius Copner.

A few Baptists settled on Oldman's creek as early as 1665; they were companions of Robert Carr. It does not appear that they had any regular meetings for a number of years after they first settled in Salem county. At a subsequent period they became members of Cohansey Church, it being at the time the nucleus around which the Baptists in West Jersey centered. It appears, by the care of the mother church, those scattering members residing on Oldman's creek and in Pilesgrove were constituted a branch of the Cohansey Church, at Daretown, in 1743. At that period there were several families from New England by the name of Reed, Elwell, Cheesman, Paullin, Wallace, Champney and Mayhew. Many of their descendants are still living in Pittsgrove at the present time, and most of them, I have been told, still adhere to the religious sect of their forefathers. Robert Kelsay was their pastor soon after the branch was organized, and continued to be until 1754. According to their record, the Baptists on Oldman's creek, in 1740, purchased a piece of ground near the head of tide water, near what in after time was known as Sculltown, for a burial ground, on which they erected a log meeting house in 1771. It has gone down, and the lot is used as a common burying ground by the neighboring inhabitants. In 1771 Pittsgrove Baptist Church became a distinct Gospel Church. The following minute made at Cohansey Church 9th of 5th month, 1771, says, "We conclude that all such of our members as shall join in "said intended constitution are fully dismissed from us. So, "recommending you to God, and the words of his grace, we "rest your brethren in the Faith and Fellowship of the Gospel." It was signed at their monthly meeting in behalf of the whole church by David Bowen, Clerk. They further stated that the members dismissed from Cohansey Church, who became members of Pittsgrove, were John Mayhew, Sr., William Brick, Jacob Elwell, John Dickinson, Cornelius Austin, Samuel Brick, Johanna Mayhew, Eleanor Nelson, Esther Hewes, Hannah Elwell, Matthew Aarons, Pamannah Garton, Fulida Hudson, Mathias Dickinson, Phebe Nelson, Keuhama Austin, and Rachel Brick. The church was incorporated in 1786, and John Mayhew, William Brick, William Dickinson, John Kelley, Samuel Rose, David Nichols, and Jacob Wright were made Trustees. As was the custom in the first organization of the Protestant Societies in this colony, the first Baptist meeting house in Pilesgrove was built of logs. It stood in their grave yard on the same spot where, in 1743, the frame meeting house was built. This last was of moderate size, but was a substantial structure, and remained over a century. It was sold in 1844 to the colored people for a house of worship, and the present brick house was built the same year (1844) at a cost of $2,200. They have a parsonage situated about two miles from their church, near Pole Tavern, containing, at the present time, a comfortable dwelling house, thirty acres of land, and other buildings. In 1762, when Pilesgrove embraced the present township of Pittsgrove, John Mayhew, Jr., in consideration of £80 proclamation money, did give and convey 60 acres of land, lying near Pole Tavern, to Jacob Elwell, John Mayhew, Sr., and John Dickinson, in trust, for the use and benefit of such person as shall be minister or teacher amongst us, and for the Ana-Baptist congregation in Pilesgrove, aforesaid, and only during his official connection with them. It seems, from a want of legal authority in said person to receive the trust, it was deemed necessary by the future generation that a deed of confirmation of said trust should be made by the surviving heirs of the original grantor. The last deed was given in 1809, by John Mayhew, Sarah Worth, Susannah Smith, and Lydia Davis, heirs of John Mayhew, the elder, to Jonathan Elwell, Stanford Mayhew, Samuel Aarons, Uriah Elwell, John Coombs, Joseph Saxton, and John Dunlap, trustees of the Baptist congregation of Pittsgrove. At a subsequent period part of the said land was sold, leaving about 30 acres. William Worth was received into fellowship of the Pittsgrove Baptist Church, and became their pastor in 1771, and continued in that capacity for twenty-two years, during which time there were sixty-five new members added to the congregation by baptism. From the year 1788 the aged Pastor Worth imbibed doctrines contrary to the fundamental creed of the Baptist faith. The effect of such doctrines enunciated from the pulpit, was the cause of many of his congregation attaching themselves to the neighboring Presbyterian Church, whilst a number of male members of the Baptist Church imbibed his doctrine. The conflict between the two contending parts of the congregation was sharp and very persistent, and their historian states that, in 1803, after a struggle of ten years, two deacons and William Worth were excluded for heresy, Worth being deposed from the ministry. He remained a Universalist until approaching death induced him to renounce his error.

After such severe contention the congregation was rent in twain, the male members adhered to their pastor, whilst many of the female members maintained the doctrine of the mother church at Cohansey. Their names were Susanna Elwell, Catharine Harris, Reuhana Austin, Ann Roberson, Tabitha Mayhew, Priscilla Blue, Abigail Joslin, Reuhama Moore, Rachel Robison, and Rachel Brick. Being deprived from meeting in the church by the apostate pastor, and, which was more trying, by their husbands and sons, these sterling women frequently held their meetings in private houses, and in pleasant weather, in a contiguous grove. Ancient Rome was saved at one time by a heroic band of women, and the fundamental doctrines of the Baptists were maintained at the Pittsgrove church by those faithful women, whose names, I have no doubt, are held in grateful remembrance by the congregation up to the present time. From the year 1803 the congregation gradually increased, and in the year 1876 they numbered two hundred and thirty-one, Levi Morse being pastor.

The Dividing Creek Baptist Church was constituted 30th of 5th month, 1761, by permission of Cohansey and Cape May churches. The following are the names of the members at the time of its organization: Jonadab Sheppard, Thomas Sheppard, William Paullin, William Dallis, Temperance Sheppard, Ann Sheppard, Patience Paulin, John Terry, Sarah Terry and Eve Sockwell. Their first meeting house was erected on a lot donated by Seth Lore, in 1751. Edwards writes that their first meeting house was destroyed by fire, in 1770, and was rebuilt in 1771. The size of the building was 30 by 22 feet; they continued to occupy the new building up to 1821; when like the former church it was destroyed by fire. In 1823 they built a new building, 40 by 34 feet, and in 1860 there was added in the length of the building twenty feet, and the old side galleries removed and the entire building improved. It appears by the record kept by the meeting as early as 1761, before the church was regularly organized, steps were taken to secure a permanent home for their pastor. The people of Nantuxet and Dividing Creek, having agreed to build a parsonage, (it being first introduced by four men, Samuel Heaton, the pastor, Jonadab Sheppard, David Sheppard, and William Paullin,) they purchased of Alexander Moore, one hundred acres of land, on which they erected a house and other necessary buildings, for the use of their pastor. They paid two hundred pounds for it, and sold it some few years since for $2,700, and in 1850 they secured a lot in the village near their meeting house, on which they erected their present parsonage. Their pastor is H. B. Raybold. They have 291 members.

The Alloways Creek Baptist Church, known as the Canton Church, was constituted in 1818. There was a Baptist meeting held in this vicinity some years previous to the date of its organization, from the Cohansey mother church. At the decline and final close of the Presbyterian Church at Logtown, many of its members, together with the Mulford family, purchased a lot adjoining the Presbyterian grave-yard and erected a meeting house thereon. At what time they commenced holding their meetings at that place I have no means of determining. Frank Spencer is the pastor. Number of members 319.

Woodstown Baptist Church constituted in 1822. They number 172 members, and have no pastor at the present time.

Allowaystown Baptist Church was constituted an independent Baptist Church in 1830. The persons who took the most active part in the affairs of that meeting were William Walker, the Lambert family, and a few others at that period. M. M. Finch is the present pastor. There are 144 members.

A number of the inhabitants of Bridgeton, in the latter part of the last century, were Baptists. They were members of the old Cohansey Church. The advantage of establishing a meeting for their denomination in Bridgeton, was early recognized by the members then connected with the mother church at Cohansey. As a number of the members lived in the town of Bridgeton and surrounding neighborhood, they were desirous of having meetings that they could attend, nearer than the meetings of the Cohansey Church, which at that time were held in the Neck, near Sheppard's mill. About 1797 the Baptists commenced holding religious meetings every First-day afternoon in the Court House in the town of Bridgeton. The Pastor of Cohansey Church, Henry Smalley, generally attended their meetings. His services were continued, and the number of Baptists increased in the town. They soon found the need of a house of worship, and although the large edifice at Roadstown had been finally completed but a few years before, at a large expense for that time, and the clouds of war were gathering over the nation, the Baptists at Bridgeton resolved to wait no longer, and selected a suitable lot. On the 6th of 6th month, 1812, the matter was brought before the Cohansey Church, at that time removed to Roadstown, and met their approval. A committee was appointed to purchase the lot already selected, then belonging to Daniel Elmer. This committee promptly attended to their duty, and reported at a meeting held July 16th, of the same year, that they had secured a "deed" for two acres of land, on condition that a house of worship be built thereon within three years, and a street three rods in width was to be kept open between the meeting house and his lot, and on failure thereof the lot to be "forfeited." The lot cost $155, and the deed bears date July 16th, 1812. The lot is the one so long occupied by the church, bounding on Pearl, Marion and Bank streets, and is the same where is still their cemetery, and where the house stands which they built, now remodeled, enlarged and occupied by the Pearl street Baptist Church, a branch of the First Church. On July 23d, 1812, a committee was appointed to procure materials and superintend the building of the meeting house, and Moses Harris, Isaac Mulford and Moses Platts were chosen. The chief share of the responsibility rested on Mulford. But, as the result of the magnitude of the enterprise for those interested in it, and the high prices incident to the war, the building was not completed until the latter part of 1816. In accordance with the custom of the greater number of the religious denominations, the building was dedicated to the worship of Almighty God 17th of 12th month, 1816. Joseph Sheppard, pastor from Salem, preached the sermon on the occasion, and the pastor, Henry Smalley, from the First Cohansey Church, made the dedicatory prayer. The meetings that were formerly held at the Court House were transferred to the new house, and were regularly held there thereafter.

The first meeting with reference to a separate organization was held 1st of 2d month, 1827. At that meeting there were thirty-eight members, men and women, applied for letters of dismission from the First Cohansey Church, for the purpose of forming a separate church. The letters of dismission were granted at a meeting held 5th of 1st month, 1828, and the church at Bridgeton was constituted a separate body the 31st of the 1st month, the same year. The number of members belonging to the new organization was forty, and George Spratt was their pastor. He and his wife Elizabeth were from the Third Baptist Church, Philadelphia. The rest of the congregation were from the First Cohansey Church, among whom were John Sibley, Curtis Ogden, Noah Ayres, Lewis Paullin, Ruth B. Ogden, Sarah Sibley, and a number of others. The church was incorporated by the name of the "Second Cohansey Baptist Church, at Bridgeton." The first trustees elected were Smith Bowen, Daniel Pierson and Garrison Maul. Mr. Spratt continued as pastor until 20th of 10th month, 1830. He was succeeded by John C. Harrison in 2d month, 1831, who remained until 3d month, 1834. Michael Frederick became the third pastor in 12th month, 1834, and died in the pastorate, 13th of 11th month, 1837. Large numbers were added to the church during his pastorate, and the number of members at his death had increased to one hundred and sixty-eight, besides thirty-one dismissed in the fall of 1836, to form a new church at Cedarville. Galleries and a vestibule were put into the meeting house during his time, greatly increasing its accommodations. The fourth pastor was Charles J. Hopkins, who commenced his labors 25th of 11th month, 1838, and resigned 25th of 9th month, 1843. During his pastorate the church increased to two hundred and thirty-nine members, and a chapel was built on Atlantic street, near the centre of the town, for evening meetings and Sunday School purposes, which was dedicated 11th of 1st month, 1840. The fifth pastor was Charles E. Wilson, who commenced his labors 7th of 4th month, 1844, and remained until 5th month, 1852. The number of members had increased to 304 at the time of his removal. The sixth pastor was William Cornwell, who was installed 7th of 8th month, 1852, and remained until 13th of 7th month, 1856. Soon after his arrival, the subject of repairing and enlarging the meeting house, or building a new one, was advocated, and on 26th of 2d month, 1853, a meeting of the church was held to consider the subject, and a resolution was adopted to procure a lot in as central a location as possible and build a new house of worship, and a committee, consisting of James Stiles, Horatio J. Mulford and Isaac A. Sheppard, was appointed to carry out the above resolution. A lot, 67 feet front and 126 feet deep, situated on the south side of Commerce street, just above Pearl and in the centre of the city, was purchased for $1,300, of Azel and Henry R. Pierson, the deed being dated 3d of 10th month, 1853. The size of the building was 50 feet in width, and 99 feet in length. It has a basement story for evening meetings and Sunday School purposes, and the upper story is for the main audience room. The basement is built of stone, and the rest of brick. The whole building is rough-cast, with a tower in the centre of the front, surmounted with a steeple rising 140 feet from the ground. The building was completed in the fall of 1857.

Mr. Cornwell was succeeded, as pastor, by J. Spencer Kennard, 4th of 1st month, 1857; the church prospered greatly during his pastorate, which lasted until 11th of 9th month, 1859. He was succeeded by James F. Brown in 6th month, 1860, who remained until 3d month, 1868. William Wilder became the ninth pastor 1st month, 1869, and continued until 7th month, 1871, when he resigned, and was succeeded in 3d month, 1872, by E. B. Palmer, the tenth and present pastor. The walls and ceiling of the audience room of their house of worship were handsomely frescoed in the summer of 1872. A parsonage, situated on Atlantic street, was purchased in 1869, at a cost of about $5,500. The church also has three chapels, two frame and the other brick, used for Sunday school purposes. The present number of members is three hundred and sixty-six.

In 7th month, 1866, sixty-nine members of the First Church were dismissed, and were constituted a new church under the name of the Pearl Street Baptist Church, of Bridgeton. The mother church gave them a deed for the old meeting house, which they have since enlarged and handsomely improved, at a cost of about $20,000. William R. McNeil became their first pastor, and remained until 2d month, 1872. He was followed by B. S. Morse, in 4th month, 1872, who resigned in the spring of 1874. A. B. MacGowan is the third and present pastor. They number two hundred and eighty-eight members at the present time.

I am indebted to my young friend, Charles E. Sheppard, of Bridgeton, for the particulars of the first Baptist churches, and the time they were constituted in that city.

As a result of a series of meetings held at Cedarville in 1835 and 1836, by Mr. Frederick, pastor of the Bridgeton Baptist Church, a large number of persons united with that church, and on their application thirty-one persons were dismissed and constituted a church at Cedarville, 6th of 9th month, 1836. During the last year the congregation have erected a large and elegant building for a church edifice, and a building attached where they hold their First day or Sunday school, which is a very commodious room. The cost of the whole building was nearly $10,000. Wm. A. Durfee is the pastor. There are at present two hundred and thirty-five members.

The Baptist Church at Greenwich was constituted from Cohansey in 1850, and erected a plain and substantial brick edifice on the main street of Greenwich. S. C. Dare is the pastor. There are two hundred and thirty-seven members.

The Baptist congregation at Newport built themselves a good meeting house within the town a few years ago; the church was constituted in 1855. W. A. Durfee is the pastor, and they have one hundred and thirty-seven members.

Within the recollection of some of the oldest inhabitants of this section of the country, the place where Vineland is now located was a wilderness, where many sportsmen of the towns of Salem and Bridgeton, in the fall of the year, went in pursuit of deer and other wild animals. When Landis purchased the tract of land of the late Richard Wood, it was in its primeval state. He soon afterward commenced running out the land into convenient lots, and held out inducements for persons to settle thereon, and many embraced the opportunity from several states—the result is, there is no part of South Jersey that has a more cultivated set of inhabitants than can be found in Vineland. A seminary was built, and good school houses were established; meeting houses were erected of nearly all religious organizations; among them are two Baptist churches, which are rapidly increasing in members. The first one was constituted in 1865; N. B. Randall is the pastor, and has three hundred and nineteen members. The second, called South Vineland Baptist Church, was organized in 1871; Wm. W. Meach is the pastor, and it has fifty-six members.

The idea of a High School for the southern part of New Jersey, to be under the control of Baptists, originated with R. F. Young, in 1849, then pastor of the First Baptist Church in Salem. Through his influence a convention was subsequently called, connected with the West New Jersey Baptist Association, to be held at Salem. To this invitation a number of churches responded. After deliberating on the propriety of the enterprise, passed resolutions touching its desirableness and importance. No corresponding act, however, followed, and the whole project ended. It was revived again at a meeting of the West New Jersey Baptist Association, held in Greenwich in September, 1865. At that time the Association passed the following resolutions:

Resolved, That this Association has heard, with pleasure, of the establishment of a denominational school, for the education of both sexes, at Hightstown, and that in the judgment of this body, the time has come when a high school, for the education of both sexes, should be established within the bounds and under the exclusive direction of the West Jersey Baptist Association.

Resolved, That this Institution shall be located in that place which shall present the greatest inducement.

Resolved, That the minimum amount to be raised for the buildings and grounds of said Institution, shall be twenty-five thousand dollars.

There was a committee appointed at the time, to carry out the objects of the aforesaid resolutions. All the churches belonging to the West New Jersey Baptist Association were represented on the committee; they had power to act as trustees till the next meeting of the Association. The first meeting of the committee was held 3d of 10th month, 1865, at the rooms of the American Baptist publication society, 530 Arch street, Philadelphia. The following preamble and resolutions were passed:

WHEREAS, The sum of ten thousand dollars has been offered by the following individuals, conjointly, H. J. Mulford, Isaac W. Mulford, Anna Maria Mulford, Hannah Mulford and Lucy

W. Mulford, with the understanding that the proposed school shall be located in Bridgeton, their place of residence, respectively;

WHEREAS, This is the highest sum offered for the location; Therefore,

Resolved, That the school shall be located in Bridgeton, New Jersey, agreeable to the resolutions passed at the late meeting of the West Jersey Baptist Association.

Horatio J. Mulford, in 1868, offered the ground for the Institute on west side of the Cohansey, containing ten acres and forty-two rods, which was cordially accepted, as being ample in size and most eligibly located. This Institute is located on the west bank of the Cohansey. It is built of brick, with a mansard or French roof, and is a great improvement to the city of Bridgeton. The school was opened in the fall of 1870, and has taken a high rank in the community, and is in a prosperous condition.

SEVENTH-DAY BAPTIST SOCIETIES.

The Seventh-Day Baptists are an ancient religious organization in the American Provinces. As early as 1662, a large number of Welsh Baptist emigrants, known as John Miles Company, he being their pastor, arrived at Boston, and settled in Massachusetts, and named their location "Swansea," after their native place in Wales. (See Davis' History of the Welsh Baptist). Meeting with persecution from their Puritan neighbors, a large number of their children and grandchildren, with some Baptists from Scotland, moved to South Jersey, in the year 1687, and settled at Barratt's Run, Bowentown and Shiloh. This colony from New England, was known as the "Rev. Timothy Brooks," or the Bowen Company; and kept up a separate Society until 1710, when they united with the old Cohansey Baptist Church. From 1695 to 1700, and subsequently, Jonathan Davis, son of the pastor by the same name, of the Miles Company from Wales, a Seventh-Day Baptist from Long Island, (see Morgan Edward's History,) having married Elizabeth Bowen, one of the Miles Company, visited his Welsh cousins at Bowentown, Shiloh and vicinity; he gained many converts to the Seventh-Day Baptist Church. Their numbers were also increased by additions from Pennsylvania, Delaware and Maryland, and from Trenton, Bonhamtown and Piscataway, New Jersey. It appears from their old records, that in 1716 these Seventh-Day Baptists had a temporary organization, and held meetings from house to house. About the year 1700, Jonathan Davis moved from Long Island and settled at Trenton, with his brother Elnathan Davis, who was the Surveyor General of New Jersey; from there Jonathan made frequent visits to his brethren at Shiloh. Jonathan Davis, son of Elnathan, the Surveyor-General, married Esther, daughter of Isaac Ayars, Sr., of Shiloh, and located near by, and became a prominent preacher of the Gospel. On the 27th day of the 3d month, 1737, the Seventh-Day Baptist Church of Shiloh, was organized, with the following articles of faith, and agreement, and the names in the order as they are found in the old records. It commences thus: "We, whose names are hereunder written, "do join together upon the articles of agreements following "which includes nine articles of Faith. 1st. We believe that "unto us there is but one God, the Father, and one Lord, Jesus "Christ, who is the Mediator between God and mankind. We "believe the Holy Ghost is the Spirit of God." The other articles of faith I omit on account of brevity. John Swinney, his wife Deborah Swinney, Dr. Elijah Bowen, Deborah Bowen, John Jerman, now spelled Jarman, Caleb Barratt, Abigail Barratt, Hugh Dunn, Amy Dunn, Jonathan Davis, Jr., Esther Davis, Caleb Ayars, Joseph Swinney, Deborah Swinney, Jr., Samuel Davis, Ann Davis, Jane Philips, of Newtown Square, Pennsylvania, and Anna Swinney.

It should be borne in mind that many of the Seventh-Day Baptists still held their membership with the First-Day Baptists, and hesitated to become contentious members, among whom were Timothy Brooks' two daughters. Some of the consistent members had burial lots in other societies, and were not interred at Shiloh; among this class were the first two names on the list who were buried in the old Baptist burying ground of Cohansey, located near Sheppard's Mill. On a marble tombstone, still standing, are carved the words, "In "memory of Deborah Swinney, who departed this life the 4th "day of April, 1760, in the 77th year of her age." She was the daughter of John Swinney, who was one of the first European settlers at Cohansey. The inscription further states that Deborah was the first white female child born at Cohansey precinct. At the constitution of the church Jonathan Davis, Jr., was chosen pastor; ruling elders and deacons were also elected officers of the church—the former to look after the spiritual, and the latter the temporal interests of the flock. About the year 1830 the office of ruling elder was discontinued, partly from an unwillingness on the part of some to submit to the close spiritual oversight of the elders, partly on account of the belief that the deacons should attend to the spiritual as well as temporal concerns of the church. On the 24th of 3d month, 1738, Caleb Ayars, Sr., deeded to the church one acre of land, near the village, for a meeting house lot and burying ground; and a frame house for worship, size forty by thirty feet, was erected the same year. The ministers of the Seventh-Day Baptist Church were many of them noted for their learning and piety. Jonathan Davis, of Trenton, was never a settled pastor at Shiloh; his wife was Elizabeth Bowen, sister, aunt and cousin to the Bowens, Brookses, and Swinneys, who resided at

Bowentown and vicinity. On account of this relationship he frequently visited Cohansey, and preached mostly at Shiloh; occasionally at the Cohansey Church. History says he was very tall and large in proportion, and was sometimes called "great high priest." Samuel Bowen, of the Timothy Brooks' company, was colleague for many years of the first pastor, Jonathan Davis, Sr. The younger Jonathan Davis continued to be pastor of Shiloh Church till his death, which occurred 2d of 2d month, 1768, in his 60th year. He was succeeeded by Jonathan Davis, of the Welsh tract, now Brandywine, Delaware. He married Margaretta Bond, of Delaware, a descendant of the distinguished Sharpless family, of Chester county, Pennsylvania. Before settling in Shiloh he founded Newark Academy, which has since grown into Delaware College. This Elder Davis was born 7th of 7th month, 1734, ordained in Shiloh Church 1768, and continued to be their pastor till his death, which event took place in 1785. It was this man, so eminent for learning and true piety, that gave the beautiful name of Shiloh, in imitation "of the Ark of God resting at "Shiloh." Previous to that time the place was called Cohansey Corners. Jonathan Jarman was his colleague for some years, and after his death supplied the church until he moved to Cape May, where he died, but his remains were brought back to Shiloh for burial. For about two years Thomas Jones, a First-Day Baptist minister, supplied the church, and Deacon Philip Ayars, a prominent member of the church, administered the ordinance of baptism, in the absence of a pastor. In 1786 Nathan Ayars was called by the church, and ordained to the gospel ministry, and remained pastor till his death in 1810. John Davis, youngest son of Jonathan Davis, of Delaware, was ordained in 1807. He continued within the church until 1842, when he resigned on account of age. During his pastorate there were large numbers added to their church.

Azor Estee was the next pastor, who remained nearly three years; during that time, their records state, there were ninety new members. In 1844, Solomon Carpenter took the oversight of their church, but his transfer to the China mission left them without a pastor. In 1845, Samuel Davison, a convert to the Seventh-Day Baptist Church, took the pastoral charge, and was succeeded in 1848 by Giles M. Longworthy, whose sickness and premature death again left them without a pastor. Enoch Barnes, a convert from the Methodist Church, supplied the pulpit during the summer of 1850. Elder George R. Wheeler and wife, joined the church under the ministry of Davison, and he supplied the church occasionally; but living at Salem, twelve miles distant, could not perform pastoral labor. Soon after, he became pastor of the Seventh-Day Baptist Church at Marlborough, located in Salem county near Cumberland line, it being a branch of Shiloh Church.

William Jones became a convert to the Seventh-Day Baptist Church, while laboring in Hayti under the Baptist Free Missionary Society. He became the pastor of Shiloh Church in 1850, and continued there three years. During that time, the present brick meeting house was completed, and dedicated. The old building was donated to Union Academy, and fitted up especially for the wants of that institution, then so prosperous under the principalship of Prof. E. P. Larkin. Their pastor, William Jones, continued after the new meeting house was completed, to hold meetings from night to night, which resulted in a large addition to the church, principally young people. In the year 1853, Jones resigned his charge to go as missionary to Palestine, and was succeeded by Walter B. Gillette, after a successful pastorate of nearly twenty years; during his ministration the cause of education advanced, and the present Academic building was erected. He resigned the pastorate to go as missionary in the Western Association. In April 1873, A. H. Lewis was elected as pastor of their church; during his ministration a parsonage in the village was purchased and remodeled at a cost of about three thousand dollars. Lewis is above mediocrity as a pulpit orator, possesses great learning, and is affable and pleasing in his address, consequently many joined the church during the last winter. It now numbers about three hundred and seventy-five. In 1827 a Sabbath School was organized, and I have been informed it has continued ever since, uninterruptedly. The old, as well as the young, take absorbing interest in the maintenance of the schools. The first settlers of Shiloh were an intelligent people, and some were graduates of institutions of learning. They soon established a library of useful books in their village school; the higher branches were taught, as well as the rudiments of knowledge, and Shiloh became noted for its schools. In 1848, an academy was opened under the management of Prof. E. P. Larkin, which stood for many years as the leading institution of learning in South Jersey, and still continues to exert a healthful influence under the care of Prof. G. M. Cottrell. The temperance cause enlisted the feelings of the members of this ancient church. In 1833, their Elder William B. Maxson, introduced the subject in their meeting, and so great an interest was manifested that one hundred and forty signatures to a temperance pledge were immediately obtained; but none entered into the cause more heartily, nor rejoiced more to see it prosper, as I have been informed, than their venerable pastor, John Davis. Some years after the church adopted a temperance clause, and as a church has been committed to it ever since.

Although the church at Shiloh has from time to time incurred heavy expenditures in money in building their churches and academies, I have been informed that it is clear of debt. They have obtained, by legacies and from other sources, considerable sums of money. In 1774 Esther Davis, daughter of Isaac Ayars, and widow of the first pastor, Jonathan Davis, left, by will, a house and lot to the church. In 1754 Richard Sparks, a Keithite Seventh-Day Baptist, left, by will, a lot on Fifth street, Philadelphia, for a burial ground. George Keith, the apostate Quaker preacher, in the latter part of the seventeenth and early part of the eighteenth century, left the Society of Friends, of which he at one time was a consistent and useful member, and with his followers adopted the Seventh day as the Sabbath, and espoused the Baptist creed. Several of John Smith's, of Amblebury, grand-children became the followers of Keith, and others that resided within the Salem tenth, a number that belonged to Newton meeting, also many Friends that were citizens of Philadelphia and adjacent country, so much so that there were three Keithite meetings established—one in Byberry, one within the city limits, the third, I think, was located near Radnor. George Keith, within a short time after these meetings were established, returned to England, his native land, and became a member of the Church of England. Most of his followers in America, in a few years, became members of other religious denominations, generally the old Baptist organization. The city government soon afterward prohibiting interments thereon, the New Market and Shiloh churches took charge of it, and realized some $4,000 or $5,000 from the part not occupied by the graves.

In 1858 Deacon Ayars, grandson of Rev. Jonathan Davis, 3d, left, by will, $1,000 to the church, the interest only to be used. In 1873 the late Caleb Sheppard left, by will, $500 to the Shiloh Academy, and that sum, with the recent subscriptions, will free the institution from debt.

PRESBYTERIAN SOCIETIES.

From the year 1690 up to 1745 there was a large emigration from New England and New York States to Fenwick Colony. Many of the emigrants were Presbyterians, and they, like the early Friends, were satisfied with erecting log houses for Divine worship here in the wilderness. The first Presbyterian church erected in Fenwick's tenth was built at Fairfield, on the south bank of Cohansey creek, about the year 1695. It was composed of logs. The pastor of the church at that time was Thomas Bridges, who, it is said, was called away to Boston in 1702. A few years later the congregation erected for themselves a frame edifice in the old New Englandtown grave-yard, on the banks of Cohansey creek, it being about one mile from what is known at this time as the old stone church. Howell Powell, it seems, was one of the early pastors of Fairfield church. He died in 1717.

In the year 1727 Daniel Elmer emigrated to Fairton from Connecticut. He was a young man, and a clergyman of considerable note in his native State. He was a pastor of Fairfield Presbyterian church up to the time of his death, which occurred in 1755. From him originated the Elmers of Cumberland county, many of whom have been distinguished men in professional and civil life up to the present day. The ancestors of the Potter, Ewing, Fithian, Westcott and Bateman families also came from New England and settled at Cohansey in the latter part of the seventeenth or early in the eighteenth century. They have held an influential position in Cumberland county for several generations.

The Presbyterians from New England settled on both sides of Cohansey creek, and quite a number of them purchased homes in, and in the neighborhoood of, Cohansey (now Greenwich). About the year 1705 they established and organized the first Presbyterian church on the north side of Cohansey creek, which was named Greenwich Church. I am indebted to the venerable Dr. Fithian, of Greenwich, for much valuable information respecting it. It appears that the early records of the church were destroyed accidentally by fire, and the oldest record in possession of the congregation is a deed of gift from Jeremiah Bacon to Henry Joice and Thomas Maskell, for one acre of land, in trust for the people called Presbyterians, living on the north side of Cohansey creek, to build and establish a church for the public worship of God, dated 24th of 4th month, 1717. It is probable that this was a part of the thirty-two acres of land that William Bacon purchased of the executors of John Fenwick in 1688. The first pastor of the church was a gentleman of the name of Black, and he remained as pastor for about three years. In 1708 he removed to Lewes, Delaware, and in 1712 Ebenezer Goold, a native of New England, was installed pastor. The year after the installation of Goold the congregation procured a piece of land, on which they built a parsonage. The deed for the land (six acres) was from Nicholas Gibbon and Leonard Gibbon to Josiah Fithian, Thomas Maskell and Noah Miller. They made a provision in the deed that Presbyterians should build a house for their minister to dwell in, by deed dated 13th of 1st month, 1729. What a noble example the two wealthy men, Nicholas and Leonard Gibbon, set for future generations! They, though strict members of the Church of England, were willing to assist other religious denominations. The congregation did build a house on the land, in which their pastor resided until it, together with the furniture it contained, was consumed with fire, as also the early records of the church. Ebenezer Goold, soon after he went to Greenwich, married Ann Brewster, a sister of Francis Brewster, one of the elders of the church, and a descendant of Elder Brewster, who landed from the Mayflower, at Plymouth, in 1620. The congregation increased so greatly about the year 1735 that the house of worship was too small to accommodate them. They resolved to build a new church, and started a subscription for that purpose. Perhaps it would be interesting to many at this day to know who were the leading members of the Presbyterian Church at Greenwich at that period, who subscribed to the fund. They are as follows:

	£ sh.		£ sh.
Ebenezer Goold,	5 00	Jos. Simpkins,	1 00
Wm. Watson,	10 00	Thos. Wartham,	3 00
Elias Cotting,	10 00	Matthias Fithian,	5 00
Samuel Clark,	5 00	Constant Maskell,	10 00
Benj. Dare,	10 00	John Woolsey,	2 00
Thos. Ewing,	10 00	Ananias Sayre,	4 00
Abel Carll,	5 00	Aaron Mulford,	3 00
Thos. Buryman,	5 00	Chas. Fordham,	3 00

PRESBYTERIAN SOCIETIES.

	£ sh.		£ sh.
Abraham Reeves,	10 00	Wm. Perry,	4 00
Jonathan Sayre,	2 00	Jas. Carathers,	4 00
Nathaniel Bishop,	2 05	Thos. Road,	3 00
Samuel Miller,	4 00	John Woodruff,	3 00
Jonathan Holmes,	6 00	Noah Miller, Jr.,	4 00
Thomas Sayre,	5 00	Jos. Moore,	6 00
John Padgett,	8 00	Jas. McKnight,	2 00
Harbour Beck,	4 00	Ebenezer Smith,	1 00
Nehemiah Veal,	3 00	Nathan Lupton,	1 10
Balbie Sheppard,	1 00	John Tyler,	1 00
Francis Brewster,	2 00	Deborah Keith,	1 00
Samuel Moore,	5 00	John Plummer,	10
John Miller,	4 00	Elias Davis,	1 00
Joseph Peck,	2 00	Mercy Maskell,	2 00
Nathaniel Harris,	2 00	Samuel Bacon, Jr.,	15
Francis Tulies,	1 10	Josiah Parain,	4 00
John Shaw.	3 00	Thos. Padgett,	6 00
Philip Vickers,	5 00	James Crawford,	1 00
John Keith,	2 10	John Finlaw,	1 00

The subscription amounted to £234 10s. I think a number of those who subscribed were members of Deerfield Church, the members of which were in unison with Greenwich Presbyterian Church. The sum raised was insufficient to build the church, which in size was 44 feet in length by 34 feet in width, and it was not completed until 1751. It was built of brick, and has since been taken down, and a more modern edifice has been erected on the opposite side of the street.

When John Fenwick had determined upon laying out a town on the banks of the Cohansey, to be called after the Indian name of the river Cohansey; hence all the country on the north and south sides of said river was known as Cohansey Precinct. The country was known by the same name until about the year 1710 or 1720. In 1690 there were a number of emigrants from Connecticut came to Fenwick Colony, and settled at a place which they called Fairton, on the south side of Cohansey river, in Shrewsbury Neck, as it was called by the first settlers of Fenwick Colony. The name was changed by the Eastern emigrants to Fairfield, after their native township in Connecticut. There were also a number of families from the State of New York and the Eastern States emigrated and settled in the town of Cohansey and the country adjacent, such as the Denn, Miller, Maskell, Padgett, Watson, Ewing, Seeley, and several other families, who became conspicuous in the religious and civil affairs of the Colony. The great-grandson of the first Watson that settled at Cohansey removed to Philadelphia, and late in life wrote 'Annals of Philadelphia," a work that will perpetuate his name for many generations. About the time the families that I mentioned came from New England and New York, the name of Cohansey was changed to Greenwich, after the native town of some of the emigrants.

William Fithian emigrated from England to America, and settled at East Hampton, New York, in 1639, and his son, Samuel Fithian, removed from New York to Fairfield, in Fenwick Colony, in 1700, with his family. His wife was Priscilla Burnett. They had six children—John, Josiah, Samuel, Esther, Matthias and William. Josiah Fithian removed from Fairfield and made Cohansey his permanent home, in 1706, and there married Sarah Dennis. They had seven children—John, Jeremiah, Samuel, 3d, Hannah, (who subsequently married Ephraim Seeley); Esther, Joseph, Sarah and Josiah. Josiah and Sarah Dennis Fithian were the great grandparents of the present Dr. Enoch Fithian, of Greenwich.

By a deed dated 13th of 2d month, 1738, the Presbyterian grave-yard was enlarged by the addition of one acre and a quarter to its southern end, which was purchased for the sum of £25. The deed, made by John Ogden, of Cohansey, conveyed to Josiah Fithian, William Watson, and Abraham Reeves, "in trust for the sole and proper use and benefit of the Presbyterian congregation of Greenwich, for a meeting house and burying-ground forever, and to and for no other use."

About the year 1700, William Hall, of Salem, and Daniel Cox, of Burlington, came into possession of large tracts of excellent land in the southern portion of Pilesgrove township, Deerfield, and other parts of the Colony. They held out inducements to purchasers, and from the year 1715 to 1750 there was a large emigration from New York and other places to South Jersey. The Parvin, Harber Peck, Harris, Preston, Foster, and several other families, most of them Presbyterians, purchased lands in Deerfield, Cumberland county, as it is called, since the division of Salem tenth. Nearly at the same period the Newkirk, Vanmeter, Dubois, and other families bought lands of Cox and the heirs of Hall in what is now Pittsgrove, being formerly part of Pilesgrove. About 1737 the first Presbyterian Church was erected at Deerfield. It seems that the churches at Greenwich and at Deerfield were in full unity with each other, both of them being under the charge of a body of deacons and elders who were members of both churches. Their names were as follows: Andrew Hunter, their pastor, Josiah Parvin, Harber Peck, Joseph Peck, Nathaniel Harris, Isaac Preston, and Jeremiah Foster, of Deerfield Church; Jonathan

Holmes, Isaac Mills, Francis Brewster, Thomas Padgett, Thomas Ewing and Abraham Reeves, of Greenwich Church. It appears that Andrew Hunter succeeded Ebenezer Goold as pastor of those two churches. He was born in Ireland about the year 1715, and has been represented to have had great oratorical powers in the pulpit; better than all, his moral and Christian life was in accordance with his precepts. He married Annie Stockton, of Princeton, New Jersey who survived him; they left no children. Andrew Hunter died 7th month, 2d, 1775, and was buried in the ancient grave-yard at Greenwich, he being at the time of his death about sixty years of age.

The Presbyterians, like the early Friends, seem to have had dissensions among them. The old church at Fairfield adhered strictly to the old Calvinistic doctrines, while the members of Greenwich and Deerfield took a more liberal view of their modes of faith; hence there was no unity between the two oldest Presbyterian churches in Fenwick Colony. While the Fairfield members adhered to what they called the old side, the members of Greenwich and Deerfield churches strenuously advocated the new modes of faith. It appears there was not full unity between the two churches for nearly forty years. The eloquence of Hunter, however, attracted many persons from Fairfield Church, as Webster, their historian remarked, to the congregation at Greenwich.

Pilesgrove Presbyterian Church is known at this time as Pittsgrove congregation, on account of the division of the township of Pilesgrove. The said church was organized by David Evans, in 1741; it was associated at the first period of its existence with the church at Gloucester, later with Deerfield, the neighboring church, and finally with Quihawkin, located in Penn's Neck. There appears to be no definite record showing when the latter named church was founded. It is generally believed by the members of that society that it was about the time Pilesgrove church was organized. The families that were members of Pittsgrove church at its establishment were—David Evans, their pastor, DuBois, VanMeter, Newkirk and Mayhew, and at a later date the Coombs family, and a number of others that I do not recollect at this time, whose descendants generally are members of the same church that their forefathers assisted in founding in the wilderness more than one hundred and thirty years ago. The congregation at this time is said to be large, and has a large moral and religious influence in that section of the county.

Quihawkin Church was located at Obisquahasit, now Penn's Neck, on the banks of the Shanangah (now Delaware) river, near what is now Pennsville. The building was similar to the old Presbyterian Church at Greenwich, but less in size; it has been taken down for a number of years. Some of the persons that were members of it at its organization were Tobias Copner and family, and Dunn and Lambson families. Tradition asserts that the Philpot family, Thomas Miles, and his son Francis, and a number of others, were also members of said church. There is no Presbyterian meeting now kept up in that township. Joseph Copner, the son of Tobias, became a member of the Society of Friends in old age, while the large and influential family of Dunns have left the religious society of their ancestors, most of them being members of the Methodist church.

The records of the Presbyterian church located formerly at Logtown, in Alloways Creek, seems in lapse of time to have been lost. Johnson, in his history of Salem county, says that the said church was founded in 1750. The families that were members of it at the time of its organization were James Sayre, Joseph Hildredth, Richard Moore, a person by the name of Woodruff, (I think it was Thomas, whose grandparents, Thomas and Edith Wyatt Woodruff, emigrated from Worcestershire, England, to Salem county, in 1678), and Thomas Padgett, Jr. Towards the latter part of the last century Solomon DuBois, a young man from Pittsgrove, George Grier, Sr., Henry Wood, and a few others, became members of said church. I think it was not at any time large. The house of worship has been taken down more than a half century. The cemetery that once belonged to the church is now enclosed with the Baptist grave-yard, near the village of Canton, where the descendants of the former members of the Presbyterian church still bury their deceased relatives, and a number whose parents were formerly members of the Logtown Church have become members of the Baptist Society.

Bridgeton is comparatively a modern city in Fenwick's Colony. Richard Tindall, after the difficulties between Richard Hancock and the proprietor, was made surveyor-general of the province by Fenwick, in the year 1680. In 1682 Richard Hancock erected a saw mill on the south side of Cohansey, where Bridgeton is located, on a small stream that flows into the Cohansey, called Mill creek. I presume that name was given to it on account of Hancock's mill being located there. What time he remained there I have no means of determining, but Judge Elmer thinks he left that place and purchased property where Hancock's Bridge is located, and the family by that name at that place are his descendants. I am inclined to think that Richard Hancock left no children, if any they were daughters; hence the name of the family is lost. There were three persons by that name who emigrated to this country. Richard came with the proprietor in 1675. William Hancock, who purchased one thousand acres of land of the proprietor before he embarked to take possession of the province. William gave Richard Whiticar the power of attorney to take charge of his landed estate until such time as he should arrive in this country himself, which was in 1677. He died in 1679, on his allotment, leaving two sons—John and William Hancock. John Hancock was the father of William, who was killed at the massacre in his own house during the American Revolution. William Hancock, the son of the emigrant, purchased lands in Elsinborough, and was the ancestor of the family by that name in that township. John, the cousin of Richard and William Hancock, came to this province in 1680, and married Mary, the daughter of Nathaniel and Elizabeth Chambless, in 1681. Their descendants are numerous in the county at this time.

Where the city of Bridgeton is now located the first bridge across the Cohansey was built. The village, during the time of the Revolution, went under the name of Cohansey Bridge. The American Militia, under Colonels Hand and Home, was quartered there for some time in the years 1777-8. I was told many years ago by a celebrated antiquarian, the late Dalyman Harris, that a few years before the Revolution John Moore, a native of Ireland, after he arrived in this country, followed the business of a pedlar of dry goods. According to the custom of that day he carried the pack of merchandise on his back. By strict economy he soon was enabled to build a small building on the north side of the creek, near the bridge, in which he kept store. My informant further stated that he believed he married a young woman by the name of Reeve, grand-daughter of Mark Reeve. They were the grand-parents of the late John Moore White, of Woodbury. At the time of his death he was more than fourscore years and ten. He was a good lawyer, and for a number of years one of the Judges of the Courts.

Allen H. Brown, a divine of considerable eminence, gave the following of the first Presbyterian Church built at Bridgeton, in a discourse delivered in that city, in 1865 : "Sensible of the "inconvenience of attending public worship in the neighboring "churches, the people of Bridgeton determined, about the year "1774, to build a house for public worship and to form a con-"gregation on or near the lot where the old session house re-"cently stood. The revolutionary war coming on soon after,

55

"the project was relinquished. In 1778 the subject was revived, but because of disagreement respecting the location, the site was not determined upon until 1791. The work was begun in 1792, and in the same year the house was enclosed. In May, 1793, a lottery was started for raising two thousand dollars for the purpose of finishing the building, which was drawn in January, 1794. In May, 1795, the house was opened and dedicated by Davenport, the pastor of Deerfield church." Although the same author further states that they possessed a house, the people still felt unable to support the Gospel alone. They made a proposition to Greenwich church to unite with them as a collegiate church, under the name of the "United Churches of Greenwich and Bridgeton," with but one set of church officers, and one church session for both churches, and that for the present the officers of Greenwich church shall control both churches, but in filling vacancies, elections shall be held and officers chosen alternately at each church. Greenwich congregation did not agree to the proposal, and the plan was relinquished. Application was then made to the Presbytery for a separate congregation in Bridgeton, and the prayer was granted in 10th month, 1792. The population at that place at that period was about three hundred. They now number about eight thousand. I have been informed that at the present time there are three Presbyterian churches in that city, besides a large seminary called the West Jersey Academy. The said institution, if the report respecting it be correct, is extensively patronized.

I think many of the ancestors of the members of the Presbyterian churches of Bridgeton were members of the old Presbyterian church at Fairfield. It can safely be said of Bridgeton that it is a place of factories and churches, and there seems to be a general industry and talent in its population that is calculated to produce good results upon their character.

The Presbyterian church at Salem was founded about 1821. At that time there were only six members—the late Dr. James VanMeter, and his brother, Robert VanMeter, were two of the principal members, and took an active part in its organization. The corner stone of their church was laid in the beginning of 3d month, 1821, on a lot on Griffith street, which was given to the church by Robert Johnson. In 1824 the congregation increased from six to thirty-one members, and the number who generally attended their meeting was about two hundred. The congregation agreed about that time to give their pastor, Burt, three hundred dollars per annum, and his firewood, and find him a house to live in. Their record further states that "their people are mostly of common circumstances. From the attention given to their minister the congregation confidently expected, by the goodness of Divine Providence, that in a few years the Society will be so far increased in numbers that they may be able to support their minister without the aid of their brethren elsewhere." They further stated that "they will be thankful to their Christian friends for any pecuniary assistance they may feel disposed to confer upon the infant church at Salem."

Notwithstanding the Presbyterian church had erected a substantial brick edifice on the lot they obtained from Robert G. Johnson, on East Griffith street, they soon found it too small to accommodate the congregation, and a few years afterward they built an addition to it. Their pastor at that period was Daniel Stratton, a native of Bridgeton, New Jersey. He married Ellen, the eldest daughter of Morris and Sarah Hancock, of Salem. Daniel was educated for the ministry. In early life, I have been informed, he was threatened with consumption, and soon after his marriage he removed with his wife to Newburn, North Carolina, where he was installed pastor of the Presbyterian church of that town. Thinking, I have no doubt, that a warmer climate would be more genial to his weak constitution, he continued in that place for several years, and in 1852 he and his family returned to their native State. I think he was installed pastor of the Salem Presbyterian congregation the same year. He continued in that service until his death, in 8th month, 1866, which event cast a gloom over his admiring congregation, a large number of relatives and acquaintances, and the inhabitants of the city of Salem generally, by whom he was much beloved for his Christian and moral deportment whilst residing among them. He was succeeded in the pastoral charge of the congregation by Frederic W. Bauus, who continued to fill the duties of pastor for sixteen or seventeen months, having resigned the charge in 1868. He was followed by the present popular pastor, William Bannard, who was installed by the congregation the same year.

The Presbyterian Church, desiring a more eligible location for their house of worship, bought a lot of ground on Market street of the late Calvin Belden, who was a member and a liberal contributor, the lot costing $4,000. The corner stone was laid July 17, 1854, for the new church, and the house, when completed, cost $22,000, furniture $1,200; the whole cost, including the ground, was $27,000. The building is 83x49 feet, the spire is 165 feet from the ground, and in point of architecture is not surpassed by any church edifice in the city of Salem. The congregation now numbers over two hundred members.

The large and influential congregation of Pittsgrove found it incumbent to provide more ample room for Divine worship, and they resolved to erect a new church. In July 14th, 1864, the corner stone for a new building was laid. The size was 81x51 feet; including projecting tower and pulpit recess, is 91 feet in length; the tower and spire is 125 feet. The cost of the building was $21,050; the furniture $700; bell, $4,186; the whole cost, $25,836.

In 1859 the old church at Deerfield was remodeled and enlarged by the addition of 25 feet, at an expense of $3,000.

The Presbyterian Church at Millville was organized 12th of 8th month, 1820, at Port Elizabeth, under the name of the First Presbyterian Church at Maurice River, by Ethan Osborne and Jonathan Freeman, appointed by the Presbytery of Philadelphia to that duty. It began with twenty-one members, including three ruling elders. The elders were Nathaniel Foster, Jeremiah Stratton and Samuel S. Barry. The town of Millville soon eclipsed Port Elizabeth in population, manufactories and commerce. The meeting of the Presbyterians was transferred from Port Elizabeth to Millville by common consent, because the members mainly resided there. The church was erected at Millville in 1837; the corner stone was laid by Pastor Kennedy, of Bridgeton; the building, when completed, was dedicated in 1838, by Pastor Blythe, of Woodbury. The building was enlarged in 1855.

The Presbyterian inhabitants of the town of Cedarville, members of the old mother church at or near Fairton, were anxious to organize a church at that place. A meeting of the inhabitants of Cedarville was held in the Friendship school house, January 21st, 1819, when it was resolved "that it is the sincere desire of this meeting to continue united with the Presbyterian Congregation at Fairfield." The following is a minute made at the time mentioned: "Resolved, that it is the opinion of this meeting, considering the circumstances of many of the inhabitants of this place are such as to render it almost impossible for them to attend the preaching of the Gospel in the old meeting house, that the building of a meeting house in this place is necessary for the accommodation of the inhabitants. Amos Fithian subscribed four hundred dollars, and he and Amos Westcott, and Henry Howell of Cedarville, and Shephard Gandy, of Philadelphia, were appointed to solicit donations. The question was brought to a vote of the congregation, when 43 voted for and 45 against the proposition." About the time of these propositions the old church of Fairfield had united with the new school. There was eventually a Presbyterian Church organized at Cedarville, which took place 23d of 10th month, 1839, at which time there were thirty-nine members—thirteen males and twenty-six females. The church was erected in 1839; size, 51x37 feet. The house was enlarged in 1851 by the the addition of 20 feet to its length, at an expense of $2,500. The new and elegant Presbyterian Church in West Bridgeton, was erected in 1869, its dimensions being 100 feet in length by 53 feet in width, with a spire 162 feet high. The material was light Chester stone, with Trenton brown stone trimmings; cost of the building about $45,000. Samuel Sloan was the architect.

I shall now confine my remarks to the different religious organizations located within Fenwick's Colony.

I visited a short time since, in company with two neighbors, together with some of our friends in that section of the country, the old Fairfield grave-yard. It is a romantic place located on the banks of the Cohansey. To all appearances, (and the dates on the tombstones confirm it,) it has not been used as a burying place for nearly a century. A forest of trees, consisting of upland cedars and a variety of oaks, has overgrown the ancient grave-yard. There was one ancient member of the olden times still standing, a species of the oak, near the middle of the yard, which to all appearance has withstood the wintry blast for more than two centuries, and other trees of the same kind have taken root and grown to be large trees within the last century. They bid fair, ere long, to equal in size the venerable parent of the ground. There was one that we noticed in particular, on the grave of Daniel Parvin, who died in 1772, had grown to the size of nearly two feet in diameter, and in proportion in height. There was some of the early emigrants who attained a great longevity. Lulin Preston, as inscribed on the tombstone, departed this life in 1752, aged ninety-two years; and several others, we noticed by their tombstones, arrived at the age of four-score years. To me it was a solemn and interesting visit, when I reflected that here in this place the first emigrants lie buried, most of whom are the sons and daughters of New England, and here they will remain forever, their mortal bodies mouldering with the mother earth of their adopted country.

EPISCOPAL SOCIETIES.

At the first settlement of the town of New Salem, or soon afterwards, there were a number of persons who were members of the Church of England. The Vining family, Alexander Grant, James Rolph, George Trenchard, Benjamin Vining, James Sherron, and the Dunlap family were among the first families of Episcopalians. They probably held meetings in private houses prior to the year 1722, when they organized a church under the name of the St. John's Episcopal Church, of Salem. It was the second religious society in the town of New Salem, the Society of Friends being organized forty-six years previous. The following account of St. John's Church, Salem, is taken from Humphrey's History of the Society for propagating the Gospel in foreign parts. "The inhabitants of Salem wrote a
" very earnest letter to the Society, desiring that they might
" have a missionary settled among them. The Rev. Mr. Hol-
" brook was sent there in 1722. As soon as he came among
" them, the people, though generally poor, contributed very
" freely toward raising a neat brick church. They made appli-
" cation to the Church people of Philadelphia for assistance,
" and received considerable contributions from them. Holbrook
" soon after acquainted the Society that many of the inhabitants
" led more Christian lives; eight young men and women had
" desired and received baptism, and a considerable number of
" children had been baptized. That in the discharge of all parts
" of his ministerial office, he had the satisfaction of finding the
" people seriously disposed, and the number of church members
" daily increasing."

It is probable that a temporary church was built of logs, on the same lot of ground where the present church stands. In 4th month, 1728, Samuel Fenwick Hedge deeded the Society one acre of ground on the south side of Bridge street (now Market) fronting 165 feet on the said street and 264 feet in depth. The Society allowed £10 worth of books to each missionary for a library, and £5 worth of small tracts to be distributed among the parishoners. The missionaries at Salem received £60 annually. In the proceedings of the Society from 2d month, 1722, to 2d month, 1723, it is mentioned that gratuities had been given to the two Swedish ministers, Hesselus and Lidenius, for supplying the churches in Salem, New Jersey, and Apoquinomy in Pennsylvania, now Delaware.

During the year from 2d month, 1726, to 2d month 1727, Holbrook reported fourteen communicants. He had baptized one man and two women, all Quakers, also seven children and one negro woman. The ensuing year, he reported that the church was so far finished, they had met in it since the 24th of 6th month, 1728, since which time his congregation had considerably increased. Rev. Howard is stated to have been the Society missionary at Salem, in 1st month, 1725; he continued here until the year 1733, when William Pierson was appointed to fill his station. His letter, dated August 6th, 1734, informs the Society that he arrived at Salem the 30th of 1st month, and that the people belonging to the church received him with joy, and continued to express much kindness and respect for him, and great gratitude to the Society for taking them under its care; that he had commonly a congregation of a hundred on Sunday, and on some occasions hath had upwards of two hundred. In his letter of 7th of 11th month, 1737, he wrote "that he was encouraged by a more regular, orderly attendance of the people at divine service than formerly, and by an increase of communicants. The people of Salem, generally, were very ignorant, especially in regard to the sacraments, and not only neglected them but held them in great contempt, through a deep tincture of Quakerism." His name does not appear after 1747, which was about the time of his death. His remains, together with his wife and two children, lie in St. John's Episcopal Church yard. 2d month, 1748 and 1749, a person by the name of Thompson was appointed missionary at Salem, but removed the succeeding year to Chester, Pennsylvania. The Rev. Eric Umander, a Swedish Missionary, pastor of Swedesborough and Penns Neck churches, preached occasionally in St. John's Church, at Salem. This church did not again enjoy the regular services of a clergyman until the year 1792. It was so seriously damaged during the Revolutionary war, by the English troops, as to unfit it for public worship. The Episcopal Church and a house on Yorke street seem to have been the two principal houses where the British troops quartered during their stay in the town of Salem in 1778. By tradition the officers occupied those buildings during the year 1792 and part of the following year. John Gray officiated at Salem in connection with St. George's in Penns Neck. Some time after the Revolution the Legislature was petitioned to allow the members of St. John's Church, in connection with the Salem Academy, to raise by lottery the sum of $300 for its repair, giving as a reason for the request, the injury which had been done to the building by the enemy in 1778. The petition was signed by Thomas Sinnickson, William Parrot, Samuel Dick, Jacob Hufty, Richard Burchan, Edmund Weatherby, and Robert Johnson, but what was its fate was not recorded. The report of the missionary in 1813 was that the old church had been enlarged and handsomely repaired. In appendix to the journal of the convention for the year 1817, it is mentioned that St. John Church, Salem, had within a short time revived and considerably improved, and that in connection with St. George's, in Penns Neck, it enjoyed the ministration of the pastor formerly of Mount Holly—name not given.

The following is an extract of a discourse of Bishop Crocs, 1821 : "This ancient and respectable town, and these hallowed "walls, in which we have now for the first time assembled, con"stitute one, among many proofs, not only of its revival, but of "its increasing prosperity. Not fourteen years ago this temple "was in absolute ruins, and had been so for a long time previ"ously. The sparrow had literally found here a house, and the "swallow an undisturbed nest. The parish had been destitute "of a minister for at least sixty years, with the exception of a "short period about thirty-three years since, and the congrega"tion was on the point of expiring. Yet in this apparently "hopeless state God was pleased to put it into the hearts of a "few zealous Episcopalians to attempt its recovery, and they "happily succeeded. The church was enlarged and completely "repaired, a regular congregation organized, and within the last "six years they have had almost uninterruptedly the services of "a minister."

During the ministration of Henry M. Mason the members of the church decided upon erecting a new church edifice, and the corner stone was laid in 1836 by Bishop Doane; Henry M. Mason, the rector; Abbercrombe, of Christ Church, Philadelphia; McCraskey, at the present time Bishop of Michigan; and Rector J. L. Wirt, of Swedesboro. The church edifice is a large one, built of stone, and stands on the site of the old one, erected in 1728. It is the most substantial church building in Salem, and is much admired for its architectural appearance. It was finished in 1838, and was dedicated about the 5th of 2d month, the same year. The sermon was delivered on the occasion by the eminent divine, Edward G. Prescott, who was the Rector of the church at that time. The Wardens at that time were Thomas Sinnickson, Daniel Garrison; the Vestry, Richard P. Thompson, Jacob W. Mulford, James M. Hannah, Benjamin Acton, Joseph Kille, Thomas Rowan, John Sinnickson, David B. Smith, and Oliver B. Stoughton. For a number of years after the Revolutionary war there were no meetings held at St. John's Church. During that time I presume the most zealous among them attended St. George's, at Penn's Neck.

The following is a list of the missionaries and rectors of St. John's Church since 1722: The Swedish missionaries were Hesselius and Lindenius, 1723-4. In 1725 the rector was Howard, who remained until 1733. From that year until 1748 John Pierson was rector. The church was occasionally visited by Eric Anader in 1749; a short time in 1749-50 by John Craig. The church records appear to have been lost or were destroyed in the old church by the British troops. In 1817 the pastor of St. Andrew's Church, Mount Holly, occasionally visited St. John's Church. From 1820 to 1823 Richard F. Cadle was the pastor; from 1823 to 1829, Christian F. Cadle; from 1829 to 1837, Henry M. Mason; from 1837 to 1844, Edward G. Prescott; from 1844 to 1848, William B. Otis; from 1848 to 1853, John S. Kidney; from 1853 to 1858, A. B. Patterson; from 1858 to 1867, Thomas F. Billop; from 1867 to 1871, William A. Holbrook; from that date to the present time, George W. Timlow.

In the address referred to in the preceding statement as having been sent by some of the inhabitants of Salem to the Society for the propogation of the Gospel in foreign parts, after saying "That in the good Providence of God they had been "enabled to obtain a moderate supply of their temporal wants, "they depict in very earnest language their utter spiritual des- "titution, never having had any one to dispense to them the "ordinances of religion: the very name of it had almost died out "among them. Their condition, they say, is truly deplorable, "and deserving of Christian compassion, and in moving terms "they entreat the Society to send them some reverend clergy- "man, who may preach to them the truths of the Gospel, and "recover them out of the spiritual ignorance and corruption "in which they have fallen. To such a one they promise en- "couragement to the extent of their ability, and all due respect "to his office, instructions and person."

Many of the members of the Episcopal church of Salem have been conspicuous citizens in civil affairs in this section of country. James Rolph died about 1731, and many of his descendants have been useful members of society. Alexander Grant resided on Market street, and, I believe, he died about 1730. Although I have not any knowledge that he left any sons, yet his descendants are numerous at this day. His daughter, Ann Grant, married Samuel Fenwick Hedge, and their children were Samuel and Rebecca Hedge. The former married the daughter of Joseph Woodnutt, and their children, Samuel, Joseph and Rebecca, during their lives adhered to the Society of Friends, but the greater number of Rebecca Hedge Thompson's children and grandchildren attached themselves to the Episcopal Church. Rebecca, the daughter of Samuel Fenwick Hedge, married Giles Smith, of Mannington, who was a Friend, and his children likewise. Ann Grant's second husband was Nicholas Gibbon. Their children were Nicholas, Grant and Jane Gibbon, who, together with their mother, soon after the death of their father, left Greenwich and removed to Salem. They were all members of the Episcopal Church. Nicholas Gibbon died in 1758, and his widow, Ann Gibbon, in 1760, and both lie in the Episcopal grave-yard. Grant Gibbon died in 1776, aged 41 years. Jane Gibbon married Robert Johnson, Sr., and was the mother of the late Robert G. Johnson. George Trenchard, Sr., was one of the first members of the Episcopal Church at Salem. He died 22d of 9th month, 1728, and his son, George Trenchard, was one of the best educated men in this section. At that time he owned a large quantity of land in Monmouth Precinct, was an assessor for the precinct several years, and was a surveyor. His wife was a Sinnickson. I think he resided in Penn's Neck the latter part of his days. The Coleman family were among the first families of that church. Dr. Samuel Dick was also an active member of the church, and he took an active part in public affairs at the time of the Revolution. Andrew Yorke and his wife Eleanor were also distinguished members. Andrew died 23d of 3d month, 1794, and his wife in 1802. They left children, and most of their descendants adhere to the religious profession of their parents. William and Richard Parrott were members of the Episcopal Church at Salem. The late John B. Tuft's ancestors were among the first members of the church, as were also Ebenezer Howell and his sister Clarissa. The Sinnickson family formerly belonged to the Swedes' Church in Penn's Neck, but for nearly a century they have been the leading members of the Episcopal Church. Dr. Benjamin Archer was a descendant of one of the oldest Swedish families that settled at Swedesboro, as early as

1638 or 1640. He was born in 1775, and died in 1845. Soon after he located at Salem he married Rachel, the daughter of Thomas and Rebecca Hedge Thompson. They left one son, Fenwick Archer, who is a lineal descendant of John Fenwick, being of the seventh generation.

The annual meeting of the convention of the Protestant Episcopal Church in the Diocese of New Jersey was held at Salem 27th of 5th month, 1826. The Bishop, and several of the clergy and of the lay deputies, assembled in St. John's Church at 11 A. M. Morning prayer was read by Matthew Matthews, and a sermon preached by the Rev. John Croes, Jr. The Bishop then admitted to the Holy Order of Priests Christian F. Cruce, Rector-elect of that church. After the termination of the religious exercises, the Bishop took the chair, and appointed Dr. Wharton and Robert Boggs, Esq., a committee to examine the testimonials of their appointment, which should be presented by the lay deputies, and report the number of churches duly represented. The committee on examination made a report that deputies were present from 11 churches, and the lay deputies representing St. John's Church were Dr. Hedge Thompson, Dr. Thomas Rowan, Dr. Benjamin Archer, William N. Jeffries and James Kinsey; St. George's Church, Penns Neck—Aaron Wright and John Jaquett.

Hedge Thompson, the only son of Thomas and Rebecca H. Thompson, was educated a physician, and practiced several years in his native town and surrounding country with considerable success. His calling, it appears, was not congenial to his health, and before he was middle aged, having acquired a competency, he, in a great degree, abandoned his professional practice, and in some measure turned his attention to politics, but was never considered an ardent politician. He was subsequently elected to represent this District in Congress. His wife was Mary Ann, daughter of Richard Parrot, by whom he had five children—Richard P., Thomas, Dr. Joseph Hedge, Mary and Rebecca H. Thompson. Most of those children, like their parents, are members of the Episcopal Church. Hedge Thompson, their father, was the great-grandson of Samuel Fenwick and Ann Grant Hedge, and the lineal descendant of the sixth generation of John Fenwick, and the fifth from Andrew Thompson, of Elsinborough.

Jacob Hufty, another prominent member of St. John's Episcopal Church, was one that is commonly called a self-made man, he belonging to the working class of society. He inherited a good physical constitution, and his intellect was above mediocrity. In early life he learned the blacksmithing trade, and followed it for a number of years in the town of Salem. He eventually became an ardent politician, attaching himself to what was then called the Jeffersonian Republican party, and in a few years afterward was elected Sheriff of Salem county, and subsequently was chosen by the South Jersey District a member of Congress. He was twice married; by his first wife he had two daughters,—Eliza and Sarah Hufty. Sarah married a Mr. Perry, and had children, one of whom is the wife of Mr. Charles Sinnickson, of Philadelphia. Eliza married Samuel, the son of Thomas Clement, of Elsinborough, and by him had two sons, Samuel and De W. Clinton Clement. Jacob's second wife was Rachel, daughter of John and Susanna Denn, of Mannington. She died a few years before her husband, leaving no issue.

William Parrot was also a member of the Episcopal Church. He took an active part in the Revolutionary war, and when peace was declared between the two countries he returned to his native town. Being a man of wealth, he soon after purchased a house and lot of ground on the east side of Fenwick street, on the site now occupied by Rumsey's building. The property formerly belonged to an eminent Friend, Richard Johnson, the forefather of Robert Johnson. William Parrot was also the owner of a considerable quantity of land on the south side of same street, said lands extending to the town meadow. In his time, the street now known as Walnut went by the name of Margaret's Lane, and it extended through the entire length of his property. William in his old age married Clarissa Howell, sister of Dr. Ebenezer Howell, who was a young woman of superior accomplishments and had a good intellect. He died not many years after that event, leaving no issue. His widow afterwards married Edward Burroughs; they had one daughter—Clarissa Burroughs. Her second husband died a few years after they were married, and their daughter Clarissa died a young woman. Her mother survived her for many years, and lived to the advanced age of ninety-one years.

It is a singular occurrence that there have been more Congressmen elected from the members of St. John's Episcopal Church than any other church in South Jersey. Thomas Sinnickson, son of Andrew Sinnickson, of Penns Neck, was the first; Jacob Hufty, Hedge Thompson, Daniel Garrison, the late Judge Thomas Sinnickson, Joseph Kille, Thomas Jones Yorke, have since been members, and Clement Hall Sinnickson has recently been elected to the forty-fourth Congress.

At what time the Swedes Church in Penns Neck was organized remains in doubt. For a number of years the inhabitants of New Sweden, on the eastern side of the Delaware river, belonged to the Swedes Church located near the mouth of Christiana Creek, on the western shore of said river. The prominent Swedish families in this county at that period were the Neilsons. Joansons, Sinakers, Ericksons, Hendricks, Yearnis', and several others. There were some French Protestants, also, residing in that section of country; Jaquetts, and several other families. Some historians write that Swedes Church was erected on the site where the present Episcopal Church in Penns Neck is located, as early as 1714, and the ground was deeded to them by Hans Jaquett. The Swedes were Lutherans. It can readily be perceived that the French Huguenots and the Swede inhabitants could unite together in divine worship. In 1742 the Church was duly organized as an Episcopal Church, by the name of St. George's Episcopal Church, of Penns Neck. The congregation at one time was large; at the present time there are but few members belonging to it. Andreas Sandal being Provost, appointed Abraham Lidenius as the first pastor over this church, in 1714. He continued in that capacity until 1724, then Petrus Tanburg and Andreas Windouswa divided their services between the church of Penns Neck and the Swedes' church at Baccoon, as Swedesboro was then called. The Episcopal church at Greenwich was erected in 1728 or 1729, by Nicholas and Grant Gibbon; they were brothers. The house was consecrated by Phineas Bond, a clergyman from New Castle, and was named St. Stevens Church. The Gibbon family contracted with Pearson, the clergyman of St. John's Church, Salem, to officiate in their church for them as often as he could be spared from his church at Salem. The Episcopalians in a few years dwindled away. Their house of worship has been removed for many years; a few tombstones, still standing, mark the spot near where the church formerly stood.

METHODIST SOCIETIES.

The spirit of religious reformation emanated from John and Charles Wesley, the eminent Christian reformers. It appears by the record that the first organization took place at the City Road chapel, situated on Moorsfield, a kind of pleasure grounds where the people walked on their holidays, and the young men engaged in sports and games. The first Conference was held 25th of 6th month, 1774, in the vestry of the church. John and Charles Wesley and four other clergymen and four laymen attended, and the foundation of the Methodist Society was laid. Both of the Wesleys lived to the advanced age of four-score years or more. Charles had been sickly from his youth, yet his active intellect had accomplished labors scarcely inferior to those of his brother. It has been said his sermons were always attractive to his audience, and his plaintive hymns stirred the deepest feelings of his contemporaries, and are still numbered among the most popular of modern compositions. It is further stated that he lived in self-chosen poverty, and when he died, at the age of eighty years, he left nothing to pay for a modest funeral. He was buried at the expense of a few of his personal friends. The loss of his brother warned John Wesley that he too could not long hope to remain behind to guide his faithful followers, but he still preached with animation at the age of eighty-four, but at eighty-six he admitted the weight of years; his eyes, he remarked, were dim, his voice faint, but he traveled almost to the last; and was followed by the throngs who never deserted him. In the spring of 1791 he was brought to his house in City Road, stricken with a fever, and on the 2d of 3d month he died. Thus passed away one of the greatest men that England ever raised. He desired no pomp at his funeral, but only the tears of those who loved him.

With the death of its founder the opponents of the new reform foretold that it must soon pass away, yet the Wesleys had left behind them a throng of disciples of various powers and attainments whose zeal upheld the principles they had inculcated, and whose laborious lives enforced the growth of

Methodism. Of the most eminent for learning and virtuous resolution was Adam Clark, a man who was never idle, whose very amusements, his son wrote, were instructive. History tells us that he studied the Septuagenet and mastered the rarest niceties of the Hebrew while on horseback, book in hand, riding from place to place, preaching almost incessantly. He was sometimes assailed by gangs of angry smugglers in Guernsey, or frozen with the cold, and worn with fatigue, shivered in a lonely cabin as he pressed on in his studies. He composed, in the midst of his active labors as an ardent preacher, a "Commentary on the Bible," which is considered the most accurate, learned and extensive known to any tongue, a work that is acknowledged a wonder of English intellect, and fit to stand not far from "Gibbons' History of the downfall of Rome." He was at the same time employed by the English government in arranging its state papers, and enlarging the knowledge of its own history. An eminent writer said such a man could scarcely fail to bear on the banner of the Wesleyan reform, and was indeed the mental offspring, the peculiar product of the care and the foresight of John Wesley. Adam Clark was born in rude, yet honest poverty, in Ireland. He said on one occasion that he should hate his scoundrel heart if he did not love all mankind. Hence the Methodist Society began at once to teach a liberal humanity.

In that bold crusade against human slavery that agitated all England at the beginning of the present century, it is not improbable, but for the strenuous efforts of the prominent members of Friends and Methodist Societies, and the support and influence they gave, that Wilberforce, Brougham and Clarkson might have failed to reach the goal for which they toiled.

It has been said that the most pleasing preachers at the City Road Chapel, after the death of Wesley, was Joseph Benson, and probably he was one of the greatest pulpit orators that ever belonged to the Methodist Society. His biographer states he was learned, amiable, modest, and graceful in elocution, and never failed to draw large audiences, and to touch the higher impulses of his hearers. There were also among the early Methodists a noble band of women, the most conspicuous among them being Susanna Wesley, the mother of John and Charles Wesley, and Mary, the wife of Adam Clark. Their names should be perpetuated to the latest posterity for their self-sacrificing deeds in behalf of humanity. In this short sketch I think it would be right to refer to Thomas Clark, who was sent over to organize the Methodist Church in America, and who was the first Superintendent or Bishop in this country. He was represented to have been small in stature, yet ardent and active above his contemporaries. In early life he was touched by Methodism, and became the chosen companion of Wesley in his most difficult labors, and gave his fortune, talents, and his life to the cause of missions. But in his boundless benevolence he longed chiefly to extend the blessings of faith and culture to the slaves of the West Indies, the people of Africa, and the countless worshippers of idols in Hindostan; he could be content with nothing less than the consolation of the most miserable, or the elevation of the most degraded of his race, and while the hideous traffic in the bodies and souls of men was at its height, while men were making profit from buying and selling men, human nature is at least redeemed from total infamy by the God-like labors of Thomas Clark. There were a large number of negro slaves converted through his influence. He saw Ethiopia "stretching out her hands," and he was resolute enough to answer her cry. It has been stated on good authority that John Early, a native of Ireland, emigrated to this country in 1764, and located near what was afterwards known as Union church, in Gloucester county, he being the first Methodist in New Jersey. Previous to 1770 Early had embraced the doctrines of the Gospel as presented by John Wesley.

Methodism, in its ecclesiastical, owes its origin in New Jersey to Captain Thomas Webb, who was a local preacher and officer in the British army. Being stationed at Burlington, on duty, in 1770, he formed a class 14th of the 12th month, same year, and appointed Joseph Toy, a native of New Jersey, its leader. A short time previous to this Richard Boardman and Joseph Pilmoor came from England, and landed at Gloucester Point, in October, 1769; they were the first missionaries in America. The first house of worship of the sect was built in Greenwich township, Gloucester county, in 1770: it was called Greenwich Chapel, and Edward Evans was the first minister. He died after a few month's service, and Joseph Pilmoor, one of the first missionaries, at that period a resident of the city of Philadelphia, preached his funeral sermon, that was on the 15th of 10th month, 1771. When I take into consideration the early habits of Benjamin Abbott, the father of Methodism in Salem county, he certainly was one of the most remarkable men of his generation. He married in early life, and located himself in Pittsgrove township; his wife was a member of the Presbyterian church of that place, and he occasionally went with her to church. In the fall of 1772, in the fortieth year of his age, he became converted under the preaching of Abraham Whiteworth. At that time he was a hired laborer for Benjamin Vanmeter, a prominent farmer in that neighborhood, and, according to tradition, Benjamin employed him solely on account of his muscular strength, for otherwise he was very objectionable, being intemperate, and then so very quarrelsome. There lived in the same neighborhood John Murphy, a member of the Presbyterian Church, he being a man of considerable intellect and extensive reading, whose house appears to have been a home for the Methodist itinerants, and among the first preaching places of the county. After a time he became a member of the Society, quite contrary to the wishes of his former friends. At his house was formed the first Methodist Society in this county; on the same site there was erected, a few years since, a good substantial brick building, which is called on the Salem circuit plan Friendship church, Benjamin Abbott being the first member. John Murphy was one of his neighbors, and it was returning from a visit to Murphy's that Abbott's wife was converted. Methodism was introduced in the town of Salem about the year 1774. Daniel Ruff visited the town and preached in the Court House. Some two or three years after Abbott's conversion he left Pittsgrove and located himself and family in Mannington township. There was a Methodist society formed at Quinton's Bridge, at the house of Benjamin Weatherby; among the members were Henry Firth and John McCloskey; the latter became a distinguished preacher, and filled several important appointments, including the cities of New York, Philadelphia and Baltimore, and also that of Presiding Elder. In the year 1784, the first Methodist church was built in the town of Salem; Henry Firth and Benjamin Abbott and a few others were the principal members. The first named was instrumental (he having the most means) in building the church on a lot that he purchased on Margaret's lane, now known as Walnut street. They asked assistance from the members of other religious denominations, particularly of the Society of Friends. The matter was discussed in their Quarterly Meeting, some Friends objecting to contribute, believing, by so doing, it would be a violation of the testimony that the Society always held against aiding hireling ministry. It was stated in the meeting that the preachers of the new sect only received a passing support for their services, and after a general expression of opinion it was decided by the Society that such of their members as felt free to contribute might do so, which they accordingly did. After the meeting house was completed, Benjamin Abbott was baptized in the new church.

Although he had been preaching for twelve years, in consequence of the ministry having not been ordained he had not been baptized. He did not reside long in Mannington before he went to Lower Penns Neck to live, and about that time there was a Methodist society organized in that township; at the present it is a large congregation. The most reliable account that is left on record of Abbott is that his speaking was of a declamatory kind, calculated to arouse his audience. He possessed an uncommon degree of zeal, and if he had the learning of the Wesleys, Clark or Benson, it is probable he would have been an uncommon pulpit orator. He died on the 14th of August, 1796, aged 64 years, and was buried on the third day following, in the Methodist burial ground in Salem.

Henry Firth, one of the first Methodists in this county, was of a Quaker parentage. His great ancestor, John Firth, settled in the neighborhood of Salem as early as 1707, and had several children. Henry Firth's mother was the daughter of Samuel Stubbins, he having but one son, Henry Stubbins, who inherited his father's estate in Elsinborough, and married, in 1737, Rebecca Daniels, daughter of James Daniels, Sr. They had no issue, and Henry Stubbins Firth became the adopted son of his uncle, and eventually the owner, by will, of all the real estate that belonged to Henry Stubbins, in the township of Elsinborough. His wife was Sarah, the daughter of Charles and Sarah Bassett Fogg, of Alloways Creek. Henry subsequently purchased the Preston Carpenter property in Mannington, and perhaps that purchase, together with his liberality to the new religious sect, was the primary cause of his eventually losing his estate, and becoming unable to pay his just debts. John Wistar, whose heart was always filled with the milk of human kindness, with a few other friends, interceded for Henry and his wife, and succeeded in having a tenant house and about ten or twelve acres of ground attached, set apart for them to occupy whilst they lived. Henry soon after was appointed one of the Justices of the Peace of Salem county, he being well calculated for the office. He had a large patronage, and he and his wife lived comparatively comfortable to old age. They had three children—Stubbins, Ezra and Clara Firth. These children were greatly assisted in school education by those persons that took an interest in them. John Wistar soon discovered that the eldest son, Stubbins, possessed more than common abilities, and he accordingly gave him a liberal education at his own expense. The celebrated Dr. Casper Wistar, of Philadelphia, by the solicitations of his brother John, gave him studies, and soon after he graduated he removed to Charleston, South Carolina, where, in a short time, he had an extensive practice, and married a young lady of wealth, belonging to the old aristocratic families of that city. Stubbins died when he was about middle aged, without issue. John Firth, a younger brother of Henry, also left the religious sect of which he was born a member, and became a member of the Methodist Church. He married in 1793, Margaret Taber Sparks, of the county of Gloucester, in which place I think he resided mostly the remainder of his life. He was the author of the life of Benjamin Abbott.

In 1788 the name of the circuit was changed from West Jersey circuit to Salem circuit; James O. Cromwell was appointed elder, and Joseph Cromwell, Nathaniel B. Mills, and John Cooper appointed to the circuit. About the year 1800, or a short time prior, the Salem church was largely increased in numbers. Among those new converts were three brothers, Jacob, William and Maskell Mulford; they came to Salem from Greenwich, Cumberland county. Their parents were members of the Presbyterian church of that place; their mother's name was Maskell. That family were among the first Presbyterians that emigrated to Fenwick Colony from New England, as early as 1700. William, the second son, married the daughter of Elijah Cattell, who was the son of William Cattell, and Ann, his wife, born 27th of 7th month, 1751. He took an active part in the Revolutionary war, by which he lost his membership in the Society of Friends. He was a merchant, and his place of business was at the corner of Market and Broadway streets. After the death of E. Cattell, the property was sold to Isaac Moss, and he conveyed it to Thomas Jones.

The Methodist congregation in Salem increased rapidly, so much so that the Society found that the old frame building on Walnut street was not large enough to accommodate them, and in 1826 they concluded to erect a brick meeting house, which was completed and dedicated in 1838. Abraham Owen was at the time pastor of the church; since then there have been several eminent clergymen stationed there; among them was Jefferson Lewis, who was considered more than an ordinary pulpit speaker. The present popular pastor, Willis Reeves, I have been informed, attracts large audiences; so much so that the Society has it in in contemplation to enlarge the present house. The church has about 334 members. In 1858 there was a number of the congregation, who belonged to the old church, believing it would be an advantage to the Society to have two separate congregations, resolved to build another church. Accordingly 114 members purchased a lot on Broadway street at a cost of $4,000, and erected a large brick church there in 1859, at a cost of $18,000, size 55x80 feet. At the time of the organization of the new church, the following persons named were the trustees: James Newell, Benjamin Lloyd, Ebenezer Dunn, John C. Dunn, Robert Newell, and T. V. F. Rusling. The two first named trustees, however, soon returned to the Walnut street meeting. The different ministers that have been stationed at the Broadway church since it was established were William H. Jeffery, two years; R. H. Chalker, two years; C. E. Hill, two years; Caleb Fleming, two years; J. S. Heisler, three years; G. K. Morris, three years; William H. Pearne, two years. The present pastor is C. W. Heisley. There are about 300 members belonging to the church at the present time.

There are now more than twenty Methodist congregations within Fenwick Colony. Although their first religious organization in this country being not much over one hundred years old, they are one of the most numerous Protestant sects in the United States. It must be admitted by every unprejudiced mind that they, in a society capacity, have done great good in promulgating moral and religious sentiments among mankind.

AFRICAN METHODIST SOCIETY.

The African Methodist Church in Salem was organized the latter part of the last century on Fenwick street. The late Robert G. Johnson deeded a lot of ground for the purpose, for their meeting house, and grave-yard. The Society purchased the old frame house that was formerly used as a Baptist Church at Mill Hollow, and moved it on Johnson's lot. It was used as a place of worship until within a few years. It is now used as a school house for colored children, and the Wesleyan Society of colored have erected a brick church in its stead. About 1820, there was a division among the colored Methodists in the town of Salem. Richard Allen, a colored preacher from Philadelphia, contended the colored church should be governed by Bishops of their own race. By far the greatest number that belonged to the Salem church adhered to his principles of church government, and withdrew, and erected a meeting house for themselves. Consequently there are ten African churches in the city of Salem. There is one at Marshallville, in the township of Mannington, one in the township of Quinton, and one at Bushtown, in Pilesgrove township.

ROMAN CATHOLIC SOCIETY.

In the early part of the present century there was a considerable emigration from Germany and Ireland to Salem and Cumberland counties. The greater number of those persons who came were members of the Roman Catholic Church. In the year 1850 the Catholics organized in the city of Salem a church, calling it the St. Mary's Catholic Church. There was erected about that time, on Oak street, a large church building. It was built of stone. The Catholic congregation at this time is considered one of the largest in the city. Father Pattle is their priest. It is generally considered that he exerts a moral and religious influence over his large congregation.

TOWNSHIPS.

John Fenwick, soon after his arrival, in 1675, wrote a code of laws for the government of his colony, being republican in form, and laid out a town which he called Salem, on a point of land bounded on the east by a tributary of Salem creek, which he called Fenwick creek, on the south by Amblebury creek. The number of acres, including the town marsh, was about 1700. His plan seems to have been for his colony to be governed by a Legislative body, distinct and separate from the other inhabitants of West Jersey. But the most eminent men that resided within the Salem tenth, and large owners within the same, opposed his plan in that particular. They insisted that the inhabitants of the whole of West Jersey should be governed by one Legislative body. The result of their disagreement was that the inhabitants of the infant colony were governed by the different justices of the peace, created by the proprietor, and located in the different precincts of the county until 1683. At that time William Penn, being one of Edward Billings' trustees, took a great interest in the affairs of the people of the whole of West Jersey, and in 1682 he purchased the whole of John Fenwick's right in the Salem tenth, the proprietor reserving 150,000 acres for himself and heirs. In the spring of 1683 there was an election held for the first time in this section of Jersey, to elect three members to the Legislature of West Jersey, to meet at the town of Burlington the following winter. John Fenwick was elected as one of the members, but he died the same fall before the time of the meeting of the Assembly.

The principal and leading inhabitants of the town of Salem, from 1675 to 1770, were James Nevell, Thomas Killingsworth, Hippolite Lefever, John Pledger, Edward Wade, Edward Bradway, Richard Johnson, William Hall, Alexander Grant, James Rolph, Benjamin Acton, Samuel Hedge, Jr., and his son, Samuel Hedge, 3d, Robert Rumsey, John Goodwin, Robert Conarroe, Henry Wilkinson, James Champney, John Adams, John Fenwick, the proprietor, Edward Keasbey and John Test. The latter had a son, John Test, who resided in Pilesgrove; also a son, Francis Test, who married and settled on the south side of Cohansey; he had nine children. The present Joseph Test, of Salem, is a lineal descendant of Francis Test, Jr. Thomas Hill was a leading and influential man in the town of Salem in the fore part of the last century.

The precinct of Elsinboro, although the smallest in the colony, by the original survey contained only 800 acres. It was first called Elsborg, after the fort built by the Swedes about 1640. Elsinboro is a historical precinct, for in that place the first English settlement was made by a colony from New Haven, Connecticut, as early as 1640. It was not a permanent settlement, for in 1642 they all returned to New England again. The township is also noted for having some of the most conspicuous men in the first settlement of the colony that purchased lands and resided within its boundaries; such men as Samuel Nicholson and his two sons, Samuel and Abel Nicholson, John Smith of Amblebury; Robert Windham and his son-in-law, Richard Darkin; John Mason and his son Thomas Mason; John, Andrew and Thomas Thompson; Rudoc Morris, and his three sons, Joseph, Lewis and David Morris; Isaac Smart and his son, Nathan Smart; George Abbott and his two sons, George and Samuel Abbott; Samuel Stubbins and his son, Henry, and John Firth. In the third generation there was Samuel Nicholson, son of Abel Nicholson, who was an eminent philanthropist in his generation. Perhaps he did as much or more than any other person of his time towards assisting the poor in Salem county. As early as 1760, Col. Benjamin Holme, who is well known in the history of this county, became a resident of Elsinboro, and died there in old age, full of honors; and his great-grandchildren are the owners of the patrimonial estate, and reside thereon. As early as 1700 William Hancock, the son of the emigrant, purchased a large tract of land in Elsinboro, and, with his son, Thomas, and grandsons, William and Thomas Hancock, held a large influence in that place.

Monmouth precinct composed at the present time three townships—Alloways, Quinton and Upper Alloways Creek, and originally contained 64,000 acres. In the year 1760 an act was passed by the New Jersey Legislature giving the inhabitants of Alloways Creek power to divide the township. Benjamin Thompson, in the upper district; John Stewart, of the lower; and Elnathan Davis, of Cumberland, were appointed commissioners; the latter also was the surveyor. They set off 34,000 acres to the upper district, and it was called Upper Alloways Creek, and leaving 30,000 acres to the lower portion, it retaining the original name, Alloways Creek. A few years since there was an act passed by the Legislature to set off another township from the territory of Upper Alloways Creek, which is called Quinton, to commemorate Tobias Quinton, who was one of the first emigrants that located a large tract of land where the village of Quinton is situated. The descendants of the first and the most conspicuous men that first resided in the ancient Monmouth District became historical characters: Christopher White, Samuel Wade, Neal Daniels, William Hancock and his son, John, John Hancock, cousin of William, Nathaniel Chambless, his son Nathaniel, William Tyler and his son, William, Charles Oakford, William Bradway, son of Edward Bradway, of Salem, John Malstaff, James Denn and his son, John Maddox Denn, Joseph Ware and his son, Joseph, George Trenchard 1st, George Deacon, who removed to Burlington county in 1690, (where some of his descendants are still living,) Jonathan Smith, the son of John Smith, of Almsbury, Tobias Quinton, Daniel Smith, son of John Smith, William Willis, William Penton, John Holme, William Thompson, the eldest son of Andrew Thompson, William's four sons—Joseph, William, Samuel C. and Benjamin Thompson, Joseph Fogg and his three sons—Joseph, Daniel and Samuel Fogg, William Oakford, Jeremiah Powell and his two sons—Jeremiah and Samuel. John Maddox, the son of Ralph Maddox, was born near London, in 1631, removed to the city of London, in 1669, and resided in the parish of St. Sepulchre. His business was that of a tallow chandler. He married Elizabeth Durham, widow of Joseph Durham, a citizen of London. John and his wife, Elizabeth Maddox, and their daughter, Elizabeth, with two or three servants and a number of other passengers, sailed from London in the ship Surrey, Steven Nichols, Captain, on the 24th of 6th month, 1678, for the province of West New Jersey. John and his family resided a short time in Salem. In 1680 he purchased of Isabella Hancock, a widow of William Hancock, 500 acres of land on the south side of Monmouth river. Their daughter, Elizabeth Maddox, married James Denn; they had two children—Margaret Denn, born 29th of the 4th month, 1689, and John Maddox Denn, born 1693. John Maddox, in 1700, sold all his real estate in the Monmouth precinct to Jeremiah Powell and John Hancock. (The latter was the son-in-law of Nathaniel Chambless, Sr.) It appears by the records that James Maddox and Elizabeth, his wife, had only one child, Elizabeth Denn. James Maddox died at Alloways Creek, in 1701; his will was executed in the year 1700.

The precinct of Mannington contains, by the original survey,

28,000 acres. It appears to have been the favorite township of the proprietor. In Upper Mannington he had his country seat, called Fenwick's Grove, which contained 6000 acres. Adjoining the said tract on the south, Fenwick had two thousand acres laid off to his favorite daughter, Annie Fenwick, and her husband, Samuel Hedge; it was called, for several generations, Hedgefield.

John Pledger and his wife, Elizabeth, were married in 1672; they lived in Portsmouth, Southampshire; he was a ship carpenter. They had one son born in England, Joseph Pledger, on the 4th of 6th month, 1672. Their son, John Pledger, was born in Salem, 27th of 9th month, 1680. Hypolyte Lefevre, it has been stated, was a French Huguenot. He left his native country on account of religious persecution, and went to England. He and his wife, Mary Lefevre, were residents of St. Martins in the fields of Middlesex, London. Being a man of considerable means he was known as a gentleman. He and John Pledger purchased 6,000 acres of John Fenwick in the fall of 1674. They, with their families, arrived in West New Jersey several months before the proprietor. In the summer of 1676 their lands were surveyed by Richard Noble and were located within the bounds of Mannington township. I think neither Hypolyte or John Pledger, Sr., ever resided on their large allotment, but lived and died in Salem. Hypolyte and his wife, Mary Lefevre, had one son, Hypolyte, who married Hannah Carll, of Philadelphia. Hypolite, the elder, died previous to 1698. The principal landholders and residents of the township of Mannington, in the latter part of the seventeenth and the fore part of the eighteenth century, were John Smith, of Smithfield, and his sons Joseph, David and Samuel, William Hall, Jr., Bartholomew Wyatt, and his son Bartholomew; James Sherron, who was killed by Hagar, his slave; John Hedge, Jr., Richard Woodnutt and his two sons, Joseph and Richard; James Whittan, Thomas Mason and his four sons, Jonathan, Samuel, Aaron and James Mason; Benjamin Cripps, John Vining, Ezekiel Peterson, Jedediah Allen, Benjamin Wyncoop, Henry Wamsley, Thomas Hackett, Edward Weatherby, Giles Smith. Samuel and Anna Fenwick Hedge resided in the township of Mannington up to 1684. After the death of their father, John Fenwick, they removed to Salem. The precinct of Pilesgrove formerly contained 87,000 acres. It derived its name from Thomas Pyle, who was a citizen and upholsterer in the city of London. He purchased 10,000 acres in said township.

Thomas Pyle probably died before 1690. I find no record of

him after that time. The Sharps were among the most conspicuous men that resided in the precinct at the first settlement. They located on 2,000 acres of land, the greater part of which was in the township of Pilesgrove, but some portions were in the township of Mannington. The Salem County Alms House farm is the part that was formerly of the Sharps; also, their family grave-yard was located in the same township, where the mortal remains of John Fenwick were buried. The Colson family were among the first inhabitants of Pilesgrove; likewise John Davis, who emigrated from Long Island with his four sons—John, Isaac, Malachi and David Davis. The latter became active and useful in civil and religious life, and was a Judge for many years in the Salem Courts. There were also the Bassetts, Lippincotts, and Dunns. Zaccheus Dunn had a large family of children. He was the son of Zaccheus and Deborah Dunn, born in Pilesgrove in 1698. The large township of Pilesgrove was divided about the time of the American revolution; there were about 27,000 acres which is now known as Pilesgrove. The new township was named by the patriots of that day Pittsgrove, in memory of William Pitt, Earl of Chatham, who advocated the rights of the colonies in the British Parliament. Among the active and influential persons in the new township were the Duboises, Newkirks, Elwells, Coombs, Johnsons, Mayhews, VanMeters, Swings and Hitchners. About 1832 there was an act passed to divide the township, which was done, one part retaining the old name, Pittsgrove, the other, Upper Pittsgrove. Penn's Neck was settled by Europeans earlier, perhaps, than any other portion of Salem county. The Finns and Swedes settled there as early as 1638 or 1640. The original survey of the township amounted to about 54,000 acres. Many of the early Swedes and Finns took deeds for the land they settled on from the Indian chiefs. When the proprietors arrived the said tracts of land were re-surveyed, and each one of the former inhabitants agreed to pay Fenwick and his heirs a certain amount annually, called quit-rents. The names of most of the Swedes and Finns were Andrew Sinaker, Fop Joanson, Gille Joanson, Mat Neilson, Abram Vanhyest, the Petersons, Engsons, Vanculans, Shonons, and others. The first English emigrant that purchased lands there of John Fenwick was Roger Pedrick, in the fall of 1674, being one thousand acres; it was surveyed to him by Richard Noble in the spring of 1676. There are a number of the descendants of R. Pedrick living in the township of Upper Penn's Neck at the present day. The said land was bounded on the east by Old Man's creek. The village of Pedrickstown stands on part of the Pedrick tract. Michael Baron was also a large landholder there; his tract contained one thousand acres in the lower district. The Adams family owned the greater portion. The sapona, in this township, not far from Salem, was Tindeldale. Richard Tindell, the surveyor-general of the province, owned and resided there, while the deputy surveyor, John Woolidge, lived in the town of Salem. The house that he built and lived in is still standing on Broadway, near the old wharf, opposite Edward Bradway's brick building.

The Jaquetts were French Hugnenots, who emigrated to West Jersey, and became large landholders in Penn's Neck. Thomas Dunn purchased land as early as 1689, and many of his descendants are residents of the township at the present time. Edward Mecum, Cornelius Copner, Thomas Lambson, Thomas Baldwin and William Hewes were among the first English emigrants that purchased lands in the upper district bordering on Old Man's creek. His great grandson, Hezekiah Hewes, was a cabinet maker and undertaker in the town of Salem as early as 1780; he continued in the business for more than twenty years. He purchased a farm in Elsinborough when he was past middle age, and went to farming. Towards the close of his life he returned to Salem, and carried on the trade again. Not being able to work much himself he employed Japhet Somers as his journeyman. It is probable that Hezekiah buried more persons in the ancient grave-yard of Friends in Salem than any other person. His wife was the daughter of Benjamin Wright, of Mannington. There were two children—Thomas and Jane Hewes. Samuel Hewes was also a descendant of Wm. Hewes. He was born in Penn's Neck, and learned the hatting business of David Smith, Sr., of Salem. After he became of age he and David Smith, the nephew of his former employer, carried on the trade near Concordville, Delaware county, Pennnsylvania. The partnership did not last long. David Smith, the uncle of David, died in a short time after they went into business together, leaving the greater part of his estate to his nephew, and consequently returned to Salem; but Samuel Hewes continued in business and was prosperous. He was one of the directors of the Bank at Chester for a number of years. He resigned his office when the afflictions that attend old age came upon him. He lived to be nearly 92 years of age. He was twice married. By his first wife he had two children—John and Sarah Ann Hewes. His second wife was Mary, the daughter of Benjamin and Mary Shourds, of this county; they had one son, Charles

Hewes. The Somers family left Egg Harbor a century or more ago. One of the brothers purchased a large farm bordering on the Delaware river, not far from Old Man's creek.

William Summerill and Tnomas Carney (of whom mention has been made before) and their descendants, were large landholders, and had great influence in the township; likewise the Philpot family. The township of Penn's Neck, a number of years ago, was divided. The lower section contains about 22,000 acres, and retains the original name, Penn's Neck. The upper district is much larger in territory and in population, and is called Upper Penn's Neck.

The territory belonging to Fenwick Colony, now Cumberland, was called in the first settlement of the county, and up to nearly the middle of the last century, North and South Cohansey precincts. That section was peopled largely by emigrants from New England, and also from East Jersey and the state of New York.

The names of some of the most prominent families that located in the North and South Cohansey precints were Obadiah Holmes, Sheppards, Ogdens, Sayres, Fithians, Moores, Bucks, Woods, Bricks, Batemans, Prestons, Whitaker, Harris, Maskell, Ewing, Swing, Mulford, Butcher, and Padgetts. Samuel Bacon, probably, was one of the first Europeans that purchased lands in the North Cohansey precincts, now known as Bacon's Neck. He purchased it of an Indian chief, and the deed is still in possession of one of the branches of the Bacon family. A considerable portion of the land is held at this time by some of Samuel's descendants, being the sixth generation. William, Joseph and John, sons of Samuel Bacon, were prominent men. John was one of the Judges of the Salem Courts for a number of years. Mark Reeves located at the town of Cohansey in 1685, and in a short time afterwards he removed to Fairfield township, where he died about 1709, leaving three sons—Charles, Mark and Joseph. The large family of Reeves, of Cumberland, Salem and Burlington counties, are the descendants of Joseph, the youngest son of Mark Reeves, Sr. I think it probable that Charles, the eldest son of Mark, died single. Mark Reeves, Jr., married and had a daughter, who subsequently married Alexander Moore; they were the grandparents of the late John Moore White, of Woodbury. There was a large conspicuous family located in the South Cohansey precinct, by the name of Alexander, in the fore part of the last century. Daniel Elmer emigrated from Connecticut, and was pastor of the first Presbyterian church, near the New England town, South Cohansey; his descendants are numerous in the county at the present day.

About 1720 Nicholas and Leonard Gibbon emigrated from England, settled at Cohansey, and took possession of a large tract of land that was conveyed to them by Francis Gibbon, their father. The tract contained 5,500 acres and was situated in three townships—Greenwich, Stoe Creek and Hopewell, as the county is divided at this time. Leonard took the eastern portion and Nicholas the part next to Greenwich.

The first Court of Records was held at the town of Salem the 17th of 9th month, 1706. The Judges were Thomas Killingworth, of Salem, and Obadiah Holmes, of Cohansey precinct. Justices—Joseph Sayres, Cohansey; Samuel Hedge, Jr., Salem; James Alexander, Cohansey; Walter Husted, Salem; Samuel Alexander, Cohansey. The Grand Jury called were Joseph Eastland, foreman; John Paine, Isaac Pierson, John Sheppard, Isaac Bonner, John Williams, Edward Mecum, Henry Corneilson, Thomas Lambson, John Swing, Samuel Fogg, James Barret, Henry Fisher and John Lackey. Sheriff, William Griffin; Micheal Hackett, under sheriff; Isaac Sharp, deputy sheriff, and Elisha Bassett, constable for Salem. In 1707 Court held at Salem had the same officers of the preceding year. The Grand Jury being called were Henry Buck, foreman; Samuel Curtis, Benjamin Bacon, Joseph Bacon, Richard Whitaker, Thomas Alderman, John Brick, Samuel Fogg, Jacob Garrison, Jeremiah Nickson, Gabriel Davis, Edward Mecum, Isaac Pierson, Mark Elger, William Thompson and Thomas Wallin. It was the law at that time for the Court to appoint overseers of the poor for the several districts of the county. The Court appointed the following named persons as overseers of the highways: For Salem—William Holoway and Samuel Hedge; Elsinborough—Abel Nicholson and Thomas Thompson; Monmouth precinct—Joseph Ware and Jonathan Smith; Mannington—Thomas Hackett and John Culver; Penn's Neck—William Neilson and Thomas Lambson; Pilesgrove—Isaac Davis and George Colson; Northern Precinct of Cohansey—John Williams and John Miller; South Cohansey Precinct—Henry Buck and Francis Alexander. Overseers of the Poor in the several precincts: Salem—Robert Rumsey and Robert Brothell; Monmouth—Nathaniel Chambless and Ephraim Allen; Elsinborough—Richard Darkin and Thomas Thompson; Penn's Neck—Jeremiah Nickson and Harris Shoval; Mannington—James Sherron and Daniel Rumsey; Pilesgrove—Jacob Sharp and Thomas Wallin; North Cohansey—Richard Butcher and Samuel Woodhouse; South Cohansey—Richard Whitaker and Thomas Sheppard.

In the year 1747 the precincts of North and South Cohansey was set off from Salem, and was called Cumberland county. It has been stated the name was given to it by Jonathan Belcher, at that time Governor of New Jersey, out of respect to the Duke of Cumberland, which decision was confirmed by an act of Assembly in 1747.

It appears it was the intention of the commissioners to divide the county of Salem into two equal parts; their first proposition was to make the mouth of Stoe creek the starting point, follow up the creek until they came to a small tributary, on which Seeley's mill pond is located, thence up to the head branches, and then by a direct course to the Gloucester county line. John Brick, Jr., at that time one of the Judges of the Salem County Courts, and a man of great influence, was desirous that his possessions should be included in the new county, and insisted that the lower branch of Stoe creek (called at this time Gravelly Run) should be the line between the two counties, which, after considerable excitement, was made the boundary, thereby giving the new county a much larger territory than Salem.

EARLY MARRIAGES.

An account of some of the early marriages in Salem, Newton and Burlington meetings: Samuel Hedge married Ann Fenwick, 1676; Abraham Strand to Parabol Nicholson, daughter of Samuel and Ann Nicholson, 1677; Thomas Leeds, of New York, to Margaret Collins, they were married at Newton in 1678; Robert Zane, of Salem, to Alice Alday, of Burlington; they were married in Burlington meeting. She was the daughter of an Indian chief. Judge Clement, in alluding to the marriage says: "It may fairly be concluded that Robert became enamored of the bronzed beauty in some of his perambulations among the natives of the soil. Perhaps some hunting expedition found him at nightfall hungry and footsore, near the hospitable wigwam of an Indian chief, where he was invited to rest and accept what the good chief set before him. With the assurance of welcome he delayed for the night, and when he noticed a daughter of his host,

> "What though the sun with ardent frown
> Had slightly tinged her cheek with brown,"

could see in her comely, and to his youthful eye an attractive person. The talk by the evening fire, when the old Chief would question him about "the story of his life," to which the dark haired damsel would listen, and with a greedy ear devour his discourse, and which gave him a chance to watch her interest in his words, and draw from her at least a look of sympathy. Perchance in the sad story of the wrongs that drove him from his home, and of those who were soon to follow, he beguiled her of her tears, and won her love." The residence of Robert Zane in Salem brought him in contact with John Fenwick. He purchased two 16 acre lots on Fenwick street, Salem, of the proprietor, and was one of the members that organized the Friends' Meeting in 1676. As as artisan he was a worker in wool, manufacturing a kind of material that bears the same name to this day, and is used for the same purpose. About 1680 he left Salem and purchased a large tract of land near the head of

Newton creek, within the Irish tenth. He was considered the pioneer of Newton Meeting, and was elected to the Legislature in 1682, and again in 1685. He sold one of his town lots in Salem in 1689, and one of his sons became the owner of the other lot, upon which the old house is still standing on Fenwick near Yorke street. Robert Zane was twice married, and had issue by both of them. One of his great-grandsons went to Ohio, a territory then, and there settled. He was the founder of Zanesville in that State. His second wife's name was Elizabeth. Robert died in 1694. 17th of the 1st month, 1679, Richard Whitaker, of Salem, married Elizabeth Adkin, of Monmouth precinct. In 1680 Thomas Fairman to Elizabeth Kinsey, at Burlington. In 1684, John Abbott to Elizabeth Nicholson, at Salem, daughter of Samuel and Ann Nicholson, of Elsinboro. Married at Salem, in 1685, Israel Harrison to Hester White, daughter of Christopher White. At Salem, George Haselwood to Margaret Butcher, widow of John Butcher, in 1681. Married, at Burlington, in 1680, Thomas Borton to Ann Borton, daughter of John Borton. In 1680, Freedom Lippincott, son of Richard, to Mary Curtis, of Burlington. At Burlington, 1681, John Woolson to Hannah Cooper, daughter of William Cooper, and sister of William Cooper at Salem. Married, at Burlington, 1682, John Snowden to Ann Barrett. Married, at Salem, John Antrim to Francis Butcher, 1682, daughter of John Butcher, the emigrant. At Burlington, Seth Smith to Mary Pancoast, in 1682; she was the daughter of John Pancoast, Sheriff of the London tenth. At Newton, 1682, William Wood, of New York, to Mary Parnell. At Salem, Lawrence Morris to Virginia Cripps. In 1685, at Burlington, William Satterwaite to Ann Bingham, late servant of Thomas Olive. At Salem, Mark Reeve to Ann Hunt, in 1686. John Shinn to Ellen Stacy; 1695, Joseph Nicholson, of Elsinboro, son of Samuel, to Hannah Wood, of Newton. 1696, at Salem, Edward Buzby, of Pennsylvania, to Susan Adams, daughter of John Adams. 1703, at Newton, Stephen Newby to Elizabeth Wood. 1702, at Newton, John Estaugh to Elizabeth Hadden. 1705, at Newton, Joseph Bates to Mercy Clement, daughter of James Clement, and sister of Sarah Hall. At Salem, 1704, John Mickell to Hannah Cooper, daughter of William and Mary Bradway. They were married at Newton. 1706, Joseph Brown, of Philadelphia, to Mary Spicer, daughter of Samuel Spicer, and sister of Jacob Spicer. They were married at Newton. At Salem, Joseph Ware Jr., to Elizabeth Walker, 1707. 1711, at Salem, Samuel Dennis to Ruth Tindell, daughter of Richard Tindell, of Penns Neck. 1714, at Burlington, John Cox to Lydia Cooper, daughter of Joseph and Lydia Cooper. 1718, at Salem, Samuel Sharp to Martha Hall, daughter of William Hall, Jr., of Mannington. 1730, at Haddonfield, Bartholomew Wyatt, Jr., of Mannington, to Elizabeth Tomlinson, daughter of Joseph Tomlinson. 1731, at Burlington, William Borton to Deborah Hedge. 1731, at Burlington, John Cripps to Mary Eves. 1732, at Salem, Philip Pedrick to Hannah Bickman. 1733, Samuel, the youngest son of George Abbott, of Elsinboro, married Hannah Foster, of Burlington county. 1734, at Burlington, Josiah White, grandson of Christopher, to Rebecca Foster, sister of Samuel Abbott's wife. 1737, John Jessup to Margaret Whitaker, grand-daughter of Richard. 1744, Solomon Lippincott to Sarah Cozzins. William Rumsey and Ruth Gave were married 17th of the 1st month, 1679. William Warner of Alloways Creek married Jane Curtes, 10th month 2d, 1680. Richard Hancock of Alloways Creek married Elizabeth Denn, sister of James Denn, November 28th, 1680. Thomas Smith, of Cohansey, married Ann Pancoast, 14th of 3d month, 1681.

ANCIENT BUILDINGS.

I think it probable that Salem county has as many or more ancient buildings standing at this time, according to her population, than any other county in West Jersey. The oldest building standing at this time is in the city of Salem. It was built by Edward Bradway in 1691, and stands on Broadway street, which, at the time the building was erected, was called Wharf street. At the latter part of the last and first of the present century it was tenanted, and the doors and windows were gone. Thomas H. Bradway, son of Aaron Bradway, lineal descendant of Edward, repaired it by putting new doors and windows into it, and Sarah Ann, daughter of Thomas Bradway, inherited it. John S. Wood, her husband, made farther improvements to the ancient building, and had a piazza built to it fronting the street, and rented it a number of years for a boarding house. There is another ancient brick building standing near, on the opposite side of the same street, built on what was formerly the fair grounds, which land was given by John Fenwick for that purpose in 1676.

The inhabitants of Fenwick Colony continued to hold their public fairs at that place. Officers were chosen yearly in the different towns and precincts within the Colony, whose business was to attend and keep order, and dispose of the grain and stock of various kinds which was brought to the fair ground for exhibition, and, if the several owners desired, to expose them for sale. It was the duty of those men, appointed as before mentioned, to superintend the selling at public auction. The fair generally lasted four or five days. The brick building, I have no doubt, was built about the year 1700, although some old men I have conversed with on the subject think it was built at an earlier period. John Mason's brick house on the same street, from the most authentic account, was built before he purchased in Elsinborough, which was about the year 1692. The house and sixteen acres of ground was purchased of John Mason, the grandson of the emigrant, in 1756, by Thomas Goodwin. The ancient mason building was taken down by A.

Naudain Bell, whose wife was a lineal descendant of Goodwin, and some three or four years ago he built a large building upon its site; in the upper apartment is the "National Standard" office. Samuel Hedge, the son-in-law of John Fenwick, built a brick dwelling in 1684, in which he and his wife, Annie Fenwick Hedge, resided until his death. It was taken down by William F. Miller, a few years ago, who built a more modern brick dwelling on the site of the old one, which had been standing about 156 years. In this ancient dwelling died Samuel and Joseph Hedge, being the fourth generation from the first Samuel Hedge in this country; about one hundred years after the death of their ancestor. Benjamin Acton, Sr., built a brick dwelling on East Broadway, in 1727, which is still standing. The house of Robert Zanes, Jr., on the same street, was built, as near as can be ascertained, about 1715, of hewn logs, and the roof was called a hip roof. The Edward Keasbey house being brick, nearly opposite the Zanes house, is also a very ancient building. On the same street stands what was once the Baptist church, which stood at Mill Hollow, about two and a half miles from Salem, and was built in 1743; it was subsequently moved to Salem, and is used at this time as a school house for colored children. It is one of the oldest frame building in the county. Alexander Grant's brick dwelling on Bridge, now Market street, is still standing, and was built early in the last century. James Rolph's dwelling stood near to Granr's, and was built about the same time; it was taken down about twenty-five years ago. Edward Wade's house, which stood at the corner of Griffith and Market streets, was one of the first houses of any size in the city of Salem. By tradition it was built about the time John Fenwick and John Adams were on Ivy Point, about 1678. Wade's house was taken down by William N. Jeffers, who had previously purchased it, together with a large lot of ground, and he erected the commodious house on the spot, which is owned by Albert H. Slape, Esq., who resides there. Within fifty years the dwellings of John Fenwick, and his son-in-law, John Adams, on Ivy Point, were standing, it being upon an elevated piece of ground, about two hundred yards west of the line of Market street, near Fenwick creek; they were built in 1677. It is probable that the proprietor had two reasons for choosing that spot for his domicile—it being near to a navigable stream, likewise a good view of his favorite Manto or Mannington, where his country seat, Fenwick Grove, was located. In Cow Neck stands an ancient one story brick dwelling. From the most reliable information I have, it was built by William

Wilkinson, in 1692, and it is still in tolerable repair, and is owned, at this time, together with about forty acres of land, by Hugh L. Tyler. Ancient tradition, concerning this property, says at one time the Cow Neck farm was large, and the land was considered of an excellent quality. The daughter of William Wilkinson became the owner of it, together with other large tracts of land in the county. She lived to be quite aged, and when on her death bed she sent to the town of Salem for a person to write her will, she devised her different tracts of land as she desired, but not mentioning her homestead the writer asked her how she was going to dispose of her Cow Neck farm. That appeared to affect her: she gave a sigh, and then told him she believed she would hold on to her Cow Neck farm another year. How often the human family have their attachments so strongly on the things of this world, that even when death draweth nigh they still cleave to them; thereby, in a great measure, preventing that quiet and peaceful close of life, which is so desirable. Samuel Stewart, the eldest son of John and Mary Stewart, of Alloways Creek, bought their property about 1770, and there he and his wife, Sarah Tyler Stewart, lived and ended their days; they were greatly respected for their many virtues.

Elsborg, now Elsinborough, is one of the first places where Europeans landed and settled in West Jersey, being coeval with Obisquahaset, now Penn's Neck. It was there a small colony of English, from New Haven, Connecticut, landed in 1640, and lived about three years. It appears that they never gained the confidence of the Indians or the Swedish settlers, by whom they were greatly harassed, but a greater scourge even than that was an epidemic called pleurisy. A historian writes that more than one-half of their number died with the fatal malady, and those that escaped the disease returned to the state from whence they came. When Fenwick arrived with his colony the point of land called Asamhocking was purchased by Robert Windham, but he died soon after that event, and left a daughter who married Richard Darkin, a young man of much promise. Richard and Ann W. Darkin had two sons and two or three daughters. Richard dying about 1714, their landed estate was divided between their two sons, John and Joseph Darkin. About 1720 John removed the old log domicile of his father and built a substantial brick dwelling, which is still standing, and owned at the present time by Amos Harris. Joseph Darkin, the younger brother, erected himself a brick dwelling on the southern portion of the Windham estate. The said building has been repaired recently, but most of the old walls are remaining. Isaac Smart located on a tract of land of about 500 acres called Middle Neck, whereon he built himself a brick mansion in 1696, and a few years later his son, Nathan Smart, built an addition to it; the house is standing and in good repair, and owned now by Richard Waddington.

John Mason, the emigrant, built in 1696 a brick dwelling on his property in Elsinborough, and in 1704 he built a large addition to it. The house is still standing, with some alterations made within a few years past by Richard M. Acton, whose wife inherited the property from her father, Thomas Mason, who is a lineal descendant of John Mason.

Abel Nicholson, the youngest son of Samuel Nicholson, built himself a brick dwelling, in 1722, which is in tolerable repair at the present time. Samuel Nicholson, the youngest son of Abel, inherited it, and lived there until about 1755. He then built himself a large brick mansion on the north end of the Nicholson allotment, on what is called the Amblebury Road, and there ended his days. The property is owned at the present time by Thomas Fogg, and the ancient house is in good repair.

George Abbott came from New England about the year 1696, and purchased a large tract of land of Joseph Nicholson, then a resident near Haddonfield, Gloucester county. George Abbott built a dwelling on the property near Monmouth river, as it was called at that time, in 1706. In 1725 he built an addition to it; the house is still standing, in good repair, and is owned by Andrew Smith Reeve. On the adjoining plantation stands another ancient dwelling, built by Henry Stubbins in 1745 or 1746. George Abbott, Jr., purchased part of the allotment of John Smith, of Amblebury, and built himself a brick dwelling, in 1730. The house is located in Alloways Creek Township. Charles Fogg became the owner, and he and his wife, Sarah Smith Fogg, resided there during the remainder of their lives.

Near Hancock's Bridge is a hip-roof brick dwelling, built in 1742 by Richard Smith, the son of Jonathan Smith, who was the youngest son of John Smith, of Amblebury. On the south side of Alloways Creek, near Hancock's Bridge, stands a large brick building in good repair, built in 1734 by William and Sarah Chambless Hancock. In this building the bloody massacre took place in 1778, at the time of the Revolution. It is now owned and occupied by Lucetta, the widow of Richard Mulford. About half a mile down the creek stands a brick dwelling built by John Maddox Denn, in 1725. The present owner is William Bradway, who, on his mother's side, is a descendant of John M. Denn. Quarter of a mile further down, within a few rods of Alloway's Creek, stands a brick dwelling built by Joseph Ware, Jr., in 1730. It is now owned and occupied by myself and wife, both the descendants of Joseph Ware, I on my mother's and she on her father's side. A mile farther down still, stands a brick dwelling, being hip-roof, built in 1745 by Charles Oakford, Jr., the grandson of Edward Wade, of Salem. It is owned by James Baker. On Alloways Creek Neck is a large brick building built by Nathaniel Chambless, the 3d, about 1730. The house erected by Daniels the elder is standing at the head of Stoe Creek, near the village of Canton, built prior to 1700. There has been within a few years an addition built to it of frame.

William Bradway, son of Edward Bradway, the emigrant, built a brick dwelling on Stoe Neck as early as 1700, which is still standing at this period; the property is owned by Jonathan Ingham, of Salem. On the same neck of land stands the ancient brick dwelling built by Bradway Stretch, the grandson of Edward Bradway, which was erected about 1745.

There are a number of ancient dwellings standing in Mannington. About a mile from the city of Salem is a large brick house, with a double roof, built by John Pledger, Jr., in 1727. In Upper Mannington, on the property which is now owned by James J. Pettit, is an ancient brick dwelling, built in 1722 by Samuel Mason, son of Thomas Mason, who bought the property of Samuel Hedge, 4th, in 1720, being part of Hedgefield. Further up the Mannington creek there is another brick mansion built by William Nicholson, son of Abel Nicholson, about 1730. Near this ancient dwelling once stood the house of Samuel Hedge, and the place where the building formerly stood is quite visible at the present day. It is a venerated spot, because there, in the autumn of 1683, John Fenwick left this world of care and perplexities. The property is now owned by Dr. Thomas and his wife Joan Dickinson. Not far from the Nicholson house stands a large brick house on the southern part of Hedgefield, built by Samuel Smith, son of John Smith, of Smithfield, about 1718. The said house stands near the King's Highway, laid out from Salem to Burlington. Near the straight road from Mannington Hill to Woodstown, about five miles from Salem, stands a large brick dwelling built by William Hall, Jr., in the year 1724. According to the record in the family Bible of the Halls, John Smith, of Almesbury, died in that house. Elizabeth, the wife of William Hall, Jr., was his grand-daughter. He was 106 years old and a few days over at the time of his death, which event took place in the beginning of 1731. He was born in the county of Norfolk, England, 20th of 3d month, 1623, and lived in his adopted country nearly fifty years.

One mile and a half from the Hall dwelling stands a large brick dwelling, built by the eminent Friend, Isaac Sharp. I have no record when it was erected, but I think, judging from the time Isaac Sharp was an active man in the public affairs of this colony, (he being one of the Justices of the Salem Courts early in the last century,) it would be safe to fix the time it was built as early as 1700. Not far from this ancient dwelling the mortal remains of John Fenwick lie mingled with its mother earth in the Sharp family burying ground. David Davis' mansion is still standing in Pilesgrove, near Paulding station; also, the house of Elisha Bassett, Jr. About a mile from Woodstown, in the township of Lower Penn's Neck, is Fenwick Adams' brick dwelling, built in 1728, now owned by Elias Buzby. Thomas Miles, the eminent surveyor, built himself a dwelling near the Delaware river, nearly opposite New Castle; it is more than 140 years old. The farm was inherited by his son, Francis Miles, and at the time of his death he devised the property to the township of Penn's Neck for educational purposes.

There is a large brick building located on Fenwick Point, as it was formerly called, built by Andrew Sinnickson in 1740, one hundred years after the first Andrew Sinaker emigrated from Sweden and settled on the eastern shore of the Delaware. During the last season the old mansion has been thoroughly repaired, but the ancient walls are left as formerly. The improvements were made by Charles Sinnickson, of Philadelphia, the great-grandson of Andrew Sinnickson, who built it. In the same neighborhood stands Sinick Sinaker's dwelling, built of brick. I presume it was built about the time of his brother Andrew's. The Sinnicksons were leading men in the township of Penn's Neck as early as 1725, and were large land-holders.

Daniel Smith, Jr., built a log dwelling with a hip roof at Mill Hollow, about 1730; it is now in good repair, and owned and occupied by James Tyler. Not far distant from the one mentioned stands a house where Daniel Smith, Sr., lived. The house was of brick, but was rebuilt within a few years past. At what time it was built I have no definite means of determining, but it was called an old house in the time of the American revolution, and in it the French soldiers secreted themselves until such time as the American militia crossed Alloways creek at Quinton's Bridge. John Smith, the eldest son of Daniel, became the owner. He married and had three sons— John, (who was the eldest, and was one of the Justices of Salem Courts for a number of years,) Benjamin and James Smith. The latter became an eminent merchant in Philadelphia, and was the senior partner of his brother-in-law, Jacob Ridgway, for a number of years. He retired from mercantile business some time previous to his death, and located himself and family in the city of Burlington.

John Pledger and Hippolit Lefevre purchased a tract of 6,000 acres of land, 2,000 acres of which is now known as Quaker Neck. The latter erected upon the tract a large brick residence in 1707. The building is still standing, and is owned at the present time by George Griscom, of Salem. The property was sold by his family to Benjamin Wyncoop, an Englishman. At the beginning of the war of the revolution Wyncoop sympathized with England, and the property was partially confiscated. John Mountain purchased the homestead, and the residue of the property was bought by Lucas and Richard Gibbs, Ebenezer Miller, Mark Miller, William Abbott, Benjamin Wright, Richard Ware and George Hall. Tradition says Wyncoop became very much reduced in circumstances, and died in the Pennsylvania Hospital a few years later.

William Tyler's brick mansion was built prior to 1730, and is located in Alloways Creek township, an addition having been added some years later. It is now owned by William Robinson. James Tyler's brick mansion is still standing, built about 1750; it is now owned by Richard McPherson. There are a number of dwellings which have recently been taken down. William Hancock, son of the emigrant, built quite a large brick house in Elsinborough, in 1705. Richard Grier became the owner, and took the old house down and erected a frame dwelling in its place.

Christopher White, who landed at Salem in 1677, built himself the largest and most substantial brick dwelling of any that was built in Fenwick Colony prior to 1700. It was erected in 1690, and located in Monmouth River precinct, about three-quarters of a mile from the present Hancock's Bridge, on his allotment of 1,000 acres, purchased of John Fenwick in 1674. Tradition says he sent to England for the bricks and an architect. The walls were eighteen inches in thickness; the floors were laid with two and a-half inch heart yellow pine; the cellar was covered with square English brick, and likewise the yard around the house. After standing 160 years it was taken down—the walls of the building even at that time were in a good condition.

Samuel Wade, who arrived in this country in 1675, built a

one-story brick dwelling in Alloways Creek in 1688. The house had four rooms, together with an entry the whole length of the house. Samuel Wade died previous to the eighteenth century. He and his wife, Jane Smith, the daughter of Thomas Smith, had three children born in England—Henry, Andrew and Anne. I presume those three children died minors, as there is no record of them after their parents arrived in this country. Samuel Wade, their third son, born at Alloways Creek 1st of 6th month, 1685, inherited his father's property in Monmouth precinct, and soon after he arrived at the age of twenty-one he married, and had five children, two sons and three daughters. He met with a great loss by losing both of his sons in 1730, it being two years before his death. John Stewart, who had emigrated from Scotland a short time before, married Mary, the eldest daughter of Samuel Wade, Jr., and they became the owner of the homestead. They raised another story on the ancient building in 1763, being seventy-five years after it was built by Samuel Wade, Sr. Man being more destructive than time, it was taken down about twenty-five years ago by John D. Stewart, a lineal descendant of Samuel Wade, being of the seventh generation, after the ancient domicile had withstood the wintry blasts of more than 160 years.

Redroe Morris' brick mansion was built on the shores of the Delaware, in Elsinborough. Samuel Carpenter, of Philadelphia, purchased five hundred acres of land of Richard Guy, and built a brick dwelling in 1688. The following year he sold it to Redroe Morris, at that time a resident of Salem. About that time he married Jane Baty, and in the spring of 1690 they removed to Elsinborough on the property he had recently purchased. To corroborate this statement, the Monthly Meeting records state Jonathan Morris, their eldest child, was born in Elsinborough, 6th of 12th month, 1690. This property has been in the possession of the Morris family for six generations. The present owner, Clement Hall, a descendant, within a few years past, rebuilt the old dwelling, and I think some of the ancient walls are still standing.

Nearly a mile from the river, on the Amblebury road, that leads to Salem, stands a large brick dwelling, built by Lewis Morris, son of Rodroe Morris, in 1725; it was rebuilt by the present owner, William B. Carpenter, about fifteen years ago; some of the old walls were left standing. William, on the side of his mother, is of the fifth generation from Lewis Morris. Bartholomew Wyatt, Jr., built himself a large brick dwelling in 1723, in the township of Mannington, on the twelve hundred acre tract that he inherited from his father, Bartholomew Wyatt, who came to Salem about 1690. The brick dwelling was taken down a short time previous by the late Andrew Thompson.

Of the ancient churches that are standing at this time, I think the Friends' meeting house at Hancock's Bridge perhaps is the most ancient. It was built on a lot that was deeded to them by William Hancock, and was erected in 1756; an addition was built to it in 1784. The prominent male members of that meeting, when the first was built, were James Daniels, Jr., Jonathan Bradway, Joseph Stretch, Jr., Bradway Stretch, Bradway Keasbey, John Denn, Charles Oakford, Nathaniel Chambless, 3d, James Chambless, Jr., Solomon Ware, John Ware, Joseph Ware, Jr., Samuel Hancock, John Hancock, Jeremiah Powell, Jr., John Stewart, Aquilla Barber, James Butcher, and quite a number of younger men.

In 1740 Jonathan Waddington, Sr., son of William Waddington, purchased about three hundred acres of land on East Thoroughfare creek, in the lower part of Lower Alloways Creek township; the year following he deeded the said tract to his fon, Jonathan Waddington, Jr. In the year following, 1742, the latter named built himself a large frame dwelling; it is still standing, in tolerable repair, being one of the oldest frame dwellings standing in the county at the present time. The property remained in the Waddington family until about 1790; at that time Jonathan Waddington, 3d, sold it to one of the Padgett family. Ephraim Turner is the present owner. Respecting his parentage I have no knowledge. Ephraim is an active member of the Canton Baptist Church, and one of the deacons of the same for a number of years; his wife was a Bradway, a lineal descendant of Edward Bradway, the emigrant.

SLAVERY.

Before the year 1700, African slavery was introduced in the Fenwick Colony, and the next generation of landholders were the owners of slaves generally. When such labor is employed to do the menial services on the farm and in the house, its effect is to produce idleness amongst children of the slave-holders, and idleness is the stepping stone to vice and immorality. Slavery continued in the county until 1772. That year was a remarkable epoch in the history of the colonies of Pennsylvania, New Jersey and Delaware. The yearly meeting of the Society of Friends, held at Philadelphia in that year, passed a rule of discipline that a member of the society who belonged to said yearly meeting should not forever afterwards hold human beings in bondage. Friends in the county submitted to the decision of the yearly meeting, and emancipated their slaves. They likewise furnished homes for the aged and infirm, and assisted them during the remainder of their lives.

The Quakers, like other religious denominations, held no principles against African slavery at the early organization of their Society. After William Penn purchased the province of Pennsylvania he, in 1677, visited Holland and parts of Germany, inviting emigrants to his new possession in America. There was a company formed composed partly of Hollanders and Germans, known as Frankfort Land Company. The company's agent was a rising young lawyer, Francis Daniel Pastorius, son of Judge Pastorius, of Windshire, who, at the age of seventeen, entered the university of Altorf. He studied law at Strausburg, Basle, Jena, and at Ratisbon, the seat of the Imperial Government, where he obtained a practical knowledge of international polity. Successful in all his examinations and disputations, he received the degree of Doctor of Laws, at Nuremburg, in 1676. He emigrated to America in the year 1683, in company with a number of his countrymen, members of the Frankfort Company. The said company purchased 2,600 acres of land of the proprietor, bounded by Delaware and Schuylkill rivers. The towns of Frankford and Germantown were founded on the company's land. Among the German emigrants that purchased land of said company was Wiggert Levering and Geohardt Levering, and William Rittinghuysen, as it was then spelled, but now spelled Rittenhouse. William was the grandfather of the celebrated American astronomer, David Rittenhouse. The mother of Dr. Thomas R. Clement, of this county, was a Levering, a direct descendant of Wiggart Levering, of Germantown. A short time after Francis Daniel Pastorious arrived in Pennsylvania he became a member of the Society of Friends. He married about that time, Anna, daughter of Dr. Klosterman, of Muhlheim. He was one of the first who had any misgivings about the institution of slavery, and in 1788 he wrote a memorial against slave-holding, which was submitted to the meeting of Germantown Friends, and by them approved of, and Pastorius was appointed to lay the memorial before the yearly meeting held in Philadelphia the same year. It was the first protest against negro slavery submitted to a religious society in the world. Whittier, the poet, who had an opportunity of seeing the original manuscript, says it was a bold and direct appeal to the human heart. The memorial found but little favor with the yearly meeting, and it was said that Pastorious returned to his home at Germantown with sadness depicted on his countenance. By that act the seed of liberty was sown, for in the year 1698 Germantown Friends again sent a memorial by the hands of Pastorius to the yearly meeting held at Burlington, and it was received with more respect and consideration than it had been ten years previous, and was directed to be put on the books of the meeting, and had during that time gained a number of advocates for the measure. In 1701 the yearly meeting petitioned the Legislatures of Pennsylvania and New Jersey to pass a law to prohibit any more importation of slaves in the colonies. There was such a law passed in Pennsylvania, but it was abrogated, and became null and void by the order of Queen Anne, of England. Westcott, the historian, says the first person that wrote a book showing the evils of slavery was Ralph Sandeford, a young merchant on Market street, Philadelphia. He had resided for some time in one of the West India islands, and had witnessed the cruelties inflicted upon his fellow-man, and in the year 1728 his book was published, showing the evils of the system, and for so doing he was disowned by the Society of Friends. In 1732 Benjamin Ley, the hermit, wrote a book on the same subject. A few years later Anthony Benezet arrived in Philadelphia, he being a French Hugenot, who left his native land on account of religious intolerance. He was a Quaker and a man of great learning and benevolence of character. His residence in Philadelphia was on Chestnut street, corner of Fifth street, and there he kept a school for colored children many years. Marshal Girard, the first ambassador from France, made his home with Anthony Benezet during his stay in this country. Benezet corresponded with the philanthropists in Europe on the evils of slavery, likewise with eminent men in this country, such as Washington, Jay, and Franklin, and many others. John Woolman, a native of Burlington county, an eminent minister of the Society of Friends, traveled extensively and visited most of the meetings within the compass of the yearly meeting, pleading the cause of the enslaved with great effect. It could not be otherwise, if it be true, as one of England's favorite sons says of him after reading the history of his life, which was published after his death: "His religion is love. His whole existence and all his passions were love. If one could venture to impute to his creed, and not to his personal character, the delightful frame of mind which he exhibited, one could not hesitate to be a convert. His Christianity is most inviting, is fascinating." And after seventy years' labor by some of the greatest minds that the Quaker society ever had among them, they abolished slavery within the compass of Philadelphia yearly meeting. Pastorious, the originator of freedom, died at Chesnut Hill, a short distance above Germantown, where he owned 500 acres of land, in the year 1720, and was buried in the Friends' burying-ground, at Germantown, a town he had founded over forty years before. There is no stone to mark the spot where he lies. His descendants live at Germantown at the present day. I close this sketch of him by quoting a few lines of Whittier respecting him, after the proclamation of freedom made by President Lincoln:

> " And the fullness of the time has come,
> And over all the exile's western home,
> From sea to sea, the flowers of freedom bloom.
>
> " And joy bells ring, and silver trumpets blow,
> But not for the Pastorious! even so
> The world forgets, but the wise angels know."

BEVERAGES.

It had long been the practice in England, Germany, and in parts of Northern Europe, prior to the settlement of the North American provinces, to use as a common beverage strong beer, and when the English and German emigrants came, they straightway busied themselves in erecting breweries for manufacturing beer for common drink. There were four of them in the small township of Elsinborough : John Thompson's, Nicholson's, Morris', and George Abbott's. There were also several more throughout the county. It seems to have been considered at that period one of the essentials of life. William Penn, the eminent apostle of Quakerism, and one of the greatest statesmen in the early settlemement of this country, had a brewery erected at his country seat in Penn's Manor, a few miles above Bristol, which is still standing. It was also made in large quantities in this section of the country, not only for home use, but a large portion was shipped to Philadelphia and New York. The succeeding generation planted large apple orchards, and when they became in full bearing order, distilleries for manufacturing cider into alcoholic liquors were erected, and that in time became the common drink of the people in the place of beer. It appears by the most reliable authority that all classes, both the rich and poor, and members of all religious organizations, made use of it as a common drink. Less than a century ago it was the custom at funerals for liquor to be handed out to those who had met to pay their last respects on earth to their departed friend. It has been daily used in many families and handed out to their workingmen until within a short period, and there may be a few at the present time who adhere to the old custom, but the number is diminishing yearly. Some persons ask if the present generation is more moral and better than our ancestors were, who used strong drink so freely, and likewise did not see any crime in holding their fellow creatures in bondage. I have no doubt that they did not see the great evil such practices produced, hence they in some measure were not accountable for it. But we, of the present generation, having seen the great wickedness arising from those two causes, should exert all our moral and religious force to expel the great evil from our land. Figuratively speaking, it has slain the first born of every family in this section of the country. From habitual drinking of the parent, it produces a settled disease of the nervous system, and is transmitted from father to son for several generations. Many an aged father and a loving mother, who have cared and waited upon their offspring in infancy with ardent solicitude for their temporal and moral welfare, have gone down prematurely to the grave with sorrow on account of their sons having become vagabonds by the use of intoxicating drink. The Friends were among the first who introduced malt and spirituous liquors in this country as a common beverage, but greatly to their credit they were the first who took a firm stand in a meeting capacity against the use of it as a common drink. Within a few years most of the other religious societies, and especially the Baptists and Methodists, are taking active measures in the cause of temperance among their own members, and their labors extend to all classes of society.

GENEALOGY.

Genealogy has arrested the attention of persons in all ages of the civilized world. William Blackstone, the son of a silk mercer, was born in London in 1723. He became an eminent lawyer, as well as a writer on English law. Since his time every student of law, both in England and America, who is desirous of becoming eminent in legal knowledge, is under the necessity of giving his days and nights to the study of Blackstone's Commentaries on English Law. Blackstone wrote largely in regard to genealogy.

The following considerations will serve to show how wonderfully men and families are knit together by the ties of blood: "When one reflects that his ancestory doubles in each assent; or, to speak more correctly, increases in two-fold geometrical progression, he will easily see this. Thus as everybody has one father, two grandfathers, four great-grandfathers, and eight great-great-grandfathers, and so on; the case being, of course, the same on the female side. If we go back to the time of King John, which, (allowing three generations to a century) would be about nineteen generations, we shall find that in the space of little more than six centuries every one of us can boast of the astounding number of 524,288 ancestors; that is to say that the blood of more than 500,000 of the human race flows in our veins." This calculation supposes, however, that all are male ancestors, having married strangers in blood, which has probably not been the case in any instance. A few matches with cousins or remote relations reduces the number. The same eminent lawyer long since called attention to the multitudinous number of ancestral relations in his commentaries, where he gives a table of numbers extending to the twentieth genealogical remove. At the fortieth remove, a period extending over about sixteen or seventeen hundred years, the total number of man's progenitors amounts to more than a million million! The same eminent writer also shows from the most satisfactory data that we have all now existing nearly two hundred and seventy millions of kindred in the 15th degree, and if this calculation should appear incompatible with the number of inhabitants on the earth, it is because of intermarriage among the several descendents from the same ancestors. A hundred or a thousand modes of consanguinity may be consolidated in one person, or he may be related to us a hundred or thousand different ways, and without being aware of it. It is thus that I account for the extraordinary resemblance, both personal and mental, often occuring between persons not regarded as being related to each other. We know how both physical and intellectual characteristics are transmitted. A due consideration of these facts would be of great moral advantage to mankind, as serving to induce a kindness of feeling to all, whether lowly or exalted; since we know not by how many ties of blood they may be connected to us, in a stronger sense than is usually affixed to the words "all men are brethren." I append here an illustrative anecdote about seventy or eighty years since. A shepherd named Tuppin was sent by his mother who resided near Eastbourn, Sussex county, to drive some sheep into South Devon. This man having discharged his commission was returning homeward from his somewhat toilsome pilgrimage when, on passing a cottage about two hundred miles from his own habitation, on a spot which he had before visited, he was greeted with the familiar words "How do you do, Master Tuppin?" The shepherd, with a rather bewildered air, turned round and found that the salutation had been addressed to him by a peasant's wife, the tenant of a cottage, a person of whom he had not the slightest knowledge. He told her as much, whereupon she apologized by saying that she had mistaken him for one Master Tuppin, a man who lived in a neighboring hamlet, but of whom the surprised shepherd had never heard. There can, however, be no doubt of the common origin of the two Master Tuppins, though all remembrance of kindred was lost.

EDITORS.

At the beginning of the present century there was not a newspaper published in Salem county, and the people depended upon the daily and weekly papers published in Philadelphia for news. There was the "Saturday Evening Post," published in Philadelphia, and edited by Samuel Atkinson, had a large circulation in Salem county up to 1820, or later. The editor was a native of this section, and a lineal descendant of John Smith, of Amblebury; his mother was the daughter of Richard and Rachel Dennis Smith, of Elsinborough. Rachel was the daughter of Philip and Lucy Dennis, born in Greenwich township 6th of 4th month, 1742.

The first newspaper published in Salem was in 1816. Isaac Pollock was the editor and publisher. He was the brother of the late Sheppard K. Pollock, who was pastor of the Presbyterian church at Greenwich, Cumberland county, for fifteen years. The Salem "Gazette," as Pollock's paper was called, became obnoxious to the party that should have sustained it in what was known as the Court House election, in the year 1817, when the test was made relative to the removal of the court house and county building from off the one acre lot that was given by John Fenwick, and surveyed and set off for the county for the inhabitants of Salem county to build a court house and prison on by an order given by Samuel Hedge to John Worlidge, deputy surveyor, in 1688. The majority of the inhabitants in Pilesgrove, both Pittsgroves, Upper Penn's Neck, and Upper Alloways Creek were in favor of removing the county buildings from Salem to some central location in the county. Where the place should be there was a diversity of opinion; some thought the village of Thompson Bridge (now Alloways-town) would be the the proper place, whilst others were in favor of Woodstown. By a survey of the county the almshouse farm was found to be the most central. The election was held to remove the county buildings to the south end of said farm, or for them to remain at Salem. It was decided by a large majority of voters for them to remain at Salem. The Salem

"Gazette," for the part it took in the election, lost much support, and its publication ceased.

In the early part of the year 1819 the Salem "Messenger," published by Elijah Brooks, followed the "Gazette." The "Messenger's" first number appeared in September, 1819, and was continued by Brooks until 1833, when the late James M. Hannah bought out the office. James had previously bought out the "American Statesman," edited and published by the late Henry H. Elwell, a native of Pittsgrove. The first number of the "Statesman," edited by Elwell, appeared during the Presidential canvass, when General Andrew Jackson was one of the candidates. James M. Hannah, as before stated, having purchased both the "Messenger" and "Statesman" merged both in one, and called his paper the "Union." Previous to that, however, during the canvass for the Presidency, in which William Wirt was the candidate, Elijah Brooks published from the "Messenger" office a paper called the "Anti-Masonic Courier." The late Dr. James VanMeter, and also the late Alphonso L. Eakin, were contributors and supporters of the "Courier," which, when started, was designed to be permanent, but upon the failure of the Anti-Masonic party to show much strength, it ceased to be published. James M. Hannah continued the publication of the "Union" until 1836, when he disposed of his interest to Samuel Prior, who at that time was the publisher of the "Freeman Banner." The "Freeman Banner" appeared April 1st, 1834, Sisty & Prior publishers. Sisty in a few months ceased his connection with the paper, and the "Banner" was continued by Samuel Prior until November, 1840, when he sold the paper to Charles P. Smith, who changed its name to "National Standard."

Samuel Prior is a native of England. His grand-father, John Prior, was a miller and baker in the town of Coggeshall, in the county of Essex, England, and was born in 1746. He was a warm partisan with William Pitt, Earl of Chatham, in opposing King George III. and the British Parliament in their measures against the American colonies. The part the eminent statesman and orator took in behalf of the colonies was calculated to arouse the sympathies of many in England in favor of America, and John Prior was one of the number. He became a marked man by the supporters of the war of the American revolution, and subsequently when the difficulties occurred between the United States and England, out of which grew the war of 1812, John Prior, with still more tenacity, opposed the cause of England as inexcusable and unjust. He continued to reside at his childhood's home until 1845, when he died, aged 99 years. One of his brothers emigrated to the United States in 1790, and settled in one of the southern states. Samuel, son of John Prior, was born at Coggeshall, Essex, England, June, 1779. He emigrated to the United States, and landed at Philadelphia in May, 1816, and subsequently came to Salem to live. His wife was Rosamond Gardner. Samuel and Rosamond Prior had five children who lived to the age of twenty-one years—Samuel, Rodamond, John, Maria and Ann. The last three are deceased, leaving children who are residing in Philadelphia. Samuel Prior, Sr., died July, 1865, being in his 87th year. Samuel Prior, his eldest son, was born May 29th, 1812. With but a short intermission he has resided in Salem county since he was brought to Salem by his parents when in his fourth year. He was apprenticed to and learned the printing business of Elijah Brooks, publisher of the Salem "Messenger." On becoming of age he started a paper called the "Freeman Banner," and published the same for more than six years. On account of ill health he quit the printing business and went to farming, but after regaining his health went into the steamboat business between Salem and Philadelphia, in 1845, and continued in that business until within a year or two, when he retired to the oversight of his farm, which is located in the township of Mannington. Samuel's first wife was Cornelia, daughter of Thomas E. and Abigail Mulford. By that connection there was one daughter, Elizabeth Prior, who died in her 17th year. Samuel's second wife, who is still living, is Mary Ann, daughter of Henry and Hannah Hilliard. Their children were Lavinia Dunlap, (who married Charles W. Casper, the son of Thomas Jefferson and Mary Ann Anderson Casper, late of Mannington,) and Frank O. and Cornelia Prior. Frank married C. A. Wilson, daughter of Dr. W. Wilson, of Bethlehem, Pennsylvania. Frank died in June, 1874, leaving two children—William W. and Samuel. Cornelia, the youngest daughter of Samuel Prior, remains single.

In 1840, as before stated, Samuel Prior sold his interest in the "Freeman Banner" to Charles P. Smith, and the name of the paper was changed by Smith to the "National Standard." He was the editor and proprietor for several years, and was subsequently elected to the State Senate. Whilst a member of that body, or soon after his term expired, he was appointed by the Governor, Clerk of the Supreme Court. I think he is a native of Philadelphia. His father was George W. Smith, of Virginia, and married Hannah, the daughter of John and Mary Smith

Ellet, of the County of Salem. Charles is a lineal descendant of John Smith, of Smithfield, on the side of his mother. Mr. Smith sold his interest in the "Standard" to William S. Sharp and Sinnickson Chew. The latter in a few years left Salem, removed to the city of Camden, and became the editor and publisher of the "West Jersey Press," which is one of the leading papers published in that city. William S. Sharp continued to be the editor and publisher of the "Standard" during the late rebellion. About the close of that struggle he left Salem and removed to the city of Trenton, where he opened an extensive printing establishment, and commenced the publication of the "Public Opinion," a large illustrated weekly newspaper. The "National Standard" was bought by S. W. Miller, Jr., who is the editor of the paper at the present time. He is the son of Samuel W. Miller, of Allowaystown, in this county, who is the son of John Miller, a native of Germany. The latter emigrated to this country and settled near Greenwich, Cumberland county, and married Mary Hitchner, by whom he had several children. Samuel W. Miller located at Allowaystown soon after he became of age and engaged in the cabinet making business, which he subsequently abandoned and embarked in the lumber business, in which he is still engaged. He married Elizabeth, the daughter of John G. and Mary Edward S. Ballinger, who were among the first settlers of Allowaystown. They had seven children—Sarah, John B., William B., Samuel W., Richard C., James R. and Anna R. John B. is deceased. Sarah and William are married. The former is the wife of Sinnickson Chew, editor of the Camden "Press," and the latter married Wilhemina, daughter of Almarine Woodruff, of Deerfield, Cumberland county. The other children are unmarried.

The Salem "Sunbeam" was started in July, 1844, by Isaac Wells, who was a native of Burlington county, and who died in Trenton about 1849. Robert Gwynne and Nathan S. Hales succeeded Wells in March, 1849. Hales retired in April, 1850, and became one of the proprietors of the Sunday "Republic" in Philadelphia. Robert Gwynne continues to this time, having applied himself diligently to his calling for nearly twenty seven years. The "Sunbeam" is a good family newspaper, and is ably edited. The circulation at this time is about 1200. Robert is a native of Ireland, coming to this country at the age of thirteen, and graduated in the office of the "Pennsylvanian," a leading newspaper in the city of Philadelphia, under Hamilton and John W. Forney. His ancestors were Welsh, and the family is associated with some of the leading families of Great Brit ain, the Gwynne Company of London and Londondery, in Ireland, being founded by his ancestors. Leading bankers of the same name and family have done business for generations in the cities of Baltimore and New York. Robert Gwynne married Mary Jane, daughter of John Camp, an old citizen of Salem county. She died 1st of the 12th month, 1865, leaving four children—Jennie, Robert, Bella and Helen. Robert Gwynne also published a paper at Woodstown in 1852, called the "Franklin Herald." This was continued only a short time. Soon after the "Herald" the Woodstown "Register" was published by J. R. Schenck. The "American Eagle" and "Jersey Blue," were published at the same town: they had a short existence. In 1870, William Taylor, who for several years had been publishing a paper at Clayton, Gloucester county, removed his establishment to Woodstown, and continued the publication of the paper at that place as the Woodstown "Register." The "Register" is well sustained by the people of Woodstown, and is a credit to the publisher. The editor, William Taylor is, I believe, a member of the ancient and respectable Taylor family of Chester county, Pennsylvania, and of the State of Virginia.

I have been informed by an aged inhabitant of Salem that the first newspaper published in Salem was the "Observer," which was edited by an Englishman by the name of Black. He married Elizabeth, daughter of Richard and Rachel Smith, of Elsinboro. After a short period Black moved his press to Dover, Delaware. My informant did not give the date when the paper was published, but I presume it was two or three years before Pollock started his paper, which was first published in 1816.

FARMING IMPLEMENTS.

The early agriculturists of Fenwick's colony, likewise all of West Jersey, labored under great disadvantage, as we should think at the present day, respecting their agricultural implements. The plough they used in breaking up the virgin soil was made almost entirely of wood. Instead of plantation wagons, as used at the present time, sleds constructed in the rudest manner were the only vehicles for carting their grain and hay, and other products of the farm. As early as 1720, carts were gradually introduced in the place of the wooden sleds. About the year 1740, the plantation wagons were first used by some of the ablest farmers, and in a short time became common. There were no fan mills in the early settlement of this country, for cleaning the grain. The usual way of separating the chaff from the cereal, was to choose a windy day, in an elevated place, and then get a person with a large wooden scoop to winnow it by the wind. About the time of the American revolution fan mills were gradually introduced, from Lancaster county, Pennsylvania, although we of the present generation would consider these Dutch Fan Mills (as they were called) tedious in cleaning grain. But our ancestors appreciated them highly, as being a great improvement, and appreciated them greatly as labor-saving to the agriculturist.

PUBLIC CONVEYANCES.

The only way by land our forefathers traveled for more than a century from the first settlement of the colony was on horseback—men, women and children. I was told, when young, by an antiquarian who has long gone to his resting place, an amusing anecdote respecting that ancient and valued friend, Bartholomew Wyatt, 2d, of Mannington. His son-in-law, Richard Wistar, of Philadelphia, sent him a one-horse chaise in which to ride to meeting held at Salem, about three miles distant, Richard thinking his father was too old a man to ride on horseback. Bartholomew tried his new vehicle, and rode in it to Salem, and when asked how he liked it, his reply was, "I thought it would kill me before I reached the meeting house." Such is the effect of habit. Vessels were early used to convey merchandise and travelers to and from the towns of Salem and Greenwich to Philadelphia.

In 1819 the steamboat "Congress" with a party of gentlemen from Philadelphia, came to Salem, being the first steamer that ever entered Assamhockin, or Salem creek. In 1824 the first regular line from Philadelphia to Salem was advertised by B. & B. Cooper, merchants of Philadelphia, when the steamboat "Lafayette" made a few regular trips, and then discontinued them. The steamboat called the "Albemarle" in 1825 was put on the line from Philadelphia to Salem. She made but a few trips, when she was completely destroyed by fire at night, while at Arch street wharf. Captain Enoch Boon, who formerly was a citizen of Bridgeton, at that time a resident of Salem, had an interest in the steamer "Albemarle." And in 1827 the same Captain Boon, the father of the present Boon family of Salem, succeeded in selling sufficient stock to the citizens of Salem, and farmers of the country, to purchase the steamer "Essex," of New York. Captain Enoch Boon ran the boat a few weeks. Owing to a disagreement with the directors he sold his stock, and another captain was chosen. The "Essex" ran about two years from Philadelphia to Salem, when the line was sold to the Philadelphia and Baltimore Company, which

Company discontinued the "Eesex," and put on a small boat called the "Salem," which ran from Salem to New Castle, connecting there with the large boats of the Philadelphia and Baltimore line. In 1835 George Boon and brothers, sons of Captain Enoch Boon, purchased the steamer "Flushing," and run her from Salem to Philadelphia up to 1838, when they exchanged her for the "Clifton." In 1836 the "Pioneer" was built by a chartered company, and run to Salem until 1848. A continuous line of steam navigation has been kept up between Salem and Philadelphia since the "Essex" commenced in 1827. The names of the boats on the line at the different periods were as follows: "Essex," "Salem," "Lenneas," "Flushing," "Pioneer," "Clifton," "New Jersey," (the latter called the "Huckleberry,") "Proprietor," "Portsmouth," "Hudson," "Antelope," "Wave," "Napoleon," "Burlington," "Cohansey," "Miantinomie," "Express," "Major Reybold," "John S. Ide," and "Perry," and a freight boat "Cynthia." Several of the boats ran to Salem but a short time. The "Major Reybold" and the steamer "Perry" are still on the line and in the summer season make daily trips.

Doubtless there were mails from Salem to Philadelphia under the colonial government; by whom carried, and how often, there is no means of ascertaining with much certainty. The first post office established at Salem, by the post office department of the United States government, was on the 20th of March, 1793; and Thomas Jones, a citizen of Salem, was appointed the same day post master. William Harvey, by an authentic authority, was the first contractor to carry the mails from Salem to Philadelphia, twice in each week, for $300 a year. Harvey continued to carry the mails until about the year 1809 or 1810. Atkinson Conrow about that time took the contract, and William Swing drove the stage principally for him. That was during the war of 1812. In 1815 John Tonkins, at Carpenter's Landing, in Gloucester county, took the contract for carrying the mails from Salem to Philadelphia, and Adam H. Sickler was his driver; however, Tonkins held the contract only one year. In 1817 Adam Sickler and George Loudenslacker took the mail contract to carry it from Salem to Philadelphia three times in each week, for the sum of $600 a year. They continued carrying the mails until 1824; Adam Sickler was the principal driver.

It is justice to record that it was generally admitted by the best horsemen that lived on the line of the road from Salem to Philadelphia, at that time, that Adam Sickler took more care and drove a better team than any of his predecessors. Adam is still living in the city of Salem, he being in his eighty-ninth year, and is highly respected by his fellow citizens. About that time, 1824, there was a daily mail established, and Benjamin Reeve, of Philadelphia, was the contractor, and Andrew McCready drove the stage.

About 1858 there was a company formed for the purpose of building a railroad from Salem to connect with the West Jersey Railroad at Elmer. The cars commenced running on the Salem road in 1861, and have continued twice a day up to this time. The mails leave Salem twice in each day by the railroad. We certainly ought to feel thankful for the many priviliges we have in this generation, compared with our early ancestors when they first settled in this wilderness country.

QUIT RENTS AND WARRANTS.

The point or neck of land bounded on the west by the Pantuxet river, as it was called by the Indians, now known as the Delaware river, on the south by Asamhocking creek, now Salem, was called by the natives Obisquahosit. When John Fenwick arrived in this country with his English colony, to take possession of his tenth of West New Jersey, he found a settlement of Finns and Swedes, who had emigrated from their fatherland, as early as 1638 or 1840, in company with a number of their countrymen, who had settled on the opposite side of the river, about the mouth of the Christiana, and along the said river, as far as where the city of Philadelphia now is. Many of the Finns and Swedes had purchased their lands of the natives and taken deeds from the Indian chiefs, but they early acknowledged that Fenwick was the rightful owner, and had their lands re-surveyed and deeded to them. For this they were to pay to the proprietor, or his heirs, certain sums for quit-rents, to be paid yearly, according to the number of acres each owned. Samuel Hedge, Jr., in 1690, made out a duplicate, or role as he called it, of what each landholder should pay quit-rent for that year. The said lands, I presume, were part of the reserved 150,000 acres, made by John Fenwick when he sold his proprietory right to William Penn, in 1682.

The following are the names of the inhabitants of Penns Neck who paid quit-rents:

Matt Neilson, Fopp Neilson, Peter Onson, 1040 acres, 2s. 1d.; Steven Yearneans, Stacy Hendrickson, Matthias Spacklesson, 1,040 acres, 3s.; Evick Yearneans, 300 acres, 3d.; John Yearneans, 300 acres, 3d.; Matt Joanson, 150 acres, 3d.; Andrew Anderson, 150 acres, 3d.; Stacy Corneilinson, 250 acres, 5d.; Ann Hendricks, 150 acres, 3d.; Andrew Seneca (now Sinnickson) 226 acres, 1s.; Hance Shershell, 100 acres, 3d.; Claus Joanson, 100 acres, 3d.; Jones Scoggin, 200 acres, 2s.; Woley Woolson, 200 acres, 20 shad, or 2s.; Roger Pedrick, 140 acres, 1s.; Barce Jacobson, 200 acres, 4s.; Peter Halter, 200 acres, 2s.;

A. C. Bronson, 250 acres, 1s.; Jarvis Bywater, 200 acres, 2s. 2d; Richard Tindall, 230 acres, 3d.; Thomas Waltson, 200 acres, 1s.; James Vickory, 300 acres, 2s. 1d.; Peter Wilkinson, 400 acres, 1s. 1d.; Andorcas Barleyson, 400 acres, 1s.; Richard Marcy, 150 acres, 1s.; Renier Vanhyost, 400 acres, 3s.; John Cullin, 200 acres, 1s. 2d.; Barnard Webb, 250 acres, 2s.; Mary White, 500 acres, 5s.; John Perkins, 300 acres, 3s.; George Garrett, 300 acres, 3s.

Lands in Pilesgrove township: Richard Tindall, 195 acres, 1s.; Mary Holman, 2,000 acres, £1; Nicholas Winton, 500 acres, 2d.; John Derickson, 500 acres, 2d.; Thomas Potter, 500 acres, 1s.; Richard Lippincott, 1000 acres, 1s. 1d.; William Shotlock, 500 acres, 1s.; William Worth, 500 acres, 1s.; Thomas Smith, 250 acres, 1s.; William Jonson, 250 acres, 2s.; Lewis Morris, 1,000 acres, 2s.

Lands in Alloways Creek subject to quit-rents: Edward Wade, meadow 100 acres, 1s.; John Hancock, 100 acres, 1s.; Thomas Smith, 300 acres, 5d.

Lands at Cohansey: Obadiah Holmes, 4 acres, 1d.; Anthony Woodhouse, 80 acres, 5d.; Samuel Hunter, 80 acres, 5d.; Richard Tindall, 100 acres, 2s.; John Clark, 16 acres, 2d.; Alexander Smith, 16 acres, 2d.; Thomas Watson, 16 acres, 2d.; Mark Reeves, 16 acres, 2d.; John Mason, 16 acres, 2d.; Thomas Smith, 16 acres, 2d.; William Bacon, 32 acres, 4d.; Joseph Bronson, 16 acres, 2d.; John Bacon, 16 acres, 2d.; Edward Hurlbert, 32 acres, 4d.; Job Holmes, 22 acres, 4d.; Joseph Dennis, 32 acres, 4d; Enoch Moore, 16 acres, 2d.; Francis Alexander, 32 acres, 4d.; Peter Craven, 2 acres, 1d.; Thomas Stuthem, 2 acres, 1d.; Joseph Bacon, 16 acres, 2d.

The quit-rents of Salem town were as follows: William Milton, 10 acres, 1d.; Thomas Smith, 6 acres, 1d.; Christopher Saunders, 10 acres, 1d.; William Wilkinson, 8 acres, 3d.; C. Lumbley, 10 acres, 1d.; Richard Daniel, 10 acres, 1d.; Joseph White, 10 acres, 1d.; R. Johnson, 10 acres, 1d.; Anthony Dixon, 10 acres, 1d.; James Nevil, 20 acres, 3d.; Thomas Woodruff, 10 acres, 1d.; John Harden, 16 acres, 1½d.; John Snooks, 10 acres, 1d.; Edward Champneys, 10 acres, 1d.; John Rolph, 10 acres, 1d.; William Wilkinson, 10 acres, 1d.; Thomas Johnson, 10 acres, 1d.; Thomas Kent, 10 acres, 1d.; Thomas Woodruff, 17 acres, 1½d.; John Snooks, 16 acres 1½d.; 2d lot of William Wilkinson, 10 acres, 1d.; Joseph Canloyd's lot, 20 acres, 2d.; John Worledge, 20 acres, 2d.; Thomas Yorke's lot, 5 acres, 4d.; Eleazar Dovberry, 2½ acres, 2d.

It appears the emigrants that came with Fenwick, and a number of others, that did not arrive until two or three years afterwards, who had purchased land of him before he left England, were exempted from paying quit-rents to the proprietor, or his heirs. Such men as Robert Windham, John Pledger, Samuel Nicholson, Isaac Smart, Robert and Edward Wade, James Sherron, the two John Smiths, Richard Guy, Christopher White, Edward Bradway, William Hancock, and several others, together with William Penn, who bought sixty acres of the proprietor at the same period. The said land was surveyed for him by Richard Hancock, in 1676. It was situated within the precincts of the town of Salem. The reader will perceive by the role of the quit-rents that were collected by Samuel Hedge, about the year 1690, for the heirs of Fenwick, it being eight years after William Penn purchased the so much talked of twelve mile circle of land and water of James, the Duke of York. There is no reliable evidence that William Penn ever attempted to claim any lands in West New Jersey except by purchase of the Jersey proprietors. It would be derogatory to his great name to think otherwise.

Lands disposed of and surveyed by order of John Fenwick's executors; Richard Tindell and John Worledge, surveyors:

5th month, 1684.—A warrant to survey 400 acres of land for Ranier VanHirst, near Cranberry Point, Mannington.

5th month, 6th.—A warrant to lay out for Charles Angelo 10 acres of land for town lot, on Nevel street, town of Salem.

5th month, 27th.—A warrant to lay out for John Jacobson 200 acres of land, near Peter Johnson's plantation, on Salem creek.

2d month, 7th, 1685.—A warrant to lay out for John Harding 16 acres, a town lot on Nevel street, in Salem.

3d month, 5th.—A warrant to lay out for James Clark 16 acres of land for a town lot at Cohansey.

3d month, 25th.—A warrant to lay out for Alexander Smith 16 acres of land for a town lot at Cohansey.

3d of 4th month.—A warrant to lay out for John Clark a town lot in Cohansey.

18th of 11th month, 1685.—A warrant to lay out 32 acres of land for town lots at Cohansey for Joseph Brown and John Mason.

3d month, 10th, 1685.—A warrant to lay out 16 acres of land, town lot in Cohansey, for Thomas Smith.

4th month, 1685.—A warrant to lay out 16 acres of land at Cohansey for Richard Danger, of Cohansey town.

10th of 5th month, 1684.—A warrant to lay out 500 acres for

Richard Tindell, to be next to Thomas Pyle's 2000 acre tract, it being a legacy.

1685.—A warrant to lay out 2000 acres for Samuel Jennings, of Burlington. Said lands lay at the head of Mannington creek.

5th month, 1684.—A warrant to lay out 500 acres for Samuel Hedge, to lie next to Richard Tindell, it being a legacy.

2d month, 1686.—A warrant to lay out 500 acres for John Smith, of Smithfield. Land to be in Alloways Creek. A legacy. And a warrant to lay out three town lots for John Smith, of Smithfield, of 16 acres each, in the town of Cohansey, it being a legacy.

A warrant to lay out 200 acres for James Vickery, next to James Webb.

2d month, 1685.—A warrant to lay out one town lot in Cohansey, to contain 16 acres, for Mark Reeve.

13th of 6th month.—A warrant to lay out a lot of 16 acres for Thomas Watson, in Cohansey.

A warrant to lay out a lot of 16 acres, a town lot in Cohansey, for John Nichols.

A warrant to lay out for Roger Smith 10 acres of land in the town of Salem.

A warrant to lay out for Thomas Johnson 10 acres of land in the town of Salem.

26th of 6th month.—A warrant to lay out for John Snooks a town lot containing 10 acres in the town of Salem.

28th of 6th month.—A warrant to lay out 10 acres of ground for Thomas Kent, in Nevell street, in the town of Salem. The street is now known as Kent street. It extended in a straight line to Nevell's landing on the branch of Fenwick creek known at the present day as Keasbey creek; it was navigable up to James Nevell's land. The said land was recently owned by Joseph Test. It originally contained 29 acres. On that property James Nevell lived. Perhaps he disposed of more land than any other man who ever lived in Salem county. He was William Penn's agent.

In the year 1690 there appeared some dissatisfaction among some of the Swedish inhabitants of Penn's Neck, they doubting the right of William Penn to the lands in that township. He, accordingly, directed James Nevell to prepare a public dinner at his house in Salem, and invite them on a certain day to meet him there, and he would endeavor to explain to them his legal rights. They accepted the invitation and generally attended. He made a speech to them, and they were well satisfied with his statements, and went home contented after enjoying a bountiful dinner at the Governor's expense. On that occasion is the only reliable account that I have ever seen of William Penn visiting the town of Salem.

In the Autumn of 1682 John Fenwick sold all his lands in the Salem Tenth, which had been previously disposed of, to Willim Penn, proprietor of the province of Pennsylvania, except 150,000 acres. Penn, soon after the purchase, appointed James Nevell, of Salem, to be his agent in disposing of said lands. Nevell belonged to the Society of Friends, and was a lawyer, and a man in whose ability and integrity John Fenwick appears to have had implicit confidence. I presume on that account the great law-giver, William Penn, chose such a man as James Nevell to the responsible office, and Richard Tindall was continued surveyor-general, and John Worlidge his deputy. The following are the names of the persons that purchased different tracts of land in the Salem Tenth:

1684, 7th month, 10th.—A warrant to lay out for Isaac Peterson 100 acres in Penn's Neck. Signed, Richard Tindall.

16th of 9th month.—A warrant to survey for Isaac Saroy 125 acres, allowing two acres for roads adjoining John Hendrickson's land in Penn's Neck. Signed, Richard Tindall.

A warrant to lay out for Abraham Vanhest 100 acres, adjoining lands of Michael Barron, on Finn's Point, Christiana Neck. Signed, Richard Tindall.

A warrant from William Penn to survey 300 acres of land, swamp and marsh for Fopp Johnson, the said land being on the Delaware river. Signed, Richard Tindall.

1684.—A warrant from James Nevell to survey for Michael Barron 500 acres of land on one of the branches of the Alloways creek, in lieu of 500 acres purchased from John Maddox, contracted for Governor William Penn.

1685, 27th of 3d month.—A warrant to survey a tract of land in Penn's Neck for Wooley Jonson, lying between Andre Jonson and James Seaugin's plantation, being 178 acres on the Delaware river. Subscribed by Richard Tindall. Examined by James Nevell.

6th of 9th month.—A warrant to lay out 100 acres of land for John Erigson and Powell Lawson, the said land lying adjoining Bouttown in Penn's Neck. Richard Tindall, surveyor.

24th of 1st month, 1686.—A warrant to Richard Tindall to survey and lay out for Henry Jeans, of Swart Hook, 540 acres of land, marsh and swamp, lying in Penn's Neck.

16th of 7th month.—A warrant to Richard Tindall to survey

for Joshua Gillett 100 acres of land adjoining Andrew Sennick's plantation.

A warrant to Richard Tindall to lay out 110 acres of fast land marsh on Oldman's creek, for William Hughes, as part of 500 acres granted by Governor Penn to William Fleetwood. There was at the time $100 due for quit rent on the 500 acre tract.

Same date.—A warrant to Richard Tindall, surveyor-general, to lay out 110 acres of fast land and marsh on Oldman's creek, for William Fowler, as part of William Fleetwood's 500 acres granted by Governor Penn.

1686, 18th.—A warrant to Richard Tindall to lay out or survey for Thomas Naisitar, at Oldman's creek, 300 acres of fast land and meadow, being part of the land granted by William Penn to William Fleetwood.

6th month, 19th.—A warrant to Richard Tindall to lay out 20 acres of marsh for the widow Vanhuyst, lying next to Michael Barron's marsh, so as to be convenient for the purchaser and not prejudicial to the proprietor, and make a return within a month at my office at Salem. James Nevell.

1687, 1st month, 27th.—A warrant to Richard Tindall to lay out for William White 200 acres of land adjoining Hance Oulson's land at Oldman's creek, not already taken up, and not predudicial to the proprietor, make a return within three months after date hereof at my office in Salem. James Nevell.

2d, 14th.—A warrant to Richard Tindall to lay out that parcel of marsh adjoining Samuel Wade's fast land, to begin where Edward Wade's marsh ends, to 37 acres running to a small creek to Nathaniel Chambless' land, and to make a return to me in three months. James Nevell.

2d month.—A warrant to Richard Tindall and John Worlidge, his deputy, to lay out for Edward Bradway, at Alloways Creek, 100 acres of marsh, not already taken up, nor prejudicial to the proprietor, and make a return within three months from date hereof. James Nevell.

5th month, 10th, 1686.—A warrant to Richard Tindall and John Worlidge, his deputy, to lay out 100 acres of land for Hance Shahara and Martin Shahara, to commence at a crooked tree between Fopp Johnson's and Michael Barron's and adjoining lands of Andrew Sennick.

A warrant to Richard Tindall to lay out 150 acres of land for Joel Bailey, next to William Flowers, on Oldman's creek, and 10 acres of marsh, convenient as may be, but not predudicial to the proprietor, and make a return to me within three months at my office in Salem. James Nevell.

1687, 15th of 8th month.—A warrant to Richard Tindall and John Worlidge to survey for Richard Wilkinson 50 acres of fast land, lying between Hance Sahara and Andrew Sennaker's plantation, not prejudicial to the proprietor, and make a return of the doings at my office in Salem six weeks from the date. Signed, James Nevell.

1687, 2d of 2d month.—A warrant to Richard Tindall and his deputy to lay out for Benjamin Goodman, (for non-payment is now sold,) to William Handley 150 acres of land, lying and being bounded by lands of John Jonson and Henry Ivans' plantations, and make a return within three months. James Nevell.

1688, 2d of 4th month.—A warrant to Richard Tindall to survey all of the parcels of land lying between the little creek next above Fopp Johnson's plantation, and to lay out one moiety or half thereof for the orphan children of Dirk Albertson, and make a return within three months from date. James Nevell.

Lands disposed of and surveyed by order of John Fenwick's executors. Each of his executors was to have 500 acres of land as a legacy, and all of them accordingly had that quantity of land surveyed to them by John Worlidge, by order of Richard Tindall, the Surveyor General, excepting Gov. William Penn, who did not accept the legacy.

1684, 5th month, 5th.—A warrant from Richard Tindall to John Worlidge, Deputy Surveyor, to survey 400 acres of land and marsh for Ranier Vanhist, lying between Quietly Point and Richard Mazey's line, taking in the small point by the Cranberry Swamp.

8th month, 6th.—A warrant to lay out for Charles Angelo 10 acres of land, a town lot lying in Nevil Street, Salem.

8th month, 27th.—A warrant to lay out for John Jacobson 200 acres of land near Peter Johnson's plantation, on Salem creek.

1685, 2d month, 7th.—A warrant to lay out for John Harding 16 acres for a town lot on Nevil street, in Salem.

3d month, 1st—A warrant to lay out for James Clark 16 acres of land for a town lot in the town of Cohansey.

25th.—A warrant to lay out for Alexander Smith 16 acres of land for a town lot at Cohansey.

3d month, 1st—A warrant to lay out 16 acres of land for a town lot for John Clark at Cohansey.

11th month, 18th.—A warrant to lay out 32 acres of land for

two town lots at Cohansey (now Greenwich) for Joseph Brown and John Mason.

1685, 3d month, 11th.—A warrant to lay out 16 acres of land for a town lot at Cohansey for Thomas Smith.

4th month, 8th.—A warrant to lay out 16 acres of land for Richard Danger, at Cohansey Town.

1684, 10th month, 5th.—A warrant to lay out 500 acres of land for Richard Tindall, to be next to Thomas Piles' 2,000 acres, a legacy.

Same date—A warrant to lay out 500 acres for Samuel Hedge, to lie next to the above mentioned tract of land, it being a legacy.

1686, 2d month, 4th.—A warrant to lay out for John Smith, of Smithfield, 500 acres of land, to lie next to Mark Elgar's land at Alloways Creek, a legacy.

1684, 1st month—A warrant to lay out three town lots for John Smith, of Smithfield, to lie at Cohansey; 32 acres left to him by John Fenwick as a legacy; one lot of 16 acres which he purchased whilst he resided at Smithfield, England.

2d month, 18th—A warrant to lay out for Mark Reeve 16 acres for a town lot in Cohansey, the said lot to lay on Cohansey River.

1685, 23d of 5th month.—A warrant to lay out to James Vickory 200 acres of land next to Edward Web's.

5th month, 18th.—A warrant to lay out for Thomas Watson 16 acres of land at Cohansey, a town lot.

6th month, 12th.—A warrant to lay out for John Nicholas 16 acres of land at Cohansey, a town lot.

6th month, 13th.—A warrant to lay out for Roger Smith 10 acres of land in New Salem, a town lot.

6th month, 26th—A warrant to lay out for Thomas Johnson 10 acres of land in Salem Town for a home lot.

Same date—A warrant to lay out for John Kylett 10 acres of land in Salem, a town lot.

26th—A warrant to lay out 10 acres of land in the town of Salem for William Wilkinson, a town lot.

Same date.—A warrant to lay out 10 acres for John Snooks as a town lot in Salem.

26th.—A warrant to lay out 10 acres of land in Salem Town for Thomas Woodruff.

28th.—A warrant to lay out 10 acres of land for Thomas Kent in Nevil street, where he now lives, in the town of Salem.

1685, 7th of 2d month.—A warrant to survey to James Nevil the plantation in the town of Salem where he then dwelt, containing 29 acres. (The said property was recently owned by Joseph Test, of Salem.)

1687, Jan. 9th.—A warrant to Richard Tindall reserving the 500 acres of land called White's Vineyard, at that time belonging to Thomas York and Mary White.

1688, 5th month, 2d—A warrant to Richard Tindall to survey for George Proud 16 acres of land for a town lot at the town of Greenwich.

Same date.—To Richard Tindall and John Worlidge, his Deputy, a warrant to lay out for Joshua Barkstead two 16 acre lots at the town of Greenwich.

1688, 12th of 2d month.—A warrant to Richard Tindall and John Worlidge, his Deputy, to lay out two town lots in the town of Greenwich for William Bacon. The said lots, or part of them, is where the Presbyterian Church and cemetery is.

When John Fenwick directed that there should be a town laid out on the Cohanzici river, in 1678 or 1679, he gave it the name of Cohansey, and it continued to be called by that name until the year 1668, about four years after his death. About that date there was a considerable emigration to Cohansey from Connecticut, and many of them were men of influence and wealth, who changed the name to Greenwich, after their native town in Connecticut.

1685, 14th of 12th month.—A warrant to Richard Tindall to lay out 16 acres of land in the town of Cohansey for Roger Canary for a town lot, part of John Adams' 2,000 acre tract.

1686, 14th of 2d month.—A warrant to lay out 2,000 acres of land for Samuel Jennings, of Burlington, purchased of John Fenwick by Thomas Beekbane. The said land lay at the mouth of Mannington creek, adjoining lands of Rynear Vanhyest in Mannington.

26th of 2d month.—A warrant to Richard Tindall to lay out 2,000 acres of land for Thomas Hutchinson of John Fenwick's, to be laid out in some convenient place not already taken up.

100 acres to John Eaton, in the year 1734, £30; 135 acres to Martin Shere, £40; 200 acres to Garret Vanneman, £50; 100 acres of marsh to Margaret Bilderback, £25; 50 acres to Timothy Rain, £12 10s.

1735.—282 acres to William Vanneman, £70; 70 acres to Sinnick Sinaker, £11 15s.; 120 acres to Harmenus Alricks, £24; 12 acres to Sinick Sinaker, £3 15s.; 270 acres to John Wilder, £67 10s; 100 acres to William Philpot, £25; 150 acres to Erick Shere, £45.

1736-1737.—100 acres to Thomas Proctor, £25; 100 acres

to Archibald Taylor, £25; 60 acres to Thomas Miles, £12; 61 acres to John Urison, £17 15s.; 162 acres to Andrew Boon, £40 10s.; 200 acres to Paul Camp, £50; 50 acres to James Butterworth, £12 10s.; 120 acres of marsh to William Mecum, £30.

1737, Gloucester county—1,370 acres on Mantua creek sold to Thomas Spicer and Alexander Morgan for £220, but on examining the lines and boundaries the quantity found was but 1,100 complete, whereupon the proprietors were pleased to abate £20 in the deed, £200; 120 acres of land near Mantua creek to Matthew Tonkins, £30; 244 acres of land in two tracts in the forks of Mantua creek to John Hashen and D. Worthington, £73 4s. Salem county—102 acres of land in three parcels to John Eaton, £25 12s. 06d.; 117 acres to Thomas Miles in two parcels, £23 08s.; 90 acres of land and swamp to Dobson Wheeler, £25; 40 acres of land and marsh to William Mecum, £10; 200 acres of land and marsh near Oldman's creek, to Thomas Miles, £45.

1738.—403 acres in Penn's Neck to Jonathan Helms, £29; 131 acres in Penn's Neck to Samuel Linch, £32 15s.; 55 acres of land and swamp in Penn's Neck to Thomas Gilchrist, £13 15s,; 50 acres of land in Penn's Neck to James Butterworth, £12 10s.

1739—20 acres of land in Penn's Neck to Daniel Bilderback, £5; 100 acres in Penn's Neck to William Philpot, £25; 156 acres in Penn's Neck to Thomas Miles, £31 04s.; 100 acres in Penn's Neck to Samuel Linch, £25; 28 acres in Penn's Neck to John Eaton, £7 02s. 06d.; 87 acres in Penn's Neck to Cornelius Corneiluson, £21 17s. 06d.

William Penn purchased, in 1674, sixty acres of land of John Fenwick, and it was accordingly laid out within the bounds of Salem township by Richard Hancock in 1676. The land was re-surveyed by Richard Tindall in 1686, together with 25 acres of the town marsh that William Penn subsequently purchased. His heirs sold the land, together with other lands, making in all 120 acres, called the Cow Neck Farm, to Isaac Saterthwait, in 1737, for £200. J. Eldridge and Edmund Warner, of London, loaned John Fenwick money for the purpose of aiding the establishing of his Colony, for which he gave them a lease, or would be considered a mortgage, which gave rise to a considerable trouble to the proprietor and uneasiness to a number of persons who had purchased lands. Warner finally came to this country to try to effect a compromise, and purchased 32,000 acres of land in lieu of the debt. He sold 10,500 acres out of the 32,000 to the following named persons: Edward Gibbon, 500 acres; William Tarrent, two separate deeds, 500 acres each; Edward Bradway, 1,000 acres joining Henry Salter's lands on the south, known at the present day as Stoe Neck; John Smith, Esq., 1,000 acres; John Mason, Esq., 5,000 acres; Roger Pedrick, of Oldman's creek, 1,000 acres, Edward Matthews, 500 acres; Richard Morgan, 500 acres. All of the said land, excepting Edward Bradway's, was laid out in what is now Cumberland county. When, 1682, Penn purchased the right and title of all the lands in Fenwick's Colony which had not already been sold, (Fenwick reserving for himself and heirs 150,000,) it appears he assumed the debt Eldridge and Warner held against the Salem Tenth. In the settlement of James Nevell with William Penn, 26th of 5th month, 1686, Penn was credited with the amount that the 10,500 acres had brought, although it was sold by Eldridge and Warner previous to Penn's purchase.

2d of 8th month.—An order from James Logan to Benjamin Acton, to survey to Joseph Gregory a point of vacant marsh, lying between his 100 acre lot of Michael Barron and a small creek, for which he is to pay at the rate of 20 pounds a hundred, clear of quit-rents.

There follows an account of James Nevell of what he received for the different tracts of land he sold for Gov. William Penn in Salem county, and in parts of Gloucester county, and what he paid.

1685—William Penn, Dr., to Nathaniel Lumly, £23; to Roger Canare, £2 1s; to Isaac Savoy and David Hendrickson, £30; to Maughhauskey Indian chief and sixteen other Indians when they expected to meet Gov. William Penn here to purchase their lands, 11s; to James Atkinson, by a bill on J. Smith, £12; to James Adkinson, for 1977 ℔s. of beef, £20 11s. 10½d.; to two bushels of salt, 10s.; for bringing a cask of meat from Elsinburg, 8s.; to James Atkinson, for 87 ℔s. of pork, 18s. 1½d.; to John Grub, by order of James Harrison, £2; to George Emly, for two cows, £8s.; and driving them to Philadelphia, 18s.; to James Williams, at New Castle, order from James Harrison, of Philadelphia, £3; to 42 ℔s. of fresh beef, received by Thomas Holme, £4; to one hogshead of beef, 738 ℔s., and 480 ℔s. of pork, at 20 shillings per hundred, £12 3s. 7d.; to freight by Henry Grub, £1 11s. 6d.; to seven barrels of pork, 1726 ℔s. £17 5s. 3d.; to four bushels of salt, 16s.; freight to Pennsbury, by Seth Smith, £2 6s. 8d.; to thirty skepples of Indian corn and ten fletches of bacon, £14 1s. 6d.; to carriage to Pennsbury, by

Seth Smith, £1 17s. 4d.; to Griffith Jones, 14 bushels of Indian corn, £1 17s.

1686—To Samuel Carpenter, by an order of James Harrison, £20; to four barrels of pork at 2s. 15d., £11; to 50 skipples of Indian corn, by Seth Hill, £5; freight to Pennsbury, £1 8s. Total £200 7s.

1685—Gov. William Penn, Cr., by Hance Oulson, for land, £14 10s.; by John Grice, do., £15; by John Vanjining, £16; by Hance Shehere and Lucas Johnson, £13 10s.; by Yeallis Gill Johnson and Garret Vanjining, £17 1s. 8d.; by William Gill Johnson, £18 12s.; by John Lecroy, £12 8s.; by Michael Lecroy, £18 12s.; by John Hendrickson, £36 11s.; by David Hendrickson, £5; by Lucas Peterson, £18 13s.; by Joseph Erigson, £12; by Powell Powelson, £14 13s.; by Isaac Savoy, £10; by Abraham Vauhest, £10; by Henry Jeans, £16 17s.; by Fopp Johson, £11 14s.; Johanes Shays, £3; by Andre Johnson, £12 5s.; by Richard Pitman, £5 5s.; by Woolly Tauson, £14 10s. Total, £295 1s.; Joshua Gillet, £10; William Hanby, £5; Edward Bradway, £10; Martin Shehere, £10; Peter Bilderback and Andrew Anderson, £12 10s.; Richard Wilkinson, £5 6s.; Isaac Savoy, £3; Michael Barran, quit-rent for 500 acres, £1 10d. Total, £62 16s. 10d.

1687—Gov. William Penn, debtor—George Hutchinson and James Budd, £5; John Harding, by order of J. Harrison, £4; tax on his land in Salem Town, 1s. 6d.; Samuel Carpenter, by an order of James Harrison, £20; 11 barrels of beef, sent by Seth Smith, £27 10s.; freight to Pennsbury, £1 13s.; Samuel Carpenter, by order of Capt. Markham, £10.

1688.—Sent by Seth Smith 100 bushels of Indian corn, £10; 1 barrel of beef, £2; 6 flitches of bacon, 201 ℔s. £5 6d.; freight £2 5s.; S. Carpenter by John Cornelius; £10; John Worlidge, surveyor, by an order of James Marshall and Thomas Gardiner, for running a plantation, £13 10s.; James Atkinson, 1 barrel of pork for Samuel Carpenter, at Philadelphia, £2 15s. Total, £115 3s.

	£	s	d
1688.			
Governor William Penn, Cr.,	358	18	06
Governor William Penn, Dr.,	315	10	10
Balance due,	43	07	08
Dr. for my stipend from 1682 to 1688,	60	00	00
Tax on his 60 acres of land in Salem,	00	02	00
	16	14	10

1689.—William Penn, Dr., to balance, £16 14s. 10d.; six flotchers of bacon, 178 pounds, £3 14s. 02d.; 20 bushels of wheat, @3s ⅌ bushel, £3; Richard Russell, order of Captain Markham, £10 6s.; to re-survey Barron's land, 1,000 acres, there being 200 acres surplus, £3 7s.; to re-survey Bout town land, and found 549 acres overplus, £5; surveying and laying out 469 acres of orphans' land near Fopp Johnson's, and making an equal division in two parts, £1 10s.; Henry Taylor, for going with the surveyor running the Picton line, by order of Thomas Gardiner, £4 15s.; the expenses at Barrons and the Governor's tenants summoned by me to agree on a certain place where they should pay their quit rents, £1 4s.; 6 barrels of beef, by George Haslewood, £12; freight to Philadelphia, 13s. 4d.; making a ditch in William Penn's town marsh within Salem township, £2 05s.; to my stipend for one year, £10; summoning the Swedes of Penn's Neck to meet William Penn Salem, £1 08s. 09d. Total, £76 10s. 07d.

1689.—Governor William Penn, Cr.—By John Erickinson, £2 13s.; William Hanby, £5; Thomas Dunn, £5 09s. 07d.; Widow Hendrickson's land at Finn's Point, £3 04s. 06d.; Wooly Tourson, £3 06s.: Richard Wilkinson, £4 14s.; Henry Cornelius, £4; Samuel Wade, for 37 acres of marsh, £3 14s.; Steven Yearns, £3 10s.; William Shute, £4; Lucus Peterson, £4; 8 bushels of barley, from Widow Hendrickson, 16s.; William Hewes, for quit rent, 05s.; Richard Wilsonson, quit rent, 06s.; wheat, Mary Hendrickson, £2 05s.; Steven Yearns, £6 05s. 07d.: Jacob Hendrickson, £2 17s. 09d.; William Hanby, £3 15s.; Jacob Saroy, 2 years quit rent for 450 acres, due 29th of 7th month, 1686, £1 05s. 06d.; 8½ bushels wheat by David Hendrickson, £13 15s.; do, to 4 bushels of wheat, and quit rent due 1686, 12s.; William Hanby, 3 bushels of wheat for quit rent, 09s.; Jacob Henderson, his purchase, £4; Lucas Peterson, his purchase, £3 10s.; Richard Pitman, by Thomas York, £5; received of Steven Yearns by Edward Champney, £2 06d.; received from Joseph Erickson 6 bushel of wheat for three years' quit rent 29th of 7th month, 1688, 18s.; John Hendrickson, six bushels of wheat for quit rent, 18s.

6th of 7th month, 1691.—William Penn, Dr.—To my stipend for one year, £10; 10 barrels of beef, to Samuel Caapenter, £20; freight to Philadelphin, by William Hall, £1; a year's salary, £10.

1691.—Governor William Penn, Cr.—Joshua Gillett, 100 acres of land, £5 10s.; Steven Yearns, £2 19s.; Lucas Peterson, £1 14s. 06d.; Mary Hendrickson, £1 05s. 11d.; Steven Yearns, quit rent, 04s. 11d.; Richard Wilkinson, quit rent, 06s.; Tobias Gillet, £2 10s.; Joel Bailey, £8; Mary Hendrickson, £4 05s. 11d.; Ephraim Herman, for the widow of Dick Albertson, called Orphans' land, £11; Matthias Johnson, for Isaac Savoy, £2 10s.; Edward Goodwin, £3 10s.; Thomas Galipeng, for Joel Bailey, £2 10s.; Lucas Peterson, quit rent, 15s. 06d.

Deeds signed by William Penn's heirs, being proprietors for lands in Salem county, the principal part of the land being laid out in Penn's Neck and Gloucester county.

Gloucester county.—650 acres to Thomas Spicer, dated 1st of 9th month, 1734, £—; 550 acres to Joseph Coles, same date, £320; 50 acres to Jeremiah Baker, same date, £15. Salem county.—41 acres to Edmund Weatherby, same date, £10, 07s. 06d.; 150 acres to Samuel Linch, 1734, £37, 10s.; 60 acres to Thomas Miles, same date, £12; 350 acres to John Dunn, 1734, £105.

1688—A warrant to Richard Tindall and his deputy, to lay out for Henry Cornelius 100 acres of land lying next to the creek, bounds of Finn's Point, running from thence toward Cranberry Swamp; lay it out not prejudicial to the proprietor, and make a return in six weeks. James Nevell.

19th of 2d month, 1688—To Richard Tindall, Surveyor General, and John Worlidge, his deputy: At the information of Thomas Arnold, Michael Barron hath more than one thousand acres of land and marsh in the bounds he claimeth on that side of Salem creek where he now liveth: This is to authorize you to resurvey the said one thousand acres of fast land and marsh, beginning at the side of Delaware river and up Salem creek, and backward in the woods as convenient for length and breadth as may not be prejudicial to the proprietor and make a return of the survey to me at my office in Salem within three months from date. For your so doing, this shall be your warrant, at the charge of said Thomas Arnold. Signed by James Nevell.

1689, 20th of 11th month.—A warrant to Richard Tindall and John Worlidge to survey for Joshua Gillet 100 acres of fast land and marsh, as it is most convenient for him and not prejudicial to the proprietor, and make a return of your doings at my office in Salem within three month's date. Signed, James Nevell.

18th of 7th month, 1688—A warrant to Richard Tindall and his deputy, John Worlidge, to lay out 100 acres of fast land and marsh lying between the line of Finn's Point and Thomas Budd's Island, not already taken up, nor to be prejudicial to the proprietor, and make a return of your doings at my office in Salem. Signed, James Nevell.

22d of 11th month, 1688.—A warrant to Richard Tindall and John Worlidge, his deputy, to resurvey for Steven Yearans, at his request, all that land that lies within the old bounds of the 1,000 acres of land and marsh formerly surveyed by Richard Hancock for the Finns, at Finn's Point, and make a return of your doings at my office in Salem Town, within three months after date. If a vacancy happens between 1,000 acres, if it is not convenient to the former owners, but beneficial to the proprietor, to make a plantation for others, then crave such land at my disposal. Signed, James Nevell.

7th of 11th month, 1688.—Order from John Fenwick's executors: A warrant to Richard Tindall, Surveyor General for the county of Salem, and John Worlidge, his deputy, to lay out one acre of land in Salem Town, given by John Fenwick, on which to erect a court house and prison.

1689.—A warrant to Richard Tindall, Surveyor General for the county of Salem, to lay out for John Worlidge a lot 200 feet front, adjoining the lot laid out in Salem Town for Edward Champneys, and running back to the marsh. Fenwick's executors.

May 2d, 1689.—A warrant to Richard Tindall, and John Worlidge, his deputy, to resurvey for Thomas Bubb 500 acres of land, formerly laid out by Richard Hancock, beginning at the first bounds.

1686, January 10th.—A warrant to Richard Tindall to lay out a piece of vacant land for John Snooks, lying next to his town lot in Salem Town.

20th.—A warrant to lay out for John Worlidge, the deputy Surveyor, a piece of vacant land lying between John Smith's and John Pledger's lands, at Alloways Creek or Monmouth Precinct.

1687, 18th of 6th month.—A warrant to Richard Tindall to lay out 16 acres of land for a house and lot in Cohansey for John March.

1687, 16th of 9th month.—A warrant to Richard Tindall, Surveyor for Salem Tenth, and John Worlidge, his deputy, to lay out for William Wilkinson 10 acres, part of the vacancy between Gov. William Penn's 60 acres in Salem Town which he bought of John Fenwick and Strickly Marshall's land.

1690—A warrant to Richard Tindall to lay out 200 acres of land for Wolly Wagson, being part of the manor of Fenwick's Grove.

1691, 15th of 3d month.—A warrant to Richard Tindall to lay out and survey 16 acres of land in the town of Greenwich for John Ketcham, late of New York Colony, out of the estate of John Fenwick, deceased.

1691, 20th of 8th month.—A warrant to Richard Tindall and his deputy to resurvey, regulate and subdivide all the tracts of land formerly surveyed by Richard Hancock, on Shrewsberry Neck, south side of Cohansey, excepting John Gillman's 400 acres, which is to be left as formerly, and to make a return within three months at my office in Salem. Signed, James Nevell.

1st of 2d month, 1690.—There being a common report that Governor Penn had never any interest in land in Salem county, I desired the inhabitants of Penn's Neck, to whom I had sold lands, to give me a meeting at Barron's, where I gave them a dinner and explained to them; they appeared to be satisfied, and it stopped the current report. James Nevell.

23d of 1st month, 1690.—A warrant to Richard Tindall, surveyor-general of Salem county, to lay out for Powell Jaquette 15 acres of land or marsh, as allowance for roads through his 300 acres purchased from John Fenwick, beginning on the north-east side of Henry Jeans, his bounds next to the river Delaware, so as to be convenient to the purchaser, not prejudicial to the proprietor, and make a return of your doings to me at my office in Salem. Signed, James Nevell.

May 12th, 1691.—A warrant to Richard Tindall and his assistant to survey and lay out for Edward Godwin of land and marsh, allowance for roads in Penn's Neck, as convenient 100 acres as the purchaser shall direct, not prejudicial to the proprietor, nor already taken up, and make a return at my office in Salem, of his doings three months after date. Subscribed, James Nevell.

June 20th.—A warrant to Richard Tindall and his assistant to survey and lay out all the vacancy of fast land and meadow that lies between William Hanley and Lucas Peterson, and make return to me, at my office in Salem, within three months from date. Subscribed, James Nevell.

May 13th, 1691.—A warrant to Richard Tindall to lay out 4000 acres of land for Roger Milton, attorney for William Milton, his brother, who purchased 4000 acres of Francis Harding, and to lay the same out as follows: 100 acres joining lands taken up by John Tirack, including cedar swamp; 600 acres, joining on Joshua Berkstead lands, and the remainder where it is not already taken up. James Nevell.

7th of 8th month, 1691.—Whereas, I granted a warrant to Roger Milton, as above mentioned, for the laying out 4000 acres, and to make a return thereof to me at my office, in Salem, within three months, and no return is yet made. At the request of said Roger Milton, these are to authorize Richard Tindall to lay out and survey the said 4000 acres of land and marsh as convenient as may be, not already taken up, nor prejudicial to the proprietor. If it may be convenient let the 4000 acres be joined upon the lands of Joseph Berkstead, George Hazlewood, Robert Hutchinson and John Mason, leaving no lands nor cripples between, so the 4000 acres may be as entire as may be, and make a return of your doings here to me, at my office in Salem, within three months from date. Subscribed, James Nevell.

29th of 4th month, 1692.—A warrant to John Worlidge to re-survey all of the 500 acres of land laid out by Richard Hancock for Roger Huskins, to begin at the bounds of land formerly laid out for Richard Hancock, now in possession of William Tyler, and to run the old courses as near as may be, without coming into other lands, until you complete 468 acres, there being two 16 acre lots allowed out of the 500 acres.

1692.—A warrant to John Worlidge to survey for Benjamin Clark, son and heir of Thomas Clark, deceased, beginning by and joining Thomas Hutchinson's land, near Gravelly Run or Stoe Creek, and make a return to me, at my office in Salem, within three months. Subscribed, James Nevell.

18th of 1st month, 1712.—An order from James Logan to Benjamin Acton, to survey 150 acres of marsh for William Hall, adjoining his plantation. The land formerly belonged to Michael Barron, for which William Hall pays £25 clear of quit rents.

18th of 1st month, 1713.—An order from James Logan to Benjamin Acton to divide the 500 acres formerly granted to Michael Barron, into several parcels, to William Hall 100, to John Smith 100, to Joseph Gregory 100, to Abraham Vanhest 200 acres, the said 500 acres having never been confirmed to Michael Barron, the several persons before mentioned, who all derive a right from him are now to pay respectively £25 of current money per hundred acres, excepting William Hall, to whom £5 are abated clear of quit rent.

The point or neck of land bounded on the west by the Pautuxet river, as it was called by the Indians, now known as the Delaware river; on the south by Asamahocking creek, now Salem, was called by the natives Obisquahosit. When John

QUIT RENTS AND WARRANTS.

Fenwick arrived in this country with his English colony, to take possession of his tenth of West New Jersey, he found a settlement of Finns and Swedes, who had emigrated from their fatherland, as early as 1638 or 1640, in company with a number of their countrymen, who had settled on the opposite side of the river, about the mouth of the Christiana, and along the said river, as far as where the city of Philadelphia now is. Many of the Finns and Swedes had purchased their lands of the natives and taken deeds from the Indian chiefs, but they early acknowledged that Fenwick was the rightful owner, and had their land re-surveyed and deeded to them. For this they were to pay to the proprietor, or his heirs, certain sums for quit rents, to be paid yearly according to the number of acres each owned. Samuel Hedge, Jr., in 1690, made out a duplicate, or role as he called it, of what each landholder should pay quit rent for that year. The said lands, I presume, were part of the reserved 150,000 acres, made by John Fenwick when he sold his proprietory right to William Penn, 1682.

The following are the names of the inhabitants of Penns Neck who paid quit-rents: Matt Neilson, Fopp Neilson, Peter Onson, 1,040 acres, 2s. 1d.; Steven Yearneans, Stacy Hendrickson, Matthias Spacklesson, 1,040 acres, 3s.; Evick Yearneans, 300 acres, 3d.; John Yearneans, 300 acres, 3d.; Matt Joanson, 150 acres, 3d.; Andrew Anderson, 150 acres, 3d.; Stacy Corneillinson, 250 acres, 5d.; Ann Hendricks, 150 acres, 3d.; Andrew Seneca (now Sinnickson) 226 acres, 1s.; Hance Shershell, 100 acres, 3d.; Claus Joanson, 100 acres, 3d.; Jones Scoggin, 200 acres, 2s.; Woley Woolson, 200 acres, 20 shad, or 2s.; Roger Pedrick, 140 acres, 1s.; Barce Jacobson, 200 acres, 4s.; Peter Halter, 200 acres, 2s.; A. C. Bronson, 250 acres, 1s.; Jarvis Bywator, 200 acres, 2s. 2d.; Richard Tindall, 230 acres, 3d.; Thomas Waltson 200 acres, 1s.; James Vickory, 300 acres, 2s. 1d.; Peter Wilkinson, 400 acres, 1s. 1d.; Andorcas Barleyson, 400 acres, 1s.; Richard Marcy, 150 acres, 1s.; Renier Vanhyost, 400 acres, 3s.; John Cullin, 200 acres, 1s. 2d.; Barnard Webb, 250 acres, 2s.; Mary White, 500 acres, 5s.; John Perkins, 300 acres, 3s.; George Garrett, 300 acres, 3s.

Lands in Pilesgrove township: Richard Tindall, 195 acres, 1s.; Mary Holman, 2,000 acres, £1; Nicholas Winton, 500 acres, 2d.; John Derickson, 500 acres, 2d.; Thomas Potter, 500 acres, 1s.; Richard Lippincott, 1000 acres, 1s. 1d.; William Shotlock, 500 acres, 1s.; William Worth, 500 acres, 1s.; Thomas Smith, 250 acres, 1s.; William Jonson, 250 acres, 2s.; Lewis Morris, 1,000 acres, 2s.

Lands in Alloways Creek subject to quit-rents: Edward Wade, meadow 100 acres, 1s.; John Hancock, 100 acres, 1s.; Thomas Smith, 300 acres, 3d.

Lands at Cohansey: Obadiah Holmes, 4 acres, 1d.; Anthony Woodhouse, 80 acres, 5d.; Samuel Hunter, 80 acres, 5d.; Richard Tindall, 100 acres, 2s.; John Clark, 16 acres, 2d.; John Clark, 16 acres, 2d.; Alexander Smith, 16 acres, 2d.; Thomas Watson, 16 acres, 2d.; Mark Reeves, 16 acres, 2d.; John Mason, 16 acres, 2d.; Thomas Smith 16 acres, 2d.; William Bacon, 32 acres, 4d.; Joseph Bronson, 16 acres, 2d.; Samuel Bacon, 16 acres, 2d.; John Bacon, 16 acres, 2d.; Edward Hurlbert, 32 acres, 4d.; Job Holmes 22 acres, 4d.; Joseph Dennis 32 acres, 4d.; Enoch Moore, 16 acres, 2d.; Francis Alexander, 32 acres, 4d.; Peter Craven, 2 acres, 1d.; Thomas Stuthem, 2 acres, 1d.; Joseph Bacon, 16 acres, 2d.

The quit-rents of Salem town were as follows: William Milton, 10 acres, 1d.; William Milton, 10 acres, 1d.; Thomas Smith, 6 acres, 1d.; Christopher Saunders, 10 acres, 1d.; William Wilkinson, 8 acres, 3d.; C. Lumbley, 10 acres, 1d.; Richard Daniel, 10 acres, 1d.; Joseph White, 10 acres, 1d.; R. Johnson, 10 acres, 1d.; Anthony Dixon, 10 acres, 1d.; James Nevil, 20 acres, 3d.; Thomas Woodruff, 10 acres, 1d.; John Harden 16 acres, $1\frac{1}{2}$d.; John Snooks, 10 acres, 1d.; Edward Champneys, 10 acres, 1d.; John Rolph, 10 acres, 1d.; William Wilkinson, 10 acres, 1d.; Thomas Johnson, 10 acres, 1d.; Thomas Woodruff, 17 acres, $1\frac{1}{2}$d.; John Snooks, 16 acres, $1\frac{1}{2}$d.; 2d lot of William Wilkinson, 10 acres, 1d.; Joseph Cauloyd's lot, 20 acres, 2d.; John Worledge, 20 acres, 2d.; Thomas York's lot, 5 acres, 4d.; Eleazer Dovberry, $2\frac{1}{2}$ acres, 2d.

It appears the emigrants that came with Fenwick, and a number of others, that did not arrive until two or three years afterwards, who had purchased land of him before he left England, were exempted from paying quit-rents to the proprietor, or his heirs. Such men as Robert Windham, John Pledger, Samuel Nicholson, Isaac Smart, Robert and Edward Wade, James Sherron, the two John Smiths, Richard Guy, Christopher White, Edward Bradway, William Hancock, and several others, together with William Penn, who bought sixty acres of the proprietor at the same period. The said land was surveyed for him by Richard Hancock, in 1676. It was situated within the precincts of the town of Salem. The reader will perceive by the role of the quit-rents that were collected by Samuel Hedge, about the year 1690, for the heirs of Fenwick, it being eight years after William Penn purchased the so much talked of twelve mile circle of land and water of James, the Duke of York. There is no reliable evidence that William Penn ever attempted to claim any lands in West New Jersey except by purchase of the Jersey proprietors. It would be derogatory to his great name to think otherwise.

SURVEYORS.

Names of the most eminent surveyors in Fenwick Colony from the time of the first English settlement:

Richard Noble was the first surveyor appointed by the proprietor. It appears by the most reliable record that he died a short time afterwards. Richard Hancock succeeded him. He surveyed large tracts of land for different individuals, but owing to his incompetency John Fenwick, in 1680, removed him, and appointed Richard Tyndell as surveyor-general of the province and John Worlidge as deputy-surveyor. After the death of John Fenwick (which event took place in the autumn of 1683) they were continued in office by his executors; and James Nevell, of Salem, was appointed by William Penn as his agent to dispose of his lands in the Salem Tenth. Nevell employed Richard Tyndell and John Worlidge to do the surveying, likewise to re-survey large tracts of lands that had previously been surveyed by Richard Hancock. After the death of Tyndell and Worlidge, which took place in the early part of last century, Benjamin Acton was the principal surveyor in the colony; likewise was appointed by James Logan, agent of William Penn and heirs, to survey large tracts of land that remained unsold within the Salem Tenth. Joseph Miller, and his son, Ebenezer Miller, who had recently come from the state of Connecticut, settled at the town of Greenwich, in North Cohansey precinct, were both land surveyors. Joseph, however, died in a short time afterwards. His son, Ebenezer, became eminent in his calling and did an extensive business in surveying, both in Salem and Cumberland counties. He died at Greenwich in 1774, aged 72 years, leaving a large family of children.

Thomas Miles, of Penn's Neck, was an eminent surveyor, and became conspicuous as such as early as 1725. He also did considerable surveying for the heirs of Penn, lands lying within the bounds of Penn's Neck, Mannington, and the lower part of Gloucester county. It is probable he died about 1760. I have not seen any of his public acts as surveyor after that time.

George Trenchard, Sr., by tradition, came from East Jersey,

and settled in the township of Alloways Creek, in this county, as early as 1725. He soon became an active and useful man; was assessor for the Monmouth precinct for some years, and did a large amount of surveying throughout Salem and Cumberland counties. In regard to his penmanship it has seldom been equalled in this section of country. He left children—his son George Trenchard, Jr., married a daughter of Andrew Sinnickson, of Penn's Neck; he and his wife resided in that township. Their daughter married James Kinsey. James Trenchard, the surveyor, residing at Bridgeton at this time, is a lineal descendant of George Trenchard, Sr.

Elnathan Davis, of Shiloh, was considered in his time the *"Captain General of the public surveyors," both in Cumberland and Salem counties. He did a large amount of surveying, not only in his own county, but in all West Jersey. It was done so accurately that it was seldom or ever doubted by future surveyors. He left three sons—Jedediah, Jeremiah, and Ebenezer Davis, all three of whom were practical surveyors. After the death of the Davises they were succeeded by Hosea Moore, who was the leading practical surveyor of Cumberland county.

William White was born at Pilesgrove about the year 1751. He became an eminent surveyor in Salem county, particularly in the upper part, and the lower section of Gloucester. During the great land trial some fifty or sixty years ago, he was generally subpœnaed to attend the courts at Salem to point out the different lines laid down on the maps, showing conclusively that the courts had full confidence in his practical abilities as a surveyor. That peculiar talent in that branch of mathematics, it seems, was transmitted to some of his descendants. His son, Samuel White, was a surveyor, as was also his grandson, the late William Haines, of Gloucester county. The latter was considered in his native county a very good mathematician and surveyor. His son, Job Haines, has now taken his place. Josiah Harrison, late of the town of Salem, was a lawyer, but during a part of his life he did a large business in surveying. Edward, the son of John and Temperance Keasbey Smith, was a public surveyor in Salem county for a number of years. He afterwards removed with his family to one of the western States, and was succeeded soon after by Joseph E. Brown, who soon became conspicuous in the profession. The maps of his surveys are considered by the best judges to be equal if not superior to any of his predecessors. His health, however, declined, and

---

*So styled by the late venerable Josiah Harrison, Esq., of Salem.

John N. Cooper, of Salem, took his place. He has done a large amount of business in that line for a number of years. He was employed about eight years ago as one of the Commissioners, and also surveyor, to survey all the meadows and low lands above John Denn's canal, up to the head tide waters of Salem creek, for the purpose of taxing the same to defray the expense of cutting the canal. There was included in the survey seven or eight thousand acres. His map of the meadow and the several courses and distances of Salem creek, from the before mentioned Denn's canal, in accuracy and workmanship (as deposited in the Clerk's office) is of a superior order. Belford M. Bonham, of Cumberland, has a mathematical talent of a superior order. He commenced as a public surveyor in early life; his surveying has been very extensive, not only in his native county, but also in Salem; and has frequently been called on in difficult cases in other sections of the State, the public having confidence in his accuracy, particularly so in running ancient lines, he having in his possession most of the surveys of the renowned Elnathan Davis, that alone giving him a great advantage in his line of business. The late Ellis Ayares, who resided in Upper Alloways Creek, did quite a considerable business as surveyor for several years. George R. Morrison, son of the late William Morrison, resides at Salem and does an extensive business in surveying. He, in early life, manifested a mathematical turn of mind, which he inherited from his grandfather, on his mother's side, the late Dalymore Harris, of Hancock's Bridge, who had also been a surveyor. I have been informed by those that knew him when young that his memory was so reliable that when surveying small tracts of land he made no field notes.

APPENDIX.

BOWEN FAMILY.

It is proper that I should refer to the ancient family of the Bowens. They evidently belonged to an ancient family of Wales. Judge Elmer thinks that the name has been corrupted from Bowmen to Bowen, that is warriors armed with bows. I think he is correct in his assertion, for Jonathan Davis, the Baptist clergyman that settled at Trenton, when he left Long Island, married Elizabeth Bowen, of Bowmantown. I presume the family in Wales were numerous. About the year 1662, (some antiquarians think it was in 1664), quite a number of Bowens and Davises left Swansea in Glamorganshire, Wales. The Bowens settled in Massachusetts, and called the place Swansea, after their native town. They were Baptists, and consequently were obnoxious to the rigid Puritans. The Davis family soon left and located on Long Island. Part of the Bowen family, agreeably to their history, left Massachusetts and formed a settlement in East Jersey, and called the place Bowmantown. I think their stay was of short duration, for as early as 1687 a number of the family purchased of the original proprietors, lands within Fenwick's Colony, known at that time as North Cohansey precinct, some two miles southwest of the present city of Bridgeton, and at that place they made a settlement and called it Bowentown, which name it has at the present time. Why it should receive the name of town I am unable to understand, although it is probable several of them built themselves small log dwellings contiguous to each other, similar to the first New England settlers on the south side of the Cohansey, which went under the name of New England town. The Bowens and others located and became large owners of as fertile lands as there are in West Jersey. This fertile land commences on the north side of Cohansey river, includes what is known as Dutch Neck, (formerly Cohansey Neck), the general course is northeast, embracing all of Hopewell, part of Stoe Creek, and the whole of Deerfield township, the eastern part of Upper Alloways Creek, and all of Upper Pittsgrove, in Salem county. In this fertile vein of land there are not less than one hundred and fifty thousand acres. Judging from the timber still standing upon this tract, it must once have been covered with extensive forests of the best quality timber, such as white and black oak, walnut, hickory, chestnut and other kinds of trees adapted to the soil and climate. I have no doubt when the early settlers first cleared the land, and put the soil in order for cultivation, the land yielded abundantly, for several generations. The inhabitants lived a long distance from the meadows that lie along Delaware Bay, likewise meadows on the creeks. After about one century, their once fertile lands became much reduced, so that hundreds of acres were thrown out in commons. Many sold their lands for whatever they could get for it, and emigrated to the far West. They knew not what inexhaustible mines of wealth in the form of marl lay in the bowels of the earth near the surface, with very little labor to obtain. The said marl is found on the head branches of Stoe creek, which is near the centre of the large and fertile lands I described. What a change the free use of marl has made on lands that fifty or sixty years ago were not worth over ten or twenty dollars per acre, now selling at one hundred, and one hundred and fifty dollars per acre; some desirable locations for a much higher price. Besides the marl which is so extensively used with such good effect, the great English grass, known as red clover, has been introduced within the last sixty or seventy years. Its usefulness is not confined to the large amount of hay it produces, but by its strong tap-root it prepares the soil for the two staple crops of cereals, wheat and Indian corn. There is a general thrift among the farmers in this fertile region, their lands producing as well as when in their virgin state. Large and convenient dwellings and outbuildings everywhere abound, and their churches and school houses are kept in good repair, and a high state of morals pervade the community generally.

If we include the lineage of the female line of the Bowens, they are one of the largest families that ever inhabited Cumberland county. The grandmother of Elnathan Davis was Elizabeth Bowen; her descendants are numerous. The Bowens and the ancient and large family of Swinneys intermarried. Ethan Swinney's, (who is at present one of the ruling elders of the Seventh-Day Baptist Church at Shiloh) great-grandmother was a Bowen. Those by that name that first came to West Jersey were David, Richard, Jonathan, Noah, Dan and Elijah. It is probable most, or all of them belonged to the Seventh-Day Baptist Church. Timothy Brooks was their pastor. The next generation of Bowens attached themselves mostly to the Cohansey

Church; a few of them, however, still adhered to their original faith. Richard Bowen married, had one son—Joseph Bowen, who subsequently married, and had two or more sons. Richard was the eldest, born in 1734; he had a brother who enlisted in the army of the Revolution, and served under Col. Hand and Holme, and was killed in the skirmish at Quinton's Bridge. When Captain Smith made an attack on the British troops that lay about half a mile off in Judge John Smith's house, Smith crossed the bridge, contrary to the orders of his superior officers, they being at that time at Thompson's Bridge. Richard Bowen, his brother, married, and had children; one of them, Joseph Bowen, married Mary Gill.

Joseph Bowen and his wife, Mary Bowen, had four children, all of whom grew to mature age. Their names were Hannah, Joseph, Elizabeth and Robert Bowen. Hannah, the eldest, married Andrew Bell; they had twelve children. Their names were Samuel, Benjamin, Mary, Robert, Joseph, Sarah, Hannah, Ann, Lydia, Andrew, and Harriet Bell; all of them are living. Joseph, the son of Joseph and Mary Bowen, was born in 1802; he subsequently married Lydia Carll, daughter of Jesse Carll, Jr.; they have no children. Elizabeth, daughter of Joseph and Mary Bowen, married David Madcliff; they had two children, both of them deceased. Robert, son of Joseph and Mary Bowen, died unmarried. Mary, the wife of Joseph Bowen, Sr., died in 1847, aged more than three score years and ten. Joseph, her husband, died in 1859, aged about 87 years. His father, Richard Bowen, died in 1822, aged 88 years. I shall not attempt to give the descendants of David Bowen; sufficient for me to say, many of them were conspicuous members of both civil and religious societies, and most of them strictly adhered to the religious sect of their forefathers.

It is generally believed that Elijah Bowen was the first physician in that part of Salem county, and was one of the founders of Shiloh Church. This Elijah Bowen was the son of Jonathan Bowen, one of the first emigrants to Bowentown. His wife was a Bowen also, a distant relative; their eldest son was Jonathan Bowen, 2d. Jonathan Bowen, 2d, inherited the homestead of his father at Bowentown; he had several children. One son, named David Bowen, was appointed Sheriff of the county by William Franklin, at that time the Royal Governor, that being in 1775, but was superseded by Joel Fithian, elected under the provision of the new constitution by the people. He built the house occupied by John S. Holmes, and owned the farm. He married Ruth, daughter of Samuel Fithian. He died in 1808, leaving one son, Jonathan Bowen, 3d. David Bowen, son of Dr. Elijah Bowen, was born 6th of 9th month. 1762. He married Jane, the daughter of Matthew Potter; she was born 28th of 1st month, 1772. They had two children—Daniel and Harriet Bowen. The daughter married Ephraim Holmes; she left descendants. David Bowen died in 1797, aged about 34 years; his wife, Jane Potter Bowen, died in 1837, aged about 65 years. Jonathan Bowen, 3d, appears to have been a man of great energy of character. He became a member in early life of the Cohansey Baptist Church; was a member of the Convention that adopted the new constitution of the State in 1776. About the commencement of the revolution he removed from the home of his ancestors to Bridgeton. He soon became one of the most enterprising citizens of the place; was elected eight years in succession to the State Legislature. He left one son—Smith Bowen. Smith Bowen, son of Jonathan, born May 26, 1763, was married three times. His first wife was a young woman of Cape May, by the name of Hand; by her he had two children—Mary, who married William Bacon, of Greenwich, and a son, Daniel Bowen. He was a physician and married Elizabeth, daughter of Jonathan and Hannah Shourds Smith, of Woodstown. Daniel and his wife had three children—Smith Bowen, born in 1818; Mary Elizabeth, born in 1820; and Hannah S. Bowen, born in 1822. The two youngest are deceased. Smith Bowen is a merchant in the city of Philadelphia. He married Anna Bispham; they have eight children—Maria Elizabeth, Augustus Bispham, Anna S., Alice, Samuel, Susan Doughton, Laura, and John Bispham Bowen. Smith's third wife was the widow of David Bowen, and daughter of Matthew Potter. He had by her three children—Jane P., who married John Buck; Dr. William S. Bowen, born in 1802; died 1872. He was a practicing physician in Bridgeton for 49 years. Dr. William S. Bowen's first wife was Ellen, daughter of Thomas Lee, of Port Elizabeth; they had two children—William S. Bowen, Jr., and Jane P. Bowen, who married Dr. Joseph C. Kirby. Dr. William S. Bowen's second wife was Martha, daughter of John Buck by his first wife. They had three children—Dr. John B. Bowen, who married Hannah, daughter of Jonathan Elmer, and granddaughter of Robert McLean. They have two children—Sydney E. and William Cortland Bowen. The names of the other two children of Dr. William S. Bowen are Charles M. and Mary B.; both are deceased.

CARLL FAMILY.

In writing the history of Jesse Carll, Sr., and his descendants, at that time I mentioned that there was a family of Carlls located in Cumberland county. One of that family has written a sketch of the Carll family in said county, and forwarded it to me. John Carll, it appears, emigrated with his elder brother Jesse Carll, from Germany, in the fore part of last century. Jesse is well known; located in Monmouth precinct, while his brother John Carll settled in the north Cohansey precinct. There was another brother who came in company with the two before mentioned. There is a tradition in the family that his name was Ephraim Carll. I think it probable, for the reason that the name of Ephraim is common in the Carll family. Ephraim Carll, the emigrant, located in the State of Delaware, married and left a large family of children. John Carll purchased a tract of land in the Cohansey precinct, four and a half miles northeast of the present city of Bridgeton, on the Parvin's Mill road. Part of the ancient domicile of John Carll is still standing. His wife's first name before marriage, is known to have been Phebe, but her maiden name is not now remembered. They had five children; their names were Jeremiah, John, Lot, Josiah, Catharine and Theney Carll. It appears that John Carll, Sr., survived his wife four years, and died in 1810, at the advanced age of four-score years.

Jeremiah, the eldest son of John and Phebe Carll, married Ruth Woodruff, daughter of John Woodruff, Sr., who lived in the same neighborhood. Jeremiah and his wife Ruth had ten children; their names were Ephraim, David, William, Eli, Jeremiah, Lot, Ruth, Phebe, John and Theny Carll. Jeremiah Carll, Sr., died on the 13th of 6th month, 1811, aged forty-four years. John Carll, Jr., son of John Carll, Sr., and his wife Phebe Carll, married Nancy Woodruff, sister of Abraham Woodruff, Sr., of Bridgeton. John and Nancy W. Carll had six children, whose names were Mary, Nancy, Lydia, Samuel, Hannah and Rachel Carll. John Carll, Jr., the father of those children, died on the 28th of the 7th month, 1811. Lot Carll, son of Jeremiah Carll, Sr., married Mary Gifford, and emigrated to Pennsylvania, and his family never heard of him until seven years ago, when his son was seen in Philadelphia. Josiah, son of John Carll, Sr., always remained single, and made his home with his brother-in-law, John Moore, Sr., who married his sister Theny Carll. Catharine Carll married Samuel Nichols on the 26th of 4th month, 1806; they had eight children—Isaac, Thomas, John, Judah, Samuel, Phebe, Abigail and Theny Nichols. Theny, the daughter of John Carll, Sr., married John Moore; they had five children—Hannah, Phebe, Keziah, Patience and John Moore. Theny, the wife of John Moore, died 12th of 7th month, 1838, in her 73d year.

Ephraim Carll, the eldest son of Jeremiah Carll, was born on the 11th day of 12th month, 1790; married Damaris Garrison, widow of Thomas Garrison, on the 21st of 9th month, 1811. Ephraim was a wheelwright; he lived at Carll's Corner. The ancient name of the place was Facemire's Corner; but the name was changed to Carllsburg, after Ephraim Carll purchased the property, in about 1812, and was thus inserted in the maps, and went by that name until after the construction of the West Jersey Railroad, when the Company transiently made a station there and called the station Carll's Corner. It is two and a half miles north of Bridgeton, on the West Jersey Railroad. Ephraim carried on farming, wheelwrighting and blacksmithing; also, about fifteen years he kept what was called the Carllsburg hotel. He had the misfortune, in about eight years, of losing his wife. He subsequently married Esther Preston Davis, daughter of Benjamin Davis, of Deerfield. That was in 1820. Ephraim had by his first wife Damaris Garrison, two children, both sons—Jeremiah and Ephraim Carll; he had by his second wife, four children; their names were Hiram Davis, Richard Davis, Edward and Robert Bruce Carll. Ephraim Carll, Sr., the father of those children, accumulated a large real estate; he owned 150 acres at Carllsburg, being his tavern property, besides a considerable tract of land in Salem and Gloucester counties, and houses and lots in the city of Bridgeton. He died 17th of 6th month, 1840, in the fiftieth year of his age. David Carll, son of Jeremiah Carll, Sr., was born 27th of 7th month, 1792; he married Catharine Souder, daughter of George Souder, Esq.; by whom he had six children—George, Maria, Jane, Emily, Sarah and Mary Carll. George and Emily emigrated to the West; Emily recently died in Wells county, Indiana, aged about fifty years; her brother George Carll is still living in Fort Wayne, Indiana. Mary, the daughter of David Carll, died in infancy; the rest of the family are still living, and have families. David, their father, died of pleurisy, in 1833, aged forty-one years.

William, son of Jeremiah and Ruth W. Carll, was born 19th of the 2d month, 1794; he married Lydia Nichols, (sister to Ephraim Carll's first wife, Damaris Garrison,) on the 7th of the 10th month, 1815; they had eleven children; their names were Abigail, Francis, Damaris, Phebe, Maria, Charles, Jonathan, Lydia N., William, Elias and Enoch Carll. Their fathers William and Ephraim Carll were in the war of 1812, and were musicians when the army lay at Billingsport. William, after his marriage, lived and owned a small farm of fifty acres about one and a half miles north of Bridgeton, where he lived until death. He came to an untimely end, by the falling of a bucket, striking him on the head, breaking his scull, while engaged in digging a well in Bridgeton. This occurred when he was in the sixtieth year of his age, being in 1853. His wife, Lydia, died in 1868, aged seventy-three years. Eli Carll, son of Jeremiah, Sr., was born the 31st of 10th month, 1795; married Margaret Ott, the 26th of 4th month, 1816; they had six children—Eliza, Ruth, Henry, George, David and Lydia Carll. Eli, their father, died in 1845, aged about fifty years. Jeremiah, son of Jeremiah Carll, Sr., was born the 26th of 1st month, 1798; married Louvisa Burt, daughter of Moses Burt, of Fairfield township, Cumberland county, by whom he had two daughters. They emigrated to Cincinnati, and are all deceased at the present time. Lot, son of Jeremiah Carll, Sr., was born the 7th of the 8th month, 1800; he resided in the city of Bridgeton; he was thrice married; his first wife was Miriam Doughty; they had three children—Mary, Francis and James Carll; his second wife was Henrietta Knappey; they had five children—Charles, Samuel, Hiram, Josiah and Eli Carll. The last three died in infancy. Lot's third wife was Sarah Russell, widow of Jeremiah Russell; they had no issue. Lot Carll died in 1872, aged seventy-two years. Ruth, daughter of Jeremiah and Ruth Woodruff Carll, was born 22d of 10th month, 1802; married Alpheus Loper, in 1821; they had eight children; their names were Elizabeth Vance, Ruth, Rhoda, Ann Elizabeth, Ephraim, Charles, Jacob Frank and Howard Loper. Ruth Carll Loper died in 1872, aged seventy years. Phebe, daughter of Jeremiah and Ruth W. Carll, was born the 11th of 6th month, 1805; she married David Brooks; they had nine children; their names were Jonathan, Phebe Ann, Enoch, Jane, Reuben, Maria, Joseph, Elizabeth, Mary Frances, and David Brooks. Phebe is still living, the only surviving child of Jeremiah and Ruth Woodruff Carll.

John, son of Jeremiah and Ruth W. Carll, was born 8th of 7th month, 1807; married Martha Harris; they had six children—Josiah, Lot, Triphene, Jacob, Jason, Phebe and Hiram Carll. John Carll emigrated to Indiana over forty years ago; in 1861 was elected Auditor in Huntington county, Indiana, for four years. He died in 1869, of paralysis, aged sixty-two years. Theny Carll died in infancy.

Ephraim, son of Ephraim Carll, Sr., was born on the 18th of 2d month, 1815; he emigrated to Cincinnati, Ohio, in 1837; married Jane Campbell, of Covington, Kentucky; owned and kept the hotel called the Temperance House, located on the corner of 7th and Western Row, Cincinnati, for fourteen years; he and his wife had two sons—Ephraim and Thomas Carll. Ephraim died young; Thomas is still living. Ephraim, their father, accumulated large real estate, consisting of several large buildings in Cincinnati. He died of consumption, on the 2d of 3d month, 1853, aged thirty-eight years. His widow subsequently married Dr. James B. Campbell, of Cincinnati; she is still living.

The name of Carll is very numerous in this section of the State. I have been informed it is a very common name in Germany; so much so it is frequently used as the first name in that country; for example, Carl Shurz, the eminent German statesman of the United States, his adopted country. There is a tradition in the family that Carll was originally spelled with one l, and that its signification is Charles.

CLARK AND HILLMAN FAMILIES.

George Clark's ancestors probably first located in the county of Gloucester. However that may be he became a large landholder in the neighborhood of the village of Auburn, formerly known as Sculltown. Thomas, son of George Clark, was born 27th of 11th month, 1742. He subsequently married Deborah, daughter of Thomas Denny. She was born 17th of 4th month, 1747. Thomas and Deborah Clark had eleven children; their names were: Elizabeth, who was born 13th of 8th month, 1768; John, born 6th of 11th month, 1769; Henry, born 30th of 9th month, 1773; Samuel, born 4th of 9th month, 1775; George, born 18th of 6th month, 1777; Rebecca, born 9th of 2d month, 1780; Sarah, born 17th of 12th month, 1781; Thomas, born 18th of 2d month, 1784; William, born 13th of 4th month, 1787; and Robert Clark, born 12th of 9th month, 1789. Elizabeth, daughter of Thomas and Deborah Clark, married Eleazer Fenton. They settled on Caoney's Point, in Upper Penn's Neck. They had issue, two sons; one of them died young; the other son lived to mature age, married, and settled in the city of Philadelphia. George, son of Thomas and Deborah Clark, married Jane Chattin; they settled on his father's property, located between Sculltown and Sharpstown. Their children were Deborah, who was born 7th of 9th month, 1800; Mary, their second daughter, born 17th of 11th month, 1802; Elizabeth, born 2d of 9th month, 1804, she died young; George, born 8th of 11th month, 1806, died the following year; Jane Ann Clark, born 6th of 6th month, 1810. Deborah, daughter of George and Jane Chattin Clark, married Thomas McCaliston, of Pilesgrove, in 1810. They had several children; all of them grew to maturity, married, and settled in different parts of Salem county. Mary, daughter of George and Jane C. Clark, married Elijah B. Holmes; they had five children. Jane Ann, daughter of George and Jane C. Clark, married John C. Turner; they settled in Gloucester county; they had nine children—Ann W. Turner, their eldest child, was born 14th of 9th month, 1830; George Clark Turner, born 17th of

7th month, 1832; Sarah Jane, born 30th of 8th month, 1834; Mary E., born 2d of 8th month, 1831; Charlotte, born 25th of 11th month, 1839, she died in 8th month, 1859; Isaac H., born 14th of 12th month, 1841; Clark C. Turner, born 28th of 8th month, 1845; Isabella H. Turner, born 25th of 6th month, 1848; Maria T. Turner, born 28th of 8th month, 1851.

Francis Hillman was born 7th of 5th month, 1760. His parents were members of the Society of Friends. Every man has some trait of character which distinguishes him through life. Francis Hillman in early life turned his attention towards the domestic animal, the horse. This trait increased as he advanced in years, and many years before his death he had the name of being the greatest horseman in the county of Salem. There is an anecdote related of him: At one time when he was returning from the town of Salem to his home near Sharpstown, he overtook a woman on foot who was traveling the same way; he invited her to get in and ride as far as she went, which she accordingly did. She soon noticed his horse being uncommonly fat and spirited, and remarked, "Your horses put me in mind "of what people say of Frank Hillman,—That he makes his "wife and children live on Indian bread, whilst he gives his "wheat to his horses." Hillman remarked to her, in a good humored manner, he thought Frank Hillman must be a very singular man, to think more of his horses than he did of his wife. He frequently afterwards told the circumstance to his associates with much pleasure and merriment. His wife was Phebe Padgett. She was also a member of the same religious society to which her husband belonged. She was born 6th of 9th month, 1762. They were married 16th of 9th month, 1782. They had seven children: Letitia Hillman was born 21st of 10th month, 1783; Charlotte Hillman, born 30th of 11th month, 1784—she married a young man by the name of Riley, they removed to the State of Illinois; Aaron Hillman, born 1st of 11th month, 1786; Elizabeth Hillman, born 30th of 9th month, 1788; Ephraim Hillman, born 25th of 12th month, 1790; Samuel Hillman, born 21st of 8th month, 1793: he married Jane Long, they located in the township of Pilesgrove; David Hillman, the youngest son of Francis and Phebe Hillman, was born 20th of 3d month, 1795.

Francis Hillman lost his first wife about the year 1795. His second wife was Sarah Philpot; they were married 26th of 3d month, 1797; they had no issue. Samuel, son of Francis and Phebe Hillman, married Jane Long; they had four children— Alwood, Ann, Charlotte, and Phebe; the latter died young.

Alwood Hillman married Mary Gregory. Ann Hillman, daughter of Samuel and Jane Hillman, married Thomas Steward. Charlotte Hillman, daughter of Samuel and Jane Hillman, married James, son of Aaron and Ann Pancoast, of Sharpstown; they have children. David, the son of Francis and Phebe Hillman, married Catharine Caoney, 16th of 9th month, 1815. Francis, their eldest son, born 9th of 6th month, 1816, died in 1834; Phebe, born 25th of 2d month, 1818, died in July, 1819; Samuel, born 11th of 1st month, 1820, died 7th month, 1837; Ann Mary Hillman, born 15th of 12th month, 1821, married Samuel M. Harris; David Hillman, son of David and Catharine Caoney, was born 10th of 6th month, 1824; John C. Hillman, son of David and Catharine Caoney, was born 17th of 4th month, 1827, he married Annie Derrickson; Hannah J. Hillman was born 8th of 4th month, 1830, she married Dewitt C. Bowen; Harriet Hillman, daughter of David and Catharine Hillman, was born 28th of 9th month, 1833, she married Martin B. Holton; Martha Caoney Hillman was born 4th of 12th month, 1836, she has been twice married; her first husband was Samuel Sparks, second husband, Rusling Dalbow. David, son of David and Catharine Caoney Hillman, has been twice married; his first wife was Elizabeth Norton, his second wife is Ann W. Turner, daughter of John C. and Jane Ann Clark Turner. They now reside in Lower Penn's Neck, near Pennsville. They have had six children—George C. T. Hillman, born 12th of 6th month, 1852; Catharine C., born 27th of 5th month, 1854, died in 1856; Francis, born 10th of 6th month, 1856, died 1870; Jane Ann W., born 7th of 9th month, 1859, died in 1862; Laura Belle, born 29th of 5th month, 1862; H. Sandford Hillman, born 6th of 2d month, 1874.

George C. T. Hillman, son of David and Ann W. Hillman, married Sallie A. Mitchell, in 12th month, 1874. They reside in Lower Penn's Neck; they have no issue. George C., son of John C. Turner, married Elizabeth Mitchell; they have issue. Sarah Jane, daughter of John C. and Jane Clark Turner, married Nathan Steward; they have six children—Mary E., daughter of John Turner, married John Locke; they have five children, none married. Isaac H., son of John Turner, married Mary V. Linch; they have issue. Clark C., son of John Turner, married Martha Peterson; they have two children. Isabella, daughter of John C. Turner, married Joseph Stretch. Maria, daughter of John C. and Jane Clark, married Alexander Burt.

ELNATHAN DAVIS FAMILY.

The ancestors of Elnathan Davis, the great surveyor of West Jersey. He was the grandson of Jonathan, the eminent divine, who was born on Long Island, whose father, together with two or three other brothers, had emigrated from Wales and settled in the New England States as early as 1664. However, some of them soon afterward located on Long Island, whence Jonathan and his brother Elnathan Davis came to New Jersey in 1700, and settled at Trenton. Elnathan's occupation was that of a land surveyor. He was soon appointed surveyor-general of the State of New Jersey. Jonathan Davis, his brother, was a conspicuous Seventh-day Baptist minister. His wife was Elizabeth Bowen. Her relatives residing in Cohansey precinct, he made frequent visits in that section of country. It has been stated he preached occasionally in the Cohansey Church, sometimes among the Seventh-day Baptists that lived near the Cohansey Corners, in one of their private houses. Soon after the Church at Shiloh was organized, Jonathan Davis, Jr., was chosen their first pastor, and Elnathan Davis, the eminent surveyor of the lower counties of West Jersey, was the son of Jonathan Davis, 2d, the first pastor of Shiloh Church. I have no doubt his life was worthily spent in the new county of Cumberland. He was born some years before that event of dividing Salem county. Hence he was a Salem county born. His physical strength and great endurance excelled most men, with his great mathematical genius, which he inherited from his ancestors. He in early life was noted, not only in his own county, but in all West Jersey and the neighboring provinces, as being the most competent and accurate land surveyor at that period of time. Hence his life was a busy one. An anecdote is extant of him as a surveyor. He was often employed in the province of Maryland. After a time his trips to that place became so frequent as to be noticed by his friends, who inquired of the business that occupied him so often. To each inquiry he would, with a smile, give the following reply: "Interest on a bond to be attended to." It is said that none of his friends suspected that the loadstone that drew the man of the compass over there until he came bringing home to Cohansey his bride, Susannah Bond. Elnathan and his wife had seven sons and three daughters—Susannah, Margaret, Jonathan, Jacob, Ebenezer, Jedediah, Jeremiah, Samuel B., and Elnathan Davis. Most of his sons were also practical surveyors. They, too, have passed away. A few of their children are living, and a large number of grandchildren and some great-grand-children. Of those seven sons and daughters from the date of their respective births, between the years of 1760 and 1776, the revolution came and passed in their early youth.

In the late rebellion of a number of their grandsons a noble record is written. Harrison Davis, who marched with Sherman down from Atlanta to the sea, and John B. Ayres lies in a patriot's grave. Argard E. Swinney laid his young life as a sacrifice on the altar of his country. Jonathan Davis Morgan, of Illinois, volunteered during the war. Thomas B. Davis volunteered in Co. F, 3d New Jersey; at the expiration of two years he enlisted in the service of the 2d U. S. Artillery; was through two of the Penninsular and Bull-Run disasters; he was also in the battles of Antietam, Gettysburg, Wilderness, Cold Harbor, six engagements in all. After which he was honorably discharged. He, at the present time, resides in Florida.

I was requested by one of my correspondents, a lady of considerable literary attainments, who is desirous of ascertaining the name of the Indian name of the Delaware River. The late Steven Baldwin, the eminent shipper of the city of Philadelphia, over forty years ago found an old manuscript in which he ascertained the Indian name of said river to be Shenangah.

DAVIS FAMILY.

There are two distinct families of Davises in the county of Cumberland, the descendants of Jonathan and Elnathan Davis, who were born on Long Island. Their parents were natives of Wales. There were also John Davis, native of the same; he first resided on Long Island. He, some years afterwards, together with his sons, came to West Jersey, and purchased a large tract of land in Pilesgrove township within the Salem tenth. I have written the history of this large and interesting family in another part of this work. Daniel Davis, which I have no doubt belonged to the same family of John and Jonathan Davis, emigrated to America with his wife, Mary Johnson. She was a native of Ireland. They landed and settled in the State of Connecticut about 1660. Benjamin Davis, their son, was born in Connecticut, in the year 1670; he was probably the only one of Daniel Davis' children who ever emigrated to West Jersey. Benjamin soon after he became of age, enlisted in the British service in the war against the French and Indians, commonly called King William's war, which began in the year 1690, and ended in 1697. It is related that Benjamin deserted from the army, and traveled through the wilderness to the State of New Jersey, and finally located within Fenwick's Tenth, now Cumberland county. By the account he left behind him, he must have endured great suffering by hunger and cold; for nineteen days during his travels in the wilderness, part of the time he subsisted on the head of a horse which he found by the roadside in his travels. Within a short period of time after he arrived within the Salem Tenth, he married Margaret Riley, she being a native of Ireland. They settled between Morris river and Cohansey, on the Delaware Bay. It is called at the present time, Ben Davis' Point; at which place he and his wife resided for twenty-eight years; during that time, they had five sons and two daughters born; their names were Margaret, Benjamin, Uriah, James, Daniel, Esther and Arthur Davis. About 1725 Benjamin Davis purchased one thousand acres of land in North Cohansey precinct of Daniel Cox, the great land speculator, a resident of Burlington, for which he paid ten shillings per acre. The price which he paid Cox was considered by the inhabitants of the precinct very dear, hence they called it Dearfield; why the name has been changed to Deerfield, I can't imagine. In after time, that and other lands adjacent, was set off as a township called Deerfield. It is as a fertile tract of high table land as can be found in West Jersey. It was truly a wilderness country when Benjamin Davis and family moved from Ben Davis' Point to Deerfield, in 1726. At that time their nearest neighbor was two miles distant, next nearest, four miles. Margaret, eldest daughter of Benjamin and Margaret Davis, was born in 1700; she married William Clark; they had one son and three daughters; their names were James, Sarah, Margaret and Percilla Clark. Benjamin, son of Benjamin and Margaret Davis, was born in the year 1702; he married and had four sons and two daughters; their names were Benjamin, John, Rufus, James, Margaret and Esther Davis. Uriah, son of Benjamin and Margaret Davis, died when a young man. James, son of Benjamin and Margaret Davis, married Mary Lummis; they had five sons and five daughters; their names were Abisha, Sarah, Othaneal, Elizabeth, Rachel, Jonathan, Johanna, Esther, James (grandfather of the late Edmund Davis, of Bridgeton), and David Davis. Daniel Davis, son of Benjamin and Margaret Davis, married Mary Bradway; they had two daughters— Mary and Patience Davis; by his second wife he had four sons; their names were Amon, Uriah, Joseph and Arthur Davis. Esther, daughter of Benjamin and Margaret Johnson Davis, married Benjamin Perry; they had two children, son and daughter. Arthur, son of Benjamin and Margaret Davis, was born 13th of 6th month, 1713; married Martha Moore, in 1736; they had four children—Phebe, Jeremiah, Elijah and Daniel Davis.

Phebe, daughter of Arthur and Martha M. Davis, was born 18th of 8th month, 1737. Jeremiah, son of the same parents, was born 2d of 9th month, 1739. Elijah, son of Arthur and Martha M. Davis, was born 2d of 9th month, 1740, and Daniel, son of Arthur and Martha M. Davis, was born on the 2d of 1st month, 1743. Martha Moore, first wife of Arthur Davis, departed this life in the 1st month, 1743, aged 37 years. Esther Preston was born 20th of the 6th month, 1723, and married Arthur Davis, in 1743, being his second wife; they had nine children; their names were Levi, Martha, Ruth, Arthur, Esther, Charles, Naomi, Benjamin, and Abijah Davis. Phebe, daughter of Arthur and Martha M. Davis, married Benjamin Thompson, and had nine children—Amon, Jeremiah, Phebe, Patience,

LANING FAMILY.

The family of Lanings are of Welsh origin. David Laning, their ancestor, emigrated from Wales in 1705, and settled in Burlington county, New Jersey. He married a young woman of the same place about the year 1732 or 1733. They had two or more sons—Samuel and John Laning. A tradition in the family is,—"That David Laning, their father, was killed by a tree falling upon him." Samuel, the oldest, was born about 1735. He subsequently married and had children. His son, James Laning, was born 15th of 6th month, 1770; he married Hannah Trench, born 20th of 2d month, 1774. James and his wife had thirteen children, ten of them lived to mature age, married, and had children. William, the eldest son of James and Hannah T. Laning, born 27th of 2d month, 1797; he married Ann Peterson, of Philadelphia; she was born 4th of 10th month, 1794. They had three sons and three daughters; their names were—Charles, John, William, Jane, Locera, and Ann Laning. Charles, the eldest son of William and Ann P. Laning, was born 24th of 4th month, 1824. He married Hope Allen, of Gloucester county; she was born 28th of 3d month, 1828; they have had eleven children, nine of them are living at this time. Emma, the eldest, was born 10th of 12th month, 1850; S. Allen Laning, born 10th of 8th month, 1852; Janey Laning, born 28th of 9th month, 1854; C. Howard Laning, born 4th of 8th month, 1856; Mattie Laning, born 17th of 9th month, 1858; May, born 3d of 6th month, 1860; William and Francis Laning, born 23d of 9th month, 1862; Elmira Laning, born 5th of 3d month, 1866; Lizzie Laning, born 20th of 12th month, 1870. Charles, the father of these children, is a house carpenter, and resides in the city of Bridgeton.

Isaac, son of James and Hannah Laning, married Ann Miller; they had four children—John M. Henry, Isaac and Henry Laning. John M. and Isaac are clock and watch makers, both in Bridgeton; Henry Laning is a dentist.

John, the son of David Laning, the emigrant, was born in the county of Burlington 19th of 1st month, 1738. He married had one son—Benjamin Davis. Amy died 10th of 6th month, 1823. Benjamin's fourth wife was Deborah Fithian; they were married 24th of 10th month, 1827; they had no issue. Benjamin Davis departed this life 25th of 2d month, 1837, in the 75th year of his age. Deborah, his fourth wife, died 21st of 2d month, 1873, in the 93d year of her age. The following gives the time when Benjamin Davis' wives were born : Thomasin Lummis, his first wife, was born 4th of 5th month, 1758. Ruth Reeve, his second wife, was born 3d of 10th month, 1772. Amy Davis, his third wife, was born 22d of 10th month, 1771. Deborah Fithian, his fourth wife was born 12th of 9th month, 1780.

Marriages of the children of Benjamin Davis: Jane, daughter of Benjamin Davis, married George Bush, 17th of 10th month, 1818; they had five children—Franklin, Mary Jane, Anna Maria, Martha and Sarah Jane Bush. Esther Preston Davis married Ephraim Carll 6th of 5th month, 1820, and had three children—Hiram D., Richard D., and Robert Bruce Carll. Alfred Davis married Sarah Steelman, of Tuckahoe, 7th of 1st month, 1830, and had seven children—Emiline, Benjamin, Ruth Reeve, Sarah, Ellen, Maria, Eleanor and Mary Davis.

Births of the children of Ephraim Carll and Esther Preston Davis: Hiram Davis Carll, their eldest son, was born 23d of 10th month, 1821; Richard D. Carll, was born 2d of 9th month, 1824; and Robert Bruce Carll, was born 16th of 6th month, 1829.

Births of the children of George Bush and Jane Davis: Franklin Bush, son of George Bush and Jane Davis, was born 8th of 11th month, 1819; Mary Jane Bush was born 22d of 8th month, 1821; Annie Maria Bush was born 23d of 10th month, 1825; Martha Carrall Bush was born 4th of 1st month, 1831; Sarah Jane Bush was born 30th of 5th month, 1833; Mary Jane Bush, daughter of George and Jane Davis Bush, died 2d of 2d month, 1832, in the 11th year of her age; Martha Carrall Bush died 2d of 10th month, 1852, in her 21st year.

Births of children of Alfred Davis: Emiline, daughter of Alfred and Sarah Steelman Davis, was born 14th of 4th month, 1831; Benjamin Davis, son of Alfred Davis, was born 27th of 7th month, 1833; Ruth Reeves Davis was born 29th of 11th month, 1835; Sarah Ellen Davis was born 2d of 2d month, 1838; Maria Riley Davis was born 25th of 3d month, 1841; Eleanor Steelman Davis was born 6th of 10th month, 1843; Mary Anna Davis was born 28th of 12th month, 1849.

had one son—Benjamin Davis. Amy died 10th of 6th month, 1823. Benjamin's fourth wife was Deborah Fithian; they were married 24th of 10th month, 1827; they had no issue. Benjamin Davis departed this life 25th of 2d month, 1837, in the 75th year of his age. Deborah, his fourth wife, died 21st of 2d month, 1873, in the 93d year of her age. The following gives the time when Benjamin Davis' wives were born: Thomasin Lummis, his first wife, was born 4th of 5th month, 1758. Ruth Reeve, his second wife, was born 3d of 10th month, 1772. Amy Davis, his third wife, was born 22d of 10th month, 1771. Deborah Fithian, his fourth wife was born 12th of 9th month, 1780.

Marriages of the children of Benjamin Davis: Jane, daughter of Benjamin Davis, married George Bush, 17th of 10th month, 1818; they had five children—Franklin, Mary Jane, Anna Maria, Martha and Sarah Jane Bush. Esther Preston Davis married Ephraim Carll 6th of 5th month, 1820, and had three children—Hiram D., Richard D., and Robert Bruce Carll. Alfred Davis married Sarah Steelman, of Tuckahoe, 7th of 1st month, 1830, and had seven children—Emiline, Benjamin, Ruth Reeve, Sarah, Ellen, Maria, Eleanor and Mary Davis.

Births of the children of Ephraim Carll and Esther Preston Davis: Hiram Davis Carll, their eldest son, was born 23d of 10th month, 1821; Richard D. Carll, was born 2d of 9th month, 1824; and Robert Bruce Carll, was born 16th of 6th month, 1829.

Births of the children of George Bush and Jane Davis: Franklin Bush, son of George Bush and Jane Davis, was born 8th of 11th month, 1819; Mary Jane Bush was born 22d of 8th month, 1821; Annie Maria Bush was born 23d of 10th month, 1825; Martha Carrall Bush was born 4th of 1st month, 1831; Sarah Jane Bush was born 30th of 5th month, 1833; Mary Jane Bush, daughter of George and Jane Davis Bush, died 2d of 2d month, 1832, in the 11th year of her age; Martha Carrall Bush died 2d of 10th month, 1852, in her 21st year.

Births of children of Alfred Davis: Emiline, daughter of Alfred and Sarah Steelman Davis, was born 14th of 4th month, 1831; Benjamin Davis, son of Alfred Davis, was born 27th of 7th month, 1833; Ruth Reeves Davis was born 29th of 11th month, 1835; Sarah Ellen Davis was born 2d of 2d month, 1838; Maria Riley Davis was born 25th of 3d month, 1841; Eleanor Steelman Davis was born 6th of 10th month, 1843; Mary Anna Davis was born 28th of 12th month, 1849.

LANING FAMILY.

The family of Lanings are of Welsh origin. David Laning, their ancestor, emigrated from Wales in 1705, and settled in Burlington county, New Jersey. He married a young woman of the same place about the year 1732 or 1733. They had two or more sons—Samuel and John Laning. A tradition in the family is,—" That David Laning, their father, was killed by a tree falling upon him." Samuel, the oldest, was born about 1735. He subsequently married and had children. His son, James Laning, was born 15th of 6th month, 1770; he married Hannah Trench, born 20th of 2d month, 1774. James and his wife had thirteen children, ten of them lived to mature age, married, and had children. William, the eldest son of James and Hannah T. Laning, born 27th of 2d month, 1797; he married Ann Peterson, of Philadelphia; she was born 4th of 10th month, 1794. They had three sons and three daughters; their names were—Charles, John, William, Jane, Locera, and Ann Laning. Charles, the eldest son of William and Ann P. Laning, was born 24th of 4th month, 1824. He married Hope Allen, of Gloucester county; she was born 28th of 3d month, 1828; they have had eleven children, nine of them are living at this time. Emma, the eldest, was born 10th of 12th month, 1850; S. Allen Laning, born 10th of 8th month, 1852; Janey Laning, born 28th of 9th month, 1854; C. Howard Laning, born 4th of 8th month, 1856; Mattie Laning, born 17th of 9th month, 1858; May, born 3d of 6th month, 1860; William and Francis Laning, born 23d of 9th month, 1862; Elmira Laning, born 5th of 3d month, 1866; Lizzie Laning, born 20th of 12th month, 1870. Charles, the father of these children, is a house carpenter, and resides in the city of Bridgeton.

Isaac, son of James and Hannah Laning, married Ann Miller; they had four children—John M. Henry, Isaac and Henry Laning. John M. and Isaac are clock and watch makers, both in Bridgeton; Henry Laning is a dentist.

John, the son of David Laning, the emigrant, was born in the county of Burlington 19th of 1st month, 1738. He married per acre. The price which he paid Cox was considered by the inhabitants of the precinct very dear, hence they called it Dearfield; why the name has been changed to Deerfield, I can't imagine. In after time, that and other lands adjacent, was set off as a township called Deerfield. It is as a fertile tract of high table land as can be found in West Jersey. It was truly a wilderness country when Benjamin Davis and family moved from Ben Davis' Point to Deerfield, in 1726. At that time their nearest neighbor was two miles distant, next nearest, four miles. Margaret, eldest daughter of Benjamin and Margaret Davis, was born in 1700; she married William Clark; they had one son and three daughters; their names were James, Sarah, Margaret and Percilla Clark. Benjamin, son of Benjamin and Margaret Davis, was born in the year 1702; he married and had four sons and two daughters; their names were Benjamin, John, Rufus, James, Margaret and Esther Davis. Uriah, son of Benjamin and Margaret Davis, died when a young man. James, son of Benjamin and Margaret Davis, married Mary Lummis; they had five sons and five daughters; their names were Abisha, Sarah, Othaneal, Elizabeth, Rachel, Jonathan, Johanna, Esther, James (grandfather of the late Edmund Davis, of Bridgeton), and David Davis. Daniel Davis, son of Benjamin and Margaret Davis, married Mary Bradway; they had two daughters—Mary and Patience Davis; by his second wife he had four sons; their names were Amon, Uriah, Joseph and Arthur Davis. Esther, daughter of Benjamin and Margaret Johnson Davis, married Benjamin Perry; they had two children, son and daughter. Arthur, son of Benjamin and Margaret Davis, was born 13th of 6th month, 1713; married Martha Moore, in 1736; they had four children—Phebe, Jeremiah, Elijah and Daniel Davis.

Phebe, daughter of Arthur and Martha M. Davis, was born 18th of 8th month, 1737. Jeremiah, son of the same parents, was born 2d of 9th month, 1739. Elijah, son of Arthur and Martha M. Davis, was born 2d of 9th month, 1740, and Daniel, son of Arthur and Martha M. Davis, was born on the 2d of 1st month, 1743. Martha Moore, first wife of Arthur Davis, departed this life in the 1st month, 1743, aged 37 years. Esther Preston was born 20th of the 6th month, 1723, and married Arthur Davis, in 1743, being his second wife; they had nine children; their names were Levi, Martha, Ruth, Arthur, Esther, Charles, Naomi, Benjamin, and Abijah Davis. Phebe, daughter of Arthur and Martha M. Davis, married Benjamin Thompson, and had nine children—Amon, Jeremiah, Phebe, Patience,

Anna Wheaton, the mother of these children, died March 1st, 1829, in her forty-fourth year. Rhoda, daughter of John and Ann Laning, married Ephraim Mulford; she was his second wife; they had issue, four children—Ruth, Alford, Ellen and John Mulford; the latter deceased. George, son of John and Ann Laning, married Rebecca Webb; they shortly after removed to Steubenville, Ohio; they had several children; George and his wife Rebecca Laning are deceased. Richard, the eldest son of John Laning, Jr., and Judith his wife, married Violet, daughter of John and Elizabeth Whitacar. John, her father, was a lineal descendant of Richard Whitacar, who landed at Salem in 1675, in company with John Fenwick. Richard and Violet Laning have had eight children, six of whom are living— John W., Samuel, Elizabeth, Julian, Richard, Rhoda, Ebenezer W., and William Westcott. Samuel, son of Richard Laning, married Ann Eliza, daughter of Joab and Mary Sheppard; they had two children—Saria B., and Jerusha Laning. John Whitacar Laning, the eldest son of Richard and Violet Laning, married Emily, daughter of Jehiel and Phebe Westcott; they have four children—Elizabeth W., Milton W., Enos W., and Franklin N. Laning.

David, second son of John Laning, Jr., married Catharine Ewing, daughter of Thomas Ewing; she was born 18th of 1st month, 1816. David and his wife Catharine Ewing Laning, have one son—Charles Ewing Laning. David resides in the city of Bridgeton; has an iron foundry; his eldest brother, Richard Laning, is a farmer, and is one of the most successful agriculturalists in the county of Cumberland. Ruth, the daughter of Ephraim and Rhoda Laning Mulford, married Dr. Benjamin Rush Bateman, of Cedarville; they have no issue. Alfred, son of Ephraim and Rhoda L. Mulford, married a young woman by the name of Flanigan; they reside in Hopewell township; have three children. Ellen, daughter of Ephraim and Rhoda Laning Mulford, married Mahlon Dickinson, of Pilesgrove, Salem county; they have issue.

MORE FAMILY.

The name of More, it is said, originated as a surname in a Scottish Highland clan, eight centuries ago, signifying in the Scotch dialect, Great in prowess and reprisal. Down through the times of the Covenanters, and the scenes in which Popery received such telling blows, we follow the name ever in the van of Protestantism. In the troublesome times of James II., Jacob More, it appears, was a native of the north of Ireland, and emigrated to America in the first decade of the eighteenth century. He first settled on Long Island, and from there he came to the North Cohansey precinct, now Cumberland county. He soon afterward married Abigail Peck. Jacob More purchased a considerable tract of land, being part of the Wasse survey. I think at that time it belonged to Daniel Cox, of Burlington. Said land that Jacob purchased lay on the north side or head of the stream that has long been known as Beebe Run; said run empties in the lower branch of Unknown or Stoe creek. About twenty years afterwards Cumberland county was set off from Salem, and the township where Jacob More's land was located in Hopewell township, Cumberland county. In the year 1738 Jacob built himself a large log dwelling. Jacob and his wife, Abigail P. More, had six children; their names were John, Azariah, Joseph, Martha, Bathsheba and Mary. The last named died young.

Bathsheba, daughter of Jacob and Abigail P. More, married Preston Hanna. They had one son, the late Dr. Charles Hanna, of Salem. Martha, the daughter of Jacob and Abigail More, lived to advanced age, and died unmarried. Joseph More, son of Jacob and Abigail More, died in 1800, having been a ruling elder in Deerfield Church a number of years. Azariah, son of Jacob and Abigail More, was a weaver by trade; by his strict attention to business he soon accumulated a sufficiency to secure him a good home. When the revolutionary war commenced Azariah More was an ardent Whig, and highly approved of the measures of the Continental Congress. He early enlisted in the army. The following letter he sent home to his friends, dated Haddonfield, at 11 o'clock at night.

"25th of November, 1777.

"DEAR BROTHER—We have had an engagement with a party "of the enemy this evening, near little Timber Creek, in which "we have lost Lieutenant Mulford, as brave a man as ever lived. "He was mortally wounded first, as the action began, which "was about 4 o'clock, was brought to this place, and died about "7 o'clock at our quarters. We have no other loss in our "Company, except Thomas Harris, who had his arm broken. "What our loss is in general is uncertain. It was night when "we left the ground, but I am certain it was small compared "with what the enemy has lost. We must have killed many of "them in the time of action, for we took the ground on which "they first engaged. We have ten or twelve prisoners with "three artillery horses branded G. R.; our light-horse took "nine grenadines yesterday, with no loss on our side. We have "Col. Morgan's Riflemen with us, I believe as fine a body of "men as any on earth. We have been expecting re-enforce-"ments several days, sufficient for a general action, but they have "not arrived, and it's now reported, and I am ready to believe, "that the enemy are crossing the river at Gloucester Ferry, and "that it is expected we shall have none of them in Jersey by "to-morrow morning. If it should prove true, I shall conclude "they have taken a fright at our torpedoes. If you received "my letter of the 22d instant, you will soon have the opportu-"nity to send me the money I wrote for, which I shall be glad "to have, with a line or two to let me know how you all are, "and what is come of our deserters, and why they are not sent "to us. I think they are proper persons to make examples of.

"Remember me to all friends.

"AZARIAH MORE."

Azariah More never married. He lived to a serene old age, on the homestead he had worked to earn. His household affairs were presided over by his sister Martha. The accounts that are recorded of him give him an excellent character. He was a Justice of the Peace, and was well known in his day and generation as a man of sound judgment, and very methodical in all his doings, was characteristic of him. A few aged persons in the early part of this generation remembered him in the dress of the time; they were never weary of speaking of his kindness and benevolence to the widows and orphans. He died where he had lived so long, in the old homestead one mile above Shiloh, on the west side of the road leading to Friesburg, and for more than half a century has slept in the old Presbyterian graveyard at Greenwich. John, the son of Jacob and Abigail More, died 22d of 2d month, 1800; he settled half a mile east of his brother Azariah. He also was in the army of the Revolution; he married Rachel Moore, a different family from the More family, although many suppose them to be of one family. John and his wife, Rachel More, had eleven children; eight of them reared to manhood and womanhood; five left descendants, four of whom, great-grand sons of John More, volunteered in the service of the United States against the rebellion, viz.: one from Pennsylvania, (died in the service), one from Ohio, one from Iowa, and in the county of Cumberland, the costly sacrifice of an only child, John More Tyler.

Lewis, son of John and Rachel More, married Susanna Shull; they had five children—Ruth, Jacob, Lydia, Elmer and Eliza More. Ruth married Archibald Minch; no issue. Jacob died a young man unmarried; Lydia, daughter of Lewis and Susanna More, married Theophilus P. Davis; they had three children—Ruth M., Samuel B. and Leonard W. Davis. Elmer, son of Lewis More, married Kitty B. West; they have two children—Lewis and Marietta Moore.

Azariah, son of John and Rachel, married Lydia Dare; they had children—David, Abigail, Enoch, Josiah, Henrietta, George, Elizabeth and Robert More. David married Deborah Cook; both are deceased, having no issue. Abigail married David Veal; the names of their children were David D., Lydia M., Enoch, Henry and Francis Veal. Enoch married Elizabeth, daughter of Hosea Moore; their children were David, George and Hosea Moore. Robert, the son of Azariah and Rachel More, was twice married; his first wife was Emily Bevan; they had issue, one daughter, Caroline, who married William Riley his second wife was Elizabeth Cake; by her there was Robert, Azariah, Richard, John, Winfield, and Elizabeth More. Robert More is quite a distinguished public man; has been a member of the State Legislature two or three different times; he is now one of the freeholders, and trustee of the Cumberland county Almshouse.

John, the son of John and Rachel More, married Phebe Moore, his cousin; they had two children—Mary M. and Emily More. Mary died a young woman unmarried; Emily was twice married; her first husband was George, son of Samuel and Rachel Tyler; they had one son—John More Tyler; her second husband was Charles Seeley; they had no issue.

SHOURDS FAMILY.

Samuel, son of Daniel and Christiana Belangee, was born at Tuckerton, New Jersey. He married Hannah Grey; they had eleven children, nine of whom lived to mature age. The names of their children were: Grey, Thomas, Samuel, Benjamin, John, Asa, Job, Daniel, Charlotte, and Elizabeth Shourds. Samuel and his wife, Hannah G. Shourds, removed to Cayuga county, State of New York. Elizabeth, daughter of Samuel and Hannah G. Shourds, married Solomon Hull, of Cayuga county, New York. They had four children. Solomon and his wife and children left Cayuga, and settled near Arculusa, in Iowa. Charlotte, daughter of Samuel and Hannah Shourds, married David Mitchell; they had four children—Joseph, Hannah, George and Louisa Mitchell. Thomas, son of Samuel and Hannah Shourds, married Eveline Warner; they had issue—Eliza, Smith, and Hannah G. Shourds. Daniel, son of Samuel and Hannah G. Shourds, married Mehitable, daughter of Judge Goodrich, of Connecticut; they had eleven children: Samuel, Chester G., Ephraim Hammond, John G., Charlotte, Ruth H., Job H., Mary Jane, Jesse N., Ann Eliza, and Martha Jane Shourds. Jesse, son of Samuel and Hannah G. Shourds, removed to the State of Ohio. There he married; he was subsequently killed in a coal mine, leaving a wife and four children. One of his sons was named Jesse Shourds. Asa, son of Samuel and Hannah Shourds, was twice married. His first wife was the widow of his brother, Thomas Shourds. She died leaving no issue by him. Thomas' second wife was Eunice Landon; they had four children: William, Abbie and Maria were twins, and Sarah Shourds. Job, son of Samuel and Hannah F. Shourds, is married; they reside at Spencer Port, near Rochester, New York. They have three daughters.

James, son of Samuel and Hannah Shourds, married. They have five children; their names are Jesse H., Phebe, Clayton, Hatty and Lucy Shourds. James and his family reside at this time in Chicago, Illinois. His wife is deceased. Benjamin, son of Samuel and Hannah Shourds, and his wife, Phebe Ann Shourds, reside in Chicago, Illinois. They have five children—

Charles, Havaline, Imagin, Elliott, and Lazelle Shourds. Chester G., son of Daniel and Mehitable Shourds, married Harriet Lode; they had one son, Giles Shourds. Dr. Ephraim Hammond Shourds, son of Daniel and Mehitable Shourds, married Almira Cleavland, of Canada; they had three children: Clara, Emma J. and Effie. Clara and Effie are deceased. Ephraim Hammond is still a resident of Canada. John G., son of David and Mehitable Shourds, is unmarried. Charlotte, daughter of Daniel and Mehitable Shourds, married Stephen Boalt. They have issue: Eben C., Elizabeth, Clara Augustus, Arthur, Elmer Eugene, and Ralph Boalt. Ruth, daughter of Daniel and Mehitable Shourds, married Josiah Southerland; they have issue: Alvin J., John G., Caroy, Addie, Frank, Jay, Fred, Grant, Mattie and Jesse Sutherland.

Job H., son of Daniel and Mehitable Shourds, resides in Huron county, Ohio, on the homestead of his parents. His father, some years before his death, left New York State, with his family, and purchased a home in the State of Ohio. Job H. Shourds has been twice married. His first wife was Jane Mixten; they had one son, Harry Shourds. His last wife was Mary Jane Henderson; she is deceased, leaving no children. Mary Jane, daughter of Daniel and Mehitable Shourds, died unmarried. Jesse, son of David and Mehitable Shourds, resides in Cleaveland, Ohio. He is attached to one of the Life Insurance Companies of that city. He married Harriet Laylin; they have no issue. Martha Jane, daughter of Daniel and Mehitable Shourds, married Franklin Campbell; they have one daughter—Ida May Dell Campbell.

JAMES NEVILL.

OPINIONS ON ENGLISH LAW AND TRIAL BY JURY.

James Nevill came to America in company with John Fenwick. He was a weaver in his native land, followed his trade in the Parish of Stepney, London, Middlesex. The executors of John Fenwick conveyed him about thirty acres of land in the town of Salem. He was a man of much talent, and had the confidence of William Penn. He was Clerk of Salem courts, I think, up to the time of his death, and held other positions of trust. He was a married man when he emigrated to this country. There is nothing in the record showing that they had children to perpetuate their name.

It appears that James Nevill possessed by nature a legal mind; and turning his attention to it he became an able counsellor. The following is a copy taken from the Salem records at Trenton, of his opinion on English Law and Trials by Juries, which I consider well worth publication in this connection, in view of the early date it was written—nearly two centuries ago:

Extracts from the Salem records (Salem surveys, N. J.), Trenton, of entries made by James Nevill in 1687.) Proverbs 28, 4. "They that forsake the law praise the wicked, but such as keep the law contend with them." As fundamental laws may continue the people in peace and tranquility, so the extirpation may cause future disturbance.

It is worthy of observation that to ye mind of reason (directing himself to the subordinate courts or seats of justice), saith that they should assuredly prosper and flourish in the distribution of justice, if they desired all their powers and strength from their proper roots, advising them not to fear to do right to all and to deliver their opinions justly according to law, 4 Inst. Epilogue.

It cannot be but that as these laws, which reason at first introduced and experience afterwards approved, do settle and fortify States, to the manifest neglect of the same, should make weak again and crazie, which, being duly considered, magistrates ought not in any thing to be more than watchful and vigorous than to keep in life those laws by which ye State at first came to be exalted; for let ye be assured that ye same are still, and shall be the foundation and base of future prosperity.

Moderation is the continuance of estates and kingdoms. Such as reckon themselves the wheels in ye engyne of a State, ought to move so effectually as that ye end and purposes of ye lawmakers may be rightly considered and pursued, which is for ye good of ye whole people.

I remember a maxim of Sir Walter Rawleigh—"To take heed of small beginnings, and to meet with them even at ye first, as well touching the breaking and altering laws as of other rules which concerns the continuance of every State, for the disease and alteration of a commonwealth doth not happen all at once, but grows by degrees.

Actions of the State are like the billows of the sea, one design drives another forward as they are agitated by the Prince's breath. The fairest flower that now grows in ye garden of Englishman's liberties is a fair tryall by peers or twelve men of his neighbourhood, which so much artifice is used by some of this age to pluck up by the roots. Justice ought to be measured by the straight meta-wand of the fundamental laws of England, and not be the crooked lines of discretion.

A greater inheritance (saith Judge Cooke) is derived to every one of us from our laws than from our parents, for without the former what would the latter signify, and this birth-right of England citizens shines more conspicuously in two things,

first, Parliament,
second, Jurys.

By the first (the people by choice representatives) in the Legislature or law-making power, for no laws bind the people of England, but such as are by common consent agreed upon in that great council. By the second, they have a share in ye executive part of ye law; no causes being tryed nor any man adjudged to lose life, limb, members or estate, but upon the verdict of his peers or equals, his neighbours and his own condition.

Judge and ministers of Justice are to allow the great charter to be pleaded before them in all points, and they are to keep in all points.

No freeman shall be taken or imprisoned or be disseized of his freehold or liberties or free customs, or be out-laws or exiled or any others may be destroyed; nor we will not pass upon him nor condemn him but by lawful judgment of his peers, or by ye law of ye land, &c., &c.

On the 29th chapter—Institutes—Cooke hath many excellent observations. I shall here write one. No man shall be disseized that is put out of seizure or dispossessed of his freehold, that is land or lively-hood or of his liberties or free customs as belong to him by his free birth right, unless it be by the lawful judgment of his peers, that is, verdict of his equals, that is, of men of his own condition or by the law of the land; that is to speak it once for all, by the due course and process of law, for so the words are expressly expounded by ye statues of 37 Elizabeth, chapter 8; and these words are especially to be referred to those foregoing to whom they relate, as none shall be considered without a tryall by his peers, so none shall be taken, imprisoned, or put out of his freehold without a due process of ye law, that is, by indictment or presentment of good and lawful men of ye place in due manner or by writ original of ye common law. The law is called Rectum, because it discovers that which is tort, crooked or wrong; for right signifieth law, so tort signifieth crooked or wrong, signifieth injuries. Injury is against right. A right lyne is before declaritory of itself, and the oblyque, hereby crooked cord of discretion appeareth to be unlawfull, unless you take it as it ought to be. Discretion is to discover by ye law what is just. It is called right, because it is the best birth-right the subject hath, for thereby his goods, lands, wife, children, his body, life, honor and estimation are protected from injury and wrong; that's for ye very words of ye oracle of ye law ye safe and learned Cooke.

Nevertheless, I have known that a person hath been tryed and judgment passed against ye law by the rule of three, not direct, but was backward or reverse, called equity, alias discretion. I accuse no man, for things may be sometimes mistransacted, by surprise, but not of ye province. I hope I shall not be blamed for taking notice of some casual failings, viz: ye judge whispering on ye bench with ye Attorney-General; that is absolutely against ye laws, when the Attorney was pleading a cause. Judges are not to speak with any one upon ye bench unless it be openly, audibly and avowedly, not in any clandestine, whispering way. It is necessary for magistrates to observe the laws of their country, and not to encounter them with their prerogatives, and not to use it at all where there is law, but govern the people by just laws, justly constituted, and their infringement on the common law ought to be evidence to the innermost sensible understanding parts of twelve good and lawful men as well as the Judge, before the party be condemned to suffer either in person or estate.

It is my opinion that a jury of twelve good and honest men of the neighborhood are as good judges of the equitable sense of the law and the intent and meaning of the law-makers as they are of the letter of the law.

Equity is of two sorts, differing much one from another, and are of contrary effects; for the one doth abridge, diminish, and take from ye letter of ye law—the other doth enlarge, add, and amplify thereunto. The first is thus defined: Equity is correction of a law, generally made in that part it faileth, which correction of the general words is much used in our law. As if for example,—When an act of Parliament is made that whosoever doeth such a thing shall be a felon and shall suffer death, yet if a mad man or an infant of young years that hath no discretion do ye same thing, shall be no felon nor suffer death therefor. Also if a statute were made that all persons that shall rescue, or give meat or drink, or other succor, to any that shall doe such a thing, shall be accessory to his offence and shall suffer death, if they did know of the facts. Yet notwithstanding one doeth such an act and cometh to his wife who knoweth thereof doth rescue him and give him meat and drink, she shall not be accessory nor felon; for in the generality of the words of the law he it is mad, nor the infant, nor the wife were not included in meaning, and that equity doth correct the generality of the law in these cases, and the general words are by equity abridged and by the same.

The other equity is defined after this sort. Equity is where the words of the law are effectually directed and one thing only provided by the words of the law, to the end that all things of the like kind may be provided by the same; and so when the words enact one thing, they enact all other things of the like degree.

As the statute which ordains that in an action of debt against executors, he that doth appear by distress shall answer, doth extend by equity to administrators, for such of them as doth appear first by distress shall answer by equity of ye said suits, because they are of like kind. So likewise the statute of Gloucester gives the action of waste and the pain thereof against him that holds for life or years and by ye equity of ye same a man shall have an action of waste against him that holdeth but for one year or half a year, and yet he is without the words of the statute; for he that holdeth but for one year or half a year, doth not hold for years, but that is the meaning and the words that enact ye one by equity enacts the others.

If our predecessors had thought the arbitrary determination

of a bench of justices had been as equal a judgment as that of our part, surely in vain did they expend so much blood for the reprizing the latter and extripating the former.

Arbitrary judgments are against the statutes of ye 25th Elizabeth, which saith that justices, sheriffs, and mayors and other ministers, which under us have the laws of the land to guide, shall allow ye charters to be pleaded before them in all their points. This is a clause, saith Cooke, worthy to be written in letters of gold, " that the laws are to be the judge's guide and therefore not the judges to guide the law by their arbitrary glasses."

Has the law of England presumed that a judge or justice had been more knowing, and so more perhaps judges who might give better and more equal determination (of such facts which for decision came before them) than a jury of twelve men could or would do. Surely the law would then have left all controversies to their sole arbitrary determination, and never have required and commanded tryall by jurors, which are not only chargeable to the jurymen by reason of their attendance and expense, but a troublesome delay and of no use in determining rights and money, and therefore the tryalls by them may be better abolished than continued; which was a strange new-found conclusion after a tryall so celebrated for many hundred of years. But the law presumes that each man best knows his neighbor's action, therefore the most proper judges. Who can know the law that is bound up only in the judge's breast? Surely the law cannot be said to be common but uncertain, and Cooke says : Miserable is that servitude when the laws are uncertain and unknown. Of what value are the grants of Princes for themselves, their heirs, and successors confirmed by solemn engagements, bonds and seals, and what trust is in them if they may be made void at ye will and pleasure of those who are in power, and often as they find the vacating of them will be their advantage.

We see and observe that every land's and this country's fountains of justice were clear and wholesome, although the rivulets and lesser streams might be troubled and corrupted. The laws of Pennsylvania say that all tryalls shall be by twelve men, and as near as may be peers and equalls, and of ye neighborhood, and men without just exception. In cases of life there shall be first twenty-four secured by the sheriff for a grand jury, of whom twelve at least shall find the complaint to be true, and then the twelve men or peers to be likewise returned by the sheriff, shall have judgment.

That there shall be at no time any alterative of any of those laws without ye consent of ye Governor, his heirs and assigns, and six parts of the seven freemen in Provincial Council and General Assembly.

That all other methods and things not herein provided for shall or may concern the public justice, peace and safety of said province, shall be and are hereby referred to ye award, prudence and determination of ye Governor and freemen in Provincial Council and General Assembly, to be held from tyme to tyme in ye said province.

Here it seemeth to me that it is the judgment of the twelve freemen of England and of Pennsylvania which gives the cast and turn of the scales of English justice. Nor can the Governor and Provincial Council alter it nor the General Assembly cannot alter any of the fundamental laws without the consent of the Governor, his heirs or assigns, and six parts of the seven of ye freemen in Provincial Council, and General Assembly.

And now to conclude, I hope that in any age of so much light, mere will or resolution will not be held forth against it, but that what reason or righteousness there is in what is here set down, will be considered and followed, nor let it find prejudice with you from any disdain toward him from whom it comes, that no failing in circumstances or expressions may prejudice either ye reason or justice of what is tendered.

I remain a true bred English freeman, obedient to ye just laws; an earnest endeavourer of ye public peace; a friend to my country and a true lover of just priviliges, liberties and freedoms.
JAMES NEVILL.

The laws are no defence nor protection of any man's rights; all are subject to that thing by some called equity, alias will and power.

Those that shall do any thing whereby the title and interest of the subject to these lands is destroyed, must needs be guilty of a very grave crime, which I say of necessity must be if they be deprived of ye benefit of ye law, the free course of justice according to ye known laws of ye land.

Those that have made large pretences and promises and resolutions to preserve the people from bondage, vassalage and slavery.

A river's mouth is bigger than its head,
So would the mouth of Pennsylvania spread
Over superiors; over all his peers,
Over English, Finns, Swedes and mine heirs,

Most horrible, monstrous, and most barbarous he!
Renders known and common law to be.
His will is right or wrong, be it plaintiff or defendant,
Should have the cause, if gold be at ye end of it.
For avarice and pride he's not the least;
Money's the thing, in the bear's nose a ring,
'Tis that commands the beast.

My heart a matter good indites, then
What hand shall I invite to guide my pen?
And set in order unto each man's views
The privileges to heirs due
The envious nature.

Standing water will breed corruption and be offensive if it be not sometimes changed, and for men to be too long in offices of government it is to have too little regard to others or to the dignity of the State.

INDEX.

	PAGE.
Introductory,	3
John Fenwick,	9
Acton Family,	18
Abbott Family,	28
Bradway Family,	35
Brick Family,	42
Bassett Family,	45
Carll Family,	50
Chambless Family,	57
Cattell Family,	61
Coles Family,	64
Davis Family,	70
Dubois Family,	75
Elwell Family,	78
Guy Family,	80
Goodwin Family,	82
Hancock Family,	85
Obebiah Holmes Family,	87
Holme Family,	91
Hall Family,	93
Richard Johnson Family,	103
John Johnson Family,	111
Jennings Family,	119
Keasbey Family,	122
Lippincott Family,	132
Lawson Family,	139
Griscom, Maddox and Denn Families,	143

Mason Family,	150
Miller Family,	153
Morris Family,	161
Nicholson Family,	164
Ogden Family,	167
Oakford and Moss Families,	173
Plummer Family,	176
Preston Family,	178
Reeve Family,	179
Rolph Family,	185
Sinnickson Fam.	188
Sheppard Family,	202
Scull Family,	218
Smith and Darkin Families,	224
Sayres Family,	227
Shourds Family,	233
Summerill Family,	239
Sharp Family,	244
John Smith (of Smithfield) Family,	250
Stretch Family,	255
Tyler Family,	268
Tindall Family,	282
Thompson Family,	283
VanMeter Family,	301
Christopher White Family,	308
Joseph White Family,	325
Ware Family,	329
Wade Family,	342
Waddington Family,	347
Whitacar Family,	349
Wyatt Family,	359
Whittan Family,	365
Woodnutt Family,	368
Woodruff Family,	374
Yorke Family,	376
Locke and Rocke Families,	385

History of the Religious Bodies of Fenwick's Colony:
  Friends Society, ... 392
  Baptist Societies, ... 405
  Seventh-Day Baptist Societies, . . 422
  Presbyterian Societies, . . . 427
  Episcopal Societies, ... 438
  Methodist Societies, ... 446
  African Methodist Society, . . . 453
  Roman Catholic Society, . . . 454
Townships, ... 455
Early Marriages, ... 464
Ancient Buildings, ... 467
Slavery, ... 476
Beverages, ... 479
Genealogy, ... 481
Editors, ... 483
Farming Implements, ... 488
Public Conveyances, ... 489
Quit-Rents and Warrants, . . . 492
Surveyors, ... 512
  Appendix.
Bowen Family, ... 517
Carll Family, ... 521
Clark and Hillman Families, . . . 525
Elnathan Davis Family, ... 528
Davis Family, ... 530
Laning Family, ... 533
More Family, ... 538
Shourds Family, ... 541
James Nevill—Opinion of English Law and Trial by Jury, 543

ERRATA.

On the 93d page, 7th line, instead of "Elizabeth Pyle," read Elizabeth Plumbsteid.

On page 374, 5th line, after Wyatt, should have been inserted "gentleman. Edith was a relative of Bartholomew Wyatt."

On pages 496, 497 and 498, and throughout quit-rents and warrants, James Nevell should be spelled "Nevill."

JOHN FENWICK'S RECEIPT
TO
RICHARD GUY,
FOR
Ten Thousand Acres of Land, for his friend, Thomas Pyle.

Received, the one and thirtieth day of the Third Month, called May, One thousand six hundred seventy and five, of and from Richard Guy, of the Parish of Stepney, alias Stebunheath, in the County of Middlesex, Cheesemonger, the full sum of fifty pounds Sterling, which is the same sum of fifty pounds mentioned and expressed in a certain Deed Poll bearing even date herewith, and made from me, John Fenwick, late of Binfeild, in the County of Berks, within the Kingdom of England, Esquire, and cheif proprietor of the one moyetie or halfe part of the Tract of Land within the Province of New Cesaria or New Jersey, in America, to the said Richard Guy.

WILLIAM CARPENTER.

Born 1792.   Died 1866.

JACOB MORE'S LOG RESIDENCE.
Built 1740.

www.ingramcontent.com/pod-product-compliance
Lightning Source LLC
Chambersburg PA
CBHW070005010526
44117CB00011B/1428